ROSELLA, OR MODERN OCCURRENCES

Chawton House Library Series

Series Editors: *Stephen Bending*
Stephen Bygrave

Titles in this Series

Eliza Haywood, *The Invisible Spy*
edited by Carol Stewart

Isabelle de Montolieu, *Caroline of Lichtfield*
edited by Laura Kirkley

Mrs S. C. Hall, *Sketches of Irish Character*
edited by Marion Durnin

Sophie Cottin, *Malvina*
edited by Marijn S. Kaplan

Charlotte Dacre, *The Confessions of the Nun of St Omer*
edited by Lucy Cogan

Mary Brurton, *Discipline*
edited by Olivia Murphy

Marguerite Blessington, *Marmaduke Herbert; or, the Fatal Error*
edited by Susanne Schmid

Elizabeth Hays Lanfear, *Fatal Errors*
edited by Felicity James and Timothy Whelan

Dorothea Du Bois, *Theodora, a Novel*
edited by Lucy Cogan

Celia in Search of a Husband: By a Modern Antique
edited by Caroline Franklin

For more information about this series, please visit: www.routledge.comhttps://www.routledge.com/Chawton-House-Library-Womens-Novels/book-series/CHLWN

ROSELLA, OR MODERN OCCURRENCES

By Mary Charlton

Edited by Natalie Neill

LONDON AND NEW YORK

First published 2023
by Routledge
4 Park Square, Milton Park, Abingdon, Oxon OX14 4RN

and by Routledge
605 Third Avenue, New York, NY 10158

Routledge is an imprint of the Taylor & Francis Group, an informa business

© 2023 selection and editorial matter, Natalie Neill; individual owners retain copyright in their own material.

The right of Natalie Neill to be identified as the author of the editorial material, and of the authors for their individual chapters, has been asserted in accordance with sections 77 and 78 of the Copyright, Designs and Patents Act 1988.

All rights reserved. No part of this book may be reprinted or reproduced or utilised in any form or by any electronic, mechanical, or other means, now known or hereafter invented, including photocopying and recording, or in any information storage or retrieval system, without permission in writing from the publishers.

Trademark notice: Product or corporate names may be trademarks or registered trademarks, and are used only for identification and explanation without intent to infringe.

British Library Cataloguing-in-Publication Data
A catalogue record for this book is available from the British Library

ISBN: 978-1-032-00772-4 (hbk)
ISBN: 978-1-003-17558-2 (ebk)

DOI: 10.4324/9781003175582

Typeset in Times New Roman
by Apex CoVantage, LLC

CONTENTS

Series preface   viii
Acknowledgements   x
Introduction   xi
Bibliography   xxvii
Note on the text   xxix

Rosella   1

Volume I   3

Chapter I	Rage for adventures	5
Chapter II	Rage for adventures persisted in	12
Chapter III	Rage for adventures rather abated	21
Chapter IV	Two heroines taken down from their stilts	27
Chapter V	Heroic hopes revived by adventures in perspective	36
Chapter VI	A glimpse into the regions of sublime distresses	43
Chapter VII	Rage for refinement	51
Chapter VIII	Palsy – gout – and rage for improvements	60
Chapter IX	A heroine travesty – and a heroine unhorsed	67
Chapter X	Rage for education – a well-conducted fête	76
Chapter XI	Rage for accomplishments – soft manners in a lady of fashion critically illustrated	86

Volume II — 97

Chapter I	Rage for casemented cottages – for wandering in wilds obscure – a mysterious stranger	99
Chapter II	A storm, and a discovery. – a hero's retirement	108
Chapter III	An heroic epistle – rage for moonlight walks, à la lanterne	118
Chapter IV	Insanity and death	127
Chapter V	The fascination of a high-born beauty analyzed	137
Chapter VI	Rage for sublime evasions – the mysterious disappearance of two heroines	145
Chapter VII	Rage for discovering entombed charmers – a humiliating rencontre	153
Chapter VIII	A lapse of memory succeeded by an adventure	162
Chapter IX	A pleasant travelling companion gained *à bonne marchée*	171
Chapter X	A disaster – symptoms of attachment	180

Volume III — 189

Chapter I	A history, and a rencontre	191
Chapter II	The Scots drover – darkening prospects of a scandalized heroine	199
Chapter III	A parting scene – a heroine's retreat *champêtre*	210
Chapter IV	An ungracious housekeeper at an old castle – a decisive meeting	219
Chapter V	Mama tears away the mysterious veil thrown aver the affinity between herself and her daughter	227
Chapter VI	The elegance of the cottage sullied by ignorant rusticity – a captive hero reduced to despair	235
Chapter VII	A botanical journey – and an elucidation of a little quiet menage	245
Chapter VIII	A mysterious manuscript – musical travels	254

Chapter IX	A moonlight walk productive of alarm in vulgar minds – a meeting	262
Chapter X	A parting – a rich relation non compos – and a careful heir	270

Volume IV   279

Chapter I	A Scot cozened – a journey renewed	281
Chapter II	Domestic subordination – and domestic discipline	290
Chapter III	Credulity, as in time immemorial, an easy conquest for artifice and hypocrisy	296
Chapter IV	Farewell wishes – a rescue from the tyranny of very humble friends	304
Chapter V	A physician's fiat – reformation in the household of a lady of sentiment	312
Chapter VI	A heroine's memoirs corroborated by grave testimony – a death-bed	322
Chapter VII	A recantation of error – a disaster productive of a rencontre	330
Chapter VIII	Maiden perseverance – and an unfashionable young woman of fashion	341
Chapter IX	Incertitude – a husband's sketch of a decorous wife	348
Chapter X	A touch of heroics – and a final adjustment	360

Endnotes	371
Glossary of repeated terms	396

SERIES PREFACE

The Chawton House Library (CHL) Series republishes rare novels, travel writing and memoirs by women from the long eighteenth century. Mark Pollard of Pickering & Chatto approached us in 2005 about a series of reprints and reset editions of some volumes in the library's collections of around 9000 volumes (there was an existing Novels Online project hosted by the library). Both of us were committed to extending the range of women's writing, and we agreed to act as general editors for a series which is now a hundred volumes and counting – if only we'd known all our work wouldn't be eligible for the Research Excellence Framework audit.

Helen Scott, then the librarian, and Jennie Batchelor, who had then just left CHL, knew the collection better than anyone. With their help and in consultation with Isobel Grundy of the University of Alberta, we came up with three main strands: Novels, Travel Writings, and Memoirs. (We found that these were not necessarily discrete categories; for instance, one of the works appearing in an early travels set we edited ourselves could easily have appeared rather as a memoir.) Stephen Bending and I took responsibility for the first two, and we were joined by Jennie Batchelor, by then at the University of Kent, for the Memoirs strand. The Memoirs and Travel Writing strands of the series included sets of four or five facsimile volumes introduced and edited by experts in the field.

The novels are published as separate works in reset editions. We worked initially from a wish list for the series prepared by Isobel Grundy, who was then heavily involved with launching the Orlando Project; in those days the catalogue wasn't online, so Isobel worked just from a sense of what desirable texts hadn't had modern editions. Selection of the texts for inclusion in the series was based on the twin criteria of rarity and scholarly interest.

The first novel in the series, the anonymous *The Penitents in the Magdalen House*, edited by Jennie Batchelor and Megan Hiatt, appeared in 2006, and the second, *Adelaide and Theodore*, by Stéphanie-Félicité de Genlis, edited by Gillian Dow, was published a year later; so both of the Chawton House Library Fellows inaugurated the series. We couldn't have produced subsequent volumes without the informed help of the next librarian, Jacqui Grainger; the education officer, Sarah Parry; and more recently, the current librarian, Darren Bevin. Other novels to appear early in the series were related to Austen or comprised continuations or parodies of novels.

Some of the novels on Isobel Grundy's list weren't in the Chawton collections, which was a third criterion until the takeover of Pickering and Chatto by Routledge in 2015, which was followed by the withdrawal of funding from CHL by the Bosack-Kruger Foundation. After a hiatus, Kimberley Smith was appointed by Taylor and Francis and took over responsibility for the series. We decided with her and Gillian Dow (by then CEO of Chawton House, as it became) that the continuing life of the series was likely to be in the novel strand. (By that point we'd added alongside the three strands of the series a series of editions of essays on editing women's writing.) Rachel Douglas, an editor at Taylor and Francis, took responsibility of the series from Kimberley Smith in early 2019. Soon afterwards, we were able to remove the stipulation that proposals for the series should be of texts in the CHL collection, and we are now keen to accept interesting, neglected novels of the period from any source.

Stephen Bending and Stephen Bygrave,
University of Southampton

ACKNOWLEDGEMENTS

I would like to express my deep gratitude to everyone at Routledge who made this edition possible. Grateful thanks to Ian Balfour, Elicia Clements, Alison Halsall, Lesley Higgins, Jennifer Judge and Kim Michasiw for supporting my work on Romantic-period Gothic parodies over the years. A warm thank you to Anjalee Nadarajan, PhD student extraordinaire in York University's English Department, for her valuable assistance in proofreading the text of *Rosella*. Thanks also to Diane Woody and Hilary Davidson, to whom I turned for guidance about matters of French literature and fashion when preparing the endnotes. I wish to thank my 'English Romantics' students at York University for the enjoyable and enlightening discussions every Wednesday. Finally, and always, my love and appreciation go to my husband, Paul Cnudde, and to my dear parents and extended family.

INTRODUCTION

To avoid spoilers, some readers may wish to treat this introduction as an afterword

Mary Charlton's *Rosella, or Modern Occurrences* (1799) tells the story of two enthusiastic novel readers, Sophia Beauclerc and her friend Selina, who try to mould Sophia's adolescent daughter Rosella into a heroine of Gothic romance. Part parody of circulating-library fiction and part travel narrative, *Rosella* recounts Sophia's and Rosella's journey through northern England and Scotland, during which Sophia proves herself to be an eccentric and inadequate chaperone to her daughter. First published by William Lane's Minerva Press, *Rosella* parodies precisely the kinds of popular fiction that Minerva Press specialized in. It was arguably Charlton's most successful novel because it could be enjoyed by both fans and critics of such fiction. A second edition was printed in Dublin in 1800, followed one year later by the publication in Paris of a French translation, *Rosella, ou les effets des romans, sur l'esprit des femmes*. *Rosella* garnered positive reviews in the *New London Review* and *Anti-Jacobin Review and Magazine*, with the reviewer for the latter commending the author for interesting the reader in Rosella's adventures while at the same time mocking 'the impossible events, unnatural incidents, and indecorous situations of contemporary writers'. The reviewer concludes: 'even the mere novel-reading Miss, who sees nothing "in the bent of the tale" beyond the story, will find her heart engaged in it'.[1]

The author of *Rosella*, Mary Charlton, was prolific in her day, and yet we do not know much about her. As Gillian Dow notes, details about her life are 'sketchy' and information about 'her career as a popular novelist has only been traced through her publications'.[2] According to M. O. Grenby, Charlton was active as an author and translator between 1794 and 1824, but she was best known for having written several novels 'in the Gothic mode' for Lane at the end of the eighteenth century and turn of the nineteenth century.[3] Charlton's Minerva Press novels include *The Parisian; or, Genuine Anecdotes of Distinguished and Noble Characters* (1794), *Andronica, or, The Fugitive Bride* (1797), *Phedora, or, The Forest of Minski* (1798), *Ammorvin and Zallida* (1798), *The Pirate of Naples* (1801) and *The Wife and his Mistress* (1803). Charlton also wrote translations and 'alterations' from the French, German and Italian for Minerva, including *The Philosophic Kidnapper. A Novel. Altered from the French* (1803), two translations of works by August Lafontaine – *The Reprobate* (1802) and *The Rake and the Misanthrope* (1804) and *The Homicide. A Novel. Taken from the Comedie di Goldoni* (1805). After a hiatus of several years, she prepared a collection of poetry for children, *Mrs. Charlton's Pathetic Poetry for Youth* (1811), and wrote two final novels, *Grandeur and Meanness, or, Domestic Persecution* (1824) and *Past Events: an Historical Novel of the Eighteenth Century* (1824). Although her last works were not published by Minerva, Charlton was affiliated with the press for most of her career. Her reputation as a Minerva Press novelist was such that she is listed among the press's 'particular and favorite Authors' in a 1798 publisher's advertisement.[4]

Despite her success as a novelist, Charlton's work is now obscure and understudied. Her 'novel upon novels',[5] *Rosella*, is mentioned in several twentieth-century studies of the Gothic, but it is only beginning to attract sustained critical interest as a work offering insights into the dynamics of the Romantic literary market.[6] *Rosella* deserves attention because it increases our understanding of Gothic parody in the Romantic period and sheds light on better-known satires on Gothic reading like Eaton Stannard Barrett's *The Heroine* (1813) and Jane Austen's *Northanger Abbey* (1818). *Rosella* is also significant because of the new insights it may provide into the Minerva Press, the leading publisher of Gothic fiction in the 1790s. As Charlton's novel illustrates, Minerva Press authors were willing to make fun of the genre in which they worked, and William Lane was willing to publish their comic Gothic texts. However, *Rosella* is not merely a Gothic spoof. Charlton uses Gothic parody to engage in broader social satire: her novel mocks female readers and writers of the Gothic, but it also engages with contentious debates of the 1790s about the role of women. Ostensibly a didactic literary satire about the dangers of overactive imagination and female overreaching, *Rosella* is fascinating for the way that it brokers between conservative and feminist ideas, humour and horror, and ridicule of and indulgence in sentimental and Gothic tropes. With its mix of conservative and liberal views, *Rosella* exemplifies the complexities and ambivalences that characterize parodies of popular fiction and attitudes towards women in this period.

A 'novel upon novels': Rosella *as Gothic parody*

Rosella is one of many parodic Gothic novels published in the Romantic period when early Gothic was at its peak.[7] In addition to those by Austen and Barrett, examples include Bullock's *Susanna; or, Traits of a Modern Miss* (1795), William Beckford's *Modern Novel Writing* (1796) and *Azemia* (1797), R. S.'s *The New Monk* (1798), F. C. Patrick's *More Ghosts!* (1798), Eliza Parsons's *Anecdotes of Two Well-Known Families* (1798), Bellin de la Liborlière's *The Hero* (1799; English translation 1817), Edward Du Bois's *St. Godwin* (1800) and *Old Nick* (1801), Ircastrensis's *Love and Horror* (1812) and Thomas Love Peacock's

INTRODUCTION

Nightmare Abbey (1818), to name just a few. Although it is rarely noted, many of the Gothic parodies from this period were published by Minerva Press, a publishing house whose name is now nearly synonymous with Romantic-era Gothic. Charlton was not the only parodist who wrote Gothic novels for the press before turning to parody. For example, *Anecdotes of Two Well-Known Families* was published by T. N. Longman, but its author, Eliza Parsons, is best known today for having written Gothic novels for Minerva, including two of the seven 'horrid novels' listed in *Northanger Abbey*: *The Castle of Wolfenbach* (1793) and *The Mysterious Warning* (1796). Henry Tilney is able to send up such novels on the carriage ride to Northanger Abbey because he has 'read hundreds and hundreds' of them (as he tells Catherine Morland with Gothic exaggeration).[8] Similarly, novelists like Charlton and Parsons were well positioned to write parodies because they knew the genre so well. The conventions they mocked were ones they had employed in their own Gothic texts.

The parodies clearly benefit from the familiarity and success of earlier Gothic novels. For example, as its title suggests, the Minerva Press parody *The New Monk* by R. S. is a scene-for-scene rewriting of Matthew Lewis's scandalous 1796 novel *The Monk*. Although the preface frames the parody as a moral corrective to *The Monk*,[9] the author and publisher were undoubtedly attempting to cash in on the popularity (and notoriety) of Lewis's text, even as they appeared to share concerns that moralists had expressed about it. The Minerva parodies were advertised alongside the more 'serious' Gothic novels by the press and even worked to promote them. In *Rosella*, Charlton takes aim at various specific texts from the 1790s including the novels of Ann Radcliffe, Charlotte Smith's *The Old Manor House* (1793) and Lewis's *The Monk*, but, importantly, many of the authors whose works she targets (e.g., Regina Maria Roche, Anna Maria Mackenzie and Anna Maria Bennett) are popular Minerva Press novelists whose names are included alongside her own in the 1798 list of Lane's 'particular and favourite Authors'. Charlton's joking allusions to bestselling Minerva novels like Bennett's *The Beggar Girl and Her Benefactors* (1797) illustrate the self-conscious intertextuality that Elizabeth A. Neiman and Hannah Doherty Hudson associate with Minerva.[10] Moreover, readers familiar with Charlton's earlier novels would have realized that *Rosella* parodied elements the author had formerly used with seriousness. As Amelia Dale notes, even the title page of *Rosella* invites such comparisons because Charlton is identified as the 'AUTHOR OF PHEDORA', a sentimental novel much like the ones 'Sophia consumes and encourages her daughter to emulate'.[11] Clearly, Lane had no fear that self-parody would lessen his readers appetite for Minerva novels. Just as authors like Charlton and Parsons wrote Gothic novels and Gothic parodies, the readers of Gothic and Gothic parody were not separate audiences, for the success of a parody always depends on the reader's familiarity with the targets.

Like other parodists of the period, Charlton laughs at the Gothic for its formulaic predictability even as she offers initiated readers the pleasure of recognizing the parodied tropes. Charlton is also like most other parodists in that she focuses on the conventionality of so-called women's Gothic (works written in

INTRODUCTION

a sentimental vein, like her own *Phedora*). Lewis's *The Monk* notwithstanding, popular Gothic fiction of the 1790s had strong feminine associations. As Angela Wright has observed, Gothic was widely regarded as a kind of writing by and for women even though many men wrote and consumed Gothic novels.[12] Professional female authorship was on the rise in this period, and the parodies reflect common attitudes in the day about the unoriginality of women's writing. For example, Beckford assumes female pseudonyms in his Gothic parodies to mock the supposed repetitive sameness of literary productions by women. The fictional author of *Modern Novel Writing*, Lady Harriet Marlow, boasts that her 'bold originality' does her credit as a 'daughter of the Muses', and yet this claim is contradicted by the work itself, which is a pastiche of well-worn conventions rewritten in a comical register.[13] The unoriginality of women's fiction is likewise derided in humourous novel 'recipes' from this period, which list conventions of mass-market fiction for the mock purpose of providing a template for aspiring writers. In her 1799 poem 'A Receipt for Writing a Novel', Mary Alcock clearly identifies women as the producers of formulaic Gothic fiction: after providing a long catalogue of Gothic conventions she observes, 'These stores supply the female pen,/Which writes them o'er and o'er again'.[14]

Apart from a passage in *Rosella* that singles out *The Monk* for ridicule (II, ch. 3, p. 122), Charlton likewise associates the Gothic with the 'female pen' by making female-authored texts like those by Radcliffe and Bennett the main objects of her parody. More generally, Charlton satirizes generic conventions typically associated with Gothic texts by women, including long-suffering heroines of sensibility, faithful and superstitious servants, explained supernatural, sublime descriptions, picturesque cottages and courtship plots. Scattered throughout *Rosella* are Gothic lists like those found in the novel recipes. These often appear in narratorial digressions that poke fun at the sentimental Gothic novels that Sophia and Selina enjoy reading. One example appears in an early chapter in which Selina takes up a Radcliffean book and

> enter[s] into all the sublimity of pale moons, blue mists, gliding figures, hollow sighs, shaking tapestry, reverberating voices, nodding pictures, long corridors, deserted west towers, north towers, and south towers, ruined chapels, suspicious vaults, damp charnel-houses, great clocks striking twelve, wood embers expiring, dying lamps, and total darkness.
>
> (I, ch. 3, p. 21)

The list suggest that this kind of fiction is written to formula, and yet Charlton's narrator observes that Selina's 'imagination' is so deeply 'occupied by so brilliant a succession of interesting subjects' that she loses track of time:

> had not [the] maid entered to enquire where she chose to have the cloth laid for her dinner, she would not have recollected that it was rather necessary to eat, to enable people to gaze with rapture upon fine prospects,

which fade terribly upon the eye that is longing to fix upon a loaf of brown bread with the homely accompaniments of ale and cheese.

(I, ch. 3, p. 21)

The scene highlights the conventionality and simultaneous lack of realism of Radcliffean Gothic. Charlton suggests that although this kind of fiction offers imaginative escape from everyday domestic realities, it is not 'imaginative' in itself. The idea is emphasized in a later scene of reading that involves Rosella: when she picks up one of her mother's novels to pass the time, she finds that she is 'going over and over the same ground – always the castle and ghost before her, let her peep where she would' (II, ch. 3, p. 121).

Gothic Quixotism: Female readers and writers

As readers in 1799 would have readily recognized, *Rosella* belongs to a large subset of parodies inspired by Cervantes's *Don Quixote* (1615) and Charlotte Lennox's *The Female Quixote* (1752) in which impressionable readers get into trouble because they expect their lives to follow the patterns set by their favourite books. Quixote tales like *Susanna, or Traits of a Modern Miss*; *Anecdotes of Two Well-Known Families*; *The Hero*; Maria Edgeworth's 'Angelina, or L'Amie Inconnue' (1801); Sarah Green's *Romance Readers and Romance Writers* (1810); *The Heroine* and *Northanger Abbey* satirize Gothic's lack of realism by juxtaposing the world of romance with the world of the internal reader. Catherine Morland's Gothic hopes are repeatedly disappointed by mundane reality: her trip to Blaise Castle is aborted (and the castle is just a folly anyway), and the mysterious manuscript she discovers at the abbey turns out to be an 'inventory of linen' that a servant has left behind.[15] In *Rosella*, a similar pattern of comic deflation is introduced in the scene discussed earlier, in which the image of Selina feasting her imagination on sublime ideas is contrasted against the prospect of the 'homely' meal that her absorbed reading nearly causes her to miss. Bathetic comparisons between Gothic fiction and 'real life' appear most often, however, in scenes featuring Sophia, the work's most important Quixote figure, during her travels with Rosella. A 'long and dreadful groan' that raises Sophia's alarm is revealed to be a man singing on the road (II, ch. 3, p. 124), and a Gothic maiden in distress whom she tries to rescue is just a statue (II, ch. 7, p. 155). Sophia's expectations are shaped by her reading but she is often let down, such as when she finds that a humble cottage in Scotland is not like those depicted in her books: 'she wondered much that the hut was not exquisitely neat and white-washed' and that there was no 'inner apartment, ornamented with drawings and wooden-shelved bookcases, ... and a lute hung carelessly by a plaid ribbon upon a cane-bottomed London cottage-chair' (III, ch. 2, p. 201).

The Gothic Quixote tales of the late eighteenth and early nineteenth centuries make fun of the fad for Gothic fiction and what the reviewer for the *Anti-Jacobin* more generally calls the 'circulating-library mania'.[16] The parodies also satirize uncritical readers – usually women – who lack the life experience and judgement required to read novels with appropriate detachment. Some Gothic Quixote tales, like the French parody *The Hero*, feature male Quixotes, but the majority by far satirize female readers. These works reinforce the Gothic's association with the feminine by depending on stereotypes about the typical reader of the genre, namely the 'novel-reading Miss' mentioned in the *Anti-Jacobin Review*, who enjoys reading but cannot be trusted to understand 'the bent of the tale'. As Jacqueline Pearson has argued, it was not just male critics who perpetuated the idea that women were inept, credulous readers; the female Quixote fictions by Bullock, Charlton, Edgeworth, Green and Austen seem to show that '[e]ven women writers internalised the association of bad reading practices with the feminine'.[17]

The female Quixote tales also reflect pervasive concerns about the supposed deleterious effects of novels upon female readers. Critics and parodists disparaged Gothic fiction for being unrealistic, but even so, they expressed fears about the genre's influence on real readers. Gothic reading was often construed as a threat to female domesticity. For example, the anonymous author of the anti-Gothic essay 'Terrorist Novel Writing' asks reproachfully, 'Can our young ladies be taught nothing more necessary in life, than to sleep in a dungeon with venomous reptiles, walk through a ward with assassins, and carry bloody daggers in their pockets, instead of pin-cushions and needle-books?'[18] Kerstin-Anja Münderlein argues that the Gothic parodies of the Romantic period fall into two kinds, 'Didactic' and 'Autotelic', with the former cautioning against the dangers of the Gothic and the latter offering a more '"wholescale" ridicule' of fiction conventions.[19] The parodies featuring quixotic female readers are almost always in the former group, according to Münderlein, due to their expected pattern of female improvement and reform. In *Rosella*, *Northanger Abbey*, 'Angelina', *The Heroine* and others, the female Quixote's book-fuelled fantasies lead predictably to a crisis that teaches the misguided reader the error of her ways. In *Rosella*, the romantic adventures of Sophia conclude with her being incarcerated in a madhouse by a male relation, an ordeal that precipitates her contrite renunciation of novels of '*sentiment and mystery*' (IV, ch. 10, p. 370). Even more so than other Romantic parodies, it would seem, works like *Rosella* catered to two reading audiences simultaneously by offering the enjoyments of mock Gothic adventure, as well as a denouement that anticipated the objections of reviewers who tended to evaluate novels on a moral basis.

It is important to note that the Quixote formula was already familiar by the late 1790s when Charlton wrote her novel and when Austen completed *Susan*, the work that would be published many years later as *Northanger Abbey*. As I have argued elsewhere, evidence suggests that Austen uses the formula with irony. At the end of *Northanger Abbey*, when the narrator invites the reader to consider the 'tendency of this work', the effect is to call into question the didacticism of Quixote narratives.[20] Charlton likewise takes up the Quixote formula and uses it with the awareness that not just her Gothic targets but also the expected reformation of the Gothic Quixote would be well known to her readers. When Charlton wrote *Rosella* she was mocking tropes she knew well and had employed in her own Gothic texts. She was also working with another set of conventions: those associated with Romantic-period Gothic parody.

Charlton reworks the Quixote plot in one important way: in *Rosella*, the Quixote is not an adolescent girl the same age as the Gothic heroines she so admires, but rather the Quixote is a middle-aged woman and mother whose romantic ambitions are for her daughter and not herself. Charlton opens her work by focusing on Sophia and Selina as young women: in the space of a few short chapters, Sophia enters into a clandestine marriage, runs away, gets pregnant and is widowed. The narrator observes, 'The abrupt termination of her own adventures, she was reconciled to; and fancied herself one of those celebrated mamas, destined to bring forth beautiful and tender-souled creatures, devoted for a given time to misfortune' (I, ch. 5, p. 41). In effect, Charlton imagines what happens when the female Quixote grows up and becomes a mother. Unlike in *Susanna* and 'Angelina', the eponymous young woman is not the instigator of romantic escapades; instead, Rosella is forced into those escapades by her fond, ill-judging parent.

Charlton's decision to turn the Quixote into a mother has several implications. For one, it allows Charlton to make fun of maternal figures in women's Gothic ('those celebrated mamas'), as well as the common trope of the long-lost mother, for Sophia conceals her true relationship with Rosella for most of the work. Radcliffe's *Sicilian Romance* (1790) and *The Italian* (1796), Roche's *The Children of the Abbey* (1796), Eleanor Sleath's *Orphan of the Rhine* (1798) and Mary Wollstonecraft's *Maria: or, The Wrongs of Woman* (1798) are just a sample of the many works from the 1790s that feature maternal heroines or absent mother figures, important targets of Charlton's Gothic parody.

The characterization of the Quixote as mother is also key to the moral dimension of Charlton's work because Sophia's book-generated fantasies are shown to have a harmful effect on her daughter. Charlton emphasizes Sophia's Gothic delusions by juxtaposing them with Rosella's far more practical outlook. For example, Rosella tries to convince Sophia to shorten a long romantic ramble across the countryside by 'talk[ing] of her own hunger, and her friend's wet shoes' (II, ch. 2, p. 108). Also, recalling the reproach to young ladies in 'Terrorist Novel Writing', Rosella is willing to pick up her work in her spare time instead of a novel, even though (as Charlton's ironic narrator remarks) mending clothes is 'a vulgarity a heroine is scarcely ever caught at, her elegant and simple wardrobe being composed of such sublime materials as never to require alteration or repair' (III, ch. 5, p. 232). It is important that Rosella does not share her mother's enthusiasm for Gothic romance. Rosella

> could with great patience cry through a dozen pages, and tremble through as many more. But then a continuation of crying and trembling, according as the superb pen of the writer varied from pathos to horrors, and from horrors to pathos, throughout several volumes, she found far exceeding any curiosity she could feel, to learn in which of the damp

dungeons, all over-run with spiders and black beetles, the most lucky of the heroine's three or four dozen lovers found a clean spot to throw himself at her feet.

(II, ch. 3, p. 121)

As Dale argues in her discussion of this passage, Rosella models a more appropriate approach to reading than that represented by her quixotic mother. Rosella 'does not lack sensibility' but 'she recognizes formulae and repetition' and is a 'skeptical, distanced, evaluative' consumer of novels.[21]

Over the course of their travels through England and Scotland, Rosella often plays Sancho Panza to Sophia. When Sophia addresses the statue whom she mistakes for an imprisoned heroine ('Much-injured and patient being . . .! No longer shall the iron hand of oppressive Tyranny immure your half-sainted form in this desolate spot –'), Rosella interrupts her: 'Good Heaven, Madam! . . . who are you thus addressing? I see no human figure but that marble one stretched over the tomb' (II, ch. 7, p. 155). Rosella recognizes and becomes increasingly alarmed about how Sophia has been affected by her Gothic reading. When Sophia insists on setting out one evening for a moonlit adventure without a male guide,

Rosella was thunderstruck: walking in the dusk of the evening without an attendant, unacquainted with the way they were to pursue, and what was still worse, returning after night-fall, which must be the case, wholly unprotected, was a thing she could not have had an idea of, but from the fearless rambles of those gentle creatures, whose marches and counter-marches she had perused in Miss Beauclerc's library books.

(II, ch. 3, p. 122)

Whereas Sophia scorns social conventions and norms, Rosella grows concerned not only about her mother's sanity but also about how her own reputation and prospects will be compromised by the romantic schemes into which she is repeatedly drawn. And her fears are well founded. On their late-night walk, for example, the ladies meet a carriage on the road whose driver mistakes them for prostitutes (II, ch. 4, p. 131). Sophia and her abetting friend Selina do not safeguard Rosella from harm; instead, they rather hope that Rosella will meet with misfortune, for this is just what it means to be a heroine. The idea is stressed in an early scene in the novel when Rosella goes out riding. We are told that Selina

almost wished the horses to take fright (a little) or the carriage to overturn (gently) that an accident so opportune might create heroic services, an obligation of eternal gratitude in return for them, and all those tender sentiments which a charming heroine and a handsome hero must experience from such a touching adventure.

(I, ch. 8, p. 65)

One is reminded of the scene in *Pride and Prejudice* in which Mrs. Bennet, another foolish mother figure, sends Jane to Netherfield without a carriage on a rainy day so that she will have to stay the night. Yet, Mrs. Bennet's main goal is to see her daughters safely married and financially secure, whereas Sophia and Selina scorn practical considerations. Their romantic schemes are undertaken purely for the sake of adventure.

This leads to a final point about Charlton's decision to turn the Quixote into a mother: namely, doing so contributes to her (self-)satire on female authorship. Satirical portraits of female novelists are found in many Gothic parodies by male and female writers. For example, as previously mentioned, Beckford uses feminine authorial personae to ridicule female novelists and their works. In Edgeworth's moral tale 'Angelina', the titular heroine finally overcomes her addiction to romances when a meeting with her favourite author, the ludicrous 'Araminta', punctures all her romantic illusions. In *Rosella*, the Quixote is not just an impressionable reader, she is also a satirical representation of a female Gothic writer to the extent that she 'plots' heroinic adventures for her daughter. As Hannah Doherty Hudson observes, Charlton 'emphasises the active, writerly role [that Sophia and her friend Selina] take in creating their own novelistic tale' in a way that accentuates the 'story's potential for metanarrative'.[22] Charlton renders explicit Sophia's status as a Gothic writer. Sophia is often found 'at her writing-desk . . . journaliz[ing] herself into a violent fit of enthusiastic heroism' (III, ch. 8, p. 254). She writes an autobiographical novel titled '*Memoirs of the hapless Mother of Rosella*', which she presents to a bemused Rosella in the third volume (III, ch. 8, p. 255). Sophia's writing is clearly linked to her reading. For example, we are told that Sophia passes one evening at a hôtellerie according to her wont: she 'wrote her interesting narrative, and read another equally interesting from the large packet of books she had brought with her from her Circulating Library' (II, ch. 1, p. 107). In Barrett's later work, *The Heroine*, the Gothic Quixote likewise turns to writing: *The Heroine* is an epistolary novel ostensibly penned by the Quixote, Cherry Wilkinson, herself, who adopts the penname 'Cherubina' to record her Gothic adventures. The humourous suggestion in both *Rosella* and later *The Heroine* is that women who read too many novels are at risk of becoming novelists themselves. These satires on female authorship reflect the reality of women's increased visibility in the period's expanding literary market. As Kathleen Hudson observes, the '[m]oral panic that women would effectively be consumed by the very Gothic texts they read' had 'an unexpected basis in reality – the Gothic, perhaps more than any other literary mode up to this point, inspired many women to respond to and create their own works'.[23]

'the bent of the tale': (Anti-)Feminism and the Gothic turn in Rosella

Much of the humour in *Rosella* comes from the mise en abyme that is created by Charlton's satirical mirroring of her own Gothic readers and herself as a female writer within the diegesis of her text. Charlton's status as a Gothic novelist confounds any straightforward reading of *Rosella*. Certainly, self-parody entails an apparent conflict of interest. As Bullock remarks in her reader's address at the beginning of *Susanna*, 'Shall she, who points the shafts of ridicule against novel readers, expect her novel to be read?'[24] The reviewer for the *Anti-Jacobin Review* suggests that young female readers of *Rosella* are likely to miss 'the bent of the tale', and yet the work's ideological and moral 'bent' is not so clear cut. There is much to indicate that *Rosella* is a conservative, moral text, including its endorsement by the *Anti-Jacobin*; and yet Charlton's satire on female authors and texts is necessarily ambivalent.

At first glance *Rosella* seems conservative and even anti-feminist due to its harsh punishment of the Quixote. Like other Quixote tales, the work connects Gothic reading to madness. 'Margaritta' in Green's *Romance Readers and Romance Writers* reads novels until 'she almost ma[kes] herself sick and blind'.[25] Charlton's comic novel takes a Gothic turn when Sophia is captured and imprisoned in an asylum for being, as her cousin puts it, 'as mad as a March hare' (III, ch. 10, p. 277). Sophia's quixotism imperils Rosella, but it also causes her (Sophia) to suffer a fate that is common among Gothic heroines; namely, imprisonment at the hands of a ruthless male relative. Yet there is nothing 'romantic' about Sophia's imprisonment. When she is released from the asylum at last, she is not only pale and emaciated (which is only to be expected of a suffering heroine), but also, 'she had lost her hair' (IV, ch. 7, p. 331) – an indignity utterly foreign to heroines of Gothic fiction. It is only after experiencing a truly Gothic ordeal that the Quixote is cured of her romantic delusions.

It is easy to read *Rosella* as a cautionary tale about the troubles that women invite when they do not conform to expectations surrounding feminine conduct. Charlton emphasizes the many dangers that lie in wait for women, particularly those who try to exercise the same freedoms that men do and who scorn their protection. In *Rosella*, the Quixote's reformation marks the end of the travel narrative. As in Barrett's *The Heroine*, women's wanderings away from home are linked to their wandering reason. In Barrett's text, Cherry runs away because she worries that she is 'doomed to endure the security of a home, and the dullness of an unimpeached reputation'.[26] Sophia's mad insistence on wandering abroad without a male protector is also a rebellious bid for freedom. Just before Sophia is seized by her cousin, Rosella says that she hopes Sophia will regain her sanity when she 'is settled in her residence, and no longer harasses herself by moving from place to place' (III, ch. 10, p. 271). In the end, both Sophia and Cherry are made to suffer for their acts of transgressive independence and are recuperated into the private, domestic sphere. As Dale puts it, Sophia is 'disciplined and learns to exchange her quixotic maternity for a more hegemonic, domestic maternity'.[27] Sophia learns to mistrust the truth of Gothic romances and 'respect the prejudices of the world' (IV, ch. 10, p. 365). For this reason, Grenby groups Charlton's book with conservative satires on novels and novel reading that criticize modern novels for 'encourag[ing] readers to disregard customary practices and values'.[28] He argues that the moral

INTRODUCTION

of Charlton's story is articulated by Rosella's legal guardian Mr. Mordaunt, who remarks of Sophia: 'I trust that her past danger will henceforth teach her to pay a little more deference to the established usages of society than I hear she has lately done' (IV, ch. 5, p. 313).[29]

Charlton's mockery of intellectual women also supports the idea that *Rosella* is a conservative work. Sophia is basically good natured, if misguided, but another female writer, the bluestocking Mrs. Methwald, is depicted with less sympathy. Like Sophia, Mrs. Methwald spends much time at her writing desk, where she occupies herself with making 'incomprehensible extracts from incomprehensible authors' (IV, ch. 9, p. 352). She pores over not Gothic novels but works of science, modern philosophy and systems of female education. Her daughter, the restrained and fashionable Mrs. Cressy, is also a butt of Charlton's satire. Mrs. Cressy's natural charms have been cultivated out of her thanks to her mother's mishandling of her education. Rosella's artless and lively manner is clearly preferable to Mrs. Cressy's artificiality; however, due to her indecorous upbringing, Rosella lacks the ease and social graces of another character, Lady Lucy. Through these and other characters, Charlton explores ideas about female education and character formation. Charlton emphasizes the importance of properly regulated imagination and sensibility, but she mocks women of learning. Rosella goes to live with Mrs. Methwald when Sophia is in the asylum, and at the end of her stay she eagerly leaves her 'and her simpering daughter to astronomize, botanize, and philosophize at their leisure' (IV, ch. 9, p. 359). Charlton's ridicule of botanizing women is especially interesting because it seems to connect her with anti-Jacobin satirists like Richard Polwhele, who in addition to deriding 'unsex'd' radicals like Wollstonecraft and Mary Robinson, argued that botany was an improper area of study for women.[30]

Although *Rosella* can be read as a conservative satire, there are tensions in the text that complicate such a reading. First, as previously suggested, the purported moral of *Rosella* is undercut by the sheer conventionality of the ending involving the Quixote's anticipated crisis and conversion. Moreover, Charlton calls into question the didacticism of her work by directing satire at the moralizing Mrs. Methwald, who spouts 'apophthegms on decorum' (IV, ch. 9, p. 352) at every opportunity. Charlton also satirizes didactic works of literature. For example, she pokes fun at the soporific effects of Tillotson's *Sermons*, a text that Rosella reads out loud to Sophia's mother. Rosella reads on with resignation, keeping careful track of the number of pages left, while Mrs. Beauclerc dozes (I, ch. 6, p. 45). In some Quixote tales, moral and religious texts are offered as an antidote to Gothic reading, but not in Charlton's novel.

Additionally, the supposed moral about the dangers of Gothic reading is diminished by the parody's 'ambivalent dependence'[31] on the very Gothic texts Charlton supposedly holds up for ridicule. As Hannah Doherty Hudson notes, '*Rosella*, like many Minerva Press novels, is a difficult novel to categorise'; Charlton's parody 'reads for long stretches as a persuasively didactic sentimental novel, and in others could very easily be taken for a thoroughly gothic one'.[32] Indeed, the Gothic episode which sees Sophia forcibly confined by a cruel and covetous male relative

xxi

INTRODUCTION

should confirm rather than shake her belief in the reality of her favourite novels. It is ironic that, following Sophia's incarceration, the story unfolds much like a Gothic romance would. Sophia is ridiculed for credulity and rebukes herself for 'the many chimeras I have absurdly indulged' (IV, ch. 7, p. 331), and yet the final volume of *Rosella* includes all the elements of a serious Gothic tale: wicked men who try to steal women's money and property, meetings with long-lost relations, true birth discovered, inheritance and marriage. Charlton mocks the well-worn long-lost mother plot, yet the tearful reunion between Rosella and Sophia at Avelines is all a fan of Gothic fiction could wish from such a scene (IV, ch. 7, p. 331). And throughout the final chapters, as Deborah McLeod notes, Sophia assumes 'the role of penitent',[33] a character as much at home in a Gothic romance as a Quixote tale. The great joke of the final volume is that real life turns out to be much like a novel after all.

Further complicating our understanding of *Rosella* is the way that it opens itself to feminist counter readings. At the end of *Rosella*, Sophia's friend Selina remains unrepentant and unchanged; in this respect and others, she can be compared to Austen's Isabella Thorpe. However, Sophia seemingly embraces a quiet, retired life. As she tells Rosella, 'I shall be pleased to avoid quitting my own enclosure, which *at present* I do not wish to pass' (IV, ch. 10, p. 364; italics added). Yet not only does Sophia's phrasing leave open the possibility that she might wish to quit Avelines *in the future*, but also her reluctance to go abroad is only natural given how much she has suffered at the hands of the cruel male relative who used her eccentricity as a pretext for taking possession of her property. It is not surprising that Sophia wishes to remain close to home at Avelines because she came so close to having the estate taken from her. As McLeod notes, for a comic novel, *Rosella* offers a remarkably 'realistic and unflinching portrayal of violence against women'.[34] Charlton illustrates the tyranny of men not only through the pitiless cousin who places Sophia in the asylum, but also through Macdoual, the Scotsman who keeps Sophia's aunt, Mrs. Delaval, a 'virtual prisoner' while siphoning off her fortune.[35] The feminist concerns explored in this section of the novel are emphasized in the chapter titles (e.g., '*Domestic subordination – and domestic discipline*') (IV, ch. 2, p. 290). Although Sophia's retreat to the private sphere suggests the curtailment of her freedom, Charlton defends women's autonomy in plotlines that show women rescuing other women from the control of men. Rosella helps Mrs. Delaval escape from Macdoual, and Mrs. Delaval in turn helps to clear Sophia of the charge of insanity so that she can be freed from the asylum. Charlton offers a vigorous defence of women's property rights. She lifts this theme from women's Gothic, but she does not parody it. The happy ending of her work consists not only in Rosella's marriage to the amiable Oberne, but in Rosella's establishment as the rightful heiress both to Sophia and Mrs. Delaval. In fact, one could argue that the true moral of *Rosella* is a feminist one because in order to protect this matrilineal inheritance the women must band together. In the end, Charlton condemns women who fail to care for and protect other women. Through characters like Rosella's friend Lady Lucy and Mrs. Delaval, Charlton promotes the value of a female solidarity rooted in care and mutual responsibility.

INTRODUCTION

Even more specifically, Rosella can be read through the lens of Wollstonecraftean feminism. For example, it is possible to understand Mrs. Cressy as a mockery, not of an educated women per se, but of superficial accomplishments of the kind that Wollstonecraft scorned. In fact, with her 'false-refinement', Mrs. Cressy may exemplify Wollstonecraft's argument that improper education turns women into '[w]eak, artificial beings'.[36] Moreover Charlton aligns her work with central tenets of Wollstonecraft's thought by promoting female rationality, especially the importance of rational motherhood. Even in targeting sentimental literature, Charlton accords with Wollstonecraft and other radical women like Mary Robinson and Mary Hays who criticized sentimental fiction for romanticizing and perpetuating feminine weakness. As Michelle Faubert argues, Wollstonecraft associated women's lack of rationality and freedom with 'the culture of sensibility' fuelled 'by sentimental authors and the women who buy their novels'.[37] When the reformed Sophia declares that she 'must watch over every start of what is falsely called sensibility' (IV, ch. 12, p. 331), is Charlton parodying, or is she echoing the kinds of cautions against 'false sentiments' and 'false sensibility' found throughout *A Vindication of the Rights of Woman* (1792) and in other works by Wollstonecraft?[38]

There are particularly suggestive links between *Rosella* and Wollstonecraft's feminist Gothic novel *Maria*. Charlton borrows much from the earlier work. Both texts feature mothers who are torn from their daughters when they are unjustly consigned to asylums by men. And in both, the women pen tender and instructive memoirs addressed to their daughters.[39] It is tempting to see *Rosella* as a conservative mockery of Wollstonecraft's Gothic text, and yet the same warning is dramatized in both narratives, namely, that sentimental women are especially vulnerable to male oppressors. As Michelle Faubert argues of Wollstonecraft's novel, Maria's problems begin when she mistakes George Venables, 'her husband- and gaoler-to-be', for a hero of sentimental fiction.[40] Like *Rosella*, Wollstonecraft's *Maria* can be read as a work of Gothic quixotism.

I will conclude by mentioning an interesting sidenote to the study of *Rosella*: the sidenotes left by one real reader of Charlton's work. As stated at the outset, parodies like *Rosella* depend for much of their humour on the readers' prior knowledge of Gothic conventions. Hannah Doherty Hudson refers to the marginalia found inside the British Library's copy of Charlton's book to show that early readers recognized 'the novel's intertextual references' and responded to them by adding the titles and authors of the parodied texts in the margins.[41] The reader whose marginal notes are found in the British Library copy, although not identified by Hudson, is Scottish aristocrat Elizabeth Rose (1747–1815), an avid reader of popular novels and other forms of literature and a keeper of commonplace books.[42] What is known about Elizabeth Rose as a reader may help us to understand how *Rosella* was received in its day. Mark Towsey uses Rose's commonplace books to argue that she regarded reading as a form of self-improvement. 'She believed fervently in the fundamentally moral implications of reading', he writes, 'and her extracts usually took the form of moral aphorisms, easily applicable to the circumstances of her own life'.[43] Towsey records that in one of her three surviving commonplace books, Rose copied the passage from Frances Burney's *Cecilia* (1782) describing 'the importance of books to young ladies intent on self-improvement'.[44] This may suggest that Rose sought out Charlton's work of Quixote fiction not just for its Scottish setting but also for its edifying moral message. Rose's status and education mean that she is far from being a stereotypical 'novel-reading Miss'. Her marginal identifications demonstrate that although she is well versed in the popular fictions that Charlton targets, she is no passive reader. For example, Rose assumes the role of editor by correcting Charlton's use of Scots dialect on several occasions.[45] Indeed, Rose's active engagements with the text are so interesting because they call into question the very cliché of the uncritical female reader that Charlton invokes in her parody.

Ultimately, *Rosella* accommodates many interpretations and ways of reading. Charlton takes aim at multiple satirical targets from botanizing women, lawyers and the dissipated upper classes to Romantic tourism, adolescent girls and Gothic and sentimental fiction. The fact that Minerva published the work offers no definite clue as to the parodist's moral or political aims. Lane's works are often associated with social and political conservativism, and yet as Terrence Allan Hoagwood and Kathryn Ledbetter note,

> The political valence of the Minerva Press novels is not always straightforwardly clear: for example, the press published novels praised by *The Anti-Jacobin Review*, a propaganda tool of the Pitt administration, including Mary Charlton's *Rosella; or, Modern Occurrences* (1799), but it also published Jacobin novels including Robert Bage's *Man as He Is* (1792) and *Hermsprong, or Man as He Is Not* (1796).[46]

The conservatism of many of William Lane's publications must be weighed against the 'profit motive' that drove his press.[47] The multivalence of *Rosella* can be understood as a canny strategy to appeal as widely as possible to the period's new mass readership. The multivalence of *Rosella* is also one reason why it continues to hold interest for readers and scholars today. It is hoped that this new edition (the first ever modern, non-facsimile edition) will prompt further study of this rich and enjoyable work and help to bring deserved attention to its author, Mary Charlton.

Notes

1 Anon., Review of *Rosella*, *Anti-Jacobin Review and Magazine* (January 1801), pp. 59–60; quotation on p. 59.
2 G. Dow, '"Genuine Anecdotes": Mary Charlton and Revolutionary Celebrity', in K. H. Doig and D. Medlin (eds), *British-French Exchanges in the Eighteenth Century* (Newcastle, UK: Cambridge Scholars Publishing, 2007), pp. 149–65; quotation on. p. 149.
3 M. O. Grenby, 'Charlton, Mary (*fl.* 1794–1824)', in *Oxford Dictionary of National Biography* (Oxford: Oxford University Press, 2004). Hereafter *ODNB*.
4 Grenby, *ODNB*. The 'General Prospectus' of 1798 is reprinted in D. Blakey, *The Minerva Press, 1790–1820* (London: Printed for the Bibliographical Society at the University Press, Oxford, 1939), pp. 309–10.

INTRODUCTION

5   Anon., Review of *Rosella*, *Anti-Jacobin Review and Magazine*, p. 59.
6   For twentieth-century discussions of *Rosella*, see Blakey's *The Minerva Press, 1790–1820*, pp. 61–2; D. P. Varma's, *The Gothic Flame* (London: Arthur Barker Ltd, 1957), p. 181; F. S. Frank's, *The First Gothics* (New York and London: Garland Publishing, Inc., 1987), p. 52; W. Huber, 'Forgotten Novels of the Romantic Era, Part II: Mary Charlton, *Rosella* (1799)', in G. Ahrends and H. Diller (eds), *English Romantic Prose: Papers Delivered at the Bochum Symposium* (Essen: Die Blaue Eule, 1990), pp. 39–49; and D. McLeod, 'Doth a Single Monk a Gothic Make? Constructing the Boundaries to Keep the Fictional Hordes at Bay', *Lumen*, 16 (1997), pp. 35–51, on pp. 44–7. Very recently, *Rosella* has been analyzed in three studies: A. Dale, 'The Quixotic Mother, the Female Author, and Mary Charlton's *Rosella*', *Studies in the Novel*, 52.1 (2020), pp. 1–19; H. D. Hudson, 'Imitation, Intertextuality and the Minerva Press Novel', *Romantic Textualities: Literature and Print Culture, 1780–1840*, 23 (2020), pp. 149–67, on pp. 156–61; and K. Münderlein, *Genre and Reception in the Gothic Parody* (New York and London: Routledge, 2021). The only other work by Charlton to attract scholarly attention is *The Parisian; or, Genuine Anecdotes of Distinguished and Noble Characters*, which Dow discusses in her 2007 essay, '"Genuine Anecdotes": Mary Charlton and Revolutionary Celebrity'.
7   For recent work on Gothic parody in the Romantic period, see D. H. Thomson, 'The Earliest Parodies of Gothic Literature', in G. Byron and D. Townshend (eds), *The Gothic World* (New York: Routledge, 2014), pp. 284–96; N. Neill, 'Gothic Parody', in A. Wright and D. Townshend (eds), *Romantic Gothic* (Edinburgh: Edinburgh University Press, 2016), pp. 185–204; and K. Münderlein, *Genre and Reception in the Gothic Parody* (New York and London: Routledge, 2021).
8   J. Austen, *Northanger Abbey*, ed. M. Gaull (New York: Longman, 2005), p. 86.
9   R. S. explains, 'My aim is to set in a ridiculous and a disgusting light, a style of writing, which only waited for toleration to become general'. See R. S., *The New Monk*, ed. E. Andrews (Chicago, Valancourt Books, 2007), p. 2.
10 See E. A. Neiman, *Minerva's Gothic's: The Politics and Poetics of Romantic Exchange, 1780–1820* (Cardiff: University of Wales Press, 2019) and Hudson, 'Imitation, Intertextuality and the Minerva Press Novel', pp. 149–67.
11 Dale, 'The Quixotic Mother, the Female Author, and Mary Charlton's *Rosella*', p. 7.
12 She writes that the Gothic parodies 'seemingly insisted upon the formulaic and derivative nature of Gothic writing by women, and the dangerously overheated responses of its female readership' even though 'neither the readership nor the authorship of Gothic romance was straightforwardly female'. See A. Wright, 'The Gothic', in D. Looser (ed), *Women's Writing in the Romantic Period* (Cambridge: Cambridge University Press, 2015), pp. 58–72; quotation on p. 67.
13 W. Beckford, *Modern Novel Writing*, ed. R. J. Gemmett (Gloucestershire: Nonsuch, 2008), p. 36.
14 M. Alcock, 'A Receipt for Writing a Novel', in *Poems, &c. &c. by the Late Mrs. Mary Alcock* (London: C. Dilly, 1799), pp. 89–93; quotation on p. 92.
15 Austen, *Northanger Abbey*, p. 136.
16 Anon., Review of *Rosella*, *Anti-Jacobin Review and Magazine*, p. 59.
17 J. Pearson, *Women's Reading in Britain, 1750–1835: A Dangerous Recreation* (Cambridge: Cambridge University Press, 1999), p. 5.
18 Anon., 'Terrorist Novel Writing', in *The Spirit of the Public Journals for 1797* (London: James Ridgway, 1802), vol. 1, pp. 227–9; quotation on pp. 228–9.
19 Münderlein, *Genre and Reception in the Gothic Parody*, p. 70.
20 Austen, *Northanger Abbey*, p. 198. See Neill, 'The Horror and Humour of Women's Rights: Early Gothic Parody and Anti-Feminism', in A. Horner and S. Zlosnik (eds), *Comic Gothic* (Edinburgh: Edinburgh UP, forthcoming).
21 Dale, 'The Quixotic Mother, the Female Author, and Mary Charlton's *Rosella*', p. 13.

INTRODUCTION

22 Hudson, 'Imitation, Intertextuality and the Minerva Press Novel', p. 158.
23 K. Hudson, 'Introduction', in K. Hudson (ed), *Women's Authorship and the Early Gothic* (Cardiff: University of Wales Press, 2020), pp. 1–19; quotation on p. 9.
24 [Bullock, Mrs.] *Susanna; or, Traits of a Modern Miss*, 4 vols (London: Minerva Press, 1795), vol. 1, p. 2.
25 S. Green, *Romance Readers and Romance Writers*, ed. C. Goulding (London and New York: Routledge, 2010), p. 92.
26 E. S. Barrett, *The Heroine*, ed. A. Horner and S. Zlosnik (Kansas City: Valancourt Books, 2011), p. 9.
27 Dale, 'The Quixotic Mother, the Female Author, and Mary Charlton's *Rosella*', p. 14.
28 Grenby, *The Anti-Jacobin Novel: British Conservatism and the French Revolution* (Cambridge: Cambridge University Press, 2001), p. 18.
29 Grenby, *The Anti-Jacobin Novel*, p. 18.
30 R. Polwhele, *The Unsex'd Females; A Poem* (New York: Wm. Cobbett, 1800), p. 10.
31 M. A. Rose, *Parody: Ancient, Modern, and Post-Modern* (Cambridge: Cambridge University Press, 1993), p. 51.
32 Hudson, 'Imitation, Intertextuality and the Minerva Press Novel', p. 156.
33 McLeod, 'Doth a Single Monk a Gothic Make?', p. 46.
34 McLeod, 'Doth a Single Monk a Gothic Make?', p. 46.
35 McLeod, 'Doth a Single Monk a Gothic Make?', p. 46.
36 M. Wollstonecraft, *A Vindication of the Rights of Woman*, ed. D. S. Lynch, 3rd edn (New York: W. W. Norton & Company, 2009), p. 11.
37 M. Faubert, 'Introduction', in M. Faubert (ed), *Mary, A Fiction* and *The Wrongs of Woman, or Maria* (Peterborough: Broadview Editions, 2012), pp. 11–50; quotation on p. 35.
38 See Wollstonecraft, *A Vindication of the Rights of Woman*, p. 12. See also M. Wollstonecraft, 'The Female Reader', in J. Todd and M. Butler (eds), *The Works of Mary Wollstonecraft* (London and New York: Routledge, 2016), vol. 4, pp. 53–352, quotation on p. 135.
39 See Wollstonecraft, *The Wrongs of Woman, or Mary Wollstonecraft*, ed. M. Faubert, p. 210.
40 Faubert, 'Introduction', p. 40.
41 See Hudson, 'Imitation, Intertextuality and the Minerva Press Novel', p. 162. As Hudson notes, the British Library copy is available on Gale's *Eighteenth Century Collections Online* (*ECCO*). It is the online text that I used in conjunction with the 1800 second edition (digitized by Archive.org) to prepare the present work.
42 Elizabeth Rose was the 19th Baroness of Kilvarock. She lived at Kilvarock Castle, the historic seat of Clan Rose, near Inverness in the Scottish Highlands. Her copies of the first three volumes of *Rosella* were digitized by Gale's *ECCO* from the originals at the British Library. We know the books were hers because the title pages are signed 'El. Rose Kilvarock 1811'.
43 M. Towsey, '"Observe her heedfully": Elizabeth Rose on Women Writers', *Women's Writing*, 18.1 (2011), pp. 15–33; quotation on pp. 21–2.
44 Towsey, '"Observe her heedfully": Elizabeth Rose on Women Writers', p. 20.
45 For example, in her copy she corrects 'dunna' to 'dinna' (II, ch. 8, p. 168) and 'brae' to 'braw' (III, ch. 2, p. 200). The latter correction is discussed in note 286.
46 T. Hoagwood and K. Ledbetter, *'Colour'd Shadows': Contexts in Publishing, Printing, and Reading: Nineteenth-Century British Women Writers* (New York: Palgrave, 2005), pp. 26–7.
47 E. J. Clery, *The Rise of Supernatural Fiction, 1762–1800* (Cambridge: Cambridge University Press, 1995), p. 137.

BIBLIOGRAPHY

Alcock, M., 'A Receipt for Writing a Novel', in *Poems, &c. &c. by the Late Mrs. Mary Alcock* (London: C. Dilly, 1799), pp. 89–93.

Anon., Review of *Rosella*, *Anti-Jacobin Review and Magazine* (January 1801), pp. 59–60.

Anon., Review of *Rosella; or, Modern Occurrences. A Novel*, *New London Review* (August 1799), p. 180.

Anon., 'Terrorist Novel Writing', in *The Spirit of the Public Journals for 1797* (London: James Ridgway, 1802), vol. 1, pp. 227–9.

Austen, A., *Northanger Abbey*, ed. M. Gaull (New York: Longman, 2005).

Barrett, E. S., *The Heroine*, ed. A. Horner and S. Zlosnik (Kansas City: Valancourt Books, 2011).

Beckford, W., *Modern Novel Writing*, ed. R. J. Gemmett (Gloucestershire: Nonsuch, 2008).

Blakey, D., *The Minerva Press, 1790–1820* (London: Printed for the Bibliographical Society at the University Press, Oxford, 1939).

[Bullock, Mrs.], *Susanna; or, Traits of a Modern Miss*, 4 vols (London: Minerva Press, 1795).

Charlton, M., *Rosella, or Modern Occurrences. A Novel*, 4 vols (London: Minerva Press, 1799).

Charlton, M., *Rosella, or Modern Occurrences. A Novel*, 2 vols (Dublin: P. Wogan, E. Porter and T. Burnside, 1800).

Charlton, M., *Rosella, ou les effets des romans, sur l'esprit des femmes. Par M****, 4 vols (Paris: Chez Fuchs, Libraire, 1801).

Clery, E. J., *The Rise of Supernatural Fiction, 1762–1800* (Cambridge: Cambridge University Press, 1995).

Dale, A., 'The Quixotic Mother, the Female Author, and Mary Charlton's *Rosella*', *Studies in the Novel*, 52.1 (2020), pp. 1–19.

Dow, G., '"Genuine Anecdotes": Mary Charlton and Revolutionary Celebrity', in K. H. Doig and D. Medlin (eds), *British-French Exchanges in the Eighteenth Century* (Newcastle, UK: Cambridge Scholars Publishing, 2007), pp. 149–65.

Edgeworth, M., 'Angelina', in E. Eger and C. ÓGallchoir (eds), *The Novels and Selected Works of Maria Edgeworth* (London and New York: Routledge, 2003), vol. 10, pp. 255–302.

Faubert, M., 'Introduction', in M. Faubert (ed), *Mary, A Fiction* and *The Wrongs of Woman, or Maria: Mary Wollstonecraft* (Peterborough: Broadview Editions, 2012), pp. 11–50.

Green, S., *Romance Readers and Romance Writers*, ed. C. Goulding (London and New York: Routledge, 2010).

Grenby, M. O., *The Anti-Jacobin Novel: British Conservatism and the French Revolution* (Cambridge: Cambridge University Press, 2001).

Grenby, M. O., 'Charlton, Mary (*fl.* 1794–1824)', in *Oxford Dictionary of National Biography* (Oxford: Oxford University Press, 2004).

Hoagwood T., and K. Ledbetter, *'Colour'd Shadows': Contexts in Publishing, Printing, and Reading: Nineteenth-Century British Women Writers* (New York: Palgrave, 2005).

Hudson, H. D., 'Imitation, Intertextuality and the Minerva Press Novel', *Romantic Textualities: Literature and Print Culture, 1780–1840*, 23 (2020), pp. 149–67.

Hudson, K., 'Introduction', in K. Hudson (ed), *Women's Authorship and the Early Gothic* (Cardiff: University of Wales Press, 2020), pp. 1–19.

McLeod, D., 'Doth a Single Monk a Gothic Make? Constructing the Boundaries to Keep the Fictional Hordes at Bay', *Lumen*, 16 (1997), pp. 35–51.

Münderlein, K., *Genre and Reception in the Gothic Parody* (New York and London: Routledge, 2021).

Neill, N., 'Gothic Parody', in A. Wright and D. Townshend (eds), *Romantic Gothic* (Edinburgh: Edinburgh University Press, 2016), pp. 185–204.

Neiman, E., *Minerva's Gothic's: The Politics and Poetics of Romantic Exchange, 1780–1820* (Cardiff: University of Wales Press, 2019).

Pearson, J., *Women's Reading in Britain, 1750–1835: A Dangerous Recreation* (Cambridge: Cambridge University Press, 1999).

Polwhele, R., *The Unsex'd Females; A Poem* (New York: Wm. Cobbett, 1800).

Rose, M. A., *Parody: Ancient, Modern, and Post-Modern* (Cambridge: Cambridge University Press, 1993).

S., R., *The New Monk*, ed. E. Andrews (Chicago: Valancourt Books, 2007).

Thomson, D. H., 'The Earliest Parodies of Gothic Literature', in G. Byron and D. Townshend (eds), *The Gothic World* (New York: Routledge, 2014), pp. 284–96.

Towsey, M., '"Observe Her Heedfully": Elizabeth Rose on Women Writers', *Women's Writing*, 18.1 (2011), pp. 15–33.

Wollstonecraft, M., 'The Female Reader', in J. Todd and M. Butler (eds), *The Works of Mary Wollstonecraft* (London and New York: Routledge, 2016), vol. 4, pp. 53–352.

Wollstonecraft, M., *A Vindication of the Rights of Woman*, ed. D. S. Lynch, 3rd edn (New York: W. W. Norton & Company, 2009).

Wollstonecraft, M., 'The Wrongs of Woman, or Maria', in M. Faubert (ed), *Mary, A Fiction* and *The Wrongs of Woman, or Maria* (Peterborough: Broadview Editions, 2012), pp. 161–288.

Wright, A., 'The Gothic', in D. Looser (ed), *Women's Writing in the Romantic Period* (Cambridge: Cambridge University Press, 2015), pp. 58–72.

NOTE ON THE TEXT

In preparing this edition of *Rosella, or Modern Occurrences*, I consulted both the first edition published in 1799 by Minerva Press and the second edition printed one year later in Dublin for P. Wogan, W. Porter and T. Burnside. Copies of these texts have been digitized by Gale's *Eighteenth Century Collections Online* (*ECCO*) and Archive.org, respectively. The present edition follows the 1799 text except for the following minor emendations: first, inconsistencies in spelling, capitalization and the italicization of foreign words and loan words have been silently corrected, and second, some of the small changes made in the 1800 text have been adopted.

Inconsistent spellings within the 1799 text include

    adviseable/advisable
    analyze/analyse
    atchievement/achievement
    bed-side/bedside
    chaperon/chaperone
    contemn/condemn
    controul/control
    corredor/corridor
    farewel/farewell
    good-humour/good humour
    good-nature/good nature
    green-house/greenhouse
    house-keeper/housekeeper
    inclosure/enclosure
    limitted/limited
    mal-à-propos/*mal à propos*
    moon-light/moonlight
    non-chalance/nonchalance
    œconomy/economy
    recal/recall
    stept/stepped
    teazing/teasing

NOTE ON THE TEXT

terra-firma/terra firma
to-morrow/tomorrow
villany/villainy
and words ending with -or and -our.

This edition standardizes spellings by using the most modern English spelling that appears in the 1799 text unless doing so would create new inconsistencies. For example, 'to-morrow' is retained to match 'to-day', which never appears unhyphenated. This edition handles street names as follows: 'St. James's-Street' (as opposed to St. James's-street or St. James's Street, variations that are also found in the 1799 text). Original spellings have been kept if they appear consistently across the first and second editions. Readers of this edition will encounter such archaic spellings as 'her's', 'your's', 'vallies', 'biassed', 'enterprize', 'journies', 'rince', 'every thing', 'any where', 'plaister' (instead of 'plaster') and 'waved' (instead of 'waived'), to list just a few examples. 'Befal', 'befel' and 'forestal' have been modernized to be consistent with 'farewell' and 'recall'.

The only significant difference between the 1799 and 1800 texts is that the former is in four volumes and the latter in two. There are some slight differences in spelling and punctuation. This edition follows the 1800 text by using 'choose' (instead of 'chuse'), 'dulcinea' (instead of 'dulcina'), 'indispensable' (instead of 'indispensible') and -our endings (instead of -or endings) (even if the change was applied unevenly in the 1800 text). This edition also follows the 1800 text in the occasional replacement of colons with semicolons: if a colon was replaced with a semicolon in the 1800 text, a semicolon was used in this edition. The emendations outlined in this section are made without comment. Other minor textual variations between the 1799 and 1800 texts are indicated in the endnotes.

ROSELLA

VOLUME I

Chapter I

RAGE FOR ADVENTURES

MISS SOPHIA BEAUCLERC, a handsome young woman who possessed an independency, was the only child and reputed heiress of a man of very respectable fortune, whose winter residence was in one of the fashionable streets at the west end of the metropolis. She was nearly of age – a period to her not at all desirable, unless the previous interval of time were marked with some interesting occurrences she had in contemplation to facilitate, by suppressing a few suggestions of prudence, which occasionally arose in spite of Lover, Novels, or Confidante.

Miss Beauclerc had therefore consented to meet a very good-natured, very thoughtless, very extravagant, very pleasing, very well-made, very dissipated young man at St. George's, Hanover-Square,[1] where banns had been published in the names of each; with very little probability that the circumstance should reach the knowledge of the lady's parents; for though they were not people of high rank, they had sufficiently practised the usages of high life, to dismiss every idea of attending the church of their London parish. Mr. Beauclerc had indeed enquired for a pew, because, to possess a thing, and to use it, are distinct circumstances; and a tolerably commodious one was most obsequiously offered him, at the reasonable price of twelve guineas a year, and a douceur[2] of five more for the favour of immediate attention – a favour which the gentleman as immediately declined receiving; but his Lady had the address to profit by her husband's economy, and adroitly placing her share of a box at the Opera in opposition to a box at St. – 's,[3] attained her object by pleading for the one which was procured with the least money.

Miss Beauclerc had only one small difficulty to encounter in keeping her appointment, which was comprised in the singularity of walking out without an attendant, or getting rid of him when he had followed her two or three streets, which she thought the more eligible plan; and on the morning proposed, she sent the footman who accompanied her, into a shop to make some enquiry which she indicated, then very dexterously glided round a turning into another street, and was in the church before John could have given his message, and received an answer: there, in a deep veil, which hid some very decorous blushes, and what was still more convenient, the face they crimsoned, she exchanged vows with. Mr. Raymond, or as the called him in her confidential correspondence, her amiable and beloved Augustus; and whilst in the vestry he arranged the important business of seeing the clergyman and his satellites, which he performed with his accustomed liberality, the fair bride had leisure to indulge some very deep-drawn sighs, and a copious shower of tears at the *rash step* which her passion for the most engaging and best of men, and the too well-known *obduracy* of her parents impelled her to commit, against the duty she owed them.

The *best of men* caught a glimpse of her streaming sorrows through the cloud that obscured them, and experienced a keen pang of self-abhorrence and reproach upon recollecting how well they would be founded, could she but be sensible of a fatal event he had been vainly struggling to drive from his memory, that he might appear upon this occasion with tolerable composure at least, if he could not attain that gaiety of aspect, for which he was generally noted.

This circumstance was merely an accidental investment which the imprudent Raymond had made on the preceding night at a gaming-house, not only of every guinea he could command, but of several thousand pounds he had no means of paying, but with the expected fortune of Miss Beauclerc.

He did not rise from the Faro-table[4] until four in the morning; having for the last three hours called incessantly for bumpers of Burgundy to assist his judgment, and accelerate his better fortune: and then finding that every person declined his bets, he took the advice of one of his kind companions, and reeled to his lodgings, where he was put to bed by his servant, who had heard him mention whilst he was dressing, that he had an appointment of *some consequence* at ten the next day. From this intimation the man ventured to wake him at a quarter after nine, when Sophia's amiable and beloved Augustus started from his miserable slumbers with an aching head, nerves unstrung, and a mind in which confusion, hated recollection, torturing regret, irresolution, and anguish warred with inconceivable tumult. In this mood, he twice walked forward with the determination of confessing the whole of his mad folly to Miss Beauclerc, and decline, what he was certain she would even then persist in, permitting her to share the poverty and disgrace into which he had plunged himself; but reluctant shame, and the dread of beholding the distress this avowal must occasion, twice arrested his steps, and he resolved to write what he was convinced he had not the power to utter. As he was hastening back to his lodgings the second time, he happened, as he turned into Piccadilly, to cast his eyes upon the dial of St. James's church, and saw that it was already considerably past ten. The situation of Sophia struck upon his recollection like a flash of lightning, waiting in a suspense too mortifying and distressing to admit of further deliberation on his part, and a third time he faced about to complete his evil destiny. In striding up Sackville-Street with hasty and agitated steps, he remembered, for the first time, that he had not a guinea in his purse, and with a half desperate smile of self-ridicule, he knocked at the door of a friend whose abode he passed, to borrow twenty pieces. This companion in dissipation was at the breakfast table; and as Fortune had been as favourable to him the evening before as she had been cruel to Raymond, the sum in question passed from the hands of one extravagant to the other with much facility: not but the lender had heard the whispered ruin of the borrower, but he happened to possess a heart which required a longer time in the school of the world to harden, than that of a tonish[5] lounger usually takes.

Raymond threw the money into his waistcoat pocket, shook the hand of his friend, and declaring that he was upon business of *some consequence,* flew out of the house, and without admitting any more reflection, marched to his station at the steps of the church, where however he arrived as soon as Sophia, who having read of the numberless accidents which harass the soul of a beautiful young creature, and impede her progress in adventures of this kind, did not think it expedient to be punctual to the time appointed.

Under these threatening auspices were the ill-boding nuptials of Raymond performed. His bride, bidding him adieu before he quitted the church, tripped to the house of a visiting acquaintance in a neighbouring street, as had been preconcerted, and complaining of an accident that had separated her from her attendant, borrowed a servant to follow her home, where she found John already arrived, to whom she manifested great displeasure for remaining so long in the shop, by which means, she said, he had not observed her turn into Brook-Street with her friends.

Sophia then withdrew to her dressing-room, exulting extremely at the charming perspective that presented itself, of a train of incidents most delightfully interesting, and sweetly romantic. She threw up her veil as she walked to and fro before a large mirror; not from the ordinary vanity of admiring her face or figure, though they were both really engaging, but from the more elevated pleasure of beholding *in propria persona*[6] a heroine in the bloom of youth, emerging into those delightful, mysterious, and sentimental situations which so agreeably occupy the imagination, when viewed within the enclosure of a tremendous breadth of margin, and cased in a surtout[7] of marbled paper, extremely soiled by the devotion of the curious.

Poor Raymond meantime, who was momentarily recovering from the confusion attending an intoxication not sufficiently slept off, was alive to the horrors of his fate, which the folly, the madness, and, in the eye of the world, the villainy of his concealed marriage completed most effectually. He grinned with rage and despair, stalked about his apartment as if he meant to crush a giant at every step, and cursed himself alternately for a fool, a dolt, an ideot, and a scoundrel. At length, in spite of the energy of his anguish and regret, he began to feel extremely weary and exhausted with this unprofitable exercise; and having sketched in his distempered fancy a hasty plan of future conduct, he sat down to write a farewell letter to his unsuspecting bride, in which very little was to be understood but that he quitted her for ever because her generous confidence in his honour and the fascinating graces of her person had made a lasting impression on his heart; and finally, that being already a wretch beneath the regard of every honest man – sunk into the lowest pit of infamy, he left her because he could not endure in her eyes to be a villain. Having sealed up this eloquent, but very incomprehensible epistle, he dropped it into his pocket, with some papers relating to his deranged affairs, and walking to a coach stand, threw himself into a hack,[8] and was carried by his directions to – Street, the residence of Mr. Mordaunt, an upright man of the law, who had been one of his guardians, and had manifested an interest, almost paternal, in his welfare. To this honest man he unfolded a long tissue of imprudence and infatuated extravagance, ending in the unfortunate incidents of the preceding night, but carefully concealing the event of the morning. He had, when his fortune was little impaired, avowed to Mr. Beauclerc his admiration of his daughter, who in his rejection of such a suitor, veiled an incorrigible reluctance to part with money under the anxious foresight of a parent, and to the claims of poor Raymond opposed his well-known failings and follies. Piqued at the old man's too just representations, he affected to continue his suit without seeking his approbation, till its full success with Sophia taught him the prudence which alone could conciliate her father. But Mr. Beauclerc's prejudice and aversion were now too completely fixed to be removed by forbearance or submission, and the young people consequently consulted only their mutual prepossession. Raymond knew that the fortune of Sophia would little more than satisfy the demands of his plunderers, and under circumstances so aggravating to the feelings of her irritated father, from him they could hope nothing: when therefore he was silent on the subject of his marriage, his motive was not want of ingenuousness, but a fear lest in disclosing it, he should crush his too confiding wife in the ruin that annihilated him.

Mr. Mordaunt heard his narrative with a steady look of concern, and prepared, at his request, to make out a double lift of debtor and creditor to the estate of Augustus Raymond, who, of fifty thousand pounds bequeathed him by his father, contrived to point out to his silent hearer, two thousand in the sum in the five per cents, and three hundred more in the hands of a banker, besides a few sums scattered as loans amongst his quondam friends and companions; a couple of saddle-horses at a livery stable, where they had stood till their master was indebted double the sum they were worth; and a curricle with a pair of bright bays not paid for, completed the list.

On the contra side of the account stood – Imprimis – To the Honourable Thomas Estcourt five thousand three hundred pounds – To Major Hangon four thousand – and to Lord Quye three thousand five hundred. – Lodgings for six months, eighty guineas. – The valet three months' wages, ten pounds ten. – Mr. Mordaunt uttered a peevish ejaculation. – The groom, the taylor, the mercer,[9] the hatter, the bootmaker, the hosier, the shoe-maker, the perfumer. – "Fools! puppies!" exclaimed the old man in a rage he could no longer suppress, "contemptible madmen that you are! disgusted with your frivolous beings before you have well quitted your leading-strings, and affecting the apathy of sages before you have well attained the age of manhood – fixed, bent upon no earthly object but galloping on to ruin with all the frantic energy of hydrophobia![10] What is your aim – what is your end? – You know not; but you rush forward with fury to escape from yourselves, and woe be to the unwary whom evil Fortune places in your path!"

The wild impatience of Raymond was irritated by this effusion; he frowned, bit his lips, and dashed the papers which had occasioned it to the further corner of the room. Mr. Mordaunt took his hand as he seemed preparing to rush out of the house.

"Raymond," said he, "do you not suppose I am interested for your well-being?"

"Yes, yes," returned the young man; "have the compassion, however, not to demonstrate it at this moment by useless lectures."

He then declared that his intention was to quit England immediately, if the friendship of Mr. Mordaunt would induce him to undertake the arrangement of his desperate affairs, as far, at least, as they could be arranged.

Mr. Mordaunt argued and reasoned against precipitation with much perseverance; but at length finding that Raymond was deaf to persuasion, he offered to furnish him with recommendatory letters to some gentlemen he had formerly well known, who were at present high in the Council at Bombay.[11] The young man eagerly caught at the proposal which soothed his sickening heart with the idea of leaving far behind him all those scenes of regretted dissipation in which his happiness had been wrecked, and of hiding himself for ever from his former associates, whose scorn or compassion he could not endure to be the object of. In the present state of his mind, every thing was to be done in a moment, every plan put in practice at the instant it was formed; and he urged Mr. Mordaunt to dispatch the promised letters without delay, as he meant to leave London before sunset.

The good man was startled by this declaration; but a moment of reflection determined him not to oppose it, and he promised that his credentials should be ready when he was prepared to demand them. Raymond then left him, proceeded in his hack to the India-House,[12] to endeavour to secure a passage in the first vessel expected to sail to Bombay, and found that the last ship taken up for that settlement, had left the Downs a fortnight back: he learned however that the purser of an Indiaman[13] bound for Madras, had just received his final dispatches, and would set off for Portsmouth the next morning at daybreak. The letters of Mr. Mordaunt were totally forgotten – for Madras, Cochin-china, Peru, or the Coast of Africa were equally desirable to him at that instant, and he determined to hasten to Portsmouth when he had packed up some baggage, and possessed himself of the three hundred pounds in the hands of his banker, to whose house he immediately drove, and received the money.

He was now obliged to return by appointment to Mr. Mordaunt, to execute a deed which invested him with the power of receiving the sums due to him, and to liquidate as far as possible every demand upon him; and to this steady friend Raymond imparted his new destination. In vain did Mr. Mordaunt very gravely represent that recommendations addressed to people at Bombay, could be of little service at Madras; still however he would not withhold them, in the hope that they might be of service on a future emergency.

Raymond, supported by the fever of his mind, then flew to his lodgings, where with indefatigable perseverance, he assisted his valet to put up such of his effects as he thought necessary to take with him – a task he undertook both to hasten the man, and to drive reflection from himself.

His servant imagined he was accompanying a flying party upon some mad excursion – a surmise that was strengthened, when his master refused to let him step to the laundress, to demand some linen she ought to have brought home the day before; and he obeyed all the directions of Raymond without perceiving in his tumultuous hurry, any thing more extraordinary than unsubsided intoxication. A post-chaise[14] was then ordered, part of the baggage attached to it, and the remainder disposed in the inside of the carriage. Raymond ordered it to – Street, telling his valet as he quitted him, to desire the people of the house to apply for the money due to them, to Mr. Mordaunt, who would likewise discharge him and the groom. The fellow now, for the first time, guessed the situation of affairs, but was too much confounded by the sudden intelligence, and was too well acquainted with the impetuosity of his master, to give way to the insolence he felt well disposed to utter.

Mr. Mordaunt was at dinner when Raymond paid this final visit; and as the unhappy young man equally loathed society and food, he could not be prevailed upon to take a seat at the table, but left his chaise in waiting at the door, whilst he walked into Oxford-Road to deposit his letter to Sophia in the post, now that he was assured he should have quitted London before she could receive it. Shocked however on reflecting upon the sudden anguish she must experience at a communication so abrupt, his intention fluctuated; he again took possession of a coach for the greater dispatch, and ordered the man to hasten to Berwick-Street: the fellow required the number, and receiving two or three oaths for an answer, mounted his box with infinite celerity, and drove off at a full canter.

In Berwick-Street resided the confidential friend of Sophia, who having acquired sentiments equally romantic, and not being in a situation quite so elevated as that of Miss Beauclerc, undertook, with equal pride and pleasure, the task of forwarding the correspondence of the lovers. A dangerous illness which had seized her mother, prevented her attendance at the ceremony of the morning; but Sophia had very kindly relieved the *ennui* of a sick chamber (where no adventure could possibly be presented to her by her better destiny, except in the guise of an *amant medicin*)[15] by the precaution of dispatching a billet to notify that the die was cast, and her fate accomplished. When the bridegroom, therefore, appeared before her with a countenance portraying much of the anxiety and perturbation of his distracted mind, her silent suggestions allowed him time to inform her that his imprudence had undone him, that his fortune was annihilated, and himself an outcast. He entreated her to break the disastrous tidings with tenderness to her friend, and when she put the letter, he now produced, into her hand, to conjure her for her own sake, never to think of him more. The confidante was for a moment thunderstruck at this intelligence; but shortly recovering herself by a recollection of the charming, interesting distresses all this must inevitably occasion, she very carefully treasured in her memory what the self-banished wanderer incautiously uttered relating to his destination; and when he had wrung her hand, and bid her farewell, she scarcely waited till the street-door had closed upon him, before she wrote to her *beloved* and *ill-fated* Sophia, abruptly informing her of her husband's flight, and urging her to follow him without hesitation; which if she resolved heroically to do, this amiable and tender daughter proposed to leave all that was dear to her, that she might perform the *duties* of friendship in accompanying the interesting fugitive. When the epistle was dispatched, the confidante waited in great anxiety the effect of her prudent advice, now almost assured of its success, and now fearful that the timidity of Sophia would disconcert a step so essential to her adventurous career.

Raymond, little suspecting the mischief his tender precaution had endangered, hastened back to Mr. Mordaunt, who still entreated him to postpone his hasty journey for one day at least, that his departure might be rather better arranged; but finding both prayers and remonstrance vain, he sighed as he gave him his good wishes, intermixed with some sage advice, and saw him depart with a dejection of which Raymond more than partook, when he pressed his hand, and leaped into the chaise.

Chapter II

RAGE FOR ADVENTURES PERSISTED IN

HE arrived at Portsmouth without accident, having been compelled however to rest several hours upon the road, from a want of post-horses to carry him forward; so that his intention of travelling all night was frustrated, and it was rather late the following morning when he quitted his last chaise at the Crown, whither the driver took him. Having refreshed himself, with renewed impetuosity he hastened to a boat, and desired to be rowed to the Indiaman. As the men leisurely pushed off, one of them made some enquiry, to which Raymond replied at random, and then sunk into a deep reverie, from which he awoke at the expiration of two hours, to find that he had been taken to a foreign vessel from Bengal. In an excessive ill-humour he gave new directions, and at length found himself on board the — Indiaman. Here he met with a fresh exercise of patience; the Captain had just gone on shore, and he was informed by the first mate that every birth was occupied, and not a nook left to swing another hammock, unless the commander would consent to pare off a bit of his own cabin, which had already undergone an operation of the same kind. It was conjectured that the Captain would remain on shore till the arrival of the Purser;[16] and the Hotel he frequented was mentioned to Raymond, who declined an invitation to drink a bottle of wine in the cuddy,[17] and was rowed back to Portsmouth in a most unenviable state of mind, accompanied with an inveterate head-ach.

Almost despairing of succeeding in his application to the Captain, and exhausted by fatigue and anxiety, a sulky despondence supplied the place of the indefatigable exertions he had used: instead of seeking out the man who would instantly end his suspense by granting or refusing his request, a dread lest it should terminate as he feared, made him resolve to defer his enquiry, whilst he took a solitary dinner, that he might not faint for nourishment rather than in obedience to the calls of hunger.

It was near seven in the evening when he threw himself into a clumsy old-fashioned couch, that ornamented the apartment to which he had been introduced; and whilst the people of the house prepared what he had ordered, unconscious of the lapse of time, he remained a prey to the most torturing reflections, till a more than usual bustle throughout the house awakened his attention; and starting up, he rung the bell with such violence, that the handle and part of the rope remained in his hand, unsustained by the broken wire; but no one answering the signal, he threw open the door of the apartment, and called to the waiters in a loud tone of angry impatience; yet had a legion obeyed the summons, poor Raymond would no longer have heeded them, for his whole attention and every faculty were engrossed by the figure of Sophia's confidante, who attracted by the well-known sound of his voice, issued from a neighbouring room, and beckoned to him in silent dignity to enter it. But a presage of the scene which there awaited him, and a full recollection of his delinquency, made him a coward, and his motion was rather retrograde, until the lady urged him forward, by exclaiming that her poor friend would expire if he persisted in deserting her. Miss Beauclerc, or rather Mrs. Raymond, had really fainted from fatigue and the agitation of her spirits, upon receiving, on entering the house, an answer to the enquiries she had till then vainly made, which revived her almost extinguished hopes.

The meeting was on either side very tender, and had not the confidante Miss Selina Swinney, been present to note down in the tablets of her memory every sentence that was uttered – every entreaty of forgiveness on one side, and promise of forgiveness on the other, neither Raymond nor Sophia would probably have recollected six words of a scene so interesting.

The fugitive forgot for the present the purport of his journey: he removed his wife and her adventurous friend on the following day to the Isle of Wight, and at their request, went in search of lodgings, where they might remain a week or two, with the least chance of attracting the attention of travellers or inhabitants. He soon found some pretty apartments to be let, at a neat cottage looking building, about half a mile from Steep-hill, in a situation too beautifully romantic however, to allow of the retirement he was conscious would be prudent; but he was satisfied that it would delight Sophia, and that consideration prevailed.

They removed to this little habitation the next day, and Raymond found that he had perfectly well consulted the taste of his fair wife, who was in raptures with her new dwelling. His own mind was far from being in a state to relish the most attractive scenery, or the most sublime forms that have ever decked the surface of the earth: the immense cliff, at the side of which the cottage appeared to cling, though it afforded the most rich and picturesque prospects, – or the varying ocean that rolled beneath it, gave him no delight, whilst his heart reproached him with having clouded the fair perspective of a prosperous and happy life, to which Miss Beauclerc had appeared well entitled to look forward. He had not yet found courage to tell her the extent of his debts, or even that his property was reduced to the contents of his pocket-book; and she very naturally imagined that if he could be contented with such a retreat as chance had then conducted them to, which was a paradise to her enthusiastic mind, the interest of her fortune might almost, if not wholly, support them in it: in a few months she should be able to claim it; – what delightful satisfaction did she not promise herself, when she could present it to him, and bid him forget the past!

At the expiration of a few days, Miss Swinney began to feel weary of her situation, in spite of her ardent fidelity, and the charm of being confidante to such an amiable and unfortunate pair. Mrs. Raymond had now another object of everlasting and unalterable affection, and poor Selina missed those strings of kind epithets and professions of fervent friendship she had been accustomed to receive from her. The ungrateful Augustus too, no longer treated her with that delicate attention and brotherly regard which had formerly rendered her his strenuous advocate: on the contrary, when Sophia was not present, he invariably sunk into a gloomy reverie, and sometimes so far forgot himself, as to suffer exclamations of regret and despair to escape him: nay, when she reminded him of her critical and well-timed interference to prevent his cruel banishment from the bosom of love and friendship, he cursed this boasted interference with vehement execration, and said it had rendered him a miserable, abject, and dishonoured wretch.

All this was very strange to the gentle Selina, who conjectured, and fancied, and feared, and trembled at the dubious fate of her charming friend. But as Raymond invariably struggled against his secret chagrin and anxiety in the presence of his wife, and not only seemed, but really was much attached to her, Miss Swinney left to time and circumstance to unravel the dark emotions of the *mysterious* Augustus, and sat down well satisfied with the efforts she had made to conduct him and Sophia to the greatest of all sublunary good, which she believed to consist of a mutual attachment, within the romantic walls of a charming cottage; – they had likewise a magnificent prospect of mountains ending in grey hills and blue mists, occasionally irradiated by a pale and majestic moon, whose beams *might* serve to throw a light upon the broad shoulders and awkward gait of some sheep-stealer, or hen-roost stripper, whom imagination *might*, upon an emergency, convert into the leader of Banditti; and finally, the dashing of impetuous waves to regale at once the eye and ear.

With such desirable objects before her, had Miss Selina been blessed with two or three tender lovers, she would have thought little of her sick mother, whose hand she had kissed with great energy the night she had been impelled by sacred friendship to desert her; and twice, after she had quitted the good lady's apartment, she turned back to water it with tears. After the due observance of these customary ceremonies, she felt her compunction considerably abated, and fulfilled the generous purposes of her soul with great composure. Mrs. Raymond, on the contrary, in spite of the romantic enthusiasm of her sentiments, the persuasions of her adviser, and her anxiety to prevent the purposed emigration of her husband, could scarcely be induced to quit the house of her father clandestinely; and after a residence of a week in the Isle of Wight, her remorse was highly stimulated upon reading the following advertisement in the newspaper Mr. Raymond took in.

"ELOPEMENT.

"Whereas a young lady has lately deserted the roof of her unhappy parents, as they suppose from an attachment they appeared to discourage, they are induced thus to solicit her return to her home, where she will be received with kindness and indulgence. If the young lady will write a few lines to her mother, should she not be willing to rely wholly upon this declaration, it will much relieve the anxiety and affliction that has been, and is still experienced. The companion of her flight will be likewise forgiven by her relations, should her persuasions prevail with her friend to comply with the earnest entreaty of her parents, who will not fail to acknowledge the benefit she will have then conferred upon them."

Sophia read these lines with great emotion, and pointing them out to her husband, watched his countenance whilst he hastily ran them over: he changed colour twice, and made no immediate reply.

"This is more than I had dared to hope," said Mrs. Raymond timidly, after a short pause: "Dear Augustus, will you not suffer me to avail myself of such kind concessions?"

"You are not certain," replied he, in painful confusion, "that you are the person meant by this advertisement."

"Oh yes, yes, I am quite certain that it can be no other."

"I have no doubt of it," cried Miss Swinney, who had been reading the paragraph two or three times with great attention; "but I cannot divine what acknowledgment your father alludes to, my dear friend, unless indeed Mrs. Beauclerc means to adopt me instead of her darling Sophia, who will now, she must necessarily think, reside with her husband: and you know, Sophy, this would be a very natural plan, as you and I are so congenial in sentiment and disposition; for it must needs be a great consolation to your tender mamma, to converse daily with one who flatters herself she is the counterpart of her daughter."

Raymond, who was walking hastily up and down the room, was strongly tempted to dispute this assertion; but the tears of his wife, who softly ejaculated, "My poor mother!" now claimed all his attention.

"Sophy," cried he, "I am distressed, Heaven knows how much, that I cannot fulfil the expectations this advertisement has raised in your affectionate bosom! I told you that I was an undone wretch, but I did not tell you all: – it is impossible that I can appear in the world; situated as I am, I would not again enter London for what the whole universe could offer me."

Mrs. Raymond was shocked: his vehemence had startled her, and she wept bitterly.

"But," continued he, "I am not such a villain as deliberately to drag you into the ruin I have brought upon myself: return to your father's house, where an affectionate welcome awaits you; tell him you have married a beggar, who has too much pride to owe his subsistence to the bounty of a man who rejected his alliance in a situation of comparative affluence; and if future circumstances will allow it, preserve your unhappy connection with me a secret from the world, and endeavour to forget it yourself."

"Do you cast me off?" exclaimed she in an agony: "if you are a beggar, so am I – I ask no better fate than you must experience: I wish for no greater happiness or higher fortune than to share your destiny! Suffer me only to write to my mother to beg her forgiveness for having left her so precipitately."

"I am not barbarian enough to refuse it," returned he: "yet, dearest Sophy, let me conjure you to adopt my plan, and do not believe for a moment that I would consent to part with you without being compelled by a dreadful necessity. Do not write by this post; perhaps I may acquire courage to inform you of the extent of my imprudence – worse than imprudence – it was ingratitude and dishonour when you had committed your happiness to my care!"

"What do you mean?" she asked in great alarm.

"Don't question me now," cried he, in an accent of impatience; "perhaps I may shortly tell you all – at present I cannot – I am greatly disordered, my head throbs to distraction – I must try if the air will relieve me."

Before Mrs. Raymond could reply, he flew out of the house. Miss Swinney, who had been a very attentive observer of this enchanting scene, and had almost enjoyed the interesting distress and unfeigned misery of either party, now thought proper to console her weeping friend, declaring at the same time, that she had never beheld any thing so gracefully pathetic. "I am convinced, my beloved Sophia," continued she, "that you were born to shine in adversity: no – I never yet saw anguish so delightfully attractive! You are quite a heroine – don't wish, my dear, to be a happier one, for distress quite becomes you; so be comforted, my dearest friend; I am sure your adventures are infinitely interesting!"

"Ah, Selina," interrupted Mrs. Raymond, "I cannot find the charm in what we used to call adventures, which I had foolishly promised myself; and I would forego them all, to find myself established in my father's house, and poor Augustus high in his favour, and reconciled to himself."

Miss Swinney reprobated such tame degenerate sentiments, and after a few anxious conjectures from her friend, concerning the nature of the confession Raymond had promised to make, and some expressions of solicitude for his indisposition, they sauntered into a small garden adjoining the house. From this spot the eye could wander over the country to a considerable distance on the one side, and had only the ocean and the horizon for a boundary on the other. Miss Swinney seated herself in the attitude of a pensive heroine, on a bench the former inmates of the house had erected; and Sophia took two or three thoughtful turns to the extent of the enclosure, her mind still occupied by the intended discovery of her husband, who in an hour was seen half way up the cliff on his return home. His appearance did not denote great cheerfulness, but he seemed much more composed than when he had quitted her, and she was only restrained from flying to meet him by the fear of being importunate. His approach was much retarded by the winding of the road, intersected here and there by a cross path; and as her eyes followed the figure of Raymond, which was sometimes obscured at a sudden angle by a fence of blossoming myrtle, she observed a party of gentlemen on horseback, taking the bridle way[18] to some pleasure grounds surrounding a neighbouring seat.

Raymond did not regard them, till a loud halloo, followed by his own name most audibly pronounced, effectually awakened his attention. Sophia saw him start with great apparent emotion, and she fancied too, that the beheld the colour forsake his cheeks, and eagerly endeavoured to catch the accents she indistinctly heard as they floated on the breeze. Raymond spoke with gestures of violent agitation, and her bosom beat with redoubled alarm. He had said that the universe should not tempt him to approach the metropolis – "Perhaps," thought Sophia, "these men are from thence, and the meeting a most unpleasant one."

The event but too well justified this supposition; for almost at the moment it was formed, Raymond levelled a blow at one of the party, that threw him from his horse: terror prevented her from discerning any thing further, and the shriek it extorted from her, brought Miss Swinney to her assistance, as she was sinking to the earth; but whilst her arms supported poor Sophia, her tongue added to the anguish and horror she experienced.

"Oh my God!" exclaimed she, "is Raymond mad? He is struggling with four or five men! – Lord, I hope they are not Bailiffs!"

"Bailiffs!" repeated Sophia, in a faint accent.

"Oh no," resumed her inconsiderate companion, "I see now that they have the appearance of men of fashion. Good Heavens! he will certainly have twenty affairs of honour[19] upon his hands. – What will become of us!"

"Which way did he go?" cried Mrs. Raymond, starting wildly, "I will follow him!"

"Certainly," rejoined Miss Selina in a quick accent, "we ought to follow them; perhaps the adventure will not prove at the denouement so unpleasant – at least I am sure it must be interesting."

Sophia was already at a little gate that opened into the public path, which she flew down with such incautious swiftness, that a loose pebble rolling under her foot, twisted her ancle so violently, that the fainted with pain and sickness. Miss Swinney, whose form was not so light as that of her fair friend, and whose mind was far from being stimulated with the same anxious eagerness, had not moved with such celerity, and was at some distance when the accident happened; so that it was wholly attributed to excess of fine feeling, and the agony of a strained ancle not even suspected to have any share in the catastrophe.

The gentle Selina seated herself, therefore, by the side of the prostrate sufferer, and pronounced a soliloquy so moving, that it brought the tears into her own eyes: the more lovely ones of Sophia opened ere it was entirely ended, and scarcely knowing what she said, she entreated that a messenger might be dispatched to Raymond, to implore his immediate return.

When Miss Swinney discovered that she was unable to move, she sent a girl who had approached from curiosity, to desire assistance from their lodgings; but in answer to the request of her friend, professed that she knew not which way Raymond had taken. A man and woman servant, who had been hired since their residence in the island, ran hastily to the place on receiving the summons, and with their assistance Sophia was conveyed to her habitation, from whence a medical person was sent for.

The confinement thus procured by her anxiety and impatience, was insupportable to her, whilst she remained ignorant of the fate of her imprudent and hasty-tempered Raymond. She had dispatched different people in search of him, who returned without any intelligence, and at midnight he was still absent.

Miss Swinney, in spite of her wishes to achieve something sublime at a crisis so momentous, could not but be extremely touched at the watchful uneasiness of her friend, and sat by her bed-side talking of patience and composure, till poor Sophia, wearied almost beyond endurance, was tempted to quarrel with her, as well as with the unlucky destiny that pursued her.

At daybreak the invalid was extremely feverish, and the apothecary again sent for, who practised the usual ceremonies in such a case, and promised to compose a febrifuge[20] that would perform wonders. The ancle was found to be quite discoloured and extremely swelled, and Mrs. Raymond was wholly unable to endure the most trifling motion: but her agitation of mind was yet infinitely more painful; the epithets of barbarous, inhuman, and savage were levelled without economy at her husband by the gentle Selina, and again was every creature round the place, of whatever age or sex, dispersed in search of him.

At about nine in the morning he made his appearance, and Miss Swinney, who ran out to meet him, was shocked at his wild and haggard looks.

"They tell me," said he, "that my poor Sophy is dangerously ill – that she has fallen, and is much hurt; nothing, I think, but such intelligence could have again brought me here."

"Good God!" exclaimed Selina, "surely you could not have meditated to desert her! Where have you been?"

"In hell," replied he, fiercely, "a hell I might have escaped, had you not persuaded that dear unfortunate girl to follow me hither!"

He then flew past her, and entered the chamber of Sophia; his countenance was now rather flushed, and no longer appeared so terrific; and as she was assured of his safety, his presence considerably calmed her inquietude. He evaded giving any account of himself until she had taken some rest, which the servants had informed him she had passed the night without; and Sophia, soothed by the affection he evinced, soon sunk into a refreshing slumber. Raymond then no longer retained the small appearance of composure he had assumed, but gave himself up to the emotions that overpowered him, whilst Miss Swinney watched him with increasing apprehension and curiosity.

At length he left the room in an agony, and she hastily followed him in defiance of his reproaches, which she began very seriously to dread would be her portion from every party. Raymond had thrown himself on a chair, where she found him agitated by contending passions, every muscle of his face convulsed, and the whole countenance suffused with a deep crimson. Alarmed at the spectacle he exhibited, she burst into tears; and when he took her hand, and begged her forgiveness of any hasty expression he might have used in his anxiety and distress, she found that he was burning with fever. This discovery completed her terror, and her questions, tears, and commiseration produced a confession from Raymond that he had been insulted and challenged by a gentleman he had unexpectedly met the day before, whom he had, about an hour back, severely, but not dangerously, wounded in the *rencontre*[21] that ensued: he then conjured her to keep the circumstance from the knowledge of Sophia, which she promised, and in return entreated him to retire to an apartment which should instantly be prepared for him, that he might endeavour to repose; but this he peremptorily refused, alledging as a reason, that Mr. Estcourt, his friend, who had only the week before purchased a villa not half a mile distant, had extorted from him a promise to return and dine; and that it was most essential to his welfare not to disappoint his expectation: but as he was distressed to leave Sophia so much indisposed, he would overcome every obstacle, and be at home early in the evening.

Miss Swinney observed to him that it was yet only eleven o'clock.

"Is it so early?" exclaimed he, much surprised: "I will go immediately then, and settle some business I have to transact with him; perhaps he may release me from my engagement, and I shall then return before Sophia misses me."

Without waiting for a reply, he left the house, and hastened to that of Mr. Estcourt, who who had come down but two days before with some of his associates to view his purchase. Major Hangon was of the party, and in their ride the preceding morning, had recognized Raymond in a manner neither tinctured with goodwill, or even common civility. The unpaid debt of honour assailed the recollection of the fugitive, and shocked his pride; his answer was therefore dictated by his feelings, and partook of the disdain and contempt with which at that moment he viewed himself. The retort was too galling to be endured, and produced the fury which had urged Raymond to treat the Major with a violence not to be overlooked. Mr. Estcourt had endeavoured to divert the coming storm; but the personal insult rendering all interference vain, it was agreed that the parties should defer the meeting they both eagerly sought, until the next morning. Raymond, unable to return to his wife, withdrew to a house of public resort,[22] where he employed the remainder of the day and the whole of the ensuing night in writing letters, which he carefully sealed and directed, and deposited them in his pocket-book, that if he fell in the contest, they might not be overlooked. At length the hour of rendezvous arrived, and Raymond hastened to a retired part of Mr. Estcourt's grounds, which had been previously marked out to him. Hangon was wounded in the breast, and his opponent immediately desired a moment of private conversation with Mr. Estcourt, to whom he lamented his inability to discharge the debt due to him, and referred him to Mr. Mordaunt, as the person in whole hands his affairs were placed. Estcourt interrupted him with a declaration that he could never apply to the old fellow for a shilling, and desired, with great appearance of generosity, that the subject might never more be mentioned, unless Raymond should at any future time amply possess the power of liquidating the debt, and he find himself in a situation to want it. "When that is the case, my good fellow," continued he, "when you are at the top of the wheel, and I at the bottom, I shall very freely remind you of our agreement:

until that moment we will talk no more of it. – Stay, I have thought – suppose I pay Quye, and this sordid fellow Hangon, that you may come among us again."

Raymond rejected this uncommon proposition with warmth, as he had not the power, he said, of requiting such friendship, or even reimbursing the money.

"Oh, damn the money!" returned the other; "this plan, or some other like it, must do."

Raymond still however had fortitude to refuse his concurrence to this disinterested urgency, and Estcourt as firmly refused to take his negative.

"You shall dine with me," said he; "we shall be alone, and we will discuss the subject."

In short, he was not suffered to leave the house until he had promised to return at the dinner hour; he then wandered back to the place where he had passed the night, and on his way learned the accident and indisposition of Sophia, which overwhelmed him with still keener anxiety and remorse.

Chapter III

RAGE FOR ADVENTURES RATHER ABATED

WHEN Raymond left Miss Swinney, to keep his appointment, she returned to the chamber of her friend to watch by her; for Sophia had not yet awakened from the well-timed sleep into which she had fallen, and the gentle Selina taking from her pocket a new Novel which she had had the precaution to pack up with the clothes she had brought from home, entered into all the sublimity of pale moons, blue mists, gliding figures, hollow sighs, shaking tapestry, reverberating voices, nodding pictures, long corridors, deserted west towers, north towers, and south towers, ruined chapels, suspicious vaults, damp charnel-houses, great clocks striking twelve, wood embers expiring, dying lamps, and total darkness.[23]

So much was the imagination of the romantic Miss Swinney occupied by so brilliant a succession of interesting subjects, that she forgot the flight of time; and had not Mrs. Raymond's maid entered to enquire where she chose to have the cloth laid for her dinner, she would not have recollected that it was rather necessary to eat, to enable people to gaze with rapture upon fine prospects, which fade terribly upon the eye that is longing to fix upon a loaf of brown bread with the homely accompaniments of ale and cheese, for the lack of better cheer.

The short conversation that passed, though uttered in a low voice, awakened the invalid, who asked if Raymond were in the room, and receiving a negative from Miss Swinney, enquired if he had gone out. The woman replied that he had come home about an hour back, to dress, and hearing that her Lady was sleeping, would not suffer her to be disturbed, but left word that he was unavoidably engaged to dine out, and should return early.

Sophia endeavoured to be satisfied with this intimation: the repose she had taken had much refreshed her, her feverish symptoms had disappeared, and she begged her friend would send up her dinner from the eating-room. When it was announced to be ready, the gentle Selina descended, and sat down to table with a mind entirely divided between the situation of her imprudent, but interesting companions, and the situation of the still more imprudent heroine, the second volume of whose captivating adventures she had popped into her pocket to supply to her the absence of Raymond and Sophia. Having attended to Mrs. Raymond's wish respecting her share of the repast, she dismissed the servant, and read and ate by turns, till at length she was surprised, on looking at her watch, to find that she had remained nearly two hours with the dinner before her. She therefore rung to have it removed, and with the fascinating book still in her hand, walked with great dignity to the sitting-room, that she might, undisturbed, descend with her heroine down some very dark and broken stairs, which communicated with the young lady's bed chamber by a supernumerary door she generally found open in the morning:[24] a circumstance of such mysterious yet striking import engrossed every feeling of Miss Swinney's heart, and she resolved to finish the chapter before she ascended to her sick friend. This humane intention was however prevented by the appearance of a very fashionable looking stranger, who without much ceremony entered the room from a sashed door that opened into the garden.

The fair reader looked up, and the fictitious heroine vanished from her imagination, to give place to the heroic Selina, thus on the point, she fondly hoped, of commencing her own career of adventures. The intruder wore an air of ton, and expressed himself with elegance, that is, he was not troubled with any embarrassment in introducing himself to his admiring auditor; and in the explanation he condescended to give, he uttered, par hazard, the most brilliant and novel terms and methods of arranging sentences which had been gathered from the finest speeches in the very last Session of Parliament, and the most florid harangues at the bar, dashed with an occasional cant phrase or expression, picked up God knows where.

Miss Selina on her side, imagined that she listened to him with blended dignity and softness; that the majesty of conscious virtue was meliorated by the blushes of modesty; that her mien was so engaging that it invited love and admiration, whilst it repelled every idea which was not consonant with the most profound and pure respect and veneration – in short, that she possessed every magnetic and repellant grace, which always belong to heroines of the first class.

She was not indeed so wholly occupied by these reflections as not to understand, from the avowal of her visiter, that his name was Estcourt, and a sudden fear struck her that all was not right with Raymond; but the apprehension vanished with equal promptitude, amidst a train of the most seducing expectations, which the adulation of the gentleman produced. He told her that her irresistible beauty, joined to the charming generosity, fortitude, and good sense her aspect denoted, perfectly well announced her to him.

"My friend," added Mr. Estcourt, "is well justified in having so suddenly abandoned his former associates for such fascination: for my own part, I find it already but too *obtaining*.[25] But I will, not *commit myself*, and incur your displeasure, by laying my envy open to your observation. I presented myself here merely to inform you that Raymond found himself indisposed soon after dinner, and I would not suffer him to walk home till he had dissipated his head-ach by repose: so I stole hither myself to adjust any uneasiness you might suffer from his absence."

During this harangue, Miss Swinney gave the rein to the most animated and but ill-suppressed delight, which her conception of his meaning created in her romantic mind: she had no suspicion that she was mistaken for Mrs. Raymond, but imagined that the friend who had given up all his former associates for so much fascination, was some secret swain who was perfectly contented to keep himself *incognito*, and to feed his moonlight love with walking round the house she occupied, alone, at midnight, stretching out his arms towards her window, and catching a glimpse of her shadow as she approached it; a piece of good fortune he might very probably often have enjoyed, as the gentle Selina always chose that hour to indulge her most pleasing reveries, in imitation of some very illustrious patterns; nor did she fail to loosen her long tresses, both those which had originally grown upon her own head, and those which had grown upon the heads of other people, and become her's by purchase. – With her loose tresses therefore, flowing over her shoulders, and a loose white robe flowing round her person, Miss Swinney was wont to fix herself near her window, which she threw up to enjoy the cool breeze; and having forgot herself in the enthusiasm of her ideas, would often stand an hour, with hands folded over her bosom, and her eyes cast up, till at length, no form being seen to issue from behind any thicket, or glide from under any plane-tree, she recovered her recollection, and shut her window, as other heroines do, almost perished with cold.

She was extremely eager to learn who this gentle love-lorn shepherd was; but to enquire would have been the height of indecorum, and she settled in the exultation of her triumph, that he was not to be the successful swain by half a dozen at least. Her imagination had already carried her amidst cloud-capped hills covered with lofty pines, and gorgeous palaces, where amidst ranges of massy pillars stood dozens of lamps, all of them on silver tripods, and each so disposed as to cast a picturesque light upon some statue of exquisite workmanship.[26]

The similarity of her own hastily imagined adventures, to those of which she had been reading but a few minutes before, made her cast her eyes upon the book that still remained in her hand; and almost unconscious of what she did, she drew from her pocket a card, and placed it in the volume, to mark the page at which she had been interrupted. Estcourt remarked the circumstance, and taking up the book, opened it in a careless way, and read the ticket, which contained her own name and address. His curiosity did not escape the vigilance of the lady, and she instantly concluded that the *fascinated friend* would profit by the discovery, had not his own diligent and eager enquiries already forestalled it.

Mr. Estcourt in a few minutes departed, and Selina, in a flutter of spirits, reviewed all that had passed: her visiter had mentioned his envy of the unknown swain, which at first, rather puzzled her, but she recollected almost instantly that he had himself almost avowed his love, and as this passion is invariably accompanied by jealousy, it was quite natural that Mr. Estcourt should despond, and suspect a rival of superior good fortune.

In short, the lady had now fallen into such a train of thinking, that it is impossible to say where her surmises would have ended, had not Mrs. Raymond's bell made her recollect that such a person existed. Ashamed of having neglected her so long, she flew upstairs, and replied to a half-grave, half-jesting rebuke from the invalid, with the most animated and enthusiastic expressions of eternal friendship; and was proceeding to inform her of the visiter who had unexpectedly detained her below, when Sophia's maid entered to announce the return of her master, who almost immediately followed her into the room.

Mrs. Raymond, who had been very anxious to see him, was shocked at his appearance; for his countenance was extremely flushed, his eyes heavy, and his gait unsteady: yet she had no other suspicion than that he had been prevailed upon to circulate the bottle too freely at Mr. Estcourt's table.

After some affectionate and solicitous enquiries into the situation of Sophia, he declared himself rather indisposed, and withdrew to the apartment prepared for him, making a sign as he left that of his wife, that Miss Swinney should follow him; and as the fully expected some tender remembrance either from her lately known, or her unknown admirer, she eagerly obeyed the intimation.

Before they had time to descend the stairs, her patience was exhausted, and she demanded what embassy he was charged with.

"Embassy!" repeated Raymond, "I cannot understand you; but I perceive that you, as well as Sophia, suppose me to be in a state of intoxication. You are mistaken; but I do not wish her to be undeceived at present, lest her consequent anxiety should procure a return of fever. I was ill in the morning, but could not resist the pressing invitation of Estcourt, who is," he added vehemently, "the most generous and disinterested of men! such hearts as his the world is far from abounding with. I endeavoured while with him, to conceal my indisposition; but the effort was a vain one, and he insisted, before we transacted the business for which we had met, that I should try to procure an hour's repose, which he well knew I had neither leisure nor inclination to attempt last night. – Believe me, Selina, instead of having passed the afternoon as you suspect, I have spent the last four hours in an agony of mind and body, society, instead of alleviating, would have increased. Do not mention this to Sophia; continue your generous attentions to her, I beseech you; and when the apothecary calls, let him step to me when he has seen her."

Miss Swinney assented, and Raymond, quite exhausted, hastened to his chamber.

Sophia still continuing in her error, was satisfied on hearing some time after that he was in a found sleep – a report which he desired might be made to her; but in fact he was too ill to quit his bed, and when the medical person saw him, who attended Mrs. Raymond, he appeared to think his indisposition attended with considerable danger. The following morning justified his apprehensions, and he desired that more attendance might be called in. The patient had lost blood on the preceding evening, and the apothecary thought it necessary that the operation should be immediately repeated; but the effect was not so satisfactory as he had expected.

Miss Swinney, completely frightened from her heroism, readily attended to the hint of obtaining the opinion of a Physician, which she begged Mr. Astell would procure: she just retained recollection enough to desire the servants would agree with her in telling Mrs. Raymond that their master had been compelled to hurry to Portsmouth before she awoke, and had desired her to be informed that business of the utmost importance would detain him, he feared, several days.

She then flew to the chamber of poor Raymond, both to see that he was properly attended, and to induce him if possible, to write a line in confirmation of the excuse she had invented, to quiet Sophia's apprehensions. She found him however, raving in a strong delirium, in which he had almost overpowered his servant and the apothecary, who had been obliged to call in the man of the house to his aid.

Miss Swinney beheld his outrageous struggles with horror; and fearing that the loud exclamations and threats of vengeance which accompanied them, would reach the ears of Sophia, felt at once all the anxious misery of her situation, conscious as she could not help feeling that her advice and persuasions had dragged her friend from the peaceable roof of her parents, and endangered the life of the unfortunate husband. A man on horseback had been dispatched to Cowes for a London Physician of eminence who happened to be there; and as he was not expected for some time, the terrified Selina was obliged to quiet her impatience to learn what his fiat would be, and endeavour to compose her countenance, to lull the suspicions of Mrs. Raymond, whilst she told the preconcerted tale: and so well had she practised the art of throwing her features into every form caprice had dictated, that she succeeded tolerably in the effort. Sophia was far from being at ease however, respecting her husband, whose promised confession, whose reluctance to suffer her to write to her mother, and subsequent conduct, tormented her recollection, and rendered her suspicious.

At length the Physician arrived; and Miss Swinney followed him into the chamber of poor Raymond, with all the real tremor of suspensive terror she had often assumed on much less important occasions. His sense of the danger of his patient even exceeded that of Mr. Astell. The disorder was a violent inflammatory fever; and short as the period was, Selina learned that the following day would most probably determine the fate of this unhappy young man, whose wild unconscious ejaculations accused her of having murdered him. The Physician observing her consternation, and having heard the aggravating circumstance of Mrs. Raymond's indisposition, advised her, after a preliminary apology for the freedom he was taking, to write immediately to the natural friends[27] of the young couple, that their presence might lighten the anxious talk which had so unexpectedly fallen to her, and that they might be satisfied, if the crisis should be what he feared, that every advice and attendance which their own solicitude would have pointed out, had been procured for the benefit of the patient.

The urgent gravity of the Doctor co-operated with her own reflections to urge her compliance with this advice, and she immediately wrote to Mr. Beauclerc, enclosing the note in a letter to her father, imploring his forgiveness for herself, and conjuring him to forward the lines to Mr. Beauclerc, which she left unsealed for his perusal, should he not be in town.

The Physician took the charge of the packet, which he considerately promised to send instantly to Portsmouth, and to procure it to be dispatched by an express the same afternoon. He would return, he said, early the next morning, to see what further could be done for the invalid, and having conferred with Mr. Astell in private, hastened away.

The apothecary at her earnest intercession, remained with poor Raymond the whole night, attended by both the servants; and as the chamber of the patient was only separated from that of Miss Swinney by a partition of deal,[28] she found it impossible to close her eyes, from his vehement ravings. She eagerly listened for coherence in his sentences, but heard only the wildest effusions of delirium, in which real distresses and real subjects of accusation were so blended with imaginary horrors and injuries, that she was doubly shocked to hear them: fortunately however, he appeared uncommonly to dread the presence and reproaches of his unfortunate Sophia, so he called her, and on that account scarcely ever suffered his voice to rise much above its usual pitch, so that Mrs. Raymond could not distinguish any sound to alarm her.

At length towards the dawn his accents sunk into a murmur, and then wholly ceased. Miss Swinney hoped that he had fallen into a slumber, and found herself impelled by an irresistible anxiety to discover if her flattering expectations were well founded, but hesitated entering his room from the fear of disturbing him. She had thrown herself upon the bed without undressing; and after some moments of irresolution, on hearing Mr. Astell speaking to the servants, she ventured to steal in. A few hours had changed poor Raymond almost beyond belief: no hectic now flushed his burning cheek, no treacherous fire sparkled in his distempered eye; but all was pale, ghastly, and inanimate, save a convulsive spasm that, at short intervals, distorted his features.

The apothecary looked very grave, and in answer to her enquiring motion, shook his head. She wept from the compassion such an object could not fail to inspire. – She had beheld the same man but one short month back, elated with youth, health, and affluence – the envy of some, the admiration of others; flattered by the high consideration of his equally thoughtless companions, by the more sedulous and artful adulation of those who studied to dash him from this height to scorn and poverty, and finally by the success of his concealed addresses to Miss Beauclerc, which gratified at once his vanity, his inclination, and his revenge upon her family, who had harshly rejected his more open pretensions.

Seduced by the force of pernicious examples, by the sanction of a too pervading practice, and by the insinuations of those who had perhaps themselves been the dupes to anterior villainy, he turned over his inheritance to gamblers, and plunged into a vortex which engulphed his probity, his humanity, his honour, peace, and life.

Chapter IV

TWO HEROINES TAKEN DOWN FROM THEIR STILTS

EARLY the next morning, the physician's post-chaise again stopped at the garden door, from whence Mrs. Raymond could not be disturbed by the sound of the wheels. Miss Swinney learned from him, that her packet had by this time reached the metropolis, and felt at once relief and terror from the intelligence. When he walked up stairs to examine the situation of the patient, her anxiety overcame all attention to form, and she accompanied him to the bed-side of poor Raymond, who was entirely insensible, and she saw that the convulsions were stronger and more frequent.

The physician wrote, but avowed that he was almost hopeless as to the effect of the prescription, declaring that he had scarcely ever before witnessed so rapid a progression of dangerous symptoms. Selina shuddered, and Mr. Astell increased her wretchedness by saying, that he had been sent for to a case of urgency, and hinting that he could no longer wholly neglect his general business. He told her that he must leave the gentleman for a few hours; but he would lend his assistant to attend him in the interim, and undertook to procure a nurse to relieve Mrs. Raymond's maid, who would be obliged to attend her mistress in the day. This was scarcely arranged, and the physician departed, when Sophia's bell announced that she was more watchful than had been expected. As Miss Swinney sometimes rose with the sun, because heroines are always matinal, she did not fear alarming her unhappy friend by appearing dressed at so early an hour, and answered the summons instead of the attendant, whose looks of fatigue, and countenance of terror might have betrayed the mournful secret.

After a hasty salutation, Mrs. Raymond enquired if she had not heard the step of her husband about five minutes back, descending the stairs. Miss Swinney coloured at this unexpected question, but almost instantly recollecting herself, replied, that it must have been William whom her friend had heard, for she had seen him descend the staircase, and open the garden door at the time mentioned. Sophia looked dissatisfied with this explanation, and after a pause, expressed a strong inclination to rise. Miss Swinney was now so much alarmed, that her caution forsook her, and she opposed the wish with an earnestness that confirmed poor Mrs. Raymond's vague suspicions.

DOI: 10.4324/9781003175582-6

"Something dreadful has happened to Augustus!" exclaimed she. "I will see him, even if you refuse me your aid – I will crawl to him without assistance!" and to execute this threat, she suddenly threw herself on the floor, with only a thin wrapping gown about her.

Miss Swinney still more frightened, rung the bell with violence, and the maid appeared, with a countenance bursting to disclose what the presence of her mistress restrained her from uttering. The efforts of poor Sophia soon yielded to the superior strength of her woman and Selina, and she was again placed upon her bed, almost fainting with pain and anxious terror.

The attendant fancying that she was insensible, because her eyes were closed, exclaimed to Miss Swinney, in a tone rendered louder than usual by an hysterical tremor – "Lord, Ma'am, my poor master is going off in the vi'lentest convulsions I ever see! Oh Christ! here's my poor dear mistress too – there's death in her face!"

Sophia had indeed for a time ceased to breathe; for the first part of the woman's speech had reached her ear, and the sudden intelligence had banished all sensation of wretchedness and even of existence. The assistance of Miss Swinney and the maid was for some time ineffectual; and when with difficulty they had recovered her to life, they were again obliged to restrain by force her frantic efforts to fly to her dying Augustus. The result of the contest was a succession of faintings, which left her unable any further to express her wishes or intentions; and after a tedious interval, Selina ventured to leave her unhappy friend, that she might learn from the medical assistant, if she could still cherish a lingering hope of Raymond's recovery.

Mr. Astell had again returned to him; but far from lessening her inquietude, he expressed his apprehensions that the patient could not possibly hold out till the friends she had written to, arrived. This idea completed the misery of her situation: reflections the most harassing and unwelcome rushed upon her; – but for her instigations, Sophia would never have consented to leave the house of indulgent parents, to marry against their advice and wishes – but for her persuasions, Raymond would now most probably have been on his projected voyage to India, in good health, and with reasonable hopes of returning to Europe, and seeing better days – but for her, his wife would then have been still under the protection of a mother, who, whatever might be her characteristic foibles and follies, had endeavoured to extend to her child a mother's cares, and of a father, who shutting his hand to all the world beside, forgot his avarice to see her happy. In short, Miss Selina felt a dreadful consciousness that her influence over her friend had been exerted to conduct her to misery, perhaps equally with her husband to an untimely grave; and that the result of her extravagant flights and pernicious advice had brought sorrow and anguish upon the heads of those who had weakly listened to her, and remorse, perhaps opprobrium, upon herself. Stung with such ideas, the young lady, ever hasty in forming her resolutions, dropped upon her knees, and took Heaven to witness a hasty vow to abandon her romantic opinions, and conform to those of her parents, who could not as yet boast of the due obedience and subjection of their hopeful daughter.

The predictions of Mr. Astell were justified by the event: poor Raymond expired in the presence of the physician, two hours before a hack-chaise brought his father-in-law and Mr. Swinney to the door; and Miss Selina took refuge from the interview she had sufficient reason to dread, in the apartment of her widowed friend, whom she found half dressed – a task she had without assistance resolutely undertaken, that she might learn the worst her apprehensions but too well whispered. But the extreme pain and inconvenience of her lame foot had compelled her to rest for a moment before she could crawl to the door, and in this interval, the entrance of Miss Swinney prevented the effort.

"Oh my dear creature!" exclaimed she, rushing forward, "I shall die with fright and alarm – your papa and mine are arrived – how shall I appear before them?"

"My father!" repeated Mrs. Raymond in a faint accent of surprise, and with increased agitation of spirits.

As she was speaking, he entered the room, presenting a countenance in which compassion and distress were strongly marked; and folding his daughter to his bosom, called her his dear Sophy, his poor widowed girl. She started at the last appellation, and after a severe struggle with her anguish at thus having her worst surmises confirmed, burst into a flood of tears that considerably relieved her; and soothed by the tenderness of her father, her grief was more calm, than from her former violence of emotion might have been expected.

She wished much to take a last farewell of her luckless Raymond, but the entreaties and representations of Mr. Beauclerc prevailed over this inclination, strong as it was; and at his earnest intercession, she suffered herself to be removed in two days to a retired lodging at Hithe,[29] to escape from the curious observation, which the almost inevitable circulation of some part of the story produced.

Mr. Swinney remained at the cottage, to ensure proper respect to the remains of the deceased, and to arrange all pecuniary affairs. The letters Raymond had written on the night preceding his duel with Major Hangon, had been given to the care of Miss Selina, with other papers apparently of some consequence, taken from his pocket by the attentive kindness of Mr. Astell, who could not avoid observing that they might have fallen into improper hands but for this precaution.

Mr. Mordaunt was written to for instructions concerning the interment of his late ward, whose father having resided near thirty years in Lisbon, to attend to some commercial concerns, had lost all traces of the different branches of his family, with whom he never corresponded; and having sent his only child Augustus to England, to receive his education, and imbibe the principles and language of his own countrymen, the young man found himself at the death of his father, totally destitute of family connections: a circumstance Mr. Mordaunt accounted for, by informing him that the nearest relations of his deceased parent had emigrated to America. His mother, who had not survived his birth, was a Portuguese orphan of considerable beauty, but of an obscure family, with whom the elder Mr. Raymond preserved no communication. Mr. Mordaunt therefore was the only person who appeared to take any interest in the fate of Augustus; and he had discharged his trust with an integrity and zeal that procured him the dislike of the thoughtless young man, and occasioned an estrangement between them when he became of age: yet this upright man of the law heard of his destiny with unfeigned sorrow, and prepared to perform the last duties of friendship, though that friendship had been chilled by neglect, and repelled by unkindness. He left his own affairs to the management of his agents, and hastened to the place where Raymond had breathed his last. He was buried in the island, and a modest stone marked the name and years of the youth thus snatched from a world, in which his fate a few months back had appeared so enviable.

This mournful ceremony over, Mr. Mordaunt, who had already received the letter which the writer had meant to be a posthumous one, was assisted by Mr. Swinney in adjusting the pecuniary demands upon the young people. On examining the papers of the deceased, a memorandum was found, in a hand scarcely legible, which intimated that he had that day executed a bond in favour of Mr. Estcourt, for £9400; and as the nature of the debt was too well guessed at, Mr. Mordaunt was highly exasperated with this pretended friend, for the considerable share he appeared to have had in the plunder and ruin of the imprudent Raymond. His coadjutor, who knew that no settlement could have been made of the lady's fortune from the privacy of the marriage, consulted whether it would not be advisable to preserve it, if possible, a secret, that so considerable a property might not be wrested from Mr. Beauclerc's family, or to prevent any litigation and unpleasant exposure of circumstances which would be better buried in oblivion.

Mr. Mordaunt did not immediately reply to this proposition, which he said was of a very delicate nature, and required much consideration; but every hope of putting it in practice had nearly been frustrated by the unlooked-for appearance of Mr. Estcourt two days after the interment of his dear friend, who demanding to see Mr. Swinney, addressed him by his name, and condoled, in the language of ceremonious regret, for his recent loss.

"I have had the honour of introducing myself to your fair daughter, Sir," continued he; "and I was induced by her merit and amiable qualities, to ensure poor Raymond the enjoyment of his good fortune, by taking all his debts of honour upon myself. They appeared indeed to be to an alarming amount, but my humanity overcame all prudential motives, and in return I had this bond forced upon me as a recognition of the obligation, as he foresaw perhaps, that I was likely to become the sacrifice of my friendship for him and his lovely wife. Raymond's death is an inexpressible inconvenience to me, for I am called upon to pay on his account, five thousand pounds more than I at this moment possess, and I have actually only a week allowed me to raise the money in. – I am far from wishing at such a moment, to make any distressing claim; but I am urged by the unlucky predicament in which I find myself, to make use of some intelligence which reached me by mere accident, that your daughter, Mr. Raymond's widow, is possessed of a very ample independent fortune, and I should hope she has too much respect for the memory of the deceased, to suffer –"

Mr. Swinney interrupted him, and was on the point of making some warm reply, both to reprehend the honourable gambler, and to undeceive him, but Mr. Mordaunt prevented him, and entreated that he would withdraw for a few moments – a request the supposed father-in-law complied with. He then remonstrated with Mr. Estcourt upon the indelicacy of introducing such a business in a moment so distressing, and promised upon his word, that he would endeavour to enforce any legal claim he might have upon the fortune of Mr. Swinney's daughter when they met in town: and in less than a month, he added, he trusted the affair would be settled to the satisfaction of every honest man.

The character of Mr. Mordaunt was well known to the man of fashion, in whose family he was esteemed for his equity, and the able and diligent manner with which he transacted all their concerns in the line of his profession; and Estcourt of all men, least wished or expected to encounter him at the present moment. He yielded therefore very readily to his representations, and relying upon the promise given, withdrew extremely rejoiced that he had so well begun a negociation, of which he felt, all bronzed[30] as he was, rather ashamed, and in truth, not without much reason: for not satisfied with having bought up the play-debts of poor Raymond for a mere song, which he did on hearing that he had privately married a City heiress, he had taken advantage of the indisposition, the confusion of mind, and half distraction of the unfortunate young man, and fearless of premature detection, had caused the bond to be drawn up for nineteen thousand four hundred pounds, instead of the sum marked in Raymond's memorandum, which, ill as he was, he had made on returning home, that his generous and worthy friend might have that additional testimony superadded to the other, of the reality of his claim, should his indisposition prove fatal, of which he felt a presage.

In the evening Mr. Mordaunt passed over to Hithe, where Mr. Beauclerc was enabled to give a better account of the health and spirits of his daughter than he had hoped to hear. He was then informed of the claim made by Estcourt, and of the memorandum of his son-in-law, which appeared to be ten thousand pounds less than the nefarious bond he had seen; and concluding with the information of the mistake which had arisen not unnaturally, as to the lady recently widowed, he advised Mr. Beauclerc to suffer the affair to rest until they met in town, when he hoped to adjust it properly. He then bade him farewell, saying that he must travel all night, as his presence was urgently required at home.

The avarice of Mr. Beauclerc was alarmed at the intelligence he had received, and he very much approved the plan of Selina's father, to profit by the mistake which had gone abroad, and preserve with the fortune of his own daughter, the secret of her connection with poor Raymond. He immediately communicated his wishes, and the circumstance which had given rise to them, to Sophia, lest she should unadvisedly betray herself; but it had a very different effect upon her than he had intended, for she insisted that the memory of her beloved Augustus should be preserved, free from blemish, and therefore she declared that the debt should be discharged, as far at least as her fortune could liquidate it.

Miss Swinney was alarmed at the indication of such a measure, as she dreaded the effect it might have on the mind of Mr. Beauclerc, whose good offices, she learned, had been very requisite to induce her father to receive her again into his house and favour. She now wished the initiatory adventures of her friend to terminate as smoothly as possible; that her share in promoting them might not be too prominent in the recollection of all those who felt themselves aggrieved by it. Since the discovery of poor Raymond's desperate affairs, she had secretly loaded his memory with the charges of selfishness and duplicity, entirely forgetting that he meant to have acted differently, had not her officious and never-sleeping zeal at once forwarded his destiny, and the misery of his wife.

Sophia warmly urged her father to write to Estcourt, and undeceive him; and Miss Swinney to avert a storm, suddenly resorted to the letter of Raymond, the only one of those found in his pocket-book, which had not been delivered according to the address, in the hope that its contents would furnish argument in favour of the opinion of Mr. Beauclerc; an expectation founded on the earnest and repeated advice of Augustus to his wife, to preserve their marriage a secret, if possible, from the world. This letter had been hitherto detained from her, in the fear that her affliction would be increased by reading his posthumous adieu; and her father now consented that it should be produced, in the idea of finding some clue to discover the evident villainy of his supposed friend.

Mrs. Raymond received it with much emotion, and having retired to read it, left Miss Swinney in a pitiable state of apprehension and curiosity. It was two long hours ere this agitation was quieted, for so long she suffered poor Sophia to remain unmolested in her own apartment: and then, unable to endure the torture of further suspense, she tapped at the door for admittance. Mrs. Raymond opened it after an interval of a few seconds, and her eyes gave evidence of the manner in which those two hours had been passed by her. Those of the gentle Selina betrayed so pointedly the eager wish she experienced to learn the parting sentiments and injunctions of Augustus, that Mrs. Raymond could not fail to understand them; but being desirous of paying the compliment of a first communication to her father, she begged Miss Swinney to take the letter to him, and to excuse her appearance at the dinner table.

Whether the folds of the epistle were conveniently pliant in the hands of the ambassadress, Miss Selina alone could disclose; she entered the sitting room however, in which she had left Mr. Beauclerc, with a countenance of exultation, and possibly from a prophetic inspiration, informed him that her dear friend's overstrained notions of probity would now be happily combatted by the dying request of her husband, which no doubt would have a proper weight.

Miss Swinney had not guessed wrong, for poor Raymond having written the letter before he went forth to encounter the vengeance of Major Hangon, had strongly prohibited Sophia from publishing their connexion.

Mr. Beauclerc was so much delighted with the prospect of retaining his daughter's fortune, that he overlooked two or three hints which the posthumous letter contained, to the prejudice of Miss Swinney's prudence, and assured her with renewed energy, that he would settle her re-admission into the house of her father, to her satisfaction.

In a week Sophia was able to travel, and Mr. Beauclerc conducted her immediately to a summer villa he had purchased about a year back at her request, between Teddington and Hampton-wick,[31] where her mother was waiting to receive and pardon her; and Miss Swinney, at her earnest entreaty, was accompanied to town by Mr. Beauclerc himself: yet whatever influence his superior fortune and consequence might give him with her family, the fair Selina could only obtain the entire forgiveness of her justly offended mother, by consenting to espouse a suitor she had hitherto rejected with disdain, because he was an odious middle aged man, of a plain person, and moderate income depending upon his industry, and because he was an attorney, and lived in Chancery-Lane.[32] All these circumstances, so shocking to her refined ideas, would still have been irremediable bars to her obedience, had she not fortunately recollected her hasty vow to conform to the future wishes and injunctions of papa and mama. This timely remembrance immediately altered her mode of conduct; she signified her submissive resignation, and decked in all the subduing paraphernalia of pensive woe, assumed a downcast look, and was the gentle victim to tyrannic commands.

In three weeks she became Mrs. Ellinger, and was rather consoled on the occasion, when she reflected that her new name was much preferable to the former, which had too often wounded her ears from its common and vulgar sound. But alas! the abode of the husband, far from being decorated with elegance to receive the bride, exhibited in the dingy wainscoted apartment the mortified Selina chose to call her drawing-room, a set of old-fashioned, worn-out, horse-hair, mahogany chairs; and an antique black escrutoire,[33] with red tape sticking out at the loose hinges, to denote the profession of its owner.[34] She considered however, that it would not be decorous to begin an immediate innovation, and consoled herself with writing a narrative of her vexations and distresses to her widowed friend, who had not yet visited the metropolis, but remained with her mother at Avelines, which was the name of their house.

Mr. Beauclerc had left them, to consult Mr. Mordaunt in town upon the means of evading the payment of the bond in the possession of Estcourt: but though the man of law was unwilling that he should succeed in obtaining so considerable a sum as must be given up when Mrs. Raymond became of age, he was delicate as to the method which might be taken to withhold it. He rather wished that an open discussion should take place, of the circumstances relative to the business, and he had then little doubt, he said, but that the family of Mr. Estcourt, who were people of strict honour and probity, would interfere to accommodate the affair, and bring the debt within the limits of reason and probability; that is, that the young man should be reimbursed what sums he could prove to have paid for the deceased, no matter on what pretence, for he had reason to suppose the amount would not be considerable; and thus any unpleasant public discussion or accusation relating to a character and conduct which humanity should now be silent upon, would be avoided; and what was yet more important, Mrs. Raymond might then reject the ridiculous plan of a mysterious concealment, which would almost infallibly blight her character after the decided step she had taken.

Mr. Beauclerc listened to this proposition without any inclination to put it in practice; for he suspected that it would occasion him to disburse more money than he was willing to part with, and any chicanery and concealment was to him much preferable, if it promised to be the means of saving even a few hundred pounds. In proportion as his daughter recovered her health, his tenderness gave place to the ruling passion, and he secretly execrated and fretted at the sum this cursed freak[35] of Sophy had already, and was still likely to cost him.

Before the affair was in the least settled, Mr. Mordaunt was unexpectedly compelled to leave town; and in his absence, as Estcourt did not wish for his interference, he called at the house of Mr. Swinney, and again presented his bond, with a hint that, in consideration of immediate payment, he would not insist upon the entire sum stated in it. In this emergency Mr. Ellinger was applied to, to negociate the business, who, with some management of incident, contrived to get the bond in his possession upon the payment of eight hundred pounds, which was stated with truth to be the whole of Miss Swinney's fortune – a fact Mr. Estcourt was too well assured of, as he had only the day before examined a will in Doctors Commons,[36] which bequeathed to Sarah Swinney (for alas! Selina was merely an embellishment) eight hundred pounds, to be given into her own possession at the age of twenty and one years, as a mark of the regard and affection of her aunt, Dorothy Swinney, of Barbican.[37] And though this sum considerably exceeded what Mr. Estcourt had parted with on speculation, yet he was so much enraged with Raymond's London valet, at a discovery so little tallying with his officious information, that he discharged him roughly from his own service, into which he had taken him, not only to reward this intelligence, but in consideration of many useful hints he had previously favoured him with. But his anger and disappointment were not alone excited by the unexpected failure of this resource; for a decided torrent of mischances overtaking him at once, and the spotted cubic gods[38] who had hitherto been propitious, becoming invariably adverse to their votary, the house and grounds in the Isle of Wight were parted with in the same style of dispatch they were purchased in, and the bond given up for the sum specified in the will of Mrs. Dorothy Swinney, of Barbican: Mr. Beauclerc eagerly produced the money; Mr. Ellinger, as attorney for the young lady, very gravely paid it, and both parties separated, tolerably well satisfied that the individual efforts of each to impose upon the credulity of the other, had not entirely failed.

This important affair settled, Mr. Beauclerc returned to Avelines, which he found both his wife and daughter still unwilling to quit, that they might avoid the sneering enquiries, and the half-pointed impertinence of the circle in which they had been accustomed to move in London. At Avelines, Sophia had leisure for reflection, and the present tone of her mind did not allow her to repel those which her situation gave rise to: in compliance with the last request of her regretted Raymond, which alone could have influenced her, she had reassumed her father's name, and locked up her wedding-ring, with the picture of her husband, and a few lighter memorials of his attachment. The natural vivacity of her character seemed to have sunk under the disappointment of her first hopes, and she appeared to have no further wish, than to pass the remainder of her life in her present quiet abode.

The fair Selina, on the contrary, was almost in despair at the humiliating insipidity of her existence: her husband, far from being refined by his alliance with her, seemed to have acquired a double portion of impenetrable stupidity, and her utmost eloquence could not banish the old escrutoire from her drawing-room, nor could she prevail so far as to procure an exchange of the detestable clumsy mahogany chairs for modern *fauteuils*.[39] As for Chelsea hangings, pier glasses, girandoles, Rumford stoves, Lucas's screens, turtleshell work tables, and canopied sofas, they were entirely unattainable, to the utter annihilation of her refinement;[40] Mr. Ellinger too, talked very seriously of wearing a close curled black bob.[41] Selina almost sunk under such an accumulation of misfortunes, and was only recalled to a pleasing consciousness of delicate exigence by her correspondence with her dearest and most hapless friend, the mysterious widow.

Chapter V

HEROIC HOPES REVIVED BY ADVENTURES IN PERSPECTIVE

FATE had not, however, dealt quite so hardly by Mrs. Ellinger, as she had found reason to fear; for as she was on the point of giving up the most glimmering prospect of future sentimental and elegant distress, she received a pressing entreaty from Sophia, that she would fly to Avelines on an affair of the most serious import. Her husband, who now transacted a considerable portion of business for Mr. Beauclerc, did not think proper to oppose the summons, which was sanctioned by Sophia's mother, and Mrs. Ellinger obeyed it with alacrity.

At Avelines she learned a secret, which Mrs. Beauclerc had hitherto desired her daughter to conceal from every one, that no whispered rumour might steal abroad, and in the hope perhaps that accident might prevent the necessity of bringing it in any degree to light: in short, the gentle Selina found that her widowed friend was on the point of becoming a mother. This delightful intelligence set every heroic faculty in motion. – What was to be done? – was she to persuade Mr. Ellinger to suffer her to adopt the dear baby, and bring it in due season into the family as her own? – Was she, as her own time of confinement approached, to withdraw, and produce herself again to the world with twins? Whatever was to be done, she would do; she only entreated that she might be allowed an interest in the dear lovely infant, and that she might likewise be permitted to give it a name, with the approbation of her amiable Sophia, who could not return an immediate assent to the proposition, because she was not present at the conference, lest it might too much agitate her spirits.

Mr. Beauclerc gently checked her flight of fancy, by reminding her that whatever she obligingly undertook to do, in order to accommodate to the peculiar situation of his daughter, must receive the entire approbation of Mr. Ellinger, without which he could not form any plan; and as he was now satisfied of her readiness to serve Sophia, he would write to her husband to require his presence.

The ardour of poor Selina was rather diminished by this remembrancer, for her *caro sposo*[42] had the brutal quality of having opinions of his own, and of choosing to abide by them in defiance of entreaty, persuasion, or argument. His arrival confirmed the fears which had succeeded to her heroism; for he positively refused to receive as a child of his own, the offspring of another, which he said, he considered to be an unjustifiable imposition upon the world in general, and a more unpardonable breach of faith to every individual of his own family. Nor was he insincere in his protestations; though the craft with which he had more than tacitly deceived Mr. Estcourt, induced Sophia's father to think otherwise. But that transaction was merely in the course of business, and Mr. Ellinger had witnessed others of a hue so much more inclining to knavery, that his rectitude had not once revolted from it; but the circumstance in discussion was wholly novel to him, and custom had never settled this species of deceit easily upon his conscience. The only concession that could be obtained, was that at the expiration of three years after its birth, the child, whether male or female, should be received into his house as an orphan ward – but with this proviso, that a sum of money should be settled upon it, sufficient for the purposes of decently educating and settling it in the world; as a never-failing resource, should any accident or accidents combine to leave it wholly upon his hands.

Mr. Beauclerc was compelled to acquiesce in this arrangement, for Sophia refused to part with her child upon any other terms than that Mrs. Ellinger should be allowed to give it those attentions it was denied to her to bestow, and that it might be so placed that she herself could frequently see it.

In a few weeks after, she brought into the world a girl, having been previously removed to an obscure village at a considerable distance from town, where she assumed the name of Montresor, which, from its signification, she had determined her little orphan should be called, since she could not give her the family appellation to which she had a natural right. Every circumstance was attended to, that could secure the secrecy required, and Sophia returned to Avelines six weeks after her accouchement, having previously had her baby conveyed to Mrs. Ellinger's care, who placed it to nurse, with her approbation, at a neat little dwelling at Kilburn, on the Edgware road: and Mr. Beauclerc consented that his family should return to London at his daughter's earnest entreaty, that she might be within a walk of Selina's little charge.

The child was baptized Rosella, for so Mrs. Ellinger had predetermined, and it was not judged prudent to oppose her; the mother merely stipulated that Augusta should be added, in commemoration of the unfortunate Raymond. To remove the objection Mr. Ellinger had raised, Sophia, who was now of age, placed fifteen hundred pounds in the funds, in the name of Rosella Augusta Montresor – a sum she had no inclination to raise the displeasure of her father by increasing, as she was firmly resolved never more to marry, and had privately executed a will, by which she constituted Rosella the sole heiress of her property, with the exception of a legacy of five hundred pounds to her friend Selina.

According to the tenor of the agreement, at the end of three years the child was taken into the house of Mr. Ellinger, as his orphan ward, very much to the satisfaction of his wife, who appeared infinitely more fond of little Miss Montresor than of a son and daughter she had presented her husband since their marriage, which was generally attributed to the superior beauty of Rosella, whose opening graces struck every eye.

In this interim Miss Beauclerc had amused the heavy hours in visiting this beloved child, in making purchases for her, and working for her;[43] and the whole time which was not thus employed, or in attending to the increasing infirmities of her mother, was passed in reading the novels of the day – a practice which was too much confirmed into a habit before her marriage, not to be renewed when retirement and leisure invited her to pursue it.

Rosella was now occasionally taken to Avelines, and insensibly her visits were extended every successive time she quitted Mr. Ellinger's dingy looking mansion, from days to weeks, and from weeks to months. The hundred tongues of rumour had long since been telling each a different tale, at the sudden disappearance of Miss Beauclerc from the house of her father – her very quiet return to Avelines, her seclusion, and the succeeding transformation of a fashionable lively girl, to a dull moping young woman: consequently a hundred different reasons were given for all this, and it was almost impossible but amongst them the true one should escape.

Fortunately for Mr. Estcourt, he had not the mortification of learning that he had been duped; for the extreme disorder of his affairs had compelled him to accept the charge of secretary to an embassy, and at his return Miss Beauclerc was no longer talked of, except in the narrow circle of visiting acquaintance her mother still kept up, where indeed the continual appearance of Rosella gave birth to much epigrammatic scandal.

This child of sentiment, as Mrs. Ellinger chose to call her, discovered great affection for her unacknowledged mother, which was a very natural consequence of the perpetual *agrémens*[44] she was the means of procuring her, and the unlimited indulgence by which a fond and admiring parent gratifies her own feelings, and conciliates the love of her offspring. But Mrs. Ellinger imputed the circumstance to the mysterious workings of Nature, and Sophia was highly flattered by the attachment of her daughter, whose return to the house of her guardian, after a long visit at Avelines, was at length attended almost invariably by passionate regrets and fits of crying, which after a sufficient repetition, began to ruffle the temper of the gentle Mrs. Ellinger, and induce her to suspect that her endearing caresses, and enthusiastic attachment did not entirely compensate to her young charge for the morose formality of her husband, the teasing jealousy of her son and daughter, and the dreary gloom of their habitation, which was indeed far from boasting that air *riante* that Marmontel recommends to surrounding objects, in order to form an infant mind to cheerfulness and gaiety.[45]

This supposition recurring too often, piqued the vanity of the good lady, and weakened her violent regard for Rosella, who had soon little more to recommend her to the romantic Selina than her features and figure, which she predicted would be enchanting, and likewise the secret of her birth, which she hoped and trusted, would lead to many interesting adventures. As her fondness for the child had been rather inconvenient to Miss Beauclerc, by sometimes depriving her too long of her little Rosella, the effect of her growing coldness was highly gratifying both to mother and daughter; and by the time Miss Montresor had passed her thirteenth year, she regularly spent ten months out of the twelve either at the house of Mr. Beauclerc in town, or at Avelines.

Her mother spared no expence in procuring her the usual acquirements of her sex, and often laid aside a most interesting volume, to repeat with her the lessons of her masters. Mr. Beauclerc fretted and remonstrated at an expenditure he thought unnecessary; but as the income of Sophia's fortune was at her own disposal, she entreated him to allow her the only satisfaction she could derive from it; and he usually gave up his argument after a trifling cavil, except when he recollected that his daughter had, in her twenty-sixth year, declined the alliance of a family of distinction for the sake of Rosella – the child of a man not worth a groat.[46] He condescended however, to be amused with her little sallies and girlish frolics when the business of the day was over; and Mrs. Beauclerc, who had, since her daughter's seclusion, retired on her part from "cards and scandal,"[47] sometimes deigned to employ this disowned grandchild in reading Tillotson's Sermons to her, with now and then a variation of Young's Night Thoughts, and the Whole Duty of Man:[48] so that the loss of Rosella's society was much regretted by each of the trio at Avelines, when decorum obliged them to send her for a week or two to Mrs. Ellinger.

This lady, without losing the idea of being a principal actress in the foreseen adventures of the charming orphan, was labouring to render her daughter Livia a sweet interesting child of exquisite sensibility and promising loveliness; and her son she hoped to behold in a few years, a most graceful and manly youth, intelligence beaming from his fine eyes, and tender fondness exhibited for dear mama in every action, whilst excessive love should be conveyed in every glance to the enchanting Rosella Montresor. Unluckily however, Miss was unconquerably froward,[49] obstinate, pert, hard-featured, and ricketty;[50] circumstances very easily accounted for, from her too perfect resemblance to papa, and from her having been nursed by an idle servant girl in the atmosphere of Chancery-Lane, with the relievo of an airing into Holborn[51] every day, that Betty might meet her sweetheart, and bring home vegetables for cook; and in these excursions Miss Livia was stuck upon a green-stall,[52] to gnaw a bit of turnip, whilst the lovers coquetted at their leisure. Her temper, which would have been sour and resolute, like that of Mr. Ellinger, had she been of the same age and sex, was improved by frequent reproofs and slaps on the face for being idle, vain, and untoward like her foolish mother; and on the other hand, she was often deprived of her playthings, cakes, and finery for frowning, pouting, and snapping like her insupportable father: whilst the servants caressed and applauded her for taking off master and mistress when they scolded and quarrelled togither, "jest as natral as if 'twas them 'emfelves."

The young gentleman, her brother, was remarkable only for a most oafish stupidity, and a disgusting assortment of features; and this engaging pair were the associates of Rosella's younger days, whose patience and ingenuity had often been exercised in preserving herself from the effects of Miss Ellinger's dislike and envy, and in rescuing poor William from her sudden fits of wrath and indignation. When with them, her own wishes and inclinations had been invariably sacrificed to an ardent desire of keeping the peace, any breach of which, on arriving at the knowledge of Mr. Ellinger, was followed by a formal complaint to her good friend Miss Beauclerc, and the next visit was unhappily abridged. But this frequent exertion of forbearance, and the disappointments which sometimes awaited her, prevented Rosella from degenerating into a spoiled child; and as she met with indulgence only from one quarter, and either constraint or vexations from every other, she soon learned to appreciate properly the unabated kindness of her mother, and to repay it with gratitude and affection instead of capricious exactions and peevish whims.

A subject of contention had however lately arisen from the envious petulancy of Miss Ellinger, which put to flight all the philosophical endurance of Rosella: it was occasioned by the appearance of Mr. Mordaunt, who sometimes called in Chancery-Lane to see her; for he had much disapproved the conduct of Mr. Beauclerc, and thought the child, thus disowned and cast from the bosom of the family which ought to have cherished her, most unjustly dealt by, and a coolness of intercourse had taken place between him and the inhabitants of Avelines: but to the little Montresor he had transferred all the regard he formerly felt for her father, superadded to a jealous sort of compassion for her wrongs.

Rosella's little tormenter, seized with avidity upon an opportunity to give her pain, by speaking with childish, but outrageous disrespect of Mr. Mordaunt, whose paternal solicitude had won the heart of her grateful companion, and she could not then forbear retorting Miss Livia's sarcasms with uncommon warmth; she even defended with eagerness the cut of her old friend's shoes and coat, and the form of his hat and wig, all of which were in turn the source of animadversion and contempt.

The increasing countenance and favour of Miss Beauclerc at length withdrew her from a scene she abhorred; and at the age of sixteen, Rosella considered Avelines as her home, Mr. Beauclerc's house in town as a convenient residence to receive the instructions of her masters, and the habitation of Mr. Ellinger a disagreeable place, where form obliged her sometimes to appear, and where she was to purchase a short-lived peace by repeated presents, which the unbounded liberality of her kind friend enabled her to make.

In proportion as Sophia and her mother forgot the gay circle they had so abruptly quitted, they became enamoured of their peaceful villa, and Avelines was now the date of all Miss Beauclerc's letters to Mrs. Ellinger, who was delighted that her *imagination* at least might wander in the fascinating regions of romance, though her person was confined to the horrid purlieus of Chancery-Lane: to the mysterious widow she constantly remitted three times a week, a long sheet of paper filled with chimerical expectations, supernatural fancies, and wild suppositions concerning the future fate of Rosella, which, if any reasonable mother had believed, they must have driven her to desperation: but alas! Sophia had read of castles, banditti, invisible music, rugged mountains, and murderous daggers, and indulged her fancy in giving the features of Rosella to all her airy heroines, had conducted her in their persons, through such horrid adventures, had so often seen a sword at her breast, a blunderbuss at her temples,[53] and a terrific vision appalling her senses, that she thought little of such inevitable incidents, as they must infallibly lead her at length, to unheard-of happiness. The abrupt termination of her own adventures, she was reconciled to; and fancied herself one of those celebrated mamas, destined to bring forth beautiful and tender-souled creatures, devoted for a given time to misfortune.

The world had now ceased to concern itself with the conduct of Miss Beauclerc, and she was recognized only as a very quiet stupid kind of old maid, who had formerly met with a disappointment, and had consoled herself with novels and religion. That the latter part of the supposition was strictly just, is not certain; she had, however, indulged her early bias, by charging her memory with every production of fancy that had appeared in the last fifteen years, and it must be imagined, that such an uninterrupted series of images, soothing and encouraging a romantic imagination, must operate with considerable force. At length every pretty young woman she saw, was immediately supposed to be a damsel suffering under the pressure of excessive sensibility, and every haberdasher's journeyman who trudged on Sundays across a road skirting her father's grounds, was transformed into a love-lorn swain in search of his caged divinity. Every letter addressed to *her Selina*, exceeded the former in extravagance of idea and opinion, and evinced that she believed Rosella, both in mind and person, the most perfect of all the perfect young ladies that ever waved a white handkerchief to a banished lover, or sighed her pure flame in extempore verse to the whistling winds and raging ocean: – and indeed, if the fondness of a widowed mother, and the effusion of a flighty imagination may be allowed for, the supposition was not so extravagant as many of her fancies; for Rosella possessed a countenance and mien that stole universal good-will, and a character and deportment that secured the conquest. She was all that imagination can form of captivating in adolescence – gay, artless, forgiving, sedulous to please, soon piqued, much sooner reconciled, ardent in her pursuits, compassionate to excess, credulous because she was unsuspicious, warm in her attachments, less warm in her antipathies, fond of walking, fond of riding, of dancing, of her new harp, of laughing, of sometimes talking without the trouble of measuring her words, fond of looking for the Guinea-hen's eggs at Avelines, fond of the neighbouring shepherd's little blue-eyed son, who had once given her a nest of chaffinches, and passionately fond of Miss Beauclerc, that dear best of friends, who made her life so happy: in short, fond of every thing, for every thing then interested and amused her, excepting Tillotson's Sermons and Mr. Ellinger's household.

At length she grew formed and womanly, much to the satisfaction of her mother, who now eagerly looked forward to her progress in celebrity and heroism: these she knew, were not to be attained in the odious metropolis, where the most heavy and disgusting fetters must of necessity be put upon the sublimity of romance, and Rosella was therefore almost wholly confined to the grounds of Avelines, where she frisked about in that dubious style of dress which flatters the ambition of young girls, by making them appear like women, and gratifies the folly of women, by giving them the semblance of young girls.

As the summer advanced, Miss Beauclerc usually spent the mid-day in a little thatched hermitage,[54] raised amidst a cluster of flowering shrubs, upon a lawn which descended to the Thames-side: in this spot she relished more particularly the descriptive progress of the loves of all the Ethelindas, the Jemimas, the Fredericas, and the Georgianas, with all their panics, their castles, and their visions;[55] and now that Rosella was of an age to figure with some consideration amidst these groupes of beautiful saints in folio, Miss Beauclerc had a peculiar pleasure in making her read aloud, whilst she contemplated her picturesque figure, and watched the zephyr stealing amidst her light brown tresses. Every wish of the admiring mother then appeared to her, certain of being realized: her Rosella would be the admiration of the multitude, the little deity of unnumbered lovers, and the distinguished choice of some matchless swain.

Chapter VI

A GLIMPSE INTO THE REGIONS OF SUBLIME DISTRESSES

IN the beginning of a lovely Autumn, when the heat rendered the favourite retreat of Miss Beauclerc delicious, she was sitting in it with Rosella, who had, in obedience to her commands, opened a novel, and was reading a splendid account of a celebrated day-break; when she had arrived however, at the interesting epoch where black and grey quit the field for purple and saffron, she found her eyes attracted from her book, which they constantly were by every moving object, by a large pleasure-boat glittering with decorations. The pillars which supported the canopy were of gilt wood, the curtains of green silk, fringed, tasselled, and festooned, and the ornamented stern exhibited an Earl's coronet embossed and gilt, over an emblazoned crest. The poor novel fell into the background, and Rosella eagerly sprung forward to contemplate so gay a spectacle, when remarking the showy livery of the servants seated in the stern, "Do come and look," exclaimed she, laughing, "dear Miss Beauclerc, do look! here are the colours of Edelferinda's magnificent Aurora upon Lord Morteyne's footmen!"[56]

Miss Beauclerc smiled, notwithstanding this attack upon the most tender of all subjects; for she was delighted to observe that Rosella had attracted the attention of the party in the boat.

"I declare," continued she, in a voice of ecstacy, "they have horns and clarinets! How delightful! Do you think they are going far? I dare say they will return in the afternoon – I would watch here all day but I will see them return!"

One or two of the ladies, pleased with the animation her gestures expressed, bowed to her good-humouredly, to repay the evident admiration with which she viewed them, and Rosella returned the salute with equal ease and vivacity. Half a dozen glasses[57] had been already levelled at her, which she endured with great unconcern, because she had not the least suspicion that she was individually the object of so much curiosity.

When the boat had passed the grounds, she heard the clarinets, and having listened for some time with charmed attention, she turned to Miss Beauclerc, exclaiming –

"How happy they must be! There was not one in the whole party that did not smile and seem pleased!"

"Not so happy perhaps as you may imagine, my Rosella," returned her friend: "I suspect there are some aching bosoms in the groupe."

Rosella protested against this idea, repeating, "They all looked so happy!"

Miss Beauclerc secretly persisted however in her supposition, as she believed, with an exceeding good reason: for she had caught the eye of Lord Morteyne fixed upon Rosella with some degree of earnestness, one day that her father's carriage and his Lordship's happened to pass on the road: a circumstance which had been communicated to Mrs. Ellinger with such annotations and presentiments, that the good lady had from that moment impatiently awaited some very surprising catastrophes and *denouements*.

But accident had never put it a second time in Miss Beauclerc's power to ascertain how far Lord Morteyne had advanced in the belle passion until this morning, when he certainly did turn from a very pretty woman, to whom he had been talking, to survey the lively hermit – an appellation the party had given her; and he only resumed his conversation with his fair neighbour, when he could no longer with perfect convenience gaze at Rosella. And though on this occasion his deportment did not entirely please Miss Beauclerc, yet she was tolerably certain, to use her own language to Selina, that the arrow rankled at his heart.

The imagination of Rosella was so occupied by the ideas of gaiety and happiness she had annexed to the object which had so much pleased her, that she scarcely allowed herself time to swallow her dinner, that she might run back to the hermitage, sincerely hoping that no stupid people would drop in before tea to recall her to the house. Miss Beauclerc remained in the drawing-room with her mother, who was indisposed, and could not take her afternoon airing; but as the windows of the apartment gave on to the lawn, she watched the motions of Rosella, and saw her sometimes standing at the extremity of the bank, looking earnestly up the river, and sometimes beguiling the moment of expectation, by frolicking with an Italian greyhound, who was a great favourite; an exercise that rather discomposed her attire, but increased the animation and vivid bloom of her countenance.

At length her presence was required at the tea table before any boat, except watermen's wherries,[58] had appeared; and with her fancy still hovering round the hermitage, she returned to the drawing-room, and thought Mr. Beauclerc unusually slow and tedious in sipping his coffee.

"This pamphlet," said the old gentleman, turning the leaves of a political publication, "is pleasantly written, the principles and sentiments just, the language, clear and perspicuous: I really don't remember that I ever before met with an author whose opinions so exactly tallied with my own."

It was full half an hour after having made this observation, that he drank his cold coffee, and retired to his study to read and admire this excellent author, who had the good fortune to write exactly his opinions.

Mrs. Beauclerc, who had before appeared inclined to doze, now desired Rosella to take down a book, and read to her.

"Yes, Madam," replied she, endeavouring to speak with alacrity: "what book shall it be?"

Though Miss Beauclerc participated in her disappointment, she was much pleased with her good-humoured compliance: "I always told Selina," thought she, "that this dear girl had an unequalled sweetness of disposition."

"I think," said the old lady, gaping, and speaking with her eyes almost closed, "that as we have almost got through that fine discourse of Bishop Tillotson, we may as well conclude it: there cannot be many more pages I should suppose."

"About two or three and twenty, Ma'am," said Rosella, turning over the leaves.

"Very well, my dear; then we shall have time to finish it before I take my draught."

Rosella resigned herself to her destiny with a tolerable good grace, and instantly began the lecture, keeping a very exact account of the leaves as they faced about to the left. – "Five, six – very well," whispered she to herself, "I have not many more to get through – I shall soon have done."[59]

On looking up at the close of the next paragraph, she saw Mrs. Beauclerc in a profound state of repose; and her daughter smiled encouragement and consolation to Rosella.

After an uninterrupted pause of a few seconds, the good lady drew a long breath, and half opening her eyes, "Bless me," exclaimed she, "I believe I almost forgot myself – yes, indeed, that is an excellent discourse – mark the page, my dear – I feel rather heavy. – Sophy, you had better take your evening walk – I shall ring for my draught when I awake."

Rosella felt much relieved by this emancipation, though she concluded that by her detention she had missed the gratification she had promised herself, as the sun was now nearly beneath the horizon, and the breeze swept cool over the river. Miss Beauclerc was of the same opinion; but when they strolled out together, Rosella led to the hermitage, and she followed.

"You have been very obliging, my dear child," said she, "to the inclinations of my poor mother; and to console us both for our confinement in the house such a sweet evening as this has been, you shall order your harp into our retreat, and give me my favourite ballad by moonlight."

Rosella had scarcely received this permission, than she flew back to the house, and having desired a servant to bring the harp to the hermitage, returned to her friend with the same speed. The instrument soon followed her, and the charming ballad, "Lady Alice,"[60] was performed in a style that enraptured Miss Beauclerc: she had had the voice of her *protegée* highly cultivated, because heroines are always infallibly fine and pathetic fingers,[61] and the voice of Rosella was not unworthy the expence and the trouble which had been bestowed upon it; so that the gentle correspondents prided themselves upon her possessing every requisite to shine in the heroic page, except a pensive countenance; they hoped however that this deficiency would be no more, after an initiation of a few months into the sublime distress of a gentle, fervent, everlasting, but apparently unfortunate prepossession.

Rosella continued to sing, with a few intermissions, that were filled up, by her, in admiration of the workmanship of her dear new harp, which was a foreign one, and was ornamented with several figures exquisitely finished: but at length perceiving the generous friend who had made her this superb present, in a deep reverie, she endeavoured to draw her from it by repeating "Lady Alice." Miss Beauclerc listened attentively, and a remembrance of the termination of her own hapless love, made her tears flow. A lighterman[62] was dropping down the river, and the rude bawling of the men was in a moment hushed in motionless surprise, and almost unconscious admiration of the fair Syren, whose dulcet tones might have "created a soul under the ribs of death."[63]

But these rough auditors were not the only captives to the harmony of Rosella, which father Thames had borne towards the hermitage: the noise of the lightermen had prevented her from observing the beautiful boat so anxiously watched for, which had glided to the bank of the lawn, and was there fixed by the magic of sweet sounds.

A few minutes after the pathetic exit of poor Lady Alice from this mortal coil, Rosella turned her eyes towards the river, and its undulating motion caused a part of the gilded stern of the boat to glitter on her eye.

"Ah, here it is!" exclaimed she; "it is empty – where can they all be? – no, here are the rowers!"

She was then running to the water-side; but before the could reach it, a scream from Miss Beauclerc recalled her steps, and on regaining the hermitage, she stopped at the entrance, from whence she saw with surprise and consternation, that her friend was surrounded by a party of gentlemen, who were tumultuously addressing many compliments to her, under the influence of a mistake the twilight occasioned.

"Charming creature!" exclaimed one of the set, who had seized the poor lady's hand, and thrown himself upon his knees with all the gallant inspiration of Champagne; "divine girl! whose ecstatic notes may silence with envy the seraphic host!"

"Bravo! bravo!" echoed through the place from different mouths; "well said, Ainslie!"

Rosella remained trembling and confounded at the uproar, and just distinguished the voice of Miss Beauclerc, who endeavoured to be heard, when a tall figure advancing to her, said, in a tone scarcely audible –

"On a wrong scent, by G – d, the whole pack!" then seizing the arm of Rosella, he burst into a half-smothered fit of laughter, and enquired if they were deifying the crabbed old maid, or her mother. "As for myself," continued this witty personage, "you see I can distinguish a Hebe[64] from a tabby cat, though encompassed in the shades of night."

"Let go my hand, Sir," said Rosella, endeavouring to disengage it.

"Not I, faith," returned he, trying to catch the other.

She was terrified at this determined insolence, and called to Miss Beauclerc in a voice of affright, which attracted the attention of another individual of the intruding party, who hastily stepped forward, and discovered to Rosella the countenance of Lord Morteyne.

"Forbear, Estcourt!" said he, in a tone of authority: "how will you justify or excuse this conduct? If your riotous companions refuse to listen to me, you, at least, shall not disgrace yourself in my presence."

He then seized the offender by the collar, a liberty of action this discerning gentleman resented, and a struggle ensued, when he, probably from having drank more wine than Lord Morteyne, was soon thrown to the ground: but, alas! he encountered the unfortunate harp in his descent, and it fell with him upon the pebble-paved floor with a violent crash. Rosella flew to examine if it had sustained much injury, and found, to her inexpressible mortification, that it was so battered in one place, and wholly beat in in another, that she had little hope the mischief could ever be repaired.

"You have broken my new harp to pieces!" exclaimed she, in an agony of grief, the tears springing to her eyes.

"I feared so," returned Lord Morteyne; "and how I may deprecate your anger, I know not: I can only entreat you to believe, Madam, that I feel the utmost indignation for the insolence of this intrusion, which I hope Miss Beauclerc will believe I endeavoured to prevent: but after having spent the afternoon in too much conviviality perhaps, she will not be surprised that I had little influence in restraining a set of thoughtless young men, when I could scarcely myself resist the attraction that drew them to this place."

Rosella attended little to this fine speech; she had, assisted by him, raised her demolished lyre, and was shedding tears over it, when her friend advanced to her, and enquired earnestly why she wept, and the rest of the party demanded the same information of Mr. Estcourt, who was half stunned by his fall, and was leaning in a very sullen posture against the entrance of the hermitage.

"Heaven and earth!" exclaimed one of the intruders, "who has been committing this sacrilege?"

"No more she'll tune the vocal shell,
"To hills and dales her passion tell,
"A flame which time can never quell –"[65]

A burst of applause interrupted this amusing quotation, which[66] completely overcame the patience of Lord Morteyne, who had perhaps no inclination to incur the public or private enmity of Mr. Beauclerc, whose grounds adjoined to his own, and in whose power it would have been to have annoyed him extremely.

The indignation of Miss Beauclerc, which had hitherto slumbered in the cherished idea that Rosella would at least gain three or four passionate admirers in the fray, was now equally roused; but as she attempted to give it utterance, she was interrupted by his Lordship –

"Gentlemen," said he warmly, "I insist that you immediately retire; this conduct is insolent and unmanly. Permit me, ladies," added he, "to attend you towards the house."

"My Lord," replied Miss Beauclerc, with an air of infinite dignity, "however your associates may have deviated from the dictates of propriety and good breeding, I am not so unjust as to implicate your Lordship in their transgression, and I thank you for this considerate proposal; but as I imagine these gentlemen are now satisfied with the alarm they have given Miss Montresor and myself, I will not trouble your Lordship to accompany us."

They then quitted the hermitage without opposition from the intruders, and soon gained the house; Miss Beauclerc making no answer to the lamentations of Rosella for the poor harp, but repeating internally, with a rapture she could scarcely restrain, "Yes, this is an adventure!"

In their absence, Mrs. Beauclerc feeling her indisposition increase, had retired to bed, and her husband being still in his study, Rosella and her friend found the drawing-room empty. Miss Beauclerc, discovering by the lights, that the eyes of Rosella were red with weeping, endeavoured to console her by saying, that the poor harp might not be in so hopeless a state as she supposed: "and if so," added she, "we will contrive to get it repaired without mentioning the disaster, or the circumstance that occasioned it, to my father."

Rosella was now composed enough to dread Mr. Beauclerc's animadversions upon the folly of lavishing expensive presents upon careless young girls, and readily acceded to the proposal. Orders were issued to the old butler to convey the unlucky instrument into Miss Beauclerc's dressing-room without being seen by his master; and as Simpson had, on former occasions, had the honour of being a confidential agent, he nodded, looked wise, and withdrew, but soon returned with the petrifying intelligence that the harp was no where to be found.

Miss Beauclerc dismissing old Simpson, endeavoured again to diminish the chagrin and consternation of Rosella, by representing that Lord Morteyne had most probably carried it away, with the hope of having it repaired; though in fact, she imagined he meant to indulge the tender sentiments that had taken possession of his soul, by preserving it as a relique which had once been near the divinity at whose shrine he worshipped.

"I wish," exclaimed Rosella with some vehemence, "the boat had been sailing on the Black Sea! and then this misfortune would never have happened."

"But some other of more consequence might," observed Miss Beauclerc with a smile: "do you wish too that all the party had been in it?"

"No," replied Rosella, recollecting herself, "not all the party – nor any one of them indeed; but I hope you will allow that I have reason to be very much vexed, and so have you to be displeased: I should be glad to know what Lord Morteyne would have thought of Mr. Beauclerc, if he had taken half a dozen rude men into his grounds to frighten his sister, Lady Lucy?"

Her friend laughed internally to see her so much piqued. "Ah! my poor Rosella," thought she, "'tis the loss of thy heart, and not of thy harp, that so much discomposes thee!"

Miss Beauclerc then left her to her regrets, real and imaginary, that she might attend the invalid, whom she found unusually languid and fretful; and she excused her appearance at the supper table, by saying she would sit up stairs till she went to bed, as her mother was much indisposed and very low.

Rosella, thus left *tête-à-tête* with Mr. Beauclerc, and not so much inclined to chat as usual, suffered him to conduct the conversation, which turned upon the very youthful and cardinal virtues of prudence, steadiness, and economy, all of which he hoped to see her one day possess. Rosella thanked him, and in her turn, wished she might merit her generous friend's kindness and indulgence to her.

"Yes," returned the old man, "Sophia is indeed indulgent to you – too much so, I often tell her; however, I hope you will always be a good girl, and remember what you owe to her affection for you, and be prudent, and economical, and steady; in short, be a good girl, and we will take care of you – that is, we shall not disapprove what Sophy does to render you an accomplished and happy young woman: though I must say, I think that harp was an unnecessary purchase; the old one would have done perfectly well. Seventy guineas only last year for a grand forte-piano! and now as much more for a harp! Oh, it's absurd, it's extravagant! however, be a good girl – Sophy will not be controlled – but be a prudent girl, and I shall not he displeased at what she does for you."

Rosella coloured, and hung her head; her spirits already agitated, were painfully affected – the harp, this regretted extravagance, was demolished, and appeared to justify the complaints of Mr. Beauclerc; whilst the secret consciousness of it gave her a sensation of criminality, joined to the mortification she experienced for the first time, at receiving benefits which parsimony would fain have withheld from her, and she burst into tears.

He had not intended to give her pain, and hastened to relieve her distress by assuring her of his own affection for her, and that of Mrs. Beauclerc, desiring at the same time, that she would not take notice to Sophy of any thing he had said, which Rosella readily promised.

The next morning she was still much out of spirits; the enticing curvets of poor Flirt,[67] who was her constant companion, could not allure her to the usual race upon the lawn, nor could she endure to amuse herself with her forte-piano, with the economical observations of Mr. Beauclerc still fresh in her memory. Her absence and dejection were remarked by her fanciful friend, who concluded after breakfast, a long *narrative letter* to *her Selina*, by observing that Rosella had become pensive, and even melancholy.

"I too well guess the cause of this change," continued she, "her fate now hangs upon this noble youth: the shaft was mutually felt, and both Morteyne and Rosella act under its influence."

Mr. Beauclerc had announced his intention of going to town, and returning before dinner, and enquired who would accompany him. Mrs. Beauclerc was too much indisposed, Sophia remained at home with her, and at length it was settled that Rosella should take the opportunity of paying a visit of a few hours, to her guardian and Mrs. Ellinger. She felt very reluctant to renew her *tête-à-tête* with

Mr. Beauclerc, but had not the courage to form an objection, when her friend desired her to execute a few commissions which she mentioned, and gave the packet to Selina in charge with her. Miss Beauclerc then embraced her, bade her good morning, and Rosella followed her grandfather into the chariot.

Fortunately however, he was very busily employed in examining a memorandum-book, and minuting down some recent expenditures; and as he was going to settle with his banker, and receive some dividends from his funded cash, his spectacles were never absent from his nose, his pocket-book from one hand, and his pencil from the other.

Rosella was pleased to be spared the repetition of his lecture upon prudence, economy, and steadiness, and endeavoured to amuse her mind with the passing objects; but the recent animadversions of her companion, and her vexatious loss, would occur to harass her spirits, in spite of her efforts to drive them from her recollection.

Chapter VII

RAGE FOR REFINEMENT

AS Mr. Beauclerc was going into the City, he left Rosella in Chancery-Lane, telling her he would call for her in three hours. She bade him farewell, and walked up stairs, with a gloomy remembrance of the many unpleasant hours she had passed in this den of parchments and perplexities.

Rosella opened the sitting-room door, and seeing it empty, proceeded up another flight of stairs to greet Mrs. Ellinger, who she concluded was dressing; but before she had entirely finished her peregrination,[68] she met a servant maid, who informed her that Mistress and Miss Livy was sot off to see ould Madam Swinney, who had been took vilent ill, and ispicted to die, as she was already noteless.[69] – Rosella expressed her sorrow at this event, and measured back her steps to speak to Mr. Ellinger at the office door.

He evinced more surprise than pleasure at this visit, which she soon learned was not very *à-propos*.

"My dear," said Mr. Ellinger, tying up a bundle of papers very carefully with the goose quill's regimental insignia, red tape,[70] "my dear, you are unlucky in coming to-day, for my wife and daughter are not at home, and I am going to Gray's-Inn Coffee-House[71] to dine with a country client, so that we have only a bit of scrag of mutton for clerks and servants; but I will tell you what you shall do – Mr. Mordaunt cannot go out I know, for he has been confined to his house with a bilious complaint, and he was saying a few days ago, that he had not seen you for a long time, so you can go and pay him a visit, which will look attentive and pretty, and perhaps he will ask you to dine."

Rosella was on the point of replying that she was expected to return to Avelines to dinner, but she was fearful that she might then be made to remain at Mr. Ellinger's, entirely alone, and without the smallest resource against the *ennui* which had already taken possession of her; and she was besides really anxious to see her old friend, and she readily assented to the saving plan proposed to her.

"Let me see," said Mr. Ellinger, "you can't find your way alone, I suppose – and there again, William is not at hand – stay, you shall have Mr. Povey to show you to Mr. Mordaunt's house."

Mr. Povey was one of the articled clerks, then sitting in the office upon a high stool, facing a very dirty grim window, looking into a little paved court, where weeds and grass thrust up their presuming heads between the crevices, to balk in the oblique rays of the morning sun, which condescended to visit them for about ten minutes, and then retired behind an immense high wall. In this court, the attention of Mr. Povey and his fellow scribes could only be diverted from business by a marvellous foul cinder heap, which the elevated notions of the lady of the mansion prevented her from observing: item an old wig block, item a dust tub, whose diurnal peregrinations generally terminated there to save trouble;[72] so that it is not to be wondered at if Mr. Povey, on hearing his destination, jumped down from his stool, wiped his pen, snatched his hat from peg marked P. and bowed to Rosella with more alacrity than if he had been called from the employment of smoking the Hooka with houries[73] in Mahomet's paradise.

She returned his salutation with her usual good humour, and professed herself sorry to give him trouble; he was opening his mouth to reply with some gallantry, when Mr. Ellinger cut all complimenting, by desiring him to call at his friend the counsellor's, for them 'ere cases; "and stay," added the phlegmatic lawyer, "take these briefs, and that 'ere will and codicil back to Furnival's Inn,[74] that is, after you have conducted Miss Montresor."

Mr. Povey thrusting the cases, briefs, will, and codicil into a green stuff bag,[75] prepared with a less elated aspect to attend Rosella. After they had proceeded two or three streets, he shook his ears,[76] hemmed, and placing his green burthen as much as possible out of sight, assisted his fair companion over a kennel,[77] now choked with dust, old mortar from a repaired house, odoriferous cabbage leaves, and putrid herrings.

"It's charmingly pleasant, Ma'am," said the young man, with a simper; "I think it is a pity not to walk out and take the air such a day as this."

Rosella made no reply, for they had just then entered an alley, and she was intent upon preserving her eyes from a puff of wind that was whirling through it, and gathering into its vortex all the filth and ordure which strewed the pavement.

"Are we almost arrived at – Street?" asked she, on removing her hand from her face.

"Oh dear no, Ma'am; we have near a mile yet to walk – we cross this street into that passage, and then –"

"Another alley!" exclaimed Rosella, again preparing to guard against the inconvenience of the first. The precaution was however useless, for no air could circulate at that moment through this abode of closeness and stench, on account of a mob collected to hear a loving pair from the distinguished atmosphere of St. Giles's,[78] roaring alternately the stanzas of a popular ballad.

"We must turn back," said Rosella, hastily.

"No, no, Ma'am," replied Mr. Povey, pushing forward, "we shall soon get through; I never turn back for such a handful of people as this."

Rosella tried to follow him; but not possessing either the strength or the expertness of her conductor, and not understanding the arts of shuffling, hitching, and elbowing through a crowd, Mr. Povey was obliged to divide his attention between her and his parchment treasure, and wholly overlooked a boxing match which suddenly began between the female warbler and her associate, to favour the dexterity of some diving acquaintances who were mixed in the audience. Rosella, terrified at the blows, which resounded in her ears, and the language that defiled them, was now driven about at the will of those who surrounded her, and soon lost sight of the green stuff bag and its master. At length, without any effort of her own, she found herself disengaged from the crowd, and pushed into a spacious street, the name of which was hidden from her view by a projecting sign that covered it.

Several moments passed before she recovered sufficient recollection to ask of a woman passing by, the way to – Street. The dame looked round her with tedious imbecility, and whilst Rosella watched her countenance in eager enquiry, she declared "she did not know – she could not tell for her part – she was a stranger herself, and knew no more what all the turnings and the streets were called, not she, than the babe unborn."

Rosella, much disappointed, walked on at the hazard of going wrong, but could not at that moment see any one near her to whom she could summon courage to apply. There was not a coach-stand in sight, and wholly unused as she had been to walk in London without a companion or attendant, her embarrassment was visible both in her countenance and manner. At length, fearing that she should not have time to see Mr. Mordaunt if she wandered far from the way, she collected resolution to ask information of a boy who was passing, with an immense pile of pewter pots strung upon his back: for she had looked into several shops, and unluckily saw no person at leisure to attend to her; some were, or seemed to be empty, others were tenanted only by children, there was but one occupied by a person who appeared to be the master of it, and he looked at her as she peeped in, with such a savage mien of suspicion, that she withdrew in haste.

"The way to – Street," repeated the boy, turning round, "ay – it's a good way though – but I'll show you," returned he, swinging the pots off his back, and dashing them on the pavement with a most stunning clutter.[79] Before he could execute his intention however, or utter another syllable, he received a shower of blows from the cane of a man, whose feet his pots had aggrieved, accompanied by such a roundelay of oaths and execrations, that Rosella stood aghast in the utmost surprise and horror, wholly unable to account for the uproar: but the outcries of the poor boy soon gathered a circle of enquirers about him, and she left him to his fate, because she was unable to endure the heat and pressure of the people about her. She now felt uncommonly thirsty, and was much perplexed how to act, when a confectioner's shop greeted her eyes, and she recollected that she could at once enquire her way, and recompense the people for any little civility she might require of them, by laying out some money. A glass of capillaire[80] was given to her at her request, and she took likewise some biscuits, of a sort she recollected Miss Beauclerc was fond of. But lo! on seeking for her purse, she found that it had vanished; her distress and confusion at this discovery were insupportable, and while the colour rushed into her cheeks, she made known her unexpected loss to a very showy lady, gaily dressed, who condescended to officiate behind the counter, and expressed her concern at the same time, that she could not immediately pay for the capillaire.

"Oh dear Ma'am," said the dame, with unlooked-for urbanity, "pray don't mention such a trifle; I am only sorry for you, Ma'am – I hope you have not lost much?"

"Only a guinea and a few shillings," replied Rosella, "I had no more in my pocket."

"Well, Ma'am, that's too much to lose, as people say; but pray don't mention it on my account; I dare say when you come this way again, you will not forget me."

"No, indeed," cried Rosella; "I will discharge my debt, and remember your civility with much gratitude."

She then enquired the way to — Street, and this polite shopkeeper stepped to the door to slow her the next turning, with as much complaisance as if she had just received an order for a superb dessert.

Whilst Rosella was listening with great attention to her instructions, a voice close to her ear exclaimed –

"Tis herself, by G – d! the Syren, the little hermit, the fair harper!"

She started with renewed confusion, and wholly forgot in a moment which way she was first to turn.

"Dear me, Ma'am," said the dame, glancing a pair of keen black eyes upon two fashionable looking men who were gazing with *nonchalente* satisfaction at the distress of Rosella, "you are not recovered yet; you had better walk in again, and sit down a little: I am sure if I had met with such an accident, I should have been quite fluttered."

"What, another accident!" exclaimed one of the gentlemen in a voice Rosella recollected to be that of Mr. Estcourt; "what an unfortunate fair one!"

He spoke with an air of disdainful raillery, which the remembrance of the last evening's disgrace perhaps promoted, and the lady confectioner began to suspect that this was far from being the first time that her moneyless customer had unexpectedly lost her purse; and abhorring the idea. of being so grossly imposed on, she drew Rosella, who was ashamed to rest, into her shop, saying –

"Come, Ma'am, you had better take another glass of capillaire, and then these young gentlemen, who seem to be friends of your's, will pay for both glasses, and you can return the money you know, when you find your purse again."

"No," replied she indignantly, "I will send a servant in less than half an hour with the money."

"Very well, Ma'am, as you please, Ma'am," returned the dame, with re-assumed complaisance, on finding that her hint was not taken by either party; "you are to take the second turning on your right."

"I thank you," returned Rosella, hastily leaving the shop with unassured steps.

One of the gentlemen, as she hurried forward, accosted her with tolerable politeness, whilst his companion, Mr. Estcourt, by several rude innuendos, recalled the circumstance that had so much shocked her, with added mortification to her mind. The colour in her face heightened to the deepest crimson, with heat and agitation; but the confusion of her mind prevented her from attending to personal inconvenience. At length her progress was impeded by a number of idle people gathered round the window of a caricature shop; and as the insolence of her uncivil tormenter increased with her increasing anxiety, she felt unable to endure it any longer, and looking round, rushed suddenly into a haberdasher's near her, and unmindful who regarded her, sat down, and burst into tears. He had followed her; but on observing a very engaging and elegant young woman gazing at Rosella with strong marks of commiseration, he suddenly stopped with an air of surprise and confusion, which did not escape her. The young lady shook her head with a countenance of reprehension, and advancing to Rosella, offered her a bottle of salts[81] with an air of such gentle compassion, that its influence revived her.

The people of the house, from her example, brought a glass of water; but the amiable stranger observing that Rosella was much heated, would not allow her to take it, and on seeing her more composed, she made a sign to Mr. Estcourt, who approached her, and having converged with him in a whisper for a moment, at the entrance of the shop, he suddenly disappeared, and she returned to Rosella.

"My name is Estcourt, Ma'am," said she; "I have a carriage in waiting, and if you will do me the honour to use it, it shall attend you to any part of the town you wish to visit."

Rosella expressed her gratitude for this generous attention.

"No acknowledgments are due to me," replied Lady Lucy; "I ought rather to apologize to you for the impertinence of my thoughtless brother."

Rosella, with renewed thanks, said that if a hackney coach could be procured, she should feel an equal obligation, without the fear of occasioning any inconvenience: but this proposition would not by any means be admitted, and Lady Lucy, on hearing that she was going to the house of Mr. Mordaunt, led her to her carriage, and ordered it thither.

"Mr. Mordaunt," said she, as it drove away, "I am well acquainted with: he has transacted business in my family near thirty years, I believe, and notwithstanding his gravity and precision, he is a great favourite with me."

Rosella joined very warmly her approbation and respect to that of Lady Lucy, who enquired if she were on terms of intimacy with Mrs. Methwald, his sister: her young companion replied that she was scarcely known to her. A momentary smile passed over the countenance of Lady Lucy, who remained silent, and Rosella took advantage of a pause, to explain the accident by which Mr. Estcourt had met her unattended. His amiable sister again assured her that she blushed for his conduct.

"This is not," said she, "his first offence towards you, Miss Montresor, and that you should this morning suffer renewed uneasiness from his folly, gives me much concern."

Rosella supposed that the broken harp was alluded to, and she asserted, with truth, that the accident was much overbalanced by the flattering condescension of Lady Lucy. The carriage now stopped at the house of Mr. Mordaunt, who happened to be at home, and Rosella parted from her fair protectress with an undefined but deep impression of esteem and admiration, which was likewise experienced by Lady Lucy, though not in so enthusiastic a degree.

"Philip," said Rosella to the servant who opened the door, "how is Mr. Mordaunt? I was much hurt to hear that he has been ill: may I see him?"

"I am partly sure, Miss," replied the man, who was a very old domestic, "that my master would be gladder to see you than any body, almost. But Mrs. Methwald is here, and if you please I will shew you into the drawing-room, and let my master know you are there."

Rosella, who had been used to run to him in his study, felt restrained: she had seen Mrs. Methwald in her childhood, and still retained a confused recollection of her, though it was by no means a pleasing one. As Philip announced her, the old lady looked up, but without attempting to rise: she had been writing, and with the pen still in her hand, and her *secretaire*[82] before her, she surveyed her young visitor very earnestly through her spectacles. Rosella, much abashed, expressed her fears that her intrusion was ill-timed.

"Is it possible," exclaimed Mrs. Methwald, "that you can be Rosella Montresor?"

Rosella, not knowing in what manner to prove her identity, remained silent.

"You are grown out of knowledge,"[83] continued the lady: "but," added she, recollecting herself, "my surprise has betrayed me into giving you a strange reception – sit down, my dear – I am happy to see you."

She graciously held forth her hand, which Rosella received with some diffidence of deserving the honour, and then she ventured to ask if Mr. Mordaunt was recovered from his indisposition.

"Not entirely," Mrs. Methwald said; "Philip told him," continued she, "of course, that you are here, and when he is entirely disengaged, he will no doubt see you."

She now arranged the papers in her *secretaire*, and taking up a book, from which she appeared to have been making extracts, she marked the page, and placed every thing aside; but in a manner that plainly told Rosella she had been disturbed from her employment by her presence, and meant to resume it the instant she was relieved from it. From this moment, to the entrance of her brother, she laboured to keep up a conversation with her young guest, who not being acquainted with the chit chat reports of the day, and not being imagined qualified for any superior subject, did not make a very brilliant figure. The entrance of Mr. Mordaunt, who welcomed her with his usual frankness and affection, relieved her from a situation, of all others the most unpleasant, herself refrained, and conscious of being a *gêne*[84] to others.

"You have before seen this good child I think," said he to his sister; "but you had no idea that you should so suddenly renew acquaintance with such a tall, handsome girl?"

"Miss Montresor is certainly much grown," returned the lady, coldly, "and I suppose – I believe much improved in appearance; she is vastly like her father."

"How is poor Mrs. Beauclerc?" demanded Mr. Mordaunt, hastily; "I hear she is ill."

56

Rosella confirmed the report. He then enquired how long she remained in town; and having heard until three o'clock, observed that it was already near half after two, and asked why she had not called sooner. She took this opportunity of telling the tale of her disasters, and Mr. Mordaunt, much provoked with the conduct of her guardian, in entrusting her to such an incompetent protector as Mr. Povey, relieved one part of her inquietude, by sending Philip to the confectioner, to perform the promise she had given: and then recollecting how short a time remained for her stay in town, he ordered his carriage to take her back, and whilst it was getting ready, demanded what the larder could produce.

"Rosella will not dine," said he, "probably till six, and Miss Beauclerc will not trust her here again, if I send her home hungry and sick."

Mrs. Methwald said she would ring for something; but observed at the same moment, that she believed there were biscuits in the anti-room.

"Pho, pho," returned her brother, "a farthing biscuit for a young girl half famished! Do suffer your darling Muses," continued he, glancing his eye at the *secretaire*, "to regale for once with the smell of cold roast or boiled."[85]

Rosella interrupted him to declare that she had no inclination for either.

"Child," said Mr. Mordaunt, "I am at this time suffering a painful malady, which arose to its present height from the folly of preserving my appetite from nine in the morning until five and six in the evening; and I recommend it to you, never to suffer a foolish complaisance or punctilio, to place you in the same predicament. I shall take some refreshment myself, if it is to be had, and I hope you will not refuse to follow my example."

He then rung the bell himself, and gave orders; whilst Mrs. Methwald, with a countenance extremely disconcerted, locked up the precious contents of the *secretaire*, and sent it to her apartment.

Rosella, at this moment, wished herself at Avelines; – she wished herself any where, even at Mr. Ellinger's dismal mansion, rather than be compelled to partake of a repast that was not bestowed with cordiality, or meet a physiognomy forced every other minute into a momentary simper, which, like gleams of sunshine in a winter-day, gave way per force, to the more prevailing gloom.

Mr. Mordaunt paid no attention to the ill-concealed displeasure of his sister, but sat down to the tray which the servant brought, and obliged Rosella to share the contents with him. Mrs. Methwald would not be prevailed with to have the same condescension, but sat as far from the scene of action as possible, and the instant her brother and his copartner in this vulgar business had ended, she desired that the fragments might be taken away, and flew herself to open the doors and windows, that the smell of the meat might evaporate.

Rosella, still more distressed than at her entrance, began to anticipate with delight the moment of her departure, and for the first time since she had lost sight of Mr. Povey, reflected, that as he could not possibly guess what had become of her, he might have informed Mr. Ellinger that she was lost, who perhaps would spread the alarm to Mr. Beauclerc when he called for her in Chancery-Lane. This fear made her yet more eagerly wish to hear the carriage announced, and at length her apprehensions were allayed by the agreeable intelligence that it was ready.

"Philip, you will attend Miss Montresor," said Mr. Mordaunt.

"Thomas is below," observed Mrs. Methwald, with a nervous motion of the head, and a fretful fidget.

"I suppose so," returned her brother, provoked at her childish contradictions, "and there let Thomas remain."

Rosella hastily rose to depart. Mrs. Methwald, checking her peevishness, took her hand, and touched her cheek with her own condescending lips.

"My dear child," said Mr. Mordaunt, "you must not be frightened from renewing your visit by my sister's unlucky discomposure this morning."

Mrs. Methwald darted at him a look of anger.

"I beg you to believe," added he, "that she is very friendly and good-humoured, and I assure you has your welfare much at heart: but I suppose the truth is, that she found the hill of Parnassus steeper than usual this morning, and perhaps too, the heat of the weather has dried up the helicon fountain, at which I believe my good sister sips now and then."[86]

"Absurd!" exclaimed the old lady.

Rosella now courtesied to her, and bidding Mr. Mordaunt adieu, ran down stairs, glad to escape from the peevish precision of this ancient votary of the Muses. On arriving at the house of Mr. Ellinger, she was met in the passage by the knight of the green stuff bag, who eagerly ran out to inform her that he had with difficulty traced her as far as the corner of — Street, and seen her run into the haberdasher's; and as he then thought her safe, he turned back to execute his other commissions.

"Mr. Ellinger does not then know the little embarrassment I met with?" said she.

"No, Ma'am," replied Povey, colouring, "I thought as you was safe, there was no occasion to mention it, as perhaps he might think I ought –"

Rosella now understood him, and relieved his apprehension, by saying she was pleased to find there had not been any needless alarm; and as she had fortunately arrived safe at her destination, there would not be any necessity to speak of it. She then walked up stairs to wait the appearance of Mr. Beauclerc, and discovered to her mortification, that Mr. Povey thought it necessary to atone for his late negligence, by following her into the dining-room, because he was afraid she would be dull by herself; and for his part, he was not fit to sit down to "aforesaids and whereases," after taking such a fag[87] in such a devilish hot day.

Rosella was silent.

"After you had entered the carriage, Ma'am," continued he, "I thought –"

"Oh you saw that?" interrupted Rosella with some surprise.

"Yes, Ma'am; I was following you, but I spied the livery[88] – confound it, says I, here's my luck again! I never touch this damned green devil,[89] but I meet some of my old friends: there was Cyril Estcourt and I at Westminster school, like two brothers; we were always together at my uncle's, or at the house of Lord Morteyne, his father. But when my uncle took the whim to article me to old Ellinger, that I might understand common law, all my friends cut me, damme, or what's almost as bad, they hoax me to the devil for being a lawyer's clerk: however, they may come round again one of these days, for I shall only do business in the soliciting way – in my uncle's track, with two or three snug auditorships. Zounds! the haunches of venison and fat turtles that fall into his larder – Lord, Ma'am, he is as much courted as a Prime Minister."

"Pray may I ask on what particular account?" said Rosella, who found she was expected to speak.

"Why, he carries in the rents of such of his noble patrons who have rents to receive, and contrives that others who have none, shall live upon his wits and his credit."

"I am sorry I cannot understand you," said Rosella; "and I am so ignorant of business of every kind, that I fear I should not comprehend you even if you endeavour to explain to me."

"I cannot think," returned Povey, with an air of chagrin, "what induces me to talk upon such quizzing[90] subjects, except it is the confounded air of this house. I dare say now, if I was to meet Lady Lucy, or Cyril, or any of them, they would pronounce me already quite an altered fellow."

"Lady Lucy is extremely amiable!" exclaimed Rosella earnestly.

"As sweet a tempered little creature as any in the world," returned he: "now *I* met her once a short time after I was articled, and I felt confounded foolish to be sure – for there was a cursed load of red-taped papers[91] staring her full in the face. Mr. Povey," said she, "we never see you now: my father was remarking yesterday that you had deserted us. I could have told her that Cyril had hoaxed me off the field, but I was so chagrined that the devil of a word could I utter; however, when I meet her, she always bows, let it be where it will: and her taking you to old Mordaunt's was just like her – she would almost have done the same thing for a girl fagging with a band-box."[92]

Mr. Beauclerc's chariot now drove to the door, and Rosella, who was not much delighted with her companion, bade him good morning with great alacrity, and flew down stairs with even more than the usual eagerness she ever felt to quit the house. She found Mr. Beauclerc in extreme good humour; but the spectacles and memorandum-book were still in constant employment. She reminded him of the commissions her friend had given her, and was desired to direct the coachman as she pleased, provided she did not order him much out of the way.

Chapter VIII

PALSY – GOUT – AND RAGE FOR IMPROVEMENTS

WHEN the carriage drove round the sweep that led to the front entrance at Avelines, Rosella looked up at the dressing-room windows of Miss Beauclerc, and to her extreme surprise, this beloved friend was not watching for her return – a custom that had hitherto been invariable with her. The servant who had attended the chariot had rung twice, and the doors were yet shut against their master.

"I hope no accident has happened!" ejaculated Rosella in a low yet distinguishable voice.

"What is it – what is the matter?" asked Mr. Beauclerc, taking off his spectacles, and looking up.

Old Simpson now appeared with a face of important concern.

"I am sure Miss Beauclerc is ill!" cried Rosella, rushing into the house, and flying up stairs with a step equally rapid. The sight of the family apothecary walking down with a very solemn air, confirmed all her fears. "Oh I thought so," said she – "I feared so! Tell me, is she very ill?"

"I am apprehensive, Miss Montresor," returned the gentleman in measured accents –

"Of what?" interrupted Rosella, turning very pale.

"That the poor lady is in a very critical situation."

She heard no more, but ran with incredible swiftness to the apartment of Miss Beauclerc, which she was surprised to find wholly deserted.

"Where is she?" exclaimed the weeping girl, "where is my best and only friend?"

"Lord, Miss," said Sophia's maid, who just then entered, "you cannot mean my old Lady sure – and as for *my* Lady, why you know she is tending her."

Rosella insensibly lost her inconsolable countenance.

"There, Ma'am," continued the toilet damsel, "my old master and you hadn't been gone half an hour, before my poor old Lady was taken all in such a queer way – like – and *my* Lady shrieked out, and pulled the bell, fit to pull it down – and we all ran, and there was my poor old Lady had tumbled down upon the carpet, and was making faces – like – all in such a queer way. So Will was sent off to Hampton-Court for the doctor, and John set off to fetch back his master, and bring Doctor Watkins, and there he is not come back yet."

"Do you think I may go to Mrs. Beauclerc's chamber?" asked Rosella; "could not I do any good? – perhaps I might relieve my dear Miss Beauclerc?"

"Ah poor dear lady!" said the suivante,[93] "she has been in a pack of troubles; I'll go and ask if you may see my old Lady."

Rosella waited with impatience for her return; but the request was denied, for Miss Beauclerc wished that she might, if possible, be spared the shock of seeing her mother in her present deplorable state, and it had been recommended besides, to keep her as quiet as circumstances would admit.

The old lady languished six-and-thirty hours in a state of insensibility, and at the end of that period, a second fit released her daughter and her husband from their melancholy attendance. But the sudden alarm of her danger, and the shock of her death, affected the health of Mr. Beauclerc, and occasioned a fit of the gout, to which he had been for some time subjected; and the regret of Sophia for the loss of her mother, was much diverted by her attention to her sick father, in which Rosella joined with all the tenderness and ardour natural to her character.

A few days after the funeral of Mrs. Beauclerc, their cares were however frustrated by intelligence received by the invalid, of the sudden failure of his banker, to whom he had recently entrusted a considerable sum of money, but not enough to injure him in the slightest manner, or in the least embarrass his affairs. Yet the avarice of the old man was cruelly wounded by the stroke, and the agitation of his mind upon this event, threw the gout into his head, and proved fatal to him.

Sophia, worn with anxiety and attendance, was now herself assailed by illness; and only the tears and distress of Rosella had the power of rousing her spirits to fortitude and exertion.

The nearest relation of Miss Beauclerc on the side of her father, was a first cousin who resided in Devonshire upon a small estate, and had seldom visited his uncle, because he had no expectations from him. Of her mother's family, the most approximate to her was Mrs. Mary Delaval, the sister of Mrs. Beauclerc, who having in her youth met with a sensible disappointment, had declined some advantageous matches, and had imbibed so strong a friendship for a woman of rather an inferior situation in life, who had had complaisance enough to console the poor damsel by listening with patience to her tale of woe, and playing everlastingly at piquet[94] with her, that Miss Delaval, possessing a handsome independence, took up her abode at the house of her comforter, and followed her and her husband, a wary Scotchman, to Dumfries, where he chose to return to spend the income of a small fortune he had scraped together in England. A very kind letter was interchanged once a year between Miss Beauclerc and her aunt, and this annual correspondence was the only intercourse preserved by the good lady with her family.

Besides these relatives, Miss Beauclerc had three or four second and third cousins, with whom she was upon formal terms; and finding herself thus suddenly called upon to act from her own judgment and discretion, she wrote to entreat the presence of Mr. Mordaunt, that she might have the benefit of his friendly instructions; and at the same time desired the attendance of Mr. Ellinger in his professional capacity.

A mandate was likewise issued to Selina, that her eloquence and personal consolation might sooth the griefs of her distressed correspondent; and when this first task was accomplished, that she might join in the more delicious one of sketching out a variety of intricate and mazy destinies for the unconscious Rosella, who, entirely innocent of the forced-meat adventures[95] laid in her name upon the shelf for Fortune's better leisure, was fervently blessing Heaven that her indulgent friend was still on the surface of this trumpery globe; and wondering much, how that time would henceforth be filled, which had till then been devoted to the excellent discourses of Bishop Tillotson, to the screech-owl night-thoughts,[96] to prosing, to political pamphlets, and to the examination of account-books and cash memorandums.

The will of Mr. Beauclerc had been deposited with Mr. Ellinger, and a copy of it, sealed up, was found in his escrutoire, with an intimation where the original was placed. Mr. Mordaunt, at the request of Sophia, was present at the reading of it, as was likewise Rosella, who was supposed to be a legatee. The nephew of the deceased had been written to in form, but no answer had been received; and Mr. Ellinger proposed that the will should be opened without delay, that it might be seen if instructions had been left for the interment of the body. This expectation was not disappointed, and the testator then proceeded to dispose of his property. According to the general idea, Miss Beauclerc was the heiress of his estates and all his personals; but the sentence that followed was equally unexpected and unwelcome to her. It imported, that his daughter had lately rejected an alliance he had been anxious to obtain for her, and unless she altered her situation in favour of the Honourable Mr. Treson, or some other gentleman of family and probity, he willed that his estates should descend, at her demise, to his nephew John Bristock, of Girton-place, in the county of Devon, or to his heirs, on taking the surname of Beauclerc. Then followed a few legacies, amongst which, the most considerable was a bequest of one thousand pounds to Rosella, *commonly called* Montresor.

"Commonly called Montresor!" repeated Rosella internally: "that is a mistake, for I am most commonly called Rosella." She was extremely delighted when the conclusion of this business liberated her friend from a scene which had appeared to agitate her considerably. Mr. Mordaunt too, had seemed much chagrined, she thought, and had put on a most tremendous frown during the latter part of the reading: nor could she avoid observing, that even Mr. Povey, who had accompanied Mr. Ellinger as his *aid-du-camp*, on pronouncing her name, given with such legal gravity, looked up with an inquisitive leer, hesitated, half-simpered, then recollecting himself, hemmed, and proceeded with a repetition of the words "Rosella, commonly called Montresor."

Miss Beauclerc had an immediate conference with Mr. Mordaunt in her dressing-room, and Rosella retired to her own apartment, repeating, as the threw herself into a chair, "commonly called Montresor!" The more this form struck her imagination, the more strange it appeared; but at length she remembered to have seen the words applied to others, yet without recollecting on what occasion, and supposed they were used by formal people, either to express contempt or respect, she could not exactly define which, nor did she ten minutes after much wish to discover.

The *tête-à-tête* of Miss Beauclerc and her old friend was long, and Rosella observed that when she rejoined her, she had been in tears; but her caresses and expressions of affliction were uncommonly tender, and the returning fondness of her child soothed her affliction, which Rosella was careful not to renew, by preferring any question which would lead her mind back to the circumstance that had apparently excited it.

When Mr. Mordaunt left Avelines, he took leave of Rosella with a greater indication of friendship and regard than he had ever yet shown her; but his conduct to Miss Beauclerc was cold and ceremonious, and created such a restraint in every one, that his absence was a relief to her spirits.

Mrs. Ellinger obeyed the summons of her correspondent two days after the funeral, and their long and private conversations soon removed the chagrin that had taken possession of Miss Beauclerc from the period of the examination of the will. Fond as she was of Rosella, and delighted as Mrs. Ellinger still continued to be, to admire with prognosticating gaze the daily improving charms of the *child of sentiment*, this darling girl was invariably excluded from their confidential *tête-à-têtes*, which in less than a week, began to encroach upon more than half the time of Rosella's indulgent friend. She was therefore compelled to amuse herself as well as she could without a companion, excepting Flirt, and she hourly regretted the loss of her harp, which Miss Beauclerc had not replaced by any other. Rosella was too delicate to hint a wish, that might appear to force the further liberality of one to whom she had already such infinite obligations; and she was perfectly convinced that it would be a very useless effort to apply to Mr. Ellinger for an expensive superfluity.

Her piano-forte, and very long rambles with Flirt, who was her chaperon and play-fellow, became her principal resources against *ennui*. The anger and regret which a sight of the hermitage always occasioned, prevented her from reposing herself there after a walk round the grounds, and she preferred being half-baked under an autumnal sun, in a small tub summer-house[97] at the other extremity of the lawn, where she contrived to make room for Mr. Flirt, who lay very lovingly at her feet, panting with heat, and not able to comprehend why he was forbidden to enter the shades of the proscribed retreat.

One morning however, when the correspondents had withdrawn after breakfast, and taken with them from the library, a voluminous "Tour through Great Britain,"[98] Rosella sat down to her instrument, the sounds of which could be distinguished in Miss Beauclerc's dressing-room.

"Charming creature!" exclaimed Mrs. Ellinger with enthusiasm, "what a delightful singer – what a heavenly voice!"

"My dear Selina," said Miss Beauclerc, "do you really think she excels? To me I must confess she appears to sing enchantingly."

"And then," cried Mrs. Selina, "her figure! her hair! her eyes! her complexion! her hands!"

"I must own," interrupted the enraptured mother, "I think she is beautiful."

"Beautiful!" screamed the gentle Mrs. Ellinger in the accents of an inspired priestess of Delphos, "she must be angelic, since even that old hottentot Mordaunt says she is lovely."[99]

Poor Miss Beauclerc burst into tears of delight, and pressed the hand of the panegyrist, whose eulogiums and epithets were still flowing with unebbing fulness, when they were suddenly interrupted by sounds which seemed to resemble the chords of a harp struck in haste.

"What can this mean?" exclaimed Miss Beauclerc; and the expression being echoed by her companion, they both hurried to the apartment from whence these unexpected sounds proceeded, where they discovered Rosella almost dancing with ecstacy round a superb harp, and so much occupied with her admiration, that she did not immediately observe their entrance.

"From whence did this come?" asked Mrs. Ellinger, casting an expressive look at her friend.

"Oh my too indulgent Miss Beauclerc," cried Rosella, not attending to the question, "how kind you are! I am sure this must have been very expensive – I am afraid it cost too much money," added she, recollecting the admonition of Mr. Beauclerc.

"Not of mine," returned her friend, repaying with interest the meaning smile of *her Selina*, "I assure you I have nothing to do with the affair."

Simpson was immediately summoned: but to the numerous interrogations he received, he could only answer that a man brought the instrument in a caravan to the stable-yard door, and merely saying he had brought the young lady's harp home, made the coachman help him out with it, and went off without another word. The simper on Mrs. Ellinger's countenance almost degenerated into a grin at this recital, and Miss Beauclerc was as much delighted as when poor Raymond had first slipped a *billet-doux*[100] into her hand, after her father had rejected his overtures; whilst Rosella, far from crediting her disclaiming speech, imagined that she had thus conducted this pleasing circumstance to increase her satisfaction by surprise, and alternately caressed Miss Beauclerc and the newly-recovered treasure, until Selina, no longer able to contain her annotations, drew her friend back to her dressing-room, that they might freely congratulate each other upon this indubitable proof of the attachment of Lord Morteyne; for they could not entertain a doubt but that he was the author of this gallantry, and it had a considerable effect upon the plans they were laying down with such eager zeal.

Whatever these plans were however, it was agreed that they could not be effected before the spring was tolerably advanced; and the invention of the two ladies was now very worthily employed in finding out the best method of passing the intervening time. Miss Beauclerc, on inspecting her inheritance, found herself possessed of an income far exceeding her utmost expectations: independent of the estates of her father, he had amassed a large sum of money, which he had laid out to great advantage, and had purchased not only Avelines, but the house in town. Mr. Mordaunt never refused his advice to the mother of Rosella, and she found

Mr. Ellinger a man of professional integrity; so that her affairs were soon settled to her satisfaction.

No longer shackled in her views, she bespoke, by the recommendation of *Selina*, an elegant open carriage, and hired another for use whilst it was building. It was drawn by a beautiful pair of foresters,[101] and Rosella received instructions from the coachman, that she might become an expert charioteer. Miss Beauclerc likewise sent her twice a week to a riding-school, to learn to sit a horse with grace, and a very fine one was purchased for her at an extravagant price.

All these unlooked-for indulgences intoxicated the young mind of Rosella with a happiness never before experienced. She laughed, danced, sung, caressed Miss Beauclerc, and thought Mrs. Ellinger more agreeable in this visit to Avelines, than she could ever remember her to have been before. The keen delight attending these new occupations had not much abated, when her attention was still further amused, by learning that her kind friend had bought some meadow-land adjoining the grounds, which were to be beautified and enlarged. Nothing could now be done without a landscape gardener. R –[102] was sent for, plans were made, and Rosella suffered to have a voice in rejecting or accepting them.

It was discovered that the house must undergo a complete alteration, and that a library and greenhouse must open on to the lawn – that is, a lady's library and a lady's greenhouse. Under the shade of some fine chesnut-trees a fanciful dairy was to be erected in the form of a bungalo.[103] Rosella was already constituted dairymaid in chief, and an expensive dairy-set actually bespoke at Wedgewood's.[104]

What a variety of charming amusements all in succession! Poor Flirt, though still extremely cherished, was rivalled by the long-tailed foresters, whose wavy manes wantoned in the wind like the careless tresses of their smiling mistress, and who, flattered by the advances she had made to win their friendship, willingly obeyed the fair hand which so often patted encouragement and approbation.

At length Mrs. Ellinger, eager that Rosella should exhibit her new acquirement, trusted herself to her skill and the docility of the ponies; and as she directed which way they should take, they drove of course, immediately past the house of Lord Morteyne, near which the public road happened to sweep. The mourning of the servant, and the black dress of the young lady, Mrs. Ellinger concluded would sufficiently indicate who they were, and she expected to see the sighing swain dart from behind some spreading oak to catch a passing glance of his lovely mistress: nay, she almost wished the horses to take fright (a little) or the carriage to overturn (gently) that an accident so opportune might create heroic services, an obligation of eternal gratitude in return for them, and all those tender sentiments which a charming heroine and a handsome hero must experience from such a touching adventure.

They had almost quitted Lord Morteyne's demesnes however, without encountering him, and Mrs. Ellinger had nearly given up the hope of beholding the passionate lover, when at an angle in the road they met a jaunting car,[105] filled with a very lively party, some of whom were leaping from the machine, and on to it again, as it rolled forward: and, Oh degeneracy of the age! the man, who ought to have employed his solitary moments in wafting innumerable sighs to the broad-faced moon, was conducting this care-killing party, and joining in their mirth!

The road happened to be narrow where the carriages met, and Lord Morteyne very politely drew up his horse, to give Rosella more room, who feeling the timidity of inexperience, checked her foresters, and gave the whole party an opportunity of surveying her as she slowly passed. Mrs. Ellinger was all observation, all ear, but she was not so much occupied as to forget to act a distinguished part in the scene: not content with performing the interesting matron, she undertook to personate likewise the woman of distinction, and made herself so extremely conspicuous in both characters, that it was impossible she could be overlooked.

The opposite groupe were divided into two parties of gazers; the men criticized Rosella, and the women amused themselves with the airs of her companion, whose growing indignation was rather qualified by observing some expressive glances of approbation cast towards the heroine.

Lady Lucy, who was in the car, bowed to Rosella with her usual complacency; and she feeling gratified and happy by this mark of recognition, returned the compliment with a cheek dimpled over with smiles.

When the enemy were out of sight, "Miss," said the coachman, with an air of chagrin, "you mought have passed that queer thing without pulling up; there was a foot or two to spare I know."

"Yes, John," replied Rosella, "but I was afraid."

"No," thought Mrs. Ellinger, triumphantly, "no, my amiable Rosella, it was not fear you experienced, it was *sentiment*; and shortly your infant passion will develope itself to your conviction!"

The infant passion was however yet so extremely in embryo, that Rosella was not at all conscious of it; but conversed with her usual freedom and gaiety for the remainder of the ride, only recurring to the adventitious meeting, by expressing a warm admiration of Lady Lucy Estcourt.

"Estcourt!" repeated Mrs. Ellinger: "humph – drive home, my dear; I have recollected something which I wish to communicate to your friend immediately."

Rosella, accustomed to this lady's singular mode of speaking, paid no attention to her exclamation, but complied with her request.

Miss Beauclerc had been really anxious for their return, as it was the first time Rosella had displayed her new acquirement on the public road; she trembled lest they had met with an accident, and was looking out for them when they stopped at the door.

"Don't come down," cried Mrs. Ellinger eagerly; "I wish to speak with you in your dressing-room."

Miss Beauclerc smiled, and cast a glance of satisfied approbation at the unconscious object of all this mysterious solicitude.

Chapter IX

A HEROINE TRAVESTY – AND A HEROINE UNHORSED

THE workmen soon began their operations both on the house and grounds; and Rosella finding herself extremely interested in their progress, was soon *à portée*[106] to act as overseer and directress. When the alterations began to be apparent, the curiosity of the people in the neighbourhood, induced them to visit as much of the place as was open to their inspection; and at length, a billet was given to Miss Beauclerc from Lady Lucy Estcourt, requesting permission to walk over the improvements with three or four friends.

An assent was immediately returned, and Rosella desired to pay attention to Lady Lucy's party – a mandate which she readily promised to obey. That day however, and two more passed over, and not a creature from the house of Lord Morteyne availed themselves of the circumstance, to improve their growing flames with a nearer view of the object that inspired them. The gentle Selina then became very impatient, and even rather indignant, that Lord Morteyne himself should miss so fair an opportunity for an impromptu declaration of everlasting tenderness and attachment; and even Miss Beauclerc began to fear that she had, in marking down this conquest, paid too high a compliment to the charms of her beloved girl; whilst Rosella herself, having expected with some eagerness the promised moment of renewing an intercourse, however transitory, with Mr. Povey's *best little creature in the world*, forgot her disappointment on the third day, and pursued her office of superintendent of the works, with her accustomed ardour.

The wind was high, and besides disordering her hair, had wafted her hat into the urn of the river god which was flowing near her: a nail in an old plank had caught her muslin dress, and having rent it the whole length of the skirt, retained a large fragment of it, which waved like a banneret to and fro in the air, and the rest trailed after her in sullen state; and to conclude with her disasters, she had, in jumping from a ha! ha![107] into the newly-purchased meadow-land, popped one of her feet into some black mud, which had communicated from her shoe to her petticoats, and extremely discoloured them: but unmindful of such trifles, Rosella continued to amuse herself, and was helping a little boy belonging to one of the workmen, to wheel some loom in a hand-barrow, when she was suddenly overtaken, and most unexpectedly, by Lady Lucy and her three or four friends, amounting to nearly a dozen, including her two brothers, Lord Morteyne and Mr. Povey's *ci-devant*[108] friend Cyril Estcourt.

Rosella hastily quitted her occupation, and the blood flew to her cheeks, as she surveyed with a momentary glance the disorder of her adjustment. Lady Lucy seemed fearful of distressing her by subjecting her to the regards of her companions, and with a courtesy was passing on, when the following disjointed phrases caught the ear of Rosella from the train that followed her.

"A confounded handsome hoyden[109] – the Jordan[110] might take a lesson here – devilish pity – a fine girl, faith – rustic you must own – yes yes – *a belle sauvage*." Accompanied by an assortment of shrugs and grimaces to denote contempt, compassion, or faint admiration.

Her pride was piqued, and her resentment roused by such a string of comments, uttered just loud enough for her to catch the sense of each phrase. Hoyden! rustic! savage! repeated she indignantly, as she surveyed herself once more. The situation in which she had been discovered then recurring to her, and the accidents which had discredited her toilet, all catching her eye, made her almost admit the justice of the remarks; and forgetting the insolent affectation of superiority which had dictated the utterance of them in her hearing, she advanced to Lady Lucy, and apologizing for the dishabille to which her morning's ramble had reduced her, offered, with returning good humour, to point out the improvements and alterations which had not yet been made apparent.

The overture was received with politeness, and accepted with acknowledgments by the amiable Lady Lucy and her elder brother: but Mr. Estcourt and another young man of fashion chose to amuse a very bold-looking, deeply-rouged, middle-aged woman, of apparently high pretensions, who was leaning familiarly upon an arm of each, by half-whispered witticisms and observations upon their fair conductress, which obtained peals of laughter from all who walked within six paces of them.

Rosella, consoled by the solicitous attention of Lady Lucy, endured this polite persecution with tolerable fortitude, till hearing the name of Miss Beauclerc mentioned in accents she disapproved, she listened more attentively to the distinguished *hoaxers* who were so obligingly honouring her with their derision, and hearing her best friend not very ceremoniously treated, she turned to the party, and with some vivacity exclaimed –

"I am indeed rustic enough to imagine that such conversation as I have this moment heard, would have been more proper on the other side of Miss Beauclerc's gates: and besides, Sir," added she, addressing Mr. Estcourt, and gathering resentment as she spoke, "you would display your judgment in returning to your first subject, for I am surely a much greater object of ridicule than Miss Beauclerc, who is one of the best and most amiable of women."

The whole party paused at this unlooked-for warmth; the principal offender made no reply, and Rosella immediately repenting that she had given way to the impulse of the moment, had the additional mortification of observing that Lady Lucy appeared exceedingly chagrined at what had passed. Lord Morteyne too, who had no share in the offence, seemed hurt, and Rosella would have given the most cherished of her possessions to have recalled her words. She determined to endure any further impertinence the witty groupe chose to inflict upon her, rather than increase the vexation, perhaps too the secret censure, of Lady Lucy, and resumed the office she had taken upon herself, with redoubled alacrity, resolutely endeavouring to shut her ears against the titters, hints, and innuendos which still escaped from the well-bred set, who chose to regard her in the first place as a dependant, and secondly as a child, in compliment to a woman of high rank who was present, and with well-founded claims to admiration from personal beauty, was actually wavering whether she should or should not forward a match in agitation for her favourite granddaughter, by disclosing to her the ingredients of a pomade known only to herself, which possessed, she was fully persuaded, the most sovereign efficacy in heightening the charms of a youthful complexion, and in preserving a loveliness of a riper date. This never-fading flower, this American aloe, had laughed exceedingly at the pertness of the silly girl, who presumed to comment upon the conversation of people of fashion, and dashed any rising fame the unadorned beauty of Rosella might have attained, by remarking with a careless air, that she was just such a pretty unformed thing as Lady Agatha's *femme de chambre*, and much resembled her.

"Does Miss Beauclerc," asked Lord Morteyne, to divert the attention of Rosella, "remain much longer at Avelines?"

"All the winter, I believe, my Lord," replied she.

"And do you stay here all the winter?" said Lady Lucy, in a voice of kindness.

"Oh I hope so!" returned Rosella, "I hope I shall be with my good and kind friend."

Lady Lucy smiled, but without any trait of irony or disdain, and her brother smiled with the same expression.

They had now nearly reached a swing-gate that opened to the road, and Lady Lucy making towards it, thanked her fair conductress with great sweetness, and Lord Morteyne made his acknowledgment with an air of being really obliged. Rosella had so far recovered her usual spirits and vivacity, as to receive unmoved the half nods, half courtesies of some of the party as they quitted the grounds, and the intended mortification of being wholly and disdainfully overlooked by the rest. More pleased with the notice of Lady Lucy, than chagrined by the impertinence of her associates, she ran to the house, and flying up stairs to the dressing-room of Miss Beauclerc, hastily informed her to whom she had been doing the honours of Avelines.

Her friend surveyed her figure with surprise and consternation, and Mrs. Ellinger, who was present, eagerly exclaimed –

"Good heavens, Rosella! by what accident could you possibly have become this object?"

Rosella had almost forgotten the state she was in, but thus reminded, she recounted the misadventures of the morning, and extended the narrative to the little *brusquerie* with which she had retorted the rudeness she had experienced.

The gentle Selina looked extremely disconcerted at the history she imparted, and some glances were interchanged between her and the mysterious widow, expressive of excessive vexation; for in fact it was rather uncouth that a beautiful and interesting young heroine should be surprised by a tender and disconsolate lover, whilst she was wheeling a barrow of loom, in petticoats fringed with black mud, and a robe whose fractured drapery embraced the wanton pinions of every zephyr that fluttered by. Nor had they, in the course of their extensive reading, met with one instance of an insulted charmer ever noticing the most outrageous obloquy or taunt that envy, pride, and malice could inflict, except by distilling from her dark and fringed eyes a shower of pearly drops upon her pale and pensive cheek.

Yet however shocked Miss Beauclerc might be at the indecorum of Rosella, she was too fond of her to suffer a harsh reprimand to escape her lips; and though Mrs. Ellinger might long to read her a lecture upon the drooping loves and patient graces, she was obliged by her example to confine herself to an entreaty that Rosella would in future pay proper attention to her exterior. She was then dismissed by the ladies to repair her toilet, and they entered into a long and very interesting conversation concerning the expediency of her continuing the character of a lively and thoughtless, but very captivating girl, or whether the more subduing, though beaten track of pensive dignity should be recommended and enforced? They had been some time debating whether Lord Morteyne would prove the boisterous, unprincipled, daring, disliked, yet persevering lover, who was destined to traduce her, torment her, carry her off, and marry her, in spite either of inclination, law, gospel, or the favoured swain; or whether the sequel would prove him the favoured swain himself, who would respect her, venerate her, trust her, confide in her, sigh for her, and die for her, in contempt of the most intricate, threatening, mysterious, black, and unpropitious appearances. The account, given by Rosella of his conduct that morning, determined the point in his favour; he was to be the perfect and happy lover, and they now put in practice two or three expedients, to discover if he, or any one of his family, possessed any tumble-down castle either in the north of England, in Wales, Scotland or Ireland.

In a short time Rosella was pronounced a good horsewoman: a very beautiful animal had been bought for her use, and Miss Beauclerc having two or three times feasted her eyes, and fed her hopes, with a view of this beloved girl in her equestrian character, and being convinced of the gentleness of her horse, sent her forth, attended only by a groom lad, really and literally in search of adventures. Uncertain of her powers, and though delighted, a little apprehensive at being thus left to her own guidance, Rosella, for the first day or two, confined her rides to the neighbouring common; and then gathering courage, she extended them by degrees, till she was tolerably well acquainted with the country for ten miles round. Every time she returned home, and hastily dismounting, ran to embrace her indulgent friend, the accustomed question of "Who did you see?" was generally answered by "Nobody I knew;" and the two matrons growing impatient, as they very reasonably might, at this chasm in adventures, it almost occurred to them that the figure of Rosella, and the figure of her horse, though they were both admirable, must by this time be pretty well known, and by ceasing to excite curiosity, cease to excite any vivid admiration.

Mr. Ellinger, *en attendant*,[111] began to think that his wife had given up quite enough of her time for the consolation and comfort of her fanciful friend, and had written to require her return home, setting forth in forcible terms the inconveniences of her absence; amongst which the more prominent were, the impudence and laziness of Molly, their cook, who spoiled the dinner regularly every day; the disappearance of several of his shirts; the deplorable state of his daughter, who walked about the house slipshod, and had not a whole frock to her back; and, lastly, the filthy condition of his mansion, where it was impossible to move without disturbing a bushel of dust, and brushing down a dozen cobwebs at every step.

Miss Beauclerc found it too difficult however, to part with her confidante and adviser; shirts, frocks, and shoes were procured at ready-made warehouses at her expence, and sent to Mr. Ellinger to qualify his impatience for the return of his refined Lady, who accompanied her dear Sophia to town, and assisted her in choosing a very handsome piece of plate, as a sop to her growling Cerberus.[112] The friends then ventured to his den, and presenting their offering, received a sullen permission that Mrs. Ellinger might revisit Avelines for another month: and this amiable mistress of an amiable family, having corrected her deserted daughter, lectured her son, and sufficiently stormed at her servants, returned with a light heart to the residence of taste, sentiment, friendship, and Sophia.

Rosella, who had not been of the excursion, because she did not wish it, saw her re-appear without pleasure, and only endeavoured to see it without pain; for she could not reconcile her judgment to the affected manners of Mrs. Ellinger, or subdue something like contempt and dislike which her absurd language and ridiculous deportment often created, and for which Rosella invariably condemned herself, because she believed her to be friendly, and to possess a good heart.

Miss Beauclerc, delighted to have carried her point with Mr. Ellinger, continued to trace with her invaluable Selina, her summer tour, and project each day different adventures for Rosella in the course of it, who in compliance with their injunctions and her own inclinations, continued her daily rides; and still the same question, and the same answer, were duly repeated, till one auspicious morning she mounted her horse in high spirits, and still more animated by the fineness of the weather, which was unusually favourable for the season, she extended her peregrination rather further than usual, and was hastening home, when the cry of hounds and the horn of the huntsman saluted the ear of the spirited animal on which she was seated, who snuffed the air, and laying his ears close to his head, set off without further notice, followed by the horse on which the groom was mounted, and soon joined in the chace.[113]

Rosella, startled at her want of power to restrain him, and terrified by the deafening yelping of the dogs, and the confused cries and shouts of the almost frantic crew, amongst whom chance had thrown her, trembled, and scarcely kept her seat, which was several times endangered by the flying leaps which her courser[114] chose to take. At length he thought proper to ford a brook that immediately obstructed his progress, and about a dozen more horses and riders plunging in at the same time, Rosella was in a moment nearly as wet as though she had been drawn through the stream.

She was scarcely again landed on a fine pasture, when her agitation of spirits overcame her, her trembling hands refused to retain the bridle, and half fainting, she fell to the earth, where stunned by the concussion, she lay insensible to the danger with which she was surrounded from the impetuous animals who were behind her, and pursuing their course, successively leaped over her whilst she was stretched upon the ground. One of the gentlemen of the hunt, either more compassionate, or more observant than others, threw himself from his horse at a considerable hazard, and scarcely waiting till the tumultuous crowd had gone by, flew to aid the luckless being who appeared still unconscious of the accident that had befallen her. He saw that she was "fair and young;"[115] but her eyes were closed, her lips pale, and her features void of expression, so that every person (Mrs. Ellinger excepted) might have well excused any deficiency of rapturous admiration at the brilliant charms of his inanimate charge, whom he nevertheless endeavoured to restore to life with more humanity than success.

Distressed at the failure of his efforts, the stranger looked round for an *aid-du-camp*, and very opportunely discovered one in the person of a labourer, who was carrying a truss of hay from a stack at a small distance, to a public-house by the road-side. With the assistance of this man, Rosella was conveyed to it; but before she was lodged in the house, the stranger was accosted by a person on horseback, who enquired what had happened.

"Ah, my Lord, is it you?" returned he: "you have arrived very *à-propos*[116] to assist me in a d—mned troublesome charge I have been Quixote enough to undertake. This fallen Diana,"[117] continued he, as he pursued his way, "was dismounted during our chace this morning, and I begin to fear she is more seriously hurt than I had imagined."

They had now gained the house, and the women belonging to it being called, Rosella was given to their care, and a surgeon sent for by Lord Morteyne; for it was even him the stranger addressed, and he dispatched his own servant upon the errand.

When Rosella had been placed upon the best bed the *hôtellerie*[118] afforded, the gentlemen walked before the door of the house, impatient for the arrival of the medical person who would relieve them, they hoped, from an anxiety the most indifferent man must have experienced in the same situation.

"So this is the fair Syren whom Ainslie raves about," said the stranger, continuing a conversation which had begun in the house: "but who the devil is she?"

"An orphan, I am told," replied the other: "she is allied to the family of old Beauclerc who is lately dead – the people, I mean, who live at Avelines."

"Oh, aye – the melancholy old maid Lady Lucy was speaking of."

"Yes; this poor girl seems left to her management, and is suffered to ride about the country with no other protection than the attendance of a lad."

"She appears to be a charming creature."

"She is one of the loveliest young women I ever beheld: but like other wild flowers, might be vastly improved by cultivation, I believe."

"I do not think so," cried the gentleman of the chace; "I should prefer her fresh from her "native woodlands wild."[119]

"Then she would at this moment exactly meet your taste; for no Arabian untamed filly ever scorned the whip and spur, as she scorns the forms of decorum and etiquette usually practiced by girls of her age and situation in life."

Lord Morteyne then proceeded to relate her appearance when she was surprised by his sister and her visiters in the grounds at Avelines: "And yet," added he, "she checked the criticisms of Cyril with such spirit, and after the little ebullition[120] of resentment, endured the ill-natured sarcasms of some, and the incessant tittering of others, with such invincible patience and unaffected good humour, that Lucy has become her firm champion, and will not suffer her to be censured or ridiculed in her presence."

The stranger laughed at the recital, and commended the urbanity of Lady Lucy, who was, he said, a good creature, and unfit to live in this world of selfishness and uncharitableness.

Long before the surgeon could arrive, Rosella recovered her recollection, and hearing from the woman who attended her, what had been done by the gentlemen for her benefit, earnestly declared that she was not at all hurt, and insisted upon rising from her bed. The good people, who were not willing to give up so suddenly what they thought would turn out a profitable job, ran to inform Lord Morteyne and his companion, that the lady would have it she was very well, and that she would get up.

"Oh, if that be the case," cried the stranger, hastily, "I shall place her in your protection, my Lord, leave my congratulations for her safety, and be off: for faith, I left my famous new mare to her own discretion, and I begin to be uneasy lest Miss Jenny should have taken as little care of herself as your sister's handsome favourite."

He then flew away without waiting the reply of Lord Morteyne, and the women asked what was to be done. Rosella, however, spared them any further deliberation on the subject by making her appearance; and she no sooner beheld whom they were addressing, than uttering an exclamation of surprise –

"Ah, my Lord!" cried she, "how much I am indebted to your charitable assistance! But Miss Beauclerc must express my acknowledgments. Will your Lordship add to the obligation, by informing me how I can return home, for I am very anxious that she should not be alarmed at my long absence?"

After a short conversation, he dismissed the idea which the women had excited, by insinuating that Rosella was light-headed; and finding her rational, and apparently unhurt, he sent to the nearest inn for a post-chaise. But the surgeon arriving in the interim, Rosella was obliged to suffer him to examine her pulse, and with much entreaty on her part, the ceremony of losing blood,[121] which he pronounced to be proper, was deferred till the returned to Avelines.

Lord Morteyne felt himself interested that so young and amiable a creature should not lose her life by neglecting this precaution, and determined to accompany her home, that he might enforce the opinion of the surgeon, which appeared reasonable. He contrived to see him without the knowledge of Rosella, who was too eager for the arrival of the chaise, to remember that it was necessary to do so; and at length, to the great relief of her impatience, the messenger who had been dispatched, returned successful. Before she stepped into it, she recollected that the people of the house ought to be rewarded for their attention, and left her purse with them – a liberality Lord Morteyne did not oppose. She then took her leave of him with a simple, yet earnest expression of gratitude, which however he disclaimed any title to, and the chaise drove off; but it was stopped again in two minutes by his Lordship, who meant to have followed her on horseback, until he discovered that the knight-errant of Rosella had borrowed his steed, that he might pursue his Jenny with greater celerity.

Lord Morteyne entreated that Miss Montresor would allow him a seat in the chaise, which was very readily complied with, and he had now leisure to remove the error she had been in, in imagining he had rendered her the service of conveying her to the place where she had received assistance: though he could not persuade her that she did not owe him obligation for his generous attentions.

He felt the interest he had already taken in her welfare increased by the artless energy of her gratitude, and was irresistibly prompted to hint, distantly indeed, and with great delicacy, at the impropriety of a lady so young, and so engaging as Miss Montresor, venturing so far from home without a chaperon or companion.

Rosella comprehended the full force of the rebuke, gentle though it was, and was thunderstruck at the facility with which she had been suffered to err.

"Is it possible," thought she, "that Miss Beauclerc should not have been aware of this?"

Lord Morteyne saw her consternation, and was hurt to have occasioned her so much mortification as it was evident she felt: it was impossible however to enlarge on the subject without increasing her emotion, and he conversed upon indifferent and unimportant themes, till the chaise stopped at Avelines: but Rosella could not detach her mind from the slight and half-expressed censure he had betrayed, which rendered her silent and thoughtful, until he forced her attention by enquiring if she would not wish the driver to take her to the back entrance, that Miss Beauclerc might not be alarmed by feeing her return in a carriage, before she was assured that no material accident had happened.

Rosella thanked him for the caution, and assented.

"You will pardon me," continued Lord Morteyne, "if I desire a servant to inform Miss Beauclerc that it has been strongly recommended you should have a vein opened as soon as possible; for I should imagine I had very imperfectly performed the office my friend Oberne delegated to me, if I neglected to give her this intelligence."

She again thanked him, and asked if he would not do her the honour to accompany her into the house: but he declined the invitation.

Lord Morteyne's servant now opened the chaise door, and old Simpson, who happened to be walking across the stable-yard, hastened to it in great surprise. To quiet the apprehensions of the old man, Rosella briefly mentioned her disaster, and Lord Morteyne having twice repeated the injunction of the surgeon, desired him particularly not to fail communicating it to his Lady, and making his bow to Rosella, ordered the postboy to drive on.

After two or three moments of reflection, she turned in silence from the minute enquiries of Simpson, and ran up stairs to the dressing-room of her friend, where she was sure to be found till dinner time in close conference with Mrs. Ellinger, surrounded by maps, tours, and roads, from the folio Atlas to the pocket volume.

Chapter X

RAGE FOR EDUCATION – A WELL-CONDUCTED FÊTE

"YOU have been an unusual long ride, my love," said Miss Beauclerc, as Rosella entered the room; "we have been uneasy that you did not return sooner."

Mrs. Ellinger confirmed the assertion as far as it related to her, by rehearsing the cruel anxiety she had suffered; and Rosella, after a little preface, related as much of the misadventure that had befallen her, as she herself knew.

Miss Beauclerc trembled at the peril she had been in; but the ladies interchanged very significant regards when the much-admired hero appeared on the canvas; and they considered his denial of being the fortunate man who had rescued the fair one from danger, as an ingenious device to spare her tender heart the weight of such a load of gratitude.

But in giving the narrative, Rosella could not prevail upon herself to repeat the hint Lord Morteyne had let fall, of the impropriety she had so innocently been guilty of; because it appeared to reflect either upon the judgment or the prudence of Miss Beauclerc.

Mrs. Ellinger's unnumbered questions were now interrupted by Simpson, who having rehearsed the adventures of the post-chaise in the housekeeper's room, recollected the injunctions of the young Lord, and entered the apartment to fulfil them.

Miss Beauclerc instantly caught the alarm; and fancying her beloved child had received some dangerous contusion, notwithstanding her earnest assertions to the contrary, sent instantly to the family apothecary, and to the London physician, and insisted that she should immediately be put to bed.

The absent groom and his horses, who had not yet been heard of, were wholly forgotten in the hurry that ensued, and every pleasurable sensation which the intervention of Lord Morteyne had excited in the bosom of Miss Beauclerc, vanished in terror for the event, which might deprive her of all that could, in her eyes, render life desirable. Rosella, who really felt stiff and indisposed, submitted at length to the discipline and confinement preparing for her; and the next day, in spite of every precaution, she was discovered to have a violent cold, sore throat, and considerable fever. The last fatal illness of her father recurred to the recollection of Miss Beauclerc, who tormented herself by imagining that the disorder of his daughter was of the same nature, and would terminate as horribly. In vain did Mrs.

Ellinger exhaust her invention in prognosticating future adventures and future greatness; she was not to be diverted from her fears but by some very interesting intelligence the consoling Selina accidentally procured: this was no other, than that Lord Morteyne was actually at that moment confined to his bed by the same malady that had seized their dear suffering Rosella.

"What wonderful sympathy!" exclaimed Mrs. Ellinger, continuing her harangue, "what a striking and mysterious similarity of destiny approaches these amiable, charming, and well-matched young people to each other. Is it not improbable, my dear friend, that fate should, after a series of incidents so remarkable, fail to render them happy in each other? But certainly we must prepare for many unfortunate and intricate adventures to delay their tender union, which trust me, Sophia, we shall live to congratulate each other upon."

Miss Beauclerc viewed this sublime effusion in a prophetic light, and suffered hope and gladness once more to visit her heart; little suspecting that this wonderful and mysterious sympathy in the destinies of Lord Morteyne and Rosella, was occasioned by the intolerable dampness of the hack post-chaise, which having been out the day before for several hours in a heavy rain, had been incapable of resisting the gravity of the torrent that penetrated into every part of it, and assisted the shower-bath Rosella had received in the chace, to disorder her, and had been the only cause of the indisposition of his Lordship, who had been dancing the whole of the preceding night, and having taken his hat off, that he might recline with greater ease, had rode twelve miles in this dangerous machine, in a very sound sleep.

The winter was considerably advanced before Rosella had wholly recovered the effect of this adventure, and her resolution never more to venture upon the back of her runaway steed, was not thought very strange or mysterious even by Mrs. Ellinger. The animal had been recovered by the groom, who returned home in safety, and the important incident was settled when Rosella grew convalescent, by a very strenuous letter of thanks from Miss Beauclerc to Lord Morteyne and his *unknown* friend. This *politesse* had been retorted by a note of enquiry concerning the fair invalid, which produced a second on the part of Miss Beauclerc, trusting, hoping, and wishing that his Lordship himself was recovering, or would soon recover: and there the intercourse ended, to the extreme astonishment and mortification of Mrs. Ellinger, who thought the man was either crazy, or had entangled himself in some unfortunate engagement, which now tortured his mind, and rived his heart: on this score alone she could forgive and pity him.

Avelines had now almost lost its attractions with the departure of the foliage and warm weather. Lord Morteyne had deserted the neighbourhood, and Mrs. Ellinger could no longer be suffered to neglect her household; so that Miss Beauclerc, leaving her improvements to the proper superintendent, established herself at her house in town. Her chariot was then sent three or four times a week for the indulgent Selina, who quitted every thing to assist in perfecting the charming plan, which, amidst innumerable consultations, had been sketched out at Avelines; and in return for this proof of uncommon attachment, Miss Beauclerc could not avoid sending Rosella sometimes to Chancery-Lane. As for herself, she had originally disliked the manners and person of Mr. Ellinger, and by an extreme indulgence of what she called natural antipathy, had now an unconquerable aversion to him, in which the gentle Selina assuring her of her entire sympathy, Miss Beauclerc never troubled herself to ruffle her delicate soul by enduring his society if she could avoid it, and Rosella almost always made her visits unaccompanied by her friend. Those which she more assiduously paid Mr. Mordaunt, whom she very sincerely loved and reverenced, were scarcely less irksome to her, from the minute, teasing, and fretful disposition of his sister, who insisted with great perseverance, that Rosella was most pitiably brought up, for that she had no reason in her arguments, and no method in her actions.

"What is it that you disapprove in her?" asked Mr. Mordaunt, rather angrily: "in my opinion she is a very good girl, and a very clever girl; but if you mean to lament that her genius was not put in a go-cart till it could never creep without one, I must assert my dear sister, that I think she is benefited by the neglect. I am no friend to the fine system of trying and condemning without mercy the little indiscretions and natural ebullitions of youth. I cannot endure to see the mind of a young woman suspended in the chains of grey-headed prudence and circumspection, till like a gibbetted criminal, there is nothing left to indicate what the original figure was, but the tattered disgusting skeleton which the hangman's accoutrements hold together."

Mrs. Methwald was much offended by this speech, which she thought an attack upon a subject, of all others she could least bear to have rudely handled. This lady having lately lost her husband, had taken up her residence with her brother, that she might save the principal part of her income for the use of a daughter, who had some years before married an expensive man of some fashion, chiefly it was supposed, for the pleasure of seducing him from a matronly beauty, whose most devoted cicisbeo[122] Mr. Cressy was; and to render the eclat of the defection complete, the deserted dame was called the most intimate friend of Mrs. and Miss Methwald. Mrs. Cressy was idolized by her father; and against his judgment, he at length assented to the match. The bride was furnished with jewels, and presented; but unluckily her fortune, which had been called immense, proved to be considerably less than Mr. Cressy had computed it at, and in resentment for such perfidy, he resolved to run through it as fast as possible, that the old man might see he was not to be fettered and stinted with impunity.

The education of the young lady, his wife, had been conducted entirely under the eye of Mrs. Methwald, who had indefatigably collected every publication upon the "delightful task" of rearing "the tender thought,"[123] which had ever appeared; from the grand, minute, superb, sentimental, overbearing, manoeuvring lady of doubtful fame, Madame G—l—s, to the pretty, natural, easy, and instructive moral of Mrs. Trimmer.[124] But all this could not suffice – Mrs. Methwald had determined to form a phoenix, and had alike devoured essays, sermons, posthumous advice, and posthumous letters. The *fortitèr in re*, and *suavitèr in modo*,[125] struck her imagination as a maxim wonderfully sublime and beautiful, and became the ground-work of the superstructure she wished to raise. Unluckily however, the object of her cares and hopes was a being of uncommon mould, alike without affections and without passions. The *fortitèr in re* with her consistent in self-gratification, without regard to the feelings and the mortifications of others; and when she most displayed a cold-blooded superciliousness, void of those little attentions and endearments which form the charm of domestic society, the unfortunate beings who were destined io be her companions, were most certain of beholding her broad white countenance puckered into simpers – this was the *suavitèr in modo*. She was like a stinted cucumber from an early hot-bed, which of its own nature retains only the coldness, and tastes only of the manure that reared it: her person corresponded with her mind, and her complexion was so uniformly death-like and inanimate, that her husband in reforming her toilet, insisted upon introducing the rouge-box.

This lady Rosella met at the house of Mr. Mordaunt, who in compliment to his sister, treated his wonderful niece with attention and politeness; yet on many occasions she had much offended and disgusted him, and did not efface any unpleasant impression he might have received when he presented to her his little friend, Miss Montresor: Mrs. Cressy imagined that her uncle intended to request of her to introduce Rosella into her circle of acquaintance; and to crush such an expectation, she received the introductory courtesy of Mr. Mordaunt's insignificant *protegée* with a stiff inclination of the head, gazed at her attentively for half a minute, threw her eyes on the ground, closed them with a quick motion, and drawing her mouth into a half-prim, half-insidious simper, abruptly turned to her mother, to enquire if the Demainbrys had lately called in upon her.

Mama, who discerned nothing in this but an agreeable air of fashion, began a very minute answer to the question; and Mr. Mordaunt, who saw every thing in it which he did not wish to see, would not urge Rosella on to the notice of others, but contented himself with marking the most benevolent attentions to his young favourite during the remainder of her visit – a circumstance that provoked the indignation of both the ladies.

The day after this pleasant introduction, Rosella was to pass with Mrs. Ellinger by previous appointment, to commemorate the birth of her daughter Livia, who was now so seldom in the society of her former companion, that the rivalry and constitutional animosity by which Rosella had two or three years since so much suffered, was now confined to the coarse mockery with which she spoke of her to a few favourite intimates, and to Betty the house-maid, who was her principal confidante.

The evening of this auspicious day was to be enlivened with a ball, to which the reluctant consent of Mr. Ellinger had been almost forcibly obtained: he insisted however, that he would quit the house until it should be again sobered, that his brains might not be addled by the folly and uproar to which his family consigned themselves: and Mrs. Ellinger, as it may be imagined, readily assented to the preliminary.

Rosella very unwillingly quitted the house of Miss Beauclerc at two o'clock, because it had been stipulated that she should go early. The carriage set her down in Chancery-Lane, and was to be in waiting for her between twelve and one, when Mr. Ellinger brutally insisted that the festival should end. About two hours after her entrance, the dinner was announced, and it was discovered that Mr. Povey, who took his meals in the house, was absent. Miss Livia declared it was very hard he should stay out so on her birth-day; and observing that no one else appeared much chagrined at the circumstance, she was offended, and resolved to be very sulky till he returned. In vain did Rosella, by every little attention in her power, endeavour to divert her ill-humour, which completely annulled the purpose of the *fête* – no Povey, no smiles! Mrs. Ellinger was mortified at this public exhibition of the perverseness of her daughter, and her vexation was considerable increased by the unhappy plight of the dinner, which was meant to be superb and was found not to be eatable. How unfortunate! Did any one ever hear of a spoiled dinner at a heroine's entertainment? No! – even though the heaven-dropped food of an *elegant distressed* should be cooked by an infirm old nurse, or an ignorant cottage damsel at the foot of a sequestered mountain, the meal is invariably exquisitely neat and delicious, and the table always flows with milk and honey.

Fate, unpropitious to the serenity of Miss Livia, had destined that Mr. Povey should on that morning, whilst in the act of conveying some papers of importance to a lawyer who unfortunately lived within the atmosphere of Bond-Street, meet Mr. Estcourt and a knot of loungers, with most of whom he had been on terms of intimacy at Westminster; and the consequence was, a general resolution to *hoax* the quill-driver,[126] who was surrounded in a moment, and so much occupied in shaking hands with three or four *ci-devant* friends all at the same moment, that the green bag fell to the ground, and was instantly kicked into a kennel, whilst several open fists slapped his shoulders with energetic zeal, and the epithets of my good one, my fine fellow, &c. climaxed the salutation.

After a few lurking scruples, which he did not dare avow, Povey, overcome by the unusual and flattering condescension of Mr. Estcourt and his companions, consented to dine with them at an hotel; but recollecting the consequence of the commission with which he had been entrusted, he had just enough strength of mind to endure the raillery of the party, whilst he raised from the pavement the badge of his detested occupation, and carried the papers to the appointed place, accompanied by all his new associates, who would not quit him. Povey, having thus relieved his mind from any anxiety that might have clogged his gaiety, instantly assumed the vacant, lolloping, striding, unsteady gait of his companions, leant on the arm of Mr. Estcourt, contrived to occupy the whole pavement, and elated with his unexpected good fortune in being so delightfully noticed in spite of his degradation, compelled all the women he met to make a circuit into the carriage-way, and instantly laughed aloud at some opportune sally of wit.

It was therefore little to be wondered at, that at nine in the evening Miss Livia was still in the sullens; for Mr. Povey, who had so unaccountably absented himself, had engaged her for the dance, and nobody could prevail upon her to forget the neglect, and take another partner.

Rosella felt dispirited and fatigued from the effect of her continued ill-humour, teased by the riotous familiarity of young Ellinger, who was swallowing all the wine he could seize from the servants, and tormented by the folly of his mother, who laboured very hard to produce sentimental situations and interesting scenes from conversations and manners very opposite to general ideas of refinement.

The *ennui* which now overpowered Rosella, notwithstanding her painful efforts to seem lively and amused, by giving her an air of constraint and gravity that sat awkwardly on her features, subjected her to the censures of the assembly for being proud and fastidious; whilst the superiority of her appearance, and the attractions of her figure, excited the universal indignation of all the females who were present, and she became the object of perpetual whispers, tittering, and offensive glances, which Mrs. Ellinger could not observe, because she was now extremely busy in urging forward the tardy refreshments, already much diminished by the incessant pilferings of Master William and his sister, who, angry though she was, still condescended to take rather more than her share of the good things provided for her guests. The servants, teased and goaded on either side, watched the dexterous movements of the young gentleman; and Mrs. Betty, the superintendent of the stores, catching him in the act of conveying away a basket of cakes, thumped him without scruple or mercy. Miss Livia, who have likewise stolen into the back-room for some nefarious purpose, applauded the punishment.

"That's right," exclaimed she; "he deserves to be well beat for his greediness!"

"Hold you your tongue," retorted Betty, "you are as bad as he every bit: I'm sure there isn't such another two among the whole company, big and little."

"How cross you are!" replied the young lady; "havn't[127] I done all I can to help you?"

"Help me, quotha! let it alone and welcome," cried the serving dame, raising her voice; "you've helped off ever so many tumblers of orgitt, and I seed you carry away myself, a whole bottle of caterpillar."[128]

"What a story!" exclaimed Miss, in a tone equally exalted: "but I don't care – I'll make William remember stealing the cakes however!"

Unfortunately, William happened to grin at this threat; and he immediately received a glass of wine in his face from the hands of his virago[129] sister, and struggling for breath, he roared out that his new waistcoat was spoiled: the little remnant of patience which Mrs. Betty and her coadjutors had, by the favour of heaven, till then preserved, entirely vanished, and a most horrible uproar ensued, that soon awakened the attention of Mrs. Ellinger and her guests. She flew to learn the cause of so indecent an interruption of the amusements of the evening, and in her absence from the ball-room, some of the dancers, under pretence of wanting space and fresh air, which indeed might very well have been the fact, opened the door, and listened to the contending parties.

Rosella was shocked at the improper language the heard, and blushed both for the violent mother, and her delinquent children. She endeavoured to draw the attention of the listeners from so disgraceful a scene, but in vain: they enjoyed it too much to give up the delights of it without absolute necessity, and were soon further regaled by another, and still more outrageous riot of a different kind, from below stairs. It seemed to approach by degrees, and Rosella eagerly listening, more from inquietude and terror than from curiosity, distinguished scraps of Bacchanalian songs, roared out of tune and out of time; vollies of oaths half uttered, and convulsive peals of loud laughter, whilst every other minute was signalized by a most uncommon lumbering noise, accompanied by shouts of exultation, outcries, and curses.

A pair of wretched violins, and an accompanying tabour[130] and pipe entirely worthy of them, which made up the orchestra for the dancers, were hushed by the still more discordant noises that overpowered all their efforts; and the whole assembly awaited in impatient trepidation, the unfolding of this *mysterious* business.

At length it was *elucidated* by the entrance of Mr. Povey,[131] much intoxicated, supported by two young men in a situation very little better than his own, and followed by several others, who made a variety of ingenious efforts as they advanced, to preserve the centre of gravity. The head of Mr. Povey was decorated with a counsellor's wig, put on in so cavalier a style, that one of his eyes and half his face were concealed under it, and his person was decorated with a pleader's gown, not so well adjusted as it might have been.

"Damme, hold up!" exclaimed one of his gentlemen ushers; "stand steady, my neat one!"

"Open the cause, confound you," cried another; "don't be brow-beat, my fine fellow."

"Zounds, man," bawled a third, "he has not got his brief."

Then snatching some lemonade from a salver, he poured it very deliberately upon the wig of the mock barrister, which distilled it on to his face, and closed up his disengaged eye.

"I'm blind!" stammered Povey, reeling violently, "blind – as justice – so seat me – on the bench."

"Aye aye," vociferated three or four voices, "seat him on the bench."

One of the party looking round, observed that there was a very full court; then seizing Rosella by the arm, who had been driven near him by the curiosity of those behind her –

"Are you plaintiff or defendant?" continued he. She struggled to escape from him, and as he could not stand with any firmness, she soon succeeded.

Mrs. Ellinger now advanced with an air of dignity; and irritated as she had been by the scene she had just left, it was not very probable that she should tolerate the contemptuous insolence of the intruders –

"Mr. Povey," said she, indignantly, "your conduct of to-day is insufferable – I desire that you will quit the room, and that your impertinent companions instantly leave the house. How dare you, Sir, intrude these vulgar fellows amongst my friends!"

"Vulgar fellows!" repeated Povey, who appeared to awake as from a dream; then wiping the humidity from his face, he gazed with blinking eyes at his obliging attendants. "Ma'am," added he, "you – you – mistake, Ma'am: this is Sir Belmeis Ashmore – no – there he stands – I believe – and that honest fellow is Lesley – and here is my friend Estcourt – and that is – faith I can't see exactly – but he is – somebody."

The misses simpered, and the young gentlemen, comprehensively included in Mrs. Ellinger's friends, thought Povey a fortunate dog, and envied him such dashing associates; whilst the gentle and prudent lady of the mansion paused a moment to consider in what manner she should suffer this adventure to terminate. Povey had named a young man of fashion, a Baronet, and the brother of a Nobleman, intelligence that entirely changed the face of affairs; and she was now very well disposed to think the frolic that introduced them under her roof, a very harmless and agreeable one. All the ladies of the party appeared equally willing to tolerate it, and at length Povey was hastened to his own apartment, and Miss Livia recalled from a hasty banishment, to which her misconduct had doomed her, that her fair hand might be bestowed by her decorous mama upon the Baronet, who was so far however from being *en train* to dance, that he was scarcely able to walk.

Rosella, disgusted, frightened, and reluctant, was compelled to stand up with Mr. Lesley, who was not in a situation to understand that she chose to decline the honour he was solicitous to confer upon her. The rest of this disordered groupe very prudently preferred being spectators of the dance, and Mrs. Ellinger, affecting to preserve great dignity, yet inwardly exulting, gave the word of command to the magnificent orchestra.

The partner of Rosella contrived, with a little assistance, to walk the figure without much deranging his neighbours; but inebriated as he was, his ear was grievously hurt by the horrible discord that assailed it –

"May I be black-balled eternally," cried he, "if I ever dance again to a hurdy-gurdy!"

"There's a conceit!" exclaimed Mr. Estcourt, who happened to hear him; "the devil a hurdy-gurdy is there but in your brain: I tell you it's a jew's-harp and a kettle-drum."

This amendment created an almost universal laugh, in which however neither Mrs. Ellinger nor Rosella could join; for the good lady was offended in behalf of her musicians, and Mr. Lesley's fair partner felt humiliated and displeased. Fortune indeed had hitherto favoured her so far, that she had not been much incommoded by the attention of either gentleman; but unluckily Miss Livia, who had now recovered the utmost extent of her good humour, and was giggling and chattering without restraint, exclaimed to one of her companions –

"Only look at Miss Montresor, how glum she is!"

"Miss Montresor!" repeated Mr. Estcourt, gazing round him; "where is that charming little Iroquois?"

"Lord, there she is to be sure," returned Miss Livia; "that fine lady in the pouts, who thinks none of us are good enough to wipe her shoes."

"Ho, does she so?" said the gentleman; "when I saw her last, by G – d I believe no one would have been solicitous for that honour. Lesley," continued he, affecting to whisper, "don't you remember that fine girl digging potatoes at Hampton-wick, with flowing locks and rent garments?"

"Loose were her tresses seen, her zone unbound!"[132] exclaimed Mr. Lesley, in an heroic accent; and staggering to Rosella, who had run to Mrs. Ellinger, to beg that she might be permitted to sit down, he seized her hand, swearing that she was a divine creature, and deserved a civic crown for her achievements.

Again she appealed to Mrs. Ellinger, who having now no hope of deriving any thing interesting from such horrid brutes, who appeared in more danger of falling asleep than of falling in love, and fearing to be censured for tolerating such unqualified impertinence, she again assumed her most sublime mien, and with infinite solemnity expostulated upon such ungentlemanly conduct. But as soon as they discovered that she was the Lady of the mansion, her remonstrances, instead of subduing, increased their insolence, by the prospect of hoaxing Mrs. Latitat,[133] and quizzing the handsome potatoe-digger at the same time.

The whole party seconded this noble purpose by encoring the witticisms, roaring out bravo at every capital hit, and finally, when the enemy were totally discomfited, the men retreating and the women fainting, this frantic crew, some of whom were British Legislators, began hallooing most vehemently to signify their victory, and celebrate their triumph.

At this moment Mr. Ellinger entered the room, fury and revenge lowering on his brow, and several constables in his train. The conduct of Mr. Povey and his companions had attracted the notice of a very grave and indefatigable personage who superintended in the office, who in defiance of the noise and confusion around him, had, till within the last hour, been writing his six words in a line, and his six lines in a page, with wonderful perseverance and unabated attention: but though he would have been an excellent secretary to the mad hero of the north,[134] it was not in human nature to hear unmoved, the abominable jar of horrible sounds that began to assail his sturdy ears when the truant was conducted home: the scribe was enraged to find, for the first time, his quill curvetting, and his eye wandering from the parchment to bring intelligence to his distracted brain; and perceiving that it was wholly impossible again to fix his roving attention, he snatched his hat, and flew with all the energy of revenge, to several places where he thought it probable he should meet Mr. Ellinger. Having at length succeeded in his search, he made out such a charge against *Povey and others aiding and abetting*, that Mr. Ellinger collected his judicial attendants, and stumped home, firmly resolved to lodge all the conspirators in the watch-house.[135]

His wife, shocked at so vulgar and plebeian an idea, which he announced on entering the room, and inexpressibly mortified at the events of the evening, that for a month past she had been planning to render uncommon and delightful, endeavoured to palliate what had happened: but Mr. Ellinger imitated those barbarous husbands who cruelly maltreat a gentle, lovely, and faultless wife, by desiring her to check her confounded tongue, and then proceeded to execute his intention, notwithstanding the endeavours of the intruders to resist with effect.

"Good God!" whispered the disconsolate matron, "I shall be derided by all my friends! What a catastrophe! How will it sound that the principal men amongst my visitors, instead of entangling themselves in imprudent yet indelible passions for beautiful girls of mysterious birth, should make a drunken riot in spite of the awe which my presence should have inspired, and be ignominiously taken to a vulgar watch-house, when they ought to have been employed in carrying off their lovely unknowns to their sequestered castles!"

In despite of the mortifying cruelty of the circumstance, the good friends of Mr. Povey were at length led away, after the destruction of a few glasses and tumblers, and some hysteric fits on the part of a few ladies, who declared however, on recovering their breath and recollection, that they should now dance with more spirit than before, and maliciously begged Mrs. Ellinger to try to prevail with her husband to join the party; a request she was imprudent enough to comply with, and the result was a very rough refusal, the instant dismission of the superb orchestra, and a very plain hint to those who had conveyances in waiting, that the most proper thing they could do, would be to depart. Mrs. Ellinger, still more shocked, had now nothing to do but to weep over her unhappy destiny: but her guests in general regarded her tears with the most vulgar apathy; and after a most cheerless and tedious interval, the rooms were cleared of all but the family and Rosella, who waited with painful impatience to hear the chariot announced. But unfortunately, Miss Beauclerc knowing her fondness for dancing, and imagining she would be pleased with her *soirée*, delayed sending it rather beyond the time proposed, and Rosella was obliged to witness a violent quarrel between Mrs. Ellinger and her husband, and a furious recrimination on the part of their hopeful and amiable children.

Time however still moves, though slowly, and at half after one, she left the wretched habitation of morose tyranny, imprudent folly, absurd pretensions, and flippant bickering. Miss Beauclerc, who sat up for her return, was surprised to see her so lifeless and dispirited, when she had expected to behold her all gaiety and animation: but an explanation of the disasters of the evening well accounted for the cause, and her friend not only sympathized in her disappointment and vexations, but equally in her poor Selina's well-imagined mortification and chagrin.

Chapter XI

RAGE FOR ACCOMPLISHMENTS – SOFT MANNERS IN A LADY OF FASHION CRITICALLY ILLUSTRATED

TWO mornings after the fête, Mr. Mordaunt was announced to Miss Beauclerc before she had quitted her breakfast table, and as he did not often confer the favour of a ceremonious visit, she concluded that he had some communication to make relating to affairs of business. He addressed her with greater solemnity and less kindness than usual, and after a conversation of a few minutes –

"So I find that this little girl," said he, turning to Rosella, "narrowly escaped being conducted to the watch-house on Thursday night, for being suspiciously found in the company of half a dozen house-breakers."

Rosella smiled, and he continued –

"I heard this pretty anecdote from Lord Morteyne, whose foolish brother was one of the gang it seems. Lady Lucy Estcourt was uneasy for the result of the precious frolic, and I was applied to, to propose terms of accommodation to Ellinger. In the discussion of the business, I learned that Miss Montresor had grounds for complaint, and I am commissioned to offer very humble excuses, which I suppose will be accepted. And now that I have explained myself," continued he, with a countenance half-serious, half-gay, "let me never more hear that your fondness for dancing, or any other youthful folly, betrays you into a situation so distressing and extremely improper, as the account I have received gives me to understand you were exposed to on Thursday."

Miss Beauclerc coloured, and was beginning a vindication, but Mr. Mordaunt interrupted it by dismissing Rosella with good-humoured freedom to her embroidery-frame: for so antiquated and absurd were his ideas, that he fancied young ladies still employed two or three hours of the day in working: nor would he have believed Mrs. Methwald herself, had she informed him, that the rising female generation found their time wholly filled up in studying botany, modern philosophy, and the *theory* of morality – in shuffling Irish steps to the tune of *Go to the devil and shake yourself* – in playing tolerably well, or intolerably ill, upon two or three instruments – and lastly, in dressing *à la grecque*, and *practising* soft manners, or indulging in faro-table manners, according to the whim of the day.[136] Rosella did not however laugh in his face at the barbarism he had uttered, but took the hint, and withdrew.

She had felt sufficiently mortified and uncomfortable at the moment of receiving those insults Mr. Mordaunt's well-meant lecture painfully renewed the remembrance of: and now the intelligence that Lord Morteyne and his sister were acquainted with the circumstance of her being present at such a scene, redoubled her chagrin.

"What will they think of me!" exclaimed she; "they will suppose I am always going where I ought not to be, and ever acting with the same impropriety."

This idea so distressed her, that in spite of her usual good spirits, it produced some tears, and she resolved to entreat Miss Beauclerc never to accept for her any other invitation from Mrs. Ellinger, which indicated, by any promised festivity, that she might again be introduced to such unpleasant associates: and indeed at this moment she thought she could be very well satisfied to remain at home the whole year round, rather than hazard encountering such vexatious circumstances.

When Mr. Mordaunt departed, she flew to Miss Beauclerc, to prefer the meditated request; but observing her in tears, and in very apparent distress, she forgot every idea but that of offering consolation.

Miss Beauclerc in a short time recovered to tolerable composure, but was entirely silent on the subject of her agitation. She informed Rosella however, that she meant very shortly to make a tour to the northern part of the island, principally to amuse her mind by a change of scene, and that she might at the same time see her aunt Delaval, probably for the last time.

Rosella was confounded at this intelligence; for she was not by any means certain that she was to accompany her kind friend, and the chagrin of quitting her, perhaps for many months, joined to the horror she had conceived at returning to the house of Mr. Ellinger, overpowered her spirits, and the tears gushed from her eyes.

"Do *you* then object to remain with me?" exclaimed Miss Beauclerc, mournfully.

"Me!" cried Rosella; "Oh no: and shall I have the happiness of being your companion in this journey? Did you think of taking me?"

"Yes, my own Rosella," replied Miss Beauclerc, "you *shall* accompany me. I have suffered much," she added, in a faltering voice, "from the harsh reflections I have not deserved; but I could not bear to part with you now, and I will not consent to give either of us such unnecessary anguish. You shall call once more on Mrs. Ellinger before we leave town, and only once, to bid her adieu. I cannot like Mr. Ellinger," resumed she, "or his children; but I think the situation of my friend Selina so pitiable, and I have so many obligations to her, that independent of my affection, I could not be justified in giving her up."

The request Rosella had intended to make, was thus prevented; and as Mr. Mordaunt had so seriously taken up the affair, she was pleased that she had not further wounded the feelings of Miss Beauclerc by adding to his remonstrances, what on her part, would appear a complaint.

Three weeks had not elapsed since Rosella had first heard of the travelling plan, before her friend had so well arranged her establishment to admit of her absence, that she had only further to select those of her domestics she intended to take in her suite; to bid adieu to the few intimates she still retained, in defiance of the melancholy and eccentricity of which she was accused, and to fix the day of her departure.

Rosella, who had equally busied herself in preparation, almost forgot her recent chagrin in the charming prospect of visiting some of those delightful scenes she had read so glowing a picture of, both in real and ideal travellers; and Miss Beauclerc on her side, could think and dream only of wild rocks and mountains, tremendous precipices, fringing woods, gushing cataracts, romantic cottages placed on acclivities and declivities, lovely Jacquelinas, Clarentinas, Rosinas, Emmelinas, and more humble Joannas, Susannas, Cicelys, and Annas who inhabited them, playing upon their lutes, their forte-pianos and their harps, and gazing at the pale moon which never fails to dart its silver beams through their humble casements with such uncommon brilliancy, as to allow them to choose by its pale light a favoured poet from their libraries, which it is the etiquette to form of simple shelves placed against the white-washed, or neatly papered walls; no passing cloud intervening, the chaste orb of night next lends her aid to enable the beautiful recluses to distinguish and recite the most elegant passages from the most elegant authors. – Miss Beauclerc still follows them in fancy, and beholds them transported by the sublimity of their ideas, beyond the bounds of ordinary prudence or common sense; they wander forth, the volume still in their delicate hands, their mild blue eyes raised to heaven, their beautiful auburn hair escaped from its confinement, or refrained only by a simple ribbon (which, alas! would do little towards securing their lovely heads against damps and dews), their white robes flowing in beautiful drapery over their light and nymph-like figures! In this equipage they continue to contemplate and to stray, until they lose themselves in some wild and remote spot, where they gaze round them with astonishment, and start at their imprudence in venturing so far: but they account to themselves very naturally for the error, by the captivation of the surrounding scenery and the delightful stillness of the night; and the adventure never fails to produce something interesting or terrific. They return however at length, to their cottage, where some good and fond old dame is looking out in infinite anxiety for the stray sheep; she then spreads before the delicate young creature her guest, the most delicious cream and new cheese, a profusion of exquisite fruit and home-made bread, new-laid eggs, and currant wine. The gentle souls make a slight repast, because no heroine ever yet committed such an indecorum as to eat a plentiful meal; and retire to their excessively neat apartments, not to sleep vulgarly in their bed, but to ruminate on their mysterious destinies, and revolve their recent adventure.

In short, so delightfully did the imagination of Miss Beauclerc delineate the gentle wanderers of fiction, that she determined not to defer her own ramble another week, though it was now only the beginning of April; but the season, in compliance with her wishes, was uncommonly forward, the air mild and genial, the foliage rapidly bursting forth, and the grounds at Avelines ornamented with early flowers.

"My Rosella," said the fond mother, "we will defer our charming tour no longer than till next Monday: to-morrow we will take leave of Mr. Mordaunt, and this morning we will find time to call in Chancery-Lane, and bid adieu to our poor Mrs. Ellinger."

"My dear kind Miss Beauclerc," exclaimed Rosella, "how shall I repay your goodness! If you had resolved to make this sweet excursion without me, and had been now going to leave me at Mr. Ellinger's, how melancholy should I have been at the prospect of lingering a whole summer in that gloomy house, tormented by the society of the rude William and ill-tempered Livia! How grateful ought I to be to such a friend!"

"Rosella," replied Miss Beauclerc, embracing her, "you forget that I have often entreated you to spare these expressions of a gratitude you do not owe me: I cannot be happy without you; and every attention it is in my power to bestow, all the affection with which I regard you, is less than you have a right to claim – I mean from your invariable sweetness of disposition, and the tender respect you have ever evinced for me. Besides, I was well acquainted with your father, and I love you, my dear child, for his sake."

"And did you know my mother too?" said Rosella, much interested in the question: "I have often asked Mrs. Ellinger whom she resembled, and she has always told me she was like you in every respect: – was my father as amiable?"

"A thousand times more so," returned Miss Beauclerc eagerly: "but tell me, could you have loved your mother very much, as a mother, if she had been, as Mrs. Ellinger says, entirely like me in person and mind?"

"I suppose I ought to have been more attached to her," replied Rosella, "than I am to you; but I really do not think I could have loved her better than you, who have at once been the kindest friend, and the most indulgent mother to me."

The heart of Miss Beauclerc was so much softened by the affection of Rosella, that the secret of their affinity might have been at that moment revealed to her, had not the carriage, which had been ordered for a shopping expedition, been announced.

When they arrived at Mr. Ellinger's mansion, Miss Beauclerc, in contradiction to her general custom, entered it; and having drawn her faithful Selina to her own apartment, that they might discuss, uninterruptedly, their darling project, and settle the correspondence they meditated, Rosella was left in the sitting-room with Miss Livia, who had been taking a lesson from a drawing-master, and was now affecting to shade a delectable sketch from a print of Charlotte at the tomb of Werter.[137] The *outrée* dress of the German heroine, designed from the fashions of the day, and dated at least ten years back, the form without symmetry, and the features without meaning, were exceedingly improved by the joint efforts of Miss Livia and her preceptor, who had, at least, an equal share in the performance to which she was giving the *coup-de-grace*;[138] and Rosella gazed with extreme astonishment upon the wonders of her pencil.

"You did not know that I was learning to draw?" said the self-satisfied student, with a look of triumph.

"No," replied her visitor, "I had not heard it: have you learned long?"

"I think you might perceive that I have made some proficiency," returned Miss Livia: "Mr. Dawson says he never gives such sweet things as I have to copy, but to his very best scholars. I'll shew you my Innocence with her sweet little lamb – and Abelard and Eloisa: those are only little things, quite when I began, but here is Una and the Parson's Maid, and Patty and William at Eve, and Belinda with her dog Shock, and the Shepherdess of the Alps, and this is –"[139]

"Give me leave," interrupted Rosella, "to look at what you have already laid before me, and then I will examine the rest of your performances."

She then took up some of the caricatures which had been so rapidly presented to her, and unable to outrage truth so far as to bestow upon them any praise, again enquired how long the young lady had taken lessons.

"Oh more than six weeks," returned Miss Livia; "but this is not all I have done, for I assure you I have learned to paint landscapes: here is Hornsey Church and the Bell at Edmonton;[140] and here is a willow, with two swans swimming under it; and this is a castle, Mr. Dawson does not know where – this should be a tower, to look round like the top of St. Paul's, but somehow I blotted it, and it does not show so well what it should be: but mama likes this better than any thing I have done yet: she wanted Mr. Dawson to show me how to put Innocence with her little lamb, to be looking out of this old broken window, because she thought it would pass for a young lady and a fawn, and then it would seem as if some gentleman had shut her up there, and that the fawn had followed her in when she went to take a walk in the forest, which should have been just here, mama says; this bush in the corner shows where the forest should begin. – However, Mr. Dawson said it could not be done now that the picture was finished; and mama has been teasing him ever since to draw an old castle and a forest and a moon, with a young lady all in white coming out of it."

"Out of the moon?" asked Rosella, smiling.

"No, no," returned Miss Livia, "you know I don't mean that: out of the castle or the forest, I forget which. And then on one side there is to be a rock, with a cave under it, and you are to see a whole heap of – what are they called? – men who used to rob and murder people above a hundred years ago."

"Thieves and assassins, I suppose," said Rosella.

"No indeed," resumed the young lady, rather contemptuously; "who would think of putting thieves into a picture, dressed like other men, with nothing but pistols in their hands! – no, what I mean is – *banditti* – that's the word. Oh Lord! but I have another secret to tell you – you must make believe though, not to know it; for mama thinks to surprise Miss Beauclerc and you when you come back again. She has bought me a piano-*fort*[141] – it's up stairs in the garret, for cross papa must not find it out – so Mr. Strum, who lodges two doors off, gives me sixteen lessons for a guinea."

"Surely you mistake, Livia," said her auditor, who recollected that her own master only attended twice for that sum.

"No indeed: and I can play the Battle of Prague, and the Siege of Bangalore, and Hurly Burly, and the Storming of Trincomalee."[142]

"Already!" exclaimed Rosella: "I should have thought you could scarcely have had time to learn the gamut?"[143]

"Oh, Mr. Strum says it is ridiculous to perplex people who have such an ear as I have, with too much of such hum drum nonsense; but come, I will show you my piano-*fort*, and you shall hear me play the Storming of Trincomalee."

Rosella was not without some curiosity to witness the performance, and followed her to the musical garret, where Mr. Strum condescended to preside as Apollo, and was amused with a composition that sounded like harmony run mad, very vilely mangled, where noise and loud uproar saluted her ear instead of brilliancy and execution. The piano-forte, Mrs. Ellinger's secret purchase, was old and extremely battered, and in its best days had never deserved a more conspicuous situation than that in which it was now placed.

"There!" exclaimed Miss Livia, ending with a full chord, fiercely struck, "how do you think I execute? Have you the Storming of Trincomalee?"

"No," replied Rosella, "I never heard it before."

"Good gracious! it's the sweetest thing in the world! I wonder you have not got the Storming of Trincomalee; – stay, I am afraid my cross papa is come home, so I cannot play the Siege of Bangalore now; you shall hear it another time."

Rosella thanked the young lady for this kind promise.

"Let us creep down," resumed Miss Livia, "and mind you do not tell mama that I have let you into the secret."

Rosella promised to attend to the caution, and they descended to the sitting-room, where, instead of *cross papa*, they found Mr. Povey, who had walked up stairs for some papers deposited in the old escrutoire. He accosted Miss Livia's visitor with a half-confident, half-sheepish grin, and enquired if she had seen the Estcourt family lately.

"I know very little of any individual of it," replied Rosella; "they are not in any of Miss Beauclerc's parties."

"Do tell Miss Montresor," cried Livia, eagerly, "what that droll creature said of her!"

"Of me!" exclaimed Rosella: "who is the droll creature you speak of?"

"My friend Cyril Estcourt, Ma'am: but I shall not repeat his quizzing nonsense."

"Oh I am determined she shall hear it though," cried the obliging young lady: "he said you might be handsome; he did not care a – whether you was or not but that you gave yourself confounded airs to Mr. Lesley, considering you had been taken out of a brick-field, where you had spent your *tender* years in mixing up mud pancakes. And he said afterwards that his brother, Lord Morteyne, found you once lying half dead on the Reading road, for you was not the kind of young lady to be kept under any restraint."

The countenance of Rosella was suffused a deep crimson, and her eyes beamed with indignation at this unjust and insolent report, which the malicious informer repeated with equal eagerness and glee.

"Who did Mr. Estcourt tell this to?" asked Rosella, her resentment suddenly giving way to unmixed mortification.

"Lord, I don't know – to a whole room full of people."

"No no, Miss Ellinger," cried Povey, interrupting her, "no such thing; there was only Ashmore, and Lesley, and Morteyne, and Mr. Cressy, and me."

"Well, that was a room full, wasn't it?" demanded Miss Livia, in a voice of angry interrogation.

"At least," said Rosella, hardly restraining her tears, "there were enough present to answer the intention of Mr. Estcourt, if he meant that his comments should reach me."

"Lord, Ma'am," said Povey, "nobody minds what Cyril says: – now for example, there's me – if I was to kick up a row every time I was hoaxed, I should have little else to do."

He then withdrew with his papers, saying in a low voice to Miss Livia, as he passed her, "Damme, if I ever tell you any thing again!"

"You only say so," replied the young lady in a careless tone; "I know you will though."

The conference between Miss Beauclerc and her friend now broke up, and their entrance relieved Rosella from the good-natured communications and observations of her companion, with whom she parted however, in apparent civility. Mrs. Ellinger embraced her with pathetic emotion, and conjured her to supply every accidental deficiency in the correspondence of her beloved Sophia.

Rosella promised compliance, and returning her adieu, tripped down the *sombre* stairs with a light step. Her delight in quitting the house, predominated as usual over every other emotion; but on her re-entrance into that which she now considered as her home, she could not fail to recollect the mortification and chagrin she had received through the officious medium of Miss Livia and Mr. Povey, and immediately imparted the grievance to her friend, who treated the report with apparent contempt, but who was, in fact, not displeased that Rosella, beloved as she was, should become the object of transient malevolence and misrepresentation. Was there indeed a single heroine in the great circle of her reading, who had escaped them? – Not one of any celebrity; and this recollection instantly reconciled her to the impertinence of Mr. Estcourt, who had not forgotten that Rosella was the immediate cause of the disgrace he had endured at the hermitage at Avelines – a disgrace he could not revenge upon his brother, because he condescended occasionally to have recourse to his purse.

The next morning, as Miss Beauclerc had proposed, Rosella accompanied her to Mr. Mordaunt's, and contrary to the wishes of either, they met Mrs. Methwald at home, who happened at the moment to be attended by her daughter and son-in-law. Rosella had never before seen Mr. Cressy, and was in considerable confusion during the introduction; when it occurred to her that his opinion, if it was formed upon the cruel reports circulated by Mr. Estcourt, must be of a most unfavourable nature.

Mr. Mordaunt did not immediately appear, and the conversation, after the entrance of Miss Beauclerc and her companion, was continued upon the same subject their appearance had given a momentary interruption to.

"I was so extremely shocked," said Mrs. Cressy, addressing her mother, "that I resolved never more to subject myself to such a tormenting purgatory as that of pretending to introduce a young woman into public. Your sister must procure herself another *chaperon*, indeed she must," continued she, turning to her husband, with a *fâde*[144] smile, and raising up one hand with a prim motion, which extended only to the elbow; "for I would not break my resolution upon any consideration: it is unfortunate for her that I happened to be *chagrenée*[145] with this most unlucky Miss – but you are acquainted with my firmness of mind, though you cannot know half the provocation I received. As she was left upon my hands, and there happened to be a vacancy in my Opera-box, I thought I might venture to take her; I shall never forget the *horreur* she gave me! There was not a *gaucherie* she did not torture me with; she took precedence of Lady Emlin,[146] dropped her fan upon poor Brackin's nose, who was bowing to me from the pit, and because a large scene happened to fall, and a horse to prance in the grand procession of the ballet, she actually screamed. The Marquis was at my elbow – I thought I should have fainted with shame; however, I had recourse to my usual fortitude, and consoled myself with a vow, never to take her out again, were she to live twenty years in my house."

This good-natured speech was uttered in a voice scarcely above a whisper, with a monotonous tone of determined placidity; and it closed with a practised smile. But the lady was not yet satisfied with having hitherto been the only speaker, for she addressed her mother again, without suffering any other person to utter a syllable –

"Do you go to Lady Emlin's assembly Ma'am? I have nothing in the world but old dresses to wear; but I can't afford myself any thing just now; my Opera box and court-dress have absolutely ruined me."

This declaration ended like the last, with a smile that drew up her cheeks, naturally prominent, almost to her eye-brows. Mr. Cressy returned the simper with an air of approbation, but could no longer allow her fatiguing loquacity to exclude him from shining in the conversation; and he paid his court to Mrs. Methwald by a number of compliments, which he meant should be extremely insinuating, requiring her judgment upon some delicate pastoral poetry, and some elegant little fugitive pieces[147] he had lately procured for her.

His Lady was too well-bred to interrupt him, and amused herself *en attendant*, with gazing *non chalamment*,[148] alternately at Rosella and Miss Beauclerc, who felt offended at the very little attention the family party had shown to her, and had taken up the newspaper whilst she waited the appearance of Mr. Mordaunt.

Mrs. Methwald was in an agony of fidgets, which her son-in-law vainly endeavoured to remove by the most assiduous respect, and he only increased the sharpness of the thorns upon which the poor lady sat. The important subject of anxiety which was torturing her soul, was twofold – she was sensible that Miss Beauclerc felt herself treated with slight and she would have enquired into the state of her health, have recommended books to her notice, pointed out a charming *jeu d'esprit*[149] in the last week's paper, and displayed her last number of the Botanical Magazine,[150] had not her whole countenance, all her nods, smiles, and assents, been wrested from her by Mr. and Mrs. Cressy. Her daughter, the first of women, must always be a primary object wherever she went; and she could not appear to turn abruptly from Mr. Cressy's elegant attentions: men were capricious – they must be kept always in temper she knew, and Mrs. Cressy's happiness was her grand consideration. On the other hand, a guest suffering under a moment of neglect, missing those little sources of entertainment and instruction which were always to be found with Mrs. Methwald, she could not endure to think of. She recollected too, that she had seen but the day before, an embroidered muslin at Dyde's,[151] that would just make up for Mrs. Cressy, and reward her projected self-denial – the muslin was cheap and pretty, and might be fold[152] whilst she was detained at home.

Mr. Cressy had, by this time, begun to think Rosella a very captivating little nobody, and was calculating how much credit might accrue to him, if by his notice and encouragement, with an occasional oath and compliment in her favour, he should succeed in bringing her forward. "She is handsomer than Lady Elizabeth Waldon,"[153] thought he, "not withstanding her want of manner, and that she has no idea of giving her features the right sort of expression; upon my soul, with management, she might be made a most fascinating creature."

The result of this private conclusion made Mr. Cressy throw himself into a chair by the side of Rosella; he smiled upon her to lessen the embarrassment he had no doubt she would feel at an honour so unexpected, and enquired if she had been to see the exhibition of work which did so much credit to her sex.[154] Rosella answered in the affirmative, and he immediately favoured her with his opinion of its merits.

Mrs. Cressy, surprised at the uncommon condescension of her husband, hunted nevertheless for her most approving and gracious smile, and having cast it over her features, regarded him and his fair companion with steady suavity, to announce that she had too much fortitude to be jealous.

"You have not been introduced to Lady Elizabeth Waldon, I presume?" said Mr. Cressy.

"No, Sir."

"But you have met her in society?"

"I do not recollect that I have," replied Rosella.

"Most certainly you have not then," resumed Mr. Cressy, determined to begin his preceptorship immediately, "or you could not have forgotten so fascinating a woman. I would recommend to every young lady now entering the world, to study her manner; there is such a captivating vivacity in her countenance, such uncommon softness of accent, such an insinuating gentleness of motion, such harmony of action, such flexible delicacy of voice, and such refinement of sentiment –"

"If she is a woman to be held up, without exception of circumstance, to the imitation of a young lady," said Miss Beauclerc, interrupting the panegyric, "the world most cruelly defames her."

The gentleman was nettled at this unanswerable remark, which might perhaps have been made in a louder key than the simpering gabble of Mrs. Cressy.

"No one, I am certain," exclaimed Mr. Cressy, "ever heard her voice raised in anger or rustic gaiety above the silver tones of decorum: in short," added he, with considerable warmth, "were I to propose to the woman I wished most to admire, a model to captivate my approbation, Lady Elizabeth Waldon –"

"Oh, you have already heard it then?" said Mr. Mordaunt, as he entered the room: "if there is a woman I could less forgive than another, it is that specious devil – married to a man who gratified every absurd whim with doting fondness – the mother of three heavenly children, and to desert them, to abandon their father! – The unhappy babe she pretended to nourish at her flinty breast, whose food was converted to poison by her dissipations, has died in convulsions; her poor mother, whose hands I have myself seen her kiss with affected fondness, at every short absence, has been in fainting fits from the moment she learnt the intelligence, and Waldon is now actually in a strait waistcoat!"

A short but complete silence succeeded to this imperfect but well-understood account. Mr. Cressy was dumb, and his Lady, who had often experienced a secret impatience at his warm admiration for the fallen idol, now felt an equally dissembled emotion of joy.

"Are we to understand, Sir," demanded Miss Beauclerc, "that the lady has eloped?"

"I thought I heard you speaking of the circumstance as I entered," returned Mr. Mordaunt.

Miss Beauclerc smiled, and a second momentary silence ensued, which she now thought proper to interrupt by announcing her journey and the intention of her visit. Mr. Mordaunt seemed astonished at the suddenness of the plan, for he had never before heard that it was in agitation; but whatever might be his opinion, he judged it would have little weight with Miss Beauclerc, and merely desired her to bring his little girl safely back, in a tone of solicitude his pretended gaiety but ill concealed. Mr. Cressy would have buried himself in describing the most charming route, but that his recent discomfiture chained his tongue: and Miss Beauclerc having returned, with equal gravity, the ceremonious farewell of Mrs. Methwald, and the insipid half courtesy of her peerless daughter, descended to her carriage. Mr. Mordaunt accompanied her to it, and as he parted with Rosella, who happened to be a few steps behind her –

"Remember, my dear child," said he, with more than usual kindness and energy, "that you leave here a firm, sincere, and affectionate friend: one who will consider an application in any little emergency or distress, as a mark of confidence and esteem. If occasion should stimulate you to make use of this hint, recollect that I urged it."

VOLUME II

Chapter I

RAGE FOR CASEMENTED COTTAGES – FOR WANDERING IN WILDS OBSCURE – A MYSTERIOUS STRANGER

THE delightful peregrination from which Miss Beauclerc promised to herself and Rosella infinite amusement, numberless adventures, and ultimate happiness, was not, of course, delayed by her. She had settled to take with her only one male domestic, as she had agreed with Mrs. Ellinger that he might be sent out of the way if any interesting occurrence should take place which his presence could mar; and as she might sometimes have occasion for a faithful old servant, whose zeal and fidelity would induce him to expose his safety and life for the protection of his beloved Lady, she fixed upon Simpson who had lived in her family near forty years, and often talked of the joyful day that gave birth to Miss Sophy; a day on which he boasted to his fellow domestics that he drank part of a bottle of claret at his own expence, though he was only an under footman, to the health of his Lady and the little Miss.

Miss Beauclerc's own maid was a grave personage, who moved from the housekeeper's room to her Lady's apartment, and from her Lady's apartment to the housekeeper's room, with infinite dignity and importance; and the first of considerations with her, was her own proper ease and comfort, so that Miss Beauclerc thought it but too probable she would upon the first misadventure, such as being benighted in a forest, or overturned at midnight into a marlpit, consult her own vulgar safety, and demand her wages and her *congé*[155] the very next morning; a want of simplicity and affection that would reflect dishonour on her mistress, and extremely sully the narrative she intended to transmit to her faithful Selina, who well knew that a heroine's attendant is infallibly some Babette, or Jeannette, or Annette, who prattles an astonishing quantity of nonsense in the midst of the most horrible occurrences, and is always on the point of betraying her young Lady in her most important expeditions, by screaming, or sneezing, or raising a hue and cry after a ghost, or clinging to her so as to make her drop her lamp. But in the midst of the mischief, Babette, Jeannette, or Annette should be extremely intelligent, though full of simplicity, and above all other considerations she must be unalterably attached to her beautiful mistress.[156]

In vain had Miss Beauclerc cast her eye upon every *soubrette*[157] within her observation; no such personage could be found; and she was compelled, after consulting with Selina, to decline at present the attendance of a female servant, in the secret hope of meeting a more suitable one in some "deep glen,"[158] remote from the infection of a too populous neighbourhood.

At length Rosella and her friend placed themselves in the travelling post-chaise, and attended only by old Simpson on a hack-horse, left London at six in the morning of a delightful Spring day, more warm and genial than the season in general might promise. Both the fair travellers felt a renovation of spirits as the carriage whirled them from the great centre of dissipation, and left Marybone[159] behind them; and Rosella then, for the first time, thought of enquiring their immediate destination. She learnt that Miss Beauclerc had settled to proceed immediately to the northern counties of England, and then enlarge her excursion to Scotland; after which she had almost resolved to bend her steps to the charming and romantic Principality which has furnished adventurous scenes to so many modern heroines,[160] who have climbed its rugged cliffs, and reposed their beautiful heads in its delightful cottages.

Rosella was perfectly satisfied with the plan, and charmed with the prospect of becoming better acquainted with the "mountain nymph, sweet Liberty," and living in "unreproved pleasures free,"[161] without danger of being stigmatized as a hoyden, or a savage rustic. Whilst the imagination of Miss Beauclerc was filled *à l'ordinaire*[162] with

> "Russet lawns and fallows grey,
> Where the nibbling flocks do stray –
> Mountains, on whose barren breast
> The labouring clouds do often rest;
> Meadows trim with daisies pied,
> Shallow brooks and rivers wide.
> Towers and battlements *she* sees
> Bosom'd high in tufted trees,
> Where *she thinks* some beauty lies,
> The Cynosure of neigh'bring eyes."[163]

At the second stage poor old Simpson quitted his horse for a hack-chaise, a change which had previously been agreed upon, and he then proceeded with rather less fatigue to himself.

Miss Beauclerc found little to interest her attention on a well-frequented turnpike road, where the moonlight walks of fair ladies would probably terminate uncouthly, from their being run over by mail-coaches, or being knocked down and robbed in a common vulgar way by a footpad;[164] she therefore pursued her journey with eager rapidity, till the country assumed a form so diversified and lovely, that her eyes devoured every object on which they rested, and she often left the chaise, attended by Rosella, to ascend some steep, or peep into cottages whose romantic situations excited recollections and hopes which were generally lost in the disgust occasioned by awkward cunning, evident designs of extorting her liberality, and often a more open and shameless attack upon her purse, uttered in tones of whining cant and palpable disingenuousness. The children, instead of being strong and healthy, were often pining in dirt and neglect; and in place of the artless and careless graces of childhood, they almost universally teased her by extending their little filthy hands, and petitioning for *a farding*, in voices of such whimpering discordance that her ear was tortured by the sound.

Rosella, though uncommonly fond of children, could not prevail upon herself to caress these; and with her friend the generally resumed her journey in disappointment.

"I must remove still further from the murky south," ejaculated Miss Beauclerc; "I have not yet attained those regions, where noble simplicity and genuine hospitality of soul urge a peasant to set before the passing stranger his choicest flock of food and beverage, cloathe the luckless wanderer in his raiment, and serve him with the hard-earned fruit of his toil."

In consulting the book of roads[165] she had taken with her, she pursued her way in preference through Yorkshire, and arrived on the fourth day from leaving the metropolis, at Greta-bridge,[166] where the wild aspect of the country and the apparent rusticity of the inhabitants induced her to pause. From this town Rosella and herself made little excursions to the neighbouring places which could boast the allurement of natural beauty; and in one of their rides through the rich valley of Swale to Wenseley Dale, they were peculiarly charmed with a spot in which was situated a thatch-roofed inn, where they stopped to take refreshment. It was sheltered from the bleak winds that sweep over the eastern ocean, by an irregular chain of hills, rising, as Miss Beauclerc had often read in the page of fiction, majestic, wild, and romantic; at their base ran a clear and rapid stream, which loudly murmured to find its progress sometimes impeded by fragments of rock either time or the war of elements had hurled from the surrounding heights; a small bridge of a single arch rose over the river, which, a few paces further, flowed round the foot of a precipice in a pleasing curvature, and was for a time lost to the eye by an overshadowing grove of hazle-trees, the well-known haunt of all the village swains and lasses for five miles round. But these were not the sole attractions of the spot to the enthusiastic fancy of Miss Beauclerc; – the grove, when seen from the opposite bank of the stream, disclosed the white chimney and part of the roof of the little mansion to which she had been conducted, which thus viewed, might, without any indecorum of idea, have formed a retreat for the most captivating and ill-treated young lady that ever took refuge from the pursuit of lovers, or the calumnies of the world. A white chimney and thatched roof peeping out of a grove encircled by immense rocks, margined by a dashing stream!!!

"I feel so much fatigued," said Miss Beauclerc to Simpson, as she returned from a delightful ramble, "that I will have the horses again taken from the carriage; and if the people here can accommodate us for a day or two with tolerable convenience, I will lay by a little, and recruit my strength before I proceed further on my journey."

Simpson, whose old bones had been vehemently discomposed by a continued and wearying motion of so many days, excessively approved the proposal, and hastened to give orders, and make the necessary enquiries; whilst Rosella, happy as youth, health, and innocence could make her, was satisfied either to advance or repose, as her friend thought proper.

The inn, if it might be dignified with the title, was discovered to contain a tolerable lodging room, furnished with two old-fashioned beds, that appeared to have made a heavy impression upon the ancient floor, which evidently sunk in the places where they stood. This, however, might have been a fault in the grand construction of the building; for the surface of the boards was so exceedingly uneven, that a Noctambulo[167] might very well have supposed himself ascending to the turrets of an old castle, or descending to its caverns without moving from the precincts of his bed-room. This could not fail to prove an inconvenience to any fair heroine who paces her chamber after the extinction of her midnight lamp; but fortunately Miss Beauclerc overlooked the circumstance, because the window, which was a little shattered and crazy,[168] happened to be a real, original, green glassed, small squared casement, encircled by a creeping plant whose first shoots were just expanding; and though they could not be mistaken for "the sweet-briar, or the vine, or the twisted eglantine,"[169] yet at the moment Miss Beauclerc put her head out of the little window, a sparrow nestled amidst the budding leaves, and chirupped with great glee.

Such a sweet rural welcome instantly decided her stay at this charmingly retired spot for at least a week, and in a quarter of an hour Rosella and herself were completely established in their new quarters.

They arose the next morning with alacrity, to *wander* amidst the mountains that surrounded them, and gaze over the wild and deep vallies they overhung. Miss Beauclerc was now in the haven of her expectations; but not having been accustomed to these wandering delights, after having walked some time she felt much fatigued, and seated herself *en heroine* upon a fragment of rock.

A few yards beneath her the river murmured over its craggy bed, and on the further banks stood the ruins of a mill half hid by trees that grew in luxuriant wildness upon the steep ascent that formed a background to the deserted building. Miss Beauclerc drew a book from her pocket, and indulged herself in the pleasure of reading the mountainous adventures of a most mountain loving damsel, in a spot so congenial: whilst Rosella, delighted with the semblance of freedom she now enjoyed, and charmed with every passing gale that kissed her glowing cheek, flew from cliff to cliff, inhaling the freshness of the early morning, and expressing the fulness of her contentment in smiles and gestures of delight. Miss Beauclerc often raised her eyes from her book, to mark her step, now rapid from the impulse of curiosity, now arrested by wonder and pleased attention, and thought that her lovely figure highly adorned the scene. At length her friend observed her running with more than common speed; and strongly biassed by the tenor of her immediate studies, expected, with mingled horror and palpitating rapture, to see her pursued by twenty lurking banditti at least, in green velvet caps, with plumes of yellows and black doublets and hose trimmed with scarlet; she even pictured to herself the figures of the liveried spoilers all so tall and muscular, armed with arquebusses[170] and long sabres.

Rosella reached her, however, without pursuit, but so extremely out of breath, that it was several minutes before she could articulate that she had seen a man on the summit of the further rock, sometimes walking very quickly, at others as slowly, talking to himself in a very disturbed manner, and often striking his hand upon his forehead with frantic agitation. Miss Beauclerc listened in eager attention, but looked round in vain for the hero.

"I was frightened at his vehement motions," continued Rosella; "yet he has not the appearance I imagine a madman to have, nor does he look like a robber, but there was something very strange in his manner."

"Is he handsome?" asked Miss Beauclerc, hastily; forgetting, at that instant, all caution and reserve in the transporting hope of meeting with an adventure worthy the sublimest efforts of her pen.

"I did not observe his face," replied Rosella.

"Was he in the habit of a gentleman?"

Rosella believed so; "He looked unhappy," she added, "and as if he had committed an action he repented."

"No, my love," said Miss Beauclerc, sagely, "I rather think he has suffered wrong than done wrong; which way did he take?"

"I believe he came this way; shall we return to breakfast?"

Miss Beauclerc assented; but lingered so repeatedly, and looked behind her so often, that it became evident to Rosella she had no fear, at least, of the bugbear her own apprehensions had rendered formidable.

At a turning of the path they followed, which bent in sudden curves with the windings of the river, the object, whose approach was so much desired, and so much deprecated, unexpectedly appeared: he started, and regarding Miss Beauclerc and her young companion with earnest, but momentary glances, passed on. Rosella felt her heart palpitate when she discerned the moody wildness of his eye; but his quiet departure relieved her, and pressing the arm of her friend, she whispered her satisfaction at it.

The stranger turned at this moment to survey them once more, and his attention was arrested by the countenance of Rosella, which was turned full upon him: he stood a few seconds without motion, and then perceiving the alarm he had occasioned, advanced with an air of easy politeness, whilst he addressed them in a manner gentle and insinuating: "I hope," said he, "I am not a subject of terror to you, ladies?"

The unexpected change in his countenance, and the tone of his voice, which was calculated to quiet apprehension, revived the courage of Rosella, and the fugitive dimples again returned to her cheeks, while Miss Beauclerc interchanged with the stranger the compliments of the morning: and he probably conceiving that the romantic beauty of the spot which marked the *rencontre*, and its remoteness from the grand centre of etiquette and established ceremonials, would authorize the freedom of continuing the conversation, sauntered with them towards their little habitation, which Miss Beauclerc had soon an opportunity of pointing out to him as being such.

The stranger enquired how long she had honoured such a cottage by becoming its inmate, and proceeded to question her, but without any appearance of impertinent curiosity, concerning the route by which she had arrived at it. On learning that her companion and herself had recently quitted the metropolis, he eagerly asked the news of the day; but Miss Beauclerc professed to have paid little attention to the political or domestic reports in circulation at the moment of her journey.

They were now near the hôtellerie, and Simpson, who had with some difficulty procured materials for breakfast, was looking out for the return of the ladies; and the stranger on observing him, hastily bade farewell to his fair associates, and hurried back the way he came, without waiting for the invitation that hung upon the lips of Miss Beauclerc, that he would join their repast.

"This man has a very interesting countenance," said she to Rosella, when they were seated at the breakfast table; "he has certainly too the most captivating manners I ever beheld!"

He appeared good-humoured," returned she, "but I thought his gaiety seemed forced: he sometimes started and looked round him, I observed, with a very disturbed aspect."

"He was merely absent," replied Miss Beauclerc; "he has probably some painful recollections haunting his mind, or has reasons powerful and imperious, that impel him to resist the soft sensations now pervading his breast for the first time."

The entrance of old Simpson with post letters, which a messenger had been dispatched to Greta-bridge in pursuit of, prevented Rosella from obtaining an explanation of her friend's last words; and the novelty of seeing a letter addressed to her, effaced them entirely from her memory: she eagerly opened it, whilst Miss Beauclerc, unfolding a large packet of writing, exclaimed, "Amiable Selina! how active to gratify your absent friend! I could scarcely have expected such a pleasing mark of attachment until to-morrow."

The correspondent of Rosella proved to be the accomplished Miss Livia, who wrote, she said, because her mamma ordered her to do so; not that she had any thing particular to say, only that her cross papa had broke her piano-forte to pieces, and turned Mr. Strum out of the house; and that Mr. Povey had run away and hid himself, and nobody could find him for above a week; so his uncle had been in a fine fright, and had bought him a commission in the Guards, or else Mr. Povey threatened to enlist himself, to spite the old man.

All this important intelligence was read by Rosella with more indifference than the conclusion of the epistle, in which Miss Livia begged she would answer her letter, and tell her all the news she could think of, in return for her own communications; a task Rosella would most willingly have excused herself from undertaking.

When Miss Beauclerc had very attentively perused her voluminous epistle from the most amiable Selina, she prepared with more than usual glee and good-will to write her, in the words of Livia, all the news she could think of; and chose, as the most eligible situation for an occupation so important, the rural window of her own chamber, which afforded her a hint for the following amusing, novel, and most heroic paragraph: –

"I am now, my kind and gentle friend, seated at the little casement of my humble apartment, which offers the most enchanting prospect of varied beauty, the most delightful and admired landscape writer ever dissected. My beautiful Rosella, that darling girl, is now adorned with more than her usual loveliness, amusing herself by playing with the children of our honest host and hostess on the rustic lawn before the door" – this was actually the case – "I will now therefore, comply with your earnest request to learn our adventures."

Miss Beauclerc now paused in her career of narrative; and at this moment the fair subject of her eloquent pen called to her to say that she was going to walk a little way with the children, who, encouraged by her caresses, importuned her in an accent she could scarcely comprehend, to go with them to some place the could not distinguish the name of: but they pointed to the road up the hill, and entreated so earnestly, that Rosella was as eager to gratify them, as they could be to receive gratification. Miss Beauclerc readily assented, in the hope that she might again meet the *mysterious stranger*, and thus continue the adventure in style; and Rosella immediately suffered her little companions, a girl and a boy, who appeared about four or five years old, to lead her forward.

They took a path leading to an eminence that overlooked the chimnies of the diminutive mansion they quitted; and the heat of the sun, joined to the fatigue of ascending an almost perpendicular steep, made the way seem long to Rosella; but her associates climbed up very nimbly, with a fearless dexterity that proclaimed they had been accustomed to the task, and very much approved it. At length they arrived at the summit of the hill, the little girl holding Rosella by the hand, the boy leading the way in a full trot, which he was obliged, however, to slacken every other minute, that he might allow his sister and her *protectrice* to overtake him; and in another quarter of an hour they reached the goal at which their infantine wishes pointed.

It was a very forlorn little cottage, raised against a mountain's side, with a level of about six feet before it, from whence any despairing personage might, with the smallest trouble, precipitate themselves several fathoms, without danger of breaking their descent, except from a few jutting craigs, that might perchance have suspended a woe-worn lover between heaven and earth, "a spectacle for gods and men."[171]

The children ran into the hut, the door of which was open, whilst Rosella found her attention too much engaged by the tremendous beauties of the place to follow them: no poetic description of roaring cataracts, cloud-capt hills, and yawning abysses came to her assistance, or aided her to give birth to her admiration and astonishment; no elegant soliloquy, uttered in a melodious voice, directed a listening swain to the spot – her animated satisfaction was strongly but silently expressed. No touch of a die-away lute, no silver tones of a celestial flute or oboe announced the approach of the *mysterious stranger*; yet the mysterious stranger at this moment approached, to gaze perhaps unseen upon the lovely figure of the fair angel he had so unexpectedly encountered in the early morning! – Ye gods, no! he approached to deposit a dirty shirt in Molly Spanger's wash-tub, and with a mind almost wholly intent upon breaking his fast with the oaten cakes and skimmed milk in Molly Spanger's larder.

Gentle genius of romance, be appeased! The recognition was made on either side in due form; Rosella looked round, the mysterious stranger started; Rosella blushed, the stranger bowed; she smiled, and he forgot his twofold errand, approached her with courtly ease, and having expressed much pleasure at this second meeting, pointed out to her more immediate observation the most prominent features in the landscape, in the terms of an amateur of the beauties of nature, and enquired if she was in the habit of delineating them.

Rosella replied that she was not, for that she had more inclination than genius for so charming an employment; but the stranger declared himself incredulous of the assertion, and expressed a wish to see her make an essay of her art in tracing the scenery that surrounded them. Rosella had however the modest opinion of her ability which she professed, and persisting in affirming it, the stranger at length reluctantly yielded to her decision, and changed the subject of conversation from an art to a science. Music was now his theme: having spoken of those instruments in use in the female world of fashion, and gathered from her replies how far she was mistress of them – "There is," said he, "a charming echo not more than fifty paces from this spot, which I think would produce a fine effect, if called forth by the modulations of a voice such as I judge you possess: you plead guilty," continued he, smiling, "will you allow me to conduce you to the "airy cell" of the "unseen nymph?"[172]

Rosella was on the point of complying; but a sudden idea of impropriety intervened, and after a moment of hesitation, she excused herself by saying she had two little companions in the cottage, who might miss her if she left the door. The stranger bowed his head with an air that seemed to say he comprehended her motive, and allowed it. In the moment of silence that ensued, his countenance lost its tranquil ease; he gazed round him as if he had awakened out of a dream, and every feature underwent a sudden convulsion. Rosella, much alarmed, immediately entered the hut which contained only its youthful visitors; but she felt even their presence a protection, and having recovered from the panic that had seized her, she had leisure to observe their actions: the boy was mounted upon a stool, endeavouring to open an old beaufet,[173] which refused to obey his efforts; and the girl then told her in melancholy accents, that Molly was gone out, and the nuts were locked up.

"Since it is so," replied Rosella, "we will return home; for I should be sorry to be a party in carrying off the least portion of your friend Molly's treasures in my first visit to her habitation, and in her absence."

The boy very unwillingly gave up his pursuit, and at her desire followed her out of the cottage. Rosella looked round for the stranger, but he had vanished. "How odd was his conduct!" thought she; "I wish I had bidden him farewell! Perhaps he was offended, or hurt at my abrupt retreat."

At her return to the hôtellerie, she found that Miss Beauclerc had laid by her writing, and was waiting her appearance with some impatience; the fact was, that she had exhausted her materials for the narrative to her gentle Selina, and having been compelled to leave her unknown hero in the act of breathing his first complement of sighs in honour of Rosella's charms, she was eager to procure the further information she had no doubt of obtaining in consequence of this second peregrination.

Rosella having delivered the children to the care of their mother, hastened to attend the summons of her friend, and being very closely questioned, contrived to recollect the principal part of the conversation which had passed between herself and the mysterious stranger; but she was far from being able to relate every word of it, and apply the appropriate gestures, with the copious accuracy that always accompanies the astonishing narratives of those heroines with never-failing memories, who contrive to recall every thought and word of their childhood, and recollect every sentiment, sentence, and single expression of all their friends and all their foes, their papas, their lovers, their nurses, and their waiting-damsels.

Miss Beauclerc was however extremely well satisfied with the account she obtained from Rosella, and the history for the perusal of the gentle Selina went on *à merveille*.[174] The remainder of this momentous day was passed, as the lady herself expressed it, in "tranquil serenity;" that is, Miss Beauclerc wrote her interesting narrative, and read another equally interesting from the large packet of books she had brought with her from her Circulating Library; and Rosella, for lack of something better to do, played with the children, and taught them their letters.

Chapter II

A STORM, AND A DISCOVERY. – A HERO'S RETIREMENT

ON the following morning Miss Beauclerc by no means forgot to repeat her early walk with Rosella: she would not lead exactly to the same spot, but she was careful to pass near it, in the hope of surprising her newly found hero in the first delightful meditations of love. Her watch had informed her that when she quitted her chamber it was but six o'clock; and the sun had long dissolved the liquid gems that hung upon the mountain foliage, when Rosella quite satisfied with the length of her ramble, talked of her own hunger, and her friend's wet shoes. But Miss Beauclerc affected for some time not to attend to these hints, and her perseverance was at last rewarded by the appearance of the *mysterious youth*; he was accompanied by a very beautiful French pointer who gave loud notice of the approach of the ladies. His master started, turned hastily to them, and bowed with a grave air, but spoke not.

Miss Beauclerc, secretly disappointed, and rather offended that no symptom of rapture should escape him at such a fortunate *rencontre*, returned the silent salutation, and taking the arm of Rosella, passed on. The path they were descending was smooth and slippery, and Miss Beauclerc either did, pretended to make a false step, which nearly brought her to the ground; – the exclamation Rosella uttered, caught the ear of the stranger, who discerned in the countenance of the lady the pain which she persuaded herself the accident occasioned her, and he politely offered to assist her to the bottom of the hill. Of course they were not mute as they proceeded: Miss Beauclerc professed her obligation for the attention of the stranger, who in return summoned his native gallantry to his aid, and talked of being much indebted to chance for his present enviable situation. On sight of their little habitation, Rosella, unconscious of the dignity of heroism, expressed a most vulgar inclination for her breakfast; and Miss Beauclerc recollecting the haste with which her supporter had retreated the preceding day, seized the opportunity of inviting him to partake their meal. He declined the honour in terms of regret, but without assigning any motive for his refusal.

"Perhaps," said Rosella innocently, "some other time will be more convenient to you?"

He bowed in silence.

"I cannot be so indecorous," thought Miss Beauclerc, "to urge him further."

At this moment the dog, who had followed his master's steps very closely, passed him, and ran forward, barking violently: the stranger called him back in a tone of anger, and as the poor little creature returned, menaced him with a blow.

"Oh don't beat him!" exclaimed Rosella eagerly, and she stooped to caress the animal, who crouched in terror; its master coloured violently, and with a conciliating action invited a reconciliation.

"Poor Pet!" cried he with a thoughtful look, "you have not been accustomed to rough treatment!"

"Is his name Pet?" asked Rosella; "ah, I see he has been used to wear a collar; has he lost it?"

The stranger appeared confused, and answered with hesitation that he had.

Miss Beauclerc lost not one word or a single tint of the changes in the countenance of the unknown youth, and had formed a variety of conjectures concerning this Pet of declining interest, which she concluded had been the gift of some fair favourite, whose image in the stranger's heart, had been superseded by the more lovely one of Rosella. Before the ladies reached the inn, he suddenly stopped, and withdrawing his arm from Miss Beauclerc, bade her good morning, and casting an expressive glance of cordiality at her companion, left them precipitately, followed by poor Pet, who often looked back on his fair protectress as he trotted away.

"This is very mysterious!" exclaimed Miss Beauclerc; "how strange that he should again turn away exactly at this spot!"

"In spite of his vehemence in correcting his little dog," said Rosella, "he appears amiable, especially when he shakes off that melancholy which seems to attend him. He says Pet is not used to rough treatment; I should like to know if the animal has always been his."

"It will not be easily discovered, I should imagine," said Miss Beauclerc, "for he is wonderfully cautious; and the mystery of the dog is not likely soon to be unravelled."

"What mystery do you allude to?" asked Rosella, in some surprise.

"A mystery time will undoubtedly unveil to our eyes," resumed the lady, "and we must wait the elucidation of it with patience."

Rosella readily agreed to have all the patience required; and just at that moment catching a view of Simpson, demanded if the breakfast were ready. Whilst she was employed in making it, her thoughts reverted insensibly to the stranger, and after some musing, she concluded that his mind must be a little disordered – a circumstance the people of the house could ascertain, if he resided in the neighbourhood; and she mentioned her conjecture to her friend, who agreed that Simpson should make some enquiries of the landlord. No one in the house, however, could give any information of the young man, though Rosella described both the master and the dog very minutely; and as Miss Beauclerc fully expected he would still remain *the Incognito*, in spite of every effort that could be made to discover who he was, she was not surprised or chagrined that her suspicions were just. The first part of her journal, which contained numberless surmises concerning the developement of the adventure, had already been sent off by a special messenger to the nearest post-town, from whence she was now awaiting the arrival of several articles of travelling appendage, for which she had written four days back; and as the commission had been given to the indefatigable Selina, she knew the execution of it would not be delayed.

Rosella, not having the same expedient as her friend to wear out the lagging hours, and not choosing, from an intuitive motive of delicacy, to repeat her ramble with her little playfellows, began to grow rather weary of this divine retreat, in which sentiment, so little partaking of the sublimity of heroism, she was heartily joined by old Simpson, who now found himself better able to continue flying after his Lady's tantrums, as he privately expressed himself, and had quarrelled with his wretched cock-loft[175] and his forlorn pallet bed.

In the course of the morning, the courier Miss Beauclerc had employed, returned with a large trunk brought by a stage from London; and the man had hired a cart to convey it from the town where it had been left. Rosella, charmed with the prospect of passing an hour in some kind of employment, solicited to unpack it; and Miss Beauclerc readily consenting, it was taken to their chamber immediately.

Amidst a variety of books, writing-paper, sheets, pillow-cases, &c. Rosella drew out some newspapers, and recollected that the stranger had enquired the news of the day with considerable anxiety; she renewed the circumstance in the remembrance of her friend, and with her usual alacrity to confer a benefit, asked if the papers might not be conveyed to him.

"He may," replied Miss Beauclerc, "have reasons very important for concealing himself, and we should perhaps do him an injury by exposing him to the notice of any one; and yet the intelligence he might gain from these papers might be essentially useful to him. I think, my dear Rosella, you may without any danger to yourself take them to that hut you visited yesterday; and if the woman has any knowledge of him, she will take charge of the packet for him; even if she has none, you may perhaps meet him by the way."

"I hope not," said Rosella, "I think he did not seem inclined to speak to us this morning; he may think me impertinent or officious."

"What a ridiculous apprehension!" interrupted Miss Beauclerc, who, in her extreme eagerness to pursue this delightful adventure, entirely lost sight of decorum. "Take the children with you, and leave the papers at the cottage, with an injunction to the woman to present them to the gentleman, if she should see him wandering in her neighbourhood. I am fatigued and busy, or I would accompany you. It is probable that you will merit the thanks of this poor man by the effort; and I am sorry to observe that you are rather unwilling to make it."

Rosella, perceiving that her friend spoke with a gravity she seldom used to her, instantly prepared to obey her, though with a reluctance she could not conquer. She put the papers up,[176] and descended to enquire for her little companions: the boy she learned, was absent from home, but the girl, who was the younger of the two, very eagerly accepted her invitation to walk to Molly Spanger's cottage, and seizing the hand of Rosella, led the way up the path, talking all the way "of the nuts locked up in the cupboard, which Molly had promised to give her when she came to see her."

Rosella was diverted with her prattle, and almost forgot the unwillingness with which she had undertaken her commission, in the pleasantness of the walk, which received no check, as on the preceding day, from the too great fervour of the sun: the harebell and violet began to unfold their humble beauties, and scent the passing gale with renovating sweets, and the blackbird made the wooded precipices reverberate his clear and mellow note.

"This is charming!" ejaculated Rosella; "I am again reconciled to the place."

She had now reached the brow of the mountain, and her little guide looking round with much perplexity, exclaimed, "Where's Molly's house?"

"To the left," answered Rosella, "we have not come wrong, I hope."

"Johnnie knows the way," cried the child; "Johnnie always comes with Molly."

"And did not you?" enquired Rosella.

"No, only once; Johnnie knows the way best."

Rosella now began to fear that this assertion was too true; for she had turned to the left, as on her first visit to the hut, but could not observe one object which she then recollected to have remarked. "We have lost our way, Patty," said she.

The child looked gravely up in her face, but made no reply; and Rosella, rather chagrined, yet without any fear of recovering her track, endeavoured to remedy the error by turning into another path, in which she walked for some time; still, however, no cottage greeted her view. "We have lost our way, indeed," repeated she.

"Can't we never go back again?" asked Patty.

"Oh yes," returned Rosella cheerfully; "but we must have a little patience."

"I tired!" cried the child in a still more aggrieved voice.

"Already!" exclaimed Rosella; "no, no, you are not tired yet; you will not be tired till you go home."

"I hungry!" resumed Patty, half crying.

Rosella was by this time alarmed; for in endeavouring to regain the right path, she insensibly found herself in the most wild and dreary range of mountains, which seemed reared by some enchanter to guard from human eye, the agitated stream that rushed with rapid and noisy violence in the deep glen beneath. "What shall I do?" exclaimed she in extreme anxiety.

"I dry!"[177] was now the burthen of poor Patty's song.

"Have patience, my good little Patty," repeated her companion; "tell me, is there any other cottage near Molly's?"

"I don't know – I dry!"

Rosella looked round her, she looked down the precipice before her, and gazed upwards towards the mountain's summits, but neither hut nor hovel rewarded the search: she discovered, however, that the clouds rolled black and angry over her defenceless head, and thought the heard them breaking at a distance against the craggy rocks in low peals of thunder. Nor were her fears groundless; in a few moments a louder explosion saluted her shrinking ear, and the innumerable echoes of the place continued the fearful sound, till Rosella imagined the elements were returning to their original chaos. – "I frightened!" screamed Patty; and her companion could scarcely sooth her fears, for her own were almost as potent.

At length, whilst the last echo was losing itself in distant air, a vivid flash of lightning, the prelude of another shock, illumined the darkened scene, and pointed out to her view the waves of the torrent foaming against the rocks, and rising in ungoverned fury to a height incredible. The thunder was more loud and tremendous than before; and the piercing screams of the terrified child added to her distress and horror.

"What will become of us! where shall I turn for shelter!" exclaimed she; and taking the arm of little Patty, who was burying her face in her gown, she went forward, though dreadfully appalled by the forked lightning, that darted with an angled movement from one point to another of the rocks that surrounded her; in one instant it was playing over her head, in another, attracted to the craig beneath her. An immense arm of a tree, splintered off by its electric stroke, fell from the mountain's top with a dreadful crash, into the bed of the river, sweeping every thing before it.

Rosella believing that the whole mountain was giving way to the storm, flew with the precipitation fear alone could give, and which equally winged poor Patty's little feet, through the brakes that encompassed her, and left the dreadful view, both of the precipice and torrent, behind her. Still however, she ran, and the child forgetting fatigue, hunger, and thirst, with some assistance kept pace with her, and in a few moments suddenly cried out – "There's Molly's house!" The eyes of Rosella followed her pointing finger, and discovered, not Molly's, but a still more miserable hut, to which, however, she gladly hastened. Having reached it, she endeavoured to let herself in; but the door was fastened, and a dog within gave notice of the attempt. Rosella, glad to find the place inhabited, rapped for admittance. "Open a door," cried Patty, "I wet!"

Nobody obeyed this peremptory summons, and Rosella knocked harder against the inhospitable little mansion, expressing aloud a wish to stay only during the storm, which appeared every moment to increase. The dog redoubled his barking at this second application, and a hasty step towards the door announced that it was successful. It opened – and Rosella beheld the *mysterious stranger* acting as porter, and Pet *in propria persona*, as sentinel: yet it did not occur to her that the incident was at all remarkable, as she immediately supposed both dog and master had, like herself, sought shelter in the hut against the storm. She felt, however, embarrassed in what manner to make known the motive which had brought her into iso unpleasant a predicament; for the stranger, instead of expressing apprehension at the danger she had encountered, and the complete drenching of her garments, instead of congratulating her on having found a shelter, imperfect though it was, stood before her as if every faculty had been suspended, in utter confusion and dismay.

"The rain is still very violent," said Rosella in a timid accent, after a silence of some minutes, which he attempted not to break; "and I think the thunder approaches still nearer."

No reply from the stranger, who appeared unconscious that she spoke.

"You live here?" asked Patty innocently.

He started at the words, without regarding who uttered them.

"Yes," said he, turning to Rosella; "even here!"

She shuddered at the tone in which he spoke, and involuntarily looked round upon the clay-walls, and at the half-covered roof, which in several places admitted the rain, and rendered the mud floor still more forlorn, cold, and miry.

"You gaze in incredulity," exclaimed he; "well you may! – To what chance am I indebted for this visit?"

"Visit!" repeated Rosella, inexpressibly shocked, "the storm – !"

"Oh true!" interrupted he; "the storm within made me insensible to this jar of elements: well, Madam," affecting an air of gaiety that was more dreadful than the former gloom, "I am then to thank the storm for the honour it has procured me: but you see I cannot ask you to sit in this august mansion, for it does not contain a single chair or stool!"

"I am not in the least tired," said Rosella hastily, "and I prefer standing."

"It is fortunate that you do," returned the stranger, drily.

"I very tired," cried Patty; "I want to sit down."

Rosella would have seated her on the floor; but as she cast her eyes upon it, she observed that it was full of little hollow places, which the rain, piercing through the roof, had filled with water. The quick glance of the stranger followed her's. "This is not a moment for etiquette," said he; if you will condescend to follow me, your little companion may be accommodated with a seat, and yourself better sheltered."

Rosella hesitated; but without observing her reluctance, he opened a door made of reed, and exhibited a lodging-room every way worthy of his chamber of audience: it was secured however from the weather, and contained a bed of straw, on which a spencer[178] was thrown, and by the side of it a pair of half-boots and a small bundle of linen: two or three books lay upon the floor, and on a torn sheet of light brown paper was delineated a very pretty charcoal drawing of Molly Spanger's cottage and the surrounding scenery.

Rosella, who could not believe, until these evidences convinced her, that a young man of such a distinguished, nay even elegant appearance really inhabited a place so forlorn, now experienced an amazement too potent for concealment. The stranger turning from her to hide the burning blush upon his cheek, took Patty by the hand, and seated her upon the straw; amidst the torture of his mind, which was but too evident, he again attempted an air of levity, whilst he enquired of Rosella if she still continued steady in her preference of standing.

"I do not feel any fatigue," replied she: and indeed the assertion was true, for she was wholly engrossed by the reflections that crowded upon her, from the discovery she had involuntarily made, and she began to meditate very anxiously upon the difficulties of her return to Miss Beauclerc. "I think the storm abates," resumed she; "the lady, with whom you saw me this morning, will be very much alarmed at my being exposed to such weather; and as the child's clothes, as well as my own, are quite wet, I think we had better defy the rain, and return home now that the thunder and the lightning have ceased; for I am afraid my friend will not only send after me, but perhaps in her terror venture out herself."

"Does she know where to send?" demanded the stranger in great agitation.

Rosella, frightened at the sudden change of his countenance, from whence all colour had fled, scarcely knew what she replied, but stammered something of the cottage at which she had seen him the preceding day.

"And from thence they may be directed here!" exclaimed he in an agony: "Heaven and earth, what a combination of circumstances to destroy me!"

"No, I hope not," cried Rosella in such extreme terror that she trembled in every limb; "I will try to find my way back to the inn immediately."

Patty, who saw the stranger biting his lips, and stamping in half-restrained frenzy, seized the hand of Rosella, saying softly, "What will he do to us – won't he kill us?"

"Wretch that I am!" vehemently ejaculated the young man, in an effusion of anguish he could not suppress; "outcast of the earth – abandoned, condemned, proscribed – !" Then suddenly recollecting himself, "My emotion has betrayed me," resumed he; "yet I think I may dare trust to the benevolence of your disposition, that my incautious agony of mind will not lead me to destruction, though it has almost yielded up my secret to your suspicions. Your countenance expresses all that can be conceived of angelic in the human heart; – yet what have I not suffered from an aspect equally enchanting, that adorned the most depraved of your sex!"

His air was so frantic, that Rosella, too much frightened to reflect upon what she ought, or what she ought not to do, attempted a precipitate retreat, but he caught her arm, and defeated her intention; and Patty, who now imagined he was assuredly on the point of murdering both the pretty lady and herself, raised her voice to the highest pitch her little throat would admit of.

"Who is this child?" demanded the stranger; "she cannot belong to your friend?"

"No," replied Rosella in a faltering accent, "she belongs to the people of the inn."

"Then I am undone!" returned he in a low tone of anxiety; "she will report, no doubt, all that she has seen, and can recollect to have heard."

"Not if I can prevent her," interrupted Rosella, who felt herself actuated equally by fear and compassion to give him this assurance.

An expressive look spoke his thanks, and for the first time she now remembered the papers in her pocket; but that she might not seem to advert to any unhappy circumstance he had darkly hinted at, she produced them, not as inferring that they might be of any use to him, but with an expressed hope that they would afford him amusement.

He eagerly seized them from her, and his eye glancing in haste over them as they remained in his hand, he started, and striking his forehead, vehemently asked who had read them besides herself.

"I have not read a line in either paper," replied Rosella, every spark of pity in her nature awakened at his sensitive apprehensions, "nor has any person seen them since they were sent from London to the lady you saw this morning, who slightly looked over a few paragraphs in each."

"Do you think," said he, "she would allow me to retain these papers? If she could guess how important to me – how –"

He hesitated.

"I think I may be certain," returned Rosella, with more than her usual sweetness of aspect, "that my friend, Miss Beauclerc, will have no further use for them, and in her name I beg you will dispose of them as you please; indeed she desired me to put them in my pocket, in the idea that you might perhaps not dislike to look them over; and I – I imagined," continued she, confused at the earnest manner in which he at this instant regarded her, "that the woman who lives in the cottage where I saw you yesterday, might be able to convey them to you, and therefore –"

"And therefore," interrupted he, "you subjected yourself to the inconvenience you now experience, in the amiable humanity of your heart, to relieve the solitary misery of a stranger, who betrayed I suppose, the agitation of a mind at war with peace; and even now you cannot repent the shock, the alarm you have received, because you hear me declare that you have inexpressibly served me, and but for your gentle condescension I had been lost. How can I acknowledge my obligation to your friend? She appeared to me all charity and goodness, and I fear she thinks I have repaid her generous civilities but ill. As for yourself, who have deigned to become the messenger of safety to a wretch like me, – what terms can I choose to impress you with some part of the humble admiration I feel for the sensibility, the delicate compassion you have evinced? You have indeed the figure of an angel, and appear to possess every gentle attribute the imagination will, spite of past experience, give to such a form!"

Rosella, blushing at the warmth with which he spoke, turned from him without replying. She had now executed her commission, and was sensible she could not too soon return to her little habitation, which she naturally supposed would be in commotion and alarm for her safety and that of the child. The rain had ceased, and the sky was once more serene, which she observed, and uttering a farewell compliment to the stranger, led to the door, and was joyfully accompanied by Patty. But he suddenly remembered that his fair visiter had said she had lost herself in the storm; and well knowing the difficulty of finding a track in a place so wild, offered to conduct her to the path she was acquainted with, which overlooked the roof of the inn. Rosella was obliged to accept the proposal, though she feared he might encounter either Simpson or Patty's father; and after the confession of the recluse, she earnestly wished to spare him any further confusion and mortification.

They walked silently forward for some time, the stranger, from habitual politeness, affording her every assistance, which the wet by rendering the descent of the mountain very slippery made extremely necessary; though at the same moment he appeared absent, melancholy, and lost in thought.

At length when Rosella could once more discern the chimnies of Patty's little dwelling, she turned to thank the stranger for the aid he had given her, when the voice of old Simpson hallooing her name, made him start from a deep reverie, and taking her hand, which he kissed respectfully, "Farewell!" said he; "I have a request to urge – do you stay in this place till to-morrow?"

"We do," replied Rosella.

"Once more then farewell – but not for ever – I will write an eternal adieu – I cannot speak it!"

He then walked hastily away, and his dog, who had closely attended his steps, followed him. Rosella was shocked at the solemnity with which he had uttered his last words, and still more at their import. "Does this unfortunate young man mean to deprive himself of life," thought she, "that he talks of an eternal adieu?"

Patty now interrupted the course of her fearful suppositions by calling out in answer to old Simpson – "Here's Lady – I here!" *Lady* herself too replied to the vociferations in her own voice, and the poor man advanced with great alertness to ascertain her safety: – at the same instant Miss Beauclerc met her in the path; for notwithstanding the charms in her imagination, of an adventure amidst mountains, cataracts, thunder, lightning, and rain, – her affection, which was neither artificial nor acquired, had predominated over her taste for the romantic and marvellous, and had impelled her forth, as Rosella had well guessed, before the storm had quite ceased, that she might aid the researches of old Simpson and the landlord.

"My Rosella," exclaimed she, "you are quite wet! Good heavens! you have been wholly exposed to this tempest – you will catch a cold, perhaps a fever, and through my means! What will become of me if you should be ill?"

"At present," replied she with alacrity, "I feel not the least symptom of indisposition; and I hope Patty has no other ailment than fatigue and hunger."

"Yes," cried the child, "I hungry, and I tired too!"

Simpson was desired to carry her home; and Rosella then in a low voice, as she followed with Miss Beauclerc, had merely time to say that she had seen the stranger, who was very grateful for an attention which he acknowledged to be of the utmost consequence to his welfare, before Patty's mother and her household damsel overtook them in their way from Molly's cottage, whither they had run in search of the young lady and the child.

Rosella feared that the little girl would recollect the impression of terror she had received at the stranger's miserable dwelling; and repeat more than for his safety ought to be known; but fortunately all that poor Patty was inclined to articulate, was, "I dry, I hungry!" and when she was relieved from these misfortunes, having been previously put to bed, she fell into a profound sleep, which lasted sufficiently not only to allow of Rosella's communication to her friend, whilst she changed her wet garments, and drank the good landlady's posset,[179] but gave Miss Beauclerc ample time to arrange a story that might agree with that of Patty, without subjecting the hapless stranger to the curiosity of the people of the inn, who were by no means numerous, and being generally employed, had not luckily that violent thirst for gathering knowledge, and collecting amusing facts and mysterious anecdotes, which may be supposed to torment a supernumerary domestic in a house of larger dimensions: and when she contrived to mention in the presence of the woman of the house and her husband several circumstances of the vehement impatience of some person who had taken shelter in the same hut with Patty and her companion, and whose hasty progress had been provokingly impeded by the tempest, the good people listened very calmly, and did not appear to think any concealed *mystery* might be *elucidated*[180] by tracing the steps of a traveller who rated[181] the thunder, and swore at the rain, which they very likely might have done themselves, had they been going to the fair at the next town, or to a christening at any neighbouring village. So that at Patty's levee, when she discussed in her own way as much of the history as she could recollect, the only observations or exclamations it raised, were, "sure!" and "lauk!" and thus the dreaded report ended, to the generous satisfaction of Rosella, whose compassion was still excited by the remembered agonies of the unhappy stranger; as his desolate situation, whether the result of misfortune or guilt, could not fail to interest a bosom, where he had himself justly said, all the gentler attributes of innocence and goodness resided.

Chapter III

AN HEROIC EPISTLE – RAGE FOR MOONLIGHT WALKS, À LA LANTERNE

ON the following morning, before the busy spirit of Miss Beauclerc could devise any new plan to heighten the delicious pathos of the poor man's misery, by contriving for him another interview with Rosella, whose charms she was extremely certain were tearing his oppressed heart with all the horrors of hopeless love, a country fellow brought to the door of the hôtellerie Mr. Pet, the decided hero of an underplot in the tragical drama of the mysterious stranger, who, in the opinion of Miss Beauclerc, was either some young Noble, whose father had gravely betrothed him in infancy to some embryo heiress, and who was flying from matrimonial persecutions – a tale she had met with in her extensive reading; or that he was at least a Baronet, who had incautiously married some very handsome and very fashionable young lady, and now found sufficient reason to repent the precipitation of ill-judged passion, in the outrageous conduct of his wife, who after ruining his fortune and her own reputation, embroils the much-suffering husband with her gallant, or any other man, and the consequences of a serious duel had obliged him to hide his injured head – where Rosella so fortunately found him: incidents which the memory of Miss Beauclerc also furnished.

But whoever the mysterious stranger might be, he proved that Mr. Pet was, to him at least, a very important personage, by the following letter, which was given to Miss Beauclerc by the man who had charge of him.

"I believe, Madam, I hinted to your young friend that your condescension had emboldened me to meditate a request, which perhaps in a being so forlorn as she now knows me to be, you will consider as a presumption scarcely to be pardoned, still less to be complied with; yet I must augur better from the benevolence of your countenance and manner, when I had the honour of those transient interviews which have procured you the trouble of receiving this application.

"The poor little dog, whom I have delivered to the lad entrusted with this scrawl, I can no longer, for reasons very important, retain with me in my wanderings; – yet I cannot endure to deprive him of life, or drive him from me without some hope that he will be taken care of: his original owner resides near Sedgfield, in Durham.

I think you mentioned that you were travelling northward, and I cannot suppose that you will deviate so much from your route, at the request of an unfortunate stranger, who is not worthy the considerate attentions you have already bestowed upon him; but should you perchance find yourself within a few miles of Sedgfield, and should you then cast a thought upon the man you have eternally obliged, will you condescend to assign poor Pet to the care of a person to be relied upon, and instruct such an one to conduct the dog to Mr. Mompesson, whose name and family residence are well known round the neighbourhood.

"I offer no apology for the freedom I use in thus addressing you, for I know of no words that would in any degree excuse it. I trust to your generosity not to reject my application entirely; but should you attribute to presumption what is wholly the effect of misery and despair, and experience only indignation instead of the compassion I solicit, upon the gentle mercy of your charming young friend I cast my deserted companion, and I am assured she will not suffer him to perish. His master she will never see more – I hope in heaven she will never hear of him more. To you, Madam, I wish every blessing this world can give; and to your Rosella, so I think you called her, I earnestly invoke the continuance of that gentleness, innocence, and peace which now harmonize her accents, and enrich every grace of a form I can never forget.

"By what signature to design myself, I know not – to you I will not lend a fictitious one, and the name which I received from the best and most virtuous of parents, – a name I have – but I will end here – I am, Madam,

"A WRETCH."

"P.S. – Yes, you *shall* know that one of those papers you sent for my *amusement*, the first on which my eager eye fell, exposed to me the imminent danger which you have thus enabled me to escape. It was your intervention that drew me back from the precipice on which I stood; but I still wander blindfold, and may this moment be again rushing to certain death – Oh worse, a thousand times worse – to infamy!"

Miss Beauclerc twice read this very mysterious epistle, which, from the evident haste and trepidation of the writer, he had justly called a scrawl, before she recovered her recollection so far as to enquire of Simpson who waited her orders, where the person was who brought it. He was in the kitchen, Simpson replied; should he call him? Miss Beauclerc assented, and the young man appeared, who answered her enquiries in the broad Yorkshire dialect. With some effort, however, she comprehended that he had received that scrap of paper and the little beast he had got with him, from a man he met about two miles off, who was to have carried them all the way himself; but he said he had fallen lame, and could not get on, so he told him where to come, and offered him a shilling to undertake the errand, and the lady, he said, would give him another shilling if he brought the letter and the dog safe to her.

This was all she could learn; and having fulfilled the covenant which the lame man had made, whom she imagined to be the stranger himself, she dismissed Simpson who was bursting with curiosity, and communicated the contents of the letter to Rosella, who had already almost reconciled poor Pet to his fate.

She blushed at the commendation it so lavishly bestowed upon her, but soon lost every passing emotion in concern for the deplorable situation of a person who possessed such distinguished attractions. Miss Beauclerc relieved her anxiety for the destiny of the animal so solicitously recommended to her, by saying, she would comply with his master's evident wish, that he should be returned to his *original owner*, and convey him herself to Sedgfield. Indeed her own inclination to learn the imprudences or misfortunes which had operated to place Mr. Pet under her protection, joined to a strong hope of encountering some very interesting adventures in seeking to *elucidate* those of the stranger, would have been alone sufficient to have urged her to the step, without the aid of that compassion he had really excited in her bosom. Simpson therefore received orders to procure post-horses for the following morning; and Miss Beauclerc then employed the rest of the day in conversing with Rosella upon the supposed disasters of the stranger, and in writing to her friend Selina a very circumstantial history of the turn affairs had taken.

Rosella, when she bade adieu to Patty and her brother, left with them such magnificent marks of her approbation, that Molly's nuts in the cupboard were entirely forgotten; and as Miss Beauclerc's carriage drove from the door, the little girl, who had become fond of her lovely playfellow, began a cry that threatened to last the whole day.

Simpson was obliged to ride a hack-horse, not having been able to procure a second pair for a chaise, and Mr. Pet was, of course, taken into that of Miss Beauclerc, who was far from being displeased that she was compelled to shew this mark of respect to the master, in the person of the dog. They arrived at Sedgfield in time to dine; and when the repast was over, Miss Beauclerc, sending for the master of the house where she had put up, demanded if he could direct her to the house of Mr. Mompesson, and if he knew any thing of the family. The man looked with earnestness at her whilst she spoke, and after some hesitation, replied, that Eideva Lodge was about three miles further, on the Durham road; that Mr. Mompesson was a worthy gentleman as ever breathed, – that he believed he was at present very ill – and – and he had heard that he was in some trouble – but he could not tell for his part – he only knew that he was a very worthy, kind-hearted gentleman.

The manner in which this intelligence was given, very plainly indicated that the informant could say a great deal more if he chose it; but Miss Beauclerc did not wish to forestall this delicious mystery from the vulgar periods of an innkeeper, and resolved to present the dog herself to the worthy gentleman, (even if she should be compelled to the indecorum of being introduced into his bedchamber,) that she might behold the effect which the sudden sight of Pet would have upon him, and discover, from his varied emotions, his pathetic soliloquies, and heart-rending ejaculations, the nature of those troubles he was overwhelmed with, and by what interest he was implicated thus apparently in the miseries of the unhappy and self-condemned stranger. She had no obstacle to prevent her from riding or walking immediately to Eideva Lodge, accompanied by the ostensible cause of her visit; for the weather was fine, and several hours of daylight were yet before her; but undertaking a charming adventure, such as this had every prospect of becoming, by the "garish eye of day,"[182] was not to be thought of; no, by the sublime beams of the pale moon she intended to shape her pensive course towards the mansion of Mr. Mompesson, and really persuaded herself that she was under a necessity of dispatching several letters by the mail of that evening, which happened to pass through the town at twilight.

Rosella wondered what this sudden pressure of letter-writing could be caused by, and ventured to hint that the performance of the commission might be deferred till the next morning, as it could not be executed with convenience that evening: but such an arrangement not at all according with the views of her enthusiastic friend, her intimation was opposed by a plea of not wishing to lose another day by this affair; and Rosella, who had ever been accustomed to obey every wish of Miss Beauclerc, thought her reasons must be all-sufficient, at least she had neither authority nor inclination to over-rule them.

Whilst these unlucky letters were being written, Rosella found the hours very slowly move forward. The house was not enlivened by children, who, if they were tolerably attractive, had always the power of amusing her; and those books which were most adapted to the taste of her friend, and of which there was always a number very conveniently at hand, did not unfortunately agree with her ideas of entertainment; though to do justice to her sensibility and perseverance, she could with great patience cry through a dozen pages, and tremble through as many more. But then a continuation of crying and trembling, according as the superb pen of the writer varied from pathos to horrors, and from horrors to pathos, throughout several volumes, she found far exceeding any curiosity she could feel, to learn in which of the damp dungeons, all over-run with spiders and black beetles, the most lucky of the heroine's three or four dozen lovers found a clean spot to throw himself at her feet; and besides Rosella began to think with Don Quixote when he was upon his enchanted Pegasus, that, notwithstanding the variety of curvatures and prancings practised to deceive the judgment, she was only, like him, going over and over the same ground – always the castle and ghost before her, let her peep where she would. She had however, at the present moment no choice of amusement, for Miss Beauclerc continued to write with the most unwearied inflexibility; and Rosella took up a volume of charming adventures, written in the style of a magic lantern, where a dusky succession of half delineated figures dance about *à-propos de bottes*,[183] and then disappear to make way for others equally well drawn and equally to the purpose, as the first.

At seven the master of the house entered the room, to say that he was making up the bag for the mail; and as he understood the ladies had some letters to put in, he came to request that they would not detain them much longer. Miss Beauclerc, now obliged to forego her occupation of writing for the post, pleaded fatigue to delay the expedition to Eideva Lodge to a proper heroic hour, and ordered tea. Rosella was chagrined, but preserved silence, though she could not avoid watching the departing sun-beams in great anxiety. "It will be quite dark," thought she, "before we reach the house of Mr. Mompesson; what will he imagine on seeing us at such an hour, invalid as he is too!"

From reflections upon the time in which the visit would be paid, Rosella was led to others upon the purport of it; and for the first moment, it appeared to her in a ridiculous point of view, unacquainted as Miss Beauclerc and herself were with the character of their mountain friend, or what his connection was with the family whose mansion they were thus going to besiege at an hour so undue, when if sickness assailed them, they would be seeking repose, – or if in health, they would most probably be assembled in social gaiety, and neither wish nor expect the intrusion of total strangers, upon an errand that might severely mortify their pride, or shock their feelings. Yet whatever might be the secret reluctance of Rosella to become gentlewoman-usher in second to Mr. Pet, she did not think proper to hesitate when Miss Beauclerc declared herself ready to begin the expedition; but merely reminded her that neither Simpson nor themselves were acquainted with the road they were to take, and asked if he should not obtain particular directions upon the subject: for her friend had previously announced that she meant to walk.

"I will myself enquire," replied Miss Beauclerc, "for it is not my intention to take Simpson; as it must be the height of cruelty to expose the agonizing feelings we may too possibly be witness to, to the observation of a servant; and indeed," continued the lady with great solemnity, "such an indiscretion might betray the most important secrets to public curiosity."

Rosella was thunderstruck: walking in the dusk of the evening without an attendant, unacquainted with the way they were to pursue, and what was still worse, returning after night-fall, which must be the case, wholly unprotected, was a thing she could not have had an idea of, but from the fearless rambles of those gentle creatures, whose marches and counter-marches she had perused in Miss Beauclerc's library books; but then she fancied that the roads, the lanes, and the woods she read of, must universally have been appropriated to interesting adventures, or that the beautiful creatures who majestically paced through them, "all alone by the light of the moon,"[184] must have inevitably worn some distinguishing mark of sublimity which exempted them from the vulgar attacks of common accidents;* like that honest gentleman of solemn memory, who so obligingly walked this earth eight or nine hundred years (looking quite fresh and young) with a cross of fire imprinted upon his forehead, under a cilician[185] bandeau, to awe ghosts, goblins, and devils from impertinent approaches.[186]

---

* This is Charlton's footnote. The 'late most brilliant publication' is Matthew Lewis's *The Monk* (1796). See note 186.

Miss Beauclerc, who did not observe the consternation of her young companion, put on her cloak with infinite composure; and desiring Rosella to follow her example, called down Mr. Pet from the chair on which he had extended himself, and walked into the inn-yard, where from a side window she had observed the landlord talking to a servant in a grey frock with a black collar, who rode away before she reached them. Having made known her wish to be particularly informed of the road to Eideva Lodge, she waited two or three seconds for an answer; the landlord, as before, surveying her very earnestly.

"If I had known only a minute ago, Madam," said he, "that you had business with Mr. Mompesson, you could have spoken to his servant, that young man who was with me just now; but I can send after him if you choose."

"No," replied Miss Beauclerc with a dignified air, "what I have to relate is only for the ear of Mr. Mompesson himself."

"The poor gentleman is very ill, Ma'am; I hope you have not any bad news for him," said mine host with a look of doubt and reluctance: "it's very late, Ma'am – I believe it is nearer three miles than two from here to the Lodge – I question if the poor gentleman be well enough to see you, Ma'am?"

"I hope," returned she, "he will think my errand a welcome one; perhaps I can give him information that will not displease him!"

"That indeed, Madam," said the landlord, "is quite and clean another thing, and I don't think, poor gentleman, you can tell him any good news too soon; so, if you please, I will attend you."

"You are very obliging," replied Miss Beauclerc, "but I have reasons for not choosing to be accompanied by any person but this young lady."

"That young lady!" repeated he, turning his enquiring eyes upon Rosella.

"And I will thank you," returned Miss Beauclerc, "to instruct me which road I am to take, for it becomes late."

"Yes, Ma'am, it is too late for two ladies to walk so far all lonely by themselves – however you must do as you see fitting; though I must say there is not a man for ten miles round that wishes that there family better than I do; and I will make bold to advise you, Ma'am, to let me shew you the way."

"I am obliged to decline your proposal," said she, half offended at an obstinacy that so much incommoded her plan.

"Well, I say no more – I only hope you carry the poor gentleman good news. I have been his tenant thirty years, and he never once asked for his rent harshly, though God knows I have had my troubles, and havn't always been so able to pay it as I am now; but he is a worthy gentleman, and would not distress the father of a family, God help him! He will be rewarded in the next world, for he's not long for this – he's broken-hearted, Ma'am! But come, I'll just shew you into the green lane that leads to his house, for if you have good news, you can't go too soon!"

A thousand conjectures danced successively into Miss Beauclerc's brain at these hints, and she eagerly followed him into the Durham road, where he led the way at a brisk pace. Rosella attended with almost equal alacrity; for her compassion and never-failing wish of carrying consolation to the afflicted, which she imagined it would be possible to afford, by giving the worthy poor gentleman a clue to discover Mr. Pet's master, who she concluded, from the landlord's expressions, might very possibly be a run-away son, made her forget her recent reflections, until their conductor having led them about a mile and a half on the high road, turned into a narrow lane, rendered very dark by tall trees which overhung the hedges on either side.

"Have we yet far to go?" asked Rosella. "About a mile, Miss," returned the landlord: "I think I had better walk on till you get into Mr. Mompesson's grounds."

"I have not the least fear," said Miss Beauclerc, hastily; "have the goodness to direct us, and we will now pursue our walk without you."

"Well, you must do as you please, to be sure – so, Ma'am, you must go right straight on an end[187] till you get to a little bit of a pond, then please to turn to your left, and go clean across the field, and on th'other side on't you will find a six-barred swing gate, and that takes you through the Squire's shrubbery, and then when you get onto the lawn, you see the house afore your eyes."

The landlord then required instructions concerning the supper, and having received them, trudged off whistling a psalm melody.

Miss Beauclerc and Rosella continued their way through the dark lane, and Pet, now their only escort, led the van with so quick a march, that it was evident he was well acquainted with the road they were travelling. Miss Beauclerc remarked the circumstance to her companion, who had been trembling with affright from the moment the landlord had left them; whilst her heroic friend, on the contrary, felt her courage rise in proportion as the shades of night deepened round them.

"I am alarmed lest Pet should run away from us," exclaimed Rosella, advancing a few steps to allure him back; but the animal for the first time disregarded her voice, and in two minutes they wholly lost sight of him. "How unfortunate!" she continued; "had we not better return to Sedgfield, and send somebody to look for him?"

"No, my dear," said Miss Beauclerc very calmly; "it is most probable that the dog will go on to the Lodge, which he appears so well to know; and as he cannot account for his appearance, or inform the friends of his unhappy master where they may trace his wandering steps, we ought to follow him, and elucidate the mystery."

Rosella had no objection to the proposition, but she wished to elucidate the mystery in a less heroic manner – that is, she would have made her present peregrination at a more convenient hour, when the sun might have illumined her on the way: – in the present instance, unluckily, the pale moon was only a day old; and instead of exerting her mild radiance in behalf of the fair travellers, she very carelessly left the hemisphere in total darkness, in contradiction to the particular and unvaried assistance she always lends during her whole revolution, to gentle and beautiful nocturnal adventurers. Rosella, as she advanced in the lane, thought they should never arrive at the little bit of a pond which was to direct them out of it; and her fears increasing every moment, she crept close to her whimsical friend, and clung very amicably to the arm she held.

"Hark!" cried Miss Beauclerc suddenly, "surely that breeze brought a long and dreadful groan to my ear!"

Rosella listened, and the sound at that instant appeared to die away, but was almost immediately renewed with more violence.

"Merciful Heaven!" exclaimed Miss Beauclerc, clasping her hands in an attitude of sublime distress, "direct our steps to the poor sufferer!"

Rosella was in an agony.

"Perhaps," resumed her companion, "it is the unhappy stranger himself!"

Rosella listened yet more earnestly, and at length discovered that the poor sufferer was the good landlord, who had ceased whistling to end his tune vocally; and as he had been in his youth a singer at a village Church, he bellowed out his minims and semibreves with so persevering a *tenuto*,[188] that at a little distance, his tones borne upon the softening zephyr, might be mistaken without violating the judgment, for signals of distress.

Miss Beauclerc, on discovering her error, blushed with vexation; for she had prepared every tender feeling to come upon the stage with considerable eclat, and had momentarily reviewed all the admirable conduct of the most captivating damsels upon such emergencies. In the first place, she intended to fly to the succour of the groaning hero, and then call to his servant, if he had any, and with cool fortitude give the most wise and salutary directions – then brave every inconvenience to see them executed – then attend him with the care of the most affectionate sister, – and finally, on suspecting the effect her charms and her expert nursing could not fail to have upon the heart of the convalescent, she was to vanish like a dream, as a repelling hint to his flame, and leave the poor youth to gallop in search of her from Durham to Dover: – not that she meant to execute all this herself – no; Rosella, her beloved Rosella was to be the loadstone, the magnet, the attraction, the constellation; but she was very sensible that with the best heart in the world, and the most compassionate and amiable temper that ever softened at the distresses of others, Rosella still required a very well-read and able guide to instruct her in the fervent sympathies and melting pity that glow in the tender bosoms of heroines; so she placed her in the background till called for, and constructed all her allegories, *en attendant*, in the first person singular.

At length, after walking some time in the lane with a caution the obscurity of the night demanded, they arrived at the pond the landlord had spoken of, but did not discover this long looked-for object till Miss Beauclerc had walked two or three steps into it. She extricated herself by the assistance of Rosella, and they very gladly turned to the left to cross the field, which in their imagination was a level pasture; but they found they had to mount a most fatiguing ascent, and that their progress was often impeded by large pieces of rough stone that rose out of the scanty turf the neighbouring flocks were doomed to nibble at. Rosella fell over one of those, and in endeavouring to save her face from injury, severely hurt one of her hands; but not to excite the elegiac complaints of her friend, she concealed the mischance, and went forward to seek the gate they were to pass through. It was with considerable difficulty that she found it; and holding it open for Miss Beauclerc, her eyes very earnestly explored the path they were to take.

"It is so dark," exclaimed she, "that I cannot discern any track." She still continued to look for it, however, and discovered at length, within three paces of the place where she stood, a very sudden abyss, that seemed yawning to receive her: and stopping her friend, who was walking fearlessly on, she shudderingly informed her of the danger they had escaped.

"Surely," cried Miss Beauclerc, "this cannot be the shrubbery we were told of?"

Rosella thought it certainly was not; however they advanced slowly, in path flanked on one side by an almost perpendicular mountain cloathed with foliage, and on the other, by a descent as sudden, which presented the tops of the trees that were thickly planted down the steep, just on a parallel with the road, and as the eye fell over them, waving in the night breeze, they resembled the black billows of Cocytus.[189]

The ladies, creeping for security close to the mountain side, moving as slow as "foot could fall,"[190] arrived in rather more than half an hour at a second gate, which being fastened, they were obliged to climb over: and on the other side of it, they descried what they supposed to be the house of Mr. Mompesson, which appeared a tolerably spacious building but no signs of domestic occurrences or social festivity enlivened it, for only one solitary window exhibited any token of its being inhabited, by emitting through a half-closed shutter a faint reflection of light.

Chapter IV

INSANITY AND DEATH

ROSELLA was now completely dispirited.

"What can this mean?" exclaimed Miss Beauclerc: "it is impossible the whole family can have gone to rest so early!"

It was with difficulty, and after a long search, that a bell could be found; and in consideration of the illness of Mr. Mompesson, united to a presentiment which the sad stillness that reigned round the house occasioned, Miss Beauclerc rung it with great moderation. No one attending the summons, she applied to the bell once more, and after another interval, an old woman, with a light in her hand, unlocked the door, and peeped out.

"Oh Christ, defend me!" exclaimed she, in a voice of horror, and drawing back with precipitation, she threw the door in the face of Miss Beauclerc, who at that moment, advanced before Rosella, to gain admittance.

"What mystery hangs over us?" ejaculated she to her terrified companion. – "How unaccountably strange is all this!"

"Let us return," cried Rosella; "you can send here, or call yourself to-morrow morning."

"No," replied Miss Beauclerc, with a sublime air, "it may be that some important discovery will result from our perseverance in desiring to see Mr. Mompesson this evening."

A third time she pulled the bell with a more authoritative peal, and in two minutes the servant she had seen conversing with the landlord at Sedgfield, threw open a window in the first story, and holding a candle as low as he could, that he might survey the intruders, demanded what they wanted.

"I desire to speak to Mr. Mompesson," returned Miss Beauclerc, "upon business of importance."

"Mr. Mompesson! my master!" exclaimed the domestic. – "Do you mean old Mr. Mompesson?"

"Yes," returned the lady, after a pause of consideration whether, as there was a younger personage, it would not be more desirable to speak to him.

"Good God! my poor master died a little after noon to-day!"

Miss Beauclerc now began to repent her letter-writing most bitterly: – "Unfortunate!" cried she; "perhaps my intelligence might have lengthened his days!"

"What, is my young master safe in France?" asked the man eagerly.

It now occurred to Rosella and Miss Beauclerc at the same moment, that the unhappy mountaineer was assuredly the son of Mr. Mompesson.

"How will he be shocked to hear of his father's death!" thought Rosella: "poor young man – I hope, for his sake, that his conduct has not hastened it!"

Miss Beauclerc demanded of the servant what part of the family was now in the house; and learned that it contained only the body of his master, the old woman they had seen, and himself: the man adding in the most mournful tone, "Perhaps, Ma'am, you want to speak with the young ladies? They are both out of their mind, and not here. But if you can give me any news of Mr. George, I will come down and open the door; for I expect every hour the arrival of a gentleman my poor master sent me to fetch just before he was taken speechless; and this gentleman would give a thousand pounds to know what is become of Mr. George; for we are all afraid – but I will come down directly."

This promise was soon executed; but as Rosella passed the man to enter the house, he gazed earnestly at her, and turned pale.

"My mind misgives me," cried he, "that this blood is Mr. George Mompesson's."

"What does he mean?" said Miss Beauclerc: but the words had not passed her lips, before she discovered that the muslin cloak Rosella wore was almost dyed with blood. –

"Oh my God!" added she, "my child is killed!"

Rosella was terrified at her own appearance; but almost instantly recollecting that it was occasioned by her wounded hand, she re-assured both her friend and the servant by explaining the disaster.

Miss Beauclerc debated with herself whether she should entrust the domestic with the secret of young Mompesson's late retreat; but reflecting, in spite of the principles of heroism, which allow the confiding of life and fame to the discretion of strangers, that such a communication might lead to a discovery of the unhappy youth, which the question "if he were safe in France?" gave her to understand must be fatal to him, she so far governed her sympathetic overflowings, as to preserve them for the ear of the gentleman who was momentarily expected; and informing the man where she was to be found, desired him to send his master's friend to Sedgfield, where she should remain the whole of the next day, if he were anxious to hear the intelligence she could give him.

The servant appeared disappointed, but acquiesced in her decision: and when he learned that the ladies were wholly unaccompanied, he lamented that he could not attend them back, because he was obliged to await the coming of the gentleman, and could not, besides, leave his poor master's remains.

"I am far from wishing it," said Miss Beauclerc; "but I shall be indebted to you if you will furnish me with a light."

"Most willingly, Ma'am; and I am sorry I can do nothing more to serve you: the old woman is getting a bed ready for Mr. Delamere, who will sleep here, I suppose; and besides, she is so decrepid, that she could not be of much use to you."

"A light is all the assistance I either expect or desire," returned Miss Beauclerc.

"I will get it in a moment, Madam," said the man, withdrawing for that purpose.

He had left his candle with them, which Rosella took up, to examine some portraits hanging over the chimney-piece of a sort of breakfast room, into which the servant had led them from the hall they had entered at. A pair of these represented two very lovely young women; and between the frames hung another, with the glazed side turned to the wainscot: upon the back, which alone was exposed to view, were pasted four hearts cut in black crape, each one torn in two.

"What can this be?" said Rosella, after having examined this strange object.

Miss Beauclerc took the frame from the hook, and turning the glazed side to the light, beheld a most animated and correct resemblance of the mysterious stranger.

"It is himself!" exclaimed Rosella; "but more handsome."

"Yes, Madam," said the domestic, who returned whilst she spoke, "it is him indeed; but not more handsome than he was, when he was reckoned the best son, the best brother, and the best master in the whole county, and when he was indeed the best young gentleman I ever came anigh."[191]

Miss Beauclerc could no longer restrain her eager curiosity: – "Has he done aught," asked she, "to forfeit so excellent a character?"

The man looked at her in surprise, and for a few moments, made no reply. At length – "I thought," cried he, "you had known – or else, God knows, it does not become me –"

"Say no more," interrupted Miss Beauclerc, who began to fear that the dignity of her character would be sullied, by extorting so important a secret from a poor fellow, who wished to withhold it from the fidelity of his attachment to the family he served.

"Indeed, Ma'am," resumed he, "Mr. George was more unfortunate than – than any thing else."

"I always thought so," returned she, pleased to have her mountain hero raised again in her estimation; for she had begun to fear she had interested herself and her Rosella in the fate of a degenerate wretch, who had committed some vulgar sort of Old Bailey offence, and instead of sinking under the weight of a delicate woe, was flying from a cell in Newgate, and death, death, death – lying perdue in a Judge's wig.[192]

"But pray," said Rosella eagerly, "can you tell me what this means on the back of his picture?"

"That, Madam," replied the domestic, whilst the tears started to his eyes, "was done by one of the young ladies before she was removed: from the time the bad news reached us, she was always talking about despair and the grave, and singing such dismal songs so wildly – my poor mistress had fallen down in a fit, and never got up alive; and the eldest of the ladies cut up her mourning cloaths to make such fancies as these whenever they came into her head. She said Mr. George had broke all their hearts, and one of them was her papa's, and one her poor mama's, another was her sister's, and the large one was her own heart, for her's, she said, was swelled to bursting. The other young lady never spoke, or cried one single drop – but Oh! Ma'am, they were obliged to be taken to the doctor's house, for they grew very bad, and my master took to his bed!"

The poor fellow could say no more; and Rosella, whose tears flowed at the broken recital, sobbed aloud. Miss Beauclerc was much and undesignedly affected: she recollected, however, that her companion and herself had nearly three miles of very indifferent road to repass before they could repose for the night; and after having roused her mind from the momentary forgetfulness which genuine sensibility had occasioned, she relapsed into the sublimity of heroism, and taking the lanthorn from the servant with an air of repressed emotion, she repeated her message to the expected gentleman, and led the way to the hall door.

Rosella followed her, after having again hung up the portrait of their unhappy acquaintance as she had found it, from respect to the fanciful yet striking allusion made by his still more unfortunate sister.

The man gazed at them some time after they had left the house, as if he really was what he professed to be, anxious for their safe return: and it was only when they had nearly reached the first gate in what the landlord called the shrubbery, that they ceased to behold the light of his candle; for he had followed them a considerable way from the door.

"The night is surely unusually dark," said Miss Beauclerc, giving her lanthorn to her companion, whilst she climbed the gate.

Rosella's whole soul was occupied by the disjointed tale she had just heard, and she merely returned an assenting monosyllable to the observation. Their light burned so dimly, that it was with great difficulty they could explore their way so as to escape the precipice which skirted the path as far as the second gate. Rosella walked first, holding the lanthorn to the ground, and Miss Beauclerc followed her closely, entreating that she would be careful of herself. They had proceeded thus sometime, when a rustling in the trees terrified them both: Miss Beauclerc started, and directed her eyes to the place from whence the noise issued; at the same moment she heard a crash, and both Rosella and the light vanished. Every calamity their situation could admit of, assailed the imagination of her alarmed friend, who screamed her name in all the energy of despair.

"I am safe, dear Madam, I am safe," cried Rosella; "but in falling I have extinguished the light: what shall we do?"

"Oh, thank God you are not killed," exclaimed Miss Beauclerc; "I care not for any other disaster – give me your arm."

Rosella obeyed, and they crept to the swing gate, where, as they stood a moment, they were joined by the run-away Pet, who announced himself by licking the hand of Rosella, who was pleased to have recovered him, and concluded, that not being able to get in at the Lodge, he had wandered back in search of his deserted companions: she caressed him with kindness, and he, followed her very patiently.

They were more than half an hour crossing the field, and to their infinite satisfaction, at length discovered the pond at the entrance of the lane, by a faint light which the water reflected.

"We have now only level ground to traverse," said Miss Beauclerc, in a tone expressive of pleasure – a sensation in which Rosella joined, for she had begun to feel inconvenience from her accident. – Yet their terrors were not at an end: they had scarcely walked an hundred paces ere the rattling of a carriage gave a new alarm; for the darkness of the night rather increased than diminished, and they ran a considerable risk of being crushed under the wheels, from the narrowness of the lane.

Miss Beauclerc called out, but in vain: the post-chaise, for such it appeared to be, approached very rapidly, and Rosella then joined her voice to that of her friend, to deprecate the mischief she apprehended. Their united screams at length reached the driver, and arrested his speed; and at the same instant the chaise window was let down, and the voice of a man demanded the reason of the outcry. The postillion swore a tremendous oath, and levelled at the trembling Rosella and her indignant companion those delicate epithets commonly used to the most unfortunate of their sex.

"What the devil is the matter?" again demanded the voice from the carriage.

"Why, your Honour," replied the driver, "it's only a couple of —"

"How dare you," cried Miss Beauclerc, all the dignity of heroic virtue up in arms – "how dare you insult people of honour and decency with such vile language?"

"*Dessent*, quotha," retorted the driver; "yes, you must be dessent sort of folks, to be sure, to be a stroaming[193] at this toime o'night in hedges and ditches, and up sitch leanes as this!"

The person in the carriage silenced him with a tone of authority; then addressing the complainants, "Good women," said he, "are you hurt?"

"Good women!" retorted Miss Beauclerc aloud. – "Good women!" repeated she to herself, "great Heaven! was ever beautiful young heroine before included in such a term!"

"My head is giddy," said Rosella in a faint voice; "I am very sick!"

The postillion was proceeding without further ceremony, but the gentleman called to him to stop: – "Are you in distress?" asked he.

"My poor Rosella!" exclaimed Miss Beauclerc; "what will become of us!"

"Which way are you travelling?" resumed the voice.

At this moment a light appeared in that part of the lane adjoining the road.

"I hope," cried Miss Beauclerc, not condescending to attend to the questions she heard, "this is my servant come in search of us."

"Your servant!" repeated the gentleman; "good God! how could this happen!"

He then jumped from the carriage, and approaching the offended fair one, asked if she had not been at Eideva Lodge about an hour back: on hearing the reply, he entreated forgiveness for the error he had been in, and begged the ladies would use the chaise in their return to Sedgfield. Rosella, recollecting the disfigured state in which her wounded hand had put her, hastily refused the proffered civility.

"No, no, my dear Miss Beauclerc," said she, "let us walk."

The appearance of Simpson, who carried the light they had seen, was in favour of the request; but the master of the carriage strenuously opposed it.

The poor old butler instantly discovered the discoloured state of her garments, and uttering an exclamation of horror, respectfully blamed his Lady for not requiring his attendance. "Has Miss Rosella been run over?" added he.

"No, I hope not," said the gentleman hastily; "but the young lady should be immediately carried to Sedgfield, that she may be taken proper care of."

Miss Beauclerc assented to the proposition; and Rosella no longer opposing it from fatigue and weakness, the gentleman placed her in the chaise, where her heroic friend followed her, inviting the master of it to take his seat by her side. During their short ride, he told Miss Beauclerc that he was the person expected by the servant they had seen at the Lodge, who was, by a concurrence of melancholy circumstances, the only remaining domestic of a once numerous and happy household. "I understand from him, Madam," continued the gentleman, "that chance has made you acquainted with a very unfortunate young man, whom I once called – whom I must still call my friend, in spite of his errors, and the misery they have produced."

"I know not," returned Miss Beauclerc, "what those errors are: their effects are dreadful indeed! But I found it impossible to refuse my compassion to the desolate situation of this wretched youth, which became known to me in a singular manner."

She then related the circumstances attending her first and second interview with Mompesson, to which his friend listened with interest and attention; but before her narration had arrived at the period in which Rosella was driven to the forlorn hut he inhabited, the chaise stopped in the inn yard, to the mortification of her auditor, whose anxiety was much heightened to learn the sequel of the tale. Rosella failed not on alighting, to enquire for poor Pet, and had the satisfaction to hear that he had followed the carriage. She then withdrew, to her chamber, accompanied by Miss Beauclerc, who finding that her ailments were not very serious, permitted her, after having changed her dress, to descend to the supper table.

The gentleman, who had announced himself as Mr. Delamere, had sent to desire the honour of taking his meal with the ladies, which Miss Beauclerc consented to after a little deliberation. As her companion and herself entered the eating-room appropriated to them, they found him already there, and he instantly congratulated Rosella upon her present safety, with a compliment equally addressed to her friend, upon their generosity in having risked it from motives of genuine compassion and charity.

As Simpson entered with the supper apparatus, Pet seized the opportunity of making his appearance likewise. "Good God!" exclaimed Mr. Delamere, "from whence came this animal?"

"It was yesterday morning entrusted to my care," replied Miss Beauclerc, "with a request to have him conveyed to the Lodge."

"So lately!" ejaculated he: and Simpson then quitting the room, he continued – "Poor Mompesson had been traced to York, and both his cloaths and his dog particularly described by various advertisements, offering a considerable reward for further intelligence of his route. This little animal belonged to his favourite sister; and I suppose he was unwilling to part with him but upon the most urgent necessity."

Rosella, as well as her friend, instantly conjectured that this advertisement had met the eye of the wanderer when she had presented him the papers at his forlorn retreat: but no further conversation could now take place, from the attendance upon the supper table. When the servants had withdrawn, Mr. Delamere eagerly requested all the information of his unhappy friend the ladies could give; as he said he wished to convey some money to him, without which he feared, by his lingering so near the habitation of his father, he could not quit the kingdom.

Miss Beauclerc complied with the entreaty, not forgetting to paint the share Rosella had taken in the adventure of the storm, in a point of view the most favourable to her fortitude, her sensibility, and discretion. Mr. Delamere uttered some animated expressions of admiration upon the excellence of her heart; but Rosella, conscious of the unwillingness with which she had under-taken the mission so much extolled, declined his encomiums, and directed them to her friend.

Miss Beauclerc, in mentioning the embassy of which Pet was the object, described, at the request of Mr. Delamere, the person of the peasant who was charged with it. – "I must hope," said he, "that I may rescue this most unfortunate young man from further disgrace and punishment: what he has already endured is, I am convinced, sufficient to expiate his offence."

The question which had the whole evening been hovering on the lips of Miss Beauclerc, could no longer be restrained – what the nature of that offence was which had thus carried so horrible a desolation into the bosom of the family.

"The error of George Mompesson," said Mr. Delamere gravely, "without the mitigation of many extenuating circumstances, might justly be denominated a crime. You have not at this moment sufficient time to hear all that I wish to relate in palliation, and I cannot endure that in your opinion he should sink to a point too abject: let me entreat then, that you will forbear all enquiry for the present; and should you by accident become acquainted with the fatal stigma attending a name once respected and revered, let me conjure you to review his single lapse with all the indulgence your compassion and generosity may suggest."

He then rose, saying he should instantly set out for Stanmore Hills,[194] and begin his search, as he was sensible no time was to be lost. – He added, that on his return to Eideva Lodge, he should call at Sedgfield, in the flattering hope of again acknowledging the obligation he had received, in the person of his unhappy friend, and of being enabled to inform the ladies that their active humanity had been effectual.

When Miss Beauclerc and Rosella retired for the night, instead of taking the repose they so much required, they could not forbear spending some time in forming conjectures upon the wide-spreading errors of young Mompesson, and deprecating his immediate knowledge of their tragical effects. They justly concluded that the people of the house could in a moment solve their doubts, because the landlord had appeared so well acquainted with the distress at the Lodge; but Miss Beauclerc from heroic motives, and Rosella from genuine delicacy, and in compliance with the request of Mr. Delamere, would each sooner have endured her suspense for weeks, than have questioned any part of the family upon so tender a subject.

It was late the next morning when they rose; and after breakfast, as Miss Beauclerc had not yet had an opportunity of writing what she conceived to be the most interesting part of her journal, she determined to employ the rest of the morning to that purpose. – Rosella remained alone in the eating-room, which was rather detached from the house, and very quiet; and having fallen into a reverie when her friend left her, she had not been roused from it by any external object for above an hour. During that time her ideas had merely reverted from the miseries at the Lodge, to the unfortunate author of those miseries, and from him to the generous young man who was so anxious to soften the misfortunes of this distracted family, who boldly avowed himself attached by affection to a being plunged into disgrace and abject poverty, and who appeared eager to bring to notice the habitual good qualities of his fallen friend, that the dark spot which tarnished them might be the less observed. Little as she had seen of the world, this conduct was, she thought, by no means common, and she remembered with regret, how small had been her merit in acting the part that had procured her so many eulogiums. She conceived a higher idea of the judgment of Miss Beauclerc, from the opinions she had romantically hazarded concerning the *mysterious stranger*, and from her solicitude to assist him, than any she had formed since they had quitted Mr. Mordaunt, whose parting words had made a considerable impression upon her mind, and infused a kind of suspicion into it, which though Rosella regarded as treasonable to gratitude and friendship, she could not wholly discard.

She was musing still with great earnestness, when two gentle taps at the door recalled her attention; it opened, and Mr. Delamere appeared. Rosella started up – "I hope you bring good news?" cried she hastily.

"I thank you a thousand times for your solicitude," returned he. – "Yes, I bring better news than I had dared to hope."

"You have seen him?" asked Rosella.

"I have seen him: having parted with his dog, he changed his cloaths at Reeth,[195] and had the imprudence to return to the very spot where you met with him. So that I soon discovered his retreat for I was almost unaccountably carried to the place, from an idea that he would nor be far from it."

"But is he now removed?" interrupted Rosella.

"He is," replied Mr. Delamere: "I trust that he has by this time, almost reached the sea-port we fixed upon whilst I remained with him; and if he gets out of the kingdom, all will be well."

"All will be well!" repeated she, the scene at the Lodge still dwelling upon her mind.

"Very partially, and in a most limited sense, I must mean," replied Delamere: – "believe me, he is much to be pitied even where he is most to be condemned. If you could know," added he, "what he has suffered, and still suffers, you would greatly compassionate him: he speaks with energetic gratitude of the generous attentions of your friend, and pays an ampler tribute of admiration and reverence to the gentle being that appeared to him in the fury of the storm, and placed before his eyes the abyss into which he was falling. Your friend, in his presence, called you Rosella: he remembers the name, but his ear did not catch any other."

Rosella, understanding this as an indirect application, replied that she was called Montresor: Mr. Delamere bowed. – "Miss Beauclerc," added she, "will be happy to hear of your return, and the success that has attended you: I will inform her that you are here."

She then withdrew, and ran to perform her commission.

It so happened, that the good lady had at this moment brought her narrative unwarily to a point, where it was essential that she should introduce the *faux pas* of her mountain hero, and she very readily complied with the summons of Rosella.

Mr. Delamere repeated to her the substance of what he had related to her young companion, and Miss Beauclerc thanked him for the information.

"I claim your presence at our dinner table," added she; "and until we adjourn to it, the time shall be given to an uninterrupted detail of the unfortunate history of your friend, young Mompesson: I feel well disposed to listen to it with all the indulgence you have predemanded, and I beg leave to observe to you, that Rosella and myself have avoided any enquiry into the origin of those distresses represented to us at the Lodge, that we might hear it with every favourable circumstance it will admit of."

"I told you," replied he, "that many palliatives were attached to his misconduct, and certainly the fact is so: but I must yet entreat your patience, and the generous forbearance you have hitherto used, in not seeking to know, by common report, what must much excite your curiosity. The family at the Lodge are too much pitied and respected to allow me any fear that the case of their wretchedness should be obtruded upon you without any apparent solicitude on your part: and – I think will tell you that Mompesson himself conjured me not to reveal his disgrace to you, until I could reasonably conclude, from the lapse of time, that he had left the kingdom; for he protested he would never survive the simple possibility of encountering you or your young friend, in the positive character, to use his own words, which are undeservedly harsh, of a villain."

The eager wishes of Miss Beauclerc and Rosella to learn this secret, the disclosure of which was so long delayed, were now almost beyond control; but stimulated by the encomiums of Delamere to merit still further praise, they acquiesced with his proposal. – He expressed his acknowledgments for the dinner invitation, which was a pleasure he was obliged, he said, to deny himself, because he wished to ensure, by his personal attendance, every proper respect to the remains of the elder Mr. Mompesson: but if Miss Beauclerc would allow him to take his tea with her, he should think himself honoured. – And on the following morning, if she remained so long at Sedgfield, he would expose to her the horrible depravity of a fashionable and titled Circe,[196] who was the primary cause of the calamities which had so much excited her compassion and interest.

She readily agreed to the proposition, saying she was merely travelling for the improvement of her health and spirits, both of which had lately received a shock by severe losses; and it was therefore indifferent to her whether she remained a day or a week in any place where she could be tolerably well accommodated.

Mr. Delamere then withdrew; and Rosella, the next minute, beheld him on horseback, galloping in the road that led to the Lodge.

When Simpson entered to lay the cloth, Rosella remarked that he appeared indisposed, and kindly enquired if he felt unwell; he shook his head, and as Miss Beauclerc was not in the room, said, with some symptoms of ill-humour, that his Lady's fancies would soon kill him, for he had not been used to such a vagary life, and was too old to take to it now. Rosella, who had from infancy received from the old man many marks of kindness and regard, was grieved that he should have real occasion for complaint, and desiring him to desist from what he was doing, and leave the care of the table to the people of the house, begged him to repose himself, and she would inform Miss Beauclerc of his indisposition.

"No, Miss Montresor," said Simpson, "I can't do that: who is there here to lay a cloth, or put a dinner upon table as it should be? if I was to leave it to those folks, it would not be fit to sit down to."

Rosella was well acquainted with the obstinacy of the old man, and ran to her friend to urge her interference. But Miss Beauclerc interposed in vain; Simpson would not hear of seceding from his office, and after many arguments and entreaties, Rosella was obliged to give up the point.

It was late in the evening when Mr. Delamere returned: he told them he had arranged affairs at the Lodge, where he had procured the pretence of a relation of the family, as he could not consult young Mompesson, who knew not as yet the tragical events which had taken place there, and was persuaded the total silence, and seeming desertion of his natural friends, were the effects of a just anger, and an intimation that they wished to cast him off.

"And did you not even hint at any part of what had happened?" said Miss Beauclerc.

"Had I done so," returned Delamere, "he would perhaps have surmised the rest, and have become careless of his fate: and though I know his existence is a burthen to him, I think the future feelings of his amiable and unfortunate sisters, should they ever recover to a knowledge of the termination of this unhappy affair, ought to be as much attended to as possible."

After this little discussion, the conversation became less gloomy: Delamere displayed himself to great advantage on the different topics that arose, and Miss Beauclerc might possibly have fixed upon so pleasing a young man as the successful lover of her Rosella, had not that important personage, in her drama, been already immutably decided upon between herself and Mrs. Ellinger.

Chapter V

THE FASCINATION OF A HIGH-BORN BEAUTY ANALYZED

MR. DELAMERE was to breakfast with the ladies by appointment; and as Miss Beauclerc had no objection to his falling very desperately in love with Rosella, though she did not mean that his sighs should be returned, she suffered her to descend to the sitting-room some time before she chose to be ready, to allow of an interesting tête-à-tête.

The gentleman was waiting their levee when Rosella entered it, but the effect of the *rencontre* was not so interesting as Miss Beauclerc might have expected: indeed it is not to be ascertained what declarations of eternal passion might have escaped the lips of Mr. Delamere, had not poor Simpson, busy as usual, entered the apartment immediately after Rosella, whose attention then reverted almost wholly to him.

"How are you?" demanded she, with a look of unaffected solicitude: "you appear quite ill – why do you fatigue yourself with the breakfast – pray go and lie down, and Miss Beauclerc will send, I am sure, for assistance."

Simpson looked very melancholy, but made no answer; and having finished what he had undertaken, notwithstanding her remonstrances, he withdrew without replying to them. Rosella was much distressed; and Mr. Delamere perceiving it, observed that as Miss Beauclerc had no other servant with her, he hoped she would accept the attendance of his valet during the indisposition of the old man.

"You are very good," replied Rosella: "perhaps Simpson might be then induced to spare himself; I will run and inform Miss Beauclerc of his increasing illness."

She was hastening to execute this intention, but was prevented leaving the room by the entrance of her friend, who on hearing the report, very peremptorily insisted that Simpson should retire to his bed, and ordered him proper attendance: and the old butler, overcome by pain and weariness, submitted to her decision.

The breakfast was rather hurried by Miss Beauclerc, whose impatience to hear the promised narrative was become rather troublesome; but Mr. Delamere was by no means equally anxious to relate it: to him the talk was painful, and Miss Beauclerc was obliged to remind him of his promise before he thought of executing it.

"It is a melancholy history you require of me," said he; "a history in which you will find artifice and insidious vice triumphant over ingenuousness, and the firmness of habitual and tried integrity. I will give it you without preface, but I must again entreat that your judgment of my unhappy friend may lean to mercy."

Miss Beauclerc bowed, whilst Rosella, all attention to the expected tale, looked eagerly in the face of Delamere, but spoke not.

"Young Mompesson," resumed he, "is the only son of those unhappy parents, who could not survive his errors and disgrace; and his two sisters, still more unfortunate, composed the whole of a family, united equally by the gentlest bonds of affection as by the ties of consanguinity. George received the most liberal education – we met at a public school, and were both gratified by being accidentally entered at the same University. – After he had quitted it, he returned home, where he remained rather more than a year, but not in idleness: for his father was a man of genius and learning, and was anxious to improve both the natural and acquired talents of his son. From this period, the impetuosity of character which was sufficiently distinguishable in young Mompesson, could no longer be restrained to partial inactivity; he wished to enter upon some mode of life which would enable him to improve the moderate patrimony he was born to inherit, and give him at once wealth and celebrity. The bar appeared to be his election, and his father did not oppose his choice; because poor Mompesson was formed to surpass most men in a situation which calls at once for found judgment and a brilliant imagination: many circumstances however, occurred to crush the project, and he became a partner in a house of extensive interest and universal concern. There, his promptitude, his integrity, his exactness, his judgment, and various abilities were equally perceptible and equally relied upon: he was the favourite of his seniors, the idol of his dependants.

"Thus far his career was deservedly successful: the income he now possessed, enabled him to mix with the gay world of fashion and folly, and there it ensured him a welcome reception. Amongst the most distinguished of his associates for birth and rank, he was perhaps admitted and caressed, because it was known that he could command very considerable sums of money: with the more virtuous and disinterested however, his presence was courted, from the unaffected elegance of his manners, the sweetness of his disposition, and the charm which his universal genius threw into the society he frequented. Every man was then proud to acknowledge an intercourse with Mompesson, and many women, of no inconsiderable fortune, sighed to fix his attention. A female of a noble house – why should I conceal her name, who has, with the most unblushing depravity, employed every perverted charm of intellect and person, ultimately to ruin, to distract, to annihilate an amiable family, for the shameless gratification of vanity, vice, and extravagance? – Oh Madam! whilst my wretched friend wanders far from the society he was accustomed to adorn, whilst he bears – yet hardly bears his cruel disgrace, as yet unconscious of the dreadful calamities hanging over his crime, this woman hears unmoved the opprobrium she forced upon him, and audaciously expresses her indignation that his atrocious insolence should have urged him to raise his eyes to her. – Why is she not driven from the face of day, and loaded with the infamy she merits? Because her principles are not singular in the sphere she moves in, and because the virtues or the merits of her ancestors have transmitted to her in the honours she claims, a right to become degraded and vicious, without feeling the keenness of that stigma which the world affixes to the humbler offender. She is handsome, she plays deep, the bets, she lures – she is abhorred, despised, and tolerated; whilst the respectable but unnoticed family of Mompesson silently receive the poison she guided to their lips, and unable to blazon the extent of their wrongs to the world, sink into the grave; or find a refuge in the annihilation of their reason.

"This woman – this unprincipled woman, saw my poor friend, and admired him: but to her his particular attentions were not directed, for he was unconscious of, or indifferent to the sentiments she affected to display – sentiments the situation of the lady should have taught her to repel. She was married; but separated from her husband, who allowed for her maintenance merely a pittance which the law extorted from him, for she had been nearly portionless: with this, she retired to the house of an amiable, but too facile friend of the first rank, whose husband became the slave of her fascinations; but when her rapacious demands upon his fortune could no longer be complied with, without injuring his legitimate children, he refused to satisfy them, and the harpy was compelled, by her habitual profusion[197] and natural depravity, to seek other dupes to her various wiles: yet still she retained, by unknown arts, the situation from which outraged hospitality, offended chastity, and insulted dignity should have driven her; and from this conspicuous post, looked round for the victims the meant to select. George Mompesson met her eye; and his address, his vivacity of temper, his youth, and circumstances marked him for her prey. I will not offend your ear," continued Delamere, "with the detail of her Syren arts; Mompesson fatally yielded to them; and intoxicated with her favour, charmed with her beauty, her accomplishments, her treacherous wit, her insinuating manners, in which the seduction of the prostitute is veiled by the exaltation of noble birth, and by the most well-acted sweetness, gentleness, and sensibility, he supplied her with all the money he could command, because he was told that her distresses arose from the avarice of a brutal husband, who often withheld the pittance assigned her. But her demands did not stop here: as her power over his mind increased, she attempted to bend him to her purposes, by plunging him into the dishonourable acts of abusing the confidence his friends and associates in business reposed in him; – he resisted, but her tears and feigned agonies of distraction wrung his heart: she talked of being dragged ignominiously to a jail, and he flew to his father for the assistance his principles forbade him to derive from baseness. The good old man forcing himself to credit the tale he told, yet alarmed at the hurrying, the repentant confusion of his son, laid before his daughters the petition he had made, as his granting it would reduce them to an entire dependence upon their brother: these generous young women confiding in his honour for the restitution he had promised, made no scruple of sacrificing their immediate proceeds to his necessities. The elder was recently engaged to a gentleman in her neighbourhood, and as young Mompesson required the strictest secrecy, and her portion had been already named to her lover, the marriage was obliged to be protracted upon various pretences, which he had reason to suppose trivial; and piqued at the apparent inconstancy of his mistress, he entered the Army, and left the kingdom. Young Mompesson learned this distressing fact too late to prevent the misery of his gentle sister, who had insisted that it should never be mentioned to him; and stung with remorse, goaded too by the increasing demands of his infamous seductress, he assented to the plan she had often proposed, of adjourning to those gaming-tables, which the hereditary and elected legislators of the realm suffer their wives and their sisters to hold under their own roofs; where the younger and more lovely females of the family are instructed to act as decoys to the admiring, the unwary stranger. Good God!" continued Delamere, "that we should wonder at, that we should dare arraign the prevalence of licentious opinions amongst the multitude, when they must be voluntarily blind, or else behold the general licentious conduct of the titled and the rich – a conduct from which the laws of the land either withhold them, or not having power to withhold, punish with severity. The labourer must per force suffer his family to share the produce of his toil: – the idleness or the desertion of the labourer from *his* family is cognizable by the law;[198] he is sought after, brought back, imprisoned, and a better conduct enforced; whilst the profligate Noble dissipates the estates of his ancestors with impunity, and leaves the titled heir of his vices a pensioner upon the community at large, through the channel of power. The labourer is uncertain if he may not to-morrow, by the fury of fanatical reform, be forbidden to have his humble dinner baked on the seventh day;[199] and if he has ever profited by the Sunday schools those very reformers of morals have so industriously propagated, he may read in an alehouse newspaper of the magnificent dinners, concerts, card parties, collations, and suppers given by his Grace, the Countess, Sir John, my Lady, and all the Right Honourable group upon the same sacred day. Who then will dare to be indignant at this man's licentious opinions? If the anecdotes of the great do not always redound to their credit, if the daily prints will record their follies and their vices, and if the pious promoters of learning amongst the labouring poor will enable them to prose over "those pictures of the times," why do we stand astonished at the diffusion of levelling principles?[200] But pardon me – I have wandered from my subject, from the impetuous reflections it gave rise to. I left poor Mompesson in a situation of danger, in which all that can be augured of evil fortune actually befell him: at the fashionable gaming tables, the soft accents of an harmonious voice, the seducing smiles of Beauty drew his attention perpetually from the opportunities Fortune offered in her best moods; and accelerated, redoubled her persecutions when she began to frown. If perchance he was successful, salvers of liqueurs were presented with officious repetition, till his judgment was wholly obscured, and he lost his advantages; if he was unfortunate, and wished to retire, he was allured, ridiculed, sneered at till he trebled his bets, and more than trebled those debts, which the next morning he was compelled to make good.

"In the midst, however, of these desperate resources, he contrived, in defiance of the distresses which on every side assailed him, to refund the sum his family had so generously relinquished; because his heart every moment reproached him with the rupture he had unwittingly occasioned between his sister and her lover, and the consequent misery it had entailed upon her: but the effort hastened his own destruction, and equally urged forward that of beings dearer to him than life. One evening, more propitious than usual, had sent him from the Pharo table with some thousands in his possession, and with the money his situation enabled him at that moment to raise without suspicion, amounted to the sum he had accepted for a purpose so unworthy: he put the whole into his pocket-book, and was proceeding to vest it in the hands of his father's agent, when a note reached him from Lady –, for so is the wretch denominated, that she must see him without a moment of delay at the usual place of rendezvous, or her inevitable death would avenge his neglect. He flew to the appointed spot, and found her in an agony of mingled disdain, rage, and apprehension, occasioned by the threat of a jeweller to arrest her immediately, unless she paid him without hesitation, for a set of diamonds which he was well informed had disappeared a few days after they had passed from his hands into her's. Mompesson heard the story varnished as it came to his ear, with disgust, and felt his remorse redoubled that for such an abandoned extravagant, he had ruined the peace of his innocent sister: all the arts and blandishments of his mistress were insufficient to induce him to alter his original disposition of the money he at that moment carried about him, and he left her to execute his purpose. When it was accomplished however, his heart was torn with anxiety for the fate of the woman to whom his professions of inviolable attachment had been equally ardent and sincere: and his total want of power to assist her, should the menace of her irritated creditor be fulfilled, gave him horror inconceivable. In this state he remained until the following day, resolving very fully to forego his irregularities, and again become all that his fond family hoped he still was, when a second billet was given him, dated from a spunging-house.[201] He started – the contents drove him to distraction – the bane, the blaster of his youth informed him that she had a fatal vial in her possession, the contents of which she vowed to swallow in two hours, if in that time she were not set at liberty, that she might crush the flying rumours of her disgrace by her presence in the usual circles. He could not hesitate – he rushed on his destruction, became bail for her, and at her instigation, for he was compelled immediately to produce the sum in question, used the signature of his partners to a draft which he negociated, with an intention of taking it up with the first money he received, to which he subjoined a solemn vow never more to behold the face of the woman who had lured him to destroy his self-respect, his peace, and his honour.

"She saved him however, from the conflicts of love and prudence in preserving this last resolution, by sending him a letter of *congé*, in which she informed him that his backwardness to rescue her from scorn and contempt had opened her eyes to the decline of his affection, and she would not be indebted any further to compassion, for the services and assiduities she had a right to claim from fondness and gratitude: and she concluded by desiring him to return her letters and her picture, and forget that she had ever been so weak as to fancy they were pleasing to him – a request his indignant pride immediately prompted him to comply with. In fact this disgrace to her sex was alarmed at the share she had in the last desperate action of her victim, and plainly discerning that if he proceeded in the career she had forced him into, that he was inevitably undone, and if he retracted, he was no longer for her purposes – she therefore accepted the devoirs[202] of a rich, but avaricious old Nobleman, the day after her liberation from confinement had been effected at the expence of all that was most dear to the unhappy Mompesson, of whom I have little further to say, but that his fatal lapse was discovered by one of those unexpected coincidence of circumstances which it is impossible to foresee: his friends, whole names he had so unwarrantably used, would fain have hushed the transaction, and saved him from ignominy and danger; but it could not be accomplished.

"Mompesson, in the fury of despair, would have chosen instant annihilation; but his life was preserved till better thoughts prevailed, and he fled, though not till every port was shut against him, and he found himself universally proscribed and sought after. The sum he had taken with him was almost expended, and the foreign letters of credit he had received from his generous benefactors could not have extricated him from the distress that already assailed him, when you so providentially encountered him in his retreat, from whence he had dispatched an account of his perilous situation to his family, at that moment incapable of hearing or relieving his anguish by the few words of pardon he had implored. His messenger, not very intelligent, left the letter entrusted to him with the hired nurse attending poor old Mompesson, who had sent only the day before his faithful domestic to me for intelligence of the unhappy wanderer, and with an intimation that death was fast stealing him from his sorrows. The billet of his son he never read; for his senses had failed before it arrived, and the old woman wholly forgot it, until I required it of her at my return to the Lodge.

"It is therefore to your humanity alone that I have been enabled to trace him, and by which I hope he has, ere now, escaped the possibility of a pursuit."

Miss Beauclerc bowed rather coldly, in return to this compliment. – "Good heavens!" thought she, "have I then wasted so much time and sympathy upon an object who has merely committed a vulgar forgery! and whose prostituted heart was not worthy the honour of being captivated by my Rosella – a fellow whose sensibility has been blunted by running the gauntlet of those beauties so profusely exhibited by the whole tribe of little Cassinos[203] about town!"

Her indignation was roused by his presumption in having dared to direct one glance of admiration at Miss Montresor, and most seriously did she repent the many hours she had stolen from a much more important and delightful pursuit, for a man whose dying speech and confession would contain the horrible periods of Newgate eloquence, expressive of regret for being drawn in to spend his Sundays in bad company, the beginning of all evil, and giving up his time to the lewd pursuits of swearing, drinking, cards, and dice. What a history! – when compared, too, with the interesting dying speeches and confessions of repentant heroes, who discover to their attentive auditors a beautiful long buried wife shut up in one secret dungeon, and a still more beautiful discarded mistress very safely deposited in another, not forgetting the old chest in the corner, containing the mouldering bones of a murdered rival, reposing quietly upon the purloined title-deeds of his own estates, which being restored to some cottage-cradled damsel, their rightful owner, exalt her to an equality with some disinterested and illustrious lover, whose passion and valor have elucidated the whole business, and placed the saddle upon the right horse.[204]

Rosella, perceiving that Mr. Delamere was very apparently chagrined at the inauspicious reverie of her friend, exerted herself to remove the impression it could not fail to give him, by expressing the unmixed compassion the still felt for young Mompesson, and lamenting the fatal destiny which had led him into the society of such a wretch as Lady – . Mr. Delamere was much gratified that her sentiments remained unaltered; and whilst he bestowed the most animated encomiums upon her philanthropy, Miss Beauclerc recollected the ungenerous appearance her silence must have, and atoned for it by a little exertion of the hypocrisy society not only allows, but sometimes exacts: she renewed her civilities to Delamere, and made her peace by proposing that they should not separate at dinner, which he gratefully acceded to.

Rosella now withdrew to enquire into the situation of poor Simpson, which was lamentable enough, as she found him combating a strong fit of rheumatic gout with the treacherous arms of anger and impatience: the old butler had more than once before been discomfited by the same enemy; but he had always, until this time, been consoled by the auxiliaries of kind attendance, a comfortable chamber, and a good bed. The attention of Rosella, however, enforced that of others, and at her representation, Miss Beauclerc desired that a nurse should be procured, that he might not suffer from the hurry and forgetfulness incident to a house of public resort: and at the repeated request of Mr. Delamere, his servant was, *en attendant*, constituted valet extraordinary to the ladies, who would be, he supposed, detained some time at Sedgfield by the circumstance, which he was not displeased at, because he intended to remain there several days himself to settle the affairs at the Lodge, and attend the interment of Mr. Mompesson.

These ceremonials being adjusted, and there appearing to be several hours intervening between that of dinner, the gentleman proposed a rural promenade, offering himself as an escort to the ladies and as Miss Beauclerc was no longer in such extreme haste to record the unhappy narrative of the mountain hero, she assented to the plan. On beholding the immense expanse of waves which could be plainly discerned beyond the eastern coast, she immediately figured to herself the sublimity of a young heroine gazing over the mountain tops, which gradually retire from her heroic vision, till they gain the delightful and celebrated appearance of blue mists; and then the majestic ocean, rolling its superb billows from the strand where her lover was torn from her, or she was torn from her lover; but unfortunately the German ocean,[205] far from inspiring such heavenly fancies as the vicinity of a Venetian sea might have created, could raise in a common imagination, only the heavy murmurs of a Dutch fishery, or the coarse scenery of a grand bout of salmon pickling; it was cruel certainly, and Miss Beauclerc wished herself very vehemently on the celebrated banks of the Garonne, or gliding through the Rialto, encircled by dying cadencies, garnished with pauses, and swells, and ritornellos.[206]

Her companion and Mr. Delamere having left her to contemplate at her leisure, walked slowly forward; and frequently standing still to discuss with earnestness the merits and misfortunes of the Mompesson family, Rosella learned several interesting anecdotes of the culprit's amiable sisters, which heightened the interest she already felt in their fate. – When he had unwarily drawn the tears to her eyes, he suddenly checked himself, and introduced another subject; but that one which most occupied the imagination of each would still recur, and Rosella mentioned a wish of possessing the drawing traced by the recluse, in those lingering moments he would fain have urged forward, whilst not certain but the next might conduct him to annihilation.

"Perhaps," said Delamere, "he may have left it in the hut: do you suppose your friend would object to employ a day in visiting Stanmore Hills, which are well worthy her observation? If she assents, we will look once more at the habitation of the unhappy wanderer, and trace his erring steps to the scene which stole him for a moment from the recollection of misery and misconduct."

Rosella was pleased with the proposal, and her solicitations, joined to the prospect of waiting the convalescence of Simpson, induced Miss Beauclerc to concur readily in an excursion that promised a little variation from the tiresome sameness of her present life, in which her only amusement consisted of rocking the cradle of her elevated fancies; without perceiving any possibility that the inclinations of Rosella might take a bias that would frustrate all her heroic plans, which destined her as the reward of Lord Morteyne's disinterested passion, whom she represented to herself and to Selina, sighing in the extreme disconsolation of that poetic death in love – absence.

Chapter VI

RAGE FOR SUBLIME EVASIONS[207] – THE MYSTERIOUS DISAPPEARANCE OF TWO HEROINES

AT the grave of Mr. Mompesson, the most rugged cheek was watered with a tear; and there the curses of wounded humanity were raised to heaven, against the shameless depravity of those titled and untitled beings, who revel in our bloated metropolis upon the spoils of the young and the unwary.

Miss Beauclerc and Rosella had not been able to absent themselves from this scene, where the story of the young man's seduction and his wrongs, was told in various ways by many execrating tongues, and the annihilation of his family closed the tale. The effect of such a history at a moment so solemn, however rude the rehearsal might be, can well be conceived. The sobs of Rosella, who was accidentally stationed during the service for the dead, by the side of George Mompesson's village nurse, rendered outrageous by her grief, attracted universal attention: and she was by many supposed to be an intimate friend of the poor young ladies; by others it was whispered that she was a deserted sweetheart of Mr. George – a fact that was proved from her being accompanied to the funeral by the little dog he had begged of his sister. – Rosella was too much absorbed by her own sensations to hear the comments of her neighbours, and returned with her friend to their temporary residence, with a heart more heavy than she had ever before experienced.

When this painful ceremony was over, Mr. Delamere exerted himself to ensure to the Miss Mompessons the best attendance from the people to whose care they had been committed, both from motives of interest as well as of compassion; and that their still more unhappy brother, in whatever soil his errors had eternally banished him, might be secured at least from want. Several days were consumed in effecting these benevolent purposes, during which poor Simpson continued rather to decline than to amend in health, and was now perfectly unable to traverse his narrow chamber – a circumstance extremely *mal-à-propos*,[208] because it detained Miss Beauclerc from the immediate execution of a very promising project, replete with interest and adventure; and though she had half intended to drop the old butler before she reached the grand scene of action, yet she could not reconcile the barbarity of leaving him wholly to the care of strangers, with the tender and delicate feelings of those amiable pattern personages, who so often raise an old and decrepid domestic to be one of the principal *dramatis personae* in the fine-spun scene of sensibility.

When every duty was discharged at the Lodge, Mr. Delamere reminded Miss Beauclerc of their intended ramble to Stanmore Hills; and the next morning, at an early hour, Rosella and herself stepped into a post-chaise, accompanied by him on horseback. – When they arrived at the little inn, whose romantic situation had so much attracted the approbation of Miss Beauclerc, the well-remembered equipage drew the children to the door.

"Oh pretty Lady! pretty Lady come back!" cried little Patty. – "Pretty Lady come back!" echoed the boy.

"She's come back – she's come back!" they both repeated, striking their hands together with eager exultation.

Rosella, who had recognized her play-fellows with nods and smiles, now alighted, and kissed the uplifted faces of Patty and her brother after their mother had very carefully wiped each little mouth with her apron.

"I perceive," said Mr. Delamere, smiling, "that even in this remote and almost desolate spot, the merits of Miss Montresor are warmly acknowledged."

"She is fond of children, and indulgent to them," replied Miss Beauclerc, "and the natural consequence of it is, that children are universally fond of her."

"I admit the inference," returned he; – "yet if Miss Montresor had been as remarkable for deformity and sourness of aspect as she is remarkable for the reverse of both, she might have courted the affection of those little distinguishing beings a considerable time before she could have boasted of so great a portion of their regard."

"I cannot agree with you," said Miss Beauclerc, forgetting for a moment her heroism, "that the affections are naturally connected with personal graces. Rosella," continued she, "do you not remember the poor little child who was nursed by the old woman on the common? To hear it call for its own pretty Phebe – its own dear little Phebe, any one might have supposed this beloved Phebe to have been a sprightly young nurse-maid at least; instead of which, Rosella introduced me, when she led home the nursling, to a pretty little Phebe about eighty, with a person so deformed, and an aspect so forbidding, that it was curious to behold the process by which her features were twisted into an expression of something like tenderness to her orphan charge."

"I think your illustration implies a compliment to human nature," returned Delamere; "but I must still assert that the fondness which these little creatures so artlessly express for the 'pretty lady,' has much discernment in it: at least I may assert from experience, that she may very assuredly inspire admiration even before the moment when it is discovered that her benevolence entitles her to gratitude."

"This unfortunate youth is desperately enamoured of her!" thought Miss Beauclerc: she was elated however, by the equal certainty of other and still more desirable conquests; and when she reflected that this Delamere was the avowed friend of an exotic in the fashionable world, whose exploits not only *entitled* him to the honours of the platform (there he would not have been singular), but had even conducted him to the edge of it, she could not forbear betraying a chilling coldness in her manner, sufficiently observable. He saw the change in her aspect, and assumed, on his part, a distance and formality, the result perhaps of a disinclination that either herself or her young companion should suppose he had formed pretensions they felt no wish of encouraging.

After having taken refreshment, the party began to ascend the hill leading to the spot they meant to visit. Mr. Delamere suffered Rosella and her little associates, who would not leave her a moment, to pass him; and having vainly offered his assistance to Miss Beauclerc, who refused it however with complacency, he walked with an air of nonchalance by her side, till they had reached Molly's cottage. Here Rosella waited his approach; and was surprised at his silence and gravity, which yet a moment of reflection accounted for, as it reminded her that Mr. Delamere had taken an eternal leave of the wretched Mompesson at that place not long since.

Influenced by this idea, she turned back to meet him, and her efforts to chase the gloom from his countenance soon succeeded: whilst Miss Beauclerc, naturally of an inoffensive and placid disposition, as easily forgot her heroic dignity, and conversed with her usual freedom and good humour.

Molly was at home, and ran out to ax the gentlefolks if they would not walk in, a civility they declined; but the children consented to quit the pretty lady, to realize some expectations of a rural feast. Miss Beauclerc, who had never before beheld the picturesque scene around her, gazed at it with astonishment, whilst Rosella endeavoured to discover a path that might lead her to the forlorn hut lately so strangely inhabited: but it required long custom to find a scarcely trodden track in so wild a solitude; and Mrs. Spanger being applied to for assistance, called to a half-cloathed girl to lead the way to the cot, where she had sometimes been dispatched with a loaf or washed linen.

"Poor gentleman," exclaimed the woman, when she heard the request, "our landlord say, a suppose a quoined golden guineas,[209] and wad be honged for it. God help un, a never quoined any that I see; a wos more like to be crazed we love say I, and I be sure a was – for sometime a would eat a mite, and sometime a wou'd n't touch a bit – and sometime a wou'd walk about all night, so Jack say; and then sometime a wou'd tak to as bed, and not get oop all day!"

Mr. Delamere here cut short the report; but reflections would arise that, whilst Mompesson was thus dragging on existence, and deploring his blasted hopes, the companions of his fleeting, his treacherous enjoyments no longer uttered his name but to load it with obloquy and contempt, not for having committed evil, but for being betrayed into that particular species of dishonesty which the law could reach. The laugh, the jest, the trifling amusement of the moment followed the mention of his disgrace, with a harmony no regret for him disturbed; and at that table where he had been fleeced of thousands, the same harpies presided, and successive fools were cheated with equal impunity; – whilst the woman who had more immediately precipitated the unhappy youth into the gulph of infamy, affected to regret that his sudden disappearance prevented the chastisement she had charged her footman to give him: and though no one credited the innocence she aimed to establish, yet all who heard her, pretended they did, and joined with the Right Honourable Lady —, in shrugs of admiration at the audacity of young Cits.[210] When she could thus force a chorus to her recitative, she cared little for the indignation, fashion, and suavity condemned to silence.

At length Rosella once more entered the wretched asylum, where the despairing countenance of Mompesson met her eye, charged with the confusion of a soul on which self-accusation and conscious guilt did not sit easily. The straw which had served him for repose, when repose had not fled him, still lay in the corner; but the drawing of Molly's cottage either himself, or some other person, had removed.

Miss Beauclerc soon quitted the hut to survey the surrounding scenery, which was indeed extremely well fitted to inspire some of those sublime ideas that floated on her imagination; and the effect it produced heightened her impatience to proceed on her journey, in spite of the incapacity of poor Simpson to attend her. Suddenly she hastened her companions back to the inn, scarcely allowing Rosella to go in quest of little Patty and her brother, whilst she waited where the path turned towards, Molly's dwelling.

"I cannot but admire the persevering spirit of charity which governs your mind," said Mr. Delamere, who accompanied her; "whilst I perceive that of others evaporate with the emotion of the moment."

"If you allude to Miss Beauclerc," said Rosella, eagerly, "your opinion does her injustice."

"I believe not," returned he: "but may I take the liberty of enquiring if you are of her family, either by affinity or alliance?"

After a moment of embarrassment, which the abruptness of the question created, Rosella replied that she was not in the remotest degree related to her friend, but that she respected her as the most generous and best of women. Little Patty and her brother now joined them, and in a few minutes the whole party overtook Miss Beauclerc, who was returning to the inn to hasten the dinner, because she had resolved to travel back to Sedgfield the same evening; a precipitation that surprised and rather offended Mr. Delamere, as she had not long before resolved to remain in her present quarters two or three days, to explore still further the beauties of the place. Rosella appeared disappointed, but was silent upon the subject; and late in the evening the party re-entered Sedgfield.

Simpson was not improved in health since the morning, and complained very grievously, when his Lady paid him a compassionate visit whilst her supper table was being arranged: she expressed her chagrin at his indisposition, a chagrin which was heightened, she said, by the unfortunate necessity in which she found herself, of immediately resuming her journey.

The old man was thunderstruck at this intelligence; nor was he in the least consoled by the prospect of being abandoned, sick and helpless, in a place to which he was entirely a stranger, at the sight of a purse his Lady put into his hand, and her assurances that she would enjoin the people of the house to give him every attention.

Rosella was not present at this interview; and only learned, when she retired for the night, after having simply bade Mr. Delamere good evening, that at four the next morning, a chaise was ordered to convey Miss Beauclerc and herself towards Scotland. – Extreme astonishment, and an emotion nearly allied to displeasure, arose in the mind of Rosella at the unprecedented conduct of her friend. The situation of Simpson, whom it was cruelty to leave without actual necessity, and the strange rudeness of quitting Mr. Delamere in a manner so abrupt, filled her with dismay, and she vainly essayed to alter the determination of Miss Beauclerc by representation and entreaty. But she was at length silenced by a very solemn prediction, that there were mysterious reasons for such a conduct, which would hereafter justify it.

At four in the morning therefore, Miss Beauclerc descended the staircase of the inn, with all the silence and precipitation of a young beauty, flying from the power of some atrocious gentle or noble, who, in carrying her towards his never-failing chateau in Scotland, or Ireland, or Wales, good-naturedly stops short in his enterprize to loiter on the road: and then the distressed heroine, either by bribing the maid of hôtellerie, or by unlocking all the doors at midnight with a *passe-par-tout*[211] of her own peculiar invention, escapes, leaving the disappointed lover

– "To storm and stare,
"And load with curses the withdrawing fair."[212]

And in this manner did Miss Beauclerc imagine the forsaken Delamere would vent the first transports of his disappointment, until the tender remembrance of the charms of the cruel fugitive subdued his soul, and forced the hard-wrung drops of anguish from his eyes.

As the lady chose now to travel *incog.*, she left her carriage at Sedgfield, having previously ordered Simpson to use it when he received instructions to rejoin her. This arrangement was thought strange by Rosella, and she stepped into a hack-chaise in a very disconsolate mood, as she had been forbidden to see the old man before her departure, and now reflected, with considerable disquiet, that she was travelling under the sole protection of a person who, however her affection and long cherished gratitude might soften the general tenor of her conduct and conversation, appeared inclined to follow without reflection, every freak of a distempered fancy.

The farewell intimation of Mr. Mordaunt rose to her recollection, and she was tempted for a moment, so far to profit by it, as to state to him her present situation; but the well-remembered kindness and generosity Miss Beauclerc had displayed towards her from infancy, repelled all idea of appealing from her guidance: and as she sat shivering in a broken windowed chaise, breakfastless, on[213] a dark rainy morning before sunrise, the worldly idea of seeking refuge in the counsels of discretion from the adventures that appeared to await her, may be excused a young heroine not yet inured to the hardships of one campaign in the walks of romance.

Miss Beauclerc took a hasty breakfast at Durham, but declined staying to view the place, in the fear that Delamere would pursue the object of his passion, and force an explanation she chose to forego. In the same hasty manner she passed through Newcastle and Morpeth, and still occupied by her apprehensions, instead of continuing in the high road, directed the driver to Warkworth,[214] hoping, by this well-precedented manoeuvre, to elude the fond enquiries of the distracted lover. At this place she condescended to attend to her own fatigue and the entreaties of Rosella, and having ordered a dinner, sat down with great self-complacency to think of the dangers she had passed.

After having relieved, by two hours of rest, the weariness which, in spite of heroism, had assailed her, and gazed, as all sublime travellers do, with wonder and awe and rapture upon the ocean's far extending billows, which could be discerned from the apartment she was placed in, she began to sigh for amusement or occupation. In the towns she had passed, she had been repeatedly asked if she would not stay to behold this particular beauty or that particular curiosity; so she applied to the people around her, to be informed of the beauties and curiosities worthy of renown in Warkworth, and was told that the hermitage up the river was the most curiousest place any gentlefolks might wish to see.[215]

To the hermitage therefore, Miss Beauclerc resolved to dedicate the evening, provided she were not prevented by the effects of Mr. Delamere's lover-like despair, of which, notwithstanding her disinclination for an immediate *denouement*, she felt extremely surprised not to have received, by the interference of fate, any intimation. However, she did not yet give up the idea of being called to his bed-side, where her presence might be required, in consequence of a pistol ball, or a fall from his steed, pushed by the impatience of the enamoured rider, beyond his strength; for she well knew that a lover will sometimes drive his spurs into the sides of his horse, in proportion as he feels the arrows of the *tender* passion wounding his own susceptible bosom.

As Miss Beauclerc understood that the hermitage might be attained by water, she ordered a boat to take her up the river; but was informed that a post-chaise would convey her there in a much shorter time, and was advised to alter her plan upon the further doubt that arose, of there being any boat in a condition to receive ladies who were not exactly cloathed in sackcloth and ashes: but the obstinacy of Miss Beauclerc overcame all representation, and at length a fishing skiff was procured, very dirty indeed, and not very dry; yet these objections could not prove impediments to a gentle fair-one, bent upon enjoying at every event,

"The moon shining over the stream,
"Gentle harmony breathing around,
"The feathering oar reflecting the gleam,
"Beating time to the echo's soft sound."[216]

Now it was that she regretted the want of a lute, that delightful companion to all blooming damsels of heroic standard. A harp Rosella could play upon; but then a modern one was cumbrous to carry from place to place, though indeed she recollected to have read of a sublime young lady, who, in her perilous adventures, all achieved on foot, carried her Welch harp upon her back from one end of the island to the other, taking care to preserve a most graceful deportment the whole way.

Another captivating heroine she remembered to have read of, who made a pedestrian tour on the Continent of more than eight hundred miles, in pursuance of the dictates of "Plain Sense,"[217] and till more conspicuous perseverance – a feat the lady performed with her wardrobe under her arm, one pair of shoes upon her delicate feet, a chance-brought ducat in her pocket, a hurdy-gurdy depending in a string from her ivory neck, and her beautiful *frame* supported by coarse bread, or milk pottage, which *once* a day her good genius, and the charity of peasants, presented to her.

This last method of seeking adventures was extremely well accommodated to the fancy of Miss Beauclerc, and she resolved upon the first opportunity to procure a guitar or mandoline for Rosella. *En attendant*, as it was absolutely necessary that the aquatic adventure she was on the point of engaging in, should not be undertaken without music of some kind, the master of the inn was directed to enquire in the place for some dulcet-eared swain, a retainer of the olive-wreathed god.[218]

The landlord, extremely surprised at such a demand, as well as offended at the preference which had been given to a filthy boat over his neat post-chaise, made the perquisition required of him, with so little ceremony and attention to the dignity of his fair guests, that by the time a superannuated deaf fifer, formerly belonging to the Northumberland Militia,[219] had been dragged from his hovel to accompany the ladies to the hermitage, half the town were waiting with extreme impatience for a sight of the crazy woman dancing to Will Hobbes's music; for such had been my landlord's witty innuendo.

Miss Beauclerc received the devoirs of this ancient servant of Apollo and Mars with great condescension, and accepted the offered services of himself and his fife, since neither flute, lute, oboe, or clarinet could be obtained.

The owner of the skiff, who had been washing and mopping with great effort and perseverance from the moment his commission had been given him, now signified that it was ready, and Miss Beauclerc sallied forth, attended by Rosella, who appeared mortified and depressed; but the expression of her countenance was changed to consternation on seeing a number of people assembled at the inn door to behold her embarkation. – She seized the arm of her friend, and making an effort to draw her back to the apartment they had quitted, accompanied the motion with an earnest entreaty to wait till the crowd dispersed; but the adventurous dame was inflexible. Indeed she discovered nothing unpleasant in being exposed to the gaze of the Warkworth populace, because she concluded that the beauty of her young companion, and her own interesting mien of silent sorrow, had alone gathered it together: and thus poor Rosella was constrained to face the eager and rude glances of the multitude, who were however mollified into a silent curiosity by the confused agitation which her downcast eye and glowing cheek expressed.

But a general grin succeeded, when Miss Beauclerc was ushered into the boat by the fisherman and the old fifer, who, having put on his ancient finery, as being his best array, looked literally like a thing "made up of shreds and patches."[220] Rosella followed much against her inclination, shocked at the absurdity of her once revered friend, and fearing to look forward to the adventures her whimsical fancies might still further plunge them into.

Their officious attendants accompanied them a short way on the banks of the river; but as the *crazy lady* was wrapping herself up as fast as possible in sublime meditation, they could not discover, on her part, any preparation to amuse them in the manner the landlord had announced, and they fell off by degrees, and soon vanished entirely.

Chapter VII

RAGE FOR DISCOVERING ENTOMBED CHARMERS – A HUMILIATING RENCONTRE

MISS BEAUCLERC had, by this time, started from her reverie, and looking round, beheld Rosella with a mien melancholy and pensive enough to have satisfied the most refined of tastes. She was pleased with the observation. – "Now," whispered she, "my lovely child is divine! there wanted but this expression of countenance to make her perfect!"

The fifer sat in the stern of the vessel as upright and straight as a reed; his hat, exhibiting a variety of colours, and feathered on every side to the brim, had been for many years kicked and laid by, and thrown about, and taken care of alternately, till it had acquired several unintentional forms, and had lost a considerable part of its original dignity: but the wearer felt decorated and consequential, and, like an old courser in a dust-cart, still pricked up his ears, and kept his paces as well as he could.

Miss Beauclerc, having finished her thankful ejaculation, turned her eye upon the fifer, and remembering that "music is the food of love,"[221] desired him to play some pathetic air, such as doubtless he well recollected to have wept at in his youth. The poor fellow understanding some part of her command, but very far from hearing the extent of it, drew forth his instrument, which had almost been as ill-treated as his hat, though the injuries of time had been rather meliorated by the aids of industry and cobbler's ends, and set off *con molto spirito*[222] in those well-known strains entitled the White Cockade,[223] at the same time marching as he sat, a very quick pace against the loose boards that covered the bottom of the skiff; which movement not only supplied the place of the absent drum, but very unfortunately threw over his auditors a great part of the bilge-water secreted under this false flooring.

Rosella, mortified and vexed as she had been, instantly lost her *pensive mien* in an unconquerable fit of laughter, whilst Miss Beauclerc exerted her voice to arrest the career of this noisy son of Harmony; but having called and entreated to no purpose for some time, she was informed by the boatman that Will Hobbes was so dunny,[224] he could not hear his own performance.

The man was obliged to quit his oars, that he might, at the urgent request of the lady, make him sensible that she wished him to restore peace to her ears, and to her wounded sensibility; for the fifer sat with his head averted from his party, and his eyes fixed upon the water that flowed from beneath the stern. A rough salutation upon the shoulder interrupted his strains, and Miss Beauclerc, by a variety of gestures, obtained a much-desired repose for the neighbouring echoes, though not before he had, in eager wishes to earn the reward which had been promised, changed his melody, to try if he could not succeed better in "Moll in the Wad," – "the Cameronian Rant," and "the Morgan Rattler."[225]

Rosella felt for his wounded reputation, and would have endeavoured to praise his performance, but that at the first half-heard sentence of commendation he hastily put his hand to his pocket, with an intimation that he was not tired, and could blow for six hours without stopping.

Miss Beauclerc, whose serene dignity had been cruelly put to the rout, arrested him however, with a frown, and the poor fellow remained quiet till the boatman announced that they were near the hermitage, which she found worthy of her attention, and forgot, in contemplating it, her recent disappointment.

The hollow cliff overhanging the river, in whose vaulted roof the prayer and hymn of the recluse had often broken the silence of night, could not but be highly interesting: it was too sublime to be shared by her rude and ignorant conductors, and they were therefore instructed to remain in the boat, whilst Rosella and herself entered the sacred receptacle of piety and meditation.

Miss Beauclerc examined, with attention, every part of the place said to be the remains of the hermit's kitchen, and carefully sounded the ground and the walls, in the hope of discovering, like so many other heroines, either a trap-door, or a repository for family treasures, and confessions of horrible crimes and uncommon frauds locked up in inlaid or curious cabinets, by which the lands, tenements, castles, dungeons, and caverns for many miles round might suddenly be snatched from their present peaceful and unsuspicious owners, and descend, with a profusion of blushing honours upon the head of a drooping and tender-souled damsel, whom the whole world had till then combined to treat with scorn and obloquy; except indeed, the generous and manly-formed young gentleman, her happy lover, who never, for a moment, loses sight of the innate dignity of her soul, or ceases to bow down to the sublime elevation of her meek and humble deportment.

But however eager Miss Beauclerc might be in the search, no good fortune of this kind awaited her, and she passed into the chapel with a strong presentiment that she should there be more successful: at least she could scarcely fail, she thought, to discover the subterraneous passages and vaults so very generally appertaining to places of the smallest reputation in the annals of romance, where lovely and gentle creatures have an opportunity of initiating themselves into the science of tracing the histories, amours, and amourettes[226] of their forefathers, and bringing to light all the *faux-pas* of their grandmamas and old aunts, merely by walking with a solemn pace amidst their dry bones, with lamps half extinguished.

Yet a glimpse of happiness awaited Miss Beauclerc, more transporting than she had dared to hope in the highest flight of enthusiasm. At the further end of the chapel a recumbent female figure caught her eye,[227] and a blissful idea darted like a ray of light into her mind, that she should be the fortunate discoverer of some hapless good lady who might have been confined ten, twenty, perhaps thirty years in a cell adjoining this place; whilst a barbarous husband, having buried, instead of her, a curious effigy, composed of straw and old linen, very freely followed the bent of his fancies, and married some beautiful but licentious charmer, whose atrocious children seize, in due time, what they conceive to be their inheritance, and revel on the spoils, until papa's lawful and virtuous wife steps out of her enforced retirement, and places every body in their proper situations.

The imagination of Miss Beauclerc, fertile and rapid, in an instant spun forth such a web, that she remained entranced in the delightful intricacies of her own fantastic fancies. One moment the reclining dame was of the family of her deceased Raymond, who, having been forcibly imprisoned in this abode for nearly half a century, could now discover to her enraptured great grand-daughter some splendid fortune to which she could claim a right. The next instant she as hastily supposed the figure to be one of her own female ancestors, who could impart the customary information in similar cases, which must entitle her ever after to the sudden dignity of being addressed as Lady Sophia Beauclerc at least, if it should not create her a Baroness in her own right.

Under the influence of there ideas, she addressed the personage with a mixture of veneration for her supposed affinity and virtues, and of compassion for her sufferings and wrongs; and to the extreme surprise and affright of Rosella threw herself upon her knees, which had been trembling under her for some time past with agitation, and burst into the following ejaculation: –

"Much-injured and patient being, whoe'er thou art – whether, as my heart forebodes, the blood which circles in these veins derives its source from the more stagnant streams that creep through your's – or, as my wishes more eagerly point, whether you gave being to the grandfather of my love, accept the sustaining cares of your admiring and tender liberators! No longer shall the iron hand of oppressive Tyranny immure your half-sainted form in this desolate spot – no, my voice, and the voice of your fair and lovely child, my beauteous Rosella, shall proclaim to the world, which now believes you to be mouldering in the dust, that you live to bless your fond and astonished progeny: say by what miracle – by what wonderful interference of Providence have you escaped so long the fury of your relentless jailer? Alas! how often has he not raised the cup of death to your guileless lips – how often has he not held the poniard to your emaciated bosom! But Fate staid his ruthless hand, that we might thus meet – that we might thus –"

"Good Heaven, Madam!" exclaimed Rosella, who could no longer restrain her astonishment and consternation, "who are you thus addressing? I see no human figure but that marble one stretched over the tomb."

Miss Beauclerc shook her head. – "Well may you suppose," replied she, "that this dear and venerable sufferer is what you say: the immensity of her misfortunes have deadened those fine and sensitive feelings, which often made her weep the fate of the autumnal leaf torn from its parent tree by the relentless blast; but assist me, incredulous Rosella, to rise, that I may instantly succour this patient and much wronged saint, who has, I suppose, for a temporary space, lost the sensation of her former woes and present happiness by the too sudden tide of hope and joy."

Rosella endeavoured to obey the command: but alas! Miss Beauclerc now unluckily discovered that she was not capable of entering the lists with those delicately formed, but tough constitutioned heroines, who dance out of their castles at midnight, and are so often drenched with dew and rain, and pelted with hail, and scorched by lightning, and puffed by wintry blasts, and pinched by frosts, till they are absolutely compelled to steal from their briny repository a few of the sacred drops dedicated to sensibility to thaw their beautiful noses withal.

The hardships such fair creatures sustain, both corporeal as well as mental, were so familiar to the imagination of Miss Beauclerc, that she was confounded to find herself almost unable to move, after her kneeling apostrophe, from a sudden and violent rheumatic pain in her limbs, brought on most probably by evening walks and fatigue, sitting in a wet boat, and finally, prostrating herself in a distillation from the damp roof of the hermitage.

Rosella, previously terrified by the effusion of heroism she had heard, found her alarm so much increased by the agony her luckless friend appeared to be in, that she flew towards the boat, and called the man who had rowed it, and their musical appendage, the fifer, to assist in removing her to it.

Whilst they were fastening the skiff, that they might attend her summons, she returned to Miss Beauclerc, and found her again fallen upon her knees, in apparent devotion.

"Dear Madam," said Rosella, "the place is quite wet; you will kill yourself!"

"My child," replied the lady very gravely, "in your absence I heard a hollow sighing near me, accompanied by a gentle step; supposing it to be you, I spoke, when suddenly the step and the sighing ceased, and I beheld a figure glide across the remotest part of the chapel, and vanish beneath the altar. Something mysterious appertains to this place. – I cannot but believe that the fragile form I originally beheld reclining despondingly upon that tomb, has been conveyed by some machination from our sight, and that marble figure replaced in its room. My eyes did not deceive me; I distinctly saw an imploring aspect gazing upon me, and the hands raised in entreaty: but the vile monster who persecutes this poor secluded victim, has invented this expedient to prevent a discovery of his atrocity, and I plainly perceive this is not the fortunate moment to work the delivery of the hapless prisoner, who must yet languish some time ere her tyrant is forced to confers her wrongs, and disclose the secret of her confinement."

Rosella, without replying, again raised Miss Beauclerc with considerable difficulty; and the men now approaching her, she was conveyed to the boat, and taken back to the inn, where the party did not arrive till some hours after the evening had closed in. In the night, she found her indisposition increase so fast upon her, to her own infinite mortification, and the extreme distress and anxiety of Rosella, that, on the following day, she was confined to her bed, instead of passing it as she had intended, in minutely surveying the ruins of the castle,[228] where she had expected to make such discoveries of heroes recorded and unrecorded, that a perusal of the fragments she meant to have given the public in seven thick volumes, would have made the Brutus wigs and banded wigs[229] of her fair and gentle readers to stand an end with affrighted expectation. Her poor Rosella, having passed more than half the night at her bed-side, now desired permission to make Mr. Mordaunt and Mrs. Ellinger acquainted with her situation that they might send her such assistance as she required: but Miss Beauclerc absolutely forbade it in a tone so peremptory, that her companion felt unable to disobey her, though she was scarcely equal to the task of supporting her spirits sufficiently to perform, as she wished, those little offices for the invalid, which inclination and humanity equally prompted.

The people of the inn were for some time uncertain how far their inmates might be supplied with that which procures, in such places, the best and most unfeigned welcome; and as the travellers appeared totally unconnected, and evinced no intention of changing their abode for one better adapted to a sick person, they experienced a kind of sullen and cold civility, which, as the strength of Miss Beauclerc declined, degenerated very often into negligence, and a disposition to avoid executing her commands.

Rosella was sometimes compelled, after having rung the bell more than once, to descend to the bar, and make known her wishes – a task she never performed but upon the greatest emergency, because it subjected her to the impertinent gaze of every individual in the house, from the strutting landlord to John Ostler. Her situation was, by these means, rendered so insupportable, that she resolved to hazard the loss of Miss Beauclerc's friendship by communicating it to Mr. Mordaunt; for she believed it impossible that any circumstance could occur to her, where the benefit of that advice he had so impressively promised, could be more desirable. Yet a reluctance to forfeit at once a countenance and protection she had ever so highly prized, and which, for so many years back, had been her greatest boast, and the source of all the pleasant moments she had yet known, made her defer the talk, in the hope that each day would render it less necessary by the amending health of her mistaken, but ever kind friend.

Miss Beauclerc meantime, would most probably have soon recovered from her indisposition, had she not every day very imprudently, and in spite of the admonitions of Rosella, caught additional colds by sitting up in her bed for several hours to write – an employment she engaged in, in compliance with the rules she had never observed to have been violated by matronly heroines, who always, as a legacy to their beautiful daughters, leave behind them a long narrative of their youthful adventures, imprudences, persecutions, and amourettes, all written in their last moments, sealed up very carefully, and addressed to their beloved Hermiones, Jacquelinas, Geraldinas, and Phillippinas. But in the midst of Miss Beauclerc's sublime occupation to the same purpose, she was one luckless day seized with so violent a spasm, that Rosella, in the utmost terror, having rung as usual in vain, flew down stairs to procure better assistance than it was in her power to give.

It was not however, at that moment very easily to be obtained; for the inn was in commotion with a post-chaise just arrived, a gentleman's carriage, and servants changing horses; whilst a company of farmers and mechanics drinking in one room, and a party calling themselves gentlemen, devouring a haunch of venison in another, created such a rivalry for the honour of the yeomanry on one side, and for the superior prowess of Esquires on the other, that it was scarcely possible, for every individual the house could muster, to supply a sufficient quantity of nectar for these heroes of the North.

Yet Rosella pressed forward, scarcely observing the uproar that reigned around her, and arresting the steps of a waiter who was flying across a passage, demanded the instant attendance of some female to the sick lady. The man uttering the mechanical "Yes, Ma'am," pursued his way; and she had been sufficiently accustomed to this method, to understand what it meant. With increased distress therefore, she ran towards the bar, to entreat immediate assistance from the mistress of the house; but before she could reach it, she was encountered by a young man more than half intoxicated, who from her negligent morning dress, and her being without a hat, probably mistook her for the landlady's fair daughter or niece; and instantly assuming the rural gallant, he informed her with several oaths and imprecations, that she was a d – d fine girl.

Rosella, extremely terrified, looked round her for protection, and observing through a sashed door the landlady employed in making very low courtesies to her post-horse customers in the stable-yard, she rushed towards it, calling the woman by her name.

"Stay – stop – let down the step," exclaimed a voice from the post-chaise, which was driving off with furious haste.

Rosella's tormenter still followed her, and she reiterated her claims upon the attention of the landlady, who pretending not to hear her, advanced to another carriage with fresh compliments and fresh courtesies. "Good God, what inhumanity!" exclaimed she, bursting into tears: what must I do?"

At this moment she heard her own name repeated; and Mr. Delamere taking her hand, led her into a small room, and shut the door. "You surely cannot be here alone?" demanded he; "where is Miss Beauclerc?"

"Confined to her bed by illness," returned Rosella, whose tears were rather checked by surprise, and a hope of relief from her embarrassment – "and I cannot procure her proper assistance."

Delamere seemed much shocked; for he construed the sentence she thus hastily uttered into an avowal of poverty, which the treatment he had a minute before seen her experience from the woman of the house well corroborated.

"I am concerned," returned he, "that I must leave the place this hour, this very moment – Mompesson has learned the horrible news I would have concealed, and has written that he will deliver himself to his pursuers: – from this coast he was to have embarked; and I have been seeking him from the instant I received his despairing letter, that I may prevent if possible, his intention; if I miss him today, he is undone. But I cannot even at such a moment, be so wholly concerned for him, as not to feel interested for Miss Montresor, whom I must entreat, at the hazard of being thought impertinent, to have a sufficient regard for her own welfare, to place herself under the protection of any relation or female friend she may possess, rather than remain in the exposed situation, in which I have now the real mortification to find her."

When the ear of Rosella was saluted with this remonstrance, she felt as if a thunderbolt had fallen at her feet: in the suspension of her faculties she suffered him, unresisted and unheeded, to put a paper into her hand, and saw him quit the room without the power of articulating a syllable. An involuntary emotion of anger and resentment arose in her bosom against Miss Beauclerc, who had so cruelly circumstanced her, by the follies which had operated to reduce her to the helpless state she was in; but the recollection of that helpless slate, and of her sufferings, as instantly banished them from her mind, and as she found she could not obtain from the cares of others any alleviation of her malady, she returned to her chamber to offer at least her own.

She found the invalid much relieved by some drops she had given her before she had quitted the chamber, and now inclined to doze – a symptom Rosella was pleased to observe, and therefore indulged it. She had not yet recovered from the shock and consternation the reproof of Mr. Delamere had occasioned her; and as she sat silently by the side of the bed, his words, actions, and looks recurring more distinctly to her mind, she opened the paper, which she had retained almost unconsciously in her hand, and beheld a bank-note of twenty pounds.

A crimson blush suffused her whole face at this unexpected object, and it fell from her nerveless hands. Severely humiliated, her pride deeply wounded, and every idea of decorum completely outraged, she recollected the tenor of her complaint to Mr. Delamere, and guessing the construction he had put upon it, she felt as if every hope and prospect of her youth were annihilated. To be suspected of soliciting alms! Never more, she imagined, should she be able to look up – above all she could brave a thousand deaths, rather than again endure the horror of beholding Mr. Delamere.

Amidst the anguish of her reflections, she resolved, at least, to follow his disinterested advice, and snatching a pen from Miss Beauclerc's *secretaire*, which was always placed close to the bed, she eagerly began a letter to Mr. Mordaunt; but had not proceeded in it three lines before she was interrupted by a tapping at the door, and fearing the noise might disturb the invalid if it were repeated, hastily obeyed the intimation, and found that the intruder was the landlady, who accosted her with a dignified mien, and condescended to ax pardon for being so troublesome, being that she could not rest, she said, till she knew how the gentlewoman was. "And, Miss," continued the woman, "I thought I would just make bold to inform you, that you might tell your frind, that we niver strikes up no scores, so as I coomed oop stairs, I just brought wi me this little *merandam* of what the gentlewoman and ye ha had, for it's a week to day sin ye coomed here."

"You wish to be paid?" said Rosella, taking the bill which she held out to her.

"Why," returned the landlady, "we are always paid daily by our goers and coomers; but as the gentlewoman seemed quite a lady, we ha staid till the week was oop."

"Very well," said Rosella; "when my friend wakes, I will tell her so."

"Why, Miss," replied the woman, in a voice rather exalted, "I can't come oop again to-day, for I am so busy that I – and to be sure it can make noo great difference if the gentlewoman wakes now or five minutes hence, for her bit of dinner."

Miss Beauclerc, who was already disturbed by her vociferation, asked what was the matter; and Rosella, with an indignation she could not suppress, informed her.

"You must not," said the sick lady, "look for delicacy or refinement from such people as those, my love: take some money from the private drawer of my escrutoire, and pay the bill."

The landlady having listened very attentively to the conversation, on hearing these words, shut the chamber door, lest the bawling of the folks below should discompose the poor dear lady, and advanced to Rosella that she might not lose the opportunity of examining the state of this private drawer. Delamere's note, which still remained upon the floor, caught her attention and picking it up, she demanded, with a courtesy, if she should get it changed.

"No, let it be," said Rosella, rather peevishly.

"Yes, sure," replied the dame, laying it obsequiously upon the table.

After receiving the amount of her little *merandum*, without having it very minutely examined, she crept on tiptoe to the bed-side, and with a variety of condolements and enquiries, thought for her part the poor dear lady should hire a nurse to tend upon her; for in her house, God knew, she could not answer for her own mother being well tended, without petickler looking after by some person whose business it was; and she hoped the poor dear lady hadn't to complain of her folks, though, God knew, she had enough to do to get 'em to mind her guests as they ought; but if she found that any body in her house had a right to complain of them, they should all troop at an hour's warning.

"Do you know any young person you could recommend to me as an attendant?" interrupted Miss Beauclerc, who was now in hopes she might procure a waiting damsel to suit her ideas.

"Yes, my Lady," replied the woman eagerly, "as luck will have it, I have a kinswoman out of employ, who would be glad of such a hap[230] to help her on a bit; I'll send for her off hand: so now what would your Ladyship please to relish for your dinner? I can toss up a white fricassee, or boil a chicken, or get a sweetbread – and while it's dressing, your Ladyship had better have a crum of jelly to hearten you oop a bit – I've got both sweet and savoury; and this poor dear sweet young lady, as has tooked on so much – what would you please to have sent oop for you, my dear – or wad ye please for to have your dinner in the peacock? It's a mooch more airier and lightsome room, and looks such a fine perspect on to the Jarmin oshin!"[231]

The dear sweet young lady, whose disgust was rather increased than diminished by this address, replied that she should dine with her friend. "But I was told, not an hour back," continued Rosella, "that we could not have any thing but mutton chops for our dinner, because there was nothing else in the house."

"Lord bless your sweet face, who could have told you such a thing? But I know who it was – it was that cursed fellow Will waiter – he han't been sober this week – he shall troop, please the pigs, for this imperence – and there's my husband too, he's in his tantrums! – Ah, God help me, I'm well hoped oop wi 'em all! Many's the time," continued she, whimpering, "when I'm at my wit's end to keep things a going for other people's fagaries – yes sure – I'm finely beset!"

"Well, well," cried Miss Beauclerc, who was very much fatigued with her incessant gabbling, "then you will speak to your relation, and let me see her as soon as possible; and send up a chicken when you can get it ready."

My landlady, glad to escape so well from her dilemma, forgot to urge her jellies any further, and decamped as fast as she decently could, with many courtesies and self-congratulations.

The first care of Rosella after her exit, was to secrete the letter she had begun writing to Mr. Mordaunt, and her next to secure Mr. Delamere's note, that she might return it the first opportunity. She deliberated whether she should inform Miss Beauclerc of the circumstance, because she dreaded lest some heroic extravagance should retort the seeming insult; but the expectation of being assisted in some expedient to render Mr. Delamere sensible of the error he had adopted, and to put him again in possession of his unwished-for loan, determined the point, and she at length acquired courage to rehearse a scene which had given her such acute mortification; but her disinclination to communicate uneasiness and pain, induced her to soften any intimation that appeared to reflect with asperity upon the conduct, or the want of prudence in Miss Beauclerc, who listened with great attention to her relation, but expressed neither anger nor astonishment at it, merely dismissing the subject by saying she would think of a method to return the note as soon as possible.

Chapter VIII

A LAPSE OF MEMORY SUCCEEDED BY AN ADVENTURE

THE attention and respect which Rosella and her friend now experienced from the people of the house, was a remarkable contrast to the negligence and impertinence they had endured only a few hours before: the bell was never suffered to ring twice; the landlady herself attended at the door several times during the dinner to receive and execute orders, and in the early part of the afternoon introduced her relation by the name of Nancy, to the invalid as a nurse. The mien and appearance of the girl indicated cleanliness, honesty, and simplicity; and Miss Beauclerc fancying she had found an attendant, such as she had in vain looked for at the commencement of her journey, retained her at the wages stipulated by the obsequious landlady, with a voluntary promise of further encouragement.

Rosella found her situation so much improved by this arrangement, and her friend, whose spirits were revived by proper attentions, treated her with so much affection and kindness, that she destroyed her half-written letter to Mr. Mordaunt, and resigned herself to the destiny that awaited her, in spite of the admonitions of Delamere, whose note she had persuaded Miss Beauclerc to permit her to enclose in a blank cover addressed to him at Eideva Lodge, where she hoped he would meet with it – at any rate she was delighted that it was no longer in her possession, or that of her friend, as every moment that passed before she could get rid of it, added to her mortification.

Nancy, their new attendant, was found quiet, steady, and very assiduous, not only in obedience to the eternal admonitions of mine hostess, her aunt, who had been obliged to support her for a few months back, but in conformity to her own natural disposition: – and when Miss Beauclerc had fortunately finished her posthumous packet of juvenile adventures, the cares of Rosella and Nancy, and the prescriptions of the landlady and the good man she called her doctor, soon re-established her health.

The niece was consulted as to her inclination to continue with her mistress when she left Warkworth, and assented with great thankfulness, to the evident satisfaction of her aunt, whose little *merandums* being duly discharged, she accompanied her guests to the post-chaise that carried them away, in great sorrow, often applying her apron to her eyes, and protesting that she should not smile again till they coomed back, which Miss Beauclerc had promised to do, on her return to London, if Nancy altered her mind, and should wish to remain in the North.

They travelled the Berwick road to Edinburgh, in preference to the more inland one; and as Miss Beauclerc was not yet sufficiently strong to journey many miles without resting, they remained in their route two or three hours at Belford, extremely gratified by a fine coast view on the East, and the Cheviot hills rising to the West. Nancy hearing her Lady repeat a few lines of the famous ballad that celebrates Chevy Chace,[232] gave unasked a very minute history of that eventful day, which every lass in the county is perfectly well acquainted with, and even promised, in accents graced by a strong Northumberland wharle,[233] to shew the exact spot where the two chiefs were slain, if they should travel near it.

The travellers rested that night at Berwick-upon-Tweed, whose stream has been so sweetly and so simply sung;[234] and Rosella found, with a pleasure scarcely inferior to that of her romantic friend, that their ears were here saluted by accents and tones which conveyed to the mind the idea of that peculiar and national style of harmony she enthusiastically admired.

The next morning they set out for Edinburgh; and having passed Press-Inn rather early in the morning, which was dull and hazy, and seeing before them an extensive dreary heath, without one object to interest curiosity, or excite approbation, Rosella, in spite of her extreme good-will to be pleased and enchanted, felt a secret disappointment on first treading Scottish ground: but as they arrived near Peas-bridge,[235] the sun burst forth with uncommon splendour, and gilding its proud arches, as if to point out their lofty pre-eminence to the admiring traveller, gave to the deep glen beneath a bolder shade.

Miss Beauclerc felt her imagination tower, as the scenes before her opened to her view. Already she beheld Rosella the fair retiring heroine of some beautiful sequestered spot never visited by the inhabitants of the *vulgar great world*, save only by one distinguishing and distinguished young gentleman of extraordinary merit and sensibility, who chances to visit, for the purpose of hunting or shooting, the old castle belonging to his family, whose turrets, or white chimnies, or towers rise above the surrounding wood, and form a delightful object for the gentle recluse, as she catches a glimpse of them standing at her casement to gaze at the scenery by moonlight.

Certainly the powers of sympathy must be small indeed, if in such a case they cannot draw the lady to the castle, or the lover to the cottage: however, should they for the first time fail on so pressing an occasion, a never-wanting resource, Miss Beauclerc well recollected, is always ready in the Curate or Rector of the parish, who, in such a charming place, must undoubtedly be full of sentiment and sighs, and therefore doomed to languish out the remainder of his existence in a hopeless passion for the beautiful stranger, who, being decreed by Fate to reward the virtues of his patron, can never of course smile upon his hopes. The poor youth, in the fulness of his despair, talks of the paragon to my Lord, or Sir Edward (for the owner of the castle is always a titled being), and thus my Lord and the lovely recluse become acquainted, which is an important point gained.

"This landscape is sweetly captivating!" exclaimed Rosella, turning to her friend, who involved in such a comprehensive reverie as that just described, appeared not to attend to the beauties which had given birth to it. – Collecting her scattered thoughts however, she joined in the approbation Rosella expressed, but soon relapsed into the delight of castle building and cottage building, and spoke very little till the varied scenery before her forcibly claimed her attention; nor would her delighted companion suffer it again to wander till they reached Dunbar.

It was rather late the next morning when they pursued their way to Edinburgh, where they arrived to an early dinner. Rosella, impatient to survey the Scottish capital, easily prevailed upon Miss Beauclerc to accompany her in a ramble through some of the streets, and they were compelled to admit Nancy, of their party, because she would not by any means be left alone in a strange place, which, though they called it an inn, she said, was no more like her aunt's, than she was like Miss Montresor.

The landlord offered to procure the ladies a conductor, when he understood their intention; but Miss Beauclerc declined this courtesy because she was convinced that a heroine might unfortunately miss a number of pleasant adventures by being in the least protected, or having the appearance of being protected, and likewise by having only a tolerable knowledge of the path she usually wished, and meant to pursue.

She announced her readiness however, to accept his well-intentioned offer on the day following, as she certainly much wished to behold, amongst other desirable objects, the apartments at the Palace, where she had lately read a beautiful young creature had been immured from the ardent gaze of her lovers, her only relaxation being comprised in stealing glances at groupes of young men as they walked across the Calton, whilst she was eternally employed in making caps and gowns after her own exquisite taste, to adorn the persons of her envious cater cousins.[236]

Miss Beauclerc, after the example of many condescending heroines, not objecting to the company of her suivante, the whole party sallied out to reconnoitre the outside of the buildings in Edinburgh. Rosella was pleased with almost every thing that met her eye, because every thing possessed the charm of novelty; but how much more was her friend delighted, when having strolled about for some time, they found themselves on the North Bridge, which divides the old town from the new. The wind happened to be rather high, and this circumstance, joined to the spot she stood upon, brought to her recollection the sufferings of a distressed heroine, who, in wandering about, as many others are wont to do, without a place to rest her beautiful head in, lost her bonnet by a subaltern zephyr, which took up its station in her lovely hair, and drove her, with as little ceremony as a huge grenadier with a fixed bayonet would have done, full tilt upon the pathetic adventure that of course ensued.

Yet notwithstanding the sublime ecstacy of Miss Beauclerc to find herself thus upon consecrated ground, it was certainly not possible to remain on the Bridge the whole afternoon, and she therefore agreed, at the request of Rosella, to move forward, as unluckily no adventure appeared there to await her.

After having wandered about, near two hours, the wishes of all the party pointed to the hôtel where they had fixed their station: but alas! neither Rosella, her friend, nor their attendant could recollect the name it was known by; nor had they even remarked the appellation of the street in which it was situated. Miss Beauclerc secretly made light of the dilemma they were thus reduced to, as she conceived that it had something extremely pleasant and romantic in it, and must furnish some very interesting scenes. She thought proper however, to conceal from her companions that she had been in this respect more unpardonably thoughtless than themselves, because she knew the absurd timidity of Rosella's disposition would lead her to tremble at the prospect of the inconveniences it might entail upon them.

She proved how little it affected herself: for happening at that moment to catch a view of the Theatre, which was then open, she informed her young companion that she felt inclined to while away the evening, by seeing the performance. Charmed with her friend's intimation, she eagerly seconded it; for it never entered the imagination of Rosella that the *incognita* style they would be compelled to use, from their undress, and want of a male attendant, might subject them to unpleasant situations. She thought only of having experienced much satisfaction, when escorted by Mr. Beauclerc, and assisted by his servants, she had entered and quitted the London Theatres with facility and comfort.

Miss Beauclerc was more acquainted with the distresses they might have to encounter, but was more disposed to welcome than to fly from them; and with Rosella by her side, and Nancy following her very closely, she penetrated, with some difficulty, to the second tier of boxes, where she obtained two seats in the front row. The suivante seated herself in the background, perfectly satisfied with gazing straight forward, as she conceived the whole of the show to consist of fine folks sitting all of a row, with fine paintings and gildings about them, and a whole chandler's shop of candles over their heads.

The party remained unmolested until the latter act of the piece, which happening to be a musical one, and very well performed, much interested the attention of Rosella: – but her friend began to feel indignant that so charming a young creature should fail to draw into first sight fetters all the men in Edinburgh, out of whom she might have selected the libertine lover, who is always brought forward in the picture to torment beautiful heroines, and is generally a Right Honourable profligate – secondly, the pathetic submissive lover – thirdly, the grave, fatherly, disinterested, generous, middle-aged lover, who, when the fair lady is in desperate distress, advances with a solemn mien, and offers his hand, which is of course refused, that the *denouement* may be *selon l'usage*.[237]

"Insensible brutes!" softly ejaculated Miss Beauclerc, as she beheld several young men of distinguished appearance, either conversing indolently with each other, or paying court to mere fashionable looking women with handsome faces. – "Insensible brutes! unable to taste the charms of innocence and sensibility, you are not worthy that it should be exposed to your observation!"

Her opinion was however rather mollified with respect to Scottish discrimination, when the box-door was opened by one of those young gentlemen who prefer the amusement of peeping into every part of the house, excepting indeed the stage when the curtain has risen, rather than attending to the performance. The intruder began his examination, by bestowing a glance or two upon the countenance of Nancy, whose rural appearance arrested his observation; but his movements, with an accompaniment of alternate whistling and humming, in concert with the air an actor was then singing, drawing the eyes of Rosella towards him, his curiosity was satisfied with a view of her face, and his regards were instantly detached from Nancy, and fixed upon her.

Miss Beauclerc, in the interim, had taken the attitude and expression of a woe-worn matronly heroine pervaded with resignation, and the gazer turned towards her; but soon returned to his second object, who, from the moment of his unwished-for presence, began to reflect, with some disquietude, upon their unprotected situation.

When the curtain fell, the stranger, who had very patiently maintained his post, in defiance of the apparent disregard with which he was treated, listened to the conversation of his fair neighbours, and discovered, by their accent, that they were Englishwomen.

"I perceive, Madam," said he, addressing Miss Beauclerc, "that you are not of this country; and I suppose, by the observations I have had the honour of hearing, that you have not been long in Edinburgh."

The lady had sufficient fortitude to dissemble the pleasure she experienced at this opening, and assented with a mien of proper reserve. Happily however, the young man wanted no further encouragement to induce him to proceed; and having named to the stranger party, those of the actors who had never appeared on the London stage, he continued his remarks, by pointing out and characterizing every lady of distinction in the house, beginning by that eccentric Highland lassie, Lady C – .[238]

Rosella listened to his observations, which were lively and amusing, with some pleasure; but it was mixed with a painful sense of indecorum in thus encouraging the conversation of a person wholly unknown both to Miss Beauclerc and herself: yet it was impossible that she could put on the matron, and act the censor, where her friend, so much her senior in years, and her superior, it might be imagined, in discretion, appeared not to condemn.

At length the after-piece ended, the curtain dropped, the audience began to depart, and the gentleman, with a politeness but little practised at present, offered his services in any way the ladies would indicate, to assist their departure. Miss Beauclerc thanked him for his attention, and condescended to acknowledge that she had neither equipage nor servant in waiting, and would be under real obligation to him for procuring her a hackney carriage of any sort.

"Most willingly," he replied; and taking his hat from the bench, instantly left the box.

In his absence, which appeared uncommonly long, several gentlemen opened the box-door, and peeping in, took a very particular survey of the party; and at length this unpleasant ceremony was so often repeated, and sometimes by the same persons more than once, that it gave Rosella to suspect their new acquaintance of being the cause of it, and she urged her friend not to wait his return, any further, as every passing minute rendered it less to be expected.

Miss Beauclerc began to admit this opinion, and replied that she would certainly leave the house, but that she had forgotten the name and situation of their hôtel, as well as herself and Nancy, and that she had planned to have asked information of the polite stranger, which she hoped he would have been able to have afforded her, by learning the direction in which the post-boy had taken them on their entrance into the town from Haddington, and from hearing a few particulars, which she fortunately recollected, of the appearance and neighbourhood of the house.

Rosella was much shocked at such unwelcome intelligence, but preferred wandering about the streets, wretched, forlorn, desolate as they must be at such an hour, and in such circumstances, to the mortification of confessing to a young man, whose character and situation in life they knew nothing of – nay whose existence they had been two hours back unacquainted with, that they had been guilty of an imprudence so unpardonable, that Rosella could not but perceive it would invite a freedom of deportment, which the very incident that rendered them liable to it, would prevent them from resenting with any appearance of justice. She importuned Miss Beauclerc therefore, to leave the place immediately; but the good lady was extremely averse to giving up the perspective of such a charming adventure, as that of traversing the whole town with the gentle youth Fortune had presented to her, in search of the house where she had left her baggage, concerning which she meant to be very sincerely anxious, not so much for the apparel and valuables comprised in it, but for a small writing-case *of the utmost importance to herself, and the future welfare of those most dear to her.*

Rosella was too earnest however, to be denied, and continued urging her request most strenuously, whilst Nancy, who had comprehended their dilemma, now thought she should be obliged to stay in the show-room all night – a place which began to lose its charms very rapidly in her imagination, in proportion as the company vanished, and the servants of the Theatre put out the lights. One of these, approaching a lustre that hung very near the box, that he might extinguish it, she began bellowing with great violence; and when her Lady enquired her subject of complaint, "Lord help us!" exclaimed she, "we shall be left in pitch darkness in this lonesome place!"

"Be quiet, good Nancy!" said Rosella in an agony: "do, dear Madam, if you love me, let us go!"

Miss Beauclerc found herself unable to withstand this adjuration, which was almost accompanied by tears, and assisted by the fear of being shut into the Theatre, by the universal solitariness that reigned around.

Very much irritated against her apostate Esquire, she arose with dignity, and taking the arm of Rosella, marched forward, Nancy seizing fast by the train of her gown, which she supported with more care, though not with such graceful ease, as a page in a tragedy.

They met with little obstacle to their retreat, for almost every one had quitted the Theatre: but when they found themselves in the street, not knowing which turning to take, and unacquainted with any individual the place contained, even Miss Beauclerc felt embarrassed and uncomfortable; for she had not foreseen that her merit, and the charms of Rosella, would have been affronted by the indiscriminating neglect of every hero in Edinburgh.

At length when her patience, and even her courage, were extremely exhausted, she perceived a stand of coaches, one of which she gladly took possession of: Rosella and Nancy, fatigued and dispirited, followed her into it in silence.

"Drive me," said Miss Beauclerc, "to the hôtel – to – to a handsome hôtel in a spacious street near a square."

"I dunna ken what ye wad spake of," replied the coachman; "but I suppose ye wad gang tul F –'s."[239]

"Yes, yes," returned the lady hastily. The man shut the door, and mounted his box; and in ten minutes the coach stopped. Rosella, eagerly putting out her head to reconnoitre, exclaimed, "This is not the place. The man has brought us to the wrong house!"

"Dinna ye tell me," retorted he, "to tak ye aw tul F—'s, maistress?"

At this moment a party of very sprightly young gentlemen, either meaning to pass the house, or to enter it, presented themselves at the coach-door, and looking into it with perfect ease and *nonchalance*, applauded the ladies for giving the direction, and the man for executing it.

"It is a mistake!" exclaimed Miss Beauclerc, who begin to suspect the predicament in which her imprudence had placed her.

"The de'el a step did I tak but by y'er ain order," interposed the coachman; "ye told me to dreeve ye aw to a tavern, and F—'s is as gude as ony other."

"Oh better, better, ten to one," cried a gentleman, opening the coach-door, "come come, my lassie, don't be in the pouts: if some ungrateful fellow has failed in his appointment, here are we, sent by heaven and St. Andrew to avenge his perfidy."

As he spoke, he took the hand of Rosella to assist her in alighting, who, too much distressed to utter a sentence intelligibly, and unable entirely to resist the motion that drew her forward, burst into tears of terror and indignation.

"Gentlemen," exclaimed Miss Beauclerc, who now thought it time to affect her dignity, "I beg you will not insult us: we are strangers here; and though appearances may perhaps authorize your mistake of our character, you have certainly no power over our actions. Coachman, drive on!"

"And where wad ye gang noo?"

"Carry us to the place where you took us up."

The young men whispered to each other, whilst the coachman, who displayed more complaisance to their wishes, than to the orders he received from people who had declared themselves strangers, very patiently waited the result of the conference.

"No," replied one of the party aloud, "they are not worth it."

"Yes, by G—d," exclaimed another, who had gazed very earnestly in the face of Rosella, "here is one worth sighing for."

"This is insupportable," cried Miss Beauclerc, more offended by the careless manner in which this admiration was expressed, than flattered with the admiration itself: – "is this," continued she in a lofty tone, "the best impression of your politeness you choose to give to the ladies of South Britain who visit your metropolis? Gentlemen (if you are such), you will cease to molest us. Coachman, I again order you to drive on!"

Most of the party now retreated, some with contemptuous sneers, and the others with loud laughs: the champion of Rosella's charms alone remained; when the recreant hero of the theatric adventure greeted the eyes of Miss Beauclerc. He looked into the carriage, with some surprise, on hearing the latter part of her remonstrance, and recognizing his *ci-devant* companions, demanded what was the matter. Miss Beauclerc now thought proper to consider him as a protector, and entreated that he would free her from the impertinence of her persecutor.

"Do you speak of this gentleman?" returned he, pointing to the offender; "he can only be considered in such a light from misapprehension: for he is too much a man of honour to insult ladies of character."

"I hope so," interrupted the other in some confusion; "but yet, Oberne, how is this?"

"I beg, Sir," said Miss Beauclerc, addressing the mediator, "that I may have the honour of speaking to you."

Rosella was ready to sink at this prelude, which foreboded some new humiliation; and turning her aching head from the light of two large lamps which illumined the door, rested it on the shoulder of Nancy, who had fallen fast asleep the moment she was seated in the coach, and had not been in the least disturbed by the noises that had ensued. – Oberne, as he had been called, now uttered something in a low voice to the obstinate intruder, who, without further hesitation, made his bows, and vanished. Miss Beauclerc, delighted with the conduct of her Esquire, instantly informed him of the dilemma she had found herself in, from her want of thought; and Mr. Oberne, with little trouble, discovered, from her description, the hôtel to which she had been taken on her entrance into Edinburgh.

He accompanied her to it in the coach, to guard the party from further alarm or inconvenience; and during the ride, exculpated himself from the charge of deserting them, by mentioning the difficulties he had encountered in his mission, and protesting his extreme concern on finding, at his return to the box, that the ladies had quitted it. – Whether the excuse were true or false, it was entirely credited by Miss Beauclerc; and the gentleman, on bidding her adieu, had the satisfaction of receiving from her enthusiastic gratitude, an invitation to breakfast with Rosella and herself the next morning.

The people of the house had not conceived the most favourable opinion of their southern guests, from their unannounced absence till so late an hour, and their return with a gay young man, though they had intimated very plainly that they were entirely unknown in the town; and they now found the acrimony of their suspicions exceedingly increased, by the *slight refreshment* which Miss Beauclerc ordered upon the table which was spread for supper, in conformity with the invariable regimen of heroines, who take especial care never to increase their delicate and nymph-like forms with too much good cheer: it being a maxim never departed from, that though a young, pensive, woe-worn, emaciated charmer may be reduced to a pale skeleton, and yet preserve all the fascination of beauty, and still gain multitudes of enraptured lovers, yet no plump damsel can long "sigh in shades, and sicken at the sun,"[240] without becoming very bilious, and being threatened with a yellow or black jaundice. As it is therefore indispensably necessary that heroines should possess slender forms, the attention they give to ordering slight repasts is extremely proper; but people who live and exist by the extravagance, gluttony, drunkenness, and epicurism of others, will not consider this matter with an attention sufficiently serious; and it is much to be feared that, like Miss Beauclerc's Edinburgh landlord, others of the same stamp may annihilate, in wish at least, such taper-shaped guests, and in the fury of their wrath, curse them limb by limb, and feature by feature. All that is to be hoped on such an occasion is, that the gentle souls may never attain any knowledge of such barbarous and vulgar execration, and that the arms of their lovers may not undertake to avenge it, with just but relentless indignation.

Chapter IX

A PLEASANT TRAVELLING COMPANION GAINED *À BONNE MARCHÉE*[241]

IT was near one o'clock before Rosella experienced the comfort of laying her head upon the pillow: yet fatigued as she was, she found it impossible to obtain any repose. She felt mortified and degraded by the contempt and derision she had been the object of; and though far from suspecting the extent of the disastrous circumstance which had given rise to the freedom and levity of manner the young men had adopted, she could not but be sensible that in the situation to which her own forgetfulness, and the unpardonable want of caution of her chaperon had driven them there was a sufficient latitude for conclusions, not extremely favourable to women of any delicacy.

The facility with which Miss Beauclerc had, by her breakfast invitation, given the stamp of an acquaintance to this Oberne, whose first appearance had not impressed Rosella with the best sentiments of his manners or morals, she secretly condemned; and resolved, for the first time since the commencement of their tour, to contradict the wishes of Miss Beauclerc, if they led her to request her company in her intended visit to the lions[242] of Edinburgh; for she dreaded to be seen and recognized by any of the party, the recollection of whose surmises she fled from with horror; and feared that her precipitate friend would not find much reason to congratulate herself upon the acquisition of an escort, picked up in the second tier of boxes at the Theatre Royal.

In the morning a plea of indisposition, which her languid appearance justified, procured her a dispensation from attending the breakfast table – a ceremony Miss Beauclerc did not insist upon, because she was not sorry to have an opportunity of sounding the sentiments of Mr. Oberne towards the invalid, by the unlooked-for disappointment of her absence, and the touchstone of eulogiums and observations upon her virtues and her beauties, uttered from the overflowings of the fondness they excited.

At ten o'clock, the hour appointed, Mr. Oberne announced the idea he entertained of the favour extended to him, by the punctuality of his attendance: but Rosella, the supposed object of attraction, was invisible. He looked earnestly towards the door every time a step was heard near it, and at length Miss Beauclerc condescended to relieve his cruel suspense, by a certainty equally afflicting: yet, contrary to her expectation, he learned the news of his fair one's indisposition, without turning pale, or dropping his tea-cup.

Immediately after breakfast, Miss Beauclerc visited her sick companion, to propose an airing, which she thought would re-establish her health; and Rosella then heard that Mr. Oberne had very obligingly offered himself as their cicerone[243] whilst they remained at Edinburgh. This sudden partiality to a young man wholly unknown to Miss Beauclerc, very much provoked Rosella, who felt an extreme antipathy to every object that could remind her of the misadventure of the preceding evening; and she excused herself from being of the party that morning, under pretext of a violent head-ach.

Miss Beauclerc would then have made her own apologies to the gentleman; but Rosella, fearing if the project were only deferred, she must at length be included in it, rather wished it to take place immediately, and pressed her whimsical friend so earnestly to leave her to the care of Nancy, who was attentive and obliging, that she at length complied, and suffered Mr. Oberne to look forward to the honour of a *tête-à-tête* during their intended ramble, which he might perhaps have declined, had he foreseen it.

Rosella, thus left to her reflections, found them vexatious enough; and in spite of her early prejudices in favour of Miss Beauclerc, she could no longer avoid confessing to herself, that her conduct was a tissue of eccentricities, and that if they continued to increase as they had done since the moment of their quitting London, Rosella herself might be irreparably injured in the opinion of that world she was now only entering. Again did prudence suggest the measure of hinting her embarrassment to Mr. Mordaunt, and once more the gratitude and affection Miss Beauclerc had a right to challenge from her, opposed themselves to its dictates, which were likewise weakened by the appearance of versatility she should incur, by soliciting to be withdrawn from a situation she had entered into with eager and unequivocal delight.

With an uneasiness she could not suppress, and a depression of spirits she could not surmount, she met Miss Beauclerc on her return from her excursion. Mr. Oberne no longer accompanied her, and Rosella sincerely hoped she should see him no more; but how great were her chagrin and disappointment, when she was informed that her friend had consented he should become their *compagnon du voyage*[244] as far as Glasgow! She felt wholly confounded and dismayed, and received the intelligence with a silence sufficiently expressive.

Miss Beauclerc remarked it, and hastily endeavoured to remove any impression her too easy compliance with this measure might produce, by assuring Rosella that Mr. Oberne had been addressed by many people of distinction during their excursion, and had very politely introduced her to some women of rank they had met on their way to the Castle, as a lady of family with whom he had become acquainted in England.

"Mr. Oberne then," said Rosella gravely, "has no objection to deceive others into erroneous opinions, by uttering a deliberate falsehood."

"You should not view the effect of his good humour in such a light," returned Miss Beauclerc. – "Indeed he convinced me that he was better informed of some very interesting events than I had any suspicion of, by telling me he had several times heard my name mentioned at the table of Lord Morteyne, when he was in the South: so that his deception was an innocent one, as he was perfectly conscious I was really the character he represented me to be."

Rosella silently hoped the women of rank, to whom her friend had been so politely introduced, were of characters as essentially responsible; but as Miss Beauclerc had vindicated her new acquaintance rather warmly, she would not venture to give utterance to so offensive an intimation, and awaited what she meant further to say.

"I think I may affirm," continued the lady, "that he is a very estimable young man; but as our knowledge of each other commenced in a manner which some foolish people might cavil at, he would not scruple to follow the example of many worthy characters, and alter facts in a manner more favourable to the date and propriety of our friendship." – "For example," added she, willing to convince Rosella, whose disapprobation was still visibly expressed in her downcast looks, "in the charming new novel we lately read,[245] did not a very amiable, honest, and moral man introduce a very lovely young stranger to his wife and daughters, as their niece and cousin? And though in fact she was such, as he was unacquainted with the truth of what he asserted, it was not the less a falsehood from his lips; and did not the same man, on discovering accidentally a very charming female neighbour, carry his daughters and their beautiful cousin there, and carry himself there, unknown to his wife, which morally would have been very improper, only that this wife, who was indeed rather in the way, was a mere handsome woman of the world, without the least pathos of the heroine in her disposition; and therefore certainly every lover of the sublime and beautiful, must have wished her any where but in the devotional apartment of the gentle recluse, when she was surprised by her ancient admirer and her female pupils, with her grey tresses flowing, in her pathetic attitude, kneeling before her elegant crucifix and her Roman Catholic apparatus, so sweetly and fancifully disposed, and repeating in such silvery, yet fervent tones, her *confiteor*[246] out of her gilt Latin office-book. – Can we," said Miss Beauclerc earnestly, "blame the good man for being, virtuous as he was, betrayed into a passionate rally of admiration? and can we wonder, that having conducted his young companions to their home, he should be impelled, by his sensibility, to return at midnight to the interesting solitary, that he might protect her from the thunder and lightning?"

Rosella, perceiving that her friend, in the ardour of her imagination, had strayed considerably from her argument, now took advantage of a pause, to observe that the incautious conduct of this amiable, honest, and moral man, had nearly been the occasion of sending the orphan he meant to serve, to the workhouse.

"Rosella," interrupted Miss Beauclerc hastily, "never let me again hear such a low expression – a grocer's heiress could not have uttered that sentence with more vulgar spite."

"Dear Madam," returned she, almost laughing, "do you mean a grocer's heiress in a novel, or a grocer's heiress in Cheapside?"[247]

"There are many characters of that description," said Miss Beauclerc very gravely, "which I conceive to be very well delineated in many modern works: their malice towards superior beauty and amiable sensibility, their clumsy persons, and pretences to accomplishments, their immense bloated mamas, and sheepish hen-pecked fathers –"

"And their needy Right Honourable lovers," interrupted Rosella gaily. – "Oh no doubt, the portrait is a good one, as it has been so often copied."

"You are quite silly to-day!" exclaimed Miss Beauclerc; "but we will argue no further upon this or any other subject; for we have only time to put up such things as are unpacked, and take some refreshment, before the hour I have fixed upon to leave Edinburgh."

"I thought, Madam," said Rosella, "that you had determined to remain here till you received letters from Mrs. Ellinger?"

"I have already received them, my dear," replied Miss Beauclerc; "I called at the post-office, and found them waiting my arrival, owing to the punctual kindness of my poor Selina."

Rosella had indeed earnestly wished to quit Edinburgh from the moment of their unpleasant adventure; but to leave it accompanied by a gay young man – so suddenly too! Her gleam of merriment quickly vanished before the most unpleasant reflections that had ever occurred; and she assisted Nancy, in silence, to arrange their baggage.

After a repast as slight as that of the preceding evening, a post-chaise was ordered; and whilst the request was obeyed, Rosella sat in momentary expectation of the arrival of Mr. Oberne, ready booted for the journey; but to her great consolation, he came not, and she secretly hoped, as she followed her imprudent friend into their hired carriage, that he had never intended to carry his gallantry and himself out of Edinburgh. Yet Miss Beauclerc did not appear to feel the disappointment, upon which she made no comment. Indeed the conversation was extremely languid until they reached the end of the first stage, and there Rosella observed her to look round, as if for some person she awaited; and the heart of her young companion beat quick, in the expectation that her present disappointment would teach her future caution: but at the moment their driver was mounting to leave the inn-yard, she observed another hack-chaise drive furiously into it, and almost instantly, the voice of Mr. Oberne enquired if Miss Montresor had recovered from her indisposition.

The cheek of Rosella varied as she returned an answer of cold civility to the compliment, and their departure then relieved her from her embarrassment.

They continued to journey thus – the ladies in one chaise, and their knight-errant in another, merely exchanging a few sentences at each stage, until they entered the town of Airdrie, where Miss Beauclerc, finding herself fatigued, resolved to rest for the night. Rosella was more chagrined than surprised to observe that Mr. Oberne took his supper with them *en famille*, and likewise reposed his weary limbs at Airdrie; that he addressed her with the freedom of an acquaintance of long standing, invariably stiling her his charming fellow-traveller; and that he treated Miss Beauclerc as if she had had the honour of being his sister or aunt. She learned too, from his unreserved communication, that he was of Ireland, but that he had many connexions and friends in England. The latter part of the intelligence was the least welcome to Rosella, who did not feel at all ambitious of having the fame of her charms and adventures travel to the South, through the medium of Mr. Oberne.

The whole party entered Glasgow the next morning to breakfast; and Rosella would have beheld this charming city with unqualified satisfaction, had not the society of their new companion damped every pleasurable sensation: he affected to attend to their accommodations, regulated the disposal of their time whilst they remained at Glasgow, planned several excursions in the neighbourhood, and finally spoke with anticipated rapture of their intended tour to Loch Lomond.

The remainder of the day was passed in viewing the beauties of the place: the noble bridges over the Clyde, the Guildhall, the Tolbooth, the University, and the Cathedral divided into stories or distinct tiers, each forming a separate place of worship;[248] nay, even the houses in the principal streets almost universally supported by Doric columns, forming an arcade into which the shops open – every thing was a subject of admiration and amusement.

In the evening Miss Beauclerc and Rosella reposed, that they might set out with renewed spirits the next morning to visit the ruins of Bothwell Castle, and see the falls of the Clyde.[249] Mr. Oberne endeavoured to render the dulness of an evening passed at an inn less observable, by sometimes reading, and breaking the lecture occasionally with observations, enlivened by extreme vivacity of manner and idea, and tinctured with discrimination.

Rosella was amused in spite of the prudence and reflection of nearly eighteen years' residence in this sage and unerring world; – and, in the gaiety of the moment, forgot the impropriety of encouraging the lively sallies of their unknown associate. Unchecked by the dictates of wisdom superior to her own, she lost sight, for a moment, of the restrictions her native good sense had imposed, and before they parted for the night, she had laughed at the giddy flights of Oberne, had been evidently pleased at his good-humoured efforts to shorten the "tedious hours," and had even listened to the utterance of his extravagant and half-burlesqued sentiments of eternal devotion to her charms, without any idea of serious displeasure.

Reflection returned however, with darkness and the pillow: she then regretted that she had not maintained her reserve, but was convinced that she could not return to it with any appearance of consistency; and much against her more rigid plans, now felt the necessity of continuing towards her new acquaintance, an unconstrained deportment, which, without applauding, seemed not either to censure.

This did not resemble the never-receding, never-faltering dignity of a majestic heroine, who preserves, without ceasing, a proper distance towards the presumptuous man whom she suspects to have become the slave of her charms. Alas! no, not in the least; but it was extremely natural that a young woman of an amiable and lively temper should forget her sage resolutions in a fit of laughter, and approve that winning suavity in others, which Nature had abundantly bestowed upon herself.

The following day beheld Miss Beauclerc, Rosella, and Mr. Oberne on their way to Bothwell. Nancy was, with some difficulty, prevailed upon to remain at Glasgow, and one chaise therefore contained the party, who were not quite so well pleased with each other as on the preceding evening. The young Irishman, rather mortified to observe that his renewed devoirs were not so welcome as he had perhaps flattered himself with, turned from Rosella to address an invocation to the Naiades[250] of the Clyde, whose charming banks, delightfully wooded, greeted his view. But his theme was again almost as suddenly changed, to one which the name of the place they were visiting gave rise to; and he lamented, with great gallantry, the luckless destiny of the Scottish Mary, over whose admitted faults he cast the veil of oblivion.[251]

Miss Beauclerc, whose divine sympathy was awakened by his expressions of compassion, almost wept the cruel clouds which had gloomed the gay thoughtless hours of a "fair young wanton lady,"[252] who, gifted by Nature with eminence of wit and beauty, and by Fortune with a plenitude of power, lost this double empire over mankind, because over herself she had none! – a lesson which should be reverenced, not regretted. – Though Rosella's tribute of pity was ever ready, upon the slightest demand of suffering humanity, yet upon a subject where her judgment combated the compassion she could not avoid feeling, she chose to remain silent; and their arrival at Bothwell Castle put an end to the subject.

Miss Beauclerc eagerly ascended one of the turrets Time has spared of this building, "once how honoured!"[253] and though she had, in her progress, not made any discovery of sliding pannels and stalking visions, which perhaps she might have expected, yet she was rewarded for her trouble more rationally, by a captivating view of the country round. Mr. Oberne pointed out on one side, Ben Lomond rearing its lofty head, and the opposing landscape enriched by the majestic falls of the Clyde, and the wild mountains of Lanerk.[254]

Rosella had not been persuaded to leave *terra firma*; and her friend, charmed with the improvements in the scenery her elevation afforded, called to her from the height she had attained, and bade her follow the example she had given. – "I wish most sincerely," thought Rosella, "that I might, in every respect, do so with security!"

Oberne had hastily descended to assist her in obeying the summons, but forgot his errand by the way, and seemed perfectly contented to wander by her side amidst the ruins below, whilst he expatiated with much eloquence, upon the charms of solitude and contemplation.

Miss Beauclerc meantime was still perched in her turret, like a certain heroine, of whom it was said that she was beautiful, and dignified, and virtuous, notwithstanding she was the housekeeper's niece, and was wont to meet the young heir clandestinely at midnight, whilst the rest of the family were wrapped in soft repose:[255] but this history did not at present occupy the imagination of the lady in the turret at Bothwell, though she had sunk into a reverie, and was mentally drawing a hasty sketch of a sweet pensive young creature, confined by a cruel tyrant of a mother-in-law, or a father, or a barbarous uncle, in one of the deserted towers of an immense castle where the sounds of revelry, and dance, and song perpetually assail her solitary ears from the banqueting rooms below, where no doubt but some of the guests sigh, in the centre of conviviality, for her hapless fate and matchless charms, and meditate in which of the endless corridors they may watch, to enjoy a momentary conversation, when she steals out of her apartment to procure more oil to recruit her expiring lamp, or else to entreat her negligent attendant to bring a faggot for her declining fire – two things a heroine is always particularly anxious about, though she will fast, *ad infinitum*, without repining.

Whilst the imagination of Miss Beauclerc was thus occupied, she thought not of her absent companions, and would probably have remained in her present situation, until the interesting moon had risen to illumine the scenery around her, but that Rosella, embarrassed by the assiduous attentions of Mr. Oberne, sent him to inform her that the circling hours were not standing still.

Very reluctantly Miss Beauclerc left Bothwell Castle, to proceed to a celebrated Palace,[256] and if possible, to approach the falls of the Clyde before the day was too far advanced.

On entering the extensive park in which the mansion is situated, Miss Beauclerc, catching a sight of the building, immediately assimilated it in idea to that imaginary, sweet, retired, yet magnificent place in Wales, belonging to a young Nobleman, whose destined love, as she had read, having fled from an atrocious persecuting admirer, takes refuge by the instructions of her papa, exactly within the precincts of the hero's domains, at the cottage of her nurse, which her mama had ornamented according to custom (when she had fled to it likewise in *her* youth) with shelves for books, neatly papered the walls, and it may be supposed had even left an old lute in them; in this delightful place the heroine forgets not of course the amusement of wandering over the apartments at the great house, and dismantling the library of its books – a thing generally preferred to the vulgar care of looking over an heroic wardrobe, and repairing the occasional damage it may have sustained, in spite of sublimity.

Mr. Oberne and Rosella were, *en attendant*, conversing with some vivacity upon the custom of the Scottish and Irish Nobles, of almost wholly deserting their estates, and spending their time and their revenues in the metropolis of England; but the gentleman, who had himself often been seduced into imprudence by the allurements of fashion, could but feebly censure what he could not nevertheless excuse. Yet whilst Rosella expressed her astonishment that any place, such as she then beheld, could be abandoned for any length of time – "Abandoned for what?" thought Oberne; "to mix with the Nobles of a nation, who may reflect with secret pride, that the ancient Barons of this country once maintained the independence of their own crown, now a secondary jewel in that of England, from whose favour they solicit a Barony on the other side of the Tweed, that they may mingle in the legislature, by an inferior title, with the more modern and bastard descendants of the house of Stuart, from which some Scots Nobles claim an honourable lineage."

However these ideas, which were perhaps the mistaken result of prejudice, he chose to condemn to silence, and undertook to vindicate a few North Britons by imputing their conduct to that prudent reserve, which we are told certain Monarchs maintain, of showing themselves seldom, that they may preserve the respect of their subjects.

"For example," continued Oberne, "suppose the ennobled owner of this or any other place should prove unworthy of the honours to which he was born – a circumstance," said he with a smile, "I grant, very improbable   and losing sight of that respect which the established customs of society demand, bring the partner of his vices to the palace of his ancestors, to sully with brutal degeneracy the spot where their bones repose – would not this be the highest impolicy, as well as immorality; when, from the metropolis of England, the same faults and follies, were they to be committed, would be borne to the ears of tenants and vassals with a softened report, and not strike like the sulphureous bolt, falling visibly in the midst of them, with an effect no loyalty or attachment can withstand?"

"You think it better then," said Rosella, "that tenants and vassals should have to complain of the poverty which the desertion of the Nobles produces, than that they should feel the influence of a bad example over their principles and conduct?"

"What is that?" enquired Miss Beauclerc, awaking from her reverie.

Oberne repeated the purport of what he had advanced, and the observations which had given rise to the conversation.

"I do not agree with you," returned Miss Beauclerc, "in your ideas of London residence: what can be more odious than the manners of our fashionable Englishmen? How much more amiable and simple would the young men of the present age be, if they were to reside more upon their remote estates, brought up by some charming old person, the friend of the family, whose daughter, or niece, or some beautiful dependant cousin, might then engross the susceptible heart of the youth, and form by the opposition of parents and relations, a delightful series of interesting memoirs."

Rosella, who had never before known her friend to make so violent an excursion upon her hobby-horse in the presence of Oberne, coloured up to the ears, and gazed for some time without ceasing upon the little river Avon, which was meandering before her eyes. "This man," thought she, "will fancy that he is expected to be so amiably simple as to fall in love with me; and no doubt he mistakes me for the dependant cousin, who will thankfully accept any susceptible heart that offers."

"This spot is indeed so charming," said Mr. Oberne, whose eyes followed the direction of her's, "that I cannot wonder my dear little fellow-traveller is so much occupied in admiring it, as not to have heard my enquiry."

"His dear little fellow-traveller!" repeated Rosella internally, and very much provoked at his freedom; for though Oberne had uttered the expression twenty times before, it had never sounded so very impertinent as at that moment.,

"I wish to know," added he, "if your sentiments coincide with mine – if you imagine that it is possible for any man to be proof against the united beauties of person and mind in a charming young woman, though she may happen to be in a subordinate situation, merely because she is seen in the metropolis?"

"Yes," interrupted Miss Beauclerc eagerly; "and the reason is, that it is supposed she has not virtue enough to be proof against the united charms of idleness and luxury, whenever any man may think proper to offer them to her acceptance. However the young gentlemen will not give themselves the trouble to make the trial; and therefore it is, that the scenes of a modern novel cannot, if they are interesting, be laid in the metropolis; because it is no longer possible to imagine my Lord or Sir George running mad for an *innocent* beauty who appears at the public spectacles, or even when she is introduced into the circles they frequent; so that our popular writers have had recourse, and with great justice of idea, to the most remote parts of the kingdoms, for their scenes of eternal and disinterested attachment; many have crossed the channel for their personages, their plots, their castles, and their mountains, and with good effect, whilst others have been compelled to open the graves of heroes and heroines who had been sleeping quietly three or four hundred years. And really," continued Miss Beauclerc, in a tone of melancholy, "it was full time to remove all interesting adventures from London and its neighbourhood; since the air of St. James's-Street cannot be more pestilential to virtue, than suffocating to every breath of tenderness and sensibility."

Oberne, notwithstanding his utmost efforts, could not avoid smiling at this explanation; and Rosella, whose cheeks were dyed with blushes of vexation, observing that the postboy had now let down the step, jumped out of the chaise before he could offer his assistance, and hastened towards the august mansion they had rode thus far to see, that she might not be tortured by hearing any further lamentation upon the woeful decline of sentiment in the men of the present age. Fortunately however, whatever more of the sublime offered itself to the recollection of Miss Beauclerc, she enjoyed in silence; yet Rosella was in continual dread, lest many objects which passed in review, should revive heroic subjects; and much as her admiration had been excited, she was pleased when they quitted the place.

Chapter X

A DISASTER – SYMPTOMS OF ATTACHMENT

IN the town of Hamilton they took some refreshment, and then proceeded to view the falls of the Clyde. Rosella was silent and rather dejected; and Miss Beauclerc thoughtfully revolved the numberless charming incidents that might accrue to a young adventurer by being situated near Hamilton, or any other magnificent seat, where she might *wander* into the park, and *wander* into the superb gallery to view the pictures, or into the library to read the books, whenever she put on a new hat, or received a becoming and simple fashion from her female confidante.

In vain did Oberne endeavour to enliven either the one or the other; he could obtain little more than monosyllables in reply to his observations, and at length gave way to the prevailing system, and was silent.

Within a small distance of Lanerk the chaise, which was not in the best condition, being more than ordinarily shaken by the roughness of the road, by some sudden failure of the machinery, overturned with violence on the side where Miss Beauclerc sat: unfortunately they were descending a hill, and the driver, in trying to stop his horses, fell with the animal on which he rode, and appeared unable to assist himself, or even to rise.

It was some minutes before Mr. Oberne could succeed in disengaging himself from the shattered carriage, from the fear of injuring his companions in the attempt: he then drew Rosella out of the window, for in his trepidation he could not immediately open the door, and seeing her as pale as death, earnestly enquired if she were hurt.

"No, no," returned she faintly, "go and assist Miss Beauclerc."

"Tell me first that you are not seriously hurt," repeated he.

"I am quite safe," replied Rosella; – "pray go!"

He then flew back to the chaise, which he could now contrive to open, and was much shocked to behold Miss Beauclerc lying senseless on the side next the ground. With some difficulty he raised her, and with still more, lifted her from the fatal carriage.

"She is dead!" exclaimed Rosella wildly, "she is dead!"

Oberne thought so likewise; but unwilling to confirm her alarm, he asserted that she had only fainted.

"No, she is dead!" repeated Rosella mournfully.

A groan from the unfortunate postboy increased her horror, yet she endeavoured, though almost without a hope, to revive her friend: all her early kindness, her unshaken attachment, and maternal indulgence crowded to the recollection of Rosella, and she viewed herself with abhorrence for having suffered, what she now thought a slight vexation, to create a disgust however transient, against so tried, so sincere a benefactress. – Oberne assisted in rubbing Miss Beauclerc's lifeless hands, whilst Rosella chafed her temples, and applied salts to her nose. After a melancholy interval, she exhibited signs of returning life, and at length opening her eyes, asked, in a languid voice, for Rosella.

"Our dear little friend is safe," replied Oberne; "but she has been dreadfully alarmed for you."

"I fear you are much hurt," said Rosella, tenderly: "what can I do, dear Miss Beauclerc, to relieve you?"

"I think my arm is broken," returned she: "it pains me very much; but perhaps I am mistaken."

"What can be done?" exclaimed Rosella, applying to Oberne for his opinion.

"It cannot be long surely, before we are assisted by passengers," replied he: "we will then send to Lanerk for the easiest conveyance to carry Miss Beauclerc thither."

Rosella then supported her luckless friend as well as she was able, whilst he examined into the situation of the postboy, who had received a contusion on the head, and had been quite stunned by the fall. Oberne gave him every aid he could: and when the lad was tolerably recovered, returned to assist Rosella; for Miss Beauclerc was quite helpless, and leant her whole weight against her, so that it was with the utmost exertion she could prevent her from falling to the ground.

In a short time however, he was relieved from his painful embarrassment, by the approach of a returning chaise, which was driving towards Lanerk; and Oberne secured it, in the hope that Miss Beauclerc might be able to endure the motion for so short a way.

Assisted by the postboy just arrived, he put her into the carriage, though not without indications of agony on her part, that wounded the heart of Rosella, who endeavoured, by her cares, to soften the jolting, which even the footpace they went, produced. Their own driver could not be prevailed upon to leave his horses, and Oberne promised to send him assistance from Lanerk, where they arrived in rather more than half an hour.

Miss Beauclerc was taken to the best inn the place afforded, and a surgeon sent for by Oberne, who had made many vain efforts to keep up the spirits of Rosella: at her request, he likewise sent off an express to Glasgow for Nancy, and enlarged upon the commission, by desiring the immediate attendance of a professional man from that place.

Rosella was soon relieved from the poignancy of her anxiety, by being assured that her friend, though much bruised, was not in any danger; and the next morning, the Glasgow surgeon confirmed the report that no bone was broken, and that the patient would do well.

The attendance of Nancy preserved her from the fatigue she would otherwise have willingly encountered, though she still insisted upon watching half the night, and passed almost the whole day in the chamber of the sufferer. She remembered, with gratitude, the friendly attentions of Oberne, which had been of such real service, and still received those he invariably continued to offer, with complacency: but as this was not a moment to indulge his careless gaiety, which he had had the art of communicating, in some measure, to his fair associates, it could no longer operate to blind her judgment when reflection assailed her; and she could not think, without an uneasiness blended with surprise, that this man, not many days since an entire stranger to them, should now appear so completely to think himself of their party, that without very apparent presumption, he should quietly station himself in the same house, establish himself in a manner their major-domo, and not seem to have any business or plan but that which related to them.

It was in vain, she well knew, to represent these circumstances to Miss Beauclerc, nor indeed did she wish, at such a moment, to attempt either complaint or argument: but as Mr. Oberne appeared extremely good-humoured, and not deaf to persuasion, she endeavoured to gain sufficient courage to hint to him that it was evident her friend would not for some time be in a situation to continue the excursion she had planned, and she was certain it was not her wish to detain him in a place so little calculated to afford either accommodation or amusement. Yet as Rosella was conscious this would sound like a dismission, she saw Mr. Oberne twice before she could prevail upon herself to give it utterance; and he, *en attendant*, was indefatigable in procuring some luxuries and many conveniences which Lanerk was unable to produce. He had sent for quite a little library from Glasgow, and every other day, Nancy brought up a quantity of flowers and fruit for Miss Montresor, which thus early in the season must have been purchased at a considerable expence.

These assiduous attentions, whilst they pained her extremely, rendered her the less able to execute her prudent intention; till finding that she could not for a moment quit Miss Beauclerc's chamber without meeting him in the passage or on the stairs, where he actually appeared to have taken up his station, and that he never suffered her to return without a conversation of some length, she felt the necessity of adhering to her resolution.

The next time he accosted her, she permitted him to conduct her to a sitting-room within view of the stairs, which he had on that account appropriated to his own use; and this apparent mark of favour heightened the usual animation of his countenance.

"They have sent me the Airshire Bard,"[257] cried he, taking up some books which lay upon the table: "perhaps our poor invalid may like to hear his rustic lays. I should wish to listen to them too, from those lips; but I suppose I must try to content myself as hitherto, with a distant vibration of that sweet voice, when Nancy happens to open the door."

Rosella, taking no notice of his supposition, thanked him for the offered loan of the books, which she had in his presence inadvertently expressed a wish to read;

but told him that he had already sent to Miss Beauclerc's apartment, many more than she should have time to look over, whilst she imagined he would remain at Lanerk.

"Our friend is not able to remove yet?" asked he hastily.

"No," replied Rosella.

"Then why do you think I shall quit Lanerk?"

"I only supposed," said she, in some confusion, and almost forgetting the argument she had meant to urge, "that as Miss Beauclerc cannot continue the excursion to Loch Lomond, which I understood it was your intention to make, and as she is not sufficiently recovered to quit her apartment, I thought you would – that is, I believe it is not proper for me –"

"What!" interrupted he, "not even to speak to me *en passant!* Have I ever presumed to intrude upon you for a moment, or utter a sentence, but when I had the good fortune to meet with you accidentally?"

"No, certainly," replied Rosella, blushing; "but I –"

"Oh fie!" exclaimed he, smiling, "you think me such a St. James's-Street fellow[258] as to fly from friends who have distinguished me with so much condescension, because an unfortunate casualty has disabled them from immediately fulfilling intentions kindly formed."

"I am serious, Mr. Oberne," said Rosella with considerable vexation.

"And so am I," returned he, "when I affirm that I will not quit Lanerk till Miss Beauclerc is able to travel."

An idea now occurred to Rosella, that he was attaching himself to her friend with a design to marry her; and she immediately desisted from her intention of endeavouring to persuade him to a retreat, which, in such a case, would have the semblance both of vanity and impertinence; and coolly telling him he was certainly at liberty to act as he thought proper, left the room.

"Will you not take these poems with you?" demanded he, following her with the books in his hand.

"I will enquire if Miss Beauclerc wishes to see them," returned Rosella, "and Nancy shall inform you."

"You took a turn in the garden yesterday," he resumed, whilst he detained her, "will you not repeat your walk to-day?"

"No, I believe not."

She then ran up the stairs; and though he said something further, she staid not either to listen or reply to him.

Miss Beauclerc, having no inclination at that moment to read the rural strains of poor Burns,[259] Rosella, as she had promised, sent Nancy with the information, who re-appeared with a large bouquet of greenhouse flowers for Miss Montresor. She was chagrined; but as she could not return them, she made her friend participate in the present.

From the time she surmised that Mr. Oberne's more serious gallantry was directed towards Miss Beauclerc, many circumstances struck upon her memory which seemed to authorise the supposition; and she was astonished that she had so long been blind to so palpable a fact. She had read of Irish fortune-hunters, their undaunted assurance, and extreme perseverance, and it was now scarcely a matter of doubt in her mind, that Mr. Oberne was one of these; and his attentions to herself, she supposed, were directed with a design to facilitate his views, by gaining all the interest she might be imagined to possess over her friend. She resolved however, to see him as little as possible, and confined herself for two days almost wholly to Miss Beauclerc's apartment.

Mr. Oberne, who had not expected so perfect a seclusion, at length sent a note to the invalid, where after many entreaties to command his services, and employ him in any way conducive to her ease, he expressed a fear that her amiable Rosella would injure her health, by refusing herself from day to day a moment of air and exercise. Miss Beauclerc had already remonstrated with her upon the subject, and now more earnestly repeated her wishes that she would pay a proper attention to herself, and allot some part of the time she had hitherto too sedulously dedicated to the alleviation of her pain, to the preservation of her own spirits and health.

Rosella was, however, so much provoked with the officious interposition of Oberne, that she made a pretext of a trifling cold she had caught, to disappoint his intentions; and in spite of the exhortations of her anxious friend, passed two days more without allowing him an opportunity of speaking to her.

On the third morning Nancy brought intelligence that Mr. Oberne was going to Glasgow, and begged Miss Montresor would permit him the honour of seeing her for a moment before his departure.

"By all means," said Miss Beauclerc, on hearing the message; "convey my acknowledgments to him, my dear Rosella, for his many attentions and solicitude for our welfare; and tell him, as I suppose it is not in his power to wait my entire recovery, to accompany us to Loch Lomond, I beg he will send me word if he remains any time in Scotland, where I may personally thank him for his brotherly kindness."

Shocked at the idea of being compelled to solicit an appointment, Rosella most unwillingly descended the stairs, and preceded by Nancy, who announced her approach, entered the room where she had last seen Oberne. He started up to welcome her and Nancy having disappeared, he began a very serious complaint against her extreme reserve, in withdrawing herself from those momentary interviews, in which he had ever been particularly careful to avoid giving any reasonable offence to her delicacy.

"However," continued he, "since you have completely starved me out, I shall obey the intimation you have so dexterously given me, and leave Lanerk; but as I am thus compelled to a retreat, I confess I wish I had retreated with a better grace."

"I imagine," returned Rosella with a disengaged air, "that you are quite satisfied with the sample you have had of the attractions of this magnificent place, and that *ennui* has at least an equal share with what you call my intimation, which was given, I think, six days back."

"You are mistaken," interrupted he; "and I should convince you that I have at least as much perseverance as yourself, but that I fear your excessive punctilio will make you *really* ill, as well as deprive you of those little airings you occasionally took, before you thought proper to give me my *congé*."

"I have certainly no right to assume such a power over any person Miss Beauclerc chooses to honour with her acquaintance," said Rosella more gravely; "at the same time, I may surely adapt my conduct to my own ideas of propriety, when my friend is unable to direct it."

"Do not let us quarrel, my dear Miss Montresor!" exclaimed Oberne, taking her hand. "Will you have the goodness to inform Miss Beauclerc, that as I shall be equally happy to be of the least service to her at Glasgow, as at this place, I will pass three or four days there; and I hope she will consider me as her factor,[260] and employ me to execute her commissions. And tell her I shall wait with much impatience for the news of her complete recovery, which I shall consider as a recall to Lanerk, and a pleasing intimation that she has not repented her intention of admitting me in her party to Loch Lomond."

Rosella replied that she would repeat what he said.

"Well then," resumed he, "I must bid you adieu. – You do not wear," he added, "your usual aspect; and faith, if the truth were known, I believe I have much more reason to look grave."

"I suppose that chaise is for you," interrupted Rosella: "I will therefore bid you good morning, and report your message."

"The chaise can wait," said he impatiently; "you are in a violent hurry to dispatch me!"

"I thought you had uttered your farewell," returned she; "but my returning to Miss Beauclerc need not precipitate your departure, if you have not sufficiently arranged it."

She then repeated her parting compliment, and retired; and in a few moments Oberne left the inn, and Rosella very strictly performed her promise of delivering almost *verbatim* his message to her friend, who received it with a pleasure so very apparent, that Rosella believed the success of the supposed admirer indubitable; – and the idea was fully confirmed, when Miss Beauclerc the next day employed her to continue the journal to Mrs. Ellinger, in which so many panegyrics were interspersed, by her particular desire, upon their new acquaintance, that it appeared to her too certain, her ill-judging friend, who had incurred the lasting displeasure of her father for remaining unmarried in her youth, would now from caprice expose herself to ridicule and censure, by precipitating herself into an alliance with a young man, whose prevailing motive could not be personal attractions; for those of Miss Beauclerc were on the wane, as she did not resemble those evergreen ladies who flourish, and bloom, and look divinely beautiful *ad libitum*,[261] until the feebleness of extreme old age renders the trouble of adorning for conquest too painful a task. Neither could it be any characteristic excellence, which could not have been discovered when the sudden pursuit of Oberne began; though Rosella feared he had very early perceived her foibles.

Supposing her surmises to be just, there was a meanness in the conduct of this young man, which his manners and character of countenance entirely contradicted;

but they did not render his deportment less disgusting, by stamping it with hypocrisy, and Rosella conceived a prejudice against him, which successfully combated the impression his easy good humour, his assiduity, and pleasing vivacity had made.

Miss Beauclerc soon recovered sufficiently to walk in a small paddock behind the house, into which Rosella and Nancy supported her, where the gentle freshness of the air, and the sweetness of the verdure restored her strength and spirits.

The second time she was thus exercising herself, Mr. Oberne, without any previous notice, made his appearance, and was delighted to witness her convalescence: he took her hand with the freedom and cordiality of an old friend, and supplanting Nancy in her post, rattled away with such gaiety and rhodomontade, that even Rosella could not refuse the smile he sought to raise. He informed the ladies that in his first despair at being deprived so cruelly of their society, he had many temptations to fly to the depths of science for relief, and enter himself in the University of Glasgow: but that fortunately he recollected some lines importing the vanity of books, or wit, or wisdom to relieve an oppressed heart, and trusting to the experience of others, he suffered his spleen to take its course, which carried him per force on the banks of the Clyde back to Lanerk, and had there left him under such a concourse of pleasant images, that at the entrance of the paddock he had almost fancied himself mounting the wings of the wind, and directing the gentlest zephyrs to salute his convalescent friend.

Miss Beauclerc was not displeased with this flourish; but as his spirits were rather too violent to agree with her still enfeebled state, she was obliged to shorten her walk, and Mr. Oberne had the mortification of dining alone. Again he established himself in the apartment he had quitted, and as Rosella now thought it would be impertinent to oppose his easy familiarity of intercourse, she endeavoured to behold it with as much unconcern as possible: and it was the less difficult to subdue her discontent, as his deportment to herself was marked with consideration and respect.

The principal object for which this unfortunate expedition to Lanerk had been undertaken, which was to see the falls of the Clyde, Mr. Oberne prevailed with Miss Beauclerc not to give up before she returned to Glasgow; and on the fourth day from his renewed residence in the house, she ventured thither in a chaise, which he took care to examine, and as the distance was only two miles, he walked by the side of it – an exercise Rosella would willingly have partaken, but that she avoided every appearance of encouraging the advances he evidently made to overcome her reserve.

The fall that first presented itself to the view of the party, which is by far the most striking and considerable one, inspired Miss Beauclerc and her young companion with an astonishment and awe, that deprived them of utterance:[262] it is not formed of one current only, descending amidst the rocks, but possesses the violence and extent of accumulated streams, dashing with wild fury from one rugged point to another, and at length pouring in a foaming torrent into the yawning abyss.

"What a delicious spot," thought Miss Beauclerc, "for a heroine to wander to at dewy eve, and the still hour of night!"

She had quitted the chaise, and Oberne was now at her side, supporting her unassured steps, whilst Rosella hastily pressed forward to satisfy with more expedition than her friend could use, the ardent admiration and curiosity that had taken possession of her. In silence she gazed, and, in the plenitude of enthusiasm for the sublime and wonderful, felt not the *vacuum* which it is said the most perfect object will leave in the mind, if the gazer cannot exclaim to another, "How divine this is!" Rosella, on the contrary, forgot for the moment that she was not alone, and leaving her guide far behind, followed the first path that chance presented, and with a bounding step flew onward, to devour the varied beauties which every instant disclosed themselves.

Miss Beauclerc saw her hasty gesture and rapid glance as she darted out of sight, with infinite pleasure. – "Yes," cried she, with internal exultation, "my Rosella will at length catch all the sublimity and ardour of nymphs who can climb the Alps with exquisite grace and agility, clasping under one delicate arm two complete sets of Petrarch and Metastatio,[263] and under the other a lute."

She herself felt all the good-will in the world to follow so charming an example, but was soon obliged even to relax her loitering pace, and seat herself on some mossy turf, which, by extreme good fortune, offered itself when she was quite exhausted, to accommodate her weakness. Oberne then, at her request, and in compliance with his own inclination, followed Rosella; but even with the assistance of a guide, it was near an hour ere he found her: for in the first effusion of her delight, she had incautiously left recollection to attain her as it might. Fortunately however, for her, she did not find her mental illusion last so long as is generally represented in cases of similar sublimity: far from wandering unconsciously till the sun had sunk behind the towering cliffs, and left her in total darkness, she felt her imprudence five minutes after she had committed it, and endeavoured to return to her party – a task however, by no means easy to accomplish, and she had spent some very unpleasant moments, when the voice of Oberne, hallooing her name in a tone that out-hectored the thundering of the torrent, relieved her anxiety, and she ran towards the sound.

"How pleased I am to see you!" exclaimed she; "where is Miss Beauclerc?"

"More than a mile from us; but you are so much charmed to see me, and I am so extravagantly delighted to have found you, that we shall think the way towards her very short."

"Indeed I am much indebted to you," resumed Rosella; "for I had quite lost myself."

"What recompence ought I to claim for restoring you to your friend?" demanded he.

"I cannot determine," said Rosella, smiling; "if the service is to be estimated at the value of the strayed sheep, and not at the time and trouble you have thrown away, I am afraid you will be ill rewarded: but I suppose the thanks of Miss Beauclerc will be all the recompence you will solicit."

"No, Madam, I never solicit thanks; but I have the temerity to entreat, that the next time you are disposed to send me to Glasgow, or elsewhere, you will first reflect if you may not have occasion to employ me as a shepherd's cur, or in any other respectable character, as circumstances may occur."

This was said in a tone of mingled raillery and pique; for Oberne was rather offended that she should, by transferring the little service he had rendered her to the account of her friend, appear to aim equally at transferring the obligation.

Rosella was not unconscious of his lurking displeasure, but thought it prudent to notice it only as pleasantry, and, in his own style, told him, as it was impossible she could find him any employment of sufficient dignity to suit his merit, she should decline assigning him any.

"That is to say," retorted he, "whenever I volunteer my services unasked, like other officious people, I may content myself with deserving good-will without obtaining it."

"I hope," said Rosella more gravely, "I am not ungrateful; and Miss Beauclerc –"

"Miss Beauclerc," interrupted he, "is one of the best creatures in the world! If a poor fellow, who solicits her friendship, appears honest and well-meaning, she does not, like a cattish inquisitor, require other testimonials than a respect to decency and good manners."

"You have indeed little reason to complain of her too suspicious caution," replied Rosella; "but I fear, if she had found cause to repent her reliance upon your appearance as a gentleman and a man of integrity, from the little I have seen of the world, she would not have been consoled by its charitable commiseration."

"Oh my God!" exclaimed Oberne, raising his hands in affected emotion, "defend those unhappy frail dogs who are now in the nursery, from your severe scrutiny, when you shall be armed with a rigid prudence of forty years standing!"

They had now reached Miss Beauclerc, who, on hearing the facility of their return, was extremely disappointed that not one hair-breadth escape should have graced so promising an adventure.

VOLUME III

Chapter I

A HISTORY, AND A RENCONTRE

FROM this time a sort or *guerre masqueé*[264] subsisted between Oberne and Rosella, who was sometimes nearly offended by his flying sarcasms: neither did they in the least delight her friend, who was wonderfully surprised that he had not by this epoch fallen into pensive musings, and betrayed himself by casting lingering looks of adoration and despair upon his young and lovely companion, a failure she could not by any means account for.

To any sentiment of particular partiality for Oberne, of which Rosella had suspected her, Miss Beauclerc had not the smallest bias; and indeed so entirely was her imagination occupied by the charming eclat which she hoped her beloved child would make in the annals of romance, that she never gave a passing thought to the possibility of renewing her own adventures, by exciting ardent admiration (like a certain lady of devout memory, who lived like a good housewife in a small house by the side of the bourn), merely by the enchantment of matronly smiles and flowing grey locks.[265]

Every one of the party was so completely tired of their forced residence at Lanerk, that on the day following their excursion to the falls, Miss Beauclerc, not finding herself incommoded by the effort, removed to Hamilton, and the day after returned to Glasgow, where she found a packet from her faithful Selina; and Rosella was told that she had delicately hinted her sorrow that the correspondence between Lydia and her had so much languished; but that Miss Ellinger was writing a letter to her beloved young friend, and she hoped their epistolary intercourse would now be more frequent.

Rosella, chagrined to be importuned upon a subject so inimical to her ideas, as intimacy and friendship with Miss Lydia, promised, nevertheless, that she would not neglect the wishes of Mrs. Ellinger, and her friend was pleased with her compliance.

Mr. Oberne still accompanying them, they let out for Loch Lomond; but as his influence increased with the extent of their journey, he contrived, in their way to Dumbarton, to change situations with Nancy, by placing her in the chaise he hired for himself. They travelled very slowly, as Miss Beauclerc made herself believe that she was not yet able to endure the least fatigue, and were near three hours in the road from Glasgow to Dumbarton; but the scenery was so delightful, that neither of her fellow-travellers complained of their protracted progress.

Oberne, who had in his hasty arrangement with Miss Beauclerc, merely proposed to accompany her to Glasgow, and afterwards extended the plan to the lake, now became very inquisitive as to the route she intended to pursue, after having satisfied her inclination to behold the beauties of Lomond; and in reply, she only told him she meant to travel north-east.

"To Perth?" asked Oberne. "I believe I may pass through Perth in the course of my journey," returned Miss Beauclerc, with an air of reserve unusual to her; "but at present I am not quite determined."

"May I ask if you return soon to England?" resumed he.

"Most probably in the autumn; but,"[266] she added, regarding Rosella expressively, "circumstances which I cannot foresee, must alone decide."

Oberne observed the glance cast towards her unconscious companion, and ruminated with a mien of gravity and chagrin. "Perhaps," said he, after a pause of a few moments, "Miss Montresor and yourself expect an addition to your party when you quit Loch Lomond?" – She told him they did not. – "Then will you allow me to hope that you will not discard me yet?" resumed he.

Rosella, whose head was bent with an air of extreme interest towards the charming banks of the Clyde on the Renfrew side, listened very attentively for the reply to this modest proposal, and heard Miss Beauclerc say that she had no objection to visit Perth immediately after they quitted the neighbourhood of Loch Lomond; and he might from thence, if he chose, return to Edinburgh, whilst Rosella and herself pursued their tour.

This intimation was received with much gratitude by Oberne, who entered the town of Dumbarton in high spirits, and persuaded Miss Beauclerc not to proceed any further that day. At dinner Rosella found it impossible to preserve her gravity five minutes together, from the effect of his united vivacity and good humour; and when the meal was over, the Scotch landlord, understanding from Nancy that the party were to proceed the next morning on their route, entered the room to enquire "af the leddies wad na gang tul the Castle to ken what a brae place it was."[267]

Oberne seconded the motion, and asked if Miss Beauclerc would permit him to escort her thither; but to her the undertaking appeared so serious, that she declined it, in spite of the earnest yet respectful entreaties of the landlord, who was in despair that anyone should pass through Dumbarton, and not behold its bonny Castle; but she advised her young companion to accept the offered protection of their fellow-traveller, and walk to it.

Rosella was extremely unwilling to go out under the sole protection of Oberne; but, fatigued with everlastingly opposing her single and unsupported opinion against that of her friend, and afraid of incurring his philippics if she seemed to hesitate, she assented, though without that cheerfulness that usually marked her compliance, even when she wished to compliment the judgment of others at the expence of her own.

Oberne appeared gratified in being entrusted with the care of her, though while the subject was in discussion, he had not urged it; whilst Miss Beauclerc, as

Rosella quitted her, breathed a secret vow that they might not return without some charming adventure.

As they walked towards the Castle, Oberne, still in high spirits, amused her with a few historical anecdotes which his reading and his memory happened to furnish him with; but though she felt obliged to him for his communications, they did not enliven her. Having passed the house of the Governor,[268] they ascended with some little effort by the steps cut in the rock, and were let through some immense iron gates, which closing behind them with a heavy jail-like noise, rather startled Rosella, who found herself shut out, as it seemed, from the world below, and perched upon a stupendous cliff, adorned only at intervals by the habitations of the soldiers belonging to the fort.

"Now you are completely caged," said Oberne, who observed her emotion, and guessed at what passed in her mind. "Tell me, my little prudent Rosella, what has availed all your reserve to me, and your anger against your good-humoured friend, because when I sought refuge in her society against the naked terrors of the wide world, she did not drive me from the gentle umbrage to which I had crept, by a tempest of scorn and indignation! Pray observe that with all your circumspection, you have suffered me to entrap you within these formidable gates, which, for aught you know, may not readily open again to your bidding. However, when we arrive at the summit of the cliff, you will see that your prison is airy, and, unlike most others, it will not shut out your prospects."

At any other moment Rosella would have laughed at this rhodomontade, because she knew that Oberne often indulged himself in a metaphorical style of conversation; but the impression made upon her mind by the peculiarity of the spot she had attained, aided by the accidental gloom of the weather, which had suddenly shut from them the wide-spreading prospect on every side, occasioned her fears to combat her good sense, and she gazed at the countenance of Oberne in doubt and irresolution.

He laughed at her credulity, and continued to tease her by commenting upon the distress other damsels had endured from the tyranny of jealous lovers; and bade her be thankful that her good fortune had cast her into the power of such a courteous knight as himself.

At length Rosella recovered her composure, from perceiving that he merely amused himself with her perplexity, and even endeavoured to appear cheerful, to atone for having suffered herself to listen to idle and romantic apprehensions.[269]

When they had reached the summit of the cliff, Oberne, pointing to the north, exclaimed, "There is Loch Lomond, towards which we are travelling – Loch Lomond, which was to have been the extent of my journeying in your society, had not Miss Beauclerc taken pity on my forlorn state. I am more than doubly obliged to her; for when I had first the good fortune to see you, I was on the point of being very dissipated and imprudent, I believe."

"Pray will you inform me truly," said Rosella with a smile, "what reason decided you so suddenly in our favour, as to procure us the honour of your company from Edinburgh?"

"Faith, since you are frank enough to enquire in this honest manner," replied he, "I will tell you without varnish or equivocation. I made the party in a frolic; for I was at that moment *passablement* idle and *ennuyé*,[270] and did not care to which point I was steered, provided I were amused for a few hours. But I found in the society of Miss Beauclerc a charm I could not easily give up; and I determined not to forego my situation whilst I could by any means retain it. However," added he, "I had another motive – it arose from your excessive sage and repulsive aspect: when you heard that your friend had given me permission to follow her to Glasgow, you drew those charming features into such a look of dignified wisdom, and collected such a chilling atmosphere round you, that I thought you seemed resolved to freeze me off the field; the certain consequence of which was, that I equally resolved to keep my ground. When, instead of entrenching yourself as you did, if you had only attacked me openly, and said, as with great truth you might, 'Oberne, you are a d – m – d impudent fellow to fancy that, without introduction or recommendation, you are to trespass upon our good humour, and travel with us *en famille*,[271] when, for aught we know, you may be a pick-pocket, or a bog-trotter![272] Go, presumptuous dog! and find sureties who will be responsible for your unsullied lineage, and unquestionable good demeanor;' – I must, as you may well suppose, have felt defeated at such an address; and as I could not, most probably, have picked out any lady or gentleman voucher in Edinburgh, in the circle of my acquaintance, who happened to be known to you and Miss Beauclerc, I should at this moment have been idling there or elsewhere, provoked at my unlucky destiny, and envying you the undisturbed sweets of your peregrination."

"I never swear," returned Rosella, laughing; "so if you will efface the oath and the opprobrious epithets from the oration you say I ought to have made, you may, if you please, apply it at this moment, and in reply perhaps you will condescend to give some account of yourself."

"I like this plain dealing," said he; "and as we walk down the cliff, I will give you my birth, parentage, and education: I know that a dying speech and confession should properly follow,[273] but for that you must wait till we arrive at Perth. Be it known to you then, most lovely Rosella," continued he in a burlesque tone, "that I was born near Killbegan, in the sister kingdom,[274] of honest parents, I believe, – but of their industry I never heard any vaunt; on the contrary, it is reported that my honoured papa, Dennis Neil Oberne, commonly called Lord Clanallan, lost an estate because he was too indolent to search for title-deeds, – lost an election, because he was too idle to travel fifty miles to attend it, – and lost his life, because he had unluckily no employment either of mind or body to combat his chagrin for these misfortunes. Hugh Oberne, my brother, had the good fortune to scramble on to the scene before me; so that he is, of course, a gentleman of much more importance than myself: and I have heard that I shall never regain the small portion I originally enjoyed of his gracious favour, because it happened that I was at the point of death during the election I speak of, at which he ought to have been the successful candidate; – and though I was in London, and my father in Dublin, Hugh insists that his foolish concern for my insignificant life occasioned his strange negligence of the advancement of his heir, notwithstanding the express that contained the news of my danger, had not then reached him. From that moment I became, in the eyes of my good brother, a most graceless and unpleasant object: it was soon discovered that he was never entirely happy when I occupied a younger brother's apartment at Castle Oberne, or even when I took up my lodging in the third story of the London-house; so I was sent to College to make more room for poor Hugh, and from thence I was dispatched to make a tour on the Continent, with an allowance so moderate, that in a year I overstepped my credit considerably. I drew on Lord Clanallan for the deficient sum, and followed my draft to England, to assist him in the trouble of honouring it; but behold, I found my friend Hugh possessed of the title, and he sent my demand and myself to the devil. Fortunately, however, I still retained a large share of my mother's affection, who could never discover any thing very criminal in the unhappy blunder of not being a year older than Hugh, instead of the contrary; and she, good soul, assisted me in the dilemma to which I was reduced: for, independent of her jointure, to which I was entitled, I was totally destitute of inheritance, as my portion of the perishable gifts of Fortune had been bequeathed me by my deceased father in a legacy upon the lost estate, and he had never been able to gather sufficient resolution to alter his original will. When Lady Clanallan had taken up my draft, and presented me with all the cash she could spare, I was not so ready as Hugh expected to retire into obscurity, but remained some time in London after she had departed for her residence in Ireland. He would have condescended to purchase me a pair of colours in a marching regiment, but I preferred the Guards, and he was well aware of the impracticability of entering them, without having the undesired satisfaction of maintaining me afterwards. And anxious for my welfare, he kindly employed himself in looking round for some rich bride, whose English guineas would improve my Irish destiny: and having succeeded, he demanded my thanks for his fraternal attention, and my immediate acquiescence in his scheme. But the good lady he had selected, was of a mind and person so unhappily deformed, that I rebelled against his ordinations; but at length, dunned[275] on every side, and threatened with a jail, I confess to you that I contented to accompany him upon an expedition to obtain from my captivating dulcinea,[276] an implicit avowal of the partiality he pretended to have long discovered. And here my good genius prevailed: – before such a desirable explanation took place, a sister of my mother died, and considerately bequeathed me a few thousands; – so I made a low bow to my obliging brother, and a still more profound one to my intended lady, and plunged violently into every folly and extravagance which offered to a foolish fellow just escaped from the most unpalatable of evils, poverty and dependence.[277] Without much experience, my charming Rosella may suppose that my riches diminished very rapidly; and I was tormented again by my brother's renewed proposals, when Fortune once more succoured me, and I became master of a very pretty estate, exactly on the confines of his domains; and Hugh immediately obtained from me a promise that I would mortgage and sell only to him. I have religiously adhered to my obligation; but I have been so provident, that this second supply is not half gone yet, though I have possessed it almost three years."

The manner in which this was uttered drew a smile from Rosella, who congratulated him upon his remaining three years' prospect; and promised, at his request, not to forget him in his second eclipse.

They had now almost reached the Governor's house in their descent, and the frank history Oberne had just given, had so much increased the confidence of Rosella, that she had accepted his arm, and was chatting with some gaiety, when they were met by three or four gentlemen who were ascending.

"Ha! Oberne," cried one of the party, "have you only reached Dumbarton yet? Why, my good fellow, by the haste with which you fled from Edinburgh, you ought by this time to have been Philandering on the other side of the Atlantic. Come, introduce us to this charming girl, and allow her to waste a smile or two upon your friends."

"A smile or two!" vociferated another; "Oberne knows better; – a smile from those lips is worth all the treasures of the Clyde."

Oberne, who looked equally provoked and chagrined, attempted to reply; but his *ci-devant* boon companions continued the attack with such a horrible noise and hallooing, that it was impossible he could be heard.

Rosella, mortified, shocked, and frightened, turned pale, and drawing her arm from his, made a sudden effort to retreat; but was prevented by the officious intervention of a person who, repeating her name, congratulated himself upon the pleasure of such an unexpected meeting. Rosella, turning at this address, beheld the grinning countenance of Mr. Povey, who, taking her hand with an impertinent freedom, told her he hoped she would allow him the title of an old acquaintance, and recommend him as such to her friend Mr. Oberne. But had she meant to have complied with this insolent request, Oberne was far from being disposed to admit the plea; for it was scarcely uttered, before he aimed a blow at the unlucky Povey, which rolled him down the path to a considerable distance, to the infinite amusement of his companions, whose petulant ebullitions were, however, rather restrained by the achievement.

The countenance of Oberne still glowed with rage, whilst he desired the gentlemen to wait half an hour at the Governor's house. "My first care," added he, "must be to attend this young lady, whom you have so infamously insulted, to her residence; my next shall be to demand an explanation of your conduct."

He then again seized the reluctant arm of Rosella, and walked off; whilst one of the party repeated, in a loud bombastic tone,

"– Frowning he went;
"His eyes like meteors roll'd, then darted down
"Their red and angry beams; as if his sight
"Would, like the raging dog-star, scorch the earth,
"And kindle rivers in its course."[278]

Oberne bit his lips violently, and hurried on in profound silence, which Rosella was not tempted to interrupt; and bitterly did she regret that her complaisance had betrayed her to such disgrace: but the mien of Oberne, who was soothing his meditated vengeance by a soundless execration, forbade her to heighten his fury by indulging her own indignation.

When they reached the inn, Rosella flew to impart what had happened, to her friend, whilst Oberne hastened back to the Castle. Miss Beauclerc could scarcely confine her satisfaction at this adventure within proper bounds. However, as she now considered him to be most assuredly a serious lover of Rosella, she resolved to make the event a pretext to throw him from his hopes into the gulph of despair, by giving him his *congé*, and dispensing with his further attendance.

But Oberne appeared not till the next morning; and in the interim, Rosella repeated the little history he had given of himself: and Miss Beauclerc, finding her surmises just with respect to his rank and family, altered her intention; immediately slew (in idea) the unworthy elder brother, a practice much countenanced by many writers she esteemed, and giving Oberne the title of Lord Clanallan, which she acknowledged to sound as prettily as Morteyne, she carried Rosella (still in idea) most triumphantly to Castle Oberne, as the most virtuous and lovely bride in the world, after having overcome, as heroines do, the malice of her fate, and forced her enemies to confess that she was the most prudent and amiable creature that had ever walked (in idea) the surface of the globe, notwithstanding a number of very intricate and mysterious adventures, which required great ingenuity and perseverance to explain even to the satisfaction of friends and admirers.

The breakfast was not removed before Oberne claimed admittance; but then, instead of creeping, sighing, and kneeling like an offending lover, he marched into the room with his usual air, and giving Rosella a paper, told her he hoped she would accept the humble *amende*[279] of the unfortunate miscreants who had incurred her displeasure the preceding evening.

She opened it, and found a confession of extreme misbehaviour, and a solicitation of pardon and oblivion, signed by four names, including that of Povey. Rosella professed herself satisfied that this unpleasant affair had terminated; but not so Miss Beauclerc – she was extremely provoked at the seeming nonchalance of Oberne, when she had expected at least some sword and pistol business, even if she had been disappointed of the anguish and despair he ought to have exhibited. He perceived the displeasure she nourished, and exerted himself to restore her good humour; but she received his assiduities with coldness, and suddenly ordered a chaise to carry her from Dumbarton, without seeming to remember that Oberne had obtained her permission to travel with her.

He observed the decay of his interest with a chagrin he could not conceal, though he still laboured to appear unconcerned; and Rosella saw his extreme uneasiness with some compassion, for she began to imagine that he was really attached to her friend, in spite of her age and her faded charms. Miss Beauclerc having quitted the room to give directions to Nancy, Oberne advanced to Rosella, and asked if she likewise condemned him for a casualty it was not in his power to foresee or avert.

"Or perhaps," continued he, "Miss Beauclerc has heard of the meeting of last night, and disapproves it. Yet what could I do? Was I to hear your name mentioned in my presence in a light manner, and not punish such insolence? – No! – Miss Beauclerc means, I suppose, to retract the permission she gave me to accompany her to the Lake; and if so, I shall have leisure to settle this affair more to my satisfaction."

"For Heaven's sake do not think any more of it," exclaimed Rosella, alarmed at the threatened storm; "is it not already settled – have I not received the apology?"

"But I find myself dissatisfied with it," returned he. "Why is Miss Beauclerc unjust enough to make me do penance for the impertinence by which I am equally aggrieved with herself?"

"Surely you must allow," said Rosella, "that she has sufficient cause for vexation, in finding that I have been exposed to the curiosity and censure of people, who have proved that their judgment of me is neither charitable nor just. I am sorry you made my name a subject of contest, and I hope you will give up any idea of reviving it."

"I promise you," returned he, "that your name shall not be circulated in this cursed affair – no, my dear Miss Montresor, my amiable Rosella, these names are with me too sacred to be repeated flippantly in my hearing, nor shall you be censured or insulted with impunity in my presence, whilst I have breath."

Rosella supposed, from the very animated manner in which he spoke, that he was burlesquing the knight-errant; and pleased that he had recovered his good humour, which she hoped would induce him to forget his fighting scheme, thanked him with a smiling countenance, and ran to assist in arranging the writings and books of her friend, which was a task not quickly performed.

When she stepped into the chaise with Miss Beauclerc, she observed another in waiting for Oberne, who did not venture, however, to propose the exchange with Nancy, but contented himself with learning that the ladies were proceeding to the Loch, as they had intended: and in a short time they arrived at Luss, where Miss Beauclerc was far from being displeased to behold him as assiduous as ever; for the prattle of Nancy had again raised Oberne to the post of honour in her opinion, by repeating what she had heard at Dumbarton, of the duel at which he had hinted. It appeared, when he was himself questioned on the subject, that Mr. Povey either was, or pretended to be unable to rise from his bed to receive the satisfaction offered to him, and that Oberne, in the fury of his indignation, had challenged every one of the party, who drew lots for the first turn in this pleasant business; but the *coup d'essai*[280] of his pistol sending a bullet through the folds of his antagonist's cravat, the other offenders had interfered, and compromised the matter by the written apology, and a promise never to repeat the affair with the name of Miss Montresor attached to it.

Chapter II

THE SCOTS DROVER[281] – DARKENING PROSPECTS OF A SCANDALIZED HEROINE

AS it was rather late when the party reached Luss, Miss Beauclerc resolved to postpone until the next morning, a voyage on the charming expanse of water she took much pleasure in surveying. But Rosella, who was equally enchanted with the scene, could not control her impatience to stroll out after dinner, though she avoided the attendance of Oberne, that she might not again be subjected to the shocking surmises of his gay associates, should chance and her evil destiny have conducted any of them to the banks of Loch Lomond. She therefore desired Nancy to accompany her, and taking her arm, walked to the borders of the Lake, and contemplated from an eminence the charming islands scattered over its bosom, beautified by seats and villas, and enlivened by the boats passing from the one to the other: the Grampian hills rose from the north, and gave majesty and grandeur to the interesting scene.

But however Rosella might exclaim and admire, poor Nancy was entirely unable to comprehend the cause of such raptures, as she happened to have a sick head-ach, and secretly wished the whole country had been drowned in the river Coquet, before she had been pulled off her chair to see it; she was besides extremely discomposed at having been waited upon at her dinner by a Luss gentle-woman, whose bare legs and feet were not quite so clean as she thought necessary for the occasion; and to crown her displeasure, there was not a crumb of bread fit for a Christian to eat – a misfortune in which though both Rosella and her mistress participated, Nancy declared was not to be put up with, by people who had seen what was what in more genteeler and grander places.

Rosella finding that her companion was full of complaint, and observing that she appeared indisposed, would not continue to punish her for her own gratification; and tearing herself from a contemplation that so much delighted her, turned back towards the village.

A group of half-naked children with ruddy cheeks and golden hair, were playing by the side of the path the walked: she could not in the least comprehend their language, but was pleased with their appearance, and distributed amongst them some halfpence, which she borrowed of Nancy: a generosity that excited the most rapturous emotions in the little party, who hugged their bawbees,[282] and ran before her, barefooted upon the rocky ground, without any symptom[283] of pain or inconvenience, till at length a little boy scarcely more than two years old, whose only garment was a ragged piece of plaid fastened round his little body, tripped against a pointed crag, and severely wounded his head in the fall.

Rosella very much shocked, and frightened at the cries of anguish he sent forth, asked where he lived, and desired Nancy to help her carry the child home. It was some time before she could make the others understand her question, but at length they pointed to a forlorn hut not far from the place, and thither Rosella, with considerable labour conveyed the little sufferer; for Nancy pretending that the sight of blood made her sick, did not deign to assist her.

As she was toiling up an ascent with the boy in her arms, and panting with the effort which compassion alone could have induced her to make, Oberne met her, and with an air of surprise demanded what had happened. She informed him; and being then arrived at the hut, the mother ran out, and took the unlucky bairn[284] from her, with a look in which her concern for the child was overpowered by astonishment at the condescension of sic a braw young leddy.[285]

Rosella followed her into her mansion; and the child having had his wound washed with some milk and water, which they were compelled to send to the next cottage for, she had leisure to examine the furniture and appendages of a Scotch hut, which was not superior to any description she had ever met with of a Kamschatska[286] dwelling. The roof was left partly open to admit the passage of the smoke, the walls were of mud, and the floor, like that upon which George Mompesson had laid his aching head in his retreat, was of earth, uncovered, unadorned, spreading her naked bosom to cradle her unadulterated children.

"Good God!" exclaimed Rosella, "I murmured lately at the hardness of my bed, and felt disgusted that it had been soiled by the pressure of limbs perhaps exhausted by fatigue, or enfeebled by sickness!"

This apostrophe was unintentionally uttered aloud, and heard by Oberne, who unnoticed by her, stood at the entrance of the hut, and was examining her countenance and motions with great attention. As her eyes wandered round her, they were attracted by an earthen pot of oatmeal and water that was placed upon the peat fire; and from reflecting upon the lodging of the poor Scottish peasant, her ideas were now occupied in reviewing their hard fare.

She took a broken wooden spoon from a little shelf, and dipping it into the pottage, was going to taste it; but the woman prevented her, saying in the Scottish dialect, that it was poor people's meat, and she would not like it. Rosella would not however, be deterred from pursuing her intention, and finding the food unpalatable enough, sighed to reflect that hardly earned as it was, and sparingly devoured, it should be thought by many an English fine lady too coarse to wash her idle hands.

"Have you more children than this one?" asked Rosella.

"I hae ten bonny bairns as ony in Scotland," replied the woman, "and their father deed bot twa months sin, as he was ganging wi his kie to England."

"Going with what?" demanded Rosella.

The woman explained; and at length she discovered that he had been a drover, and with indefatigable labour and self-denial, having scraped together enough money to adventure a beast of his own in the English market, had sold it to advantage; but was waylaid at his return, on the borders of Scotland, and the produce of his long-fostered hopes torn from him by the hand of rapine.[287] The shock and disappointment affected his health, and his economy becoming even yet more rigid, would not suffer him to take enough sustenance to support him in his long journies, though all his meals were merely composed of a handful of oatmeal from the bag that hung at his back, and moistened in the pool by the road-side; till at length Death overtook him on the banks of the rapid Nith,[288] where he had laid himself down to rest, under the high-arched roof of Heaven, the turf his bed – a bed he had always chosen, because when he rose from it at the dawn of day, no surly landlord demanded a bawbee for the lodging of the night. Rosella was affected by the tale, and still more by the tears and hapless destiny of the widow and her ten bairns; and her hand, which was ever as prompt as the drops that now rolled from her eyes, soon testified her benevolence.

The poor woman beheld the piece of gold which had been given to her in stupid amazement; and before she recovered the recollection which so unexpected a vision had taken away, her young benefactress had vanished.

Oberne, who had stood immoveable until Rosella turned towards the door, on perceiving that she meant to retire, hastily moved away; but not before she had caught a glimpse of his figure in his retreat. She felt however no wish either of avoiding or meeting him; even the landscape which a few minutes before had captivated her fancy, she could not admire; she could think only of the poor drover expiring with fatigue and famine, his last sigh mingling with the keen inhospitable blast that whistled round his unsheltered head.

Having rejoined Nancy, who had been very composedly nursing her ailments on a rural seat near the hut, Rosella returned to her friend, and to interest her compassion and generosity, related the little history with all the pathos she was mistress of; and her design was fully answered – for Miss Beauclerc imagining the deceased drover to have been at least an *emigré*[289] Duke retired in this charming solitude from the cruel contumely of the world, and forgetting his former splendour in the delights of pastoral labour, resolved to restore the *ci-devant* beautiful Duchess to the comforts of competence and clean linen: but on a secondary consideration, as Rosella represented her speaking in a complete Scottish dialect, her opinion wavered, and she concluded that the deceased was either a young Scotch Noble, or that his wife was of high birth, who marrying from inclination, without in the slightest degree consulting prudence, had been driven by the cruelty of parents and relatives, to desolate obscurity; yet she wondered much that the hut was not exquisitely neat and white-washed, and that Rosella had not observed an inner apartment, ornamented with drawings and wooden-shelved bookcases, with a piano-forte in one corner, and a lute hung carelessly by a plaid ribbon upon a cane-bottomed London cottage-chair.[290]

She had little doubt, however, but that the elder of the bonny bairns would suddenly, on a discovery, arrive at the honour of being styled my Lord Blackcattle, or some other title, and all the little female ragamuffins become Lady Janes and Lady Jessys;[291] a revolution by no means surprising in the annals of many a fair creature's family, whose adventures she had read.

Miss Beauclerc resolved therefore to obtain a conference with the widow, and by insinuating herself with the softest compassion into her confidence, procure a disclosure of her secret history; and whilst she was revolving a plan to effect so desirable a point, without wounding the delicate feelings of the gentle cottager, Rosella repeated to Oberne, who had returned from his ramble, the good woman's lamentable situation, and the unfortunate event which had deprived her of her husband, and with him of the means of supporting life.

He had before heard the whole story, but would not interrupt her because he was enchanted with the impressive grace with which she told the tale – a grace he found irresistible, as he was assured from conviction, that it was not a well-acted energy of feeling,[292] to veil over a cold and selfish heart.

Miss Beauclerc had not yet quite resumed the cordiality she had displayed to Oberne before the fracas at Dumbarton; but his good-humoured and almost unceasing attentions insensibly dispersed the cloud, and at supper, to which he was invited, it wholly vanished, when she discovered that he had dispatched an express to Dumbarton to procure wheaten bread, which was produced at the meal, where he knew both Rosella and herself ate little else.

This instance of delicate attention reinstated him fully in his former post of avowed escort to his fair companions, and on the next morning he acted as usual, as master of the ceremonies in regulating their voyage to the islands of the Loch. But Miss Beauclerc would not set out upon this expedition, delightful though the expectation of it was, until she had made her intended visit to her unfortunate *incognita*.

To the hut therefore she went; but after a very minute and useless exordium to induce the afflicted widow to repose her private sorrows in the faithful bosom of a new but tender and affectionate friend, she found, to her unspeakable disappointment, that the poor woman was actually no other that the wife of a peasant, whose father, instead of being the ennobled Lord of a fine old castle, containing a fine old skeleton, and a fine old mysterious manuscript, was no other than a wretched fisherman, who caught and cured herrings on the Isle of Arran.[293]

This being the case, for Miss Beauclerc had never read of a gentle unfortunate refusing her immediate confidence to the first-sight sympathy[294] of a susceptible traveller, she contented herself with relieving her vulgar necessities, and leaving her to her fate; whilst the woman and her ten bairns were rendered comparatively rich from her contributions, those of Rosella, and the silent but liberal donation of Oberne.

At about eleven o'clock they took boat on the Lake, and the weather favoured their excursion. The first island they reached was Inchdavan,[295] at the summit of whose highest rock even Miss Beauclerc mounted, invalid as she had been, to have a more perfect view of the scenery round her: here it was that Oberne felt jealous of the natural beauties of Scotland, and endeavoured to extort from his fellow-travellers an engagement to extend their tour to his native shores. But Miss Beauclerc without immediately refusing his request, would not shackle herself by an absolute promise, and in this instance his rhetoric was ineffectual.

From Inchdavan they resumed their boat to strike across the Lake; but as they passed Inchmonger,[296] Rosella was so much pleased with the appearance of industry and independence it exhibited, that Miss Beauclerc consented to land the refreshments with which the boat was stocked, and take them under a spreading tree upon the turf.

As they sat, she meditated very seriously upon the indecorum of returning to *terra firma* without having encountered the least adventure, such as ought infallibly to befall every heroine, whenever she attempts an aquatic expedition: and though her affection for Rosella forbade her even to wish that she should make the slightest experiment, by hazarding a false step, or throwing herself overboard in a start of fear, yet she thought it incumbent on her to try how far the evident attachment of Oberne would carry him – for swim or not, a lover should always plunge in, and dexterously bear a half-drowned angel, or even her sinking *chaperon* safe to shore, whilst the rest of the party are wringing their hands, and shrieking her funeral knell in hopeless anguish. However as such a perilous plan required a little consideration, Miss Beauclerc for the present contented herself with re-entering the boat, after their rural repast, with sufficient circumspection to avoid any disaster, deferring her meditated achievement to a future opportunity.

As the party were proceeding to Ben Lomond, the Lake was suddenly overspread with a thick mist, that compelled them, much to their mortification, to return to shore, leaving the most pleasant part of the excursion for the next day.

At tea Miss Beauclerc and her young companion again experienced the attention of Oberne, for their breakfast table in the morning had exhibited various strong symptoms of the poverty of their host: but Rosella, far from being gratified by the interest he took in their better accommodation, was chagrined and hurt at every instance of it which he displayed at so considerable an expence.

He had told her that half his estate was already dissipated, and she feared the other half would not long remain in his possession. He had not indeed expressly said that his income was small, but he had spoken of it in so modest a style, that she presumed it was not an extensive one; and of his improvidence his own narrative had given strong instances.

She was vexed too on her own account: for it was natural to suppose he would not have been so anxious to continue in their society at so high a tax upon his time and purse, without some prospect of compensation, either by making himself an interest in her heart, or securing the fortune of Miss Beauclerc by a marriage upon prudential motives. But as the character of Oberne opened to her observation, she could not allow herself to attribute to him any mercenary views, and she was almost compelled to acknowledge, from a retrospection of his conduct, that it appeared more probable she was the secret object of his too thoughtless and expensive gallantries. Yet as this was only conjecture, and might be far from the truth, she endeavoured to continue towards him the same mode of behaviour she had hitherto adopted. When Miss Beauclerc retired however, for the night, Rosella having dismissed Nancy, could not forbear representing to her the increasing uneasiness she sustained, from the perpetual expence into which Oberne plunged upon their account.

"I am far from approving it myself," replied Miss Beauclerc, "and though I cannot but be gratified by the tender attachment his conduct evinces, I will not suffer you, my dear Rosella, to bear the imputation of receiving attentions of a pecuniary nature from any man, however amiable. I have for some time," continued she thoughtfully, "been alarmed at the increasing passion of poor Oberne; because I fear it will not be in my power to reward it as my inclination directs, and therefore I wished him to tear himself away at this place; but his earnest solicitations to continue with us till we reach Perth, my compassion unhappily yielded to, in spite of rigid prudence."

"It is even so," thought Rosella: "Oberne pretends to be in love with her – what will Mr. Mordaunt say if she marries so young a man!"

"My poor Selina," added Miss Beauclerc, "has unconsciously increased my dilemma, by informing me, that through some channel she cannot discover, our adventure at Stanmore Hills has been mentioned to Mr. Mordaunt; nay even our alarm at Edinburgh and our meeting with Oberne, have been most cruelly misrepresented by some secret but well-informed enemy, who for a sinister purpose evidently watches all our motions."

Rosella had shuddered with all the horror of timid innocence, from the opprobrium of the world; and now at the idea of a secret enemy, envenomed with hatred to a degree that could alone animate him to take such uncommon trouble to injure them, she felt her terrors rise; her head became giddy, she grew sick, and after struggling a few moments with her emotions, lost all sensation.

The agony of Miss Beauclerc at this unexpected effect of her sublime communication, cannot be described: she flew round the room in unreflecting anguish, wrung her hands, and screamed for help. The house was small, and her cries soon distinguished. The first person who rushed into the apartment was Oberne, who, on beholding Rosella extended upon the floor, pale and without motion, exhibited as many symptoms of distraction as Miss Beauclerc.

"What has happened?" exclaimed he. "Rosella, dearest Rosella, are you ill? – God of Heaven, she is senseless!"

By this time several people were collected at the room-door, and the woman of the house entered with Nancy.

"Send this moment," cried Oberne – "where's Patrick, where's my servant?"

"The gentleman's in the kitchen," returned Nancy. "Oh Lord, poor dear Miss Montresor! that ever we should have coomed to such a place! They have poisoned her with their dirt and filth!"

The landlady's red hair bristled with resentment at this affront, but she was silent.

"Be quiet," said Miss Beauclerc angrily; "get some more water; stay – rub her hands!"

Oberne, with the rapidity of lightning, did both, and Rosella revived; not to thank him for his cares, but to turn from him with a repugnance, and a look of horror, as potent as that of a fashionable lady, who unexpectedly beholds at the corner of St. James's-Street, or any other street, a disgusting picture of sickness and famine close at her well-turned elbow, imploring her to bestow what she does not possess – money, and endeavouring to excite what she never felt – charity.

Miss Beauclerc now reflected that it would be proper to dismiss Oberne, and shut the chamber-door. He entreated before he withdrew, that she would send for advice if Miss Montresor continued indisposed; and telling her that his servant, whom he had appointed to meet him at that place was arrived, and wholly at her service, enquired, with a look of solicitude, if Rosella had been alarmed.

"Yes," returned Miss Beauclerc, in a hesitating accent; "no – not alarmed, but she has been much shocked – that is – but I will inform you to-morrow."

Not at all satisfied with this broken intimation, he departed very reluctantly, to amuse, if he could, his curiosity and concern with all the conjectures a lively imagination and apprehensive mind could suggest. The person of whom he had spoken, had brought him letters from Edinburgh, by no means so pleasing or entertaining as he could have wished – letters which reflected reproach upon his understanding, for suffering himself to be drawn into the lure of two travelling adventurers; a report then passing current, from a tolerably just detail his companions had repeatedly given of the playhouse *rencontre*.

When Rosella had wholly recovered, and again found herself *tête-à-tête* with her friend, she implored her with all the eloquence her distress inspired, no longer to suffer the attendance of Oberne.

"You promised poor Simpson," added she, "to send him word when he should rejoin us: perhaps he is now able to follow you hither. If we have enemies, which Heaven forbid, will they not remark upon your travelling so far without any attendant but Nancy? and indeed I have often wished, upon his account, to be informed of his situation, when I recollect how feeble and dispirited he appeared."

"I will send to him to join us at Perth," replied Miss Beauclerc: "but, my dear Rosella, if I retract the permission I have given Oberne to accompany us there, I must give him a reason for so doing; and to dissipate any mistaken idea of capricious coldness on my part, I believe it will be best to assign the true one; for I have now received such unequivocal proofs of his tenderness, that I would not occasion him an unnecessary pang."

"Would to Heaven," thought Rosella, "we had never seen him! How can my poor friend be so weak as to think of such nonsense, when her character, through his means, is so cruelly arraigned!"

Again the humiliating sensation which the undesired society of Oberne had originally given her, recurred with increased force, and she resolved, not without a mixture of spleen in her prudence, that since Miss Beauclerc prized his boasted tenderness so as to prefer it to reputation, her presence should not often interrupt the expression of it, as she suspected it might hitherto have done.

Nay her ill-humour prompted anew the plan of writing to Mr. Mordaunt or her guardian, to propose her return to his house; but the recollection of its gloomy dulness, and of its master's economic lectures, joined to the shame of encountering the regards of people, who no doubt had joined her name with that of Miss Beauclerc in their condemning strictures, made her hastily abandon the idea.

She could not sleep; and amongst the mortifying reflections that assailed her during the long uneasy night, the remembrance of her last *rencontre* with Mr. Delamere, his strange manner, and still more tormenting gift, haunted her recollection, and she was tempted to believe that he was the author of the officious reports to her disadvantage and that of Miss Beauclerc: and to complete the chagrin she experienced, she imagined that if he had not received the note she had been so carelessly hasty in returning, he might further represent her as having solicited and received pecuniary favours from his compassion.

These surmises banished every favourable sentiment she had once entertained of him; and Oberne, who had never wounded her self-love by ill-founded reproach the effect of appearances too severely construed, but had ever seemed to regard her with the respect she coveted, was thought amiable by the contrast; but he again forfeited her esteem by aiming to gratify either a propensity to ridicule or avarice, in the particular admiration she supposed him to have avowed for Miss Beauclerc.

Harassed and unrefreshed, Rosella rose in the morning, hating the idea of meeting Oberne, but not choosing to awaken the alarm of her friend, by remaining in her chamber under pretext of indisposition. Before she descended to breakfast, he had twice enquired by Nancy if she were quite recovered, and if he might hope to greet her in the sitting-room; and she wondered this assiduity did not occasion any displeasure in his mistress, who, on the contrary, appeared only desirous to soften his anxiety.

At length Rosella attended the breakfast table, to which Miss Beauclerc had previously adjourned, and as she opened the door, she heard her say –

"Enquire of herself – here she is!"

"My dear Miss Montresor," cried Oberne, "you look pale; you are not quite well yet!"

"I feel rather indisposed," said Rosella coldly, "and will request Miss Beauclerc to leave me here whilst you accompany her to the Lake."

"It is impossible we can leave you," exclaimed he eagerly; "your friend I am sure will defer the excursion."

"Most certainly I shall," replied Miss Beauclerc.

Rosella suffered the argument to drop; for she was too languid to converse, and too heart-sick to care much what effect her silence would have. Oberne too, was far from being in his usual spirits; but as they were in him constitutional, they appeared sometimes by flashes, and it was only at intervals that he looked thoughtful and uneasy.

After breakfast, Miss Beauclerc declaring her intention of retiring for an hour or two to write letters, Rosella was careful to quit the room before she left it and then, without any inclination to occupy herself, she sat in her chamber, holding her aching temples, silent and solitary, until Nancy made her *entré* in a most extraordinary flow of spirits, apparently brimful of intelligence, which without any solicitation she soon began to pour out; and Rosella had the satisfaction of hearing that Mr. Patrick thought her exceedingly handsome, and did not wonder that his master slighted the London lady; for Mr. Patrick himself could never keep constant to an old sweetheart whenever he saw a prettier.

"I do not wish to hear such nonsense," said Rosella, with some anger.

"Lorrk-a-mighty, Miss!" exclaimed Nancy, "I never see you so cross-grained before! I am sure Mr. Patrick said no harm, or I should not have coomed to tell you – only he said, his master's brother, Lord Clinking, or Clanking, or somewhat, was very angry that Mr. Oberne had left his sweetheart, and that he had been told a heap of stories of his spending all his money upon good-for-nought minxes all round the country of North Britain – God-a-mighty knows where that is! But I told Mr. Patrick I was glad he had coomed to see it was no such thing, for his master had been with my ladies morning, noon, and night, as one may say, ever sin they coomed from Edinburgh."

"Good God, how teasing!" exclaimed Rosella.

"Lorrk no, Miss," returned Nancy, "Mr. Patrick laughed fit to crack his sides!"

Rosella now found her patience exhausted, and desired Nancy to leave the room, which the girl had scarcely done before she burst into a passion of tears, and imagining that the good opinion of the world was to her irretrievably lost, gave herself up to despair. After having remained some time absorbed in the most tormenting reflections, her solitude was interrupted by Miss Beauclerc, who was terrified at the condition in which she found her; and rightly guessing the cause of those tears, whose traces were yet visible in the pallid cheek of Rosella, she eagerly promised to dismiss Oberne, and restore her tranquility by every means in her power.

Accustomed as Rosella had been to indulgence from her fanciful yet kind friend, she was surprised at the important sacrifice so readily made to her scruples – a sacrifice she had not however insincerity or complaisance enough to oppose by the faintest contest, because her delicacy ought, she secretly thought, to have been seconded at least, even if it had not been directed by her older companion: – she therefore received the offer of Oberne's dismission with an emotion of thankfulness; and it was settled that Miss Beauclerc should immediately intimate her intention of foregoing the pleasure of his company after they quitted Luss.

She descended to their sitting-room to announce their approaching reparation, and found him in a meditation so profound, that she was well assured his volatile spirits could only have suffered such a revolution by the almighty power of heroic love. His first enquiry was for the health of Rosella, and his next for the subject of the alarm or shock she had received the preceding evening, which he had not yet had an opportunity of learning.

"The cruel and unjust world," replied Miss Beauclerc, with unusual dignity, "is never so rigid as when a young, lovely, and innocent girl is arraigned before its tribunal."

Oberne stared at this comment, and his attention to the explanation of it redoubled.

"My timid Rosella," continued the lady, "is not equal to meeting its stern inquisition or rebuke, and I would not wish her to combat its reproach, even with a placid conscience for her auxiliary!"

"In the name of God, my dear Madam, explain yourself!" exclaimed Oberne impatiently.

"To a man of delicacy," said Miss Beauclerc, "I have surely sufficiently explained my meaning; and you must comprehend enough of it not to be surprised if I decline very peremptorily the honour of your attendance from this hour!"

He made no reply to this heart-rending instance of cruelty, but appeared to reflect for a moment, and then darted out of the room with a precipitation that half terrified and half delighted Miss Beauclerc, who waited a considerable time for the report of the pistol she concluded the disconsolate hero had gone in quest of; but hearing nothing of it, she was on the point of sallying out to enquire by what method the poor youth had slipped out of the world, and eluded the peculiar anguish of his fate, when her intention was suspended from surprise, occasioned by the most violent outcries, lamentations, and oaths uttered in a strong brogue, with supplications and adjurations dancing on a Scotch dialect, accompanied by female shrieks and these again interrupted by threats of vengeance, independent of present punishment.

The last mentioned sound, though scarcely articulated from excessive rage, Miss Beauclerc fancied to proceed from the lips of the heart-broken Oberne, and what the uproar portended she was at a loss to guess: the solemnity of the present crisis could not long outbalance her vehement curiosity to learn it, and she repaired to the scene of contention, where she beheld the repulsed lover brandishing a whip instead of a sword, and Rosella, who from time to time earnestly conjured him to moderate his wrath, had only the power of mitigating the chastisement he was inflicting upon a man, whose collar he grasped: whilst Nancy wept bitterly, and tore her hair in concert with Mr. Patrick, the culprit, who seemed only intent upon stripping his head of its honours, and again applying to himself every villainous name his obliging master had before invested him with.

A Scotch lassie, who thought Mr. Patrick a vara bonny loon,[297] was in her haste to be attended to, bawling out a remonstrance in the Erse language,[298] which Mr. Patrick comprehending, bade her hould her tongue, and not be after axing pardon for him, unless she would first lend him a cord to hang himself a little, for being such a d – m – d spalpeen[299] to a better master tan ever crossed the Channel.

Miss Beauclerc conceiving this strange affray to be beneath the interference of Rosella, and not perceiving any signs of its ending in a sentimental tragedy, called to her to re-enter the house; for the scene lay in a yard, flanked on one side by the road, and on the other by a convenient horse-pond, to which Oberne had almost dragged his self-condemned prisoner.

But Rosella heard her not, and before the storm was in the least allayed, a very brilliant travelling chaise passed the road, followed by two or three others; and Miss Beauclerc obeyed an impulse of curiosity in endeavouring to discover who occupied the first, which had stopped before the little inn whilst a servant made some enquiries, when a tumult of emotions was excited in her bosom, by discerning rather unexpectedly Lord Morteyne, seated by a very pretty woman, who was regarding Rosella with looks of concern and surprise, which his Lordship did not diminish by a narrative he was apparently giving of the object thus scrutinized.

"Oh my Lord," thought Miss Beauclerc, with a mixture of disdain and exultation, "you likewise believe these calumniating stories of your once beloved Rosella! But though you imagine your horrible dereliction unknown to her, be assured you shall, like other rash and jealous lovers, bitterly repent your shocking credulity."

This prophetic idea had scarcely crossed her imagination before the carriages drove away, and Rosella remained wholly unconscious that she had been thus recognized by an old acquaintance.

By persuasion and entreaty she at length induced Oberne to leave the offender to his own contrition, which he manifested by a variety of emotions; and his master in the first moment of returning reflection, ashamed of having displayed such a want of self-control, withdrew hastily from the presence of Rosella, who by compassionating the object of his vehement anger, more than tacitly condemned it.

Chapter III

A PARTING SCENE – A HEROINE'S RETREAT CHAMPÊTRE[300]

WHEN Rosella rejoined her friend, she learned that a circumstance had occurred to urge the continuation of their journey immediately, and wondered exceedingly what event of importance could have reached her in the space of ten minutes; but recollecting how much her friend sometimes amused her imagination with suppositious affairs, she concluded it was one of those fabulous exigences which had more than once in the course of their tour guided her motions.

Oberne meantime heard the order given for a chaise for the ladies, and starting from his solitary trance, flew to enquire the reason of such an unexpected precipitation: happening to encounter Rosella in his search, he asked with rapidity whither she was going; and she declared, with truth, that she knew not.

"That is you do not wish to tell me. Are you going towards Perth?" resumed he, after a moment's pause.

"I am entirely ignorant of the route Miss Beauclerc means to take," replied she, "but I believe not."

Again he re-urged his first question, and she made the same reply. "Tell me at least," said Oberne, "the motive for this sudden movement: it is, I suppose, in consequence of the impertinence of that fellow, which reached you through Nancy?"

"Indeed you distress me," she replied, "because I cannot answer you!"

"Miss Montresor," exclaimed Oberne suddenly, "tell me with sincerity the opinion you have formed of me. I know you think me a strange mortal, incapable of reflecting seriously; foolish, extravagant in conduct and idea, giddy, fickle, impetuous, and unmeaning."

"If you know all this," said Rosella, half smiling, "why do you apply to me? Will it be any satisfaction to have this idea of your's confirmed?"

"No; I should, on the contrary, be charmed to find that my fears were unfounded."

"Well then I beg you to believe that they are; for I cannot yet think myself qualified by experience to form any decisive judgment of your character."

"I suspect," said Oberne, "that hitherto I have not had any – at least, I find myself under the influence of a new character within a very limited time. To have done however with an unworthy subject, let me quit it to inform you, that I shall not oppose the promise Miss Beauclerc condescended to make, to her present determination of discarding me, because I feel equally indignant with her at the odious imputation her generosity and candid reliance upon me have drawn upon her – an imputation I shall assuredly endeavour to wipe off before I see you again. And now, dear Miss Montresor, let me entreat that you will forgive the shock that fellow's insolence and folly, and the silly prattle of Nancy have occasioned you; and believe that from the first hour I saw you, I have not for a moment entertained an opinion I would not freely avow to your most zealous champion. Miss Beauclerc does me injustice in affecting to hide from me the route she means to take; I have too much respect for you and her to discover it without her permission; but as I am fortunately acquainted with her English residence, I will not despair of being able to renew the pleasure I have enjoyed in your society, with a better recommendation to your favour than idleness and assurance. You will be next winter still under her protection I hope?"

"I cannot decide for myself," returned Rosella; "my stay with Miss Beauclerc depends upon her invitation, and the indulgence of my guardian."

"Your guardian! I supposed – I thought you – excuse me, dear Miss Montresor, if I take the liberty of enquiring if he is the guardian of your person alone, or your fortune likewise?"

"Of both," replied she, wondering where these enquiries would end.

"Then I have been in an error," said Oberne gravely: "to deal frankly with you, I imagined you to be as destitute of fortune as you abound in every amiable quality."

"Am I to suppose then," said Rosella, rather indignantly, "that such a circumstance has influenced your conduct?"

"Certainly had I been better informed; I should not have followed you from Edinburgh."

"Followed *me!*" interrupted she, still more irritated, "do you say you followed me?"

"Yes, I have the presumption to say it; I should not have been absent from Edinburgh twelve hours, had you not accompanied Miss Beauclerc. Be not, however, angry – I acknowledged to you that I had dissipated half my fortune, not very splendid originally, and with the other half I would have offered you my unworthy self, had you been at liberty to encourage or receive me, and had you not been above my hopes: as it is, I must bid you adieu, with the additional mortification of feeling those wishes crushed which I have for some time past foolishly cherished."

Without waiting her answer, he left the room; and Rosella, from surprise and confusion, had not the power of preventing him, that she might explain from mere humility, that he carried with him an erroneous supposition, if he imagined the fortune she had spoken of even approached to mediocrity. She ran to the window in the hope of seeing him pass it, but he had wholly vanished; and Miss Beauclerc calling to her almost immediately, to enquire if she were ready, she hastened to obey the intimation, and followed her into the chaise a few minutes after, without again beholding the eccentric Oberne, whose absence she had so often wished, and now almost regretted.

Nancy was still sobbing at intervals, and secretly deploring that her too flippant tongue had caused, as she imagined, two such great disasters as the disgrace of Mr. Patrick, and the parting of Miss Rosella from her true lover; for such she considered Oberne. And her discontent was increased by an attack which had been made upon her by the landlady, who had plainly hinted that she would scorn to serve people who did not know their own minds; for her part, if she had known the leddies were going away, she might have had a great Laird and aw his family at her hoose, which would have made the fortune of her and her gude mon.

Miss Beauclerc sat immersed in the sublimity of those adventures, she was now pursuing with an avidity, that would not allow her leisure to finish her survey of the beautiful Lake she had so much deviated out of her road to see; and so rapidly did her ideas hurry her forward, that she could not even spare one look of approbation at the romantic scenery she was so eager to quit, but fixed her eyes upon the trotting hoofs of the galloways that bore her away, calculating how soon she should leave behind her Loch Lomond and its charming islands, and the lovely vale of Tarbet, with its eastern boundary of water.

Rosella had therefore full liberty to pursue her own reflections, which led her to examine the previous conduct of her friend, and the strange unpleasant situations which had been the result of it; and so far was she then from deploring the injustice of the world, that she could not but acknowledge, those reports which had reached her ear, were but the natural inferences to be drawn from a mode of acting so singular and unaccountable. She became, in consequence, anxious to learn whither the whimsical genius of her friend would point; and without any preface, made an enquiry into their present destination.

Miss Beauclerc replied that she had not any settled plan, but having much curiosity to behold the Grampian mountains, she should journey in the direction they took.

Rosella perceiving some reserve in her manner whilst the returned this vague answer, suspected an achievement *in petto*,[301] which she was not yet to be made acquainted with, and looked forward to it with apprehension and anticipated disgust. She conceived that to hesitate taking any step at the present moment, however unpleasant, to rescue herself from the malicious sneers of those, who having already learned their adventures, and poured them with cruel comments into the ear of Mr. Mordaunt, a man, whose esteem and friendship she highly prized, would be to deserve and wait for further opprobrium: and in spite of the innate affection she still retained for Miss Beauclerc, she resolved to give up the pleasing expectations she had lately found so little realized in her society, and voluntarily return to dulness and discord, as an asylum from censure.

When they rested for the night, she preferred her claim to the offered advice of her old and sage friend, through the channel of a letter, written without the knowledge of Miss Beauclerc; but she could not send it off until they stopped at some town for a few days, that she might have a chance of receiving an answer. She deprecated the opinion Mr. Mordaunt might form of her, from not receiving any appeal to his kindness, after he had heard such a detail of her journey, as Mrs. Ellinger had transmitted an account of to Miss Beauclerc, of whom Rosella spoke without disrespect, though she acknowledged that the reports in circulation, however cruelly exaggerated or misrepresented the circumstances might be to which they related, were yet not wholly without foundation: she then entreated his aid to extricate her from her present situation, without offending Miss Beauclerc, or wounding that affection which had induced her to bestow favours and benefits, she could never think of without the warmest gratitude.

This epistle Rosella reserved very carefully to the moment when she might put it into a post with a chance of catching the wished-for reply; and as her mind was rather calmed after having decided upon a step so prudent, she found herself sufficiently disengaged to remark upon the uncommon enthusiasm which had taken possession of her strange and romantic friend, who compared the Grampian hills to the Alps, the Appenines, and the Pyrenees; and the river Tay, with its distant Loch, to each sublime stream of which she had ever read. Their progress was slow, for the road was hilly and mountainous; but the almost insufferable tediousness of every ascent, was amply rewarded by a view of the intervening vales, sweetly wild, almost invariably watered by a winding stream, and generally well wooded.

In one of these, about five miles south of Dunkeld, Miss Beauclerc loitered near an hour, taking the dinner she had had the precaution to provide at the last town, at the foot of a mountain, down whose rocky bosom a natural cascade fell into the Tay, which circuited round a small but pleasant wood, to visit the spot, and receive the falling tribute into its own waves.

"I should much like," exclaimed Miss Beauclerc, "to pass a few weeks in this lovely spot; but I fear I shall not here meet with a cottage to suit my purpose."

"All those I have hitherto observed," replied Rosella, "are really not so good as English piggeries: a cottage in the environs of London, fitted up with French windows, treillage paper,[302] and cane chairs, and a cottage at the foot of the Grampian hills, are very different things I perceive."

"Perhaps we may have the good fortune," resumed Miss Beauclerc with a smile, "to find the deserted habitation of some elegant recluse, whose taste and labours may have rendered it precisely what a delicate and cultivated mind might wish."

Rosella made no reply, but sincerely hoped they might not fall into the track of any elegant recluse, who had been capable of executing so mad a scheme.

Miss Beauclerc at length condescended to resume her journey, and proceeded to Dunkeld, where she slept; and on the next morning at an early hour sent to the house of a person in the place, with whom she said she had business; and her note was immediately answered by the appearance of an obsequious North Briton, who was, he affirmed, the vara parson Maister Mac-clood had mentioned to the leddy, and after a few compliments, and many professions of devotion to the interest of sic aimable parsonages, he proceeded, as a matter of course, to describe the most charming dwelling in the whole island; a deleetful cottage, only two sitting rooms and a small kitchen below, and three lodging rooms above, but vara tastefully fitted up and furnished by an unfortunate leddy, who was prevented from finding it the asylum she had hoped for herself and her children, by the folly of a jealous loon of a husband, who made her quit her ain coontra, and follow him to another, whither he was banished by his ain extravagance and dissipation. The praspects were the most romantic in aw Scotland, and it was not more than twa miles from the rumbling brig, a majestic cascade as ony in Europe. An Edinburgh painter had taken views to the extent of five miles round, which views were hung up in the cottage;[303] and it likewise contained a piano-forte, and sundry instruments particulareesed in the leest of the furniture and appurtenances.

"I am perfectly satisfied with this account of my future residence," interrupted Miss Beauclerc; "I have already instructed my agent in London to pay the sum demanded, and I hear that I can have immediate possession."

"Maister Mac-clood," the Scot replied, "had desired him to accede to the leddy's wishes in that respect, and she might act as the thought proper as to instant residence; and even if anything intervened to prevent the agreement from taking place, of which he hoped there wad be leetel probabeelity, she, as a tenant, might sotisfee ony demand of the landleddy, by the year or the quarter."

Miss Beauclerc was evidently delighted with this prompt method of proceeding, and after settling a few necessary preliminaries, she departed the next morning from Dunkeld with Rosella and Nancy, accompanied by Maister Craufurd,[304] who undertook to escort them to the Scotch paradise he had so eloquently described. Yet Rosella had so little expectation of satisfaction from it, that she dated her letter, with a memorandum that the reply was to be addressed to her at the house of Mr. Craufurd, who was to receive and forward the correspondence of Miss Beauclerc, and then contrived to send it to the post before she left the town, with a sincere hope that Mr. Mordaunt would comply with the wish it contained.

After a short ride through a country, which it required no ingenuity of the Scot to persuade the ladies was beautifully romantic, he pointed out to Miss Beauclerc her new abode, and she found it to exceed even what her enthusiastic imagination had formed of divine. It was now the beginning of July, and the weather, which in the Scottish highlands was then little more than of a pleasurable warmth, had given fragrance to the herbage, and scented the air for a considerable distance with the shrubs and wild flowers transplanted from a more southern soil, and disposed with considerable judgment in a lovely glen, where a branch of the Tay meandered in stillness, until it was joined by a brawling stream that rushed from a neighbouring rock, and then they flowed together with an impetuous motion, and shook the freshened air with their murmurs.

The cottage itself had been newly white-washed, and partially glistened from behind a green treillage[305] covering the front and one side, and placed about half a foot from the building, that the dews hanging upon the leaves of the wild rose and honeysuckle creeping over it, might not affect the apartments with damp; the windows were casements, but very neatly glazed and leaded, and reflected very brightly the sun-beam darted against them; and a rural portico open to the inspection of the passing observer, discovered a little greenhouse, fancifully arranged with pots of flowers, so as to resemble a luxuriant arbour.

To the north, the cottage was sheltered by a gentle ascent, covered with a grove of firs, interspersed with beech; and though the rays of the rising sun could salute it from the east, yet its wintry blasts were intercepted by the angle of the wood, which terminated by degrees, till at length a few scattered trees alone shaded the plain, and waved their branches in lofty pride over the reflecting bosom of the river.

Miss Beauclerc was speechless with delight, and Rosella with admiration; and with sensations widely different from the methodical apathy of their guide, Mr. Craufurd, listened or seemed to listen to his commendation of the perfect repair of the house: he observed that the thatched roof was of reeds, and very durable – indeed it would last as long as he did; that the chimnies had not been built more than three months, and were constructed with an equal attention to strength and convenience, as well as adapted to the simplicity of the building.

He made the ladies remark a well, which the landlady had been at a considerable expence to clear of weeds and rubbish, and so conveniently situated, that the lassie instead of running every hour with her pitcher to the river, would get a bucket of water in two minutes: he ushered them in at the back door, that they might behold a little poultry yard and fuel-shed,[306] and a pig-sty, the whole being part and parcel of the building.

But Miss Beauclerc was paying much greater attention to a pretty entrance contrived from a little flower-garden on the south side: it was formed like a lean-to, having a sloping roof of rough branches of trees overlaid with rushes; the wall was raised with lath and plaister, lined in the inside with a paper to represent a rustic railing, overrun with flowering weeds and high grass, and the floor was paved irregularly with small pebbles. It led to a little study, or music-room, for it was both the one and the other, being decorated on every side with light cases of painted deal,[307] filled with books elegantly bound; and in a recess stood the piano-forte Mr. Craufurd had spoken of, of a small size, adapted to the situation it filled. Beneath it, Rosella, who followed her friend in mute wonder, saw a viola and two more instruments in cases, which she afterwards learned were a lute and an Æolian harp.[308]

"An asylum for an unfortunate lady and her children!" repeated she internally, as Mr. Craufurd's explanation rose to her recollection. "Good God! if this was the unfortunate lady's idea of an economical retreat, I do not wonder that the unfortunate gentleman, her husband, was banished from his native land by the dissipation of his property!"

Mr. Craufurd was now attending to the safe disposal of the baggage, for which he had not only engaged the assistance of Nancy, but had likewise dragged a Scotch servant-girl from the hole she had fled to, at the approach of such magnificent personages.

Miss Beauclerc, relieved therefore from his tiresome observations, fully satisfied her curiosity and expectation, by surveying every apartment with rapturous avidity. The designs of the Edinburgh painter were in the room adjoining the study, into which it opened; and when Miss Beauclerc entered it, she would certainly have honoured it with the appellation of a drawing-room, had not the fascinating epithet of *the cottage* recurred to her;[309] and she then reflected that there was no such place in a captivating retreat of that kind. She contented herself with calling it simply a sitting-room, whilst she admired the elegant neatness of the furniture, the charming lightness of the paper, and the excellent effect of the beautiful views hung over it, which she resolved however to displace as fast as possible, and substitute the copies Rosella was instantly to set about, because all heroines in such a situation should be artists.

The cabriole chairs[310] and ottomane to suit the furniture, and the carpet, which actually seemed to be the same on which "the hare-bell and violet grew,"[311] claimed each a share of approbation; but all applause was faint, to that bestowed upon the effect of the portico, which by means of a stained-glass door thrown open, became part of the room: its fragrance "stole o'er the senses like the sweet south upon a bed of violets,"[312] and every vivid hue that varies the beautiful bosom of Nature under a southern sun, peeped from the shading folds of a drapery hanging in careless festoons round the entrance; it did not however, either than the arrangement of the greenhouse plants, exclude a perspective view of the country, equally wild, but far more interesting than the subjects of Salvator's pencil.[313]

"This is surely a fairy scene!" exclaimed Rosella, after a long interval of silence.

Miss Beauclerc made no reply, for her admiration and content were too potent for speech; but she smiled at the emotions of her young companion, who continued to express her astonishment.

"What invisible being," said she, "has thus prepared every thing for our reception? These flowers are newly placed here, and the plants, far from drooping for want of care, have not even a single grain of dust upon their leaves!"

Mr. Craufurd at this moment entered the room, begging leave to introduce to the lady of the mansion a Scotch lassie, who was very ambitious of the honour of continuing at her post as drudge in ordinary, scowerer of kettles and pans, pig-feeder, faggot chopper, poultry-killer, hands and knees floor-scrubber, and had no objection to take her turn at digging in the garden when necessary.

So many accomplishments centering in one person were not to be overlooked, and Miss Beauclerc very readily assented to the humble petition of Menie Cameron, who was installed into her service in due form: but as Mr. Craufurd's wife was well acquainted with the extent of her abilities, she had now, as it was usual with her when her husband left Dunkeld to examine the progress of the workmen at the cottage, taken the precaution to send a dinner with him, upon which the whole party made a tolerable meal.

Miss Beauclerc then having written out a list of things that appeared immediately necessary to her establishment, gave it to the obliging Maister Craufurd, and commissioned him to seek in Dunkeld for a lad whom she could send thither whenever she found occasion. The gentleman promised the swiftest compliance with her requests, and departed before the evening closed in, leaving the travellers in possession of their new dwelling.

When he was gone, Miss Beauclerc proposed to Rosella to walk round her little domains, which was readily agreed to; and they rambled over a small kitchen-garden, another enclosure dedicated to flowers and shrubs, and a young plantation of no great extent, but prettily laid out, and in good order. Mr. Craufurd had obviated the surprise this might have occasioned, by informing the ladies that he had sent for a young man from Edinburgh to take proper care of the pleasure-ground; and as he happened to be acquainted with the gardener of a Nobleman's seat in the neighbourhood, he had bought the exotics at a small expence, and placed them as the taste of his more experienced friend directed.

Miss Beauclerc and her companion proceeded through the eastern extremity of the grove they had admired from the cottage-windows, and coming immediately upon a hill beyond it, they endeavoured to attain the summit before the sun had wholly set, that they might better survey the extent and features of the country.

"Rosella," said Miss Beauclerc, as she leaned upon her arm, "you appear dispirited: do you imagine that our retreat is too much secluded from the world? Yet I am much deceived if you have not too much taste to regret quitting its noisy pleasures for such a retirement as this. For myself, I can aver that in your society I could not think any solitude irksome; would but my Rosella close my eyes with her wonted tenderness, and weep over my grave with filial affection, I could die in this spot, and never send a sigh towards the tumultuous and giddy crowd upon whom I now turn my back."

Rosella could not but overlook the sublimity of this declaration from the fondness which was mixed with it, and she felt anew the remorse arising from a secret consciousness of ingratitude, which whispered to her, that to add her implied censure with the indiscriminating cry of the world against her friend, was cruel. She was unable to answer the enquiry of Miss Beauclerc with the cheerfulness she had intended, and bursting into tears, remained silent.

The good lady, not in the least suspecting the source of this emotion, concluded that Rosella regretted alone in the world, one individual, to whom she was herself anxious to unite her; and in a short sentence tenderly chiding her tears, she suffered them to subside without further notice.

When they reached the summit of the hill, Rosella forgot her self-reproaches in the scene that opened before her; a few paces from them was a fence that appeared like a park-paling, and a herd of deer darting in wild terror from a clump of trees at the approach of the intruders, confirmed the supposition. The enclosure was far from being a level broken only by gentle ascents; on the contrary, it was interspersed with abrupt and rude craggy rocks, the tops of which were thinly covered with russet and heath in bloom; but the low land was more verdant, better wooded, and winded with the stream that bent its fickle course through the dale. In the bed of the river arose a building resembling a tower, upon whose mouldering turrets some ravens waved at intervals their sooty wings, and took flight for their more airy dwelling in the tallest branches of the neighbouring trees.

"What can that place be meant for?" exclaimed Rosella, unwilling to avow that she suspected it to be a prison. At the instant however that she spoke, she observed not a great way from the place, a modern pavilion, gay, light, and Grecian, but ill according with its ancient neighbour, which looked grim and sullen upon the upstart that obscured its long standing beauties.

"I should like to know," resumed she, without waiting an answer to her first question, "to whom this park and those buildings belong."

"We will enquire," returned Miss Beauclerc: "and if the family is absent, most probably we may obtain leave of the housekeeper to see the mansion, which is not far off, I suppose, and through her medium perhaps, have leave likewise to wander over these grounds whenever our inclination and their wild beauties may impel us to wish it."

Rosella did not much approve of these *wandering* plans; for though she did not imagine the habitation could be much frequented by its owners, in so retired a spot, yet if Fortune should ordain that any part of the family unexpectedly visited it, and found Miss Beauclerc and herself, or either separately, in quiet possession of the best sitting-room in the house, or *wandering* extremely at their ease in the grounds, she thought she could not feel quite so *nonchalente* as a charming heroine she had lately read of in an admired novel, who was surprised by the young unmarried owner of a magnificent Welch mansion, in which, by favour of Mrs. Housekeeper, she had liberty to wander to her heart's content, and then took advantage of a shower of rain to *feel compelled* to sit down *tête-à-tête* with my Lord, to drink a comfortable dish of tea, not forgetting however, to display afterwards all the horror of the sublimest delicacy, because the daring youth was unfeeling enough to stumble against her ideas of decorum.

As Miss Beauclerc and Rosella leaned against the paling, surveying with a parting look the scenery it enclosed, they heard distinctly the tremendous roar of the cataract Mr. Craufurd had mentioned; and as twilight stole over every object round them, they listened with an emotion not wholly unmixed with fear, and thought of their retreat with yet more satisfaction, as their imagination represented it as a place of safety and an asylum.

Chapter IV

AN UNGRACIOUS HOUSEKEEPER AT AN OLD CASTLE – A DECISIVE MEETING

NANCY having with some difficulty found a small repository of candles, supplied her Lady with lights on her return; for Menie had vanished without any previous notice; and having been absent more than an hour, occasioned some alarm in the Northumbrian, who concluded that she had been dragged down a precipice by some haggard witch, and that she and her mistress would never more get a glimpse of the unlucky girl, excepting indeed in the unwelcome accoutrements of a winding-sheet, saucer-eyes, and marble hands.[314]

Menie returned however, in about an hour, and having on her entrance received a reprimand from Nancy, for giving her such an alarm, she said she had only been to the Laird's, to set Sawney's heart at rest, by the information that her gude leddy wad not part wi her: an excuse the other thought all-sufficient.

The supper was quite a rustic one; but alas! it was served up also in a most rustic style, but ill suited to the place in which it was eaten. Nancy, at the request of her Lady, had undertaken the office of cook; and her skill was not entirely despicable, because she had more than once taken the post of honour by a kitchen fire; but it was not now displayed to much advantage, for want of implements and materials to exercise it upon. Mr. Craufurd had indeed promised to return early the next morning, with every thing that was most urgently wanted; and Miss Beauclerc was obliged to wait with composure for the time, when the exquisite and well-managed meals of a cap-a-pie[315] heroine should grace her cottage table.

Rosella, in spite of the novelty of her situation – a novelty which appeared to have nothing unpleasant in it, was far from being at ease: she had heard the ingenuous reason assigned by Menie for her absence, and feared this Laird, of whom she spoke, might induce Miss Beauclerc to drop her plan of total solitude, and furnish those enemies she acknowledged to have, with fresh cause for censure and scandal.

After breakfast the following morning letters were to be written to Selina, to relieve her friendly heart with intelligence of their safety and their arrival, at the most lovely retirement in the world: and Rosella declining at that moment, the opportunity of addressing vows of everlasting affection to Miss Livia, and of giving her a glowing portrait of every shelf in the cottage,[316] followed the advice of Miss Beauclerc, and walked out for exercise.

DOI: 10.4324/9781003175582-29

As the way she had taken the evening before was the only one with which she was at all acquainted, she pursued it again, and arrived at the park-paling without having encountered a single being. The old building again presenting its heavy sides to her view, she was desirous to have a nearer sight of it, and jumping over the fence, which was very low, advanced towards the river, but felt at every step that she was an interloper, and pictured to herself the Laird, such a figure as she had seen Wallace, the northern hero, described by a Scots painter,[317] emerging from behind every bush she passed, to demand her business in his territories. And a figure did indeed accost her with a bow, but not so fierce looking a warrior.

This personage appeared like a game-keeper, and Rosella thought he looked like a South Briton. Feeling that some apology was necessary for her intrusion, yet not knowing how to form one, she said, in a hesitating accent, that she was a stranger to the place, but had not entered it with any sinister design.

"Oh Miss," replied the man, "my Lord does not wish nor desire any person whatsoever, to be *discluded* from our park."

He had grounded the fowling-piece which had been carried on his shoulder, as if he meant to hold a long conversation; and Rosella finding that he expected to be asked a few questions, pointed to the mansion-house, which she had just discovered from between the trees, and enquired who was the owner of it.

"My Lord, Miss, as owns this onaccountable park as it's called – my Lord Morteyne," replied he.

Rosella was vexed: "Lord Morteyne!" repeated she to herself; "so, we are again his neighbours! Surely Miss Beauclerc could not be acquainted with the circumstance; if he should happen to visit this house whilst we remain in the neighbourhood, he may suppose that we removed hither to attract his attention!"

This idea was so distressing, that she had no longer any regret at having written to Mr. Mordaunt; and bidding the game-keeper good morning, she walked back to the cottage, which had now lost every charm in her imagination, she had originally allowed it to possess. That Miss Beauclerc should have so suddenly heard of a purchase thus singularly to suit her ideas, she now thought a suspicious circumstance, and she recollected even to have seen several letters from her fanciful friend addressed to that Mr. Mac-cloud, of whom his countryman Mr. Craufurd, had spoken.

She found that Miss Beauclerc had not yet finished her journalised epistle to her Selina, and as she waited her leisure to communicate the news she had just heard, it occurred to her, that Mr. Mordaunt would most probably attend to her petition, before any *adventure* could possibly happen to make her rue this unlucky vicinity; and she likewise confessed to herself, that as Miss Beauclerc had actually concluded the purchase of the cottage, it could not be expected that she would abandon it solely in complaisance to her scruples.

These reflections calmed the perturbation, with which she had in the first moment, sought to make her friend participate in her vexation; and Rosella had recovered sufficient coolness before she rejoined her, to mention her discovery without much emotion.

Miss Beauclerc endeavoured to hear it with symptoms of extreme surprise, and was so much occupied in acting her own part, that she lost the opportunity of learning from the undisguised countenance and manner of her young companion, what effect this *accidental* and *unexpected* circumstance had upon her mind. It had been very amply discussed in the journal just written to Selina, and much astonishment had been expressed that Lord Morteyne had not yet arrived, which had been fully expected from the *rencontre* at Luss.

Rosella could not but perceive that her friend felt no displeasure from what she had heard, and auguring nothing good from the conjecture that followed, began to calculate how long it might be before Mr. Mordaunt received and answered her letter, when her reflections, and those into which Miss Beauclerc had fallen, were interrupted by the entrance of Nancy, who enquired if the young man who took care of the garden could be admitted to speak to his Lady.

"Certainly, let him enter," replied the Padrona,[318] starting from her reverie; and a sandy-haired, raw-boned, high-cheeked, thick-lipped, wide-mouthed, freckled, awkward Scotchman made his appearance, so unlike those rural swains of comely mould, who falling in love with the heroine's simple but pretty waiting-damsel, form such charming episodes in their histories, that Miss Beauclerc, entirely disappointed, resolved he should not long remain in her service, notwithstanding his taste in disposing her flowers, and his evident care of her garden. Luckily however for poor Maclean, she recollected whilst he was making his bow, and expressing his hopes that she was satisfied with his services, that Nancy's arrangement might be made from the household of Lord Morteyne, which would accommodate the difficulty in a very clever and useful manner – so that she replied to his compliment with great condescension, and announced to him, that his good fortune was equal to that of Menie, in being retained through Mr. Craufurd's recommendation, and his own diligence.

She then enquired the name of a plant in the portico, with which both Rosella and herself were unacquainted, and learned that Maclean had heard, but forgotten it; but he promised to ask his gude friend, my Lord's gardener, who had let him have it from the greenhouse at Guairdy.

Miss Beauclerc having demanded if he meant the adjoining house and park, received the expected affirmative, and asked what establishment his Lordship kept up there. He did not know exactly; but it had lately been increased, and every thing put in order, in expectation of the Lord's arrival: and it was said his Lordship was come to Scotland after a young lady he was going to be married to, and the housekeeper was in hopes he would bring his bride to Guairdy, for they had heard it was not very far from where the lady lived.

Miss Beauclerc listened with the utmost eagerness to this recital, which might perhaps have crushed all her long cherished hopes, had she not been entirely convinced that the young lady thus mentioned was only – could only be Rosella. This reasonable supposition composed a certain horror she had involuntarily begun to feel; and finding that Maclean had nothing further to communicate, she dismissed him.

Rosella entertained no such idea; and the news of Lord Morteyne's marriage reconciled her in part, to the *rencontre* she imagined it almost impossible to avoid if he were to visit the Park, as any known engagement to another woman would lessen the suspicions his family or himself might form, on seeing her transported, without any apparent cause or necessity, from Avelines to the environs of Guairdy.

When Maclean retired, Nancy entered with a very grave face, to enquire what was to be done for victuals,[319] as Mr. Craufurd had not sent the eatables, he was commissioned to convey, by the lad he was to precure at Dunkeld.

Miss Beauclerc was extremely shocked at so gross a question, applied too, at such a moment, and sent the poor girl out of the room with a more serious air of anger than she had ever before beheld on the countenance of her Lady. But alas! Rosella likewise, who was young and healthy, was so shamefully different from other heroines, that a walk generally gave her an inclination for dinner, and sometimes even before the usual hour. She had breakfasted at eight, upon the tea and bread Mrs. Craufurd had furnished the house with, for the occasional accommodation of her husband, and it was now past two, so that she very much commiserated the distress of Nancy; and in spite of the charms of a cottage, situated amidst the Grampian hills, near the winding Tay, she had reason to think there were likewise some attractives in a dinner, now that she was in evident danger of passing a day without one. Yet Nancy's disgrace prevented her from imparting such degenerate sentiments to her friend; and at about three o'clock the envoy arrived from Maister Craufurd, leading a packhorse loaded to a height more than equal to his own, which was about that of a greyhound.

Menie ran out with great alacrity to help the beast in with his burthen, and almost deliberated whether she should not carry both the one and the other into the poultry yard. But Nancy meantime took a safer method, and equally expeditious, by unlading[320] the poney as it deliberately marched forward and having discovered where the provisions were deposited, she drew forth the basket that contained them, and fled to her rural kitchen with the spoil, calling to Menie to follow her without delay.

The dinner in about an hour and a half was served up, at a time but ill suited to the simplicity of rural life; the other circumstances attending it accorded better with what might be expected in humble dwellings: but Miss Beauclerc had never read of a heroine being compelled to rise from table to rince her own glasses, call for a napkin to wipe the dust from her plate, or take up her salt with a table spoon; all this discomposed her exceedingly, for such a minutia had not even entered her head, when she had devoured, in delighted admiration, those scenes so often described, of charming young ladies retiring from the world, and taking up their abode at the cottage of some honest peasant, whose infirm wife and awkward daughter form the whole train of domestics the lovely creature can boast of.

Miss Beauclerc's present dissatisfaction led her to reflect upon the innumerable dilemmas of those matronly heroines, brought forward in the mournful pages of a Niobe-like[321] authoress, who invariably conducts them through a series of lacrymalian[322] adventures, with a prison-gate in perspective at the conclusion of them: – in the course of the history, the pathetic lady, followed by a train of half-a-dozen small children, retires to the solitude of a cheap and remote cottage, or farm-house, attended by one servant girl, deserted by her dissipated and unfeeling husband; she is here sought out by her adorer, who thinks himself happy in being admitted to play with the spirited boys, and fondle little Emma, so like mama! The fair suffering saint being usually found extended upon a sofa, weeping over the unlucky baby at her breast, and the attendant constantly employed in carrying out the other children, to exercise them, a task the girl has no objection to prolong as much as possible – how, thought Miss Beauclerc, how in the name of the household gods, can the mysteries of the *menage*[323] be conducted! who washes, who dusts, who irons, who cleans, who mends, who cooks? No matter – if through the ignorance of a rustic wench, the lovely matron cannot avoid passing an hour in the presence of her lover, and inviting him to stay dinner, an impassioned admirer will surely behold with an indulgent eye, the stirrup in her petticoat,[324] and eat with an exquisite relish, in her divine presence, hashed mutton burnt in the pot, or a smoaked[325] beef steak.

Miss Beauclerc, who had expected in her cottage the pleasant refinements of that affluence to which she had been accustomed, began to regret the loss of Simpson, whose diligence and attention to her convenience would at this moment have been so acceptable; and she mentioned an intention of writing as she had promised, to direct him where to seek her – an intention very grateful to Rosella, who had often represented to herself the old man's uneasiness at being abandoned so suddenly; and she had even feared that his anxiety, and resentment at so strange a return for his long services might be fatal to him: on his account she did not regret the stubborn stupidity of poor Menie, nor the rusticity of Nancy.

The boy who had led the horse from Dunkeld, related the several disasters which had so much retarded his appearance. He had gone only a mile, before the strap that fastened the paniers, gave way, and when he buckled it a little tighter, it broke, and he was obliged to get it mended as well as he could; and then he was directed to the factor's new house instead of the right one, and in turning into the road to Guairdy again, he had had to lead the beast up a hill so steep, that when he got to the top, he was near lying down with want of breath, so the guide was obliged to let him crop a little grass to hearten him.

Rosella thought that so many combining circumstances might well excuse the tardiness which had chagrined some of the fasting party, and would not suffer the weary poney to return to Dunkeld that night, even at the hazard of waiting for the dinner again on the following day: an effort of humanity Miss Beauclerc readily concurred in, because, independent of her natural compassion, a thatched-roofed heroine should be the most commiserating and tender-hearted of the pitying sex. The next morning therefore by daylight the boy returned with a note to Mr. Craufurd, entrusting him with further commissions, and desiring that he would enquire at the post-office for letters Miss Beauclerc expected.

Rosella could not yet hope a reply to her's; but this method of sending, inspired her with the idea of being enabled to procure it unknown to her companion, by making a practice of inspecting the load the carrier was charged with, the moment it arrived.

After breakfast, Miss Beauclerc proposed walking to Guairdy Park, and Rosella reluctantly complied: she little imagined however, that her complaisance had drawn her in to accompany her friend in a projected survey of the house; but she found that Miss Beauclerc was resolved not to return to her cottage without it. Notwithstanding the approaching marriage of Lord Morteyne, Rosella felt a few scruples in *wandering* over his dwelling, prepared as she understood it was, for his reception. But Miss Beauclerc chid her for her folly, and desired her to lay aside childish prejudices, and trust to her guidance.

She was far from willing to confess all the repugnance she experienced in doing so; and silently followed her flighty friend, who having called upon a labourer she happened to meet, to conduct her, after some difficulty procured a sight of the housekeeper, and with an air of marked condescension, such as she judged it a point of heroic etiquette to assume, she announced her will of being conducted through the apartments.

The personage thus accosted had been first *femme-de-chambre* to the Dowager Lady Morteyne, and at her death had solicited to be retained in the family, hoping to be placed about the person of Lady Lucy; but unfortunately, though she had possessed the confidence of her deceased Lady, and had been extremely useful to her, she was known to have a temper so uncommonly acrimonious, that the household which had the evil fortune to contain her, was usually changed *du haut en bas*[326] at least once in a fortnight. Lady Lucy not knowing how to deny her request, yet totally averse to having such a scourge amongst her domestics, persuaded her brother to send her to Guairdy in her present capacity. But retirement, which was on the part of Mrs. Tadpole entirely unwished for, had not in the least succeeded in correcting her foibles, or making her more indulgent to those of others.

She had heard of the new comers at the house called the cottage, and concluded, from the expence and folly it exhibited so many symptoms of, that the ladies were nothing but kept madams, who were either sent there by her Lord, or came to draw him in, because they had heard in London that he was going to Guairdy; so that instead of the charming old dame so repeatedly described in Miss Beauclerc's studies, who good-naturedly conducts people through the deserted apartments of the mansion, and tells in confidence all the secret and bloody transactions which had happened in them some twenty or thirty years back, she beheld a most forbidding-looking fury, cast in the true Zantippean mould[327] – a curved spine, a sharp bony elbow, descending on one side half a foot below the protuberant hip, a thin long nose deeply coloured at the tip, red hair, and eyes nearly of the same hue, whose beams far from being lambent, shot a fierce sparkling light, and seemed to the imagination, to crackle and hiss like the fire of a blacksmith's forge: her mouth was like a deserted cemetery, which yawning upon the horror-struck observer, displayed a variety of discoloured bones scattered in rude confusion, and mouldering in their dark asylum: her hand might have been lectured upon by an anatomist without the trouble of displacing the skin, and the fingers were so long and meagre that they looked like the claw of an immense bird.

Miss Beauclerc waited almost five minutes for a reply to her request, whilst Rosella shrunk from the coming answer, as a poor traveller shrinks from an eruption of Mount Vesuvius which he finds himself unable to escape.

Mrs. Housekeeper was, in the interim, endeavouring to collect in one furious sentence, the wrath and indignation which for a moment had overpowered every faculty.

"You wants both of you to see the house!" she screamed, in a voice that was at once both bass and treble, tenor and counter-tenor, "ho, you wants to see the house!! and you wants other people to see your gew-gaw show-box, as you have tricked up there; but you may go back to your dog-holes in London, and try to trap your fools there – there's none here as wouldn't turn up their noses at such trumpery! See the house quotha! and who'd be the simpleton to trundle after your draggle tails to show it you?"

"For God's sake," whispered Rosella, "let us go away!"

"See the house! You'll see the house of correction first – my Lord's not for such as you – he's going to be married to an honest body, one as brings honour and money, and won't bring him to want and shame. See the house!!!"[328] raising her tone to the highest pitch her voice would carry, "go see how they beats hemp, you young hussy! And you, mistress, don't think to come over your honest betters, with your mincing and simpering, to gain your wicked ends – what, you wants to see the house, do you?"

Rosella, expecting every moment to feel the claws of the termagant fixed in her eyes, was now so governed by shame and terror, that she ran off with uncommon swiftness, and darting through a court-yard, soon gained the park without slackening her pace; and even then, was still so much under the impression of the antipathy and horror the beldame had inspired, that she flew over hill and dale in her way home, with the wildness of a maniac.

And now, the destiny of a heroine hovered over her: she was not fated to reach that home without an adventure; for in five minutes she was surrounded or rather enclosed on every side by horsemen of every description, and carriages of every denomination. Her recollection suddenly returned, and with it the unspeakable confusion of finding herself an object of curiosity, of compassion, of laughter, of ridicule, or diversion, as in different bosoms different opinions respecting her prevailed.

Rosella justly imagined this cavalcade to be the bridal train of Lady Morteyne, and would have given the universe to have escaped from further notice: independently of mortification, she felt extreme inconvenience from the difficulty of regaining her breath, which her running had made her lose, and from a dryness in the throat and mouth that almost threatened suffocation; she leaned against a tree, pressing her hand to her bosom with an energy indicative of great distress, which her countenance fully corroborated, when the voice of Lady Lucy Estcourt saluted her ear, whose accents spoke commiseration.

Rosella looked up, and perceived her endeavouring to descend from her carriage; but Lord Morteyne opposed her intention, not only by whispered dissuasions, but by detaining her almost forcibly. Rosella could not attend to the issue of the contest, for the sight of Mr. Povey, who was laughing violently, and recounting some circumstance in which he often introduced her name, engaged, the next moment, all her attention: she could only distinguish however, the unconnected phrases – Irish fortune-hunter – disappeared from Edinburgh – recognized the lady at Dumbarton – cursed airs – fomented a damned scuffle – deserted in her turn.

"Good God!" thought she, "my application to Mr. Mordaunt is then too late; my reputation is gone, and Miss Beauclerc's friendship has undone me! Let me not however, stay here to witness such scorn!"

Swift as thought, she again darted forward, and unpursued, reached the boundaries of the park, which she resolved never more to enter; and then, with a less hasty pace, returned to the cottage, forlorn, humiliated, sick of her existence, and fully resolved to hide her head where the cruel surmises of the world could never reach her.

Chapter V

MAMA TEARS AWAY THE MYSTERIOUS VEIL THROWN AVER THE AFFINITY BETWEEN HERSELF AND HER DAUGHTER

SHE had waited above an hour for the appearance of Miss Beauclerc, and was much alarmed at her prolonged absence: not so much from the dread of any accident having befallen her, of which she did not think there was much probability, as from a horror of her betraying herself to the ridicule of the large party she had herself just escaped from, by exhibiting the peculiarity of her sentiments and expectations.

The anxious reflections of Rosella were interrupted at this period by Nancy, who ran in, saying that a strange gentleman wanted to speak to her. The idea of Mr. Mordaunt instantly occurred, and she flew towards the door in a transport of delight, in the hope of being relieved from her distress by his friendly advice and interference, and rescued from reproach. It was not however Mr. Mordaunt who waited admittance, but Mr. Delamere; and Rosella, who had actually spread out her arms to welcome him, in the first emotion of her satisfaction, stood confounded and immoveable when she discovered her error.

"I am sorry, Madam," said the gentleman, "that my negligence of etiquette in not sending in my name, should have occasioned a mistake of person, which seems so much to chagrin you."

She had before felt awkward and abashed, and now losing all composure and presence of mind, sunk into a seat, near which she stood, and bursting into an agony of tears, laid her head upon the arm of a sofa, and sobbed violently.

Whatever the sentiments of Mr. Delamere might be as to her conduct and principles, he was shocked at so strong an expression of anguish, and endeavoured to console her, by observing that her peace of mind was yet retrievable, if she would accept the advice and assistance of a lady, who had commissioned him to enquire if she were indeed willing to receive the most essential services.

"Tell me," suddenly interrupted Rosella, her tears for a moment ceasing, "if you received a letter, or rather an enclosure, I addressed to you, at Eideva Lodge? If you have not, you may think you acquired a right to distress me thus, from the cruel mistake I had not time to rectify when you left Warkworth so suddenly; did you receive that letter?"

"Certainly not," replied he.

"Then you have thought to this hour," pursued Rosella eagerly, "that I was abject enough to solicit your bounty, when I was anxious only to procure the loan of good offices, in a moment of embarrassment to which my inexperience was unequal. Even that indeed was a liberty for which I have your pardon to entreat; and I must further beg you will wait the return of Miss Beauclerc, who will restore the twenty pounds you left in my hands. I enclosed it instantly in a cover, and sent it by the post to the house of Mr. Mompesson; but I suppose it is lost."

"I will not ask your forgiveness," said Mr. Delamere, "for a mistake which reflected no discredit upon you: for poverty, my dear Miss Montresor, is an accidental evil, not a reproach; but imprudence and error persisted in – Let me inform you, however, that I am now deputed by Lady Lucy Estcourt, who wishes to learn if she can assist you in any way that may tend to extricate you from situations, in which a mind so ingenuous, and a heart so feeling as your's, must be ill at ease. Lady Lucy is the best and most generous of her sex, and has suffered much from seeing you this morning so greatly distressed; and she thinks your appearance here is not calculated to remove unpleasant surmises, but may be productive of insult and impertinence, which, believe me, you will find it hard to bear."

"It is this insult, this impertinence, that I cannot endure!" exclaimed Rosella, flying out of the room, and hastening to her chamber, where she locked herself in; and indulging her tears, consoled herself with the reflection that remonstrance and representation which wounded her pride, and outraged her delicacy, could not then reach her ear.

After some time her distress rather abated, and she distinguished the voice of the lad returned from Dunkeld; the expected letter was now more than ever desirable, and she ran down to examine those he might bring; but not one appeared in her address. Amidst those of Miss Beauclerc however, she discovered the writing of Mr. Ellinger, and had little doubt but that he had been prompted by Mr. Mordaunt to desire her return.

Whilst she held the letters in her hand, secretly commenting on the probable contents of that from her guardian, she learned from Nancy that Miss Beauclerc was in the music-room, and had been there above half an hour, and she ran to her, and presented the packet.

The countenance of Miss Beauclerc changed whilst she tore open the epistle of her Chancery-Lane correspondent, and the unusual paleness of her cheeks increased, when she read the mandate that was meant to snatch Rosella from her.

"Let him," exclaimed she, in violent emotion, "exert the power I foolishly entrusted him with, and I will likewise assert mine! – Rosella," added she, "my poor deserted Rosella, the malicious cruelty of the unfeeling world but renders you more dear to me; know then, sweet solace of my widowed heart, that I am – thy mother! Nor can the dying request of thy murdered father now enforce a longer obedience, when my enemies have nearly succeeded in their barbarous endeavours to separate us!"

Rosella was almost convinced from this rhapsody, and the wild air with which it was uttered, that the intellects of her luckless friend were deranged, and exerted herself to sooth her rising frenzy.

"Dearest Miss Beauclerc," replied she, "let us return to Avelines; and there if you wish for my society, I am sure Mr. Ellinger will not deny it at our joint request; there you are known and respected, and there we shall live in peace, indifferent to the injustice of the world."

"Angelic creature!" exclaimed the matron, "is it thus you retort the insolent triumph of that ungrateful man? I will further fortify your detestation, by informing you, that your dear unhappy father lost his life by the dishonourable co-operation of a part of this man's family, with a league of villains, who stripped him of his fortune, and then drove him by the basest insults to despair and death. Short and embittered was the happiness my union with him afforded; he was too soon torn from my arms, and more than expiated his imprudence by his untimely fate!"

"Good Heavens!" thought Rosella, "what will become of me! How shall I pacify her violence, and prevent those dreadful wanderings?"

"Dear Madam," continued she audibly, "Mr. Delamere did not appear, as you imagine, to triumph; on the contrary, he merely called, at Lady Lucy's request, to assure me of her good-will."

"Her good-will," retorted Miss Beauclerc, every feature beaming indignation, "what perfidious insolence! When I have learned that she is particularly delighted with her unworthy brother's alliance, and that the woman he has married is her most intimate friend."

"Surely," said Rosella, in a persuasive tone, "the marriage of Lord Morteyne is of no importance to me!"

"You are right, my child," replied Miss Beauclerc, who appeared struck by her manner, "it should not be of any: I am charmed with the dignity of mind you display; and when," she added, in an heroic voice, "your gentle heart has quite forgot the ingrate who could slight those modest beauties, the passion of the worthy Oberne will I hope be encouraged."

"Mr. Oberne!" said Rosella colouring; "I dare say he no longer remembered me when a few miles had parted us!"

Miss Beauclerc, on hearing this supposition, so far forgot the outrageous injuries she had just discovered, as to smile.

"My Rosella," exclaimed she, suddenly recollecting herself, "you have not yet given me the sweet title of mother! – Come to my arms, my daughter, and, as such, embrace your only parent!"

At this tender invitation the follies which had cost Rosella so dear, faded on her memory; she still thought her friend's mind disordered, but that affection for her should be predominant when reason had almost fled, touched her soul.

"Dear Miss Beauclerc," said she, "you have ever displayed to me the kindness of a mother, and as such I must always regard you; let us only return to England, and then I may obtain the permission of Mr. Ellinger to remain with you; but against his injunctions, you are sensible I should not have the power to act as I wish."

"Have I not told you," replied the matronly heroine, with an air bordering on displeasure, "that you are my child? And do you hesitate, Rosella, to comply with my wishes, because they are opposed by the unnatural commands of a stranger? Unfortunate that I am!" continued she, bursting into tears; "did but my beloved daughter regard me with half the tenderness I bear her, she would fly from any authority, that was exerted to tear her from the lacerated bosom of her widowed mother!"

The distress, real and fictitious, of Miss Beauclerc had now worked to such a pitch of uncontrolable emotion, that Rosella was staggered in the disbelief of her strange assertion; her mind was become the seat of confusion, of anxiety, and terror, and all she could now do was to caress her sobbing friend, and assure her of the most unlimited affection.

"I believe you," interrupted she; "promise me then, my child, that you will never desert your mother: but if the man, entrusted with the guardianship of the small sum I secured to you in your infancy, should claim you as his ward, I exact of your duty and love, that you will escape with me to some retreat, where his power cannot reach us!"

Rosella started at this wild proposal, and shrunk aghast from binding herself to perform so rash and imprudent an action: but the fear of increasing the imagined frenzy of Miss Beauclerc withheld her refusal, and she hesitated, stammered, changed colour, yet no promise passed her lips.

"Am I deceived?" cried the widowed heroine. "Is your heart so wedded to the perfidious Morteyne, that you cannot determine to relinquish the sight of him, even devoted to another?"

"What an idea!" exclaimed Rosella, with a blush of anger and indignation: "for Heaven's sake, Madam, do not mortify me in this cruel manner! Have I displayed so much forwardness towards Lord Morteyne, or any other man, that you should for a moment think so ill of me?"

"Why then," resumed Miss Beauclerc, affecting an air of gentle compassion, "why not give me the promise I ask?"

"What analogy can there be," said Rosella in amazement, "between Lord Morteyne and any engagement I may enter into with you?"

Miss Beauclerc seeing her offended; and not having any reply ready for this enquiry, desired that the subject might be waved until she had read her Selina's packet, to which Rosella assented in silence: and whilst her strange friend hurried through a lecture of eight pages, closely written, she was confirmed in the opinion she had already formed, that Mrs. Ellinger was the secret spring of those absurdities, which in Miss Beauclerc had given her so much anxiety and embarrassment.

The contents of this important packet were, as usual, kept a profound secret; and as the perusal, of it lasted until the dinner was upon the table, the subject *in petto* was of course not immediately renewed.

This meal was as unhappily conducted as the preceding ones, and Miss Beauclerc becoming impatient and out of temper at such terrible indecorum, accused Nancy of awkwardness, and threatened to discharge Menie. During this discomposure, she undesignedly discovered to Rosella, that Simpson had returned to London, and having demanded his dismission of Mr. Ellinger, who was steward in the absence of his Lady, had retired into his native county, exceedingly dissatisfied with her conduct.

The method by which Mr. Mordaunt had arrived at the knowledge of their unlucky adventures, instantly occurred to Rosella; yet she could not account for his having heard the detail of their meeting with Oberne, till she surmised that it must have reached Simpson through the correspondence of Mrs. Nancy with her aunt, which had begun before they left Edinburgh. She was not displeased to unravel the mystery of the secret enemy Miss Beauclerc had complained of – an idea that had constantly been accompanied by acute uneasiness; yet she grieved to have parted entirely from the poor old butler, with an impression left upon his mind of her unkindness and negligence.

After dinner, Miss Beauclerc was silent and thoughtful; and seemed, Rosella feared, to be revolving in her mind some new whim. At length turning suddenly towards her –

"You mentioned," said she, "the name of Delamere, and joined it to that of Lady Lucy – he is now at Guairdy, I can well imagine; tell me, Rosella, did he come hither to insult you with his perfidy, and to display the double success of her wiles? For my poor Selina has heard, with the utmost indignation at such baseness, that he is shortly to be united to that artful woman, Morteyne's sister. Good God! that men will thus "on a fair mountain leave to feed, and batten on a moor!"[329]

Rosella, who fancied she saw returning frenzy in the eye of her friend, would not contradict her too peremptorily; yet she could not endure to hear Lady Lucy Estcourt branded thus with baseness and art, or Mr. Delamere so vindictively charged with perfidy towards her, without wishing to confute an accusation so entirely unjust.

"Mr. Delamere, Madam," said she, "has not surely given me cause to speak thus of him! I can at most have merely reason to be vexed that he believes too readily those calumnies which perhaps my own imprudence may have pointed. Towards Lady Lucy, it would be in me the height of impertinence to apply to her such terms as those you have used, since what I have constantly heard of her character and disposition, and the little I have had an opportunity of observing, have displayed them not only as unoffending, but extremely amiable. Yet I am convinced, dear Madam, that the warmth of your censure proceeds from your too great partiality for me; but I am hurt that it should lead you to commit even in thought, the least injustice."

Miss Beauclerc raised her hands in admiration, and apostrophised her as a patient, dispassionate, much-injured angel, enthusiastically extolling her for pleading the merits of people who deserved only her resentment.

"In what respect, Madam?" asked Rosella.

"Did not Delamere," returned she, "display at Sedgfield, a very particular admiration of you?"

"Not to my observation," said Rosella, very much vexed: "yet even if the circumstances of the moment, and want of other amusement had induced him to pay me a few compliments, and I had been silly enough to think them of more importance than they were meant to be, surely the manner in which we quitted him, after an intercourse of apparent good-will, might justify on his side any change of sentiments, and leave me little reason to complain, if Mr. Delamere now chooses to offer a just tribute of admiration to the merits of any worthy woman, whose situation, family, fortune, and character may be exactly all he wishes."

"A man must be a sordid wretch," exclaimed Miss Beauclerc, "if in seeking a wife, he considers situation, family, and fortune!"

Rosella, who saw all the ardour of romance and sentiment sparkle in her eyes, was silent; for she had before heard her friend declare, that a man who could attach himself so prudently, must inevitably be a very cool lover: indeed a lover such as Miss Beauclerc, in the course of her lectures, had so often met with, who without any reasonable cause flies to some remote village, and there never fails to encounter, in his rambles, an incognita of pensive mien and doubtful character, whom, in defiance of common caution, and repeated warnings, he adores through thick and thin – was the lover she could alone allow to wear the myrtle.[330] But the argument Rosella had used she felt the force of, though she was unwilling to own it; nay, she even began to think that there are very few lovers whose cannon-proof constancy might be so far relied upon, after enduring three or four such freaks, as even to give hope of a return of allegiance.

Fortunately this subject at present so wholly occupied her, that she forgot to renew her enquiry of the conversation that had passed when Mr. Delamere had visited the cottage, or again to urge the topic which had been waved before dinner. The afternoon was employed as usual, when any thing important had happened, in writing to Selina; and Rosella very soberly sat down to work – a vulgarity a heroine is scarcely ever caught at, her elegant and simple wardrobe being composed of such sublime materials as never to require alteration or repair.

The mind of Rosella was not however, so peaceful as her employment seemed to indicate: she thought much of the injury her fame had sustained from her fatal journey – an injury she was doubtful if even the advice and friendship of Mr. Mordaunt could efface; and her imagination dwelt too, in spite of her incredulity, upon the strange affirmation of Miss Beauclerc, that she was her daughter.

"Should it be so!" thought Rosella; "but no, it is impossible! It could not have been preserved so long a secret from the world: Mr. Ellinger must know it, and Mr. Mordaunt. Surely they would have informed me of so important a circumstance – my unhappy friend *must* be disordered in her intellects; yet if I am indeed her daughter! – if for my sake she has refused more than one eligible alliance, and as she says, lives but for me, ought I not to endure for her, the mortification which the opinions of some censorious people might give me, and perform my duty without shrinking? But Mr. Mordaunt will decide for me – I will be guided by his judgment, and his friendship; and I think he will not neglect me, at least I will hope not."

Miss Beauclerc, who was writing during this soliloquy, with the energy which enthusiasm usually gave her pen, suddenly threw her letter aside –

"Yes," exclaimed she, "I will wring the selfish soul of this unfeeling man, and make him groan with remorse, amidst his bridal revels!"

"My God, what now!" whispered Rosella, turning pale with apprehension; "Oh that I were an hundred miles from this place!"

"My child," continued the sage matron, "all gentle as you are, and unwilling to inflict punishment for the wrongs you endure, tell me what even you will allow that monster to deserve, whose family having contributed to make an orphan of a lovely innocent young creature, he can, without remorse, have the barbarity to gain her guileless heart, and then not only leave her to scorn and derision, but deprive her of another lover, whose merits and attachment might have effaced all her sorrows?"

"Indeed, Madam, I cannot at all decide," replied Rosella; "because I never had a lover, and cannot ascertain how far a lady may be affected by the loss of one."

A heroine without a lover! Rosella without an adorer! – The idea was not to be endured.

"Yes, my dear," said the lady eagerly, "you have lovers, but they are unworthy of you!"

"Well then," replied Rosella, endeavouring to smile, "we will not, dear Madam, make them of importance to us, if they are unworthy: let us think no more of them."

"I admire your fortitude," said Miss Beauclerc, "and I will imitate it. I must however, once more see this worldly-minded Morteyne, for I have a pecuniary affair to settle with him, which I will not delay: and though," continued she with ardour, "by paying him the sum mentioned in his uncle's nefarious bond, I should be reduced to beggary, with you, my Rosella, I would rather wander from door to door than not part with it."

Rosella was much terrified by her vehemence –

"Dearest Madam," said she, taking her hand, "condescend this once to listen to me. If you have any business to transact with Lord Morteyne, let Mr. Ellinger or Mr. Mordaunt settle it: you can give them your directions."

"Mr. Ellinger," interrupted Miss Beauclerc, "has already settled it, but not to my satisfaction; and this once at least, I will pursue my own unshackled will."

She then resumed her pen, and as Rosella could not forbear observing, addressed Lord Morteyne, with a formal request to have the honour of half an hour's conversation at her cottage on the next day.

As she was folding the billet, Rosella, unable to endure her apprehensions of the result, threw herself on her knees, and entreated that the affair might rest a few days longer; but her solicitations were effectually checked by her friend's reply.

"No, my child," returned she, with a dignified air, "your fond efforts to screen this ingrate from pangs he well merits, shall not avail him; therefore urge me no more."

And almost instantly, she desired Nancy to give the note to Maclean, who was to proceed with it immediately to Guairdy.

Rosella bursting into tears of mortification and anguish, left the room, and retreated to her chamber; but Miss Beauclerc was not, on this occasion, to be moved from her purpose by the distress she exhibited, and Rosella saw Maclean, from her window, take the way to the park. She represented to herself Lord Morteyne obtruded upon at his dinner table, by the unlucky note; for Miss Beauclerc had strictly charged her messenger not to return without an answer, conceiving in the ardour of her sublime revenge, that the common usages of the world, etiquette, and good manners, must all give way before more consequential concerns; and certainly, like many other woe-worn heroines, she thought her imaginary wrongs of the highest import.

Rosella pictured to her fancy the contemptuous anger of Lord Morteyne; she saw the unfortunate scroll thrown from one to another, accompanied by bursts of ridicule, and the sneers of malice: she recollected the impertinence of the reptile Povey, and she had experienced the insolence of Mr. Estcourt; but in this mortifying scene, her candour brought forward the compassionate interference of his amiable sister, and the moderation of Delamere: – she now wished that she had had more command over her feelings, and received the well-meant offer of Lady Lucy in a different manner.

Her perturbation became extreme, and she even meditated to avoid the mortifications that appeared to await her, by walking to Dunkeld, and returning to England by the aid of that advice and assistance she had in the morning rejected. This thought was however, only the momentary effervescence of suffering pride and wounded delicacy: but though she rejected the idea of leaving Miss Beauclerc in a clandestine manner, she still proposed to herself to pretend that she had some purchases to make at Dunkeld, and entreat her friend to permit her to walk thither the next day, attended by Maclean; and thus she thought to escape the horror of seeing Lord Morteyne, should he think proper to attend the summons he would receive.

Chapter VI

THE ELEGANCE OF THE COTTAGE SULLIED BY IGNORANT RUSTICITY – A CAPTIVE HERO REDUCED TO DESPAIR

ROSELLA having in some degree composed herself, at length rejoined Miss Beauclerc, who was waiting with extreme impatience the return of her envoy; but though the distance to the great house was little more than a mile and a half, Maclean had not completed his commission in three hours; – indeed, to do him justice, it would have been impossible to listen to the histories poured into his ear by the third table gentry,[331] and in return, suffer others scarcely less instructive to be extracted from him, in a shorter time.

Nancy at last entered to announce his return.

"Where is the note," asked Miss Beauclerc impatiently, "the letter, the reply?"

Nancy disappeared to fetch it; but brought it at the tip of her tongue.

"Maclean says, Ma'am, that Mr. Johnson, the gentleman, he says, his Lord says, his Lord is sorry to send a – a verdant answer to your noate; but the reason is, his Lord is a drinking his wine[332] – but however, he'll make it up to-morrow by coming to see you."

Nancy having now performed her part, by giving the *coup de grace* to this mutilated message, retired to pursue the enquiries she had already begun of Maclean, concerning the proceedings of the grand people at the Park: and Miss Beauclerc, bursting with indignation, exclaimed to Rosella –

"I expected this, and am not surprised; I was prepared for such behaviour, by the treatment I received this morning. That horrid woman, who was tutored I suppose to insult us, had not finished her peal of abuse, when a servant rode up to the house, to announce the approach of his Lord and Lady. I was rather surprised, as you may well imagine, to hear him speak of his Lady; but concluded, after a moment of reflection, that the man meant Lady Lucy, and I resolved to see her before I returned home, that she might learn the outrageous insolence of her domestic. The abusive creature hastily retreated, muttering her discontent that she had not received any previous notice; and I waited some time before the carriages drew up to the door. When I discerned Lady Lucy, I instantly advanced to her, and representing what the conduct of the housekeeper had been, desired her immediate dismission; but Lady Lucy, with an air of confusion, the consciousness of her too successful arts might well give her, replied that she was only a guest at Guairdy, but she had little doubt her sister, Lady Morteyne, would discourage any improper conduct in her servants.

"The suspicions I had before repelled as totally impossible, were by this speech confirmed beyond a doubt; and certainly my indignation must have been very apparent. I turned, with all the contempt I really felt, towards a young woman who had, descended from another carriage, and was hanging upon the arm of the vile Morteyne, in an affected emotion of fear and distress; when this shameless man advancing to me, said, with the most undaunted assurance –

'Lady Morteyne, Madam, is at present fatigued with her journey, and will be engaged in welcoming her guests; at any other time she would attend to your complaints without hesitation – at present you must excuse her.'

"With an air of defiance he then passed me, leading the woman into the house, and calling to Lady Lucy to follow him. I believe I should have sunk with the various agitations that oppressed me, had not that artful creature pretended great feeling, and called to a person I discovered to be that foolish fellow Povey, who by her directions, offered me his arm to assist me home.

"But, good Heavens! so completely had the insolence of this family humbled me in the eyes of this despicable being, that even he added his tribute of insult to that I had already endured: his impertinence however restored me to the pride of offended dignity, and I left the place with sensations less painful, I will venture to assert, than these which agitated the bosom of the self-condemned Morteyne."

Miss Beauclerc here closed her lamentable narrative, which added considerably to the misery of Rosella, who writhed with agony at the description of her indignant friend's interview with the astonished inhabitants of Guairdy Park.

"Not for the world," thought she, would I now see Lord Morteyne, or any part of his family: if Miss Beauclerc will not suffer me to go to Dunkeld, I will shut myself up in my chamber, and nothing shall induce me to quit it."

With great doubt of its success, she made her proposition, and was much surprised to find it complied with: indeed Miss Beauclerc, who well knew that a heroine should never place her foot over the threshold of her charming dwelling without an adventure, was in hopes this expedition might furnish one, at least, to console her for the horrible defection of two men, whom in looking forward to the career of Rosella's brilliant adventures, she had marked, in imagination, for the main springs of the whole machinery. She complied with her wish, that Maclean should attend her; and desired she would return in a chaise if she found herself fatigued. Mr. Craufurd was as usual, charged with innumerable commissions, which Rosella promised not to forget mentioning to him.

As she parted with Miss Beauclerc for the night, she received a parental embrace and a tender blessing, which renewed the combat she had before experienced between incredulity and a sort of innate conviction, that much disquieted her. She had however, so little of the sublime in her nature, that it never entered her imagination to consult the pale moon till any great clock struck the morning hour, or even to stand gazing till midnight upon the pine-clad hill, marking very carefully all its inflexions by the deepening shades – no, she endeavoured to compose herself to rest, and after some time had elapsed, which the agitation of her mind stole from her slumbers, her eyelids closed in forgetfulness, merely from these physical reasons, that she was not yet quite eighteen, and was in perfect health.

The consequence was, that in the morning she was not so unfortunate as to oversleep the hour she had appointed for her departure – an accident that will happen in spite of philosophy, if people do not go to bed till the sun rises, and the birds begin to carol their morning song; a practice much to be deplored in behalf of those gentle creatures who are confined, it may be against their inclination, in an old tower of an old castle, and by such a lamentable misfortune, sometimes lose a long-projected opportunity, as their historians inform the world, of making their escape.

Rosella had determined to set out at six o'clock, when she thought there would be little probability of having her promenade interrupted by any of the Guairdy family, or their guests; and as she supposed Mrs. Craufurd would invite her to stay dinner at Dunkeld, she hoped at her return, they would be engaged at table, from which she concluded they did not rise till very late.

Having breakfasted, she called for Maclean, who appeared in his best array, with his red hair combed out to its full length, his hideous countenance shining with the rough ablution it had undergone, and grinning with complacency at the honour to which his destiny had promoted him.

Rosella satisfied herself that he was well acquainted with the road to Dunkeld, and began her expedition with more speed than it was likely she should continue, congratulating herself at every twenty steps, that she was leaving Guairdy and the cottage behind her.

Miss Beauclerc, who had performed all the ceremonies of watching, praying, gazing at the pale beams of the moon and at its shadows, and clock-counting, was not so matinal as her young companion: but she heard her depart, and recollecting that Lord Morteyne would probably call in the morning, though no time had been mentioned, she started up and dressed herself hastily, that she might have time to seek amongst her papers, which she always carried from place to place with her, and which were almost as numerous and ill-arranged as those of a Prime Minister, for those relating to the bond and money obligations of her deceased husband, to the late Mr. Estcourt.

She sought however nearly two hours in vain, and after a strong contest between hunger and sublimity, finding that hunger remained master of the field of battle, she rung for her breakfast, which was to be placed as usual in the music-room, and desired Nancy to put every thing quickly in order in the adjoining one, where she intended to receive the culprit, and overwhelm him with regret for having so basely given up the taste he ought to have cultivated, for the delicious and tranquil pleasures to be found under a thatched roof.

Nancy, who could not, as she justly observed to herself, do two things at once, and concluded that the most pressing command was that which related to the breakfast, employed herself in getting it ready, and issued her own orders and instructions to Menie to accomplish the other task.

Miss Beauclerc quite forgetting the reduced state of her rural household, and satisfied with having signified her pleasure, as if she had been surrounded by domestics as at Avelines, again resumed her employment, which lasted almost two hours longer; and the breakfast was scarcely concluded, and the necessary documents brought to light, before Nancy ran into the room in an agony of perturbation, and announced the Lord.

"Have you shown his Lordship into the portico-chamber?" asked her mistress, in some emotion.

"Yes, Madam," replied Nancy, trembling. "Oh jemini!" whispered she, as the withdrew, "now all the murder will out, as sure as thunder!"

Miss Beauclerc heard the soliloquy, and applied it to her own grievances; for she imagined them of so serious and wide-spreading a nature, that even the domestics of both families were well acquainted with them, and sympathized in the wrongs of the offended beauty. She was now however, compelled to dismiss every idea except that of assuming the most dignified attitude, and the most majestic air that ever marbled the features of injured virtue: and having at length succeeded to her wish, she threw open the door of the audience-room, and beheld – the agonized Morteyne pacing the apartment perhaps, with the pale face of despair, and the frantic motions of a madman – no! – he was very composedly standing at the entrance of the portico, thinking of the improvements he had long meditated at Guairdy, towards which his eyes were earnestly bent; but Miss Beauclerc beheld one of the frames of her drawings shattered to pieces, and fragments of glass strewed about the carpet, which near the entrance of the room had lost much of its cleanliness and brilliancy: the portico exhibited likewise some symptoms of recent disaster, for several plants had been laid low, and the earth, escaped from the pots, had not been gathered up, but mixed very cordially with the water the saucers had contained, and made the finest bed of mud in the world: yet even this Miss Beauclerc might have forgiven, but to climax the misfortunes of the day, every chair in the room exhibited a black and very perfect impression of a pair of broad naked feet, which like the crest or arms of the proprietor, appeared to have been purposely stamped there, to ascertain the right of possession.

This was too much for heroism itself to support with patience and fortitude. Surprise, anger, and confusion chased away every symptom of calm dignity from her features; and when Lord Morteyne with some difficulty, made his way towards her with the usual salutation, she found it impossible to resume any composure or presence of mind. To have pointed with silent gravity to a seat, and taken one herself, could not be done, as such a movement would have transferred the drawing of Menie's feet to her garments, and those of the gentleman.

Whether this idea, or any other still more whimsical, struck upon the imagination of Lord Morteyne, cannot be decided: he could not however forbear smiling, as he begged to be informed of her commands.

"I have no commands for Lord Morteyne," said the lady, with less severity of manner than she had originally intended to have displayed; "but if your Lordship will take the trouble to walk into the next room, I will relate the motive that urged me to trespass thus upon your time."

He complied with the request in silence, imagining he was doomed to listen to a long history of complaints, excited by the overflowing gall of Mrs. Tadpole, his Guairdy housekeeper – a mortification he chose however to endure, rather than suffer his Lady to be tormented with the trouble of settling the affair: and with this prepossession, he was extremely surprised to observe Miss Beauclerc unfolding a number of papers apparently of ancient date, which would assist her, she said, in elucidating the mystery she was then going to explain.

My Lord at this hint looked excessively grave, in proportion as the hands of the Lady began to tremble, her cheeks to flow with tears, and her bosom to sob, as the writing of her long lost love was unveiled to her fond eyes. She snatched some of the papers, and pressed them to her heart –

"Father of my Rosella!" exclaimed she. And the eye of Lord Morteyne caught the name of Estcourt repeatedly traced on most of the papers. This circumstance, joined to the ejaculation, excited a greater degree of interest in his mind than he had believed it to be in the power of Miss Beauclerc to excite, and he waited very impatiently to be relieved from some unpleasant sensations of anxiety and alarm.

"You had an uncle?" said the gentle *elucidator*, after a pause of some moments.

"I had three, Madam," returned her auditor.

"It may be," resumed Miss Beauclerc, rather disconcerted: "but the man to whom I owe all the hours of sorrow I have known – the man whose vices were destined to be a scourge to me and mine! – Alas, my Lord, I have little inclination to rejoice in the prosperity of your house, and your Lordship cannot wonder that I should suffer my anguish to relieve itself in the bitterness of complaint."

"Perhaps, Madam," said he rather gravely, "I should wonder less, if you would do me the honour to give me some intimation of the injuries you seem to deplore."

"I entreat your patience," cried the lady: "surely, my Lord, you will allow for the imbecility of grief?"

"I compassionate imbecility of whatever kind it may be," replied Lord Morteyne; "but give me the liberty to observe, that my impatience to learn the grievances you hint at, is in part the effect of an earnest wish to alleviate them."

"That, my Lord, is not in your power," said Miss Beauclerc, with something of anger in her manner.

"If it is so," observed he, "you will pardon me, Madam, that I am at a loss to comprehend why you have given yourself this trouble. You mentioned the name of the young lady who resides with you – I am unacquainted with her family or her connexions; but if Lady Morteyne or my sister, have the power of serving her, I will be responsible for their inclination."

The indignation and disdain of Miss Beauclerc at this proposition, were unbounded –

"My Lord," said she, "I will shorten what I meant to say – this bond, which I found amongst my father's papers, was granted to the Honourable Thomas Estcourt, a man without one good principle or inherent virtue."

"He is no more, Madam; and in the name of his surviving relations, I entreat that you will suffer the name of my uncle –"

"You had *three*, my Lord!" retorted the lady in great heat and agitation; "and I hope those you still boast of, amply console you and the surviving relations, for your inestimable loss in the third."

Lord Morteyne was piqued, because he was really conscious that Mr. Estcourt had by no means been an ornament to the family name.

"I take my leave, Madam," said he haughtily, and rising as he spoke.

Miss Beauclerc felt rather shocked that her resentment had been roused to a degree so far exceeding the gentle anger of a heroine, and replied, with a more subdued air –

"Take with you, my Lord, these memorials of your uncle," presenting him the bond: "take with you likewise my note for the sum marked in it, the sole inheritance of a much-injured orphan! and when next the family exploits are emblazoned, forget not to record in the name of the Honourable Thomas Estcourt, the ruin and death of a credulous but virtuous man, and the beggary of his helpless child!"

Having pronounced this sentence with proper emphasis, the lady suddenly vanished, leaving Lord Morteyne motionless with surprise and dismay, internally agitated by wounded pride, and a fear that these charges might be too well founded. The bond and note he knew not how to dispose of, but he resolved not to retain them in his possession after he had quitted the house: yet he was entirely averse to tempt a second interview with Miss Beauclerc, whose emotions, exclamations, and elucidations were too sublime for his taste, and who, to finish the scene in style, was now sobbing in the next room in so audible a key, that his Lordship could not fail to hear her.

He observed that the poor lady had locked the door of communication between them, and he could not therefore return the papers into her possession. But at length, his first confusion subsiding, he recollected that, as writing materials lay upon the table before him, he could enclose them in a wafered cover,[333] under Miss Beauclerc's address, very safely; which he hastened to do, that he might fly the house, and escape any further pathetic declamation.

This task accomplished, he endeavoured to open the door leading to the garden, and finding that it was fastened, rung the bell, to be relieved from his dilemma: but Nancy, fancying this summons was the prelude to anger, scolding, and perhaps dismission, instead of answering it in person, ran into the grove to hide herself; and Menie, who was a still greater culprit, followed her example.

Lord Morteyne rung a second time – a third time, and Miss Beauclerc still sobbed in the next room. At length his patience was so wholly exhausted, that he ventured to intrude upon her sorrows, by a humble petition stating his case, and praying relief.

"It is in vain to sue, my Lord," said the mourner, interrupting him, "I will not see you."

"But for heaven's sake *hear* me, Madam," said he; "I cannot quit the room."

"I have already heard too much," ejaculated Miss Beauclerc with a deep sigh.

Lord Morteyne was not of the same opinion, so he renewed his efforts to explain his situation.

"My Lord, I insist that you leave the house," cried she vehemently.

"I desire it equally with yourself," retorted the prisoner: "and if you would condescend to listen, I would inform you that the other door of this apartment is locked."

Miss Beauclerc was now upon her knees, invoking the spirit of her sainted husband – of course no sublunary sound could reach her ear, and Lord Morteyne, finding all explanation vain, turned to the window, in the hope of making his sortie from thence: but unfortunately, it happened to be a Gothic casement so interlaced with wood work, that he saw the attempt would be useless, unless he should be reduced to the desperate necessity of breaking a way through – an alternative he really began to fear he must have recourse to. Once more he applied to the bell, with a vehemence that soon ended every hope from that expedient, by pulling it down. He now no longer heard the voice of the lady in the adjoining room, and imagined she had quitted it, until a renewed plaint struck his ear.

"Miss Beauclerc," said he eagerly, "I believe you have not understood me –"

"Cease," exclaimed she, "cease your useless importunity – I am immoveably fixed!"

"And so it seems am I!" muttered he: then raising his voice, "Good God! will you not listen to me? I have been this last half hour endeavouring to make you sensible that I am a prisoner – the glass door is locked, Madam, as well as this, and my importunity will not cease until you have ordered one of your domestics to open it."

No answer was returned to this eclaircissement: indeed Miss Beauclerc, fully determined to stand the siege she supposed the remorse of Lord Morteyne was preparing her, had quietly retired, to import from her chamber some books and her writing-desk, which she chose to do without assistance, that she might not expose his frantic demeanor to her servants.

When she returned, she heard his Lordship laughing aloud; for the ridicule of his situation struck him so forcibly, that he forgot his recent emotions: and as he was now convinced that his captivity had been designed, he concluded that the former part of the farce had not much foundation in truth.

"Poor maniac!" sighed Miss Beauclerc, who imagined that his agonies had overset his reason: a revolution, however sudden and violent, she had read many instances of – "What will now avail your unhappy bride, that she has triumphed over an artless and lovely young creature, and planted a thorn in her guileless bosom not to be extracted?"

Lord Morteyne could only hear a few words of this ejaculation; but the mention of his bride reminding him that his prolonged absence might alarm her, he very earnestly renewed his entreaties that Miss Beauclerc would open the door, which she refused with the perseverance of a heroine; and he protested, that if she continued to treat him in so absurd and unprecedented a manner, she must excuse the consequence.

The lady returned no answer, but stepping towards the offices, espied Menie creeping into the kitchen, with all the precaution she could use, that she might not be heard. Miss Beauclerc beckoned her to follow, and returned to her post, Menie standing near the entrance of the room, hanging down her head, that she might not have the horror of beholding the devastation her awkward destiny, and the unlucky commands of Nancy, had made her commit. Her Lady remained silent, and in a few minutes a horrid crash was heard from the music-room. – Miss Beauclerc started, and her attendant stared. The noise was continued, and shortly succeeded by an outrageous knocking and thumping, as if his imprisoned Lordship had been amusing his *ennui* by applying the poker to the chairs and tables.

Miss Beauclerc was now really frightened. "Run," exclaimed she, "run, Menie, and inform his unhappy family that Lord Morteyne has lost his reason!"

"Maun I say that the deil's[334] in him?" asked Menie, in some doubt.

"Yes, yes," replied her Lady, still more alarmed on hearing the uproar increase; – "say that his mind's o'erthrown, that Reason is hurled from her seat!"

"Trath, and a does hairl 'em," thought Menie; "a hairls 'em mair than I hairl'd 'em wi my pauky feet!"[335]

She then set off with great speed for Guairdy, to give the alarm, telling every one she met, that the Laird had sauled himsel to the deil, and was deleerit and roaring doon at Maistress's hoose, looder than the roombling brig.[336]

This alarming report soon spread amongst the servants; some of whom rushed into the apartment of Lady Lucy, where unfortunately her sister-in-law happened to be, and repeated the dismal news in her presence.

Lady Morteyne fainted; and some of the most unmoved of her guests endeavoured to render her some assistance, whilst Lady Lucy, almost as distracted as her brother was represented to be, ran towards the cottage to ascertain the truth, which was *elucidated* much sooner than she could have hoped, by the appearance of Lord Morteyne walking with the utmost composure to Guairdy, with his right hand bound up in a handkerchief stained with blood. She embraced him with affectionate concern; and not seeing any other mark of emotion on his countenance than surprise at her behaviour, began to lose her apprehensions, and ventured to ask what accident had happened to him.

"The most strange and absurd," replied he, "that could possibly happen: I have been a prisoner, Lucy, to a fair lady, and could only escape her enchantments by breaking her windows and window-frames, which my impatience prompted me to do, and in the exploit I have cut my hand. That poor woman at the cottage, as she calls the place, is as completely deranged as any of Doctor W – 's patients; she ought not to be at this moment without a strait-waistcoat!"

This retorted charge of insanity appeared to Lady Lucy so much better founded than the first, that she entirely lost her suspicions of the greater evil. – "How I pity that poor girl," exclaimed she, "who accompanies her from place to place! Surely she ought to be rescued from such a situation!"

"We must leave her to her destiny," replied Lord Morteyne; "for Miss Beauclerc is equal to the absurdity of giving out that she is a natural child of the family, deserted from infancy; or of embroiling us in a law-suit for property, of which she pretends our deceased uncle plundered the father of this girl."

The exclamations of Miss Beauclerc, of which he now retained but a confused recollection, and the bond history commixed, formed in the mind of Lord Morteyne an association of ideas he thus explained.

Lady Lucy looked astonished, and so did her brother, on perceiving a number of domestics flying towards them, headed by his male guests, and followed by those of the ladies who most abounded in courage and curiosity.

"What the devil," exclaimed he, "is the meaning of all this?"

Lady Lucy could scarcely forbear laughing. – "Our friends," replied she, "have heard that your situation required assistance, and I suppose they are marching this way to offer it."

Lord Morteyne, thinking she alluded to his imprisonment, smiled at the idea of being rescued from the lady's power by a *posse comitatus*.[337]

By this time he was surrounded by his guests and his household, excepting of the former, Mr. Povey, who, having become both a great man and a fashionable man, could not possibly traverse the space of a mile and a half without his horses and servant: and whilst the groom was getting ready at a minute's notice, he amused himself with asking questions of Menie, who was in the stable-yard, and had been giving a long detail of the disasters of the morning, to a helper who was her admirer.

From her, Mr. Povey learned that Rosella was gone to Dunkeld, that she walked there, and would walk back with Maister Maclean: that Maister Maclean was the gardener, and had said they could not return till evening.

Menie now found another auditor in Mr. Estcourt, who had but then arrived at the seat of his brother; and having overtaken the numerous party in the park, just staid to hear the outline of the story which appeared to divert them so extremely, before he hastened to the house, to take some repose after having passed the preceding night in receiving a festive welcome to the North.

Happy was it for the quiet of Rosella, that she never heard the conversation which now passed between this gentleman and the worthy Mr. Povey, when they had dismissed poor Menie, whom they joined very manfully to curse to all eternity, for being freckled like a toad, and having a damned nose like the rump of a goose. Indeed the *ci-devant* attorney's clerk was one of the most valiant oath-fanciers in the three kingdoms; for he really believed that the first commission presented to him through the folly of his uncle, not only entitled him to the honours of the sword and cockade, but included him as part owner of a patent, for every absurdity and vice he so often envied his former friends for appearing to hold the privilege of committing with impunity, by their initiation into the court of fashion – that raree-show,[338] which, to the gaping and shallow-headed gazers without, seems adorned with such exquisite allurement! – Put your noses into the box, good people, and see what wretched machinery, what cut paper and gilt trumpery you regard with admiring eyes!

Mr. Povey was now no longer a Cornet of the Guards, for he wished to rise rapidly, and had purchased a company in a regiment of foot then in Scotland; meaning, by a second change, to dash again into high life, as the irresistible Colonel Povey, whom all the women ogled and died for, in vain.

Chapter VII

A BOTANICAL JOURNEY – AND AN ELUCIDATION OF A LITTLE QUIET MENAGE

ROSELLA, during the fracas at the cottage, and that at Guairdy, unconscious of the extent to which her mistaken friend meant to carry her heroism, retraced the romantic road to Dunkeld, assisted by the more habitual knowledge of her attendant, who happened perchance, to possess that intuitive genius and taste for botanical studies, which has, within a few years, so suddenly overtaken ladies of fashion in the spring, the summer, nay, even the autumn of life.

Poor Maclean had no idea of stringing rhymes to celebrate the sentimental and interesting amours of the plants,[339] but he could not pass the verdant side of a hill without noting it like a spaniel. In vain did he repeatedly observe his young Lady waiting the result of his search after the game he most coveted; a sprig of heath, with a blossom or leaf varying from what he had hitherto seen, well rewarded his trouble, and encouraged him to proceed.

At length Rosella, extremely weary of this method of journeying, when she saw him flying out of the road, demanded very exactly which way she ought to take when she arrived at the top of the next hill, or which path she ought to pursue when she reached the valley, and then walked forward, leaving him to overtake her when his aim had been, for that time at least, accomplished.

Maclean gladly received the indulgence which the good nature of Rosella allowed him: but at length the load he had accumulated, not only in his pockets, but in his hat, in his waistcoat, and in his handkerchief, which he carried with great care in his hand, and the quick march he was often compelled to use, to rejoin his young Lady, added to the warm rays of the sun, which seemed to have communicated its most glowing beams to his golden hair, made him look like those Warwickshire colliers who traverse the underwoods[340] at night, with a blazing fire upon their heads. With him however, the fire consisted of the head itself; and his countenance, the natural expression of which was surprise from the elevation of his thick red brow, and consternation from the hanging of his immense under lip, now appeared so gorgon-like, that Rosella was struck with horror every time she turned her eyes upon him – and yet, like the head of Medusa, that of Maclean was so extraordinary, that it every moment attracted her regards.[341]

As they approached Dunkeld, she began to feel some reluctance to enter the town with him, conceiving, not without some reason, that the figure of her conductor would procure her the honour of more attention than she wished to receive; but there was no remedy for the evil apprehended, except indeed that Rosella, in the hope of reducing the colour in Maclean's cheek bones, desired him to rest himself in a grove of firs near the river, whilst she took a survey of the town, and the beautiful country before her.

He was very glad to obey this injunction, from the violent heat and fatigue he endured: and Rosella, intending to let him remain half an hour where he had placed himself to arrange his treasures, ascended one of the hills with which Dunkeld is surrounded, and gazed with much pleasure upon the meandering Tay, and its lovely banks; but her recollection was suddenly recalled to her attendant by hearing a violent outcry, and beholding him at the same moment struggling in the stream, by which she had recommended it to him to repose himself.

She hastily ran towards the unfortunate botanist, but without any distinct hope of assisting him; and had the satisfaction to observe that he succeeded in extricating himself from his perilous situation, but with the loss of his hat, his handkerchief, and the fruit of his eager researches.

Rosella enquired very earnestly what had occasioned the accident, and learned that Maister Maclean instead of following her instructions, had been seeking for a peculiar sort of *mentha aquatica*,[342] and leaning too far over the bank, had felt a sudden giddiness, probably from the rays of the sun darting upon his uncovered head, and the heated state of his blood, which had caused him to lose his balance, and plunge into the Tay.

The satisfaction which his escape from death occasioned her, soon gave way to compassion for the shivering fits which now seized him; besides the more immediate anxiety to get him to the house of Mr. Craufurd with as little observation as possible.

Rosella hastily wished she had been content to have endured the mortification of the poor fellow's attendance, before his unlucky immersion had given the finishing touches to his appearance: but as it was, she resolved to wave all scruples of delicacy, and endeavour to spare him a fever, by proceeding without delay to Mr. Craufurd's, where she concluded he would be relieved from his wet drapery, which did not hang about him with so much elegance as that of some ladies of ton, the labour of whose toilet consists in putting on the appearance of very slender sea-nymphs, just risen from their coral beds.

Maclean led the way, refreshing the earth as he passed on, with his dripping favours; whilst Rosella followed, looking earnestly in the eyes of those she met, to discover the opinion they formed of herself, and her conductor, who, on his part, bitterly lamented the catastrophe that deprived him of the weeds, roots, and rubbish he had collected.

Fortunately the habitation of Mr. Craufurd was near that part of the town at which they entered; and Rosella had the consolation of reaching it, with only a moderate share of gazing and conjecturing from those who encountered her and her river god. But this momentary smile of fortune was quickly overcast, when she learned that Mrs. Craufurd was not at home; and as she had gone some miles out of the town with an intention of spending the day, Rosella could neither wish nor expect to be asked to eat her dinner at the house; – yet as the master of it was not absent, she entreated permission to rest herself, and having given him a letter entrusted to her by her friend, she ventured to mention the accident that had befallen Maclean, in the hope that Mr. Craufurd would direct his servants to accommodate him; but he merely assured her that the hide of a Scotch peasant was water-proof, and began reading his letter without giving the circumstance a second thought.

After the lecture, he offered her refreshments, which she refused, but was extremely unwilling to quit the place until Maclean could be supposed to have repaired the effects of his cold bath: – she recollected however, the purchases she had intended to make, and mentioned them to Mr. Craufurd, to account for her excursion into the town; but he, happening to be one of those personages, who in the absence of a wife affect airs of gallantry they are far from having the courage to retain in her pretence, proposed to have the honour of conducting so charming a young leddy; a politesse Rosella would willingly have excused, but that she had no pretext for declining it. She entreated indeed that she might not give him so much trouble, and professed that she should be sorry to take up so considerable a portion of his time; but these protests only furnished the gentleman with an opportunity of repeating some very flourishing comments upon her loveliness, which rendered any time employed in her service, deleetfully plaisant.

Rosella now felt so provoked and disgusted, that she would have left the house and the town immediately, had not her humanity been interested for Maclean; as it was, she suffered Maister Craufurd to continue his harangues, and lead her to the shops she had mentioned; and he then proposed to himself to do the honours of the town to the fair stranger, entirely forgetting that she might be already fatigued by her walk.

He took care to inform her, that Dunkeld was the principal mart[343] of the Highlands – a circumstance she cared very little about: but she was obliged to survey with much apparent complacency, the noble seat of "Athol's Duke," which it contains, and the ruins of the cathedral,[344] though in fact, she would at the same time have preferred the most incommodious seat in one of the peat-hovels she had passed in the morning, to have been released from the absurd strain into which Mr. Craufurd had wandered, which was the more remarkable, as he had hitherto appeared only in the character of a diligent and obliging *homme d'affaires*.[345]

It was considerably past two when Rosella re-entered his house, and as she understood that the dinner was ready to be served up, she would immediately have taken her leave, but that he would not suffer her to express such an intention; and as she had not yet acquired, by an intercourse with the world, that firmness of denial which checks importunity, the loquacious entreaties of Mr. Craufurd at length silenced her excuses, and she sat down to his table exceedingly dissatisfied with him, and still more displeased with herself.

The cloth was scarcely removed; and Rosella was already meditating her escape the first moment she should find it feasible, when the lady of the mansion, without any previous notice, made her appearance.

"So, Mr. Craufurd," cried she, swinging open the door, and filling up the entrance as she flourished into the room, "I find you keep open house in my absence; people may walk into the office, and ruin you, before you know any thing of the matter."

Then perceiving Rosella occupying her seat at the head of the table, surprise and indignation choked her utterance, and she turned, with a look of suspicious rage towards her husband, who had suddenly recovered his first character, and was once more the booing and vara obsequious Maister Craufurd.

With a mien that deprecated the rising storm, he hastened to inform her that his guest was Miss Beauclerc's young friend, who had walked from the cottage with a letter from that gude leddy, and had been much vexed and chagrined in not finding Maistress Craufurd at home.

Maistress Craufurd unknit her brow at this intelligence, for she had not immediately recognized Rosella; and whilst the ebbing of the most indignant sensations still marked her countenance, she forced it into a grin, and protested that what with her surprise at the honour Miss Montresor had conferred upon her, and what with the disappointment she had experienced, at finding the friend she had visited, too ill to keep her and the rest of the party to dinner, she hardly knew what she was about: an assertion she immediately verified, by whisking her cloak from her shoulders with such a graceful circuitous motion, that it carried two or three wine glasses, and a dessert plate from the table, to which she had unfortunately advanced when Rosella rose to salute[346] her.

The poor lady, beholding the devastation she had committed, made a violent effort to laugh at the accident, calling at the same time upon Mr. Craufurd to wonder at her ill-luck throughout the day; but he, gude mon, was much more occupied in reflecting that the black cloud of his wife's displeasure, which was passing over the head of her handsome guest with such difficulty of retention, would inevitably burst upon his own with a fury entirely irresistible.

"Well, my dear," continued Mrs. Craufurd, "I am glad you had your dinner sooner than ordinary, because I dare say this young lady was not sorry to sit down to a good joint, after her walk; but if you *had* staid the usual hour, I should just have come in pudding time,[347] which is what I thought to myself as I came along: but I began the day with ill-luck, and so shall go through with it!"

"I am very much concerned," said Rosella, whose colour had heightened during this speech, "that I –"

"Oh dear, don't say a word, Miss Montresor; it could not be any fault of your's, you know: if any body is in fault, it's Mr. Craufurd!" and then followed an attempt to make this hint sound like a badinage, by an hysterical giggle.

"Will ye have the claith laid," said the implied culprit, who was anxious to divert the attack, "and arder something to be gat?"

After a pettish refusal, she complied: and Rosella, who was now really uneasy lest she should not be at home before the twilight overtook her, had the mortification of seeing the mangled joint re-appear, which the lady turned from side to side twenty times with extreme disgust, and then declaring that she could never endure tepid meat, dismissed it with an order to bring in the cold pie: – ill luck again! the pie was entirely demolished!

"Well then I must fast!" exclaimed she, half crying. "Will you have something dressed, my dear?" enquired Mr. Craufurd, in a compassionating tone.

"No: when once I am set against victuals, I do not care for any thing."

This refusal being decisive, the husband would not venture to press the subject further, and a silence of a few minutes ensued, which Rosella took advantage of, and rose from her seat with a farewell compliment.

"I am afraid," said Mrs. Craufurd, half repenting her incivility, yet more than half inclined to add to it by further rudeness, "I am afraid, Miss, that I shorten your visit?"

Rosella was doubtful in what light this speech was to be considered; and whilst she gazed at the lady in some astonishment –

"I am sure, Miss Montresor," continued she, "I ought to beg your pardon; but if you had felt as uncomfortable as I did – dear me, are you going so soon? – well – pray present my best respects to the good lady at the cottage, and pray tell her I hope she will think of her promise, and come soon – that is, drop in in a friendly way, as you have done, and partake our family dinner – you see how we live –"

"I do!" thought Rosella.

– "You see how we live, so pray now contrive to come with her, or else I shall think our little quiet way does not suit your taste. We have always what you have seen to-day, a joint and a pudding – tell Miss Beauclerc that is our bill of fare throughout the year: but even that, with a sincere welcome, and a pleasant countenance, is to me a feast!"

Rosella waited very impatiently for the end of this oration, but it did not appear in the least likely to terminate so soon as she hoped, for the lady had now pitched into what she called a good humour, that is a talkative one; and it seemed as if she supposed her loquacity was to efface every remembrance of previous ill temper – an idea she had long been in the habit of indulging, for she was one of those dames who never feel thoroughly complacent towards their guests, until they are leaving the house.

Rosella having assented very readily to all she uttered, and had the pleasure of hearing that Mrs. Craufurd, being a native of South Britain, was her countrywoman, at length took courage to ask for Maclean, who was produced, equipped in an old hat much too small for him, which stuck upon the top of his head without covering much of his long hair, not yet nearly dried, so that it hung lank and straight; and the *tout ensemble*[348] gave him the appearance of a Puritan of the last century.

Mrs. Craufurd followed her fair guest to the street-door, still entreating that she would not fail to remind Miss Beauclerc of the honour she intended her, and repeating, that now Miss Montresor saw how they lived, she hoped she would often take a walk to Dunkeld, to dine with Mr. Craufurd and her, in their little quiet way: and not even contented with this, she stood at her door, uttering sentences of the same import, till Rosella was absolutely out of sight; who, until that fortunate moment arrived, thought herself obliged at every other step, to turn round, and bow her acknowledgments.

Maclean followed in silence until they reached the spot where he had met with his misadventure, and then, in spite of the expostulations of his young Lady, he insisted upon kneeling by the side of the stream, and stooping over the steep bank that rose beside it, to obtain a root of the *mentha aquatica* –

"You certainly wish for another accident," said Rosella angrily, "or you would not act thus!"

"Mess," returned Maclean gravely, "I wad na but ha foond this for aw Guairdy and its Laird are worth: it's the *mentha hirsuta*; and thus Maister Meller[349] descreebes it – Ment wi wharled fluors, aval, sawed, hairy leaves, and stomina langer na the patols. – Mess, I foond ance upon a time here in my ain coontra, the *mentha virticillata*, which Maister Meller says graws natrally by the seed of the reever Madway: and noo I'm luking –"

"For Heaven's sake," interrupted Rosella, do not look just now for any thing but our shortest way home!" –

"And noo I'm luking for the *mentha palufiris*."

By this time she had discovered, to her extreme terror, that Maclean was much intoxicated; and instantly formed the design of returning to Dunkeld, and hiring a conveyance to the cottage, which she despaired of reaching by his guidance: – but it was impossible to drag him from the back of his hobby horse, and as Rosella did not like the idea of revisiting the house of Mr. Craufurd, and was too timid to enter an inn-gate without an attendant, she very unwillingly proceeded, as well as she could, taking care not to leave her nominal conductor too far behind, as her humanity suggested a care in his behalf he was far from having himself.

With much difficulty and loss of time she had repassed more than half the way, and congratulating herself that the sun was not yet set, ventured to repose herself a few minutes whilst she waited the leisure of Maister Maclean. The spot she had chosen presented on every side a scene so singularly beautiful, that Rosella forgot all her recent vexations whilst she contemplated it. The road bordered one side of a river, which rolled tumultuously over a bed of rocks, many of them rising above its surface, and lying in such numbers that they appeared to oppose the flowing of the stream, which collecting its waters to overcome the check, forced its way with a violent current, and formed cascades, whose murmurs at a small distance invited the wanderer to repose.

A meandering of the river overflowed a space of lowland, and was yet shallow enough to leave a rising spot uncovered, where a group of cattle were browsing, whilst others stood mid-leg in the stream, enjoying its freshness. As the quality of the capricious soil varied, Rosella beheld the naked cliff towering abrupt over her head, or the gentler rise of the verdant hill, chequered with foliage: through the fissure of a rock, an immense pine had forced its once budding growth, and now hung oblique in waving terror over a cataract the same rock had formed below it.

Further on, the double chain of mountains appeared to meet each other; but before the perspective closed, the eye of Rosella was directed by a vivid sun-beam that darted through a break, to a bridge, composed of the body of a large oak, either felled by a tempest, or directed by human care, to cross "high in air," from the summits of opposing cliffs: a rude and irregular railing assisted the giddy passenger, who "maun na luk bot where his foot do tread,"[350] and at this moment a highlander was crossing the Alpine pass, whose tartan pladdie[351] shone right gay in the reflection of the setting sun.

A pack-horse plodding through the bourn Rosella had just passed, was led, or rather dragged along by a Scotch lassie, who at every interval of persuasion and bastinado,[352] neither of which she spared towards the animal, made the glen ring with a lively air, the burthen of which she often repeated – "Wad ye sta here out owre the day, ye pauky beastie!"[353] and then followed a thump, with part of the song.

> "He glowr'd at me as he'd been daft,
> "The loon trows that I'll hae him;
> "Hoot awa I winna hae him;
> "Nae forsooth I'll nae hae him:
> "New hose and new shoon –"[354]

"Ye're nae frisket trow! Ye wad let a mousie tak the road o'ye, ye idle carle!" and then another thump.

Rosella was much amused by observing her constant rotation of employment; but the girl's admonitions quickened her own recollection, and she started up to pursue her way, but could no where discover Maclean – a circumstance that alarmed her. She had now left the songstress and her idle companion far behind, and her anxiety increased, for not a single being enlivened the scene, or appeared to answer the enquiries she was eager to make. She continued to advance however, and judged that she was not quite a mile from home, when she perceived a well-dressed man loitering in the path, who no sooner caught a glimpse of her, than he flew to meet her, and in a tone as familiar as if their acquaintance had been of long and approved growth, reproached her for having delayed her return to so late an hour.

"However," added he, "it has had one good effect; for those puppies, Estcourt and Povey, have sounded a retreat, and left me, who was much more desirous of the *rencontre* than they were, to exult at my superior fortune."

Rosella stood aghast at this strange address and the intruder observing her consternation, resumed with the same easy air –

"Why you seem vexed at it! Surely you had not a design upon either of those blockheads? They are more capricious and absurd than Oberne, and to my certain knowledge, they are equally poor."

She experienced such a rapid succession of emotions during this second attack, and her mind was so divided between surprise, anger, fear, confusion, and resentment, that she remained immoveable. The voice and features of this familiar personage she recollected to have seen and heard before, but could not in the least remember where they had met her notice.

A suspicion crossed her mind that this adventure, as Miss Beauclerc would have called it, was of her contriving; and the idea, unconfirmed as it was, gave her such pain and mortification, that after an unsuccessful struggle with her sensations, the tears sprung to her eyes; but immediately endeavouring to recover herself, she eagerly pursued her way, passing by the stranger with so quick a motion, that he could not prevent it, though he instantly rejoined her.

She averted her head to get rid of her tears unperceived, as she expected they would merely excite ridicule; but he saw them.

"You are unhappy!" exclaimed he. "Tell me truly, were you attached to Oberne?"

Rosella coloured with indignation, and though a number of angry replies rose to her lips, she still remained silent.

"Are you dumb?" resumed he, snatching her hand.

She was much alarmed, and called out to Maclean, but with little hope that he would hear her.

"Oh, à-propos," said her new acquaintance, "what have you done with your Esquire? I expected inevitably to have had that dragon to charm to rest, before I could get at you. What not a word yet? Do, charming – (what is your name) – let these shady groves, and this purling stream, speak with pastoral persuasion in my favour!"

His knowledge of her having had an attendant, confirmed the surmise that Miss Beauclerc had planned, or at least permitted, this distressing scene; and the easy assurance of the young man's manner, and the tenor of his language and conversation, which no one could mistake, too well informed her in what light she was regarded.

"Oh Heavens!" thought Rosella, "does every human being view me with the same contempt? Who will then rescue me from reproach, since it is universally believed that I but too well merit it!"

Her companion continued talking with the same flippancy; but, absorbed in reflections that occupied her whole soul, she heard his voice without hearing the sense of what he uttered, until his impetuosity recalled her attention.

"No," cried he, detaining her, "you shall not proceed unless you answer me!"

She started as if she had now observed him for the first time, and in great agitation begged he would suffer her to go on.

"Why do you not answer me?" repeated he.

"What am I to answer, Sir?" asked Rosella trembling.

"Is it possible!" exclaimed he: "is this absence of mind real or feigned?"

"You exceedingly distress me," said Rosella, with a countenance that marked the truth of the assertion; "pray let me walk on."

"Well, you shall walk on, and I will renew my enquiry – how long have you, left Oberne?"

"Left him!" repeated she, still more shocked. All the ignominy of the reports in circulation was now openly exposed to her view, and almost sinking with agony, she exclaimed – "What will become of me?"

The gentleman appeared much hurt on seeing the tears gush in torrents from her eyes, and apologized in a hesitating voice for having unintentionally given her pain.

"If what I now feel is simply pain," cried Rosella, acting the heroine without intending it, "what then is torture?"

"I entreat you will compose yourself," said her officious companion, "I am in despair that I stumbled upon so unfortunate a subject."

What he might further have said was interrupted by a loud hallooing.

"Confound those ideots!" resumed he, "they have turned back to seek me." – Then observing the increased alarm of Rosella, who trembled, and turned very pale, "do not be terrified," he added, "they shall not insult you."

The protection of a person who, notwithstanding what had passed, appeared much more rational and humane than the young men he had named, whatever mortification Rosella might feel at being in a situation to receive it with thankfulness, a little re-assured her, when she beheld Mr. Estcourt staggering towards her, with Povey hanging on his arm, vociferating her name, to which they tacked the most absurd epithets of childish endearment, accompanying their witticisms with loud peals of laughter, the violence of which threatened to overset the uncertain equilibrium they contrived to maintain.

"D – mn this fellow," exclaimed Mr. Estcourt, when he perceived in what manner Rosella was attended, "he has jockied[355] us by G—d! Lesley, d'ye call this starting fair?"

"Curse his Brutus,"[356] continued the absurd Povey in the same strain, "we are ousted! He has been doling out his sentiment, I know it, and now he will hoax us to the devil!"

"What say you, my fair one?" resumed Estcourt, seizing the arm of Rosella, who shrunk from him with an expression of terror.

The young man he had called Lesley, had been whispering to Povey, and now interfered, telling the honourable gentleman that he was not half civilized enough to address a milkmaid; and instantly disengaging Rosella from his rude grasp, he walked on with her. But Mr. Estcourt was not sufficiently intoxicated to endure this double insult without resentment, and he almost immediately followed, notwithstanding the pretended efforts of his friend Povey to retain him; for this reptile, though he did not dare enter into a discussion with the more moderate of the three, was far from desiring that the impertinence he had meditated towards Rosella, should in the least fail, and was pleased when the enraged Estcourt, contriving with some difficulty to impede her progress and that of her champion, vehemently demanded a parley, in a tone of defiance that predicted it was not to be an amicable one.

Rosella too much agitated to know what she did, and expecting only indignity at his hands, gave him a sudden push, and darting forward, did not cease running until she saw the cottage before her. She heard her persecutors shouting violently when she began her race, and suspected that she had driven Mr. Estcourt down a steep hill, on the edge of which he was standing; for she recollected that he staggered, and thought she had seen Lesley catch at him. Their not pursuing her gave colouring to the idea, and an instantaneous terror seized her, lest the foolish young man should be injured by the fall, and this new disaster imputed to her.

Chapter VIII

A MYSTERIOUS MANUSCRIPT – MUSICAL TRAVELS

THE first person she encountered on her return home was Maclean, who had not entered the house, but was busily employed in a shed, near the flower-garden, arranging his newly-acquired treasures: his composure and extreme unconcern for her fate, diverted the distress of Rosella in some degree, by exciting her anger; but she chose to confine it to her own bosom, lest Miss Beauclerc, on learning his negligence, should resent it by dismissing him.

She found her whimsical friend seated as usual at her writing-desk, and though she generally journalized herself into a violent fit of enthusiastic heroism, Rosella had never beheld her so extremely elevated: indeed the exploits of the day, as she delineated them, would have been almost sufficient to have made of the most notable housewife, a convert to the airy doctrines of sentiment and romance: no wonder then, that the rehearsal of such pathetic and sublime scenes should almost give Miss Beauclerc the mien of a *Princesse des coulisses*.[357]

She stretched her arms towards Rosella, exclaiming –

"Come to my bosom, child of my fondest affections, sweet soother of thy mother's cares!"

Rosella was at present little disposed to humour what she supposed to be entirely a flight of fancy; yet she advanced and received the salutation of Miss Beauclerc, but without that effervescence of filial adoration the good lady fully expected, according to those charming examples she had so often wept at, of good-natured young creatures falling in a trance of fondness at the feet of these heroic mamas, who determine to make up in caresses and tenderness for the absence of discretion.

"What ails my daughter?" demanded Miss Beauclerc, in a voice of surprise, on observing her tearful eyes and dejected countenance.

"Oh Madam!" said Rosella, her heart bursting with emotion, "your favour has been most fatal to me! Yet I thank you most fervently for your long kindness, and I beseech you to believe, that only one circumstance could extort from me a wish to leave you, and that is, an earnest desire to recover the good opinion of the world."

"Is it possible," exclaimed Miss Beauclerc, "that Rosella should imagine her residence with her hapless mother can draw upon her the censure of this world, cruel as it is, of which she seems in such dread? But I will not reproach you, unhappy child; you are, I too well see, weary of this solitude!"

"If this place were really a solitude," interrupted Rosella, "I might have been happy in it – I could not then have been mortified and shocked by insults which I am not supposed to have a right to complain of, because they appear well-merited."

"What insults do you speak of?" asked the sentimental lady with eager curiosity.

"My walk home," returned Rosella, "was interrupted by Mr. Estcourt, Mr. Povey, and another of Lord Morteyne's guests. I know not who could inform them of it, but they were well apprised of my excursion to Dunkeld, and I experienced from them the most contemptuous and insolent treatment. A young man, a perfect stranger to me, but too well betrayed the extent of those injurious reports in circulation! Dear Miss Beauclerc, let me conjure you to return to Avelines!"

She made no reply; but rising with an air of dignity, rummaged in an immense portable escrutoire, and produced a large bundle of papers, which she put into the hands of Rosella.

"These," said she, raising her eyes to heaven, and producing, by the force of habit, a few tears, "these contain the history of my woes. Rosella, if you should weep over the sad and mysterious destiny of your mother, remember that you have planted a fresh dagger in her heart!"

Miss Beauclerc then walked gravely to the door, and quitted the room, leaving Rosella contemplating in silence the writing on the cover of the packet she held, which consisted of characters, blotted apparently with tears, to this effect –

"*Memoirs of the hapless Mother of Rosella.*"

She knew enough of the etiquette of heroism to be certain, that after such an exit as Miss Beauclerc had just made, it followed of course that she must shut herself up in her chamber for an hour or two, and was vexed that she had provoked the catastrophe before the tea-table had been ordered; – for in spite of her chagrin and anxiety, she was sensible of extreme fatigue; and the heat of the weather, joined to the violent exercise she had taken, had rendered her feverish and thirsty.

She acquiesced however, in her destiny, and having nothing better to do, opened the papers of memoirs which she really believed Miss Beauclerc had been amusing herself with composing, and read the following sentence: –

"When these lines meet the weeping eye of my Rosella, the hand that traces them will no longer be animated with sensation!"

The writing was that of her friend; and the agitated mind of Rosella conceived an apprehension so shocking, that without proceeding any further, the threw down the narrative, and all the letters which served to illustrate and authenticate it, and ran to the apartment of Miss Beauclerc in the utmost horror and alarm. But fortunately her fears were entirely erroneous, for the good lady sat very quietly by her bed-side, absorbed in thought: she had had it in contemplation indeed, to throw herself upon her knees, and rest her face upon the quilt, but by some means the intention was laid aside, and contrary to her design, not renewed, so that upon the intrusion of Rosella, she was shocked at being surprised in so calm a state, when every warring passion should have been contending in her bosom.

Rosella stopped suddenly on beholding her perfectly safe and quite composed; and when she was asked why she had rushed with such eagerness into the room, she stood mute and confused, and retired without an explanation.

The lines which had given her this alarm, had been written by Miss Beauclerc with the rest of the packet, whilst she was confined by indisposition at Warkworth; and as she was extremely intent upon leaving behind her memoirs, according to the established usage, she forgot that it was possible she could recover, or intended, if she survived, to have altered the introductory paragraph – a design that afterwards, in the multiplicity of her adventures, entirely escaped her memory. The circumstance however, confirmed Rosella in her opinion that the whole history was equally fabulous; and instead of continuing to read it with avidity and interest, she returned languid and listless, merely to put up the papers, and then sat unemployed, ruminating upon the gloomy prospects that presented themselves to her imagination. If she succeeded in withdrawing herself from the protection of Miss Beauclerc, without being pursued by reproaches of ingratitude, and if, by retiring from notice, she could silence the calumnies so cruelly affixed to her name, what had she to look forward to, but a hateful residence, dull and unpleasant associates, who merely tolerated her because she paid her quota of expence in their wretched establishment?

She could not hope for any eligible change of situation from marriage: for what man, who was not actuated by the desire of gaining her little property, would be hardy enough (excepting a hero in romance) to entrust to her keeping his honour and his fame, when she had been found unequal to the task of preserving her own without blemish?

These melancholy ideas of the future at length gave way to the embarrassment of the present moment: – she feared the resentment of Mr. Estcourt, and she had read malice in the eye of Povey; but as she had never offended him intentionally at least, she hoped her surmise was an unjust one; yet she could not dismiss it from her imagination, either than the more cruel certainty that she had been addressed as the cast-off mistress of Oberne.

She imagined, from the conversation of the young man called Lesley, that he knew Oberne; and a suspicion crossed her mind that her Irish acquaintance had himself given rise to this injurious report, to excuse to his gay companions the infatuation of having given so much time and attention to Miss Beauclerc, who had rewarded him only by an abrupt dismission, and left him to repent at leisure the expence and ridicule attached to his excursion. Still however, she could not but think that the character of Oberne was too open and ingenuous, to allow him even tacitly to countenance so horrible a falsehood, and at length she acquitted him wholly of the charge, from a revision of his conduct.

It was entirely dark before the confusion of her mind, and the various images that crowded upon it, allowed her to recollect that the lady of the house had not proposed the usual refreshment of the afternoon – a refreshment she had so much required. At present however, she felt too much indisposed to wish for any thing more earnestly than repose; and ringing for Nancy, desired that she would inform

Miss Beauclerc when she descended to supper, that she had a head-ach, and was gone to bed, which she immediately retired to her own chamber to do.

But the agitations of the day were not yet over with poor Rosella. Nancy followed her, and whilst she assisted her to undress, wept bitterly; and after relating the effects of Menie's stupidity and awkwardness, said they were both to be turned away. Rosella promised to intercede for them, and the girl then found spirits to relate disasters in which she had no share.

"I wiped the chairs, and washed the carpet as well as I could," continued Nancy; "but I wonders you didn't see the kindition they was in! But Lorrk, Miss! when you coom'd home, did you go into the moosic-room?"

On receiving a negative, the whole history of Lord Morteyne's visit was amply discussed, as far as it had reached her knowledge through the information of Menie, who told her that Sawney said the Laird of Guairdy was not mad, but the Laird said her mistress was mad; for she had locked him up, and swore never to let him go home to his Leddy, who was fainting away all the time, till he took wi him the young Miss, and called her his sister; and her mistress wanted to give him all her fortune to make him say ay, and had tied him to a chair, and locked the doors but the Laird fought despartly, and tore the house down, and got away.

So absurd a scheme, and such frantic proceedings, would certainly not have gained any credit with Rosella, but for the testimony Nancy spoke of, of the demolished window and frame, and that she was too well assured of the truth of the *Laird*'s assertion, that the mind of her unfortunate friend was actually deranged.

Nancy's portrait of the confusion at Guairdy, in the first moment of alarm, and the universal merriment which succeeded it, almost annihilated her. Well might the unfeeling Mr. Estcourt regard her with contempt and derision, if he imagined she had the remotest knowledge of Miss Beauclerc's plan.

After Nancy had tortured her for near an hour, with every minute circumstance she could think of to swell the tale to yet greater importance, she at length bade her agonized auditor good night: but the wish was of little avail – no sleep could visit those eyelids, which the keenest anguish forbade to close. The stillness of night could not bring repose, and the dawn of another day was still more unwelcome.

It occurred to Rosella that she might learn, through Menie, whether those apprehensions were just, which tormented her by representing Mr. Estcourt falling from the mountain side, mangled by the jutting craigs that threaten the unwary traveller whose foot should stray from the beaten path; and she resolved to be relieved from her fears, or at least to ascertain if they were founded, by the intelligence of the Scotch lassie.

At the usual hour she descended to the breakfast room, with an aspect so sad and so wan, that Miss Beauclerc was terrified, and forgot her memoirs, her displeasure, even her heroism in the shock she received: she embraced Rosella with the utmost fondness, and seeing the tears fall from her heavy eyes, her own accompanied them.

"My dearest child," exclaimed she, "you are ill! I was unkind last night; forgive me, my own Rosella; I was wounded to the soul by observing that you wished to leave me. – Forgive me, and regain your health, regain your sweet vivacity, and I will quit this place if you still desire it."

"Will you promise me, dear Madam," said Rosella eagerly, "to return to Avelines as soon as possible?"

"Oh my daughter!" resumed Miss Beauclerc, relapsing into the strain Rosella condemned, "I cannot wonder that you are earnest to quit the environs of Guairdy! But if it will restore your lost happiness, I will engage to do so."

This unhoped-for concession cheered the invalid; but it could not immediately recall the bloom to her cheeks, or the brilliancy to her eye; and when the breakfast was removed, she returned to her chamber, whither Miss Beauclerc accompanied her to assist in putting her to bed, as the pain in her head still continued very troublesome, and she was conscious of want of rest.

This indisposition however, spared her the knowledge of a circumstance that would have inflicted far greater pangs; for Miss Beauclerc had scarcely left her, and returned to the portico-room, when a very large package was announced from Mr. Craufurd. As she did not expect any piece of furniture, she could not divine what it might be; and having heard that Maclean pronounced it impossible to get it into the house, as the doors were far from being lofty, the lady, with much curiosity, walked into the poultry-yard, where it had been deposited.

Her surprise, on beholding the harp-case of Rosella, was not of long duration, as she almost immediately comprehended that her obliging Selina had had it conveyed to her, and guessed what her intention had been in this impromptu act of friendship.

Had she been at a loss however, the precaution of Mrs. Ellinger had been such, that her project would not have lain dormant; – for Miss Beauclerc espied a letter under the card of address, which she eagerly tore off to seize her prize. After reading the first lines, "I supposed so!" said she aloud. – Then enquiring how the package had arrived from Dunkeld, she learned that it had been placed on the back of a strong pack-horse, supported the whole way in a kind of equipoise, by her own errand-boy, and one of his comrades, because it was urgently directed to be forwarded without delay, and Mr. Craufurd had not been able to get any other conveyance.

The many disasters the poor harp had met, *chemin faisant*,[358] with this mode of carriage, the Scotch lads were very prudently silent about, so that Miss Beauclerc, supposing it to be a very good contrivance, resolved that it should proceed in the same state to Guairdy, which was its goal and destination. She retired to write a note of renunciation to Lord Morteyne in the name of Rosella, and after many attempts to climax the sublime and beautiful, determined to send the following billet: –

"MY LORD,

"I address you not in the supposition that my feeble pen can, by assurances of compassion the most sympathizing, carry balm to your wounded soul!

Heart-struck as no doubt your Lordship is, from the torturing conviction that you have cast from you a lovely rose to bind a thorn to your breast, you claim my pity – that of the gentle angel, whose peace you have so cruelly stabbed, has ever been your's. I mean not however, to reproach, but console you – you have my forgiveness, and may the cup of Lethe[359] be your's!

"The person who delivers this, has in charge a memorial Rosella Montresor can now no longer retain of your former attachment: pardon me if I hint that you ought not to preserve it in your possession, as it has once been in her's, that you may not introduce the bitterness of jealousy into a bosom whose quiet ought now to be your care.

"Excuse, my Lord, the liberty I take in appearing to advise, and believe that I am

"Your Lordship's sincere friend,
"S. BEAUCLERC."

Perfectly satisfied with this heroic performance, she folded, directed, sealed, and delivered it to Maclean, who was to be one of the supporters, and she meant that her errand boy should have been the other; but it was found, on enquiry, that his comrade and himself had returned in great haste to Dunkeld, upon the back of the extra horse, because Nancy had unexpectedly discovered that she had arrived at the end of her wheaten bread, and that unless she dispatched Jamie in a trice, she should not have any to produce at dinner.

There remained however, the little animal that usually peregrinated to the town and back again; and the impatience of Miss Beauclerc to send off her *chef d'œuvre*[360] of a note, would not admit of delay. Maclean therefore, aided by Menie, after many useless efforts, contrived to place the harp and case upon the back of the hobby,[361] who bent under its weight.

Yet Maclean could not undertake the care both of the beast and the burthen without assistance, and Menie was very prompt to offer her's quite on tull Guairdy; and her Lady was so much pleased with her on this occasion, that she was reinstated in her good opinion, and her fault forgotten.

The harp then renewed its travels, the little horse trembling under its uncouth load, Maclean supporting the head of the instrument, and Menie the foot; and thus they jogged on very quietly, looking like the conductors of some curious present from a Sultan to a favoured Sephi.

Sometimes, if the road was too much of an inclined plane, he or she, who had the lower end of the staff, called to the other to lean all their weight upon the contrary side; and Menie, having once squatted herself upon the huge machine she was far from comprehending the use of, with her naked feet dangling in idleness, found it so agreeable to ride, that she proposed to Maclean to follow her example, never once reflecting upon the inability of the poor little animal to carry the whole party. Indeed, as she was no great reasoner, she had no idea that their gravity would descend to the back of the poney, if they sat at the extreme angles of its burthen, but thought it would merely centre in the pauky toad of loomber.[362]

Maclean continued however, to walk, and desired her likewise to descend, but without making her comprehend why it was necessary.

After many hair-breadth escapes, and much exertion of strength, they arrived at the end of their journey, no doubt very much to the satisfaction of the poor little horse, which was no sooner descried from afar, accoutred in to strange a manner, and Maclean and Menie both recognized as the domestics of the mad lady, than the servants at the park ran out to discover what new freak, to use their phrase, was in the wind.

The affair was soon communicated from the *tiers-etat* to the second *etat*, commonly called the second table, and from thence it mounted as rapidly to the *etat majeur*,[363] consisting of my Lord, my Lady, and their associates; and in a few minutes the whole house was disgorged of inhabitants of every class, who eagerly flocked round the deputation, in full hope of some extraordinary event.

Lady Lucy was chagrined, and her brother angry; but curiosity, and a strong inclination to be amused at any rate, would not suffer a single soul to attend to repellant miens and grave faces; and when Lord Morteyne ordered his servants to retire, they merely formed a more spacious ring round those who were not to be commanded to a distance.

Maclean delivered the letter in great form; and whilst the Laird was reading it, his male guests had disincumbered the poney of its load, and finding a key sealed and tied to a cord, they disengaged it in a moment, and opening the case, displayed to the eager eyes of the ladies a most costly and superb harp, a little the worse however, for the tour it had made.

Lady Morteyne now looked grave, and changed colour: she well remembered to have seen the instrument at the house of her Lord, one morning that she called unexpectedly upon Lady Lucy, and she had supposed that it was designed for her; but when days and weeks passed by, and the transfer had not been made, to her at least, she felt disappointed, and rather alarmed that so magnificent a present should have been made to any lady but herself, for she knew it was no longer in the possession of Lady Lucy. But the preparations for her nuptials, which immediately followed, and the certainty of her noble lover's fidelity, soon banished the circumstance from her mind, where it would probably never have been revived, but for this heroic fancy of Mrs. Ellinger.

Lady Lucy perceived the emotion of her fair sister, and in her extreme earnestness to explain without appearing to explain, became so confused, that she added to the latent suspicion she meant to repress.

Delamere, who was present, was wholly at a loss to comprehend the reason of the double embarrassment he observed, and Lord Morteyne, entirely disconcerted by the accusations and obliging compassion of his correspondent, suddenly retired; whilst Mr. Lesley employed his whole attention in endeavouring to disperse the assembly, because he wished to hold a parley with Menie or Maclean without so many auditors. He reminded Captain Povey that poor Estcourt was alone, and turning suddenly to some others of the party, he enquired, with an affectation of earnestness, if the game had been decided, and if he had lost or won his bet. His address succeeded; for Povey thought he was compelled to take the hint; and the rest of the men, who had quitted the billiard-table, having satisfied their curiosity, returned thither in the hope of satisfying their avarice.

Lady Morteyne likewise retired, followed by her sister and her female visiters, some of whom had observed, with keen eyes, all that had passed, and hoped to extract a little gratification from the implied jealousy of the woman whose good fortune they envied.

Chapter IX

A MOONLIGHT WALK PRODUCTIVE OF ALARM IN VULGAR MINDS – A MEETING

WHILST this scene passed at Guairdy, Rosella, happily unconscious of it, was endeavouring to recruit her health and spirits, which had both been much discomposed from anxiety and vexation: she felt the promise Miss Beauclerc had made, very efficacious in soothing the agitation she had experienced, and eagerly anticipated the moment when she might attempt her vindication in the opinion of her ancient friend, Mr. Mordaunt, and solicit the continuance of his friendship, which at a time so critical, might form the future colour of her life.

She found herself unable to sit at the dinner-table, and therefore remained in her chamber the whole day, where Nancy seized the opportunity of Miss Beauclerc's absence, to inform her that Menie had heard at Guairdy, that the Laird's brother had broke his arm and almost killed himself, and that another gentleman had given her half-a-guinea only to tell him how her young lady was – a largesse so provoking to Nancy's envy, that she entreated very earnestly of Miss Montresor if she chose for to send back a civil word or two to the gentleman, she would make her the messenger.

At another moment Rosella might have laughed at her simplicity, but at present it excited her impatience and anger so much, that she dismissed Nancy in tears, which flowed however, as much for her disappointment, as for the fault for which she was reprehended. Her disgrace prevented the disclosure of the harp story, and had therefore the good effect of preserving Rosella from an increase of mortification and distress, which the knowledge of Mr. Estcourt's accident, and the donation of the half-guinea to Menie, had revived.

The following day her head-ach and the slight fever that had accompanied it, left her, and she sat with Miss Beauclerc, who was pleased to see her recovered, but gave no indication of an immediate removal to Dunkeld, as a preliminary step to an English journey; and Rosella was chagrined to observe that no movement or preparation was made for their departure from the cottage.

In the evening Miss Beauclerc proposed that she should walk with her in the grove near the house; but the invitation was declined, as Rosella feared to meet either the Guairdy family, or any of their guests, in the company of her whimsical friend, as she thought it too probable a ridiculous scene might ensue, to the absurdity of which she would become the principal victim.

Miss Beauclerc, whose ideas were at that moment too enlarged and noble to ebulliate without inconvenience under any roof but the high-arched one of heaven, was therefore obliged to march forth by herself, fully resolved to see what wonders patience, midnight, fortune, and a pale moon, would work for her. She was determined to pace the lawn before the house of Lord Morteyne – a ceremony which ought to have been exclusively performed by Rosella; but as her flighty friend despaired of inducing her to undertake it, the thought the next best thing was to perform it by proxy.

In the interim Rosella, who little imagined the employment her timidity had compelled Miss Beauclerc to engage in, waited her return, after the clock had struck ten, in great anxiety; and in another hour her consternation increased so much, that she sent Menie to bring Maclean to her. He had retired to a cottage where he slept for want of room in that of his Lady, and had long been in bed when Menie, with Nancy in her suite, who was too much frightened to be left alone, endeavoured to rouse him from his gentle slumbers by the rural salutation of gravel at his window: but he was dreaming of having found three or four new genus of plants, and of becoming a greater and more celebrated personage than Linnæus[364] himself; and Menie had much difficulty, as no doubt many others have, in awakening a man from a very pleasant delusion.

Rosella, restless from the impression of her fears, and wishing to do something without exactly knowing what, ran to call Nancy, that they might proceed to the grove together and search round the house, from a dread that Miss Beauclerc might have fallen into a fit, and be lying without succour: but she discovered that Nancy had vanished, after having in vain visited every part of the house to find her; and the horror that seized her mind increased, on ascertaining that at such an hour she was alone in the house, which had not one door or window shut throughout it.

At this moment she heard the trampling of horses very near, and ran to the portico, on which side the sound came, to descry the intention of the riders: there she could plainly distinguish the voices of men in conversation, who neither passed on, nor gave any signal that they wished to be discerned by the inhabitants of a dwelling they seemed to survey with an intention the terrors of Rosella could well divine.

With trembling haste she fastened the outward door, and closed the windows, and then flew to the thatched entrance to endeavour to secure that likewise; but as she crept, scarcely breathing, towards a gate that terminated it, and which alone could render it secure from intruders, she found that it had already been invaded, from the found of a step almost as cautious as her own, which appeared to meet her; at the same moment a voice exclaimed, in an under tone –

"Menie, is it you?"

Rosella was now relieved of a part of her terrors; she still trembled however, though she supposed the man, whoever he might be, was merely a lover of the damsel he had mistaken her for: but as he continued to advance, she suddenly retreated into the music-room, where the lights were burning on the supper-table.

For a moment all was quiet; yet Rosella, still under the influence of her panic, stood gazing at the door through which she had entered, and at length fancying she heard a whispering in the passage, suspected that Menie was not unconcerned in the protracted absence of Miss Beauclerc, and that the purpose of the intruder was not love, but rapine: but amidst many wild conjectures, she was far from guessing that the man she had fled from was then intently surveying her through the crevice of the unshut door; and as her eyes were fixed with an expression of dismay upon it, he very naturally concluded he was seen, and entering the room, displayed the figure and features of Mr. Lesley.

Rosella started at an object so unlooked-for, and retreated as he advanced, with a dread so marked, that he thought it necessary to assure her she had nothing to fear, before he attempted to excuse his appearance at so late an hour, in a house he had no title to enter even at a less improper time.

He informed her that, having heard on the preceding day from one of her domestics that she was indisposed, he had taken the liberty of sending to the same person in the morning, in the hope of learning that she was recovered; for though he much wished to convey his apologies to her for the impertinence of his conduct, he did not intend to give her the trouble of attending to them until she was restored to her accustomed health; that he had intimated to the young woman, that he should pass the house in the evening, and would entreat her to transmit a letter from him to her young Lady, but having been detained at Dunkeld to the present hour, he had supposed it too late to execute his intention, until the lights he had seen in the lower apartments had induced him to venture with his billet, which he was far from being certain that the girl would have undertaken to deliver, and that he wished to speak to her himself, rather than entrust the commission to a servant, because the success of it was of importance to his happiness.

Rosella, who well recollected the story of the half-guinea reward, did not believe this exculpation, lame as it was, especially when she compared it with the manner in which the question had been asked of – "Menie, is it you?" and she thought it was much more probable that Menie had consented without scruple to the request of a loan of her good offices; she did not choose however to appear to doubt any part of the assertion, but very heartily wishing her visiter away, stammered something, she scarcely knew what, expressive of her expectation that he would leave the house.

"I will go immediately," returned he; "but may I hope you will do me the honour to admit me to half an hour's conversation to-morrow? If it should be inconvenient to see me here, perhaps you would prefer a walk in the Park –"

"No, Sir," interrupted Rosella indignantly: then suddenly reflecting that she was still unprotected by the vicinity of a single being, her terrors returned, and Mr. Lesley perceiving that she was offended, was beginning a second apology, when a noise at the door of the portico interrupted it, and he hastily left the house, after having conjured her to suffer him to speak to her in the Park the next morning.

He had not been gone two minutes before Nancy rushed into the room, with a very pale aspect, vowing she had met a robber with a pistol and a blunderbuss, and she supposed he had killed her mistress, and stripped the house –

"Oh Lord, Miss!" continued she, "do let me stay till Menie and Maclean come in, if it's on my bare knees do let me stay here, for I'm sure there's more ne he that rooned away, and I shall be murdered all alone by myself, and so will you, if I go away from you!"

Rosella very readily consented, though not just then from the fear of being murdered; and immediately enquired if she had found Miss Beauclerc, or called up Maclean.

Maclean was coming, she said, and he would find her Lady, for he knew every creek and corner round the place; but for her part, she never could abide going out after dark.

The anxiety of Rosella now redoubled; it was now near twelve o'clock, and she even regretted that she had not endeavoured to interest Mr. Lesley in the search she meant to begin, both in person and by her emissaries, as soon as they arrived.

It was almost ten minutes from the entrance of Nancy, before Menie appeared, yet this delay was not for lack of speed, as she had quite lost her breath with running; but Rosella discovered that after her companion and herself had succeeded in making Maclean understand the purport of the embassy, they had returned together, but had been frightened by the shadow of a bush they had encountered in their way, and Nancy springing by it with the elasticity of terror, called to Menie to follow her example, which she so far overcame her prejudices as to do, but in the effort, feeling one of the twigs of the fatal bush strike against her petticoat, she thought the evil spirit had seized her, so she fell down from fear, and lay some time with her eyes closed, till Nancy's step could no longer be heard, and then, rather than be left all alone with the spectre, she started up in desperation, and followed with all her might.[365]

The party was soon rendered complete by the arrival of Maclean; and Rosella had regulated the movements of the campaign she was going to undertake; Maclean singly composing one column of her army, and the two damsels and herself the other, when the return of Miss Beauclerc prevented the execution of their design, and lulled their fears to repose.

The good lady had, according to her intention, walked the lawn before the house at Guairdy, without perceiving a light in any window, or a single being either in the dwelling, or about the dwelling: a circumstance so extraordinary, that she almost thought it the effect of supernatural agency misleading her senses, for, like other heroines, Miss Beauclerc extremely condemned in theory the folly of believing in the spiritual visitations of unembodied gentlefolks, but most devoutly subscribed to the doctrine in private.[366]

Having at length wearied herself almost past endurance with perambulating to and fro, without any indication of an approaching adventure, she thought it would be proper, *selon l'usage*, to explore the burial-place belonging to the mansion,[367] where she had little doubt of being able to penetrate into the most ancient vaults of the deceased Nobles, and making some notable discovery worthy of record; but in this she was equally disappointed – the catacombs at Guairdy were very unhandsomely[368] kept invariably under bolt, padlock, lock and key, besides very heavy mural entrenchments; and the person who was entrusted with the care of the place of worship which contained them, being neither subject to madness nor extreme intoxication, it was impossible to *wander* at midnight in the awful space appropriated to the deceased family of Estcourt, and examine with sublime horror their mouldering skeletons.

Miss Beauclerc, provoked at the unnecessary formality with which these matters were arranged, when she wished, and had such good authority for expecting it would be otherwise, returned home before the "witching time," and thus prevented the search her household were so anxiously and dutifully setting on foot for her.

Maclean was dismissed, the doors and windows of the house secured by the direction of Rosella, and the ladies then sat down to a light supper, which Miss Beauclerc was not averse to, because at that moment she had not any very sublime occupation for her mind.

The next morning was fated to produce a discovery not very agreeable to her, however gratifying it might be to her young companion. They learned that the whole bridal party had abruptly left Guairdy, with the exception of Mr. Estcourt, who could not yet be removed, and a friend who consented to remain in the deserted mansion, to amuse the invalid.

This kind friend Rosella had reason to believe was Mr. Lesley; and she augured nothing good, to herself at least, from this supposed proof of humanity, which vanity and apprehension whispered she might have a considerable share in.

Again Miss Beauclerc invited her to walk in the grove, or the park; but Rosella, recollecting the impertinent request of the young man on the preceding evening, steadily declined it in spite of entreaty or persuasion: an obstinacy that rather offended her friend, who might perhaps have insisted upon her compliance, had she not supposed it improbable that she could encounter any adventure, Mr. Estcourt being confined to the house, and his companion she supposed to be either a dependant chaplain, or a led Captain,[369] who would not presume to stir from his elbow.

Rosella, in her absence, lectured Menie very gravely upon her facility in listening to the requests of the strange gentleman, and Menie protesting that she meant nae hairm, vowed, with a shower of tears, that she wad na mair hearken to ony thing he saud – a resolution Rosella much commended: and she was extremely surprised after having heard it, to see the girl presenting her a letter, after she had retired for the night, which the gentleman had made her tak, she said, though she tauld him hoo angered her young leddy had been; but the gentleman tauld her he wad na do ony thing to anger the young leddy, aunly he tauld her to try gin the young leddy wad tak the lettre, and gin she wad na, there wad be na hairrm, and she maun gie it him back.

"Well then," said Rosella, much vexed, "give it him again; and be assured, Menie, if you speak to me any more of this gentleman, or any other, I will complain of you to your mistress."

Menie sneaked away with the unfortunate letter in her hand, much alarmed at this threat, and mad wi the cunning loon, that had tauld her there was nae hairm, and almost lost her her place.

Rosella, mortified by a pursuit that was far from reflecting honour upon her, counted every moment that passed over her head in a situation so exposed; yet she forbore to press Miss Beauclerc to hasten her removal, since she had learned that of Lord Morteyne, lest it might be supposed that they followed him; and she thought it would be more prudent to remain in the cottage a few days at least, to take from their journey the air of a pursuit.

But the next morning her opinion again varied, when her whimsical friend sent to hasten her appearance at breakfast, with intelligence that a gentleman awaited her coming with impatience. Hope once more revisited the bosom of Rosella, with the idea of the presence of Mr. Mordaunt, and she questioned Menie, who had been sent to her, as to the age and appearance of their guest; but she had not seen him, and Rosella hurrying down stairs, beheld, instead of her old friend, Mr. Oberne, who appeared so well pleased with the reception Miss Beauclerc had given him, that he flew to greet her with all the animation the unchecked energy of his character produced: but Rosella received his salutation coldly, and the vivacity of Oberne vanished; he endeavoured however to rally his spirits, and gratified the vanity of Miss Beauclerc by expressing much admiration of her retreat.

Rosella having recovered from her first surprise, began to revolve the means by which he had discovered it, and did not entirely exculpate her inconsequent friend from having herself given him the information: but this suspicion was discarded, from the conversation that followed.

"This then is the paradise," continued Oberne, "from which such poor devils as myself were to be excluded. You, Madam," addressing the lady of the mansion, "have so much complaisance as merely to exhibit astonishment when I show my recreant face; but Miss Montresor, who, to do her justice, never flattered me much, displays a far greater portion of consternation than welcome."

"Perhaps," said Miss Beauclerc, "she has reason to be dismayed, if she is to conclude that your society will in the future be as injurious to her in its consequences as it has been hitherto."

Rosella shocked at this opening, and fearing that these reports and suspicions, which she could not think of without the utmost confusion, would be discussed in her presence to the individual person who had given rise to them, was hastily quitting the room; but Oberne caught her hand, and entreated that she would listen to him.

"I am to conclude, I fear," cried he, "that what I have now heard is meant as a reproach: and how I am to endeavour to merit forgiveness I know not, since the censure passed upon me is not the result of my own misconduct, but of the detestable impertinence and injustice of others, over whom I have neither influence nor control. But of this Miss Montresor may be assured, that though I could not prevent the insolence by which she suffers, I will at least avenge her."

The confusion and distress of Rosella now gave place to apprehension.

"For heaven's sake, Mr. Oberne," exclaimed she, "do not increase the misery I have suffered, by a rash resentment! – You may pacify your own indignation by pretending to punish my defamers, but you can only do me injury by appearing as my champion!"

"You know then," cried Oberne – but immediately checking himself, he addressed Miss Beauclerc. "Has Lesley," demanded he, "presumed to mention my name to you in a manner to shock your delicacy?"

"Who is Lesley?" returned she: "no person has entered this house but Lord Morteyne."

Oberne, turning hastily to Rosella, saw her cheeks, which a moment before were unusually pale, flush a deep crimson –

"I see how it is," exclaimed he, "but he shall repent his treacherous villainy!"

His eyes sparkled with rage; and Rosella remembering his impetuosity at Dumbarton, now trembled at the idea of the mischiefs that might ensue.

"You terrify me," said she, bursting into tears. "Mr. Oberne, if you are really concerned for the odium you have undesignedly attached to my name, you will not add to my distress by making me a further subject for the censures of the world."

"Rosella," said Miss Beauclerc, "I grieve to observe that the momentary impertinence of a few envious women and idle men, should make such an impression upon your mind: discard your fears, and think only with contempt of the hurtless slanders you ought never to have regarded!"

The lady as she spoke, happening to cast her eye upon the breakfast equipage, recollected that neither Rosella nor herself had taken any thing; and advising her with yet more energy, to rise above the fastidious criticisms of those despicable beings who called themselves the great world, she invited Oberne to a seat on her right hand, and obliging Rosella to occupy another on her left, she drank her tea with infinite composure, and declaimed upon the advantages of a fondness for solitude and retirement.

"For example," added she, "my dear Rosella, spite of the malice of her persecutors, could surely be contented with such a cottage as this, and the society of those she loves!"

"No, Madam," replied Rosella, "not whilst I imagined one single being in the multitude I quitted, could affix to my conduct the slightest stain!"

"I adore your delicacy," cried Oberne eagerly, "and I think it is impossible that injustice can be extended so far as to deprive you for any time of that tribute of that tribute of esteem and veneration so much your due!"

"Pray," said Miss Beauclerc, after a momentary reverie, "who is this Lesley of whom you spoke a few minutes back?"

"He is," replied Oberne, "the brother of Lady Morteyne: you may perhaps remember to have seen him in Edinburgh: I mean," added he hastily, "that we passed him in the Canon-gate,[370] on the morning you permitted me the honour of being your cicerone."

Miss Beauclerc assented; and Rosella now too well recollected that she had likewise seen him, though not in the same place: for, in fact, Mr. Lesley was the young man who had been so unwilling to quit her at the door of the tavern, to which the Edinburgh coachman had unfortunately driven Miss Beauclerc and herself after their excursion to the theatre. She was surprised that the circumstance had never before occurred to her, as she had retained a confused remembrance both of his voice and features, and she no longer felt astonished that he had pursued her as he had done, or that he had thrown out those mortifying hints relating to Oberne: but that he should have the power to relate her Edinburgh adventure to Lord Morteyne's family, and his numerous guests, struck her to the heart; a sickening anguish assailed her, and her countenance gave indication of what passed within.

Oberne saw the conflict, and endeavoured to dissipate the pain he had unwarily occasioned, by every attention he could devise; but as it was easy to discover that his presence was unpleasing to her, he at length withdrew, in a temper of mind very well adapted to execute an intention he had secretly formed, of extirpating the unfortunate Lesley from the face of the earth. And whilst he was marching with hasty strides to Guairdy, Rosella employed the alternate persuasives of tears, representation, and entreaty, to induce Miss Beauclerc to hasten her departure from the cottage.

The good lady might have slighted the representation, and rejected the entreaty; but the tears of Rosella, reinforced by the certainty of retaining Oberne as a dernier resort for any future achievement where an adorer must figure in the scene, determined her compliance, and orders were given to Nancy to pack up with all possible dispatch, as her Lady resolved their removal should take place the next morning.

Nancy had but two hours back acquired an admirer, who appeared to have dropped from the clouds on purpose to console her for the sudden departure of all the fine liveried and unliveried gentlemen she had heard Menie speak of as the satellites of the brilliant constellations at Guairdy; and looking aghast at this command, she stood motionless with grief and disappointment.

"As for Maclean, and that awkward creature I found here," continued Miss Beauclerc, "let them remain in the house; and I will give my agent at Dunkeld instructions concerning them."

"Yes, Madam," said Nancy, courtesying, "and if you would please to think that I could do any good here, I should like vastly to stay too!"

"You! no certainly not!" exclaimed her mistress; "I shall take you with me to London."

"To London! – Oh crimini!"[371] whispered Nancy, "there are plenty of sweethearts to be had there, so I need not grudge to leave one behind."

With a mien entirely altered, she promised, unasked, to pack all night rather than not be ready; and Rosella, who was yet more desirous than herself that her task should be accomplished, volunteered her assistance, after having required directions of Miss Beauclerc concerning the baggage to be taken with them.

Chapter X

A PARTING – A RICH RELATION NON COMPOS[372] – AND A CAREFUL HEIR

ROSELLA had employed herself very diligently about two hours, and Nancy being then obliged to leave her post to attend to the *menage*, her ideas became more disengaged, and she recollected that it would not probably occur to Miss Beauclerc to send to Dunkeld for a carriage. The apprehension of having their journey delayed even a day by such a want of thought, made her hastily quit her self-imposed task, and run down stairs to remind her of it.

Miss Beauclerc was not however in either room; for being too sublimely idle to assist in a bustle, she had taken her usual walk. But as Rosella entered one door of the music-room, Oberne appeared at the other, and she could not avoid the *tête-à-tête* chance had conducted her to.

"Dear Miss Montresor, dearest Rosella," cried he, "how little did I divine the distress you are so cruelly compelled to encounter! I had no idea that the eccentricities I have remarked in Miss Beauclerc were accompanied by occasional derangement, or I would not have quitted you at Luss, but for the purpose of giving your friends information of your unpleasant situation. Need I tell you how sincerely I participate in any uneasiness you endure? Will you not believe that whatever happiness I may have had during the time I spent near you, I repent the blindness which made me slight your more prudent repulse, and overlook the inability of your poor friend to decide how far it was proper to indulge my wish of remaining in your society? Tell me only what I can do to serve you, to whom I may apply among your relations or connexions, to snatch you from a situation which I fear injures your health."

Rosella was silent: she had indeed suspected, and was almost assured of the unhappy circumstance Oberne thus decidedly mentioned; but to have it confirmed so suddenly – to find that Miss Beauclerc's unfortunate state of mind had been so far discussed at the house of Lord Morteyne, where she supposed Oberne had learned the intelligence, as to make it no longer a matter to be doubted, most sensibly shocked her.

"Good God!" exclaimed he, "I seem to approach you only to inflict pain! – I have been too precipitate – you will hate the sight of me, and abhor the sound of my name! But surely you must have observed the misfortune I speak of? I have not been the first to announce it to you?"

"No," replied she; "I have already thought it but too possible: yet I will only thank you for your offers of service, without troubling you to fulfil them, as Miss Beauclerc has herself determined to return to her home; and then," added Rosella, with a sigh, "I shall be conveyed to mine!"

"But you cannot travel to England without any other protection!" said Oberne: "if her dreadful malady should increase whilst you are upon the road, I should tremble for you; the shock of such an event would overwhelm you!"

"I must take my chance," returned Rosella, "for I have no friend in this country to whom I could apply upon an emergency, however pressing; and the best thing I can do, is to quit it as fast as possible. But I must still hope that this event is only temporary; I trust it will go off when Miss Beauclerc is settled in her residence, and no longer harasses herself by moving from place to place: if I had reason to imagine otherwise, I should be still more unhappy than I am at present."

"I will hope so too," said Oberne; "but I must return to the subject of my anxiety – I must repeat that you cannot travel alone with Miss Beauclerc."

"Nancy goes with us!" interrupted she.

"My dear Miss Montresor, of what service would Nancy be to you or her mistress, were any distressing event to take place, of which there is, at least, a probability?"

"I have already told you," replied Rosella, "that it cannot be otherwise; and there is cruelty in placing dangers before my eyes which I have no power to avoid."

Oberne made no answer to this observation; but, musing a moment, suddenly asked her when they began their journey.

"To-morrow morning," returned she.

"So soon! – But I thank you for the information."

"You do not mean, I hope," said Rosella, "to accompany us? Consider, Mr. Oberne –"

"I do consider," interrupted he; "I give far greater consideration to your welfare and interest, than I could ever prevail upon myself to bestow upon my own. I will follow you at a distance, but without giving up the power of assisting you, should you unfortunately require any aid: for I cannot suffer your delicacy to plunge you into difficulties I shudder to think of; nor could I endure the miserable anxiety I should otherwise be a prey to, lest you should sink under the distress I could so well imagine."

"I have no power to prevent you from acting as you please," returned she, "unless you will listen to my entreaties not to endeavour to alter my destiny, whatever it may be: but pardon me, Sir, if I say the trouble you mean to give yourself, though it certainly requires my acknowledgments, cannot, as I am situated, contribute to my interest or my welfare; and as to inconvenience or embarrassment, I regard them much less than the odium I might incur."

"You are resolved," interrupted Oberne, "that my cares shall be disinterested; by forcing me to perceive that they are entirely unacceptable, you are not reduced to the necessity of regarding me more favourably on account of my Quixotism."

"My mind is too much disturbed," said Rosella, "to allow me to excuse my obstinacy, as perhaps I might be able to do: but I cannot adopt another opinion, even though you should think me ungrateful – a charge I should of all others most abhor. Will you," she added, "inform me who gave you so confirmed an idea of the melancholy circumstance that introduced this subject?"

"I heard it from every body at Guairdy, with the accompaniment of such facts, that I could no longer doubt, as I wished to do."

"And was it from Guairdy too," she asked, "that you learned Miss Beauclerc's present residence?"

"It was," replied Oberne: "why do you enquire?"

Rosella blushed whilst she answered in a hesitating accent, that it was of no consequence.

"I understand you," said he; "and I hope you will believe that I have endeavoured to efface an idea that contributed to draw upon you the impertinence I cannot think of with patience."

The entrance of Miss Beauclerc now relieved Rosella from the confusion she suffered from a discussion so unpleasant; and both Oberne and herself examined the countenance of the lady as she accosted them, with an attention they had never before thought of employing; but they could not observe any signs of discomposure either in her features or manner: indeed she was so well pleased to see the assiduities of Oberne, and found them so consoling after the failure of the grand scheme she had been at such an immense expence to accomplish, that his presence gave her an air of placidity that could not be mistaken.

Rosella, regarding the present moment as a lucid interval, was eager to advance their journey before the prospect should be again overclouded, and mentioned the necessity of sending to Dunkeld for a post-chaise. As she suspected, the imagination of her luckless friend had been too much occupied to allow of such a recollection; but Maclean was now dispatched upon the errand.

Miss Beauclerc invited Oberne to dinner; but he declined the intended honour, by saying he was engaged to return to Guairdy: an arrangement that better met the approbation of Rosella, who now retired to pursue the task she had imposed upon herself.

As she was emptying a drawer appropriated to herself, she took up the unread memoirs of her flighty friend, which she had deposited there: she felt a momentary curiosity to examine them; but fearing to encounter painful proofs of the derangement she deplored, they were placed with some things she valued, in a small case which had been assigned to her use. She was surprised Miss Beauclerc had never enquired if she had looked over them; but imagined, what was really the fact, that her poor friend had been so engrossed by the hurry of succeeding events, that she scarcely remembered the confidence she had reposed in her. In the same drawer a memento of her own forgetfulness met her eye, in an envelope addressed to Mr. Delamere, at Newcastle, whither she had first thought of sending the note; but on recollecting that there was a greater probability of his finding it at the Lodge, she altered her purpose, and using the first cover as waste paper, it now assailed her, and brought on the unpleasant remembrance that the value of the note was still due to Mr. Delamere, as he affirmed he had never received his own, and that she had suffered him to leave Guairdy without adjusting the affair.

She was sensible that Miss Beauclerc would not hesitate to relieve her embarrassment, by immediately advancing the money; but she felt an invincible scruple in applying to her for such a sum, now that she suspected she knew not the value of the property she squandered with so profuse a hand. Mr. Ellinger, she was convinced, would never listen to such a demand upon her own small income, as he had always rigidly denied her, from that source, every superfluous expence, and had given her very frequent reprimands when he witnessed any lapse of prudence in the appropriation of the stipend he thought proper to allow her: but the circumstances had never before made any very unpleasant impression upon her mind, because every indulgence that an ample fortune and maternal fondness could shower upon a favoured child, had been her's through the attachment of Miss Beauclerc.

She reflected with anguish how changed her prospects were since six short months! She recollected what a gay, thoughtless, happy creature was then Rosella Montresor, with a reasonable hope before her of being introduced with credit, through the influence of her approved friend, into a world, which to her youthful imagination, then appeared all charming, gay, and desirable.

What now were her views? To endeavour, by retiring within the limits of the sphere to which her orphan state had reduced her, to lose the unfortunate celebrity the eccentric conduct of Miss Beauclerc had procured her; to try, by the aid of reason and prudence, to banish the remembrance of those gay hopes she had once cherished; with a perception naturally distinguishing, and an acute idea of propriety, to live in the centre of affectation, morose tyranny, absurd pretensions, and squabbling ill-humour; and with a mind energetic and reflective, to endure perpetually the prattle of folly, and the scorn of the contemptible.

To this had the romantic fervour of Miss Beauclerc reduced her, by an unsuccessful endeavour to realize some of those pictures her vitiated taste would not allow her natural good sense to analyze.

Yet however Rosella might shrink from such a perspective, she would not suffer her disappointment to ebulliate in reflections injurious to her unhappy friend: her's was a disappointment unmixed with gall, except indeed when the first emotion of keen mortification forced from her lips a half expressed[373] complaint.

She could not rest in the night for the impatience with which she longed to behold the dawn of that day that was to carry her towards the only person, from whose friendly and sensible advice she hoped assistance and comfort; and it appeared at length, without giving her any omen of the fresh distress it was to bring with it.

Oberne called at eight o'clock, and could not withstand the permission of Miss Beauclerc to partake her breakfast; but he had a head-ach, and was otherwise unfit for conversation; and Rosella, who felt concerned at his uncommon depression, tried in vain to relieve it by attentions such as she had never before displayed to him.

The chaise Maclean had ordered, appeared at the door at nine, and at the same moment Mr. Lesley sent, by Nancy, an entreaty to see Miss Montresor for five minutes: but she was little disposed to comply with this request, and before Miss Beauclerc could signify her assent or disapprobation, she returned an answer, importing that she was much engaged, and desired to be excused.

"Perhaps," said Oberne, "he wishes to offer an apology, that may likewise exculpate me from any lurking suspicion of having authorised or countenanced the liberties that have been taken with your name."

"If that is his errand," exclaimed Miss Beauclerc, who panted for a scene of pathetic sublimity, "my dear Rosella, you may as well see him."

"No, Madam," replied she, with a face of earnest entreaty, "I do not wish to hear any thing more of a circumstance so distressing to me, and I must beg to withdraw from Mr. Lesley's apologies, or whatever he may intend to say."

Oberne now left the room, and Rosella saw him advance to the gentleman in waiting, who was receiving the message from Nancy; and after a short conversation, Mr. Lesley walked away.

In another half hour every thing was arranged for their departure: Oberne assisted Miss Beauclerc into the chaise, and when Rosella presented her hand as a parting compliment, he pressed it to his lips with emotion.

"I shall see you I hope," said he, "when your journey is ended; for I too, am bound for London, whither my affairs have called me for some time past, but called in vain whilst you remained in Scotland!"

Rosella blushed, and trying to assume a disengaged air, bade him farewell.

"Farewell, dearest Miss Montresor!" returned he; "when I see you in England, do not treat me as a mere travelling acquaintance, with a cool bow and a mien of surprise, if I should have the presumption to claim the little corner I hope to retain in your memory."

This conversation passed at a small distance from the chaise, by the side of which Nancy stood, with a small escrutoire in one hand, and a dressing-box[374] in the other, both of which were to travel upon her knees; and her Lady sat, *en attendant*, very patiently, without an idea of hurrying affairs, as she well knew that it was extremely natural for a lover to make the most of a parting moment.

"Miss Beauclerc waits!" said Rosella, endeavouring to advance.

"Once more then adieu!" returned Oberne; "and recollect, if any distress, foreseen or unforeseen, should assail you, that I shall not be far behind throughout your journey: I understand that you return by the way of Carlisle?"

"I really do not know," interrupted she, "what Miss Beauclerc has decided upon: but we are detaining her."

He then suffered her to walk to the chaise, and placed her in it; then with his usual good humour, shook hands with Nancy, who made a low courtesy for the condescension, and turning to discover if Menie observed it, saw her blubbering at the door of the cottage: so she gave her a nod of protection, and bestowing another of equally marked superiority upon Maclean, who was thinking more of his greenhouse than of her, she was at length so obliging, after these ceremonials were performed, to follow the ladies into the chaise, and away they trotted for Dunkeld.

Miss Beauclerc could not thus leave her charming retreat, where she expected to have encountered so different a set of adventures, without great mortification: and sublime as were usually her ideas, she could not reflect either upon the trouble or expence it had cost her unavailingly, without feeling disconcerted. She no longer experienced so pressing an inclination to communicate every hour's employment to the gentle Selina, who on her side, was almost annihilated at the discomfiture of a plan which she had for a year back most exceedingly valued herself upon having wholly invented and arranged, and which was to have terminated, after a number of sweet interesting scenes and situations, in the marriage of Lord Morteyne and Rosella – a charming discovery, full of sentiment, of the birth of the lovely bride, and a most elegant episode to portray the immutable friendship of Mrs. Ellinger, who intended to possess the enthusiastic affection of all the parties after having done so much to deserve it.

By the direction of Miss Beauclerc, the driver took her to the house of Mr. Craufurd, who was yet to learn her sudden departure for the South.

As the chaise drew up to the door, Rosella and herself had once again the honour of beholding Mrs. Tadpole, the virago housekeeper at Guairdy: she was at that moment taking her leave of Mrs. Craufurd, who wore her very best holiday countenance, and followed her guest, as usual, into the street with smiles and courtesies.

"I assure you, Madam," said Mrs. Tadpole, turning back with a sudden motion, whilst her voice, cleaving the air like a canon-ball, distinctly met the ears of Rosella and her friend, "I assure you, Ma'am, as my account, which I have made bold to trouble you with, isn't at all *exdaggered*, it's a thing I never do."

"No, Ma'am, no;" returned Mrs. Craufurd, courtseying anew; "very true, Ma'am, very true."

The housekeeper returning these civilities with the most gracious air she could contrive to throw over her countenance for the occasion, and not thinking any more assurances requisite, stumped off, and Mrs. Craufurd had then leisure to bestow a look of enquiry upon her new guests – a look that brought her information equally unexpected and unwelcome. She darted several glances of scorn into the chaise, and retreating into her house very suddenly, shut the street door with a vehemence that made them start.

"The woman is surely possessed," exclaimed Miss Beauclerc, "to treat us in this manner!"

Rosella could very well guess what her conduct implied, and extremely doubtful if they should be able to procure admittance to the master of the castellum,[375] endeavoured to persuade her friend to retire to an hotel, and send for him there to settle her Caledonian[376] affairs. But Miss Beauclerc suspecting part of the truth, from the remnant of conversation she had overheard, was too much irritated to attend to counsels of such moderation, and having directed the driver to let her out, she rung Maister Craufurd's bell with a most sovereign peal of authority.

The gude mon's office looked into the street, and he was drawn to one of the windows by the unusual violence of the application; but instead of flying to the door with innumerable low bows and fawning salutations, he called apparently to some other person in the room with him, who came likewise to the window, and gazed earnestly at Miss Beauclerc, turning afterwards a scrutinizing regard upon Rosella.

The stranger was an elderly man, with a cold and forbidding aspect; he wore a black wig, which covered half his forehead, and was tied in a very long queue[377] behind; his whole appearance indicating little commerce with the world, much formality, and more selfishness.

Miss Beauclerc, who had hitherto been disgusted with the servility of her Scotch agent, was the more provoked at the remarkable change in his deportment, and the gross insolence of his wife; with the mien of a person highly indignant, she turned from the impertinent observation of the sable-peruked[378] gentleman, and though she now heard Mr. Craufurd bustling up the passage to open the door, she renewed the thundering summons to be let in.

"Hoo d'ye do, Madam?" said the Scotchman, in a very conciliating tone; "this pleasure is sae unexpected that I cad na believe my ees when I saw ye at the door."

"I likewise," replied Miss Beauclerc, "have been doubting my eyes; and I should imagine Mrs. Craufurd has no reason to value herself upon the excellence of her sight, or surely after surveying me very attentively, she would not have turned her back so rudely upon me!"

"Ah, she has a cauld in her heed," replied Mr. Craufurd, "and there wull gather a mist before her ees fra teme to teme, and then she canna disteenguish friends fra faes!"

The lady was rather mollified by this explanation, and having desired Rosella to wait her return without quitting the chaise, she followed her conductor, who bowed vara low, into his wife's drawing-room, where he left her for a few moments to give the good woman a lecture, and confer with the stranger, whom on his return he introduced to Miss Beauclerc as his friend, but without mentioning any name.

In a quarter of an hour Mr. Craufurd appeared at the chaise-door, and brought a message from Miss Beauclerc, to the great relief of Rosella, directing her to proceed with Nancy and the baggage to the inn they had visited on their first entrance into Dunkeld, and that she would follow as soon as possible.

Rosella obeyed this intimation, so much delighted with escaping any further civil or uncivil ill-humour from Mrs. Craufurd, that she did not reflect much upon the omission of not inviting her into the house: having waited very patiently till three o'clock, without hearing any tidings of her friend, as both Nancy and herself had risen early, they began to think their dinner would not be unwelcome; and Rosella ventured to send to Mr. Craufurd's, to learn if Miss Beauclerc was coming. A reply was returned, that the lady was endeavouring to dispose of her cottage, and would be engaged in the discussion of the business till the evening.

Rosella therefore ordered her solitary meal, but had lost much of her inclination to do honour to it, from the prospect of having her journey thus perpetually delayed: she was vexed too to find herself at a house of public entertainment, accompanied only by the simple Nancy; and to fly from unpleasant reflections, opened one of the packages for a book, and read till seven. From this hour, every step in the passage leading to the apartment where she sat, every sound on the stairs, seemed to announce the return of her inconsiderate friend; but time after time her imagination deceived her, and at ten o'clock her uneasiness increased so much, that she desired Nancy to accompany her, and determined to walk to the house of Mr. Craufurd, to learn the reason of an absence protracted so considerably beyond her expectation. But as she was preparing for the purpose, she saw the Scotchman enter the room, attended by the singular looking personage she had observed at his office window. A tremor seized her –

"Where is Miss Beauclerc?" exclaimed she.

"The gude leddy is parfectly safe," replied Mr. Craufurd, who prevented his companion from answering the enquiry; "and she desires that her luggage may be sent to mie hoose, that she may examine it for some papers relating to the cottage, which is noo beckume the praperty of this gentleman."

A secret dread stole over the heart of Rosella at this strange request, her cheeks turned pale, and she supported herself only with the assistance of Nancy, who thought the black-perriwigged man must either be a bailiff or a thief, and began to tremble for her own superb wardrobe, which she had been so long toiling to gather together.

After a pause, in which Rosella had found it impossible to break silence, she at length said with a trembling voice –

"I expected the return of Miss Beauclerc long before this hour; will you inform me what detains her?"

"Some vara parteeklar business," replied Mr. Craufurd.

She paused again; at length –

"Miss Beauclerc," resumed she, "has so often entreated me to take peculiar care, in her absence, of two or three packages belonging to her, that I think she cannot intend I should send all her baggage; – but if I should be mistaken, she will perhaps write me a note; and the distance is so small between this place and Mr. Craufurd's house, that the delay cannot be of much consequence."

"Look you, Madam," said the stranger, throwing out his hand to enforce his elocution, "I shall cut this matter short; you have seen enough of my poor cousin, God help her, to know that she is as mad as a March hare, so you cannot wonder that I, who am her heir in reason, and her heir at law, should begin to look about me, and see after my property, before the rest of it is scattered round the kingdom at the rate it has been. I am not surprised that you should be unwilling to give up your hold, and a fine milch-cow[379] she has been to you by all accounts. But this you must take with you, Miss – all the fine things you have got of her, after her insanity is notoriously proved, the law will obligate you to refund; and as to her property here, you had better give it up without more ado."

The latter part of this harangue was not heard by Rosella, who had lost all sensation in the arms of Nancy, thrown round her as much in terror for herself as any other motive.

"Oh Lord, what hae you done with my poor mistress?" cried the girl, in an agony; "and here too, as I hope for marcy in the day of judgment, you have killed poor Miss Montresor!"

This exclamation produced no effect either upon the man of law, or the heir at law, who began culling from the pile of baggage that was placed in a corner of the room, every trunk, band-box, dressing-box, and escrutoire, portable and unwieldy, that bore the name or initials of Miss Beauclerc: and that they might not by mistake leave any thing behind them to which the cousin could in any way pretend a claim, they carried off two packages without inscription, one of which appertained exclusively to Rosella: then, perfectly satisfied with their uninterrupted success, they disappeared, leaving Nancy in a consternation so great, that she would not venture to scream out for assistance till she thought them far away, lest they should return and murder her.

able IV

Chapter I

A SCOT COZENED[380] – A JOURNEY RENEWED

THE people of the house, alarmed by her cries, ran into the room, and when they heard her tale, believed that her mistress had been robbed; without recollecting that one of the supposed collectors was Mr. Craufurd, whom they well knew, and whom they had seen both at his entrance and his departure. However, the most pressing investigation at this moment appeared to be, that of learning if the poor terrified young lady was in a state to profit by their assistance; and for a long time the point was a very doubtful one. Yet at length Rosella revived – revived to lament, with bitter agony, the heavy cloud now obscuring the destiny of her first, her last, and only friend; for thus, in the deep affliction and anguish of the instant, the repeatedly apostrophized Miss Beauclerc.

The crowd in her apartment attracting her attention, after the more immediate ebullition of grief was past, she entreated to be left with Nancy, and her request was complied with.

Rosella would then have flown to the house of the unfeeling Mr. Craufurd, in the hope of beholding her ill-fated friend once more, and taking, perhaps, a last farewell of her; but Nancy represented so forcibly the lateness of the hour, and the little probability of their being permitted to see her poor dear mistress, that she unwillingly deferred the effort: and Nancy added, that to be sure her Lady must for certain be tied down in her bed, with a strait-waistcoat on, such as old John Mills used to wear, or the devil himself could not have made her stay with such people.

This afflicting image drew a torrent of tears from the eyes of Rosella, who sobbed on the bosom of her inconsiderate attendant, now her only support; – but she could not be persuaded to undress herself, nor even to lie down upon a bed; and the watchful reflections of the long and comfortless night often threw her into a fresh agony, at the moment Nancy fancied she was sinking to repose.

The sun had scarcely risen, when she resolved to ask admittance into the house where she imagined Miss Beauclerc was still forcibly detained. What her sensations must have been – what they must yet be, at a treatment so unlooked-for, and offensive to a spirit for some time past unused to control of any kind, she shuddered to think of! and the loss of her own fame, and her present forlorn situation, weighed light in the balance, against so deadly a blight as the double loss of reason and of liberty.

The people around Rosella, softened by her distress, of which they now comprehended the real cause, treated her with civility and attention, in spite of the whisperings of suspicion, that their interest would not be much forwarded by the complaisance to which they were irresistibly impelled; and they suffered her to quit the house unmolested, though they were not certain she would leave in it a sufficient security for the payment of their demand; as Nancy, in her terror and agitation, had affected that the poor dear creature was stripped of every thing she had in the world.

Rosella soon found herself at Mr. Craufurd's door, and remembering the cruel artifice which had induced her the day before to leave it without being accompanied by Miss Beauclerc, she felt her indignation almost equal to her affliction. She had not, in the perturbation of her mind, reflected upon the unusual earliness of the hour, and waited a considerable time before Nancy could persuade her that no person in the house was stirring.

When she became at length convinced of this, she preferred beguiling her impatience, by enjoying, as far as her anxious solicitude would permit her, the freshness of the morning breeze, rather than return to the inn; and when her watch informed her that it was nearly eight, she could no longer restrain it, but hastily flew back to Mr. Craufurd's, and again with trembling eagerness applied for admission.

A servant opened the door, and to her request to see his master or his Lady, replied that he believed his maister was not at home, and his maistress was engaged; but he wad luk.

"Tell them," said Rosella, following him a few steps into the passage, "that I entreat they will see me; for I have very important –"

The fellow, without attending to her, entered a sitting-room, and spoke in a low tone; she soon discovered to whom, for the voice of the lady of the mansion was very distinctly heard to reply –

"She can't have any thing to say to me – I know nothing of her; and I desire you will not trouble your master, for he can do her no service, so it's in vain for her to think of it: if she wants charity, let her go to her gentlemen for charity. – But do you keep an eye upon her, Andrew, for she's pretty revengeful. – It's not a week ago, Sir," addressing herself apparently to another person in the room, "that the girl gave an appointment to three young fellows of fashion, and then set them together by the ears, and while they were scuffling, she watched her opportunity, and pushed one of them, whom she did not like, down a craig, where he was almost killed."

"What you have uttered, Madam," said Rosella, advancing into the room, "is a cruel and malicious misrepresentation; by whom it has been thus related to you I can, I believe, guess. But I merely came here to enquire for my poor friend, and to conjure Mr. Craufurd to permit me to see her once more."

"Andrew," exclaimed the indignant gentlewoman, "why did you suffer her –"

"Your servant is not to blame," interrupted Rosella; "will you, Madam, attend to my entreaty?"

She made some contemptuous reply, which Rosella heard not; for the gentleman whom she had not yet regarded, hastily advanced, and taking her hand, in a manner that displayed respect and solicitude –"

"I have," said he, "already preferred the same request, and this woman asserts that Miss Beauclerc has been removed."

"Mr. Oberne!" exclaimed Rosella, on recognizing the person she had hitherto overlooked: "Oh for Heaven's sake! prevail with her to let me see my unhappy friend, though but for a moment!"

"No, Miss," retorted Mrs. Craufurd, "the *woman*, as he is pleased to call me, will not stir a peg for your vagaries; and since you have forced yourself in, where you have no business, I shall tell you that you have no occasion to wait here upon your pretences. – And, Miss, the next time I go out, remember I shall take care you don't take my place at the head of my table, and eat your fill at my cost! *Woman* truly!"

"Devil then," cried Oberne, in a rage, "since that suits you better!"

Rosella shrunk from such a contention, and giving up the hope of again beholding Miss Beauclerc, was retiring in great dejection, when the servant came in, and informed his Lady that her presence was required immediately in the office.

She flounced away, muttering something wholly unintelligible; and Oberne, detaining Rosella, asked the man in which apartment the lady was, who came the day before in a post-chaise with Miss Montresor?

"The leddy was ta'en awa last neight by her kinsmon and twa keepers," was the reply.

"Keepers!" repeated Rosella, turning pale, "what does he mean?"

"Attendants," replied Oberne hastily, to prevent any other explanation.

Mrs. Craufurd now returned to them with a countenance wholly changed; and condescending to beg pardon for the little heat she had been in, proceeded, unasked, to confirm the assertion of Andrew, by assuring Rosella that her poor, dear, insane friend had been hurried away from her house by her violent cousin, who would not hear a word from her or Mr. Craufurd, though they both begged she might be indulged in her repeated entreaty to be suffered to send her purse to Miss Montresor, whom she called her beloved and unfortunate girl.

A loud hem from an adjoining room, which was only separated by a slight partition, stopped the loquacity of the lady; and she was endeavouring to retract the information she had too unguardedly let fall, when Oberne, irritated by her duplicity and previous insolence, interrupted her.

"Well, Madam," said he, "I will now only repeat to you, that if I find Miss Montresor has been robbed of any part of her wardrobe, or that she misses any one of her trinkets, or any of her property, Mr. Craufurd shall be responsible for her loss."

"Robbed!" reiterated Mrs. Craufurd, "good Lord! I hope not – I hope the poor dear young lady has not been robbed – that would be sad indeed after such a misfortune! But, Sir – good Sir, how can you make poor dear Mr. Craufurd responsible?"

"He perfectly understands by what means he is so," replied Oberne, "since his accomplice has disappeared."

"His accomplice! my good gentleman, Mr. Bristock is no accomplice of his."

"Then he is an accomplice of Mr. Bristock, and that is the same thing. – My dear Miss Montresor, you appear indisposed; let me conduct you from this place."

Rosella accompanied him in silence, and he attended her to the inn, where Nancy, who had been rejoiced to see him, related all their grievances; and repeated what she had told to every body who would listen to her, that the depredators had carried off Miss Montresor's trunk, with her earrings, and necklace, and bracelets, and every thing.

"I have already heard of this villainy," replied Oberne, with indignation; "and that scoundrel Craufurd shall repent his atrocity!"

Rosella, who had not been sensible of the transaction, looked over the remnant of their baggage, and found that Nancy's intelligence was true. The trunk was a small one, and had contained all her ornaments, the gifts of her unhappy friend, some of which were rather valuable. She recollected too, that she had put a five pound note into the box, which, except three or four guineas, was all the money she possessed; and for the first time her affliction would permit her to think solely of herself: she found that it would be utterly impossible to reach London without an immediate application to her guardian, nor did she imagine it would prevent her from the too probable mortification of being pennyless in a place where she was a stranger.

Oberne saw her distress, and attempted to relieve it by assuring her he would oblige Mr. Craufurd to refund the value of the things taken from her, unless Mr. Bristock restored them.

But this was little consolation to Rosella, who was anxious to begin her long journey, and dreaded, with tenacious delicacy, the offer of a pecuniary loan on his part, should he discover the slenderness of her finances. Nancy too, whatever consolation she might derive from her attentions and attachment at such a moment, she felt to be an additional source of inquietude; for she was sensible she ought to be sent back to her aunt, lest Mr. Ellinger should refuse to consider her but as the servant of Miss Beauclerc, and refuse to pay the wages due to her, or be responsible for the expences of her journey. But she could not follow the dictates of her judgment and her probity, even by stripping herself of her last guinea; and overcome by the most cruel and harassing reflections, she threw herself on a chair, and wept bitterly.

Oberne was much affected, and reiterated his offers of service.

"Command me, dearest Rosella," said he; "will you commission me to hasten to England with the information of your disaster? – shall I send my servant with a letter to any of your friends? – will you permit me to write in your name, as you are too much indisposed to undertake it? – Tell me what I shall do."

"Nothing, nothing," replied she, her heart dying within her; "do not trouble yourself any further about me. – Pray leave me!"

"I will," said Oberne, "after I have seen you eat some breakfast. You will be seriously ill, sitting up, as I understand you did, all night, and now taking no nourishment."

"Lord! who told you that?" exclaimed Nancy, suddenly imagining he dealt a little in witchcraft.

"I called here," returned he, "a few minutes after you had left the house this morning, and having heard a detail of the misfortune of poor Miss Beauclerc, I was directed to Mr. Craufurd, as a person with whom she had transacted some business, and who, was accessary to her removal."

The breakfast Oberne had ordered as he entered the house, was now introduced, and Rosella drank some tea, that she might not appear obstinate and ungrateful for his solicitude; and finding herself rather revived from the effort, she sat down to inform Mr. Ellinger of her uncomfortable and improper situation. But in describing its extreme desolation, she suddenly recollected the aunt of Miss Beauclerc, who resided at Dumfries, and that the letters of her poor friend had more than once mentioned her as the solace of the whole family at Avelines.

This fortunate remembrance cheered her with a hope of immediate relief from her difficulties; and, as Oberne had not yet left the room, she made him acquainted with the consoling idea she had just started. He was pleased to see her look less despondingly, and entreating that she would not fail to take some rest in the course of the morning he left her to pursue his threatened plan respecting Mr. Craufurd.

Rosella then began a second letter to her guardian, in which she repeated the picture of her situation; but told him she should proceed to Dumfries with Miss Beauclerc's woman, who had been left with her, where she hoped to obtain the protection of her poor friend's aunt, Mrs. Delaval, and where she trusted he would send her his instructions and a proper remittance. She would also have given an account of herself to Mr. Mordaunt; but his silence to her application, after the ill success of Mr. Ellinger's recall, which she construed into anger or contempt, withheld her.

She had neglected to order any dinner, either for herself or Nancy; but Oberne had been more considerate, and as she was deliberating whether she ought not immediately to begin her journey to Dumfries, that her expences might not exceed her purse, Nancy entered to present the compliments of Mr. Oberne, and to know if she was at leisure to receive him.

Rosella thought she was not acting prudently in assenting to this request, but his anxiety for her welfare, his earnestness to relieve her from embarrassment, and the perpetual proofs of respect and esteem he was so eager to give, chased every idea of reserve and coldness, and she consented to see him.

He appeared with a countenance of alacrity, and told her he had obtained from Mr. Craufurd a promise to restore, or cause to be restored, the valuables, of which she had been so brutally deprived; and, as a pledge of the fulfilment of this engagement, he entreated Miss Montresor would draw upon him for any sum the might have immediate occasion for.

Rosella thanked Oberne for his friendly interference; but she could not prevail upon herself to profit by the forced acknowledgment of the prudent Scot, which indeed she much doubted the truth of, and thought it a delicate expedient of Oberne to supply her with the money requisite for travelling. And thus far she was right, that could he not have succeeded with Mr. Craufurd, he had intended to have made use of the same pretext to have advanced her a sum sufficient to have taken her to London.

But this gude gentleman, with all his coolness and artifice, had suffered himself to be hurried, into an imprudence by the still more wily Mr. Bristock, who had presented him a retaining fee of fifty pounds, to ensure his assistance in securing the person of his insane relation; and the terrified agent, trembling lest he should be too suddenly called upon for the vouchers of the expenditure of those sums he had received for the purchase of the land, and the building and fitting up of the cottage, which indeed were of a scandalous magnitude, was willing to secure the friendship of the heir, who had brought with him attestations of his identity, and a copy of his deceased uncle's will. So he walked very passively in the path chalked out for him, because he had heard from Guairdy of the positive derangement of his client; and though his cautious soul shrunk from the violence he was a party in, he still supposed himself safe on every side; as he thought Rosella a destitute orphan, for such Mr. Bristock had represented her, without a single friend or protector, save the one now torn from her.

He had accompanied Miss Beauclerc and her unfeeling cousin the first stage on their way to the south; because the gentleman was desirous of the credit of Mr. Craufurd's presence, that no effort of the prisoner to obtain assistance against the outrage she sustained, should retard his journey, or hazard the failure of his scheme. But, contrary to the expectation of both, when she found resistance vain, she wept bitterly, but at length submitted to her destiny; and her inexorable heir then dismissed Maister Craufurd, telling him at parting, to arrange all his papers relative to the cursed business of the Scotch purchase, and transmit them, per next post, to his address; and that he supposed the fifty pounds he had left in his hands, would be sufficient to answer every demand for housekeeping, &c. the few days Miss Beauclerc had remained at her new residence. – And thus, according to the old adage, the Devonshire hero "maun ha got oop betimes, and ha ta'en auld scratch for his counsellor."[381]

When Oberne, the Hon. Mr. Oberne, was announced to him, demanding intelligence of Miss Beauclerc, and appearing, as a previous note had expressed, in behalf of her young friend, Mr. Craufurd, just returned from his excursion in a state of infinite discomfiture, put off the task of receiving him to his weef; and she, good woman, labouring very hard to prove the poor ladies to be the very worst of their species, was finishing the portrait of Rosella, when Andrew peeped into the room, and said she was in the passage.

Such a *mal-à-propos* interruption very naturally excited her choler; and her husband, roused from a deep reverie by the exertion of her lungs, sent for her out to drop the hasty hint that so expeditiously altered her tone.

It was not very surprising that Rosella, ignorant of all this, should suspect Oberne of endeavouring to force a friendly imposition upon her; and he protested in vain against the injustice of her supposition, till he offered to bring Mr. Craufurd to her, to ascertain the truth of what he affirmed. – Rosella still, however, declined the expedient, telling him she had little doubt of obtaining shelter and protection of Mrs. Delaval.

"To Dumfries then I will accompany you," replied Oberne; "and, should your expectations deceive you, you will at least have a resource in this man's proposition to repair some part of his villainy."

Rosella would have opposed his attendance when she solicited the countenance of Miss Beauclerc's aunt; for some of the old lady's letters expressed a strong horror of the wiles, the perfidies, and ingratitude of men, against whom she hoped her niece, being a staid young woman, would preserve herself by prayer, faith, and fasting.

But Rosella had a double disinclination to overcome in dismissing Oberne – his and her own: for he had in truth made himself an interest in her heart by a series of good offices and attentions, the source of which could not have been mistaken, even had not his parting information at Luss opened her eyes to his sentiments. He had told her that their acquaintance had begun in a moment of frolic on his side; and he had told her too, that it had been prolonged from a far different motive. The conduct of Miss Beauclerc in encouraging his assiduities, had flattered his vanity – that of Rosella in repressing them had excited his esteem; and of those reports so injurious to her, he better than any one knew the cruel fallacy, and they called at once for his indignation and tenderest compassion. But these very reports, false as they were, operated as a motive to check any further avowal of his particular admiration, and his declining fortune was a still more powerful one.

The vague fluctuation of his views, however, could not influence his conduct; and the affection he resolved to overcome, became each day more progressive. When he parted from Rosella at Luss, he might have succeeded in forgetting that he had experienced a more than common interest for her, had not a letter from Mr. Lesley, which reached him at Edinburgh, whither he had returned, aroused his resentment and solicitude in her behalf. It plainly expressed all that the writer had insinuated to Rosella herself, and demanded to know if their separation were lasting or temporary.

Oberne flew to answer the enquiry in person, and vindicate the character of the young woman, whose prudent reserve and modesty of deportment had so ill-merited the conclusions drawn from the indiscretions of her older friend.

At Guairdy, he learned, with the calamity that was supposed to have overtaken Miss Beauclerc, the extravagance of that conduct which, in some measure, justified the surmises of his friend Lesley; and when the offender professed his concern at having added to the distress of mind Rosella endured, the interview had become an amicable one, and he had voluntarily proposed to ride over to the cottage, to exculpate Oberne from having in the least authorized his impertinence – a step he privately assured Mr. Estcourt, solely dictated by the curiosity he experienced to learn upon what terms the lady and her champion were.

Rosella was so anxious to proceed to Dumfries, that she could scarcely be persuaded to remain where she was, until the dinner Oberne had ordered made its appearance; and then she found it so much more sumptuous than she, from inclination and necessity, would have thought of, that her appetite was entirely lost in the secret calculation she made of the too probable amount of the expence.

When the tedious meal was ended, from which of course Oberne was not to be excluded, she withdrew to her chamber, and sent Nancy to ask for the bill, which she was apprehensive he would think it necessary to discharge. But he had already done so; and Rosella, much chagrined, re-entered the eating-room to expostulate with him on the subject.

"Do you think," said Oberne, gravely, "I would choose to live at your expence?"

"Suffer me to retort that question," replied she; "indeed you have much hurt me by acting thus."

"I am sorry for it," returned he; "but I must persist in my error, if an error it is, unless you will compromise the dispute by accepting the proposition of Mr. Craufurd."

"I had a small note in the box," said Rosella, "and if he will send another of equal value, until I hear from my guardian, I will venture to take it, without fearing to incur my own censure, or that of others."

"No," cried Oberne, "I will not allow this. You shall not receive less than will enable you to await a reply to your letter, or carry you to London; you may then adopt which plan you find the most eligible."

She would further have objected, but he would not hear her, and went immediately to Mr. Craufurd to settle the affair to his own satisfaction. That gude gentleman, extremely provoked at the turn things had taken, and fearful of being reduced to an unpleasant dilemma, thought proper to express a great abhorrence of the inhumanity of Mr. Bristock.

"Of his villainy, say rather," said Oberne indignantly; "the insanity of his cousin has involved a most amiable young lady in distress and embarrassment, to say nothing further; and this atrocious monster adds to both, by robbing her, with unheard-of brutality, of all her cash and valuables!"

"Cash!" repeated Maister Craufurd, looking aghast, "did the box which the young leddy misses, contain cash? – But perhaps she had it in charge for Miss Booclar?"

"No," exclaimed Oberne, in a loud key, "she had it in charge from her guardian for her own use."

"Aah!" ejaculated the accomplice, dropping his jaw in surprise and consternation, "her guardian! has the young leddy a guardian? – My gude Sir, Maister Brastick maun repant what he has done! – The mon has left in my honds a fifty poond nawte, withoot expressing hoo it is to be applied and I do nae ken hoo it can be applied better than in relieving the young leddy fra her deeficulties."

"Certainly it cannot," replied Oberne, "and you had better place it in her *honds*, and wash your own of so dark a business."

Mr. Craufurd said he should be reeght glad to do so, and followed his impetuous conductor to the inn, where Rosella awaited him, who heard, with extreme surprise, that he meant to offer her fifty pounds for her immediate use. But she would not by any means consent to receive it, either as a loan or an indemnification; and after much argument and persuasion, could only be induced to accept half the sum, which she acknowledged in writing to have received of Mr. Craufurd.

After this affair was settled, Rosella, eager to quit a place rendered hateful to her, and still more earnest to shelter herself under the protection of Mrs. Delaval, reimbursed Oberne for her share of the expences at the inn, and was assisted by him into the chaise she had ordered. She bade him farewell, and he returned it; but not with an air as if he meant the adieu should be a long one, and she felt anxious to know if he followed her.

"Perhaps," thought she, "he now thinks he has done enough to serve me; yet he said he would accompany me to Dumfries. It is better however that he should not – Mrs. Delaval would perhaps be rendered suspicious by such a circumstance, were she to discover it, and refuse to receive me."

Yet, though she internally settled that the absence of Oberne would be quite desirable, she was not displeased to catch a glimpse of his figure when she rested for the night. – She rose early the next morning, intending to travel the first stage before breakfast; but Nancy was very unwilling to move without her's, and Rosella, who fancied Oberne was interested in the circumstance, altered her intention.

Nor was she mistaken: he applied for the honour of attending her *déjeuné*;[382] and, as he had had the delicacy to forbear even announcing his vicinity to her the evening before, she would not disappoint his expectation.

With much complacency on either side, they parted; and the conduct Oberne had adopted, appeared to be now tacitly agreed to by Rosella, who saw him no more until the following morning, when he again breakfasted with her at Bield; and she would not let this opportunity pass, the only one perhaps she might have, without acknowledging, with much gratitude, the services he bad rendered her.

"We will not talk in this style," interrupted he; "besides, I intend to learn how your expectations are realized by the old damsel at Dumfries, before I finally quit you."

"But I fear," said Rosella, "your appearance alone will frustrate my hopes with Mrs. Delaval."

"I shall not appear," he replied, "at least in your suite; but you must allow me to concert with Nancy some method of discovering your destination. If the good old lady should receive you kindly, I will immediately bid you farewell; if she should not, you will then, perhaps, take my advice in what manner you may most safely pursue your journey; and I will give you the best a moderate capacity, and more than moderate good wishes, can suggest."

Chapter II

DOMESTIC SUBORDINATION – AND DOMESTIC DISCIPLINE

IT was little more than one o'clock when she entered Dumfries; and having recollected that Mrs. Delaval lived with a family, named Macdoual, she soon discovered their abode, and drove immediately to the house. It was a neat little mansion, and every thing about it seemed, as Nancy said, in such grand apple-pie order, that it gave Rosella a strong idea of that extreme attention to cleanliness and form, which usually excludes ease and rest.

The arrival of a carriage at the door, occasioned the same kind of motion in this prim box, which a child gives to the contents of its rattle: half-a-dozen girls, "bull-faced, and freckled fair,"[383] ran from window to window, and their voices, dancing in alt[384] upon a Scotch cadence, were distinctly heard by Rosella. A lassie, whose claithing was in the modern style, that is, so scanty that "if it had been less, 'twould have been none at all,"[385] peeped fra the hedge at sic a bonny sight, and little thought that Nancy, the gayer leddy of the twa, was like herself a servant.

At length another personage appeared, a good-humoured looking, little, fat woman, who scudded towards the visiters in a manner that demonstrated an unseen battle between constitutional civility and constitutional corns; and Rosella returning her salutation, said, she understood that Mrs. Delaval resided at the house, and begged to know if she might be permitted to speak to her.

"Ah poor dear creature!" returned the lady, who was Mrs. Macdoual herself, "she has fell down, and bruised her leg sadly, so she can't come out to see you; but would you choose to walk in and see her; for she sets in her great chair, dear good soul, all day long without stirring, only to go to bed, and eat her dinner."

Rosella, who could not perfectly understand, by this harangue, the rank and situation of the speaker, descended from the chaise; and choosing to err by too much condescension rather than by too little, entreated the lady to excuse the liberty she took in conveying by her a letter to Mrs. Delaval. – A letter she had previously written, that she might not have to perform the awkward ceremony of announcing herself and her business.

"I hope no bad news!" returned the little dame, endeavouring to look solemn. "You come from England, Miss? aye, so do I – we're countrywomen; – but you look too pretty and good-natured to bring us bad news. Perhaps," she continued, with an air of importance, "the niece is dead, as well as the rest of 'em."

"No, Madam," said Rosella, with a saddened mien; "but I must refer Mrs. Delaval to the letter."

"Mither," hallooed a rude voice, "why dinna ye cume in, when Maistress Deelaval screams oot for ye to gang tul her?"

"I'm coming, Jannie, I'm coming," cried the mother, running off in a great hurry.

Rosella then remained standing by the side of the chaise, gazed at only by distant spectators, who seemed afraid of venturing too near; and she augured little good from such a scene.

In the interim, a very tall, bony, rigid-looking man advanced to her, and demanded her business; adding, in a tone as solemn as if he meant to pursue the whole Church Catechism –

"And what's yere nem?"

Rosella informed him, fully expecting that "Wha gave ye that nem?" would certainly follow; and the question would have been more appropriate than she had any idea of; but the Fates decreed that the next interrogation should be –

"Wha d'ye luk for here?"

"I wait in the hope of seeing Mrs. Delaval," replied she; "I have sent in a letter for her perusal."

"Fra whom?" said the questioner.

Rosella was embarrassed; – a letter from herself, brought in person, was so like the expedient of a beggar of alms, that she hesitated; and the tall personage, with a severe frown, quitted her abruptly, and walked into the house, exhibiting, as he turned his back, a pair of tremendous shoulder-bones, that marked, by their alternate elevation, every step he took.

"What next?" thought Rosella, very much tired of such a procedure.

"I do suppose," exclaimed Nancy, "them pipple means us to stay here till nightfall."

After another five minutes, the little fat gentlewoman again hobbled out.

"Well, my dear," cried she, "so you have been in a fine sea of troubles? – So Mr. Macdoual has been speaking to you; – but never mind him – we never care for his cross looks, not we – if we can but get shut of[386] him half an hour now and then, then we enjoy ourselves."

"Does Mrs. Delaval choose to see me?" asked Rosella.

"Yes, my dear, yes; I came to tell you to come in."

So saying, the talkative dame again tacked about,[387] followed by the guest thus curiously invited. Rosella expected to be reminded to wipe the dust from her shoes, and perform all these ceremonies required in a mansion kept like a cabinet; what then must have been her surprise to find the inside of the house correspond so little with the exterior, as to make her imagine she had missed the entrance, and plunged by mistake into the piggery!

The children of the family thrust their ragged heads through some half-opened doors to survey her more narrowly, whilst the gown of her conductress hooked, by means of a rent already made in it, to a lock which was hanging by one screw, belonging to the room where Mrs. Delaval was sitting, and completed a fracture from one end of the skirt to the other.

"Here, my dear love," said the airy housewife, scarcely regarding the disaster, "here is the young lady!"

And she then introduced Rosella to a woman apparently between fifty and sixty, of a middle height, slender, neat, and old-fashioned, with pellucid grey eyes, and cheeks like the shrivelled but rosy skin of a blighted peach; her nose exhibited a blue purple tint, that marked health undermined, and her whole aspect spoke little of the character to which it belonged, except that a trait of resignation and benevolence sometimes insinuated itself amidst the vacuum.

"You are Miss Montresor," said she, after a pause, in which Rosella was painfully agitated.

"Yes, Madam."

Mrs. Delaval attempted to rise to receive her.

"My dear love, pray sit still," cried her little bustling friend, "I have told Miss Mounteresa that you have fallen upon an accident – there, there, sit ye down!"

The good lady obeyed without a comment, and Rosella finding that she was expected immediately to furnish topics for a conversation, having been pulled into a ricketty chair by the mistress of the mansion, began to enlarge upon the information her letter had slightly touched upon.

"My poor niece!" exclaimed Mrs. Delaval, and the tears started into her eyes; those of Rosella fell upon her cheeks.

"Come, come, my dear creature," said the fat personage, whom Rosella had now discovered to be Mrs. Macdoual, "you must not vex yourself; consider your poor health. There, do not now," turning to the guest, "say any more; – this love will fret herself into a fever if you do."

Rosella waited to hear this admonition approved by Mrs. Delaval; but she sat very quietly expecting another topic to be started, and Rosella then ventured to entreat her protection and countenance until she received instructions from her guardian for her return to England.

Mrs. Delaval appeared disconcerted by this request, and her friend seemed equally uneasy and undecided what reply to make. They looked several times at each other before Mrs. Delaval could frame an answer that would neither encourage the petitioner to hope an acquiescence with her demand, nor yet exhibit a semblance of inhumanity, very far from her heart.

"Why, my dear – I can't say," hesitated the good lady, "I can – very readily – for here poor Mrs. Macdoual has a house quite full. God knows, there is hardly room for me, only she won't turn me out, now I'm in a strange country."

There was such an appearance of simplicity in her countenance whilst she made this explanation, and Rosella had so often heard that the whole interest of her fortune, which was nearly twenty thousand pounds, was almost entirely swallowed up by this family, that she could not feel angry at an imbecility which had no mixture of selfish hypocrisy in it.

"Will you allow me to say, Madam," said she, "that as I cannot have the good fortune of receiving shelter under the same roof with you, it would very much serve me, if I might be permitted the sanction of your name and character, in seeking accommodation in any house in the neighbourhood, where a vicinity to you and Mrs. Macdoual's family would ensure me attention and respect."

The consternation of the two ladies was increased by this proposition; and Rosella began to despair of obtaining any civility or favour from Mrs. Delaval, who muttered that she was sorry she could not always do what she wished.

"God knows," continued she, in rather a louder key, "I am as economical as I can be; – you see, my dear, I wear a coloured linen gown and a stuff petticoat, to save washing, and yet, somehow, I can scarcely make both ends meet. And poor Mrs. Macdoual here, she denies herself every thing; so I am obliged to get a hamper of wine now and then – that is an extravagance certainly; but, poor thing, I can't see her drop for want of a little nourishment; – and then the poor children, they must go to school to be a little like others when they go out in the world, though their father thinks it is not necessary, and God knows they are wild enough now, as it is! – But it is so cruel to see children pine for a little education, and not get it, somehow. – And then, as poor dear Mrs. Macdoual says, men are so ignorant of what is wanted in the kitchen, and what must be had of household linen and clothes, and extras, that it grieves one to think a friend should be distressed."

"Ah, God help me!" exclaimed the lady of the house, "I don't know where I should have been now, if I had not had a dear good friend; Mr. Macdoual is so harsh; and indeed, my dear Miss, that is partly the reason we cannot have you here. – I hope you won't think me unkind –"

"Pray, Madam," interrupted Rosella, "do not imagine such a request is necessary; but I believe Mrs. Delaval mistakes my meaning. – I have a supply of money for lodging and accommodation; I merely entreat to be recommended to a family of credit and respectability, and to be allowed to say that my character and connections are not unknown to you."

"Ay surely, surely," cried Mrs. Macdoual, with a tone of alacrity; "yes, my dear young lady, I will do that – we will do that, my dear. – But, poor thing, you have come a long way in grief and trouble – you shall have a glass of my poor love's wine."

"Excuse me, Madam," said Rosella.

"No I shan't excuse you; it's all ready at hand."

She then opened a small closet, and took from it a bottle and glasses, which she filled with wine; and Rosella, at the earnest persuasion of Mrs. Delaval, accepted one of them: but she had scarcely raised it to her lips, before it was snatched from her by the lady of the mansion, and every thing again huddled into the closet with a haste and trepidation that spilt the wine, and broke some glasses.

Rosella was not long suffered to wonder what this strange pantomime could mean; for the voice of Mr. Macdoual, who was thundering anathemas, and horse-whipping one of his girls, betrayed the secret.

The countenance of poor Mrs. Delaval expressed pain, mortification, and displeasure; and her yet more simple friend stopped her ears very carefully, and begged to be informed when Maggy had done screaming, for to hear the poor thing, and not be able to help her, made her quiver like an aspin-leaf.

Another of the daughters now burst into the room, to say that Janet and Isabel had taken the horses from the post-chaise whilst the driver was asleep, and had rode them to water; and one of the beasts had trod upon his harness, and tumbled down, and Janet's nose was bleeding; and the other was trotting into the deep pool, and Isabel called out, but nobody came to stop him.

"Confound you all!" said the mother, raising her voice to a passionate pitch; for when the informer had run in, she let fall her hands from her head, to hear the mischief that she knew was coming – "Confound you all! this is the way you serve me. You'll all get your limbs broke, and then who is to set them, and nurse you? – And there," continued she, crying, "your father will murder those two girls, he will! – Oh Lord, that I should live to see this day!"

Mrs. Delaval now endeavoured to relieve her inquietude, by saying she would go and speak to Mr. Macdoual; and calling the girl to her, she tried, with her assistance, to limp across the room; but it was with so much difficulty that she could advance in any way, that Rosella, unasked, flew to support her.

"Thank you, my dear," said the sufferer, who had not been much accustomed to spontaneous kindness, "I will not lean too hard."

"Yes but ye do," said the imp on the other side of her, "I fal drap doon gin ye dunna haud yere hond."

"Go then," replied Mrs. Delaval, with considerable resentment, "go in your father's way, and get your deserts; and then call out to me to make him *haud* his *hond*, as you did yesterday."

"Noo I wunna then," said the girl pouting.

"You are always keeping your mother in hot water," resumed the good lady; "such a set of idle, good-for-nothing girls was never seen! you worry her poor heart to breaking amongst you – you do!"

"Ah, God help me!" exclaimed the mother, in a piteous tone.

"Mither scailded me yestreen,"[388] cried the daughter, "for randing my claiths – and noo she's brak her ain goon!"

"Hold your tongue, you pert slut," retorted the matron, slapping her face.

The young lady immediately set up a roar, that saved Mrs. Delaval any further effort, by bringing the father into the room, with the dreaded whip flourishing in his right hand; but on beholding Rosella supporting his lame inmate with kind solicitude, that hand for once forgot its office, and he gave her several ferocious glances, which Mrs. Delaval could not fail to observe.

"This young gentlewoman," said she, "comes from my poor niece, who has lost her senses, and is going to be put into a mad house, I suppose."

"Aw! and wha's the next a-kin?" demanded the Scotchman.

"Why I am the nearest relation," returned Mrs. Delaval, "and should like to see that justice is done her."

"Justice!" repeated Macdoual, "aw – but wha speirs[389] aboot the property?"

"We will talk of that another time," said Mrs. Delaval; "Miss Montresor wants a lodging and board till her guardian sends somebody to take her to England."

"Aw – wal, Mess, and what d'ye luk for at Dumfries?"

"She looks for nothing but civility," said Mrs. Macdoual, eagerly.

"Haud yere toongue," returned the husband, in a voice of thunder.

An insult offered to her little fat friend generally aroused some indignation in the bosom of Mrs. Delaval, and with a look of commiseration, she begged the silenced gentlewoman to call Mally.

When Mally made her appearance, she gave orders, in a very firm tone, to shew the young lady to Jamie Campbell's, and tell his wife to give her their best room, and wait upon her, and go to market for her whenever the young lady chose.

Rosella, extremely delighted to escape the torture of living in such a *menage* as that of Macdoual, took a respectful leave of Mrs. Delaval, and accompanied Mally, telling the post-boy to follow her, who had with some trouble rescued his horses from the Miss Macdouals.

Nancy had been walking about to stretch her legs, and now joined her young Lady; who, thus attended, proceeded to take possession of the best room at Jamie Campbell's. His house, unlike that of his neighbour, promised nothing on the outside, but had "that within which passeth shew:"[390] it was neat, quiet, and well-arranged, and Jamie's wife received her unexpected guest, not without some little bustle, but without disorder.

The best room was much approved of by Rosella, for it was clean, light, and airy, and overlooked a fine tract of country terminated by the Solway Firth.[391] She discharged the chaise with real satisfaction; and Nancy having placed in her apartment what Mr. Bristock had condescended to leave of her baggage, she no longer felt a wanderer upon the surface of the globe, but contemplated the little space appropriated to her use, and much applauded herself for thinking of appealing to the protection of Mrs. Delaval.

Nancy was far from being so well pleased: she reprobated every delay that retarded her approach to London, that most charming of emporiums for sweethearts and fine clothes; and expressed her sorrow that Mr. Oberne, that sweet-tempered gentleman, had not presided over the journey, because then it would have been performed something like the matter.

Mrs. Campbell entered into her office almost immediately, by preparing dinner for her fair inmate; and as Rosella saw no one in the house but her, she began to hope that Jamie was absent from the place: for the specimen of internal government she had witnessed at Macdoual's, had very much disgusted her against matrimonial aristocracy. But she was mistaken; in the evening the husband returned from a manufactory he superintended, and Rosella found no inconvenience from it, as he sat at his door very peaceably, whilst his wife exerted herself to make every thing look comfortable, and rubbed each piece of furniture to a double brightness, in honour of their new guest.

Chapter III

CREDULITY, AS IN TIME IMMEMORIAL, AN EASY CONQUEST FOR ARTIFICE AND HYPOCRISY

THE next morning Rosella walked to Macdoual's, to enquire if Mrs. Delaval were in better health, and to say that a letter for herself would most probably be there in a day or two, which she entreated the family would either take in for her, or send to Jamie Campbell's.

Fortunately the master of the house was from home, but, in his absence, he had left a spy upon the proceedings of his wife and her friend, in the person of his eldest daughter, who much resembled him; and this young lady was to be circumvented before Mrs. Macdoual could venture to indulge her poor love with a few minutes' conversation with Rosella – a thing the good lady much wished for, but scarcely dared to propose.

After a feint of sending the visiter away, Miss Janet was easily amused, whilst Rosella was smuggled into the chamber Mr. Macdoual condescended to allow his inmate, in return for the income of her fortune, of which, from her own account, he had almost the sole use.

The reception she received was kind, and almost tender: poor Mrs. Delaval could now speak without the interruption of her officious friend, who was fully employed in keeping her precious daughter Janet at bay.

She desired Rosella to tell her every thing she could think of concerning her sister and her niece, and the good lady wept much at the death of the first, and the strange fancies of her poor Sophy, who had always, she said, been a good girl, only a little whimsical.

"And now," added she, "I know how to value a sweet-tempered child; for here – God help us! the bairns are like young dragons! – and their father – In short, my dear, only don't let it go any further, if it was not for my good friend Mrs. Macdoual, who has been like a sister to me, I should have returned to England long ago."

"Ah Madam!" said Rosella, "how delighted would Miss Beauclerc have been to have made you happy! – Indeed she was very amiable –"

"Don't cry, my dear," interrupted Mrs. Delaval, though her own tears dropped equally fast; "I see you are a good-natured girl, and I am sure you was very obliging to me yesterday. – God knows, I have not been used to kindness much since I left England, except from my poor friend; and she is almost killed herself by those termagants and their father. I have been thinking all night – only Mr. Macdoual is so stern and passionate, that he will half kill his wife, poor thing, if I go – but I have been thinking, my dear, that I should like to die in England; – and I should like too, to see if any thing could be done to bring poor Sophy to her senses again. I perceive you are grateful for her kindness to you – I love to see young people grateful – and indeed she had a great affection for you; for she never wrote me a letter without saying what a sweet, pretty, good-tempered child you was; and I find that it is all true enough. – Mr. Macdoual is so violent! – but I should like," repeated she, in an emphatic accent, "to see England and poor Sophy once again!"

From the further conversation of Mrs. Delaval, Rosella discovered that she was actually only detained in the family, by a fear of the consequences her quitting it would produce upon the stormy passions of the tyrant husband, whose youth had been spent in practising the same servility he now imposed on others. When first Mrs. Delaval took notice of his wife, whom she had a few years before slightly known as a humble companion to a lady she had visited, every effort to gain her countenance and favour, which art and interest could dictate, he employed himself, and infused into the docile and less designing mind of Mrs. Macdoual.

The heart of Miss Delaval, wounded by recent disappointment, turned to the consolatory proofs of attachment and gratitude these people so eagerly pressed upon her; and at length she withdrew from her more gay and indifferent associates, to enjoy the snug fire-side of good Mrs. Macdoual, who was always so proud and so pleased to see her there. This distinguished visiter was, however, sometimes allured from them by a fondness for the delights of the card-table; and Macdoual, when he returned home from the duties of a small place he had in a public office, hearing her sometimes recounting with animation the history of the rubbers she had won, and the pools Fortune had snatched from her in defiance of skill, purchased a green-cloth to cover his Pembroke table upon occasion, and wrangled with a waiter of a tavern for half-a-dozen second or third-hand packs of cards; and then gave his wife her lesson, who had spent many a long evening with her first patroness, an old woman, in winning a few shillings at picquet for pocket-money.

The plan had all the success Macdoual could desire: picquet became the order of the day with Miss Delaval (for she was not yet of an age to assume a matronly title), and she was constantly seen walking towards the lodgings of her favourite, exactly at five o'clock every afternoon, to drink the tea she usually purchased herself, and to have her game at picquet with her good friend.

When the crafty Macdoual thought the empire he had gained by means of his wife, thoroughly established, he suddenly avowed a design of returning to his ain coontra, and enjoying the fortune he had realized – in his own imagination; for in fact his only fortune, at that moment, was the harvest he hoped to reap from his designs. If Miss Delaval hesitated to accompany her poor dear friend Mrs. Macdoual, he intended to make himself and her an additional merit in the eyes of his dupe, by sacrificing a plan they both seemed to be fond of, to her inclination to retain them near her. But the good lady did not put them to so much trouble; for she left her sister and her little niece, for whom she had a great affection, and attended the favoured family to Dumfries.

But lo! Maister Macdoual had scarcely passed the Solway Firth, when submission and suavity gave way to an affectation of equality, and a passion for dictating; and the poor slave, his wife, was compelled to purchase half an hour of good humour by repeated loans from her friend, who, weak as her understanding was, soon comprehended that if the tyrant threatened to murder the noisy bairns, or refused money for the wife's clothes or the children's food, she might set every thing right again by advancing the sum required; nor did she ever suffer herself to deliberate when poor dear Mrs. Macdoual lamented, wrung her hands, and asserted that she was the most unhappy woman in the world, which she constantly did, in the same manner that a child will practise upon the weak affection by which it can obtain all it wants.

But a mortification awaited Mrs. Delaval she had little foreseen. The master of the house in his ain coontra, was a very rigid disciple of his ain coontra kirk,[392] and would not suffer cards, those devilish vanities, to appear in his premises. – Mrs. Delaval however submitted, bitter as was the pill; for she considered that she was in a strange land, nor would she have ventured to travel so long a journey, even to reach London again, without the protection of more than one attendant, for the world.

But she had no attendant now, whose services she could have commanded for twenty miles; for Macdoual had quarrelled with her footman, and she had discharged him at Carlisle. She had likewise parted with her own maid, because poor Mrs. Macdoual cried, and told her that her husband could not abide any but Scotch servants in his house.

Rosella, in the course of a conversation which lasted more than two hours, learned every part of this history that Mrs. Delaval could inform her of, and felt her indignation, as well as her compassion, aroused by the half-uttered complaints of the good old lady, who repeated, when her tale was ended, that if Mr. Macdoual would but hear reason, she would accompany Miss Montresor to London.

"You seem so obliging and good-natured," added she, "that I dare say you would be so kind as to take care of me; and then poor Sophy's maid might wait upon me, and I would reward her when I received my half year's interest. But unfortunately I could not undertake the journey at present; for Mr. Macdoual wanted last week to make a purchase a little way out of the town, and I could not refuse to lend him my running cash,[393] and indeed a little sum besides that I had contrived to save, notwithstanding all the drawbacks upon my income; – because the affair was so advantageous to him, and he talked too of settling the estate upon poor dear Mrs. Macdoual, if he could but get the money to buy it."

"How much do you think, Madam," said Rosella eagerly, "would take you, Nancy, and myself to London?"

"Why, my dear child," returned the good lady, "I cannot absolutely say, travelling is so expensive. – I remember when I came here, it cost me – I almost forget – let me see, we travelled in post-chaises as far as Northampton, and then William paid every thing, and Mr. Macdoual says he cheated me of near ten pounds; – how it was I can't tell, for he gave in his accounts to Mr. Macdoual; and after that I was persuaded to get into a Diligence;[394] but then what with one extra expence, and what with another, it cost me more money than I had any idea of."

"I should hope, Madam," said Rosella, "that if you would condescend to return in a stage, twenty-five pounds would take us all there, and that sum I can command. If you will honour me so far as to make use of it in this way, you will really confer an obligation upon me; – indeed the money is not mine – it is more properly Miss Beauclerc's."

"Ah, my dear," replied Mrs. Delaval, "I am afraid by my journey hither, that double what you mention would still leave us on the road. But Jamie Campbell can very likely tell you that; and you need not mention my name, you know, when you ask him. However we will hope the best; for indeed I long to see old England once more. And, my dear child, I have near five pounds by me, which I could not offer you before poor Mrs. Macdoual, because she did not know I had it; for I can't refuse her if she asks me, and last year I left myself without money to pay for my washing, and little odd things, to preserve a little peace; so I resolved, as I don't love to be in debt to poor creatures that want it, to keep a small sum that I would not break in upon but for necessary uses. – I think, my dear," resumed the good lady, after a momentary pause – "what is your Christian name?"

"Rosella, Madam."

"Aye, I recollect Sophy called you Rosella in her letters. You put me in mind of Sophy; she was a pretty girl, but you are still prettier; – I would not tell you so if you was a vain hussy – but I am sure you are not vain."

"I hope not, Madam," returned Rosella, "and as I much wish for the good opinion of my friends, I hope I shall never become any thing they disapprove."

"Aye now, that is talking like a sensible young woman. – My dear, I wanted to tell you yesterday, only there was such a turmoil in the house – there always is, I think! – I wanted to tell you, that as you have lost a friend in poor Sophy, without any fault of your own, you shall find another in me. I am not apt to take likings to young folks – indeed Janet, and Isabel, and the rest of them have sickened me of young girls; but whether it was that you put me in mind of Sophy yesterday when you offered me your arm, or how it was I can't tell, but I have been thinking almost all night that I will be your friend."

Rosella burst into tears, and kissed the hand Mrs. Delaval held out to her, but could not articulate a syllable. The good lady pressed her in her arms, and repeated –

"Poor Sophy! I little thought, when I left her in England, I should ever hear such a sad account! – I am afraid she grieved about the inconstancy of some lover – Ah my dear child, guard your heart from the wiles of men – they are deceitful, ungrateful creatures!"

This hint brought Oberne to the recollection of Rosella, and she feared, if his attendance upon her should reach the knowledge of Mrs. Delaval, she might lose the kind *protectrice* her better fortune had so opportunely afforded her; and the heightened colour in her cheeks proclaimed that the admonition was not premature.

"Well, well," resumed the good lady, "I shall say no more now, for I am sure you are a prudent girl by your coming here to me. And so, my dear, you will consult Jamie Campbell, and let me know what he says; for I am impatient to hear if, with what you so kindly offer to lend me, and my own little mite put to it, we can get to London in any way. I am quite bent upon going with you; for I think when the winter comes on, and it's bitterly cold here, if I stay I shall catch a fixed rheumatism in my poor lame leg, and be helpless perhaps all my life afterwards."

"I fear it will be very inconvenient to you to travel just now, Madam," said Rosella, who had not till that moment thought of the circumstance.

"I shall not mind that," replied Mrs. Delaval, hastily, "I shall not mind that. I shall not die happy unless I see poor Sophy once again; and perhaps, poor thing, she will know me, and be glad to see me. – But, child, I had almost forgot to tell you that you must write what Jamie Campbell says about the costs of the journey, and give the letter with your own hands to Mally, for I can trust her – she is a faithful creature! – I am afraid to say any thing to Mrs. Macdoual; it is so natural for her to tell her husband all she knows, though the never means amiss. – When I get to England, I shall not want a supply of money; for there is a person in London whom I formerly served, who will lend me, I am sure, a reasonable sum to go on with till my dividend becomes due, which will be in less than two months; so I am easy in that respect. And when I get back to London, I shall not forget, as I said before, your kindness to me here in a strange country, where I am not well looked upon, I believe, because I was bred up differently as to religion; but I will not be brow-beat out of my own way of worship, or go to the kirks[395] here, when in my own mind I like the Church of England best, because that is the worship I have been used to. Mr. Macdoual to be sure may think –"

The lady of the house now ran into the room, saying –

"Come, my poor love, you have had a long confab; it is time for Miss Mounteresa to be gone, for my husband will be back shortly – and there's Janet as prying as an imp; I'm sure she suspects mischief, and then her tongue will be at work to tell her father all – so there will be a fine hubbub by and by amongst us!"

"I will go immediately," said Rosella, starting up to prevent the catastrophe thus foretold.

"God bless you, my dear!" ejaculated Mrs. Delaval; "I am sorry to let you go without your dinner – it seems so hard to send you away without asking you to dine."

"Oh if that be all," interrupted Mrs. Macdoual, "I can send her some porridge and a neck-of-mutton bone, without its being at all missed."

"No, I beg you will not," said Rosella; "the good woman where I lodge will get me something, for she is very obliging."

"Tell her, my dear," said Mrs. Delaval, who appeared much hurt, "that I take it very kind of her; but as to our Scotch porridge, I am sure you would not like it – it was a long time before I could get used to it myself."

Rosella secretly hoped that she would not much longer be compelled to receive ill-treatment and meagre fare; and when, after being hustled out of the house, she returned to her lodgings, she could not prevail with herself to eat her own dinner, from the idea that would obtrude of Mrs. Delaval's unpalatable and embittered meal.

She forgot not to consult with Jamie, as she had been enjoined to do, who told her that he could not at all guess at the expence of such a long journey, but he promised to enquire. When he withdrew, Nancy, who had been present at the conference, said that talking of money put her in mind that she had four guineas belonging to her poor Lady, who had given her five to keep house only the day before they left the cottage, and she had paid away twenty shillings and six-pence for things had there, which Menie and Maclean could prove.

Rosella was much pleased to hear this, but desired her to keep the money and her account till they arrived in London, and then she would have it settled. Not daring, however, to trust her with Mrs. Delaval's secret, she did not inform her that she hoped to procure her a good place immediately; and Nancy was not at all anxious upon the subject, as she thought that in London good places would infallibly shower down so fast, that she would have nothing to do but to choose the most agreeable.

In the afternoon, Rosella condescended to admit her as a companion in her promenade, which would have been a most melancholy one, had not the promised friendship of Mrs. Delaval intervened to calm her inquietudes on her own account; and her proposed journey to England inspired her with a lively hope that Miss Beauclerc, by her interference, might be rescued from the power of her hateful and selfish cousin.

She followed the course of the river towards the Solway Firth, and was much amused by the busy scene it presented; but the *delassement*[396] of the mind will not always prevent the feet from tiring, and she was at length turning back, when the well-known figure of Oberne appeared at a little distance hastening to meet her. Rosella was immediately seized with a little trepidation that rather retarded her progress, and when they met, he enquired if she had not too much fatigued herself.

Nancy recollecting what she would have expected of another, had she been Miss Montresor, followed the golden rule, and very cleverly dropped behind them to admire a fishing-boat that was passing.

"How does the fair Rosella like the old aunt?" continued Oberne; "but, if I understand right, you are not in the house with her. Has she disappointed your expectations?"

"On the contrary," returned she, "Mrs. Delaval is much more favourably disposed towards me than I had any reason to hope. But the family she is with –"

"Are devils!" interrupted Oberne. – "You find I have learned something since I entered Dumfries."

"But this circumstance," resumed Rosella, "is so far in my favour, that I believe it will be one motive to induce the poor lady to accompany me to London."

"If so," said he with abrupt gravity, "my guardianship ends here."

"But not my gratitude," replied Rosella.

Oberne turned away, and hummed part of an air.

"This scene is pleasing," exclaimed he, suddenly interrupting the melody.

"I think it is," replied Rosella rather embarrassed, and the conversation dropped.

"When do you quit Dumfries?" enquired he, after an interval of several minutes.

"I really do not know: my motions will now depend upon the convenience of Mrs. Delaval, unless my guardian sends to me in the interim; and then, perhaps, she will have the goodness to make my prescribed time her's."

"I think I have heard you mention the name of your guardian?"

"Very likely," said Rosella innocently; "it is Ellinger."

"And he generally resides in London?"

"Always."

"In the city perhaps. – I suppose he is some monied man who takes great care of your fortune."

"And very little of my person, I believe you think," returned she; "and if that is the case, his cares are not very extensive, for my fortune is a very slender one."

"Be thankful," cried Oberne, "that you are not cursed with great riches. I am much obliged to *my* destiny likewise, that such a stumbling-block to virtue never lay in my way."[397]

Rosella smiled, and another pause ensued.

"Did you say," demanded Oberne suddenly, "that your guardian, Mr. Ellinger, lived in the city?"

"He lives in Chancery-lane," replied she.

"Horrid place!" exclaimed Oberne; "I never hear the name of it but I instantly recollect an atrocious old villain, who received ten guineas for scribbling over an infernal parchment so carelessly that it more than half ruined me; and when I remonstrated upon his negligence, he afforded me the particular consolation of learning that he had never practised in that particular line, and had merely done it to oblige me!"

"I never suffered in the same way," said Rosella, smiling, "but I dislike the place, I think, as much as you do."

"Do you then live there?"

"I called it my home," she replied, sighing; "but the friendship with which Miss Beauclerc has distinguished me from childhood, withdrew me from a residence I could not love."

The enquiries he had made led her to reflect upon the peculiarities of her situation; and his surprise on finding that Mr. Ellinger's abode was her's, brought to her imagination a circumstance that had never before appeared so singular to her: – she had never heard of one relative, either of the family of her father or her mother; and some vague conjectures floated on her mind, concerning the pretended discovery of Miss Beauclerc's affinity.

"I thought when I met you," said Oberne, breaking the silence, "that we had been much farther from the town. How is it that we have already reached it?"

"I had the same idea of its distance," observed Rosella; "we were both mistaken."

"Lord! I thought for my part," exclaimed Nancy, who had now approached them, "that we should never get here; but there is nothing like chatting and pleasant company to be sure, to pass the time away."

Rosella blushed; and Oberne heard the observation in silence, which Nancy thought very odd, because he was such a pleasant gentleman that had always something merry to say.

When they were near the habitation of Jamie Campbell, Rosella turned to him, and said she must wish him good evening.

"I wish you ten thousand," returned he: "do not however imagine this farewell is to last for a year or two. I shall remain at Dumfries, I believe, till you leave it, and then we will see which of us, with equal sincerity, can outvie the other in good wishes."

He then suffered her to walk forward without him; and she could not forbear reflecting, for some time afterwards, upon the variations in his countenance and manner, which had taken place during their interview.

Chapter IV

FAREWELL WISHES – A RESCUE FROM THE TYRANNY OF VERY HUMBLE FRIENDS

WHEN she retired to her apartment, Mrs. Campbell entered, to say that Jamie had been at home, and left word for the young lady that Mrs. Fraser, the merchant's weef, had been to London, some years back, for five pounds; but that every thing was dearer now; and besides she had a large family of children, and only the shop to live upon, so she went as cheap as a prudent woman could do.

Rosella was pleased with this statement, which did not overthrow the plan of Mrs. Delaval, even if her eagerness to leave Dumfries should induce her to begin the journey, before Mr. Ellinger's economic deliberations had arrived at an active conclusion.

It was twilight when Mally stole in to say, the young leddy maun gie her the latter noo, for she munna sta, or her maister wad raise the deil in the hoose; and Rosella having fortunately just written a billet to Mrs. Delaval, gave it to the girl, with a charge to deliver it privately, which Mally already understood she was to do.

Much however as she was hurried, she could not forbear staying to tell Jamie Campbell's wife, that, e'er sin yestreen, poor Maistress Dalaval had led the leefe of a dog.

Rosella overheard this intelligence, and wished she could have applied a pair of wings to Mally's feet, that the poor old lady might the sooner learn the information she carried.

She would not venture the next morning to approach Macdoual's house, but waited at home in the hope that Mrs. Delaval would find an opportunity of sending to her; nor was she mistaken – Mally came with a note, but could not wait for an answer, not even a verbal one.

The billet informed Rosella that after receiving her's, she had plucked up courage, and mentioned her intention to Mr. Macdoual; but whether he imagined she was not in earnest, or that he thought this sudden resolution was a mere whim that would never be put in practice, she could not tell, but he had taken no notice of what she said any further than by being in a worse humour than usual; and that she was so anxious to be gone before the storm broke, that she would try to be ready on the following day, though she feared there would be some difficulty in getting out of the house.

Rosella thought so too; but she was rather encouraged in the afternoon, to learn by Mally, who returned to know if she could leave Dumfries by the time mentioned, that Mr. Macdoual had gone a journey, and his wife could not tell where, only she thought it must be to Galloway;[398] and there had been a great brawl amoong 'em aw, and she had heard her maistress cry and bewail hersel, because her maister had not left ony siller[399] to buy victuals, and poor Mrs. Delaval had nae ony to gie her.

Rosella easily discerned the meaning of this: Macdoual wished to try if his inmate had any secret hoard by her, which he imagined the distress of the moment would make her betray – a circumstance he would not long be ignorant of, notwithstanding his pretended absence; and that if he were assured she was actually destitute of money, he would stay out of the way to avoid any application, until the fancy of returning to England died away. Rosella wrote therefore, a hasty note to Mrs. Delaval, entreating her to persevere in her assertion that she had no cash by her, and to keep secret the time of her quitting Dumfries.

She had scarcely dispatched Mally back with it, when a stranger enquired of Nancy at the door for Miss Montresor; she ran in to Rosella, and replied to her questions, that he was an elderly man, very plain in his dress, and that he did not look very good-humoured.

"Who can this be?" thought Rosella; and the scene at Dunkeld rushing into her memory, she dreaded the malice of Macdoual, and trembled lest this person should be an emissary of vengeance. She imagined however that she must see him, and desired Nancy to introduce him into a little parlour she occupied.

As he entered, she beheld a man in the decline of life, as Nancy had described him, of a very sedate aspect, who presented her a letter from Mr. Mordaunt, and said he had been commissioned by him to conduct her and her attendant to London. The heart of Rosella beat with delight on hearing this propitious sentence, and she hastily tore open her letter, which she found to be kind and even paternal. He promised to explain when they met why he had not replied to her application, which had not nevertheless been neglected; he lamented the many unpleasant circumstances that had befallen her, mentioned that Mr. Ellinger had communicated her last letter to him, and desired her to return immediately to England, when he hoped to arrange matters upon a better plan in future, and he would exert himself to obliterate the mischievous effects of the past.

Rosella was so charmed with this proof of the good man's regard, that even his messenger, Mr. Williams, appeared to her a superior sort of beneficent being; – she entreated that he would sit, and take some refreshment; but the latter part of the request he declined, saying he had ordered a dinner at an inn.

She then mentioned, that if he should not be too much fatigued on the following day or the day after, to resume his journey, she should wish to comply with Mr. Mordaunt's injunction of an immediate return; and that having received a proposal from Mrs. Delaval of travelling with her, she hoped she might be so far indulged as to accept it.

Mr. Williams, who was described in the letter Rosella had just read, to be the father of a family, and a confidential agent of the writer, after a moment of consideration, said that he supposed Mr. Mordaunt could not but highly approve of such a circumstance, which he thought had the appearance of being a very desirable thing.

"I was surprised, Madam," added he, "at not finding you with the lady at Mr. Macdoual's, whither indeed I have not yet been; for I happened, by accident, to enquire of a girl coming out of this house, the way I ought to take, which I could not perfectly understand from the people of the inn, and I accidentally discovered that you lodged here, which saved me an useless peregrination."

Rosella, in reply, made him acquainted with the situation of Mrs. Delaval, and the many distressing causes that forced her to return to England; and Mr. Williams listened with evident indignation and astonishment at the villainous machinations of one party, and the helpless imbecility of the other. He thought it advisable to take the poor lady immediately out of the hands of the Macdouals, and promised Rosella to accompany her the next morning to their house, to endeavour to effect this. But he much doubted, from the account of her disaster, which Rosella had not omitted, whether she would be able to travel at any rate; and he proposed, when he had dined, to look out for a more eligible and spacious lodging where Mrs. Delaval and herself might continue to reside, if his surmises were just.

Mr. Williams then withdrew, leaving Rosella much more tranquil than she had found herself for some time past.

She would not in the evening repeat her walk, lest she should appear to seek Oberne; but she felt this self-denial more forcibly than she would confess to herself, and was not in very good spirits, when Nancy suddenly introduced him without any previous ceremony, as she imagined such a kind friend should not be treated like any body one did not care for.

"I hear," said he gravely, "that your escort is arrived; perhaps you can now tell me when you leave Dumfries."

Rosella repeated the conversation she had had with Mr. Williams concerning the poor lady at Macdoual's, and added that her departure still depended upon her.

"My enquiry," resumed Oberne, "was merely from idle curiosity, I believe; for as I now consider you to be safe in harbour, I am come only with the intention of bidding you adieu. – I must hasten to London."

Rosella felt the colour fade on her cheeks.

"Are you going immediately?" asked she, hardly knowing what she said.

"I shall set off the moment I leave you," replied Oberne; then assuming a gayer air, "and yet," he added, "my business, when I arrive in London, will not be of a kind to reward such expedition; for, to say the truth, I have by some means, I cannot exactly say how, played the devil, and left myself the pleasant alternative of starving in England, or accepting a commission in a regiment ordered to the West Indies, which my generous and disinterested brother very obligingly offers to procure me."

"You are not going to the West Indies?" said Rosella, with an aspect of concern.

"You would not wish to see me sweeping the streets!" returned he, making an unsuccessful effort to appear lively.

"You shock me!" exclaimed Rosella, shuddering involuntarily.

"I will endeavour to shock you no longer," replied he, taking her hand: "receive then my parting wishes for your future undisturbed peace of mind, your happiness, and prosperity. – Do not wholly exclude the giddy, the imprudent Oberne from your recollection; and wherever his destiny or his follies shall have banished him, he will not be entirely miserable."

At the conclusion of this speech he kissed the hand he held, and suddenly left her; whilst Rosella remained in such confusion, such surprise, such regret at his departure, that she attempted no reply whilst he was still in sight, and when she could no longer discern him, she exclaimed with Orlando – "Can I not speak to him – can I not say I thank you!"[400]

All that was amiable in the character of Oberne rose to her remembrance – all that she had originally disapproved in it, had, for some time past, faded from her memory; and she wept that a disposition so unaffectedly generous, a nature so open, so frank, so undisguised, should be accompanied by such a careless and incorrigible negligence to the attention every man should render to his circumstances, if he would preserve amidst his fellow-beings of the same gradation of rank, an independence of opinion, of conduct, and of situation.

It was late before she retired to rest; and ere her eye-lids closed in sleep, a violent storm of wind, of rain, of lightning, and tremendous thunder, made her tremble for the unhappy traveller, whom she represented to herself on his passage across the Solway Firth, exposed to the heightened fury of the tempest.

The most unpleasant images troubled her repose after the subsiding of this jar of elements; and she had scarcely breakfasted the next morning, when Mr. Williams appeared to attend her to Macdoual's.

He had brought with him a post-chaise, to convey Mrs. Delaval from the scene of purgatorial discord and civil war, in which she had existed so many years; and Rosella feeling but half assured from his protection, and more than half fearful of the brutality of Macdoual should he be returned, the hyena lamentations of his wife, and the clamor of their hopeful progeny, stepped into it, to be the sooner conveyed to the scene of contention, and as she hoped, the sooner conveyed from it.

Mr. Williams rung at the bell several times unattended to; and at length, tired of an application so fruitless, he entered a passage, and opening a sitting-room, beheld Mrs. Delaval, such from the description of Rosella he concluded her to be, weeping very tenderly over her friend, whom she repeatedly promised to remember in her will, and to remit to her what sums she could spare from her yearly expenditure.

"I have taken the liberty of interrupting you, Madam," said Mr. Williams, "to inform you that Miss Montresor is at the door. She is in a carriage, which perhaps you would wish to make use of in your removal; but she desires me to say she will await your leisure, if you are not quite ready to accompany her."

"Yes," cried Mrs. Delaval eagerly, "I am quite ready!"

"Oh, for God's sake, don't go!" exclaimed Mrs. Macdoual; "I shall die with grief if I lose you; and besides my husband will kill me for letting you go!"

This double menace of dying with grief, and being killed into the bargain, appeared very much to distress poor Mrs. Delaval, who endeavoured however to console her, by saying she would write very often, and still repeating that she would not forget her promises.

"And what signifies writing," retorted the afflicted lady, "when I shan't have money to pay for your letters.[401] Oh dear, dear! Mr. Macdoual will be worse than ever; and I and my poor children won't have rags to cover us, nor victuals to put into our mouths!"

Mrs. Delaval could not hear this doleful prophecy without weeping anew; and Mr. Williams, fearing that her resolution would yield to a momentary compassion, thought proper to interpose.

"I understood, Madam," said he, addressing Mrs. Macdoual, "that this lady wished to return to her native air for the benefit of her health, which Miss Montresor thought had been injured."

"No!" replied she, in all the fury of impotent passion, to which a weak mind will yield itself, "No! it is because that Miss has wheedled herself into favour, and can't bear that I and my children should be bettered as well as herself! – I wish I had known her fawning tricks, and she should as soon have flown up to the moon, as have come into this house, mincing and carnying![402] – But I shall let her know that I have had Mrs. Delaval for my friend these twenty years and more; and every body must say I have a better right to keep her here in my family, than that girl has to take her away!"

"It appears to me, Madam," said the gentleman gravely, "that you are arguing and planning without consulting the inclinations or convenience of your friend; and indeed you are not paying a grateful compliment to the understanding of Mrs. Delaval, by supposing that, if her own affairs did not lead her to undertake the journey to England, the persuasion of a young lady, almost a stranger to her, would have sufficient weight to carry her thither."

"Then, if she is a stranger," returned Mrs. Macdoual, in a crying voice, "why does my poor dear want to go with her, away from us all? – She used to hate strangers so much, that we none of us thought of her playing us this trick. – And then, what affairs can she have in England? – Don't my husband manage all her affairs! – I'm sure she has never any trouble with her money. – But pray, Sir, who may you be?"

"I am a plain man, Madam," replied Mr. Williams calmly, "which you may easily discern; and I endeavour to be an honest man. The guardian of Miss Montresor, and another person interested in her welfare, have employed me to conduct her to them. – This, Madam, and what the message I brought from the young lady implies, is all, I presume, that you wish to be acquainted with."

"The message from her truly! Yes, a fine message from her; – and you, Sir, may take one from me – so pray tell her the is a wheedling, good-for-nothing, young viper!"

"My dear, my dear!" exclaimed Mrs. Delaval, "I must say this is not pretty! – I must say –"

"What," interrupted the poor woman, wiping the dew from her forehead, "is she to come to take the bread out of my mouth, and an't I to speak?"

Several screams, that appeared to proceed from the spot where Rosella was waiting, now attracted the immediate attention of Mrs. Delaval, who was too well enabled to guess what the outcry meant.

"Oh my God!" cried she, turning pale, "those young furies are murdering the poor child!"

Mr. Williams hastily left the room to protect her, and found that the Miss Macdouals had surrounded the chaise, armed with stones and bricks, which they had been indefatigable in collecting from the moment it arrived; and having at length procured a sufficient quantity of ammunition, they had begun the attack by a general discharge of artillery, in which the post-boy had received a contusion on the head, and one of the windows of the chaise was slivered to pieces.

Fortunately Rosella had found her attention excited by the employment the young ladies so eagerly followed from her first appearance, and thinking it a very suspicious one, had hastily put up the blinds, before she had suffered any further injury than an inconsiderable bruise on the arm.

The driver, enraged at the assault, had repelled it by force, and employed the thick end of his whip to revenge the damage he had suffered; but the Miss Macdouals had been too well accustomed to their father's discipline to shrink at this, and the man would probably have received further injury, had not Mr. Williams immediately seconded him.

Mrs. Macdoual herself likewise ran out, whose inflamed passions requiring a vent, she flew at her daughters, buffetted their faces, and tore off their hair with a violence of action that shocked every beholder, accompanying the unmatronly correction with invectives, which though they were deserved, were not the less ungrateful to the ear.

In the interim Mrs. Delaval crept to the door with the assistance of Mally, who was ever ready to attend her; and invigorated for the moment, by her terrors for Rosella, the poor lady had even approached the chaise to discover if she yet existed. Mr. Williams saw that this opportunity was not to be lost.

"You are not safe, Madam," said he, "with such people as these! Let me put you into the chaise."

"Is the young lady there?" asked she, with a trembling voice; "have they not maimed her?"

"I hope not; – but it is impossible to say what their renewed violence may not effect."

"Let us be gone," whispered Mrs. Delaval, with increasing tremor, "let us be gone! – My clothes may be sent for. – I had rather lose every thing than suffer any mischief to happen to that good young creature!"

Mr. Williams called to the driver, who instantly obeyed the summons; they raised the lady between them into the chaise, Mr. Williams followed, and they were almost out of sight before Mrs. Macdoual was sensible of the evasion of her *poor dear*.

When Mrs. Delaval no longer beheld the spot where she had lingered so many years of tasteless existence, she seemed to breathe a purer air; her spirits, lightened of an insupportable load, gave fresh animation to her countenance; and Rosella, the latent cause of her emancipation, rose in her esteem and affection in proportion as she felt a return of peace and ease to a bosom from whence they had long been banished.

Mr. Williams was, besides what he had described himself to be in answer to the enquiry of Mrs. Macdoual, a man of quick apprehension and discernment: he knew of the history of Rosella, as much as related to the unfortunate consequences of the eccentricity of Miss Beauclerc, and presaged many advantages from the acquisition of so respectable a *chaperon*, with whom her return to London would be divested of almost every unpleasant circumstance which might otherwise have attended it. He placed Mrs. Delaval and her young companion in the lodgings he had provided, and sent for Nancy to attend them, whilst he went to Jamie Campbell's to forward the baggage of Rosella to her new abode, and discharge the debt she had incurred by her residence there; from thence he proceeded to Macdoual's, to demand the trunks and packages of their late inmate, for which purpose he hired a horse and cart to follow him.

Rosella meantime, exerted herself to settle Mrs. Delaval in her apartment; and as she observed that the smallest motion of her leg was attended with a pain the poor lady could not suppress some indications of feeling, she begged to know what was usually done to relieve it.

The sufferer declined however, having any thing done till Nancy came; but Rosella would not admit of the delay, and still urging her enquiry, she at length discovered that Mrs. Macdoual had been both nurse and surgeon,[403] and that her attendance and remedies had been slight indeed. Shocked at such cruel neglect, she instantly sent for the best medical assistance the place afforded, not without opposition on the part of Mrs. Delaval, who bade her to reflect upon the expence of surgeons, and that if their stock of cash should be lessened, how should they get to England; for she was certain, she said, Macdoual would be so enraged, that he would not let her have any part of the money she had lent him.

Rosella took this opportunity of presenting her the sum she had accepted of Mr. Craufurd, which was yet entire, telling her in what manner it had become her's, and informing her that Mr. Williams would defray her own expences and those of Nancy. Mrs. Delaval was much relieved by this consolatory intelligence, and her only concern now was, the apprehension of not being able to travel immediately.

"I never felt my poor leg so bad before!" exclaimed she; "if you should be obliged to go without me, what would become of me!"

"Depend upon it," said Rosella warmly, "I would not leave Dumfries unless you are in a situation to go likewise! – No, dear Madam, after what I have witnessed, I should think myself wanting in gratitude to Miss Beauclerc if I did not attend upon you to England."

"I thank you a thousand times, my dear child," replied Mrs. Delaval; "you are so tender and so kind, that I should be very sorry to part with you, even if I did not fear that Mr. Macdoual would try to get me back. – I thought your guardian would not suffer you to stay perhaps."

Rosella endeavoured to re-assure her on this point, and at length succeeded in calming her inquietude before the arrival of the surgeon she had sent for. He ordered immediate and repeated fomentations[404] to the injured part, recommended a nourishing diet, and forbade all motion that could irritate it.

Thus was the journey positively postponed for some time, to the extreme mortification of Mrs. Delaval, who ardently desired to quit Dumfries.

It was almost three hours before Mr. Williams returned with her effects but he had brought them all, for the invalid had a friend in Mally, to whom at parting, she had been liberal in spite of apprehended poverty; and the girl would not suffer any thing to be detained by her mistress, whom she very little feared or considered in the absence of Macdoual.

Mr. Williams said he had had great difficulty in accomplishing his errand; but he declined at present entering into unpleasant details. He had heard enough however, to induce him to take up his abode in the same house with the injured lady; as Macdoual had been sent to, and his return home expected every hour.

Rosella having communicated to him the injunctions of the surgeon, he wrote the same evening to Mr. Mordaunt, stating the circumstances that detained Miss Montresor and himself and desiring instructions for his future proceedings.

He was not mistaken in supposing that Macdoual would endeavour to see Mrs. Delaval; but as she had begged that he might not have access to her, Mr. Williams took precautions to prevent him from succeeding; and when he found that the efforts of his wife, who was more fortunate, failed in the great point of drawing the poor lady back to his dwelling, he at length left her to a late repose, with a self-congratulation that he had lost no time whilst it was his good fortune to retain her in his power.

By the cares of Rosella and Nancy, and the attendance of the surgeon, every dangerous symptom was soon removed, which neglect and agitation of mind had produced in the invalid. Her general health amended visibly, and, in spite of the recollection of poor Sophy, she was sometimes cheerful.

"I seem, my dear," she often said to her young companion, "to be in heaven – I feel so calm and so easy! – I don't know what I can do to requite you for your goodness to me. – However, I will not forget poor Mrs. Macdoual; for though she is a little hasty and passionate, she is much to be pitied, and was always more civil to me than the rest of the family."

Rosella could not forbear thinking that this kind intention was but little merited; but she was far from presuming to oppose it, and generally received the intimation in silence.

Chapter V

A PHYSICIAN'S FIAT – REFORMATION IN THE HOUSEHOLD OF A LADY OF SENTIMENT

IN a few days an answer arrived from Mr. Mordaunt, who excessively approved what had been done with regard to Mrs. Delaval. He hinted at the extreme importance the continuance of her friendship would be of to Rosella, and as Mr. Williams had mentioned that she was destitute of money, from the encroachments the Macdouals had made upon her income, he desired Rosella would inform her that she must consider Mr. Williams as her banker; who had received instructions, by the same post, to supply the good lady with cash for her immediate use, and for the expences of her journey; and he was likewise directed to remain at Dumfries until she could be removed.

In Mr. Mordaunt's letter to Rosella, he further desired her to inform the aunt of Miss Beauclerc, that her guardian consented to her residence with her as long as it should be agreeable to either party. And Rosella was now so much attached to the invalid, by the mildness of her temper, the simplicity of her manners, and the goodness of her heart, that she was herself delighted with the permission, and hastened to impart it to her.

Mrs. Delaval wept from satisfaction; she no longer feared the diminution of her little stock of money. Nancy was installed into her service in due form, and in less than a fortnight she was enabled to move southward by easy stages. But when she found herself once more on English ground, the forgot all her ailments; and a letter meeting her at Carlisle from Mr. Mordaunt, to hasten her journey, by the intelligence it communicated that he much doubted the insanity of her niece from the result of some information he had been solicitous to obtain, and that her presence might be extremely useful, she would no longer be restrained by self-consideration from advancing with a rapidity highly imprudent: yet the representations of Mr. Williams, and the entreaty of Rosella, could not engage her to moderate it.

"What was her worthless life," she said, "in comparison with the hope of alleviating the confinement of poor Sophy, or freeing her from the power of a mercenary villain, if there were no just grounds for it."

By the time they reached London, the injury her leg had originally sustained, wore the same appearance, and was still more painful than it had been at

Dumfries. – Rosella was much alarmed and afflicted, and only the presence of Mr. Mordaunt, who welcomed them to England, when they arrived at the apartments he had engaged for the immediate use of Mrs. Delaval, could for a moment divert her thoughts from the melancholy presages that perpetually occupied them.

The good old man embraced Rosella with paternal affection, and congratulated her that she had replaced by her merit, the friend of which misfortune had robbed her.

"I cannot part with her," interrupted Mrs. Delaval; "you must not take her from me. I believe she has saved my life – and of this I am very sure, that she contributes much to my happiness!"

Mr. Mordaunt was pleased at this intimation of the favour with which Rosella was viewed by her ancient friend.

"This good girl," said he, "will I am sure, accept with great satisfaction the kind protection you offer her."

Rosella had no difficulty in declaring that she received it with gratitude and delight: but the regret this arrangement renewed for the misfortune of her first friend, forced the tears into her eyes, which she was careful, however, to conceal from Mrs. Delaval.

"This affair then," resumed Mr. Mordaunt, "being so satisfactorily adjusted, I must now claim a promise of Rosella, that she will steal an hour to-morrow to visit my sister, and acknowledge that I have performed a commission with which she entrusted me, to request that our young friend would favour her with her company for a few months, unless any other engagement prevented her compliance."

Rosella, who imagined this pretended request was merely the result of his own delicacy and good-will, thanked him with much energy, and promised to attend to his hint.

"I shall send Philip for you," said Mr. Mordaunt; "for you must accustom yourself to recollect that you are not in a country village, and that in this noisy place you must not indulge in contemplative rambles without an Esquire in your suite."

He then informed Mrs. Delaval that he had begun a proceeding against Mr. Bristock, in which he had taken the liberty of employing her name, and he hoped it would be successful.

"If," he added, "your niece is really sane, which I have some reason to suppose, I trust that her past danger will henceforth teach her to pay a little more deference to the established usages of society than I hear she has lately done."

Rosella coloured at the conclusion of this speech, and felt as though it had glanced at her; but Mr. Mordaunt bade her adieu with the same friendly aspect with which he had accosted her, and a sudden apprehension she had conceived, that her last interviews with Oberne had reached his ears, subsided.

The following morning, at the request of Mrs. Delaval, she wrote two or three notes in her name: one of them was addressed to a person who had formerly conducted her affairs, and the others to some female friends, with whom she had associated on intimate terms before Mrs. Macdoual had so wholly engrossed her favour.

A porter was dispatched with them to their several destinations; but, alas! it was found that only the man of business remained in the same situation in which Mrs. Delaval had left him twenty years back; and the reason perhaps was, that not being then a young man, he had already made his bed in the same corner for almost the same number of years. The ladies were either dead, or had quitted London to Tabithise at Bath,[405] or had dropped into dowager's quarters, where dowager's incomes would support them.

Mrs. Delaval raised her hands and eyes, exclaiming with a look of consternation –

"Little did I think when I left London, that at my return I should find things so changed! – But if I can but see poor Sophy once more in her senses, and you, my dear Rosella, are not tired of staying with me, I shall be happy still."

Rosella assured her, and with sincerity, of her attachment: and it was not by words only that she chose to demonstrate it; for since their departure from Dumfries she had been indefatigable herself, and as constantly directed the cares of Nancy, to fulfil the prescriptions of the medical person there; and perhaps without her unceasing attentions, poor Mrs. Delaval had never reached London. Yet spite of her efforts, spite of a night of repose undisturbed, the countenance of the invalid exhibited when she rose, those signs of half-concealed pain the affection of Rosella had taught her to discern, and she had given an additional commission to the porter, to call at the house of Dr. D – , who had attended the family of Mr. Beauclerc, and whose address she well remembered, with a request to visit Mrs. Delaval immediately.

It happened fortunately that Dr. D – recollected the name of the lady he was thus unexpectedly called upon to attend; and he obeyed the summons before Rosella was compelled to leave the house. She was present at the interview, and was much pleased to observe that the face of Mrs. Delaval brightened on finding herself addressed by an old acquaintance; but her satisfaction was completely damped when the Doctor, whom she attended into an anti-chamber, replied to her enquiries that he feared no effort of skill or attention could do more than sooth the last moments of the poor lady he had just quitted, whose constitution was too much weakened to surmount the mischief she had sustained; and he thought it but too probable that the extreme poverty of her blood might produce a mortification. He added that he would take the necessary steps that the invalid should immediately have proper attendance, and he would repeat his call the next morning.

He then withdrew, leaving Rosella thunderstruck at the suddenness of this cruel intelligence, which though she had almost foreseen, was not the less shocking to her. She repented that she had promised to visit Mrs. Methwald, and when Philip was announced to be in waiting, she meditated to send an excuse; but recollecting that Mr. Mordaunt ought immediately to be informed of the opinion of Dr. D – , and half-fearing to trust so important a communication to a note, which an accident might prevent him from receiving or reading perhaps for half a day, she determined at length to go.

She ran to the chamber of Mrs. Delaval to bid her adieu, and to charge Nancy to be very attentive to her Lady in her absence; a caution not wholly unnecessary, as the girl's senses had, from the first moment of her approaching London, rushed to her eyes and ears, and it was with much persuasion only she could be dragged from a window to take her meals.

It was now the middle of a warm autumn, and Rosella traversed the half-deserted streets with a sensation of melancholy the local dreariness of the scene increased; and Philip had knocked at the door of his master's house before she recovered from a mournful reverie, in which Miss Beauclerc, Oberne, and Mrs. Delaval had almost an equal share.

She observed a carriage in waiting, and was vexed at a circumstance which indicated that Mrs. Methwald was not alone; for she had hoped, as the season was so far advanced, that she was in no danger of meeting any person of such pretensions to distinction, as the extreme fashion and gaiety of the equipage seemed to announce.

Mr. Mordaunt issued from his study on the ground floor, to accompany Rosella up stairs, when Philip informed him of her arrival; but the distress of her countenance so much struck him, that he waved his intention whilst he enquired the reason of her uncommon depression.

Rosella, who had with difficulty repressed her tears in the street, now found herself unequal to the effort; and Mr. Mordaunt, with much tenderness of manner, took her into the room he had just quitted, where he learned the extreme danger in which Mrs. Delaval was pronounced to be, and appeared much startled by the intelligence.

"Is it so indeed!" exclaimed he; "Dr. D – is not in general a croaker.[406] I must – well, my dear – compose yourself – there, walk up stairs, my sister is quite alone, I believe. – I must go immediately. – Here, Philip, send to Mr. Williams – no, stay I will call myself in my way there – aye – My dear, don't hurry back – that is without going to Chancery-lane; – it would be proper to see Ellinger directly, and tell him how I have settled matters for your residence with Mrs. Delaval – he will understand. – There – good morning – God bless you!"

This incoherent speech excited the alarm of Rosella, who had always observed a collected calmness in her old friend entirely remarkable; but as he had disappeared at the close of it, she had no alternative but to follow his intimation, and walk up stairs to the apartment where Mrs. Methwald constantly gave audience.

She forgot to ring for a servant to announce her; for though Mr. Mordaunt had spoken to Philip, there was no Philip near to receive his commands; she forgot likewise the tears on her cheeks, and opening the drawing-room door, found herself suddenly not only in the presence of Mrs. Methwald, but subject to the astonished gaze of her peerless daughter, and the more indignant glance of a very lovely woman, to whom the other ladies, she observed, were earnestly listening, when her entrance disconcerted the party.

A silence of some moments rendered the situation of Rosella still more embarrassing. Mrs. Methwald coloured a dingy crimson, and every feature denoted vexation and unconquered confusion, whilst a thousand apophthegms rushed to her assistance, but not one that could extricate either of the party from their mute agitation.

Rosella, surprised at so uncommon a reception, and imagining that her unannounced appearance might have contributed to it, with some difficulty stammered an apology; but what could an apology avail, of which not a word could be distinguished; and what did the philosophy of the perfect Mrs. Cressy avail, since it could not, like a wishing-cap, convey her invisibly from a place where she began to apprehend, that for the first time in her life, she had committed herself? What likewise could it avail the lovely stranger, that she had gratified by a narrative she had just given in strong tints, a jealous pique her candor condemned, when the tears she now discerned in the eyes of the intruder, her conscience whispered to her she had perhaps wrung from a heart already humbled and distressed! Rosella was far from guessing that compunction had followed the scornful look she had observed, or that Mrs. Methwald was meditating how to reconcile contrary interests by being civil to her, whilst she preserved inviolate her respect for Lady Morteyne, whose condescending attentions were so grateful to Mrs. Cressy, and who promised to become the Cynosure of several seasons, from her youth, her beauty, her title, and her recent marriage; for the lovely stranger was in fact, the very thorn Miss Beauclerc so politely informed Lord Morteyne he was binding to his bosom.

Rosella feeling her spirit rise against the rude contempt with which she conceived herself to have been treated, coldly said that she was sorry her visit had been so extremely ill-timed; and shutting the drawing-room door, from which she had not advanced, she walked down stairs, and returning to the study, rung for a servant, whom she begged to procure her a chair.

Then taking up a book, she sat down, not to read, but to reflect with indignation upon the strange behaviour of Mrs. Methwald and her companions. Had she not been led by Mr. Mordaunt to suppose that his sister would receive her with kindness, she might have concluded that the reports so injuriously spread, had reached her ear, and that she did not discredit them; but he had even more than indirectly desired her to thank Mrs. Methwald for an invitation she had sent by him, to reside with her several months; and she could not reconcile such a mark of favour with the reception she had just experienced.

She had not heard the servant quit the house on the commission she had given him, and fearing she might yet be detained some time, was opening the door to enquire, when a voice in the hall, which she thought she was not unacquainted with, caught her attention: it asked if Lady (she could not distinguish the name) were not there?

"There is a lady here, Sir," replied a lad, who let the enquirer in, "but I did not hear her name. I believe the lady is in my master's study."

So saying he opened the door, and ushered into the apartment where Rosella was – Mr. Lesley.

"Ha! do I see Miss Montresor?" exclaimed he.

She wished to avoid a recognition so unpleasant, and enquired of the domestic, who appeared to be a groom, if any body had procured her a chair.

"John is gone to get one, Ma'am," replied he, leaving the room abruptly, to attend to a couple of saddle-horses that hung by the bridle to the railing before the window.

"I had almost forgot, in the unexpected pleasure of meeting you here," resumed Mr. Lesley, "that I have not received your pardon for the offence I was blind and undiscerning enough to commit at Guairdy."

Rosella, who was ardently wishing to leave the house, was listening to every sound from the hall, in the hope of hearing the chair announced; and did not at this moment so much attend to Mr. Lesley as to a bell violently rung, which she concluded was from the drawing-room, immediately followed by a female voice on the stairs.

"Good God!" exclaimed Mrs. Methwald, in a tone of agony, "there is not a creature to let your Ladyship out!" And the bell was again applied to, with still greater perseverance.

Rosella felt like a culprit: she had employed John who ought to have been in waiting; and to perfect her agitation, Mr. Lesley, who had been vainly wasting much elocution in enforcing a petition she scarcely heard, now aimed at rendering it irresistible by dropping on his knee – a movement that sufficiently claimed the attention of Rosella, however it might fail of obtaining her approbation.

"I know myself to be so unpardonable an offender," cried he hastily, as if he had feared an interruption, "that I can hardly expect the indulgence of being heard, unless you –"

The door of the study was now thrown open, and Mrs. Cressy appeared at its whose crimson-stained lips quivered with horror at so atrocious a sight as that which thus unexpectedly met her round grey eyes. Lesley, whom she had undertaken to instruct in botany, and to whom she had actually read the "loves of the plants"[407] whenever she could force him to listen to it! Lesley, with whom she had so frequently argued upon French politics and fine lady philosophy! Lesley, to whom she had one star-light night, poured out her whole knowledge of astronomy, and whom she had distinguished from the whole *parterre*[408] at the Opera, and nodded to from her box with such a fascinating air, and so many muscle-working smiles! Was it to be endured? – Yes, Mrs. Cressy endured it, and smiled once more!

"Lady Morteyne's servants said you were in the house," said she, with a simper that looked as if it was the effect of acid in the mouth, "and I imagined you must be with my uncle; but I perceive you are in more pleasing society. Your sister may be informed, I suppose, that you are not immediately at leisure to attend her."

At this instant John returned with the chair, and Rosella was relieved from one of those unpleasant scenes, in which a sensation of guilt is experienced in spite of conscious rectitude, and from the mortification of being the object of those oblique censures of malice, which must be self-appropriated before they can be resented.

She silently curtsied to Mrs. Cressy; but recollecting as she was placing herself in the chair, the kindness of Mr. Mordaunt, and his evident wish that she should preserve the good opinion of his sister, she left her compliments to Mrs. Methwald, with an intimation that she would have the honour of repeating her visit, and hoped to find her less engaged.

"My mother is perfectly alone at present," said Mrs. Cressy, advancing into the hall with an obliging air.

Rosella replied that her time was at present circumscribed from the extreme indisposition of Mrs. Delaval, and that she was compelled, by an injunction of Mr. Mordaunt, to see Mr. Ellinger before she returned home, which she wished to hasten as much as possible.

The chairmen[409] then trudged away with their burthen: but as they turned out of the house, Rosella heard the *suavitèr in modo*[410] pupil enquire of the groom if his master was going to ride; and the lad replied that the horses had been ordered at half after one, and had not yet been countermanded.

This information brought to her recollection the *impromptu* agitation in which Mr. Mordaunt had left her; and comparing it with the composure she had observed when they first met, she trembled lest the welfare of Miss Beauclerc hung upon the life of her aunt.

When she was deposited however, in the well-known passage in Chancery-lane, every gloom gave way to the habitual one with which she entered that house. She discovered from the people in the office that Mr. Ellinger was not at home, and without further enquiry walked up stairs to pay her compliments to the lady of the mansion; but was much surprised to find in the dining-room a very cross-looking old woman, seated *en maitresse*,[411] with a large basket of linen by her side, some of which she appeared to be patching very assiduously through her spectacles.

The good dame looked up on hearing the door open, exclaiming, when she beheld Rosella –

"Well, child, and what are you come for?"

"I wish to see Mrs. Ellinger, Madam."

"And pray, my dear, an't I Mrs. Ellinger?"

Rosella was embarrassed; she had never seen this personage before, but suddenly recollected that her guardian had a mother.

"It was the younger Mrs. Ellinger I wished to see, Madam," replied she.

"Ho! so I thought! what another bill, my life for it! You are a milliner's girl I take it, by your fine clothes and jaunty looks. – Well, we shall see an end to them, it is to be hoped, before my son gets into the King's Bench.[412] However, you need not trouble yourself to bring any bills run up since the second of this month; I tell you that for a warning; for the good-for-nothing, extravagant, fine lady trollop went out of these doors, bag and baggage, on that blessed day! and whilst I can keep out of my grave, she shall never set foot here again!"

"Good Heaven! has Mrs. Ellinger left her house?" exclaimed Rosella, much shocked.

"I found all these," cried she, "rotting in dirt, so I had 'em washed to see what I could make of 'em. She thought truly, nobody would pry into her doings till Madam there, her crazy friend, came home; but she came home in a strait-waistcoat, which she ought to have had when she ran away with that young fellow nineteen years ago! – I said she'd come to no good then; and there's that young

A PHYSICIAN'S FIAT

slut she took too, she has got herself into fine bread, running after gentlefolk's husbands, and playing her pranks in Lord's families."

"Is it possible," exclaimed Rosella, "that I should thus have been represented!"

The talkative old housewife now raised her spectacles, to gaze at her more attentively.

"You, child!" cried she, dropping from her withered hand the scissars that hung to her apron-string, "why surely you an't –"

"My name is Montresor," interrupted Rosella, who repented that she had been betrayed to express any emotion.

"Aye, my good child, that's the name you go by; – and so you are come back! Well, well, we must all do the best we can: howsever don't think I'm sorry. – I dare to say you can handle your needle; you look like a notable girl, so we shall agree very well, I'm sure. – But are you come now for good, my dear? because I was forced to have all the blankets washed, and the beds took'd down – Oh Lord! well it don't signify talking of it – it's well dirt don't poison; and as to the floors, I had 'em all well sluiced, and they've been all scrubbed every day since, by my own maid upon her marrow-bones, to make 'em come to their colour. – Betty's a girl that don't flinch at her work – but we've all our troubles. – I don't think this place agrees with her; she has got the violentest cold and sore throat, poor wench! I can't think what is come to her!"

Rosella was far from being at a loss to discover, but she had no inclination to discuss the point.

"Will you inform me where Mrs. Ellinger lives, Madam?" asked she.

"Oh God knows! – But, child, be advised by your elders – it will be no credit to you to herd with her; and indeed I can't have any body in this house that chooses to have any thing to say to her, or such persons as she may be with."

"Is Miss Ellinger with her mother?" resumed Rosella.

"She! no indeed – Livy is a very clever girl, and has accomplished herself in all sorts of drawing, and painting, and music, and fine works, and broidery, and such like; and she has got a place to be with the Lady Merrions, to tend upon 'em, and be their governess, I assure you!"

Rosella was much surprised at the whole of this intelligence: of Miss Livia's accomplishments she had seen proofs that perfectly satisfied her of what kind they were; – that Mr. Ellinger should suffer his daughter to reside under any roof in a menial capacity, which the old lady's expression of *tending* seemed to indicate, she much wondered at; and that the noble family into which she had introduced herself, should allow any attendant to be companion and instructor, or an instructor to perform the office of an attendant, excited still greater astonishment; nor could she forbear marvelling, when she heard how delightfully the Lady Merrions were accommodated with an attendant and a governess in one and the same person – who the inculcator of morals, and the advocate of the Virtues and the Graces, could be! – no doubt a distinct office from the other two, since Miss Livia was so ill calculated to perform this third part.

"You cannot inform me then," said Rosella, dismissing her reflections, "where I can address Mrs. Ellinger?"

"No, child, not I; but we shall know fast enough, I suppose, when her quarter-age[413] is due – she won't forget to ask for that in the midst of her fine nonsense, about not being beholden to base people who think so much of their money; she did not think of her husband's moncy, as all her bills can testify, an extravagant –"

Rosella, sick of this invective, interrupted it, to desire the good lady would present her respectful remembrance to Mr. Ellinger, and tell him she had called to say she resided for the present with Mrs. Delaval, which the hoped he would not disapprove; and then, without waiting an answer, she wished the irascible dowager good morning, and hastened out of the room.

As she passed the office-door, Mr. Povey threw it open, exclaiming, with even more than his usual pertness –

"Ha, little Montresor! what, you are come to see the old one, for a reinforcement of cash, I suppose! – Upon my soul though, I was concerned to hear that the old maid ran on the wrong side of the post so confoundedly! Why they say you was left on the road, without a guinea in your pocket!"

Rosella, with a look of anger and contempt, pushed by him; but he followed her up the passage, and as the chairmen were not in the way, she was obliged to hear a continuation of his impertinence.

"You see," cried he, "that I don't follow the example of my friend Estcourt; – upon my soul he is a fine fellow – what a cursed, hard-hearted Gipsey you must have been, to have dashed him down that rock, and broke his bones in that manner! – You see I don't cut with old friends, because they are not up to my trim! – Here I am you find! – D – n it if I can think how those poor devils in the office can sit fagging[414] the twelve hours round, like so many pack-horses!"

Rosella, who had not forgotten the time when Captain Povey thought himself happy to be called down from his stool to attend her, could not forbear smiling, with an air not to be mistaken, at the conclusion of this elegant speech; he felt the silent satire, and determined to revenge it.

"I have been so hoaxed," resumed he, "by a round of engagements to-day, that I almost forgot the scene I witnessed as I was passing Bootle's.[415] There was your old favourite, Arthur Oberne, arrested this morning in the view of about fifty of us, who were lounging up and down the street. Curse my spurs, if I ever saw a fellow fight more manfully! – but the dogs who entrapped him were up to his tricks – so a grim-looking scoundrel took him a cudgel stroke across the head, that laid the scull open, by God!"

Rosella felt as if the place turned round with her; she grew faint, and could scarcely support herself by leaning against the wainscot.

"Hollo! what!" exclaimed the unfeeling Povey, "why I thought – Oh ho! well, don't droop – he isn't done up yet! – Why an intimate friend of mine has taken five guineas to give a hundred if Clanallan sees another shooting season; so if his friends will speculate upon his carcase to such odds as that, you know, why any deep-one will bail Arthur on the same score."

Rosella did not hear a word of this pretended consolation; but, afflicted at the misfortunes of the generous Oberne, and disgusted by the impertinent ease with which the exulting Povey had treated a subject so distressing to her, she left him with contempt, to seek for some one who would enquire whither the chairmen had betaken themselves; but these gentlemen having finished a political debate at the nearest public-house, now thought proper to return, and receive her further commands; and Rosella eagerly seated herself, with just sufficient presence of mind to tell the men where to take her; whilst Povey, doubly gratified by her distress, and the subject that had excited it, saw her depart with the malicious grin of an Arabian savage.

Chapter VI

A HEROINE'S MEMOIRS CORROBORATED BY GRAVE TESTIMONY – A DEATH-BED

ROSELLA felt like a shipwrecked mariner reaching port, when she found herself once more at the lodgings of Mrs. Delaval. She ran up stairs very eagerly, and was surprised to hear from Nancy, that the old gentleman, who had made so much of her the day before, was with the invalid now, and had been with her more than two hours; and that he had sent for another queer, grave-looking gentleman, and they had been very busy; and Mistress had said nobody was to interrupt her till they rung the bell.

She concluded that the girl meant Mr. Mordaunt by the old gentleman who had made so much of her the day before, but could not divine whom the second could be. The confinement of Miss Beauclerc, however, perpetually haunting her imagination, she hoped the business in question was some preliminary to her release; and she determined to wait with as much patience as she could summon to her aid, till the signal for admittance allowed her the liberty of interrupting the congress. But in the interval the image of poor Oberne imprisoned, wounded, and disgraced, every moment obtruded upon her recollection, till at length she lost every idea but that one which the malice of Povey had forced upon her, and she was awakened from her reverie by some one tapping her shoulder.

"Rosella," said Mr. Mordaunt, who had entered the room unperceived by her, "before you again see Mrs. Delaval, I must discover to you a circumstance which would too much agitate her to communicate. Is your mind sufficiently disengaged to attend to me?"

Rosella assured him that she felt much interested in what he thus prepared her to hear.

"Your father," resumed Mr. Mordaunt, "some years back, that is, before you were born, was a young man of fortune who had been consigned to my guardianship; and I acted by him and his property in a manner my conscience has never reproached me with. But he was thoughtless and dissipated; and before he married your mother, which happened only three years after he was of age, he had parted with every guinea, and was encumbered with debts of honour to the amount of thousands. Under these circumstances, and others you will hear in future, he was privately united to a lady you are well acquainted with – you are not a stranger to your mother, Rosella –"

"My mother!" exclaimed she with astonishment; "is my mother then alive? – Ah! Miss Beauclerc is really then my mother! – how coldly, how ungenerously did I receive her caresses when she announced it to me!"

She then recounted to Mr. Mordaunt, in the bitterness of self-condemnation, her disbelief of the asseverations her mother had used to assure her of it, and that she had neglected to read some papers put into her hand for the purpose of proving the fact.

"Where are those papers?" asked he.

Rosella replied that they were in a box with her trinkets, which Mr. Bristock had taken from her.

"Taken from you!" repeated the man of law; "where did he take then from you? – why did you suffer it?"

She informed him of the effect the rough intrusion of Mr. Craufurd and his companion had had.

"But," added she, "I should not have had courage to have prevented Mr. Bristock's rapacity, had I not fainted; for I was too much hurt at his intelligence, and frightened by his threats, to have opposed him."

"Trinkets, you say! what may be the value of those trinkets? – are they worth any money?"

"Miss Beauclerc – my poor mother!" returned Rosella, sighing, "gave them all to me: there was her own picture set in a spring gold case, which cost twenty guineas; and a pair of bracelets of considerable value I believe, besides other things."

"Of the same kind, I suppose?" said Mr. Mordaunt.

Rosella replied in the affirmative; and recollecting the money, mentioned it to him.

"Well, my dear," resumed the old gentleman, with a look of exultation, "I hope your mother will soon be released but I wish to caution you not to betray the secret I have revealed to you; – it is much better for her credit and your's, as she has managed, that your affinity should not be known. Mrs. Delaval her aunt, is you know, likewise your's, and she is earnest to consider you as her niece in every respect, as your mother has already more money than she can spend with prudence. So go now to the old lady, and take care of her; and to-morrow I will call again. – But tell me, my dear child," added Mr. Mordaunt, "if this ruffian seized all your little stock of money, how did you get to Dumfries?"

Rosella changed colour more than once: the question put her sincerity to the test; for though she might have said, with truth, that she had possessed enough for the purpose, yet she was conscious of the necessity of informing Mr. Mordaunt of the loan of Mr. Craufurd; and if he learned it at all, certainly the present moment was the best opportunity she could have of introducing it. Yet to acknowledge that the interference of Mr. Oberne had obtained it, was betraying that she had some correspondence with him at least, if he had not actually accompanied her in the journey.

"What is the matter, child?" said Mr. Mordaunt, warmly; "you did not beg, or sell your clothes, I hope?"

"No certainly, Sir; but it happened, that a gentleman – that Mr. Oberne –"

"A – a-hem!" sounded in Mr. Mordaunt's throat; and Rosella, completely disconcerted, coloured a deeper crimson than before; and felt unable to proceed.

"Well, this gentleman – this Mr. Oberne, who *happened* to be travelling the same road, I suppose; what did he do to accommodate you?"

"He was so kind – that is, he was so obliging – I mean so polite, as to represent to Mr. Craufurd –"

"But pray," interrupted the good old man, "how did he *happen* to know the circumstance? – I never undertake to represent a case without being well acquainted with it; but perhaps an Irishman is not so scrupulous!"

Rosella was now plunged into fresh confusion.

"Well, well," returned he, "you are arrived in England again, by strange good fortune, and now we must retain you here; and I am not sorry a motive of delicacy respecting your mother, made me hesitate on your first application to me, to claim you, but by the unsuccessful letter Ellinger wrote at my request."

Rosella was yet more pleased that it had so fallen out.

"So tell me," added Mr. Mordaunt, "the effect of this young gentlemen's representations?"

"Mr. Craufurd offered me what money I should have occasion for," returned Rosella, "and I ventured to take twenty-five pounds, which I resigned to Mrs. Delaval at Dumfries; for I happened," she hesitated at this word, for it did not please her, "to have in my purse enough to take me there."

"Well, well, well! you are safely returned by strange good fortune!" repeated he; "go to the poor old lady – she wishes to see you."

He then left the room, and the house, much to the relief of Rosella, who had scarcely ever before rejoiced in his departure from her.

She saw, as she approached Mrs. Delaval, that she had been weeping; and when she dropped on her knees to kiss the kind hand extended to her, the good lady sobbed and embraced her, without having the power of bestowing the benediction her attitude seemed to solicit.

Several moments passed in silence; for the tears of Rosella flowed as fast as those of her newly discovered relation, who at length, with a deep sigh, articulated –

"Poor Sophy! – Ah my dear child!" continued Mrs. Delaval, "I little thought, when she wrote so kindly of you, and talked of your amiable disposition, and your pretty person, that it was my own little niece she was praising! – Indeed I must say, I think her father's will a hard one; – as things could not be altered, he should not have dealt so by a poor innocent child as you was, who had never offended him! – But he was an odd-tempered man, as I used to tell my poor sister. – Don't cry, however, my dear Rosella – I love you as much – more, I believe, than I love Sophy; – and as she does not want my fortune, because her own is much larger, I have done what I ought to do, and what I earnestly wished to do; – only before Mr. Mordaunt told me all, I was afraid Sophy might have thought ill of me for preferring any body to her; but she can't take it amiss of me, you know, for providing for her child, who has been so ill-treated amongst them all, somehow or other!"

"Do not say so," returned Rosella, "I am happy now in your protection; and if Miss Beauclerc – I mean my dear mother – were at liberty, I should have nothing more to wish."

"You are a good girl," replied the old lady, "and was sent by Providence to bring me here to die in peace, which I fear I could not have done at Dumfries. However, I have performed my promise to poor Mrs. Macdoual, so I hope her husband will now be more kind to her; but as to saving any part of my income to send her, I shall not be able to do that, I fear, before I am called elsewhere."

Rosella was unwilling to notice the melancholy intimation with which the invalid had concluded; but eager to relieve her from any anxiety, she enquired if she should apply to Mr. Mordaunt to advance a sum for the purpose she mentioned.

"No, child," returned Mrs. Delaval; "what I could do, in justice to myself and others, I would do; but I cannot get in debt myself to relieve Macdoual – it is what I never have done, though I have often been thought ill of, I believe, by refusing."

Rosella secretly commending a firmness she had not expected to have found, from the easiness of temper Mrs. Delaval displayed, and the impositions which had been practised upon her, dropped the subject, and resumed another, which much more interested her.

"Did Mr. Mordaunt," asked she, "say if he had discovered the place to which my mother had been taken?"

Mrs. Delaval, with the usual apostrophe of "Poor Sophy!" replied that he had not entered into the particulars of what he was doing to release her; but he said he hoped they would meet soon.

"Heaven grant we may!" exclaimed Rosella; "Oh Madam! I long to entreat her pardon for the cruel coldness with which I received the communication she thought proper to make to me in Scotland."

The arrival of the physical tribe, whose visits had been remitted to this hour, by the business of the morning, at the particular request of their patient, prevented any further conversation on a subject too distressing to be dwelt upon by Mrs. Delaval, without being sensibly felt.

The good lady exercised her rhetoric in vain, in endeavouring to induce Rosella to give up her post, of chief assistant, during the time employed, by the direction of the Physician, in embrocation;[416] for it was a task she would never delegate to another, less assiduous, or less tender perhaps than herself; but it was found necessary that the invalid should have a nurse to attend her in the night, and sit up alternately with Nancy; and to this Rosella, however unwilling to be superseded in her office, could not object, as the good lady suffered with the utmost reluctance, any attention from her which interfered with her rest.

But as she discovered that the catastrophe Doctor D – had so abruptly announced to her, became every hour more to be apprehended, she would not again quit her, even at the request of Mr. Mordaunt to renew her visit to his sister; for he had learned the unpleasant issue of the first, though he had not been exactly told the accidental circumstance of the narrative Lady Morteyne was at that moment giving, which rendered the *rencontre* so awkward to the whole party. The good man foresaw the almost instant decease of Mrs. Delaval; and as the mother of Rosella, under the predicament in which her imprudence had placed her, was the most improper person to be entrusted with the care of her conduct, he was anxious to secure her the good-will of Mrs. Methwald, to whose peculiarities he was not blind; that their residence in the same house, which he meditated, might be the less unpleasant to each.

The death of Mrs. Delaval, which no care or attention could avert, was even more sudden than Mr. Mordaunt had expected. The least motion soon fatigued her almost beyond endurance: after the visit of her surgeon from the sixth day of his attendance, she fell into a profound sleep; and Rosella, having watched by her for sone time, at length crept into the next room, of which the door was not shut, and to enjoy the freshness of the air, placed herself by a window which had likewise been directed to be thrown up. She held a book in her hand, more that she might not appear totally unemployed, than from any inclination to read; for in fact she sat immersed in thought, with her eyes earnestly fixed upon the pavement of the street into which the apartment looked.

At length a figure, instead of passing on like others who had walked by without attracting her attention, or disturbing her reverie, stood motionless immediately opposite to her, and Rosella instinctively regarding him, recognized Oberne! – She started – and hastily waving her hand, he returned the motion with a stiff bow, and passed on; for he imagined she had seen and disregarded the salutation he had twice vainly made.

Rosella was hurt by his manner; she looked after him, and observed that he likewise turned his head – his feet lingered a moment, and then carried him from her sight. She had no time, however, for reflections upon a distance so unusual in the manner of Oberne, for Nancy called loudly to her from the next room, and wholly occupied by terror, she flew to obey the summons, and beheld the countenance of her good old friend dreadfully changed.

The nurse coolly threw a handkerchief over it; and Rosella endeavouring to snatch it away, exclaimed –

"What are you doing – you will stifle her!"

"Let the poor lady rest," returned the woman in a solemn whisper, "she is going off!"

"Oh good Heaven!" cried Rosella, in an agony, "call, send for somebody – send for Doctor D – !"

"It is all in vain, Miss," said the nurse, "her time is come!"

Rosella insisted, however, that her demand should be complied with, and the people of the house obeyed her. She dispatched a messenger too, to Mr. Mordaunt; but the affirmation of the nurse was just – in less than a quarter of an hour Mrs. Delaval expired, sincerely mourned, by her late-found, but affectionate niece, who wished to have remained with the corpse until it was interred; but Mr. Mordaunt would not indulge her in a request, on many accounts improper; – he removed her immediately to his own house, and in the character of executor, made the usual arrangements for the funeral of the deceased, whose days were shortened by the impolitic avarice of the wretch, into whose power she had inconsiderately placed herself; – the Scotch broth of Macdoual's table had saved a few guineas for the time being, and probably deprived him of thousands.

Mrs. Methwald received Rosella, not as a young person distressed by a painful recent occurrence, but as a young lady who had just succeeded to a considerable property, which would infallibly give her the consequence she would fain perhaps have withheld: she treated her with assiduous respect, and overwhelmed her with those cold attentions, which neither excite gratitude, nor convey pleasure. Rosella felt even the operations of her mind restrained in the presence of Mrs. Methwald, and she regretted each day the death of her good old aunt even more poignantly than at the moment it happened.

It was now thought necessary that she should have a female attendant; and with much entreaty, Nancy was suffered to officiate in the capacity of lady's-maid, notwithstanding Mrs. Cressy had asked, with surprise and disgust, what awkward creature she had met as she passed into her mother's dressing-room.

Rosella soon began to be anxiously impatient for the performance of the promise Mr. Mordaunt daily renewed to her, that she should very shortly embrace her mother at Avelines; but it was accompanied with an injunction to have patience, which she every hour found a greater difficulty in complying with. He thought proper to state to her the accession of fortune she had made by the testament of Mrs. Delaval; and Rosella learned, with surprise, that nearly twenty thousand pounds[417] had devolved entirely to her. Mrs. Macdoual was a legatee for the sums Mrs. Delaval had at different times lent the husband to purchase lands and tenements, for which she had contrived to retain acknowledgments to the amount of four thousand pounds; the money was appointed to be paid into the hands of trustees, for the sole and separate use of Mrs. Macdoual, and at her death to be equally divided amongst her daughters. And Mr. Mordaunt told Rosella he had thus settled the plan, at once to gratify the wish of the testatrix to serve the woman, and at the same time to mortify Macdoual, who had conducted himself in a manner so scandalous.

At length Mr. Mordaunt announced to Rosella the intelligence she so earnestly longed to hear, that Miss Beauclerc, as she was still called, was, by his exertions in her favour, once more quietly settled at Avelines.

"Thank Heaven! – And why, why," exclaimed Rosella, "may I not immediately fly to her?"

"My dear," replied the old gentleman, "I wish you to repress your emotions, and listen to me."

Rosella was endeavouring to obey, when Mrs. Methwald, who was present, and seemed bursting with some *à-propos* apophthegm, interrupted her brother to observe, that it was not a symptom of a proper education when young ladies suffered exclamations or strong expressions to escape their lips; and that girls of fashion, who were most remarkable for quiet manners, invariably adopted the most simple and delicate phrases, and always rejected such as marked any potent wish or volition.

Rosella, who had more than once marked the countenance of Mrs. Methwald impressed with impatience and disgust towards her, which, on reviewing her conduct, she was at a loss to account for, was now enlightened as to the many offences she might have unwarily committed: but her mind was too much engrossed at this moment by a more important subject, to dwell upon this one, longer than the querulous and peevish voice of the good lady compelled her, and she turned to Mr. Mordaunt in silence, to hear what he meant to say.

"Your mother," resumed he, "has acted in a manner which her sobered judgment condemns: – I have been, I confess, uneasy lest, on her return to her home, she might claim you openly as her child; as such an avowal cannot now be made with propriety."

Rosella appeared shocked.

"But," continued he, "her natural good sense, which is no longer clouded by idle fantasies, and her earnest wish to repair the inconveniences she has occasioned you to suffer, have induced her to make a considerable sacrifice to advance your interest and future welfare. I was unfortunately absent when my counsels might have been of some service to you – I mean, when the concealment of your birth and the marriage of your mother was acceded to, from the avarice of your grandfather, the romantic ideas of his daughter, and the absurdity of that woman, Mrs. Ellinger. However they succeeded, as they imagined, in imposing upon the world; and now to publish a key to their foolish mystery,[418] and unravel it, would make more noise than a prudent and modest young woman would choose to be the subject of; especially as their succeeding politics were still more lamentably arranged and conducted, and that the will of Mr. Beauclerc excludes you from any advantage a public discovery might have given you. You now appear a young orphan of a handsome independent fortune; and the accidents which have been a momentary disadvantage to you, will not be thought the result of your own imprudence, but that of your guardian's, who entrusted you to the guidance of a person deprived, for the moment, of the power of acting with propriety."

The motion of Mrs. Methwald's head now discovered that she eagerly desired to plant a wise sentence after this observation; but her brother averted it by proceeding rather more rapidly.

"This is your mother's own remark; but if an investigation of your birth takes place – if your affinity to *her* is made known, who in spite of the utmost precaution, and the greatest activity in explaining the truth, will not escape the stigma which the most lamentable of human evils, an entire derangement of reason, affixes to a family – your future establishment in life might be much injured, and the repentance of your mother rendered still more bitter than it is. And therefore, my dear child, she has consented to your residence with Mrs. Methwald, which I am certain the good humour and good sense of each party will render pleasing to the other, until chance and your own merit present you the future partner of your life."

Rosella turned to Mrs. Methwald at the close of this speech, to thank her for her considerate and kind hospitality; but her words were arrested in their progress by observing the countenance of the lady crimsoned over with agitation, and every nerve in a tremor. She had begun to discover what these signals meant, and became so embarrassed that her intended compliment of acknowledgment faltered on her tongue, and Mrs. Methwald replied to it by a cold bow.

"May I be allowed to express my wishes," said Rosella, addressing herself to the honest and well-meaning master of the mansion, "to see my poor mother soon?"

"Yes, my dear child," returned he with a peculiar kindness of accent she well understood, "you shall visit her to-morrow, and I will accompany you."

"Oh how much I am indebted to you!" she exclaimed; then recollecting that this energy might be a transgression against decorum, she checked herself, and repeated, in a less animated tone, "Indeed, Sir, I am very much obliged to you!"

Chapter VII

A RECANTATION OF ERROR – A DISASTER PRODUCTIVE OF A RENCONTRE

THE next morning early, Mr. Mordaunt ordered the carriage, which he very seldom used himself, that he might perform his promise in escorting Rosella; and whilst they were at the breakfast-table, old Philip entered to tell his Lady that Mrs. Cressy was extremely sorry she could not let her have her chariot for he morning, as she was engaged to go to the review;[419] but she would send round to her friends to endeavour to procure a carriage; – and Mrs. Cressy hoped her mother would have the goodness to excuse the omission of writing her answer, as she was occupied in dressing. Rosella looked distressed; and Mr. Mordaunt, coolly desiring his sister to inform Mrs. Cressy that her application to her friends would not be necessary, immediately ordered a post-chaise.

The lady, who expected to have the pleasure of being distressed to death for a carriage, whilst that of her brother was employed in the service of their young inmate, was disconcerted by the new arrangement he had made, and her conscience whispered a short sentence, which her pride however would not entirely subscribe to.

When the breakfast was ended, Mr. Mordaunt enquired of Rosella if she were ready for the excursion; and she started up with alacrity to attend him.

"Shall you," hesitated Mrs. Methwald, "do you mean – perhaps you stay dinner at Hampton-wick – and if so, I will take mine with Mrs. Cressy when she returns from the review."

"Yes, yes," returned he, "we will settle it thus at every event."

He then took the hand of Rosella, who curtsied her farewell compliment to the lady, and she was led to the hack post-chaise he had sent for, which his groom attended: but Mr. Mordaunt was not long in discovering that it was drawn by a most miserable pair of horses, one of them appearing inclined to gib,[420] and the other, which the post-boy rode, was so old, feeble, and stiff that it could scarcely be forced to move at any rate: and letting down one of the front glasses, he desired to know why he had been so ill-used, and was informed by the driver that his master had let out every other horse in his stable, and would not have sent these had there been another pair to be had in London, but that every thing that could go at all, had been hired for the review.

"We had better not go on," said Mr. Mordaunt, "I much doubt if these wretched animals can take us to Hampton-wick."

Rosella, who would rather have walked the whole way than have deferred the visit, appeared however so unwilling to turn back, that he would not disappoint her hopes, and bade the lad to proceed.

They were a most tedious time upon the road; but at length, to the infinite joy of Rosella, they turned up the lane leading to Avelines, and her heart palpitated with a mixed emotion of pain and pleasure, as every well-known object met her eye. When the chaise reached the house, she looked up to the dressing-room windows, and catching a glimpse of her mother's figure, as she suddenly retreated from one of them, hastily ran up stairs, and in a few seconds found herself in her arms.

The person of Miss Beauclerc was emaciated, her countenance pale, and it was easy to discover that she had lost her hair. Rosella was shocked to agony.

"Oh my mother – my dear, dear mother!" exclaimed she, "what have you not suffered! – And I, your incredulous and ungrateful child –"

"Say no more, my Rosella," returned she, sobbing; "if I have been unhappy, this moment enables me to forget it. – Oh that my follies, which have injured my daughter, might be as easily expunged from the remembrance of the unjust world, which will not separate my imprudence and her meritorious conduct!"

"Oh Madam! think no more of the past," returned Rosella, "but let the future find us happy in the society of each other! I will forego with delight those imaginary advantages Mr. Mordaunt speaks of, which militate against my first and most cherished duty – for I cannot give up my mother!"

"You are the generous, the amiable girl I thought you," cried the tender parent; "amidst the many chimeras I have absurdly indulged, that idea alone was not imaginary! Oh Rosella! I was awakened with horror to a sense of the follies I had committed! – Let me not recall the moment in which I found myself forcibly detained from my unprotected girl; let me not reflect upon the remorse that tore my soul, when the purse I would have sent her was snatched from me, and I was goaded each moment with a horrible review of the insults to which my misconduct had subjected her!"

"No, no," interrupted Rosella, eagerly, "it must all be buried in oblivion!"

"Let me recollect myself," said Miss Beauclerc, with an air of dread, "I must no longer suffer my emotions to govern me – I must watch over every start of what is falsely called sensibility, and be thankful that the flights of imagination I have indulged, have not wholly undone me!"

Rosella, as if fearful of disturbing the empire her mother fought to gain over herself, kissed her hand in silence.

"My dear child," resumed she more calmly, "our worthy friend, Mr. Mordaunt, has informed me by whose interference you was rescued from your regretted situation at Dunkeld. – Do not be apprehensive that I am relapsing," she added, with a sedate smile; "I am no longer in the clouds, and though I still think highly of my Rosella's attractions, I do not suppose that every unmarried man she may meet, must of necessity have retained a disengaged heart for her. But I acknowledge that I think the conduct of Mr. Oberne unusually assiduous; – do not however let me mislead you by romantic suppositions perhaps," continued she, on observing a sudden change in the countenance of Rosella; "I have only to hope that my dear child may be blessed with the regard of a good man, and that she may deserve his affection and confidence by a prudence and steadiness it has been my misfortune not to have possessed. – Mr. Mordaunt is all goodness – I would to heaven I had listened to his friendly remonstrances before I left London upon that fatal expedition, which, by its effects, has deprived me of the happiness of your society!"

"And why should you not indulge your wish and mine?" asked Rosella; "believe me, dearest Madam, I would reject the consideration of what is called the world, if I must purchase it at the expence of a sacrifice so important as the fulfilment of a self-rewarding duty, and the smallest diminution of your contentment."

"Mr. Mordaunt knows my sentiments upon this painful subject," returned Miss Beauclerc; "and I must not discuss it with my Rosella. I shall at least have the consolation of reflecting, that every pang I feel will be in the reparation of my errors."

Their mutual friend now interrupted the *tête-à-tête*, which he was unwilling to suffer of too great a length, and, finding both mother and daughter more calm than he had expected, he congratulated them on a meeting so satisfactory; and to disengage the mind of Miss Beauclerc from dwelling too much upon unpleasant recollections, after enquiring her hour of dinner, which he intended, he said, to partake of, he proposed a walk upon the lawn.

She then found leisure to enquire of Rosella the progress of her acquaintance with her aunt Delaval; and dropped some tears in return for the kindness and affection with which she had ever been mentioned by her.

Miss Beauclerc congratulated her with a tender smile upon the independence she had acquired, which she rejoiced in, she said, because it would do much in procuring the favourable opinion of the world.

"But," added she, "I cannot endure that your mother, with so ample a fortune, should make no effort to render your's more respectable; and I must request the assistance of our good friend to arrange my affairs, and preserve for you at least the large legacy I received in infancy from my uncle. You will find, Sir," addressing Mr. Mordaunt, "that I have been, since the death of my father, shamefully extravagant; but I had rather blush in your presence for an avowed error, than continue unjust to my child."

"Well, well," replied the good man, "we all know that houses cannot be fitted up, and estates purchased for nothing: so at present we will say no more upon the subject."

Rosella was much pleased to be spared a discussion that wounded her feelings; and she took advantage of a momentary absence of her mother, to entreat that she might not be suffered to deprive herself of any part of those possessions she herself so little wanted.

"What she can spare," returned Mr. Mordaunt, "you are well entitled to; but she shall not inconvenience herself."

At dinner, Rosella missed the old butler, whom she had always been accustomed to see at the sideboard; and when the cloth was removed, she rather inconsiderately mentioned him.

"I am much indebted to poor Simpson, I find," replied Miss Beauclerc, "since he was indirectly the means of restoring me to a proper mode of thinking – by a violent remedy indeed, but a very salutary one. Disgusted with a servitude which had cost him so dear, he returned to his native place; and there it happens that my selfish cousin lives, who had formerly seen Simpson at my father's house, and his enquiries drew from the angry old man a recital of all the follies he had witnessed, and others which had reached him after his separation from me: Mr. Bristock immediately made a further inquisition into my conduct, and most probably thought himself well authorized to act as he did."

Mr. Mordaunt changed a subject so unpleasant to the whole party; but Rosella, much shocked that she had inadvertently introduced it, could not recover from her chagrin. The spirits of Miss Beauclerc likewise drooped as the hour of separation drew nigh. When she rose from table, she led Rosella again to her dressing-room, and embracing her with tears she could no longer restrain, gave her a key to the small trunk which had been taken from her by Mr. Bristock, and restored with other things, as she would not, by sending it to Rosella, tacitly avow a charge that had been instituted against him.

"You must take this with you, my dear girl," said Miss Beauclerc, "and you will find in it a few baubles I have no further use for; it contains likewise, a picture of your unfortunate father," added she, with a deep sigh, "whom my romantic imprudence conducted to an early grave!"

"Oh do not, dearest Madam," said Rosella, "do not render this meeting, which I have ardently longed for, so inexpressibly painful to me."

"I will not," replied Miss Beauclerc hastily, and wiping her eyes; "no, Rosella, my future study must be to improve your happiness – I have already given you sufficient pain. But I will have done – we will return to our good friend; – let me entreat you however, my love, before we join him, not to betray too much emotion when you quit me, that I may, without appearing selfish, invite you to repeat this indulgence."

Rosella promised to govern herself, and they descended to the apartment where Mr. Mordaunt awaited them, who immediately asked for his coffee; and at seven o'clock he reminded Rosella that they had a few miles to travel, who recollecting the caution she had received, avowed herself ready to accompany him.

Miss Beauclerc would have had the little coffer, of which she had given her the key, put into the chaise; but Mr. Mordaunt, who imagined from its appearance that it contained valuables, would not, he said, be, encumbered with baggage, but promised to send a servant for it the next morning; which he thought more safe than venturing it at so dangerous an hour as it must necessarily be before they reached his house.[421]

Miss Beauclerc acquiesced; and accompanying her guests to the door, she presented her hand to her old friend, and embracing his young companion, suddenly withdrew: Rosella, as the chaise drove away, vainly looked up to the dressing-room for a parting glance, whilst Mr. Mordaunt pretended to admire the landscape from the window on his side; – she so far recovered herself, however, as to present him a countenance which had some pretensions to cheerfulness, and in a few minutes conversed with calmness and coherency.

They had crept almost a foot pace for about two miles, when Mr. Mordaunt perceiving that it would be impossible to reach town till it was entirely dark, at the rate they travelled, called to the lad to push on; and he was informed in reply, that the poor beasts would do very well when they got warm.

But this favourable event not appearing likely to happen soon, Rosella enquired if it would not be better to send back the groom, and borrow Miss Beauclerc's horses.

"She would not have suffered us to have left her house in this equipage," returned Mr. Mordaunt, "depend upon it, had not that sordid villain, her cousin, instantly sold her carriages and horses when he took possession of Avelines!"

Rosella was hurt at this intelligence almost to tears, but she would not make any comment upon it.

The driver had taken them through Kingston owing to some obstruction in the other road, and with much lashing, coaxing, and swearing, had reached the middle of Putney-heath when one of the animals refused to advance, and every essay to force it forward only increased the dark aspect of affairs, by making it back the chaise into a hollow, where it overturned, in spite of the mutual efforts of the postillion and the servant who followed it.

Neither Mr. Mordaunt nor his companion were in the least hurt, but, for the first time in her life, Rosella heard an oath pass his lips; for it was now very nearly dark, and the place by no means so safe as might have been wished. He cursed the folly of the driver for bringing them that way, and as the lad made no reply, and instead of assisting to disengage the vicious beast from the carriage, stood muttering execrations on his part, he began to fear that there was more of design than accident in the circumstance, especially as in a few minutes after, he distinguished the clattering of horses' hoofs, which approached at full speed.

"Will," cried he to the groom, "have you your pistols?"

The man replied that he did not know of staying so late, and he had not brought them.

"Psha!" ejaculated his master, still more out of temper: "I shall walk forward to the next house," resumed he, taking the arm of Rosella, "when I reach it, you shall ride on, and bring me another chaise."

At this moment the horsemen, instead of passing, suddenly stopped; and Mr. Mordaunt fully expecting the usual demand, was preparing to transfer his cash without bond or obligation,[422] when a voice more courteous, enquired if he wished for assistance.

"I thank you, Sir," returned Mr. Mordaunt, "but I believe our most prudent plan will be what I mentioned."

"Is the chaise then damaged?" asked the stranger.

"I don't think it is," said the post-boy; "but I an't able to sit my horse; for that devil has almost jammed my leg with the pole."[423]

"Why did you not before say that you was hurt?" exclaimed Mr. Mordaunt in a softer accent than he had hitherto used; "if I had been aware of it, do you imagine I would have left you without assistance?"

The stranger, without any further preliminary, dismounted, and with the joint efforts of his own servant and Will, raised the fallen chaise, whilst Mr. Mordaunt held the saddle-horses. Rosella, meantime, offered the boy some hungary-water[424] to bathe his leg, which he thankfully accepted; and as she considered herself to be the primary cause of his misfortune, she put a guinea into his hand, a *largesse* that entirely consoled him for it.

He was quite unable, however, to ride but upon the bar of the chaise,[425] and Mr. Mordaunt not choosing to enter it again, resolved to walk forward as he had intended.

The stranger then bade him good night, and was mounting his horse when Mr. Mordaunt, having again taken the arm of his young charge, exclaimed –

"You tremble, Rosella, are you still frightened? – Be of good cheer – we shall soon reach a house."

"Rosella!" repeated the gentleman, walking again towards them, "is this Miss Montresor?"

Her conductor answered in the affirmative, for Rosella was dumb.

"But you, Sir," continued Mr. Mordaunt, "have no companion to announce you to us, either designedly or undesignedly; and I being literally in the dark, and figuratively in the dark, should feel a satisfaction in being enlightened a little!"

The gentleman had given his horse to his servant, and was now walking by their side.

"Miss Montresor does not recollect my voice?" said he, in a tone of enquiry.

"Yes," replied she, in a hesitating accent, "I believe – I think I do!"

"Will you have the goodness to prove it," returned he, "by introducing me to this gentleman?"[426]

Rosella was silent.

"I beg your pardon, Madam," he continued, "for my presumption. You perceive, Sir," addressing Mr. Mordaunt, "that this lady is far from being anxious to proclaim a name, which she may perhaps imagine will not make a very brilliant figure in the list of her associates; and as that is the case, I have little reason to be forward in announcing myself to any of her friends."

"You are mistaken, Mr. Oberne," cried she.

"A-hem!" issued from the lungs of Mr. Mordaunt, and Rosella no longer knew what she meant to have further said.

The groom now pointed out a light at a small distance, that seemed to proceed from a house by its being stationary; and thither they were glad to hasten for shelter from a heavy shower, which was fast coming on; but to reach it, they were obliged to quit the road, and stumble over the inequalities of a trackless waste. Rosella was still led by Mr. Mordaunt, who being booted, did not observe the various hollows filled with water through which he dragged her; and as she considered the motive from which he had taken this unpleasant excursion, she thought that at least she ought to bear the inconvenience of it with patience and fortitude.

The rain now poured down in torrents, and they were yet a considerable distance from the light, when she found herself walking apparently into a pond, and called to her conductor to stop; at the same moment Oberne, who was acquainted with the spot, caught her up, and carried her through the water, which was only knee deep – a temerity the elder gentleman very wisely chose not to hazard, but marched back again, and took a considerable circuit to rejoin his fair charge, who was scarcely landed when she heard Mr. Mordaunt hallooing to her, and would have answered the call in person, but that Oberne would not suffer it; he urged her towards the shelter, which was nearer than he had supposed it, and with some difficulty they at length reached it.

A woman who was, she said, just going to bed, and indeed it was the light in the upper apartment of her little tenement that had attracted the wanderers, stepped down, and opened the door: but alas! there was no fire in the cottage, nor had she any fuel but a bundle or two of sticks her children had picked up on the heath, and they were too wet to light immediately, because they had not been housed in the storm.

Oberne, who saw Rosella pale, fatigued, and forlorn, was inexpressibly uneasy, and waited the arrival of Mr. Mordaunt with impatience, that they might hold a council of war, whether even when a chaise was procured, she ought to venture into it with her wet garments; and she was equally anxious for his arrival on his own account, for the storm had increased to a hurricane of wind, accompanied by hail, rain, thunder, and tremendous flashes of lightning. Yet neither Mr. Mordaunt nor the men appeared, and she began to fear that he had unfortunately turned into a deeper part of the water, and that his calling had been the result of distress.

Shocked to agony by this supposition, she would have run out to seek him, had not Oberne prevented her by a superior exertion of strength.

"For Heaven's sake," exclaimed he, "pay some attention to yourself! – I will go in search of your friend, if you will promise to remain here."

"Run – fly then!" returned she; "he is drowned – I am sure he is!"

Oberne asserted that it was not possible; but he instantly left the cottage, and she heard his voice echo over the heath till the sound died away, and then her imagination was dreadfully busy in the most cruel conjectures.

The woman saw her extreme agitation, and asked if any of her company had strayed? – Rosella informing her of the accident she apprehended, learned that there was no water, for a considerable way round, deep enough to drown any body; but to counteract this good intelligence, the dame said it was much more likely the poor gentleman was beset by rogues, and belike murdered. Her guest shuddered, and the woman then proceeded to state that a man had had his throat cut, not above a month back, within a quarter of a mile of the place; and was entering into every particular of the murder, but that Rosella entreated her to forbear.

Not to be entirely idle, and in the hope perhaps of a reward, the considerate dame then undertook to make a fire with the wet wood; and after having filled her cabin with a smoke so thick that it drove her fair inmate more than once into the storm to recover her breath, she at length succeeded in kindling a blaze; but Rosella could not feel cheered by it whilst Mr. Mordaunt and Oberne remained unsheltered, and in a state of alarm and distress that almost annihilated her faculties, she waited half an hour without intelligence of either.

A violent knocking at the door then awakened her expectation; but the woman of the house began to tremble and change colour, from the recollection of the story she had been so cruelly prevented from dwelling upon in all its horrors, and she would not suffer Rosella to open it before she had made circumstantial enquiries of the person without.

"Havn't you got a young lady here, Mother Smith?" returned a hoarse voice.

"Lack-a-daisy, it's Jack Willis!" cried the dame, unbolting the entrance.

Rosella discovered the figure of Oberne immediately behind that of the man, and eagerly asked if Mr. Mordaunt were safe?

"Perfectly so," he replied; "he missed this cottage, and was admitted into another, where he has been much alarmed – You wear mourning!" exclaimed he, interrupting himself, "I hope you have not lost a very dear friend?"

"It is for poor Mrs. Delaval that I mourn," returned Rosella; "but tell me, am I to seek out Mr. Mordaunt, or will he join me here?"

"The man is gone to conduct him hither," replied Oberne.

Rosella then resumed her seat, and the woman ran out for her last bundle of wood.

As Oberne leant against the dark chimney-side, she thought, as the light gleamed upon his face, that he was much altered; and the intelligence of Povey suddenly recurring to her, she enquired, in an accent of kindness, if he had been indisposed since she had last the pleasure of seeing him.

"The *pleasure* of seeing me!" repeated he abruptly; "you had likewise the pleasure of seeing me solicit your notice for ten minutes, in vain: yet this was not according to the tenor of our compact at Dumbarton."

Rosella remembered that this compact alluded to his expected change of circumstances.

"Indeed," said she earnestly, "you mistake, and do me injustice in supposing that I could have been guilty of such rudeness to any one, much less could I have voluntarily lowered myself in the opinion of Mr. Oberne, to whom I acknowledge that I am indebted for many polite and humane attentions, at a moment I much required them."

"Then we are still good friends?" asked he, taking a chair by her side.

"Yes, I hope so."

"Well then, my amiable Rosella, I will tell you all that has happened to me since I saw you."

The woman now entered with the fuel; but, disregarding her presence, he continued –

"I was called to London upon business, which I will not trouble you to listen to; but I must mention that it was of a nature to strip me by a litigation of all that my improvidence had left. A man, closely allied to me by consanguinity, offered to take my affairs into his hands, if I would transfer for a proper consideration, my right in the disputed estate to him. But this I refused, merely, perhaps, because it was urged too warmly; and the person, offended by my obstinacy, endeavoured to force my compliance by distressing me through the means of an agent, who was instructed to lend me money to defend the litigation, and then arrest me for it." – Rosella shuddered. – "I see you are acquainted with the circumstance," resumed Oberne; "indeed it was too public for a possibility of concealment, yet I imagined it might not have reached your ear. – You know then, that by an extreme resemblance between Lord Clanallan and myself, the very people he had employed to disgrace a brother, mistakenly forced him into confinement, and treated him with considerable personal violence, which acting upon the most irritable temper, has nearly destroyed a health already undermined by dissipation. I discovered the collusion to betray me; but at the earnest request of Lord Clanallan, I forbore to punish the perfidy of his agent, and rode this morning to a small place he has taken on Norebeton Common[427] to avoid his associates, that I might see him, as he expressed himself, before he dies; but I believe his dejection operates to make him fear that his dissolution is much nearer than I apprehend it to be."

"It was not you then," said Rosella, "who was hurt in St. James's-Street?"

"Did you hear that it was me?" asked Oberne.

"Yes, I heard it with extreme regret."

"If so," cried he, "I am almost sorry that I must relinquish my claim to so kind and generous a concern."

"I will promise to renew it then," said Rosella, with more apparent gaiety than she really felt, "the next misadventure in which I may chance to hear you are engaged."

"You are obligingly provident," returned he; "but I must entreat that you will not throw away all your compassion upon a broken head or a broken fortune, since there is another still more serious evil as likely to overtake me as either."

She looked for an explanation.

"Oh Madam!" continued he, assuming an air of levity, "can it be difficult to discover that I mean a broken heart?" – Rosella smiled. – "To be more serious – I have felt a strange *vacuum* in my bosom since I quitted you – I have been most unaccountably inclined to melancholy and contemplation – I have experienced a mortal abhorrence of the thoughtless extravagance which has injured my fortune – and I have a thousand times wished to ask you, if you could condescend to live –"

Where, or in what manner, Rosella could not hear, for the return of Mr. Mordaunt interrupted what she conceived to be the most interesting epoch of the interview.

"My dear child," exclaimed he, "I am glad to find you so comfortably situated. – I expect William every moment with a chaise, and I hope you will not remain long enough in your dripping garments to catch a fever; but we must both expect a cold and sore throat at least."

"God forbid!" cried Oberne; "situated as I have been these ten minutes last," he added with his usual openness, "I had forgotten the necessity of a removal; but with such a dread as you have now inspired, I must regret the charming *tête-à-tête* Fortune has obliged me with."

"Dame," said Mr. Mordaunt to the good woman, who did not understand the compliment implied to her in the latter part of Oberne's speech, "I suppose, as it is past your bed-time, you have been sleeping in your chair."

"No, please your Honour," returned she simpering, "I han't been sleeping, only I thought the young gentleman and the young lady seemed to have so much to say to each other, that I fancied my cackle would be troublesome."

Rosella now turned from the candle, which was flaring in the socket, that her crimsoned cheek might not be discerned, especially when the well-remembered "A-hem" saluted her ear; and she was not displeased when the sound of a carriage stopping near the door of the cottage, promised to relieve her from an embarrassment that grew insupportable, from the silence that succeeded the woman's notable speech; for Oberne, recollecting the unreserved communication he had made in her presence, to which it appeared she had not been so inattentive as he had imagined, was himself rather disconcerted.

The groom opened the door to announce the chaise; and Mr. Mordaunt looking out, observed that the rain was still more violent than it had yet been, and it occurred to him that humanity must oblige him to offer Oberne a place in the carriage; a proposition he very eagerly accepted.

The disasters of the evening appeared now to be overcome; and the good woman, who had proved herself to be so patient a listener to an imaginary *tête-à-tête*, found reason to congratulate herself that her repose had been so fortunately, for her at least, disturbed.

The first mile or two was passed in silence; and Mr. Mordaunt then awakening from a reverie, addressed himself to Oberne –

"Miss Montresor has informed me," said he, "that I, with her other friends, have acknowledgments to return you, Sir, for your considerate assistance when she found herself in a very unpleasant situation; and it gives me sensible pleasure that I have thus met with an opportunity of offering them, at a moment when I have witnessed your disinterested humanity in behalf of people to whom you supposed yourself a stranger."

Oberne returned a polite answer; but Rosella silently remarked that it was devoid of that vivacity which generally characterized his replies.

As they entered Piccadilly, Mr. Mordaunt enquired where he would wish to be set down; and as Oberne did not choose to detain Rosella a moment longer than would be found necessary in the uncomfortable chilled state she must necessarily be, he begged the chaise might stop at a coach-stand.

"But will Miss Montresor allow me," continued he, taking her hand, "to enquire to-morrow, how she has endured this unmerciful soaking?"

Rosella hesitated; for the fidgets and apophthegms of Mrs. Methwald rushed to her memory, and she would perhaps have declined seeing him in spite of her inclination to the contrary, had not Mr. Mordaunt replied to the request by giving him a card of address, and saying, that young ladies of the present day were not much to be found at home; but if Mr. Oberne would take the trouble to enquire for him, he should be happy to see him at one o'clock.

Oberne, however disappointed, took the hint, and accepted the appointment; and the chaise then stopping to let him out, he pressed the hand of Rosella, which he still held, bade her good night, and repeating the compliment to Mr. Mordaunt, they separated.

"It was fortunate, my dear," observed the old gentleman, "that this good-humored fellow, this Oberne *happened* to be on the road."

Rosella, imagining from this intimation that he supposed Oberne had not been unacquainted with the expedition, was hurt that he should entertain such an idea.

"He told me," replied she, "that he was returning from a visit to Lord Clanallan."

"I never heard," said Mr. Mordaunt, "that his brother had any seat on this road; but it is of very little consequence to the world where he plants himself: for I believe he is a most worthless fellow, and I have been informed that he has used this young man very ill."

Rosella was silent; nor did her companion renew the conversation before they reached home.

Chapter VIII

MAIDEN PERSEVERANCE – AND AN UNFASHIONABLE YOUNG WOMAN OF FASHION

MRS. METHWALD was not yet returned from her dinner visit; and Rosella, delighted to escape her fastidious and formal conversation, retired immediately to her chamber, having received an injunction from Mr. Mordaunt to take care of herself; an attention he seconded by sending Mrs. Methwald's maid to see that every precaution was used to prevent her from catching cold.

The first thing Rosella discovered, on entering her apartment, was a letter on the dressing-table, which she was informed, had been placed there, in the morning, by the lady of the house. She seized it with a curious hand, and on breaking the seal, discerned the writing of Mrs. Methwald, who took this method of informing her, amidst innumerable professions of friendship, and many very wise and pretty sentences, that she could not possibly think of offering her the house where she presided, as a permanent asylum, as circumstances might arise to make her own stay there uncertain; then followed many other reasons why the thing could not be thought of, the most forcible of which was, that two people who would fly voluntarily, and with impatience, to enjoy the society of each other ten months out of the twelve, would travel to the extremities of the globe rather than be compelled to endure each other for six.

"As the lady has been married," thought Rosella, "she speaks from experience, I suppose."

"You will think this," continued Mrs. Methwald's letter, "a very frightful picture of human nature; but I fear it is a just one."

"It is a just picture of a spoiled child," repeated Rosella internally, "and it may be a just picture of the temper of a childish, capricious woman; but that it is a just picture of human nature, and may be indiscriminately applied, is I hope, only the error of a writer of sentences, who to turn a phrase smartly, would in matters of opinion, almost turn Mahometan."[428]

The conclusion of this letter, which Nancy did not suffer her to read without many remonstrances, softened extremely however; for it entreated that Rosella would consider herself as a welcome visiter in the house, where her brother would always be glad to see her, and hoped that her visits would be long and frequent; but Mrs. Methwald further added, that she would promise, in order that both Miss Montresor and herself might feel more at liberty and independent of each other, that when she was engaged to families of such rank and distinction that her young inmate, from not being used to such society, might feel uncomfortable in it, she would, with the familiarity of friendship, leave her at home.

"I am obliged to you, Madam!" ejaculated Rosella, as her memory presented her with the contents of this epistle, whilst she reposed her head on the pillow; "it is certainly a most considerate precaution, to spare those blushes my rusticity might otherwise occasion you and myself."

As she reflected upon this very prudent letter, she felt puzzled how to act. Mrs. Methwald had tacitly allowed her to accept the hospitable proposition of her brother, without urging any objection; and now, in a manner that appeared to forbid an open discussion, she put a *veto* upon it.

"What," thought she, "ought to be the extent of my visits? – What am I to understand by the indefinite terms, long and frequent? – A month is certainly a long visit; but if I am urgent to quit the house at the end of that period, what caprice and ingratitude may not Mr. Mordaunt accuse me of?"

Vexed, and uncertain of what she ought to do – with the subject of Oberne's expected conference with her old friend intervening every moment to perplex her still more, she at length sunk to rest, after having resolved to acquaint Mr. Ellinger with her dilemma, who would she imagined, hint it to Mr. Mordaunt, or assist her in deciding what it would be most proper to do. To her mother she would not complain or appeal, from the fear of disturbing her quiet, or transferring an anxiety to her bosom, she rather chose to endure wholly herself.

The next morning she rose with a cold and slight cough, but not of sufficient importance to retain her in the house, and she found that Mr. Mordaunt had escaped wonderfully – a circumstance that consoled her for the unpleasant sensation she experienced when she was left alone with Mrs. Methwald after breakfast; but the good lady found out so many subjects to expatiate upon in succession, that Rosella had as little opportunity as inclination to advert to the letter. Indeed she began, when the clock had struck twelve, to attend more to the opening of the street-door than to the conversation of her companion; and as the moment of appointment approached, her absence and anxiety increased. A carriage at length stopped before the house, but no rap followed.

"I am going to make purchases this morning," said Mrs. Methwald, "and should be glad of your company."

Rosella bowed; she did not venture to excuse herself, lest the lady, on learning the visit of Oberne, should suppose her refusal originated in indecorous motives; she forgot however, to put on her cloak and gloves, and Mrs. Methwald was obliged to wait whilst she equipped herself – a situation, she afterwards said, Mrs. Cressy had never placed her in, to the day of her marriage.

When they had driven about for nearly two hours, the business of this sententious personage had exhausted itself, and she condescended to ask Rosella if she wished to call any where in the neighbourhood, before she returned home.

"But I recollect," added Mrs. Methwald, "that my brother told me you had not seen Mr. Ellinger since your journey; and as I believe it would be right that you should not fail in attention to him, the carriage shall take you to Chancery-lane, whilst I call in upon a friend in Brook-Street; but you will have the goodness not to detain me too long. – I am sorry I cannot accompany you to the house of your guardian; for really the manners and associates of his family are so different from mine, that I –"

"To me, Madam," said Rosella gravely, "no apology can surely be necessary. – I am much obliged to you for the opportunity you so considerately offer me, of obeying any intimation Mr. Mordaunt condescends to give me."

When she had set down her unpleasant companion in Brook-Street, Rosella once more bent her way to the residence of Mr. Ellinger, who was now at home, and received her with much civility.

When the usual salutations were past; he made a grievous complaint of the scandalous imprudence of his wife, and congratulated his ward upon her acquisition of fortune.

"Mr. Povey," added he, "was here yesterday, to make proposals to you; and I think, child, considering all things, you, ought to snap at them; – a prudent match just now would set every thing right again. So I advised him to apply to your good friend Mordaunt, and told him I would give him all my interest; and he promised, if no engagement interfered, that he would call upon him as soon as he was up to-day; but I dare say that will not be till twelve or one, for he is an idle dog when there is any business in hand."

Rosella had hitherto sat in silent surprise at this intelligence; but when Mr. Ellinger mentioned twelve or one o'clock, she started up in an emotion not to be repressed, and declared her abhorrence of a man who could treat her with such insult and impertinence as she had experienced from Mr. Povey.

The dowager Mrs. Ellinger at this moment entered the room, rubbing the flour and paste from her hands with a handkerchief that bore the marks of rappee.[429]

"Bless me, my dear," exclaimed she, "why you seem in tip-top spirits! – Aye, Miss, such good offers don't happen to every body; – what though you've got your pocket full of money, let me tell you a good husband, that will take care of it, is not to be had every day in the week."

"If you mean Mr. Povey," replied Rosella, with considerable impatience in her accent and manner, "which I suppose from what Mr. Ellinger has said, I shall never give him that trouble, Madam."

The old woman raised her hands and her handkerchief in surprise.

"A-hey-day!" exclaimed she, "what maggot's in the wind now!"[430]

Rosella, rather ashamed of her warmth, contemplated a retreat; and turning to Mr. Ellinger, told him that she would take another opportunity of speaking to him upon an affair, concerning which she wished to take his advice.

"Stay, child, stay," replied he, "what is your haste? – Take my advice now, and don't turn up your nose at what I have proposed: – let me tell you that Povey will be pretty well off, marry or not marry; for his uncle is a snug old fellow, and has no other heir than him."

"Mrs. Methwald will, I fear, be displeased," interrupted Rosella, "if I detain the carriage any further."

"Well then send it away, and dine with us," cried the old lady, "and we will send for Povey, and settle matters this blessed day. – Come, come, I see you only want a little begging and praying."

"Mr. Povey's character," said Rosella firmly, "appears to me in a light so unfavourable, that no persuasion should induce me to receive his addresses; which I am convinced he would never have made to me, had he not learned the legacy of my poor friend Mrs. Delaval."

"Aye, child," returned Mr. Ellinger, "I wanted to talk to you about that. – Mr. Mordaunt can now take you into his own house, now you have got twenty thousand pounds to your fortune – when you had not two, you could be suffered to live with me; – and as to the objection of my wife being away, that's all nothing: though to be sure I expected our friend, the good lady at Avelines, would have interfered and adjusted matters a little, as there was always such an affection between them. – Here have I paid three hundred pounds, all bills which Mrs. Ellinger contracted without my knowledge! And it is, she must needs confess, very hard upon me that I should be saddled with the whole, when Mrs. Ellinger was always spared to attend upon Miss Beauclerc whenever she was wanted, and was never backward, I must say for her, to execute any commission that was given her; – and this, my dear, I hope you will represent to the good lady. – But I was saying, as to the objection of your being here – why, if Miss Beauclerc desires it, I will take Mrs. Ellinger home –"

"Take her home!" repeated the dowager; "and would you be such a fool, after what I have told you over and over, that you would be poisoned with dirt, and sent to a jail? – But I see how it is; I'll pack up my alls, and leave you to your trolloping fine lady! – The house don't hold her and me, mind that, Sam – I don't stay neither, to be the slave, and snubbed by a dawdle that can't make an apple-dumpling! – No, no – but so it is with you all – the poor mother's sent a trudging, and the wife's lady paramount all the world over! – Such a wife as your's indeed, with her milliner's bills, and all her scores unpaid!"

Rosella, shocked, frightened, and disgusted, repeated that Mrs. Methwald would be distressed for the carriage; and in the confusion of accusation and recriminating violence that ensued, made her escape, and was half a mile from the house before either party recollected themselves.

The time had, however, appeared longer than it was in reality; Mrs. Methwald was not ready to return home, and the lady of the house sent to beg Miss Montresor would walk up stairs.

Rosella was ushered into a drawing-room, where an elderly, formal-looking, very plain gentlewoman just peeped in, and making a half-curtsey, returned to an adjoining apartment, to continue a confidential communication to her dear friend Mrs. Methwald. But it happened that, as she was rather deaf, her companion was compelled to raise her voice to be heard; and the lady herself usually spoke in a loud key, that she might distinguish her own accents; so that Rosella, without any intention of listening, could hear the principal part of the conversation.

"My dear Madam," said the mistress of the mansion, "I know not how I can express my gratitude for the kind concern you take in my welfare – I fear you will be tired of my detail."

"By no means," returned Mrs. Methwald, raising her voice much above its usual querulous pitch; "I beg I may be informed of the whole, since you do me the honour to think me worthy of your confidence."

"My *dear* Madam!" exclaimed the other; "well, I believe I was telling you of the cruel slights I have received since his return to town. I no sooner heard of the selfish machinations of his brother, than I begged to speak with the faithless Oberne; for I still regard him as my betrothed husband, in spite of his desertion, as I conceive that I am not warranted in breaking through my engagements because he is regardless of his."

"Ah Madam," screamed Mrs. Methwald, "your principles are so exemplary!"

"*Dear* Ma'am! – well, but I wrote, I entreated, I expostulated in vain; – he had the heart to send me in answer, that he thought the most injurious part of his brother's conduct was that which had entangled him in the slightest semblance of attachment or engagement, where I well knew neither the one nor the other existed. – This, Madam, was cruel, and you might have supposed decisive; but no difficulty could impede my efforts to act with the utmost propriety and honour! – I told him he had tacitly plighted me his faith, though not at the altar; but I considered him equally my own, and that I was firmly his, and his I would continue to be. – The barbarian! what an answer did he send me! – His affections were engaged to a most amiable and lovely young woman, he said, at whose feet he meant to lay himself and his fortunes, broken as they were; nor should the absurd plans and iniquitous schemes of Lord Clanallan prevent his happiness, if no more potent obstacle intervened."

"Horrible!" exclaimed Mrs. Methwald.

"Admirable!" soliloquized Rosella; for she hoped that she was the object thus cherished. "This then," thought she, "is the woman whom he mentioned to me – it is singular enough that chance should have conducted me to her house!"

"But, Madam," continued the deaf *enamorata*,[431] "I hear that his brother is at the point of death; and I think I may entertain reasonable hopes that my infidel, when he has the honour of his title and family to maintain, will give up any imprudent plan he may have formed, and return to his allegiance and to happiness. – I hear too, that the creature who has fascinated him, is a little adventurer, whom he met with at –"

At this moment a violent rapping at the street-door prevented Rosella from distinguishing what this slighted but pertinacious dulcinea further said. A servant threw open the door of the apartment where she sat, and was going to announce a lady who immediately followed him, but stopped on observing that the drawing-room was only occupied by Rosella.

"If my aunt is engaged," said the new visitant, "inform her that I am not in haste."

Rosella, at the first glance, recognized Lady Lucy Estcourt; but as she was doubtful in what light she should herself be beheld, she merely bowed in silence, in return for her salutation.

"I believe I have the pleasure of seeing Miss Montresor," said the amiable young woman, extending her hand to Rosella with unaffected complacency; "and I cannot forget that I have her pardon to entreat for a very impertinent commission with which I entrusted Mr. Delamere at Guairdy. – Believe me, Madam," continued she, "when our good old friend Mr. Mordaunt, undeceived me, and I discovered the error I had adopted, however mortified I could not fail to be at my own officiousness and want of discernment, I experienced a satisfaction and pleasure, which your forgiveness will completely ratify; and if I did not fear that you would add to my list of offences, an effort to make my peace by adulation, I should venture to predict, from the amiable character of your countenance that I need not despair."

"And I too should fear," replied Rosella, pressing the hand she held, "that if your Ladyship could translate the sentiments that now contend for utterance, I should be accused of an admiration almost enthusiastic!"

"Oh you flatterer!" exclaimed Lady Lucy; "however I accept your compliment; and now you cannot refuse me your friendship without retracting."

Rosella eagerly declared that she considered this overture as the most delightful favour Fortune could bestow upon her: and whilst Lady Lucy waited the appearance of her aunt, they entered into a conversation confidential, in some degree, on either side; for though they had hitherto so little met, they experienced a reciprocal sentiment of good-will, that distanced the forms of a recent or slight acquaintance.

"Mr. Delamere informed me," said Lady Lucy, "that you much interested yourself for an unhappy young man whom chance threw in your way in the North. Perhaps you have not heard his fate?"

Rosella replied that she had not.

"He could not be prevailed upon to withdraw from the pursuit instituted against him," resumed Lady Lucy, "when he learned the destiny of his unfortunate family; but he could not endure the misery of his reflections, when in his confinement he had nothing to divert his mind from them even a moment, and he ended his life by his own hand!"

Rosella shuddered.

"Poor Mompesson!" exclaimed she.

"His sisters," added the fair informant, have not, I believe, recovered their reason; "nor do I think the circumstance at all to be desired!"

Rosella gave her concurrent opinion, and a silence of a few seconds ensued, which Lady Lucy at length interrupted.

"My good aunt," said she, smiling, "is engaged, I understand, with her confidante Mrs. Methwald; and I hope my dear Miss Montresor will excuse the inattention of a poor, deserted, love-sick lady, especially as she is herself the cause of the misfortune, I believe!"

"Me, Ma'am!" said Rosella with a deep blush.

"I am apprehensive that you will think me impertinent, a second time," resumed the other, taking her hand, and speaking in a lower voice; "yet I must inform you how the affair stands, for fear you should fancy a certain gentleman in fault in this very dark business. – My aunt Venables, who has certainly, poor lady, been rather unfortunate in her attachments, fixed upon Oberne two winters back, as her adorer for the season; and as he had then spent his younger brother's portion, and meant, like Orlando, to "go seek his fortunes,"[432] Lord Clanallan endeavoured to make him improve upon the favourable opinion of the lady; but the youth was stubborn, and with much difficulty was entrapped into one solitary visit, which was however, construed by my good aunt into a declaration. I would not," added Lady Lucy, "have hazarded your censure by this explanation, which most probably, you think it does not become me to give; only that I fear, from the long conference in the dressing-room, you may be induced to believe a different story by and by."

Rosella imagined she ought to disclaim all interest in the conduct of Oberne; but her faltering tongue and blushing cheek contradicted her words, and Lady Lucy laughed at the protest.

"To set you an example of sincerity," said she, "I will confess to you that the business which brings me to town to-day, is a compliment I think it right to pay my poor aunt, by informing her in person of a change of name that will soon take place in the family; but to say the truth, my confidence will not have the merit of being of long standing, as I could not have concealed the circumstance from you three days hence."

Encouraged by this good-humoured unreserve, Rosella mentioned Mr. Delamere, and enquired if she had guessed right. Lady Lucy replied in the affirmative, and received the sincere congratulations of her new friend, who felt concerned that the entrance of Miss Venables and Mrs. Methwald now interrupted the *tête-à-tête*.

Her *chaperon* coldly pronounced her name, and the lady of the mansion bowed in a supercilious manner, and thus passed the introduction.

As Mrs. Methwald marched gravely down stairs when she had taken her leave, Lady Lucy stopped Rosella in the anti-room, and said in a whisper –

"It is all over with you – you are discovered to be the thief! – If you should survive your repentance, I will hope to have the real pleasure of receiving you as my first visiter when I have an establishment of my own."

Rosella, highly gratified, returned a look of delighted assent, and followed Mrs. Methwald, who in a fit of spleen, to which she was rather subject, had popped into her carriage, and left her guest to follow at leisure – a slight which in her present happy temper of mind, was entirely unheeded.

Chapter IX

INCERTITUDE – A HUSBAND'S SKETCH OF A DECOROUS WIFE

IT was four o'clock when they reached home; and Rosella, spite of the satisfaction the offered friendship of Lady Lucy afforded her, could not avoid reflecting with agitation, that Oberne had had the expected conference with Mr. Mordaunt, whose prudence had perhaps annihilated his hopes: she recollected likewise, with vexation, the presumption of Povey; and longed, yet dreaded, to meet the countenance of her old friend.

Her expectations of a private conference with him, however, were completely crushed, when she learned that Mr. and Mrs. Cressy dined with the family, besides a gentleman or two. But a sudden idea struck her, that one of the other visitants, thus characterized by Nancy as a gentleman or two, might possibly be Oberne; and she hastily dressed herself, that she might be first in the drawing-room. Yet the lady of the house had already preceded her, because Mrs. Cressy was arrived; and Rosella endeavouring to restrain her expectations, sat in a state of painful incertitude and emotion.

At length Mr. Mordaunt appeared; but he accosted her without any peculiar meaning in his eye, and she eagerly watched in vain for a sentence, a word, or signal that she could translate in favour of her wishes: he slightly mentioned, indeed, their mischance of the preceding evening, but the name of Oberne did not escape his lips.

To increase her disquiet, Mr. Cressy, who was a professed man of taste, and a connoisseur of fashionable attractions, tormented her with assurances of an improved manner; and very seriously declared that her *tournure*[433] was charming.

Mrs. Cressy smiled, and nodded her approbation of these encouraging informations, and even her mother assented; but not without a change of colour, and a motion of the head that looked suspicious.

Old Philip, who acted as groom of the chambers, now threw open the drawing-room door, and announced Mr. Lesley. Rosella was disappointed; but she would not even yet give up her hopes, till they descended to dinner without evincing any expectation of an addition to the party, and her spirits then sunk in proportion as they had been buoyant before.

Mr. Cressy, who sat next her, and imagined that she was overwhelmed with timidity upon this occasion, affected to encourage her, that she might shake it off;

and Mr. Mordaunt, who liked neither his niece nor her husband, was rather silent; but Mrs. Cressy made up for his taciturnity by an incessant cant gabble, composed of shreds of incomprehensible philosophy, common-place chit-chat occurrences, *bon-mots* uttered in her box at the Opera, the brilliant achievements of English Admirals, and the Spartan harangues of the French Directory,[434] mixed up with a perpetual tide of smiles and simpers, and occasional allusions to the excellent arrangements of her own establishment, rather at the expence of that which her mother supervised.

All this was evidently directed to Mr. Lesley, who stemmed the torrent, or sailed with the stream, as well as he was able, and contrived, now and then, to call the momentary attention of Rosella, by an occasional appeal to her sentiments and opinion.

When the ladies withdrew after dinner, Mrs. Methwald retired with her daughter to her own dressing-room, to repeat the history of Miss Venables and Oberne; and Rosella threw herself into a seat in the drawing-room, well pleased to be thus left to the indulgence of her reflections, which wholly occupied her for a length of time she was so little aware of, that she was surprised to see Mr. Lesley walk into the apartment, when she could not have imagined that the dining-room party had begun to disperse.

He looked round very cautiously, as if the everlasting prattle of Mrs. Cressy were still ringing in his ears, and he feared to behold her at his elbow; but finding himself agreeably mistaken, he hastened to Rosella, and with scarcely any preliminary, dreading perhaps an interruption from the return of the ladies, or the entrance of the gentlemen, he entreated her permission to apply to Mr. Mordaunt for his countenance in addressing her.

Rosella, indignant at a precipitation that indicated a tolerable assurance of success, and confused at the nature of the demand, hesitated for an answer, when the voice of Mr. Cressy in the adjoining room added to her agitation.

"You do not forbid me then?" said Lesley.

She had not time to undeceive him before Mr. Cressy entered, who fancying he had made an important discovery, turned from the lady to the gentleman with a very significant smile, and hinted rather plainly at the style of conversation he believed he had interrupted; whilst Rosella endeavoured in vain to shut her ears against his *innuendos*, which created in her an impatience she could scarcely control; nor did Mrs. Cressy, when she condescended to re-appear, hear them with more *sang froid*.

Her husband, as much pleased with his newly possessed secret as a monkey is with a piece of looking glass, flew off after coffee, to circulate it amongst those of his associates who remained in town, and the dearth of topics from the deadness of the season, joined to his industry, had in a very short space the expected effect of rendering entirely public the approaching marriage of Lady Morteyne's brother with Mr. Mordaunt's ward; who was talked of under a variety of characters, amongst which that of the amiable and captivating young heiress began to preponderate.

The next morning her good old friend desired that she would follow him into his study; and when she was seated, he put on his spectacles in silence, and rummaged amongst some papers for nearly five minutes, exclaiming at intervals –

"Psha – that is not it – yes – no – I have mislaid it!"

"Can I assist your search?" said Rosella, with a palpitating heart; "may I enquire what you miss?"

"A letter, my dear – a letter that relates to you."

"To me, Sir!"

"Yes, yes – you are surprised, I suppose, that I should receive a letter relating to you; and I am equally, and more unaffectedly, surprised at the assurance of the fellow."

Rosella, who was thinking of Oberne, felt chagrined and hurt.

"You are no longer," resumed the old man, "Rosella Montresor, possessing merely a competency, whom the swarm of money-hunting puppies would have overlooked! – No – you are now charming, fascinating! – You are amiable, accomplished, and irresistible it seems! – And since the death of your good friend, and your acquisition of fortune, you are suddenly so improved in loveliness, that I have received in your behalf two tenders of wounded hearts, and very deep-palmed hands, which a less sum than thirty thousand pounds would not fill up."

Rosella could not reply with vivacity to this just observation; indeed she hoped that it was not just – she hoped that Oberne would have acted in the same manner, had she still been the insignificant Rosella Montresor, with only two thousand pounds to present him. How great then was her surprise to find, that poor or rich, an unprotected orphan, or a wealthy ward, Oberne thought not of her! at least he had not given any proof that he did; for the two proposals Mr. Mordaunt spoke of, were from the unthought-of Povey, and Mr. Lesley: the first by letter, the second in person before he withdrew on the preceding evening.

The countenance of Rosella betrayed a very strongly-marked disappointment; but her old friend appeared not to observe it.

"As for this Povey," said he, "you will not be displeased, I suppose, if I reject his suit, though my coadjutor, Ellinger, favours his pretensions it seems; but that is easily accounted for: he imagines that if this puppy obtains your money, he will not be in a hurry to resume his quill; and young Ellinger, I hear, has made himself useful to the uncle, who, since his hopeful nephew deserted him, has undertaken to advance the lad's interest. – But Mr. Lesley's application deserves attention and, if my advice has any weight, you will take time to reflect upon it. He is a young man of family, possesses a respectable property, and is nobly allied."

Rosella would scarcely suffer Mr. Mordaunt to conclude the sentence –

"Ah Sir!" exclaimed she, "did you not this moment say, that but for the kind remembrance of Mrs. Delaval, this man would probably not have condescended to notice me? and can I experience any gratitude for an attachment so mercenary?"

"There, there!" returned Mr. Mordaunt, "now you must sport your romance and heroics! – I thought, child, you had been surfeited of such folly. – In the name of God, do you suppose a man is to cull a wife out of a dairy or a hay-field, to prove that he is disinterested? – Or that he is to provide a race of beggars to his family name, to shew the world that he despises the dross that is to buy them bread? – If you don't mean to accept the proposals of any man till you are assured that he is wholly indifferent to your fortune, by all means divest yourself of every farthing, and wait till you are sought after portionless and destitute."

Rosella saw that he was displeased, and suppressed what further she wished to urge; yet she found in herself so great a repugnance to encourage, even tacitly, any idea that she could be induced from motives of interest, or as Mr. Mordaunt might have said, of prudence, to admit the suit of Mr. Lesley, that she ventured, when he became calm, to say so.

"Psha!" ejaculated he; "I shall not take an answer this day or two. – Stay – I almost forgot to tell you that I think you had better not mention to whom we were obliged for assistance the other night, unless indeed you are questioned upon the subject; for it may be thought singular that the young gentleman should *happen* to be on the road so opportunely, and you are not ignorant of the vile, ill-natured babble that has been circulated. – By the way, the exchange I proposed, that you might not be compelled to stay at home the whole of yesterday morning, was not approved by Mr. Oberne; for it *happened* that he forgot the appointment. I might perhaps in the interview have thought and spoken of the future and the past, and it may be that he has only a taste for contemplating the present: and besides this, I am free to confess that there *is* a trifling perceptible difference between a handsome young woman and a crabbed old fellow."

"You have not seen Mr. Oberne then?" said Rosella, in a tone of half-stifled vexation.

"Neither have I heard any thing of him," replied he.

She felt mortified, but would not venture any comment; and her old friend being compelled at this moment to attend to other business, they parted.

Wherefore should Oberne, who was all openness, avoid a conversation with Mr. Mordaunt? was a question she repeated several times. – He had been, she thought, too explicit to be mistaken; yet if her hopes should have misled her – if Oberne, in his letter to Miss Venables had alluded to another! – This supposition was too painful to be long entertained, and at length she soothed her inquietude by concluding that the report of her increased fortune had reached him, and prevented the intended application. This obstacle she ardently wished to remove, and end at once the expectations Mr. Lesley might have formed, which she would have done, notwithstanding her reluctance to irritate her well-meaning and affectionate adviser, but that the everlasting presence and watchful eye of Mrs. Cressy perpetually prevented the *tête-à-tête* which he sought, and which Rosella would not avoid.

Ten days passed in a suspense and inquietude she could ill conceal: in this interval she received her little *coffre-fort*[435] from her mother, and was surprised, but not gratified, to find that it contained all the jewels of value Miss Beauclerc possessed; but she remonstrated in vain upon the subject.

The portrait of her father excited a variety of mixed sensations, accompanied by curiosity and interest to learn his adventures and misfortunes, the more teasing, as she had once had it in her power to gratify them; and Mr. Mordaunt not only refused to impart any circumstance at present, to revive unpleasant recollections, but enjoined Rosella, as she valued the peace of mind of her mother, not to mention the subject to her.

The marriage of Lady Lucy had been publicly announced the fourth day from their meeting; and the peculiar fretful turn of Mrs. Methwald's temper and habits heightened her wishes for the moment when her amiable friend could, with propriety and convenience, perform her generous promise of claiming her as a visitant; for it was rather extraordinary that the good lady, notwithstanding her apophthegms on decorum and the wonderful effects of a proper education, actually appeared inconsolable that her daughter, the most peerless of sensible and accomplished women, should lose a dangler by the trumpery attractions of an absurd girl, who conducted herself entirely without method, who never made incomprehensible extracts from incomprehensible authors, never studied the high-sounding ebullitions of a crack-brained writer to improve her language, or looked into Voltaire or Rousseau to improve her morality.[436]

At this moment however, unpleasant as were the consequences of Mr. Lesley's assiduity to Rosella, as both Mrs. Methwald and her daughter had particular reasons not to offend Mr. Mordaunt by openly affronting his ward, their resentment was confined to trifling subjects, from which uncomfortably as she could not but feel affected by it, she had no apparent reason to complain.

Rosella was thus situated, when one morning Mrs. Methwald received a billet from Miss Venables, with whom she constantly kept up an intercourse of note-writing, independent of very assiduous visitings on either side; but this billet was of so much more importance than usual, that the good lady was agitated from head to foot on reading it; and having, very much against the inclinations of Rosella, sent her to dine with Mrs. Cressy, that she might not be placed in the indecorous predicament of sitting at a table where the mistress of it was absent, she threw herself into her carriage, and was taken to her friend's house, where she had previously declared she should spend the day.

At Mrs. Cressy's Rosella learned the occasion of this commotion; for there the master of the house, whose motions were not always regulated by profound wisdom, deferred an excursion he was making, and flew home, when he had already rode several miles, to spread the news of Lord Clanallan's death, which happened the day before.

Rosella was much affected by this intelligence. – Oberne, the generous Oberne, would now no longer be compelled to quit his country, to seek a precarious existence in another; he was now at liberty to claim her hand, and the most rigid guardian could not withhold his consent: but would he still be the same Oberne, who sought her society under the disadvantages with which she had first appeared to him – who, when others condemned and insulted, justified and defended her?

Mrs. Cressy, who adopted what she called easy manners when her own convenience was in question, had dined *tête-à-tête* with her guest, and amused her by requiring her assistance to alter her head-dress for the evening, when she really had, or pretended she had an indispensable engagement; and then desiring Rosella to make use of her books and music as she thought proper, or, if she chose to return home, to take servant to attend her, she smiled, curtsied, and stepped to her carriage.

Rosella, knowing that Mr. Cressy was not expected to return till the next day, sat indulging, in listless inactivity, the reveries that stole upon her till the twilight came on: the stillness of the evening, and a few reflections upon the rude neglect of Mrs. Methwald and her daughter, which would intrude amidst others more welcome, had given them a tinge of melancholy.

"There is but one being," thought she, "of whose affection I can be so far assured that at this moment I may venture to believe she reciprocally thinks of me; and from her I am separated by the effect of that very sensibility she indulges! – Excepting her, there is no one to whom I should dare to confide my sentiments but the amiable Lady Lucy Delamere! – Ah! when, when shall I be relieved from the miseries of forced civility, half-stifled malignity, studied slights, and a restrained intercourse with all around me?"

The opening of the door interrupted her soliloquy, and she was at once surprised and disconcerted to see Mr. Cressy walk into the room.

"My charming Rosella," exclaimed he, "you perceive that I have abridged my absence in the successful hope of finding you here at my return."

"Sir!" said Rosella, with a look not sufficiently grateful perhaps for the condescension thus announced.

"Nay," he resumed, "don't affect the dignity of the old school – those expressive eyes have not been so encouragingly cast down at my constant approach, without a cause. My dear child, you either guessed that I admired you, or wished that I should: and faith, whether it was the one or the other, you displayed some judgment in the intimation!"

This vanity and assurance almost silenced Rosella, who was tormented by an apprehension that she might undesignedly have authorized such an opinion; scarcely knowing what she meant to say, she was going to mention the permission Mrs. Cressy had given her, to be attended home by one of her servants; but when she uttered the lady's name, he interrupted her by repeating it with a horrible grimace.

"Mrs. Cressy!" exclaimed he: "a woman with a countenance, both as to form and expression, the exact resemblance of a demure tabby-cat blinking in a window! – In the name of propriety and decorum, let her mouse where she pleases; but never let me be tormented either with her velvet paws or her uncased nails!"

"These are not proper sentiments, Sir," returned Rosella, "for me to listen to; the friendship of Mrs. Cressy –"

"Her friendship!" retorted he, bursting into a fit of laughter: "you jest, my dear Miss Montresor – it is her pride and boast that she never was weak enough to profess or entertain a friendship for any woman.

"She speaks and acts ('tis said) just as she ought;
"But never, never reach'd one gen'rous thought –

"So very reasonable, so unmov'd,
"As never yet to love, or be belov'd!"[437]

"I have little interest, Sir," said Rosella, impatiently, "and I find still less satisfaction in this discussion. The character of Mrs. Cressy –"

"You are right," interrupted he, "her's is a character that cannot excite the one, or be productive of the other; let us dismiss the subject for a more pleasant one."

Rosella, without replying, rose from her seat, and rung the bell; and Mr. Cressy then endeavouring to recollect himself, assumed a disengaged air, whilst he reproached her prudery, and laughed at her ignorance of the fashionable conversation of young gentlemen, married and unmarried; and her want of practice of that excess of complaisance and good nature, with which the soft-mannered Misses of Ton were wont to listen to it. However, as importunity was a thing he abhorred to employ with others, or be tormented with himself, he readily acceded to her wish of returning home; and having, with his accustomed versatility, very strenuously recommended to her to receive the overtures of his friend Lesley with more indulgence than she had hitherto displayed, he ordered a servant to attend her, whilst he strolled to Brookes's,[438] to see who had dropped in there.

As Rosella stopped at Mr. Mordaunt's door, Lesley walked up to it, and congratulating himself upon this fortunate *rencontre*, accompanied her into the house.

Mrs. Methwald was not returned, and the drawing-room was empty; whither old Philip followed them with lights, and delivered to Rosella a letter, which she had a strong presentiment was from Oberne. The presence of Mr. Lesley was now doubly irksome to her; she ardently longed to break the seal, hurry over the contents, and know her future destiny; nor did she at that moment recollect how impossible it was that Oberne should have chosen a time so improper for the subject she surmised.

Mr. Lesley, disregarding her absence of mind, her evident discomposure, and those unfavourable symptoms which might have intimidated a less determined lover, supplicated to be heard with indulgence whilst he explained a circumstance that much occupied him.

Rosella made no reply; indeed she was very earnestly ruminating upon the probable contents of the epistle she had carefully conveyed into her pocket.

"My dear Miss Montresor," resumed Lesley, "I understand from one of your friends, that the connection between Miss Beauclerc and yourself is not of a nature to be dissolved; but that the prudence of your guardians has prevailed that the secret may remain one."

The attention of Rosella was completely arrested by this prelude.

"Permit me to enquire," said she, "to which of the few friends I boast, you are indebted for this intelligence?"

"Perhaps," returned the gentleman, "you already guess: I will inform you, however, that I heard it from the prim lips of that most insupportable of all women, Mrs. Cressy. Yet do not imagine that the communication, unpleasant as I confess it was, has in the smallest degree altered my sentiments; – you are sufficiently amiable to maintain an influence with me, too powerful to be shaken by an incident, which indeed displays your circumspection in a situation of so much difficulty as the one in which I first saw you. I have only further to say upon this subject," added he, "that I much applaud the measures Mr. Mordaunt has taken, which remove every obstacle to an alliance I earnestly wish, and to which I will flatter myself my charming Miss Montresor is not averse."

Rosella, equally mortified and incensed, was for a moment silent.

"I know not," said she at length, "why Mrs. Cressy should take the trouble to descant upon a circumstance which she acknowledges her uncle wishes to be untalked of! – I must profess myself, however, obliged to you for your favourable opinion of me; but I will, at the same time, observe, that no person shall, directly or indirectly, dictate to me the terms on which I ought to live with Miss Beauclerc, but Miss Beauclerc herself, whose pleasure it is that I act as I do: and if at this moment she were to inform me that she had altered her plan, I would subscribe to her wishes, not only with cheerfulness, but with real satisfaction."

"I admire your principles and your sentiments," replied Mr. Lesley, changing his tone; "and I hope to conciliate –"

"Pardon me," interrupted she, with earnestness, "if I say that what I have declared is merely with a view to place my conduct in a proper light, before a person who professes himself acquainted with the motives that govern it; the alliance you condescend to speak of may therefore still have with you the obstacle you supposed to have been wholly removed, and with me it has others, which I may not be anxious to remove."

"You are offended," said Mr. Lesley, "and apparently with justice; but Mr. Mordaunt, perhaps –"

"I feel no displeasure, Sir," replied Rosella more coolly, "on the contrary, I profess myself indebted to you for the example you have set me of avowing my sentiments with freedom."

She then withdrew, leaving the gentleman in a conflict of pride, mortification, anger, and involuntary admiration, vowing a mortal hatred to the first of women, Mrs. Cressy, who had, by her mischievous prattle and insinuations, involved him in this disgrace.

Rosella, meantime, flew to her own apartment to examine the contents of her letter, and was rather shocked at the formality of the address, which consisted of the solitary word

---

"MADAM!

"I have," it continued, "already directed an apology to Mr. Mordaunt for having failed to profit by the appointment with which he honoured me on Tuesday; but as you may perhaps recollect that my visit was originally intended to you – I believe, at least I hope, you will not think me officious, if I repeat the substance of what I wrote to your friend.

"A sudden and indispensable request from Lord Clanallan, who is alarmingly ill, and wished to see me again almost immediately after I had quitted him on Tuesday, prevented my attendance in – Street; and the most perplexing and urgent business has hitherto prevented the personal explanation I was anxious to give; which, from intelligence I this morning heard, I have reason to think you would find very little interest in listening to: yet I cannot, by remaining entirely silent, suffer an imputation of negligence and impertinence, I have not deserved.

"I have the honour to be, &c.
"ARTHUR OBERNE."

Rosella, stupefied by chagrin and disappointment, continued gazing at the letter some time after she had read it, and did not observe for many minutes that it was dated a week back; a circumstance that confirmed her vexation. It required no answer, and it was impossible she could have replied to it with propriety; but not to have received it before the suspicions it betrayed must be cruelly confirmed, was, she thought, extremely teasing and provoking. – And now might not he imagine, should he be undeceived as to her indifference to himself, or any engagement he supposed her to be under to another, that the change in his situation had operated to alter her sentiments? Her dolorous reflections were at length interrupted by the return of Mrs. Methwald; and she was compelled to attend at supper with very little inclination to partake of it.

Rosella, in her correspondence with her mother, which was regular and uninterrupted, had never mentioned Oberne, both in the fear of reviving unpleasant recollections, and that she might not engage her anew in what might have been called romantic ideas; but this silence she felt to be a great act of self-denial, and she was more than once strongly tempted to break it in her subsequent visits to Avelines, which were attended with more composure, and less productive of unpleasant consequences than the first, as Mrs. Methwald condescended to allow her the use of her brother's carriage, until Miss Beauclerc had accommodated herself with a new one, which was principally intended for the service of Rosella.

And to complete her inquietude, Mr. Mordaunt having arranged some affairs which had hitherto detained him in town, announced his intention of removing his family, for two or three months, to his country-seat, which was a considerable distance from the residence of Miss Beauclerc, and must necessarily prevent the personal intercourse now become her principal consolation.

Rosella had heard that Lord Clanallan, or as she preferred calling him, Oberne, had travelled to Ireland, and she could not therefore expect to see him even if she had remained in London; but she understood, from the communication of Mrs. Cressy to her mother, that Lady Lucy Delamere would pass a few days in the metropolis in a fortnight, in her way to Bognor Rocks,[439] where her brother's family *rendezvoused* for the autumn.

This intelligence rendered the notification of Mr. Mordaunt's intention extremely painful to her; as she feared, by losing an opportunity of seeing Lady Lucy, to lose also a place – insignificant as the conduct of Mrs. Methwald and her daughter made her apprehend herself to be – in the memory of one so surrounded by friends, so courted by happiness, so engaged in the enjoyment of the present, so flattered by the prospects of the future.

The day before the journey, Mr. Mordaunt took Rosella apart, and after some preliminary, enquired what misunderstanding prevailed between Mr. Lesley and herself; and with a little hesitation she informed him of the last conversation that she had had with him: nor did her old friend disapprove her conduct; and she perceived that he was much offended by the officious interference of his niece, though he was rather taciturn on the subject.

To Rosella he continued as usual, kind and attentive; but he retained several days towards Mrs. Cressy, who accompanied the party, a gravity of aspect she vainly endeavoured to soften by constant appeals to his sentiments, and submitting her own most favourite maxims voluntarily to his corrections.

He could not but perceive the inhospitable coldness of his sister, and he likewise discerned that it was felt by Rosella; but he knew of no other place to remove her to, which would carry with it the same title to respect as a residence in his house afforded her; and he pretended to be blind to the evil he could not remedy, hoping the good sense of his ward would enable her to conceal her disgust.

Rosella did indeed conquer it so far as to forbear complaint; but every time Mrs. Methwald indulged the peevishness of her querulous temper, she feared that her visit was too much lengthened; and every time she declined her conversation in favour of her pen or a book, or withdrew the whole morning to sit in Mrs. Cressy's dressing-room, where her young guest never had the honour of being admitted, Rosella fancied that it was an intimation not to be mistaken, that, according to the good lady's own words, she was ready to fly to the extremity of the globe to be rid of her.

Mrs. Cressy was however, when they met, extremely civil; indeed she was pleased with the effect she supposed her communication had taken on Mr. Lesley, as she attributed the coldness she could not fail to have observed between Rosella and him, to the discovery she had purposely made; and she could now afford to throw away a little *politesse* upon her favoured rival, without much outraging her feelings.

The spirits of Rosella sunk under the contemplation of the many cheerless moments she had yet to pass in this manner; and she began to lose that elasticity of mind, self-love and self-respect inspire, and to suspect that she must herself possess a most unsocial and repulsive disposition, since all the inmates it had been her destiny to know, were equally unpleasing to her, Mr. Mordaunt and her mother excepted.

Her only amusement consisted in solitary walks in the grounds, or in attending her kind old friend to his farm, of which he was very fond. Mrs. Methwald and her daughter were too refined to relish the common-place conversation of the principal part of their neighbours; that is, every family not recommended by some degree of rank or fashion: and unfortunately those with whom they were forward to associate, were in turn equally reserved; so that it was always the same family party, without variation, and without internal amusement; but extremely philosophical, regular, learned, quiet, and well-bred. It was indeed a most excellent household for a lethargic valetudinarian; but Rosella, who was neither of a sickly or sleepy habit, would have given all her worldly goods to have stepped out of this apoplectic paradise, and have peeped into the world she had quitted, to discover how the titled Oberne was filling up his time: if he was with eager haste, running over the same course in which he had twice before distanced reason and prudence, or whether abjuring the errors of his youth, he staid the impetuous ebullitions of a mind, where

> "Reformation comes in a flood,
> "With a strong heady current, scow'ring faults."[440]

Nor did she wish in vain: she had received a letter from Miss Beauclerc, informing her that their kind and mutual friend had so adjusted her affairs, that the trifling offering she wished to make to her Rosella of her own personal fortune, he had enabled her to do – an intelligence that communicated no additional satisfaction to her disinterested daughter, excepting when she reflected that it would render her portion more worthy the acceptance of Lord Clanallan, if indeed he had not forgotten her in the pleasant prospects he now contemplated.

As Rosella had no other correspondent than Miss Beauclerc, she felt no interest in the packet of letters laid upon the breakfast-table the following morning; but Mrs. Methwald having rather earnestly regarded the superscripture of one of them, put it across the table, repeating in a tone of surprise –

"For Miss Montresor!"

Rosella, according to the usage established by Mr. Mordaunt, immediately satisfied a very importunate curiosity by tearing it open.

"It is from Lady Lucy Delamere, Sir," said she, her eyes sparkling with delight; and she put the letter into the hands of her old friend, whilst the ladies exchanged looks of astonishment and displeasure.

"This invitation is both pleasant and honourable," returned he, "and must be attended to instantly."

With the permission of Rosella, he then passed the letter to Mrs. Methwald, who read it over in some agitation; and her daughter congratulated Rosella with a smile, upon receiving so charming a proof of the consideration of one of the most elegant and accomplished women in England.

Mr. Mordaunt had now taken up his own packet, and observing the writing of Lady Lucy addressed to him, immediately gave it the preference.

"Oh ho! here is a sop to Cerberus!"[441] exclaimed the good man: "this Syren promises to love me dearly, if I will prevail with my sister to part with Miss Montresor for a month or two; a request, she says, she feels the less difficulty in making, because she understands that Mrs. Cressy is now with her mother."

A most gracious assent was instantly given, to the infinite delight of the anxious Rosella; and according to the arrangement between Lady Lucy and Mr. Mordaunt, on the third day following she left Mrs. Methwald and her simpering daughter to astronomize, botanize, and philosophize at their leisure, whilst she proceeded towards London in the carriage of her kind old friend, accompanied by Nancy, and was met by that of Lady Lucy at an appointed place, which conducted her to the town-house of Lord Morteyne, occupied for the present moment by his sister.

Chapter X

A TOUCH OF HEROICS – AND A FINAL ADJUSTMENT

"HERE she is!" cried Lady Lucy, in an accent of pleasure, flying at the same time to meet her guest with the most enchanting suavity.

"Here she is!" echoed her husband, taking the hand of Rosella; her other hand was at the same moment seized – she turned to see by whom, and beheld –

"Mr. Oberne!" claimed she.

"No, not Oberne," said Lady Lucy, smiling, and leading her to a seat.

"I mean – I should have said –" hesitated she.

"You have said right," interrupted Lord Clanallan, "I am the same Oberne who have so often proved your patience and good humour; and with you I will know no other appellation."

Lady Lucy observing that Rosella was painfully confused, called him to order, and then enquired how she had left the good people at home.

"That is a question of course," said Mr. Delamere; "don't answer it, my dear Miss Montresor, but rather tell us how you think Clanallan –"

"As you cannot behave better," interrupted Lady Lucy, "I shall run away with my little friend; and we will sit and prose together in my dressing-room till you both cry *peccavi*."[442]

And then, in spite of promise or entreaty, she took the hand of Rosella, and withdrew with her.

When they were quietly seated *tête-à-tête* –

"You are surprised, my dear Miss Montresor," said the amiable young woman, "to find Lord Clanallan with us; but I hope you are not much displeased with me for the little embarrassment his unexpected presence has given you."

"It is impossible," replied Rosella earnestly, "that I can feel displeasure even in your Ladyship's presence, much less can I be displeased at any action of your's."

"This latitude you so obligingly allow me," returned Lady Lucy with a smile, "is a good presage for my friend Oberne! I have not, however, taken you out of the hands of the Philistines[443] to torment you myself; so I will refrain my flippant tongue, and inform you by what means you find him on your arrival, so comfortably established here: –

"When he returned from Ireland, he met by accident Lord Morteyne, and enquired when the world might congratulate Lesley upon his marriage: it happened that my brother knew so little at that moment of the intentions and arrangements of your rejected lover, that his answer did not entirely dispel those doubts our friend had formed from the officious communication of that gossip-loving Cressy; and when he learned that Mr. Delamere and myself were expected in town, he very impatiently awaited our arrival to be assured of the truth. We had been already assailed by the lamentations of poor Lesley, who execrates his own folly in not guarding against the machinations of his prim tormenter Mrs. Cressy; for, with more address than I thought her capable of, she contrived to make him the channel to communicate to you some trifling family objections raised against his suit. Mr. Delamere was therefore empowered to end the uneasy suspense of Lord Clanallan; and as we all abhorred the idea of your remaining in Mr. Mordaunt's enchanted castle, guarded by two such mountain-cats as Mrs. Methwald and her daughter, I resolved to claim the performance of the silent promise I flattered myself you gave me, to favour me with a visit. And from that time Lord Clanallan was not to be driven from the door, 'from morn till dewy eve,'[444] in the fear of missing the happiness of seeing you the first moment of your arrival."

Lady Lucy was now interrupted by a message, importing that her society, and that of her fair friend, was most impatiently wished for in the drawing-room, whither she thought proper to descend.

Lord Clanallan gave a loose to[445] his natural vivacity, Mr. Delamere seconded his cheerfulness, and his charming wife was full of those nameless attentions, those fascinating net-works that draw round the gentler affections, proceeding from a combination of polished suavity, good sense, and good humour – a charm the cold-hearted Mrs. Cressy aimed at in vain, and which, in the high-birthed seductress, degenerates into blandishment.

Rosella felt her own gaiety revive; but it revived like the slow return of health to the feeble, sensibly but not perceptibly. Her heart swam in soft contentment; and she spoke from time to time, to assure herself that she was not sleeping in the next apartment to Mrs. Methwald, and dreaming of happiness she was not destined to know.

In consideration of the fatigue she had endured from her journey, Lord Clanallan was persuaded to depart before midnight, with an invitation to breakfast the next morning.

When he was gone, Mr. Delamere approached Rosella.

"Lady Lucy," said he, "has, I find, stolen a march upon me, and received forgiveness for an error, of which I was still more guilty –"

"Let me entreat," interrupted Rosella, "that you will not renew –"

"I will not," returned he; "only permit me to say, that the paper you addressed to me at Eideva Lodge, I found there on my return from Scotland; and I should have acknowledged the receipt of it sooner, but that I was ashamed to address you when I discovered the extent of my fault. – Indeed I –"

"Now you have said quite enough," exclaimed Lady Lucy: "have the goodness to learn the exact point at which an apology should terminate – it requires at least as much judgment as to roast a pheasant; and Monsieur Servise will tell you that a turn too much *l'envoit au diable!*[446]

This sally removed the confusion of Rosella, and they parted for the night with mutual good humour and complacency.

The next day, Lord Clanallan was more than usually matinal; and Rosella was not quite dressed when she heard a double rap at the street-door, which she concluded was his. She would not however venture to peep from the window; but Nancy, whose spirits were much elevated since she had escaped from the dominion of Mrs. Methwald, felt no scruple on the subject, so she hastily put aside the blind, and thrusting her head out at the open sash, exclaimed –

"If here isn't the new Lord Mr. Oberne, God bless him! – coomed already! – And a leuks as merry as a grig,[447] for all his black coat!"

In two minutes Lady Lucy's maid came, with an entreaty that Miss Montresor would be so obliging to tell Lord Clanallan that she would descend to the breakfast-room in ten minutes: and if his Lordship chose to have any tea or chocolate in the interim, perhaps Miss Montresor would have the goodness to preside at the table till Lady Lucy appeared.

Rosella, who perfectly understood the meaning of this embassy, complied with the request, and entered the apartment where Lord Clanallan awaited her, in a trepidation he could not but observe.

"Ah! I see," cried he, "that I must thank my little friend, Lady Lucy, for this indulgence, which I should not have obtained at Mrs. Methwald's for six months, I suppose. – Encouraged and supported as I am," continued he, "by Lady Lucy's good wishes, and her promised good offices, I will hope, dear Rosella, that you still remember poor Oberne with a small degree of complacency: but may I hope too that you will forget his confessed faults and follies, and permit him to apply for a second audience of the grave and prudent Mr. Mordaunt? – whose former appointment I confess I looked forward to with some dread, ill-prepared as I was to answer stunning questions about rent-rolls and unmortgaged lands!"

Rosella was rather relieved, as he intended she should be, by this gaiety of style, and congratulated him with a smile, that his proposed emigration was now of necessity deferred a few years longer.

"Ah Rosella!" said he, "I believed that the period of indispensable banishment had overtaken me when I unexpectedly saw you in Charles-Street. I thought you refused to return my salutation; and I then felt all the misery of poverty, and the contempt it too often carries with it."

"You mentioned that circumstance when last I saw you," replied Rosella, much hurt that he should again recur to it; "did you not believe my justification?"

"I tell you why I repeat it," said he: "that you may be assured, from judging of the pain I endured at that moment, that I will never again plunge myself into a situation where my conscience may remind me, that at best I deserve the cruel pity of those whose esteem I covet."

She was silent; but a tear dropped from her eye, and he interpreted it as he wished.

"And now, my amiable Rosella," resumed he, "tell me, have I your consent to pay my compliments to your good old friend Mr. Mordaunt?"

Rosella suddenly recollected that there was another person to whom he ought likewise to apply; and all that Mr. Lesley had said upon the subject instantly recurred to her.

"Mr. Mordaunt, my Lord," said she, withdrawing from him the hand he held, with a change of countenance sufficiently visible, "is not the only one to whom I ought to account for my conduct; perhaps you do not know –"

"Yes, yes," interrupted he hastily, "I know all; and I can never forget that I am indebted to a certain dear friend of our's, for a prospect of the happiness I hope to receive her consent in obtaining."

Rosella felt a weight removed from her heart by this reply: the smile, which apprehension had driven from her lips, stole back again, and Lord Clanallan had little difficulty in persuading her to give him an explicit permission to apply both to Miss Beauclerc and Mr. Mordaunt.

He reprobated, with the generous ardour natural to his character, the idea of disavowing a mother for errors she had abjured, and encouraged Rosella to prove by her conduct the independence of her principles.

"Will you then," exclaimed she, "endeavour to persuade Miss Beauclerc to assume the name and character most properly her's, and add this more important obligation to those I already owe you?"

He was replying with much tenderness when Lady Lucy peeped into the room.

"Have you left me any breakfast?" said she, advancing: "bless me, my dear Miss Montresor," she added, on observing the *déjeuné* apparatus[448] in its original order, "what an Egyptian task[449] you have had! – I fear you will never excuse me for imposing it on your good nature!"

Rosella blushed.

"I give you notice, good people," resumed Lady Lucy, "that when my own breakfast is ended, I shall drive to Hampton-wick, to see if my brother's house is tenantable; for he has lent it to Mr. Delamere for two or three months. So if you have any inclination to accompany me, I shall be thankful, because I shall be able to find very ample employment for you."

Rosella looked her gratitude for this intimation, which she translated very justly into a wish of paying a delicate attention to Miss Beauclerc, and gratifying the feelings both of mother and daughter; and Lord Clanallan put the hand of their amiable friend to his lips, with a glance equally expressive.

Mr. Delamere almost immediately appeared, and the conversation became general. He was prevented from attending the party by having business to transact in town; and the two ladies, accompanied by Lord Clanallan, left him with a promise of returning to dinner.

When they arrived at Hampton-wick, Lady Lucy, embracing Rosella, told her that she would spare her for an hour or two; but that she would detain their mad companion as long as she could prevail upon him to attend to her injunctions.

"Perhaps," added she, in a more timid accent, "Miss Beauclerc will indulge me with an opportunity of paying my compliments to her in person; – at all events I will do myself the honour of sending my ticket."[450]

Rosella returned the embrace with sincere affection; but unable to reply, she left her in silence, and was conveyed in five minutes to the arms of her mother, who was not long unacquainted with the pleasurable change in her situation. The particular attachment of Lord Clanallan was the last intelligence that met her ear, but it was far from being the least satisfactory.

"Thank Heaven!" exclaimed the anxious mother, "my follies have not permanently injured your happiness! – Oberne, my dear Rosella, has too much good nature and generosity to reproach you in future with those imprudences to which you were yourself the victim; and if, as you inform me, he has bought experience and worldly wisdom from past lapses of discretion, you have every prospect of passing your days with as little vexation as a human being has reason to hope. And never, my dear child, diminish your comforts by an expectation of uninterrupted felicity surpassing the lot of mortality! – Perfect happiness, or happiness approaching perfection, is, I am now convinced, to be found only in fiction and romance. – Here is Lord Clanallan crossing the lawn! – Oh Rosella, can I forget what has happened since last I beheld him! – but I will think only of the future."

His entrance prevented the reply of her blushing child, and his assiduous respect to herself, his evident affection for Rosella, soon banished unpleasant recollections. She assured him of her entire approbation of his proposals, and that she derived, from the prospect of his union with her daughter, much future satisfaction to herself in the contemplation of their happiness.

Lord Clanallan had been rather shocked by the alteration still visible in the person of Miss Beauclerc; but he felt a secret gratification in observing the sedateness of her countenance, and the composed gravity of her conversation.

At length Rosella recollected the condescending message of Lady Lucy, and repeated it to her mother.

"Amiable woman!" returned she; "I ought on every account to call first upon her; but if she will have the goodness to wave ceremony in my favour, I confess I shall be pleased to avoid quitting my own enclosure, which at present I do not wish to pass."

Lord Clanallan undertook to inform Lady Lucy of her sentiments; and in half an hour he returned with her.

Miss Beauclerc received this advance with the acknowledgments it merited; and it was late when Lady Lucy reminded Rosella of the promise she had made to Mr. Delamere, of bringing back her guests to dinner. She mentioned however, that in two days she meant to return to the neighbourhood of Avelines to pass some time, and then she would hope that no circumstance could happen to prevent a lasting intercourse between the two families.

Lord Clanallan, eager to secure the approbation of Mr. Mordaunt, would not defer his application beyond the following day; and the good old man, perfectly satisfied with the statement of his *rent-rolls* and *unmortgaged lands*, and reflecting that the proposed union would completely efface every slanderous impression the former attendance of Lord Clanallan had occasioned, readily consented to the proposition; but he advised that every idea of acknowledging the very near affinity of Rosella and her friend at Avelines, by disclosing her history, should be given up.

"It is nonsense to suppose," said he, "that people will not comment upon such romantic proceedings, according to the fashion of their own opinions; and in proportion as malice, envy, and ill-humour prevail, in the same degree will acrimonious sarcasms be levelled at your peace, which, though you may affect to despise, will be unpleasant drawbacks to domestic felicity. So take the advice of an old man, and respect the prejudices of the world, whose atmosphere you condescend to breathe! – Believe me, it is only in a sentimental novel where fair ladies can Oh yes! all their perils, their follies, hair-breadth escapes, imprudences, and shipwrecks; and expect, at the winding-up of the catastrophe, to sail through the remainder of their lives so very smoothly and pleasantly, without one little breeze to whisper a remembrancer of past oblique adventures!"

Lord Clanallan smiled, and observed that it was not his province to endeavour to influence Miss Beauclerc by an indirect objection to any plan she chose to adopt; nor did he wish to oppose any determination she might ultimately form, for whatever it were, the sentiments he had avowed would remain unalterable; and he merely meant to intimate, that her own happiness and that of Rosella were with him the only consideration.

Mr. Mordaunt desired him to leave this point to his discretion; and he wrote immediately to Miss Beauclerc, to strengthen her opinion of the efficacy of her self-denial.

Mrs. Methwald and her peerless daughter received a shock by the intelligence of the approaching marriage of Rosella, which required all their fortitude, and self-command, and imaginary suavity of deportment to endure with decent composure; for the circumstance was a strong libel upon their judgment and discernment which had led them to predict that Rosella would remain the insignificant, unnoticed, mysterious little personage they would fain have thought her; and they now foresaw that they must toil hard in the trammels of forced civility and repulsed attentions, before they could induce the future Lady Clanallan wholly to forget the time, when neither maxim nor philosophy could make them overlook her offensive youth and beauty, and discover her claims to kindness.

Miss Beauclerc, whose sobered sentiments agreed with those of Mr. Mordaunt, insisted that her secret history should be confined to those who were already acquainted with it; at least she would not, by her own avowal, license the familiar comments of careless and indifferent associates, who spread, either with a malicious design, or no design at all, reports which wound the shrinking bosom of affection, and jar those interests which should never be disunited.

Whilst Rosella could occasionally enjoy her society, that of Lady Lucy, and Delamere, and was constantly attended by Lord Clanallan with assiduous attachment, she submitted with cheerfulness to the decision; nor did she repine, as he was apt to do, at the precise and tedious arrangements of Mr. Mordaunt, and count the weeks of his first mourning[451] with impatience; but she felt hurt, when she discovered that Miss Venables threatened an endless resentment to her amiable niece, for having assisted the pretensions of her young rival, and vowed that she should never possess a guinea of her fortune. But Lady Lucy laughed at her threats, and declared that she had acted the part of a dutiful relation in preventing her from marrying an Irish fortune-hunter; for so, in the fury of her disgrace and disappointment, the good lady had openly denominated her once favoured Oberne. She could not prevail upon herself to practise the philosophy her friend Mrs. Methwald preached; but highly incensed with her as with every one else, she espoused a French Marquis, who offered to engage in her service as an *aide-de cuisine*.[452]

Rosella had been about six weeks in the protection of Lady Lucy, when one morning she was called from her dressing-room by the arrival of a gentlewoman, who would not send up her name, but desired to speak to Miss Montresor immediately. In some trepidation she descended to the apartment into which this mysterious personage had been ushered, and beheld the well-remembered face of Mrs. Ellinger.

Rosella checked the surprise this unexpected visit occasioned, and advanced to her old acquaintance with a smiling countenance and an extended hand, which the lady, to her extreme consternation, seized with an heroic air, and throwing herself on her knees, kissed it with great emphasis of action, and wiped her eyes.

"I am pleased to see you in good health, Madam," said Rosella, after some hesitation; "may I enquire if you have seen Miss Beauclerc this morning?"

"No, much-injured girl!" replied the *ci-devant* heroine, with a forced agitation of features; "that lady and I meet no more; but you, whom her conduct and caprices have injured – you who are undone by her criminal concealments – you who are still ignorant to whom you are indebted for life –"

Rosella trembled.

"*You* interest and affect my heart! – Know then that this bosom possesses a secret – a secret to blast all your happiness, should it meet the ear of your lover!"

"Then, Madam," interrupted Rosella, with spirit, "I am convinced it ought to meet his ear; – if your assertion is just, my happiness is already blasted; for I practise no reserve with – with my friends. And as I imagine you have been so obliging to call upon me to communicate this tremendous secret, I shall be really thankful if you will end my suspense. Impatient however as I feel to learn it, I must first assure you that no circumstance can for a moment tempt me to suspect Miss Beauclerc of an intention to injure me, or any human being; – if she has had concealments, they are not criminal ones!"

"I would have you prepare," resumed Mrs. Ellinger, pressing her hand upon her heart, as if to still its emotions, "for a discovery I am sorry it is my lot to impart to you, ever beloved Rosella; – know then, that you are – oh Heaven! – the daughter of – Miss Beauclerc!"

"Is this *all* you would tell me?" asked Rosella.

"God of the universe!" exclaimed the poor lady, "what have I done? – Oh child of my dearest hopes, give way to your distraction, tear your hair, rend your bosom – any thing but this calm settled despair!"

"I am sorry I cannot comply with every request of your's, Mrs. Ellinger," said Rosella, with great gravity; "but as I am not really in a despairing mood, I have little inclination to act such a tragedy. – I am concerned that you have had so much trouble in seeking me out, merely to mention a circumstance I was well acquainted with."

Mrs. Ellinger gazed at her with an expression of countenance so ludicrously woeful, that Rosella could not forbear smiling.

"Acquainted with it!" exclaimed she; "my God! no *denouement* – no catastrophe!"

"No, my dear Madam," replied Rosella with some gaiety; "Lord Clanallan and myself thought it would be more novel to omit the usual ceremony of gathering together all the *dramatis personæ*, to rip up budgets of old stories,[453] and – man, woman, child, master, mistress, domestics, tenants, vagrants, friends, relations, and spectators – all cry, laugh, relate, be facetious and sentimental in the *finale* chorus!"

Mrs. Ellinger, disconcerted by the failure of her sublime scheme, and thus attacked on a favourite subject, was disposed to be heroic; but Rosella stopped the torrent just in time, by a gentle reprimand for her injustice and ingratitude to Miss Beauclerc, who had ever treated her with attention and friendship.

"I cannot however forget," continued she, "that Mrs. Ellinger, as the wife of my guardian, deported herself with much kindness towards me in my childhood."

The lady, extremely softened by this acknowledgment, recollected that it would be very desirable to preserve the favour of Lady Clanallan, whose countenance would give her a part of the consequence she had lost by quitting the roof of her husband; she therefore received the intimation with gratitude, and having declined the vulgarity of accepting refreshment, took her leave, saying she would write to Miss Beauclerc, whose affection she feared to have much diminished by the unjust accusations with which she had loaded her in a former letter; a circumstance that had never reached the knowledge of Rosella, who adopted in this instance the same prudent concealment, and by forbearing to mention the present folly of Mrs. Ellinger, avoided a retrospection of the influence she had unfortunately possessed over the actions of Miss Beauclerc at a former period; and the visit did not even reach the knowledge of Lady Lucy.

This amiable young woman displayed each day a more confirmed attachment to her fair guest, as each day unfolded to her observation the characteristic virtues and graces of Rosella; but at length they were compelled to separate, for Mrs. Methwald claimed the privilege of directing her brother's ward in the envied task of exchanging five hundred pounds for clothes and ornaments – a task Rosella left almost wholly to her, to procure peace and good-will when, for a short time, she again returned to the house of her good old friend. And whilst Mrs. Methwald was making daily perambulations to enforce the execution of her orders, she flew down to Avelines in her mother's carriage, to pass an hour with her, and another with Lady Lucy; a period generally spent by Lord Clanallan, who *happened* almost constantly to meet her on the road, in lamenting the heavy fetters of ice with which the presence of Mrs. Methwald and her daughter appeared to load the sentiments and manners of Rosella, who pleaded guilty to the charge, and conjured him to retain his patience a little longer.

Lady Lucy laughed at his woeful complaints, and rallied him upon his want of knight-errantry, in suffering his fair dulcinea to remain in such a cruel state of enchantment; but promised at length to use her influence with Mr. Mordaunt to abridge the term of his wintry punishment.

In one of these excursions Rosella unexpectedly encountered Lord and Lady Morteyne, who, in passing through town, had deviated from their road to visit Lady Lucy and her husband. She felt rather confused for the first five minutes; but the conciliating deportment of Lady Morteyne, who was much hurt at her former injustice, and wished to efface it from the memory of her sister's friend, and the polite attentions of Lord Morteyne, soon restored her to composure, and banished unpleasant recollections of the *fracas* at Guairdy.

Rosella had heard, from common report, that Mr. Estcourt was perfectly recovered from the effects of his accident, and his brother now informed her that he had very carefully concealed how deservedly he had met with it.

"But," added he to Lady Lucy, "that absurd fellow Povey, whom Cyril used to denominate your knight, either designedly or undesignedly, disclosed the secret, and our impetuous brother rewarded his officiousness by knocking him down on the Steine at Brighton; so that the poor little man, who from his original profession has a great abhorrence of breaking the peace, has been compelled to throw up his commission and, I presume, would be extremely obliged to any kind friend who would employ him to draw up marriage articles, or make a will."

This important intelligence created little emotion but of laughter; but Rosella was pleased that the affair had terminated so peaceably, as she would have been much grieved to have been again the occasion, however remote, of vexation to Lady Lucy, by endangering the safety of a brother who was beloved by her, in spite of his slender title to her affection.

"I once received very unmerited thanks," said Lord Morteyne, "for a service I was supposed to have exclusively rendered Miss Montresor; but I imagine she has long since discovered to whom the acknowledgments were due."

Rosella, with some emotion, averred that she did not comprehend his meaning; and learned from the explanation that followed, that Oberne himself was the knight-errant who had rescued her from the danger into which her runaway steed had placed her, when she had to unintentionally joined the chace.

She was much surprised at the intelligence; and Lord Clanallan at that moment making his appearance, was questioned upon his long concealment of the circumstance by Lady Lucy.

"I was unwilling," replied he, "upon a further acquaintance with our charming friend, to own that I was the stupid being who could commit her to the care of another, upon the absurd plea I urged to your brother."

"And so you suffered him," resumed Lady Lucy, "to take the whole credit of the exploit to this hour; rather than confess that having followed the impulse of humanity at the hazard of losing your life, you rejected that of gallantry at the hazard of losing your horse! – I would to Heaven," added she, "that the total absence of even politeness and attention, so much to be remarked in the present race of English *petit-maitres*,[454] could be explained in the same manner."

Lord Clanallan smiled at this apostrophe, and having thanked the good-natured Lady Lucy for the *tournure*[455] she had given to the adventure, changed the subject of conversation.

At length the moment arrived that emancipated Rosella from the dominion of Mrs. Methwald, and rewarded the faithful attachment of Lord Clanallan.

Mr. Mordaunt officiated as her father during the ceremony, and when it was ended, he embraced her with paternal affection.

"I believe," said he, "I have now done my duty as a careful and conscientious guardian: I am happy that I have not had occasion to exert my power by opposing your inclinations, my dear Rosella: and I trust that some years hence, should I live so long, I shall reflect upon this day with as much satisfaction as I experience at this moment."

Rosella kissed the hand of her venerable friend in silence; and taking leave of Lady Lucy with tenderness, and of Mrs. Methwald with polite acknowledgments, she set off with Lord Clanallan for a hunting-seat of his late brother's in Berkshire, taking Avelines in their way; where they received the fervent benedictions of Miss Beauclerc, who could not be prevailed upon to attend the ceremony, from the fear of betraying a too potent emotion, and affecting the spirits of her beloved Rosella.

To Lord Clanallan she presented all the furniture and appurtenances of her town-house, and the use of it during her life; and the cottage was purchased by Mr. Delamere.

Some time after the marriage of Rosella, her mother disclosed to her the history of her own imprudent union, and the unhappy catastrophe that ensued; and in consideration of the former friendship between Mrs. Ellinger and herself, considerably augmented her income, which the displeasure and parsimony of her husband would not allow him to make a very comfortable one.

Mr. Cressy and his Lady continued for some time to live in great apparent cordiality; but at length, to the unspeakable mortification of Mrs. Methwald, he declared, upon the refusal of her barbarous brother to make up his affairs, that a pale, prim, simpering, philosophical, deistical, botanical, astronomical, sophistical, soft-mannered, flint-hearted automaton was his supreme aversion: and his conduct evinced that an excessive rosy, open-tempered, ill-educated young lady, whose *ci-devant* employment consisted in making butter and cheeses, was not so entirely insupportable.

When the dear friends of poor Mrs. Cressy warmly resented this atrocity, in condolement and expressions of wonder and abhorrence, she still smiled in return for their obliging sympathy, retained her box at the Opera, and frequented assemblies as usual, to the admiration of her mother, who wrote a halting sonnet in praise of such fortitude and magnanimity, and sent it to be inserted with other sublime effusions, in the Lady's Magazine.[456]

Miss Beauclerc would have taken Nancy back into her own service, upon the marriage of her young Lady; but the poor girl had promised herself such felicity and honours in being *fam-de-sham*[457] to a Lord's wife, who is called my Lady all the world over, that Rosella indulged her in her wishes, in consideration of her fidelity and attachment at a moment when they were peculiarly acceptable to her.

The self-denial of Lady Clanallan's mother, in refusing herself a claim so dear to the heart of a parent, was rewarded in a few years by the society of a little grand-daughter, whose mind she was indefatigable in properly forming; and it was remarkable that the young lady understood of the words of her own language in general use, almost every one better than those hacknied expressions, *sentiment and mystery*.

ENDNOTES

Volume I

1. *St. George's, Hanover-Square*: the parish church of London's affluent Mayfair district.
2. *douceur*: a bribe or 'sweetener' (*OED*). Pew-renting was an expected practice in the Romantic period. It was also common to tip the ushers (or 'pew-openers').
3. *box at the Opera in opposition to a box at St.—'s*: Much like having one's own box at the opera, having a pew at a fashionable church like St. George's would have been a marker of social status.
4. *Faro-table*: Faro, also 'Pharaoh' or 'Pharo', is a card game that was popular during the Romantic period. In this section, Charlton introduces the first of several cautionary plotlines about the dangers of gambling.
5. *tonish*: fashionable. The 'ton' were members of high society.
6. *in propria persona*: Latin for 'in the flesh' (*OED*).
7. *surtout*: 'outer covering' (*OED*); here, the endpapers of a novel.
8. *hack*: a horse-drawn carriage for hire; short for 'hackney coach' or 'hack-chaise'.
9. *mercer*: a dealer of fine textiles.
10. *hydrophobia*: a symptom of rabies; madness.
11. *Council at Bombay*: one of the legislatures of British India.
12. *India-House*: the main office of the East India Company in London.
13. *Indiaman*: the name given to any ship operating for the East India Company.
14. *post-chaise*: a four-wheeled closed carriage drawn by two or four horses; also referred to as a 'chaise' or 'chair'.
15. *amant medicin* [médecin]: a lover doctor. This may be a reference to Molière's comedy *L'Amour médecin* (1665), in which a man disguised as a doctor prescribes marriage to the woman he loves. The 1801 Parisian edition leaves out this allusion.
16. *Purser*: an officer on a ship.
17. *cuddy*: a cabin where officers dine.
18. *bridle way*: a path meant for those on horseback or foot.
19. *affairs of honour*: duels.
20. *febrifuge*: a medicine to alleviate fever.
21. *rencontre*: French for 'meeting'. Here it means a 'fight' or 'challenge' (*OED*).
22. *house of public resort*: an inn or a tavern.
23. *a new Novel . . . wood embers expiring, dying lamps, and total darkness*: This list of Gothic tropes is somewhat anachronistic. The action to this point must take place in the early 1780s since the 'modern' heroine Rosella (not yet born) reaches adolescence in chapter V of the present volume and is seventeen for the remainder of the novel. Gothic novels proliferated following the publication of Horace Walpole's *The Castle of Otranto* (1764), yet the 'new Novel' described here is precisely the kind of Radcliffean Gothic text that was at the height of popularity in the 1790s.

ENDNOTES

24 *descend with her heroine down some very dark and broken stairs . . . by a supernumerary door she generally found open in the morning*: This recalls the predicament of Emily St. Aubert, the heroine of Ann Radcliffe's *The Mysteries of Udolpho* (1794). Soon after arriving at the castle di Udolpho, Emily discovers an insecure door in her bedroom, which leads to a secret staircase. Among the first of many mysterious occurrences at Udolpho, Emily blocks the door shut with a chair only to find later that 'it stood half open' (II, ch. 6). See Radcliffe, *The Mysteries of Udolpho*, ed. J. Howard (London: Penguin, 2001), p. 229.

25 *obtaining*: captivating.

26 *gorgeous palaces, where amidst ranges of massy pillars stood dozens of lamps, all of them on silver tripods, . . . exquisite workmanship*: possibly another allusion to *The Mysteries of Udolpho* (1794). Montoni's magnificent mansion in Venice is illumined by lamps on 'silver tripods, depending from chains' (II, ch. 2) and at the villa of the Quesnels 'Etruscan lamps, suspended from the pillars, diffused a brilliant light over the interior part of the hall, leaving the remoter porticos to the softer lustre of the moon' (II, ch. 3). As Jacqueline Howard notes, one 1797 reviewer ridiculed Radcliffe's description of suspended tripod lamps, but such absurdities would have been overlooked by an enthusiastic and uncritical reader like Selina. See Radcliffe, *The Mysteries of Udolpho*, quotations on pp. 169 and 201. For more about the silver tripods, see p. 641n5.

27 *natural friends*: family members.

28 *deal*: thin planks of wood.

29 *Hithe*: the old spelling of Hythe, a coastal town in South East England.

30 *bronzed*: hardened; 'unfeeling or shameless' (*OED*).

31 *between Teddington and Hampton-wick*: The Beauclerc summer home is in the Borough of Richmond upon Thames, a wealthy area of southwest London still known for its extensive parkland.

32 *Chancery-Lane*: a street associated with London legal professionals.

33 *escrutoire*: an older spelling of 'escritoire'; a writing desk, sometimes portable. Charlton uses the term interchangeably with '*secretaire*'.

34 *red tape . . . owner*: Red tape was used to bind legal documents.

35 *freak*: escapade.

36 *Doctors Commons*: the headquarters of a society of London lawyers. One of the annexed buildings, the Prerogative Wills office, was open to members of the public who could look up wills for a fee. See K. Tang, 'Doctor's Commons', *Bar News*, 76 (2018), p. 77.

37 *Barbican*: a neighbourhood in central London.

38 *spotted cubic gods*: dice.

39 *fauteuils*: French armchairs with carved wooden arms and upholstered seats.

40 *Chelsea hangings . . . annihilation of her refinement*: Selina pines for the latest fashions in home decor, including painted wall hangings manufactured in Chelsea ('Chelsea hangings'), ornamental mirrors ('pier glasses'), elegant candle holders ('girandoles'), state-of-the-art fireplaces ('Rumford stoves'), stylish fireplace screens (as 'Lucas's screens' presumably are, although this term has not been traced) and expensive sewing tables with tortoise shell veneers ('turtleshell work tables').

41 *close curled black bob*: 'a wig having the bottom locks turned up into "bobs" or short curls, as opposed to a "full-bottomed wig"' (*OED*). 'Bob-wigs' were considered less formal than periwigs, but wigs in general were becoming less common in this period in part because of a hair powder tax levied in 1795 to help fund the Napoleonic war. Natural hair was in fashion by 1799, although men in certain professions continued to wear wigs well into the nineteenth century.

42 *caro sposo*: Italian for 'dear husband'. In Jane Austen's *Emma* (1816), the affected Mrs. Elton uses this term of endearment for her husband.

43 *working for her*: sewing or embroidering her clothes.
44 *agrémens:* agreeable treats and experiences (French).
45 *that air riante that Marmontel recommends . . . to form an infant mind to cheerfulness and gaiety*: The reference is to 'La femme comme il y en a peu', one of Jean-François Marmontel's popular moral tales, or *Contes moraux* (1755–9). Translated into English as 'A Wife of Ten Thousand', the tale describes a young couple, Monsieur and Madame de Lisbé, whose children and household have an 'air of gaiety' due to their parenting philosophy, which 'consist[s] in treating children as children'. The story promotes natural manners in children and the natural goodness of children, ideas that are also seen in the writings on education of Marmontel's contemporary, Jean-Jacques Rousseau. See 'A Wife of Ten Thousand', in *Moral Tales by M. Marmontel*, 3 vols (London: T. Pridden, 1776), vol. 3, pp. 99–140; quotation on p. 134. (Kind thanks to Diane Woody for tracing this allusion.)
46 *not worth a groat*: worthless. A groat is an old English coin.
47 *'cards and scandal'*: possibly taken from Hannah Cowley's 1776 comedy *The Runaway* in which Bella says, 'Well, after all, men are delightful creatures; their Flattery, in conjunction with Cards and Scandal, help one through the day tolerably well' (III. ii). See H. Cowley, 'The Runaway', in *The Works of Mrs. Cowley: Drama and Poems*, 5 vols (London: Wilkie and Robinson, 1813), vol. 1: Dramas, pp. 1–99; quotation on p. 47.
48 *Tillotson's Sermons . . . Young's Night Thoughts . . . Whole Duty of Man*: These are English religious works that would have been well known in the Romantic period. John Tillotson was Archbishop of Canterbury in the late 1600s. His sermons and discourses were reprinted throughout the eighteenth and nineteenth centuries, most notably in a ponderous multivolume collection compiled by Thomas Birch in 1752. *The Complaint: or Night-Thoughts on Life, Death, and Immortality* (1742–5) is a series of nine meditations on death by the graveyard poet Edward Young. *Night-Thoughts* is now regarded as a significant proto-Romantic and proto-Gothic text due to its gloomy imagery, sombre tone and churchyard setting. Adding to the work's importance, an illustrated version of the first volume was published by William Blake in 1797. *The Whole Duty of Man* was a popular Anglican devotional work first printed in 1658. The latter work is mentioned in another Gothic parody of this period, *Love and Horror* by 'Ircastrensis' (1812): after one of his escapades, the comic Gothic hero Thomas Bailey falls asleep with a copy of the book in his hands. (See Ircastrensis, *Love and Horror*, ed. N. Neill (Kansas City: Valancourt Books, 2008), p. 10.) Charlton's Gothic parody is didactic in some respects, but she too pokes fun at the soporific effects of moral and religious works in upcoming passages in which Rosella reads the books first mentioned here to Mrs. Beauclerc. Unlike some of the other Gothic Quixote tales of this period, *Rosella* does not suggest that instructive and improving works should serve as antidotes to Gothic reading.
49 *froward*: 'disposed to go counter to what is demanded or what is reasonable' (*OED*).
50 *ricketty*: feeble in body or understanding.
51 *airing into Holborn*: An airing is a 'walk or ride outdoors to take air or exercise' (*OED*). Holborn, an area in central London, is the site of an historic street market.
52 *green-stall*: a vegetable stand.
53 *blunderbuss at her temples*: A blunderbuss is a short-barrelled gun of the kind banditti or highwaymen might use to threaten a Gothic heroine.
54 *hermitage*: a secluded rustic building, possibly a folly.
55 *the Ethelindas, the Jemimas, the Fredericas, and the Georgianas, with all their panics, their castles, and their visions*: As Hannah Doherty Hudson argues, these names are taken from real Gothic novels of the 1790s; namely, Charlotte Smith's *Ethelinde, or the Recluse of the Lake (*1789), Anne Hughes's *Jemima* (1795), *Frederica: Or the Memoirs of a Young Lady* (1792) and *Frederica Risberg, a German Story* (1793). See

H. D. Hudson, 'Imitation, Intertextuality and the Minerva Press Novel', *Romantic Textualities: Literature and Print Culture, 1780–1840*, 23 (2020), p. 160.

56 *'here are the colours of Edelferinda's magnificent Aurora upon Lord Morteyne's footmen!'*: This may be a specific allusion, but a source has not been identified. The 'splendid account of a celebrated day-break' parodies the sublime descriptions found in novels by Ann Radcliffe and her imitators. A more detached reader than Sophia, Rosella is quick to lose interest in such depictions. Her remark about Aurora reveals that she is inclined to laugh at poetic effusions rather than be inspired by them.

57 *glasses*: handheld spyglasses or quizzing glasses.

58 *watermen's wherries*: light boats used to transport passengers and goods. Wherries were a common sight on the Thames in this period.

59 *'fine discourse of Bishop Tillotson'. . . . 'I shall soon have done'*: See note 48.

60 *'Lady Alice'*: a traditional English ballad well suited to Sophia's Gothic and sentimental tastes. It is about a lady who dies the day after seeing her lover's corpse being carried by her window. The lovers are buried apart, but flowers growing on his grave spread to hers: 'Giles Collins was buried all in the east,/Lady Alice all in the west,/And the roses that grew on Giles Collins's grave,/They reached Lady Alice's breast' (lines 17–20). See 'Lady Alice' (ballad 85A), in *The English and Scottish Popular Ballads* (1882–98), 5 vols, ed. F. J. Child (Mineola, NY: Dover, 1965), vol. 1, pp. 279–80.

61 *heroines are always infallibly fine and pathetic fingers*: Here, 'fingers' means possessing 'skill or sensitivity in using the fingers when playing a musical instrument' (*OED*). Gothic heroines are typically accomplished and sensitive musicians, a trait singled out for mockery in several parodies. In *Love and Horror* (1812), for example, the would-be heroine Annabella Tit is so skilled at her chosen instrument, the Jew's harp, 'that, if she played in the fields, the cows and horses crowded around her'. In Austen's *Northanger Abbey* (1818), Catherine Morland differs from Gothic heroines in that she is not interested in practicing an instrument. In chapter one, we are told that the day on which her mother 'dismissed the music-master was the happiest of [Catherine's] life'. Rosella does not see herself in a heroic light, but she does take sincere pleasure in playing her instrument. See Ircastrensis, *Love and Horror*, ed. N. Neill (Kansas City: Valancourt Books, 2008), p. 27; see also J. Austen, *Northanger Abbey*, ed. M. Gaull (New York: Longman, 2005), p. 10.

62 *lighterman*: a lighter or lighterman is barge used to transport goods.

63 *'created a soul under the ribs of death'*: an allusion to Milton's masque *Comus* (1634). The Attendant Spirit hears the Lady singing and says, 'I was all ear,/And took in strains that might create a soul/Under the ribs of Death' (lines 560–2).

64 *Hebe*: Greek goddess of youth.

65 *'No more she'll tune the vocal shell . . .'*: a reworking of 'Lovely Peggy', a song attributed to David Garrick and included in volume two of his posthumously published *Poetical Works* (1785). It begins: 'Once more I'll tune the vocal shell,/To hills and dales my passion tell;/A flame which time can never quell,/That burns for lovely Peggy'.

66 with] 1799 text.

67 *curvets of poor Flirt*: a reference to the frolicsome Italian greyhound mentioned earlier in the chapter. A curvet is a leap or frisk.

68 *peregrination*: a tour or journey. To 'peregrinate' is to travel, especially by foot; to walk.

69 *noteless*: 'unmarked, . . . unnoticed' (*OED*). The servant girl may be thinking of the expressions 'to die noteless' or a 'noteless death'. Charlton often uses regional dialect in free indirect speech for comic effect.

70 *tying up a bundle of papers very carefully with the goose quill's regimental insignia, red tape*: See note 34. Goose quills were used to make pens, but in this instance the term also refers to the writer who wields the pen (the 'pen-pusher' or 'quill-driver').

Lawyers are a target of satire throughout *Rosella*. Here, Charlton may intend to suggest a humourous contrast between Mr. Ellinger's red tape and the dashing red coats worn by British soldiers in this period.

71 *Gray's-Inn Coffee-House*: a coffee house on High Holborn that was affiliated with Gray's Inn, one of the four legal associations collectively known as the Inns of Court.
72 *cinder heap . . . item an old wig block, item a dust tub, whose diurnal peregrinations generally terminated there to save trouble*: The cinder heap is an unsightly pile of ashes and household refuse. Presumably a servant would have used the dust tub to carry waste from the house to the pile so that it could be carted away by a dustman. However, it is suggested that the pile is left to fester in the courtyard because Mrs. Ellinger's romantic sensibilities ('elevated notions') cause her to ignore and neglect all ordinary household matters.
73 *houries*: beautiful maidens.
74 *Furnival's Inn*: one of the buildings associated with the Inns of Court (see note 71); it was used for offices, legal training and accommodations.
75 *green stuff bag*: Up until the nineteenth century it was customary for lawyers to carry green bags. According to one Victorian book about lawyers: 'On the stages of the Caroline theatres the lawyer is found with a green bag in his hand; the same is the case in the literature of Queen Anne's reign; and until a comparatively recent date green bags were generally carried in Westminster Hall and in provincial courses by the great body of legal practitioners'. See J. C. Jeaffreson, *A Book About Lawyers* (London: Hurst and Blackett, 1867), p. 1.
76 *shook his ears*: an idiom meaning 'to wake up, bestir oneself'; to evince 'pleasure in freedom' (*OED*).
77 *kennel*: street gutter.
78 *distinguished atmosphere of St. Giles's*: In the eighteenth and nineteenth centuries, the St. Giles area of London was the site of an infamous rookery (slum). William Hogarth's 1751 satirical print 'Gin Lane' is set in St. Giles and captures the disorder and squalor that was associated with the area.
79 *clutter*: to move noisily; to clatter.
80 *capillaire*: a popular beverage made with simple syrup infused with maidenhair fern; also called syrup of capillaire.
81 *bottle of salts*: a vial containing smelling salts; that is, a mixture of diluted ammonia carbonate and scent that was inhaled as a restorative. Smelling-bottles were a fashionable accessory in this period.
82 *secretaire*: used interchangeably with 'escrutoire'; a writing desk, sometimes portable.
83 *grown out of knowledge*: 'to cease to be known' (*OED*); to become a stranger.
84 *gêne*: a source of 'constraint' (*OED*); an inconvenience or bother.
85 *regale for once with the smell of cold roast or boiled*: The implication here and below, when Mrs. Methwald opens the windows to dissipate the smell of meat, is that Mrs. Methwald is a vegetarian. Ethical vegetarianism was on the rise in the Romantic period. Its proponents included Joseph Ritson, whose influential *Essay on Abstinence from Animal Food, as a Moral Duty* was published in 1802, and Percy Bysshe Shelley, who addressed the topic of vegetarianism in various works, including 'A Vindication of Natural Diet' (1813). Anita Guerrini traces the eighteenth-century idea that eating meat could be harmful to 'sensitive, intelligent, imaginative people', a notion that Mr. Mordaunt seems to ridicule. Mrs. Methwald's dislike of meat may also reflect and satirize the interest in vegetarianism taken by Mary Hays, Catharine Macaulay and other feminist writers of the 1790s. See A. Guerrini, 'A Diet for a Sensitive Soul: Vegetarianism in Eighteenth-Century Britain', *Eighteenth-Century Life*, 23.2 (1999), pp. 34–42; quotation on p. 38. For the link between vegetarianism and feminism, see M. M. Regan, 'Feminism, Vegetarianism, and Colonial Resistance in Eighteenth-Century British Novels', *Studies in the Novel*, 46.3 (2014), pp. 275–92.

ENDNOTES

86 *hill of Parnassus . . . helicon fountain. . .*: Mount Parnassus is sacred to the Muses; so too is the Hippocrene spring, the source of poetic inspiration on Mount Helicon. Mr. Mordaunt's joking allusions give voice to Charlton's necessarily ambivalent satire on female writers. Mrs. Methwald is ridiculed here and elsewhere for her interest in writing and for her bluestocking tendencies. In the second and third volumes of *Rosella*, Sophia will become the main butt of Charlton's satire on female authorship.
87 *taking such a fag*: performing such a tiring errand.
88 *livery*: the distinctive uniforms worn by Lady Lucy's servants or the emblem displayed on her carriage.
89 *green devil*: See note 75. The articled clerk Povey is ashamed of his green bag because it marks his profession and need to work for a living.
90 *quizzing*: teasing, perplexing.
91 *red-taped papers*: See note 34.
92 *fagging with a band-box*: carrying a box designed to hold collars, caps and hats.
93 *suivante*: a lady's maid.
94 *piquet*: a card game.
95 *forced-meat adventures*: Forcemeat is minced or ground meat used for stuffing or meatballs. According to the recipe for 'forc'd meat' in Eliza Smith's *The Compleat Housewife* (1727), the meat is mixed well with suet, spices, oysters and eggs and then '[kept] in an earthen pot for your use'. See E. Smith, *The Compleat Housewife: or, Accomplished Gentlewoman's Companion*, 16th edn (London: C. Hitch and L. Hawes, 1758), p. 31. Charlton uses the term here to suggest that the adventures in store for Rosella will be a mixture of plots and elements from Sophia's favourite Gothic and sentimental novels. Amelia Dale argues that '"forced-meat adventures" reiterates the novel-written-to-recipe trope', while also foreshadowing the way that Rosella's 'sexual reputation . . . becomes metaphorical meat for her mother's authorial production'. See A. Dale, 'The Quixotic Mother, the Female Author, and Mary Charlton's *Rosella*', *Studies in the Novel*, 52.1 (2020), pp. 1–19; quotation on p. 10.
96 *discourses of Bishop Tillotson, to the screech-owl night-thoughts*: See note 48.
97 *small tub summer-house*: a small building or an arbour in a garden or park.
98 *'Tour through Great Britain'*: The friends are consulting Daniel Defoe's three-volume travel book *A Tour Thro' the Whole Island of Great Britain, Divided into Circuits or Journies* (1724–6), the title page of which indicates that the book is 'Particularly fitted for the Reading of such as desire to Travel over the Island'. See D. Defoe, *A Tour Thro' the Whole Island of Great Britain*, ed. P. Rogers (London: Penguin, 1971).
99 *an inspired priestess of Delphos . . . old hottentot Mordaunt. . .*: the priestess is Pythia, the Oracle of Delphi at the Temple of Apollo. 'Hottentot' is the old Dutch and English term for the Khoisan people of Southern Africa. In extended use, it is an implicitly racist term used to imply ignorance or lack of culture.
100 *billet-doux*: love letter (French).
101 *foresters*: ponies native to New Forest in Southern England.
102 *R –* : possibly Humphry Repton (1752–1818), a leading English garden designer associated with the Romantic vogue for naturalistic landscaping. According to Tom Williamson, Repton differed from his predecessor Capability Brown in that he not only worked for the wealthy elite but 'was also employed by [those] with less spacious grounds: by local squires with smaller estates . . . and by wealthy bankers, businessmen and lawyers who might be cash-rich but were land-poor'. Repton played an important role in popularizing landscape gardening in this period. Charlton satirizes the trend for picturesque garden features below when she describes the 'fanciful dairy' that Sophia incorporates into her design. See T. Williamson, *Humphry Repton: Landscape Design in an Age of Revolution* (London: Reaktion Books, 2020), para. 4.
103 *bungalo*: a 'lightly built' structure, 'usually with a thatched roof' (*OED*).

104 *Wedgewood's*: a leading English manufacturer of pottery and fine china. Its founder Josiah Wedgwood (1730–95) opened a factory in Staffordshire in the late 1760s. A link can be made between Sophia's taste in reading and her taste in milk jugs: like the popular novels of the day, Wedgwood's ceramics were mass produced to meet popular tastes.
105 *jaunting car*: a lightweight, two-wheeled carriage drawn by a single horse.
106 *à portée*: French for 'within reach'.
107 *ha! ha!*: a sunken retaining wall used to mark the boundary of a park or grounds. Ha-has were invisible from a distance and thus provided an uninterrupted view. They were a popular feature of eighteenth-century landscape design.
108 *ci-devant*: former (French).
109 *hoyden*: a high-spirited girl; a romp or tomboy.
110 *the Jordan*: a reference to Dorothea Jordan (1761–1816), a celebrated comic actress best known for playing hoydenish characters, including the part of Miss Hoyden in Richard Brinsley Sheridan's play *The Trip to Scarborough* (1777).
111 *en attendant*: 'meanwhile' or 'while waiting' (French).
112 *a sop to her growling Cerberus*: an appeasement. The saying is an allusion to Book Six of the *Aeneid*, in which a drugged honey cake is given to the three-headed dog that guards the underworld.
113 *chace*: hunt.
114 *courser*: horse.
115 *'fair and young'*: possibly an allusion to the poem 'When I Was Fair and Young' (c. 1580), ascribed to Elizabeth I, which begins 'When I was fair and young, and favour graced me,/Of many was I sought unto, their mistress for to be,/But I did scorn them all . . .' (lines 1–3).
116 *á-propos*] 1800 text.
117 *Diana*: Roman goddess of hunting.
118 *hotellerie*] 1800 text.
119 *'native woodlands wild'*: possibly taken from Mary Heron's 1790 'Ode to Music', in which the enchanting song of a village maid is described as follows: 'Her native woodland notes tho' wild,/Have chear'd the lonely cot, and poverty beguil'd' (lines 23–4). (See M. Heron, 'Ode to Music', in *Odes, &c. on Various Occasions* (Newcastle: Hall and Elliot, 1792), pp. 34–41.) The quotation marks have been reproduced as they appear in both the 1799 and 1800 texts even though two sets of closing quotation marks seem to be needed after 'wild'. This exchange is significant because Lord Morteyne and Arthur Oberne (as yet unnamed) offer two perspectives on female education, one of the central themes of *Rosella*.
120 *ebullition:* 'a sudden outburst or . . . bubbling over' (*OED*). To 'ebulliate' is to boil or bubble up.
121 *ceremony of losing blood*: bloodletting; the outdated practice of extracting blood as a medical treatment.
122 *cicisbeo*: the lover of a married woman (Italian).
123 *'delightful task' of rearing 'the tender thought'*: taken from *The Seasons* (1726–30), a series of four poems by James Thomson. These lines from 'Spring' describe the education of young people: 'Delightful task! to rear the tender thought,/To teach the young idea how to shoot,/To pour the fresh instruction o'er the mind,/To breathe th'enlivening spirit, and to fix/The generous purpose in the glowing breast' (lines 1148–52).
124 *Madame G—l—s . . . Mrs. Trimmer*: both important educationalists in this period. Stéphanie-Félicité de Genlis (1746–1830) was a prolific French novelist and author of children's works. Her writings on education include the novel *Adèle et Théodore ou Lettres sur l'éducation* (1782), which was translated into English to great acclaim in

1783. Her intimacy with the Duke of Orléans and unconventional role as tutor to his children were the reasons for her 'doubtful fame'. Charlton's first novel, *The Parisian; or, Genuine Anecdotes of Distinguished and Noble Characters* (1794), includes a fictionalized version of Genlis. For a discussion of Charlton's representation of Genlis, see G. Dow, '"Genuine Anecdotes": Mary Charlton and Revolutionary Celebrity', in K. H. Doig and D. Medlin (eds), *British-French Exchanges in the Eighteenth Century* (Newcastle, UK: Cambridge Scholars Publishing, 2007), pp. 149–65. Sarah Trimmer (1741–1810) was an English children's writer and education reformer who founded several schools, as well as the journal *The Guardian of Education*.

125 *fortitèr in re*, and *suavitèr in modo*: a Latin expression meaning 'bold in action, and mild in manner'.
126 *quill-driver*: someone whose job involves tedious paperwork; a pen-pusher.
127 hav'nt] 1800 text.
128 *tumblers of orgitt . . . a whole bottle of caterpillar*: Orgeat is a drink made from almonds, sugar and orange flower water. 'Caterpillar' is a malapropism of 'capillaire' (see note 80).
129 *virago*: an overbearing woman; a termagant.
130 *tabour*: drum.
131 *mysterious business. . . . At length it was elucidated by the entrance of Mr. Povey*: Anna Maria Mackenzie's Gothic novel *Mysteries Elucidated* was published by the Minerva Press in 1795. Here and elsewhere, Charlton makes fun of the explained supernatural, a common trope of Radcliffean Gothic.
132 *'Loose were her tresses seen, her zone unbound!'*: taken from William Collins's allegorical poem 'The Passions' (1744), which was set to music by William Hayes. The line describes Mirth – her hair flowing and her waist free of a girdle or belt – as she dances with Love (line 91).
133 *Mrs. Latitat*: Mr. Latitat is an attorney character in Frederic Reynolds's popular 1793 play, *How to Grow Rich: A Comedy*.
134 *the mad hero of the north*: Charles XII of Sweden. The following story appears in Voltaire's *History of Charles XII* (1731): 'One day as the King was dictating to a Secretary some dispatches for Sweden, a bomb falling on the house, came through the roof, and burst very near his room. . . . In this noise and confusion the Secretary dropped his pen, and thought the house was coming down. *What ails you*, says the King very calmly, *why don't you write?* The man could only bring out, *the bomb, Sir! Well*, says the King*, and what has that to do with our business? go on*.' See Voltaire, *The History of Charles XII. King of Sweden* (London: A. Bettesworth and C. Hitch, 1734), p. 157.
135 *watch-house*: a shelter used as a station for night watchmen and a holding cell for those taken into custody.
136 *rising female generation found their time wholly filled up . . . the whim of the day*: Although it includes a gibe directed against women who study 'botany, modern philosophy, and the *theory* of morality', this paragraph playfully echoes Mary Wollstonecraft's *Vindication of the Rights of Woman* (1792) by calling attention to the superficial accomplishments and artificial manners that passed for female education in this period. Charlton also makes fun of several trends. 'Go to the Devil and Shake Yourself' was a popular jig arranged for piano by Irish composer John Field (1782–1837). It is included in *Preston's Twenty Four Country Dances for the Year 1798* (London: Preston & Son, 1798). '[D]ressing *à la grecque*' refers to the neoclassical vogue for Grecian gowns and hairstyles that emerged in the 1790s and continued into the Regency period.
137 *Charlotte at the tomb of Werter*: a scene inspired by Goethe's 1774 epistolary novel, *The Sorrows of Young Werther*, the hero of which takes his own life because of his unrequited love for Charlotte.

ENDNOTES

138 *coup-de-grace*: the finishing stroke or, as it is humourously suggested here, the fatal blow.
139 *Innocence with her sweet little lamb . . . Abelard and Eloisa . . . Una and the Parson's Maid, and Patty and William at Eve, and Belinda with her dog Shock, and the Shepherdess of the Alps. . .*: Livia copies engravings of well-known paintings and illustrations of popular stories; for example, 'Innocence with her sweet little lamb' is the subject of Lorenzo Lippi's *An Allegory of Innocence* (*c.* 1640); Abelard and Eloisa are twelfth-century lovers; Belinda is the main character of Alexander Pope's mock-heroic poem, *The Rape of the Lock* (1712) and the 'Shepherdess of the Alps' is from Jean-François Marmontel's moral tale of the same name (first translated into English in 1763). 'Una and the Parson's Maid, and Patty and William at Eve' are not identified, but possible sources include the comic verses *The Parson and his Maid* (1722) and 'Simkin, A Fairy Tale' (*c.* 1751). See *The Parson and His Maid, A Tale*, 6th edn (London: Printed for T. Payne, 1722); see also W. Kendrick, 'Simkin, A Fairy Tale', in *Poems; Ludicrous, Satirical, and Moral* (London: Printed for J. Williams, 1770), pp. 81–7.
140 *Hornsey Church and the Bell at Edmonton*: two North London landmarks. 'Hornsey Church' is the old bell tower of St. Mary's Parish Church near Hornsey High Street. The 'Bell at Edmonton' is the Bell Inn on Fore Street in Upper Edmonton, which was made famous by William Cowper's 1782 ballad, 'The Diverting History of John Gilpin'.
141 *piano-fort:* part of the satire on her dubious accomplishments, Livia mispronounces the word 'forte'.
142 *Battle of Prague, and the Siege of Bangalore, and Hurly Burly, and the Storming of Trincomalee*: 'The Battle of Prague' is a 1788 sonata by Frantisek Kotzwara. 'The Siege of Bangalore' is a sonata by Joseph Mazzinghi (*c.* 1793). 'Hurly Burly' are lyrics from Franz Joseph Haydn's canzonetta 'The Sailor's Song' (1794). 'The Storming of Trincomalee' is not identified.
143 *the gamut*: musical scales.
144 *fâde*: bland (French).
145 *chagrenée*: 'Chagrinée' is French for upset or distressed; chagrinned.
146 *took precedence of Lady Emlin*: that is, she went before Lady Emlin; she did not defer to her higher rank.
147 *fugitive pieces*: ephemera; occasional verses.
148 *non chalamment*: nonchalantly (French).
149 *jeu d'esprit*: something witty.
150 *Botanical Magazine*: Curtis's *Botanical Magazine*, later renamed *The Botanical Magazine, or Flower-Garden Displayed*, was first published in 1787.
151 *Dyde's*: Dyde and Scribe's (later Harding, Howell & Co.) was a fashionable store at 89 Pall Mall that sold muslins and other cottons, silks, furs and women's clothing and accessories. The 'embroidered muslin' may be a dress made of muslin rather than a piece of fabric.
152 *fold*: presumably a variant of 'folded'; to pin folds into the muslin, to hem it.
153 *Lady Elizabeth Waldon*: a model for Lady Waldon has not been traced, but she is the 'matronly beauty' mentioned in the previous chapter, 'whose most devoted cicisbeo was Mr. Cressy'.
154 *the exhibition of work which did so much credit to her sex*: an exhibition of artwork along the lines of the 'Public Display of Female Genius and Ingenuity in the Liberal Arts' projected for the European Museum, St. James's, in 1799. The advertisement promised that it would showcase 'exquisite Performances in Sculpture, Painting, Drawing, Needle-work, &c.' by female artists. See *The Plan and New Descriptive Catalogue of the European Museum, King Street, St. James's Square: Instituted for the Promotion of the Fine Arts, and the Encouragement of British Artists* (1799), n.p.

Volume II

155 *congé*: 'Ceremonious dismissal or leave-taking' (*OED*).
156 *Babette, or Jeannette, or Annette . . . unalterably attached to her beautiful mistress*: The loyal maidservant is a stock character of Gothic fiction. Annette, Emily's maid and companion in *The Mysteries of Udolpho* (1794), is a good example, but she is certainly not the first of this type. In fact, in his review of the novel, Samuel Taylor Coleridge observed that 'the character of Annette, a talkative waiting-maid, is much worn'. See the review of Radcliffe's 'The Mysteries of Udolpho', *The Critical Review; or Annals of Literature*, 11 (August 1794), pp. 361–72; quotation on p. 362.
157 *soubrette*: lady's maid.
158 *'deep glen'*: It is not surprising that Sophia hopes to have an adventure in 'some "deep glen"' given her taste for Radcliffean Gothic novels with their characteristically gloomy natural settings. When Emily St. Aubert is being conducted against her will to Tuscany, she passes part of the night in a 'deep glen', which is an occasion for the following sublime description 'The hollow moan struck upon Emily's heart, and served to render more gloomy and terrific every object around her, – the mountains, shaded in twilight – the gleaming torrent, hoarsely roaring – the black forests, and the *deep glen*, broken into rocky recesses, high overshadowed by cypress and sycamore and winding into long obscurity. To this glen, Emily, as she sent forth her anxious eye, thought there was no end . . .' (III, ch. 6; italics added). See Radcliffe, *The Mysteries of Udolpho* (London: Penguin, 2001), p. 383.
159 *Marybone*: Marylebone, the west-end London neighbourhood where the Beauclerc winter residence is located.
160 *the charming and romantic Principality which has furnished adventurous scenes to so many modern heroines*: Wales. Sublime and picturesque Welsh landscapes provide the backdrop for many Gothic romances of the 1790s including Anna Maria Bennett's *Ellen, Countess of Castle Howel* (London: Minerva, 1794), Isabella Kelly's *The Abbey of Saint Asaph* (London: Minerva, 1796), Ann Howell's *Anzoletta Zadoski* (London: Minerva, 1796), Sarah Landsell's *The Tower; or the Romance of Ruthyne* (London: Printed for the Author, 1798) and Emily Clark's *Ianthé, or the Flower of Caernarvon* (London: Hookham and Carpenter, 1798). As Jane Aaron points out, while some of these books were penned by Welsh writers like Bennett, most were written by travellers to Wales and reflect the fashion for tourism within Britain during a period when the wars with France prevented continental travel. See J. Aaron, *Welsh Gothic* (Cardiff: University of Wales Press, 2013), p. 23.
161 *'mountain nymph, sweet Liberty'. . . 'unreproved pleasures free'*: taken from Milton's 1645 pastoral poem 'L'Allegro':

> Come and trip it as ye go
> On the light fantastic toe,
> And in thy right hand lead with thee
> The mountain nymph, sweet Liberty;
> And if I give thee honour due,
> Mirth, admit me of thy crew,
> To live with her and live with thee,
> In unreproved pleasures free (lines 33–40).

162 *à l'ordinaire*: as usual (French).
163 *'Russet lawns and fallows grey . . . The Cynosure of neigh'bring eyes'*: Milton's 'L'Allegro', lines 71–80. The words *'she'* and *'she sees'* replace 'it' and 'perhaps'.
164 *footpad*: a highwayman who is on foot rather than on horseback.
165 *book of roads*: Sophia may be consulting *Cary's New Itinerary; or, an Accurate Delineation of the Great Roads Both Direct and Cross throughout England and Wales; with*

many of the principal Roads of Scotland (1798) by John Cary. However, there were many such books which described the roads of Great Britain and furnished travellers with maps, alphabetical lists of cities, towns and villages and their distances in miles from London. One of the oldest, *Itinerarium Angliae, or a Book of Roads*, by John Ogilby (1675), was reprinted in countless expanded and updated editions. Samuel Johnson in *The Idler* 97 describes a man whose greatest pleasure is to 'visit . . . different parts of the kingdom' in the summer months. 'When the happy hour of the annual expedition arrives, the seat of the chaise is furnished with *Ogilvy's Book of Roads*, and a choice quantity of cold tongues' (See S. Johnson, *The Idler* 97 [January 26, 1760], p. 373). Road-books only became more popular in the latter part of the eighteenth century with the rise of tourism in Britain. As Thomas Pride and Philip Luckombe observe in the Preface to their 1789 book of roads *The Traveller's Companion, or new Itinerary of England and Wales, with part of Scotland*: 'the prevailing Taste for making a Tour of this Island could not receive a more desirable Assistant than that of a correct and particular as well as comprehensive Itinerary' (p. iii). One imagines that Charlton had a book of roads near at hand when she was writing about Sophia's and Rosella's travels.

166 *Greta-bridge*: Greta Bridge is a picturesque village in the Pennine Hills in North Yorkshire. It is situated by the River Greta. Walter Scott's poem 'Rokeby' (1813) is set in Greta Bridge and at the nearby Barnaby Castle.
167 *Noctambulo*: a sleepwalker.
168 *crazy*: cracked.
169 *'the sweet-briar, or the vine, or the twisted eglantine'*: Milton's 'L'Allegro', lines 47–8.
170 *arquebusses*: guns.
171 *'a spectacle for gods and men'*: adapted from the first letter of Paul to the Corinthians, in which he refers to the spectacle of the apostles' suffering: 'For I think that God hath set forth us the apostles last, as it were appointed to death. For we are made a spectacle unto the world, and to angels, and to men' (1 Cor. 4:9).
172 *'airy cell' of the 'unseen nymph?'*: taken from the Lady's song in Milton's *Comus* (1634): 'Sweet Echo, sweetest nymph that liv'st unseen/Within thy airy cell' (lines 230–1). Quotation marks are as they appear in the 1799 and 1800 texts.
173 *beaufet*: a buffet; a sideboard.
174 *à merville*] 1799 text. 'Marvellously' or 'admirably' (French).
175 *cock-loft*: a small attic or loft.
176 *put the papers up*: 'Put up' in this context means 'to store, stow away' or 'pack up' (*OED*).
177 *dry*: thirsty.
178 *spencer*: a jacket.
179 *posset*: a drink made of hot milk, ale or wine and spices.
180 *concealed mystery might be elucidated*: See note 131.
181 *rated*: berated.
182 *'garish eye of day'*: adapted from Milton's 'Il Penseroso' (1645): '. . . in close covert by some brook,/Where no profaner eye may look,/Hide me from day's garish eye' (lines 139–41).
183 *à-propos de bottes*: 'without rhyme or reason' (*OED*)
184 *'all alone by the light of the moon'*: an allusion to a popular love song, 'Alone by the Light of the Moon' (*c.* 1789), by English composer James Hook.
185 *cilician*: Cilicia is the old Roman name for what is now Turkey.
186 *inevitably worn some distinguishing mark of sublimity . . . to awe ghosts, goblins, and devils from impertinent approaches*: a reference to the wandering Jew character in Matthew Lewis's *The Monk* (1796). In the subplot concerning Don Raymond and Agnes in volume two, chapter one, the wandering Jew wears a velvet band to conceal 'the burning Cross impressed upon his fore-head'. He tells Raymond: 'God has set

his seal upon me, and all his Creatures respect this fatal mark!'. (See M. Lewis, *The Monk*, ed. N. Groom [Oxford: Oxford University Press, 2016], pp. 137 and 131.) *The Monk* attracted criticism from reviewers for its scenes of shocking horror and depravity. In his review, Coleridge criticizes the novel on moral grounds, but he praises the wandering Jew subplot: 'the story Lewis weaves in about the bleeding nun is "truly terrific"; and we could not recall a bolder or more happy conception than that of the burning cross on the forehead of the wandering Jew'. It is likely that Charlton was familiar with this review. In her footnote she refers to Lewis (a Whig MP) as a 'British legislator', an echo of Coleridge's closing lines: 'the author of the Monk signs himself a LEGISLATOR! We stare and tremble'! See the review of Lewis's 'The Monk: A Romance', in *The Critical Review*, 19 (February 1797), pp. 194–200; quotations on pp. 194 and 198.

187 *an end*: 'to the end' (*OED*).

188 *minims and semibreves with so persevering a* tenuto: minims and semibreves are half and whole notes respectively; '*tenuto*' means to hold or sustain a note.

189 *billows of Cocytus*: the waves of Cocytus, one of the rivers in Hades.

190 '*foot could fall*': taken from the part of Laurence Sterne's *Tristram Shandy* (1759–67) in which the hero is journeying through France and trades in his carriage for a mule: 'I changed the *mode* of my travelling once more; and after so precipitate and rattling a course as I had run, I flattered my fancy with thinking of my mule, and that I should traverse the rich plains of Languedoc upon his back, as slowly as foot could fall'. See L. Sterne, *The Life and Opinions of Tristram Shandy, Gentleman*, ed. I. C. Ross (Oxford: Oxford University Press, 2000), p. 428.

191 '*it is him indeed; but not more handsome than he was, . . . when he was indeed the best young gentleman I ever came anigh*': While there is no conclusive evidence to suggest that Jane Austen read Charlton's novel, there are some noticeable parallels between *Rosella* and *Pride and Prejudice* (1813), the first draft of which Austen completed in 1797 and later revised. Here, for example, the domestic's comments about George Mompesson are much like those made by Mrs. Reynolds, the housekeeper at Pemberley, when she shows Elizabeth Bennet and the Gardiners the portraits of Darcy (III, ch. 1). See J. Austen, *Pride and Prejudice*, ed. D. Gray (New York and London: W. W. Norton & Company, 2001), pp. 160–1.

192 *instead of sinking under the weight of a delicate woe, was flying from a cell in Newgate, and death, death, death – lying perdue in a Judge's wig*: a reference to Newgate Prison in London. In the eighteenth and nineteenth centuries *The Newgate Calendar, or The Malefactors' Bloody Register* recounted the sensational exploits of notorious criminals who ended up in the prison. Sophia is momentarily alarmed by the generic turn that Rosella's adventures seem to take when it appears that George Mompesson is better suited to appear in a criminal biography than in a work of sentimental Gothic fiction.

193 *stroaming*: wandering idly.

194 *Stanmore Hills*: where George Mompesson's hut is located. Daniel Defoe describes the area as 'a mountainous Track of *Yorkshire* [that] runs, like a Promontory, up Northward a great way, Hill upon Hill, Cliffs, Rocks, and terrible Precipices, astonishing to behold. This rugged Part of the Country is called *Stanmore-hills*, which are desolate and solitary, excepting one Inn, for the Entertainment of such as may be hardy enough to go among them'. See D. Defoe, 'Letter III. Containing A Description of Part of the West-riding of Yorkshire, and of all the North and East-ridings, the Bishoprick of Durham, and the County of Northumberland', in *Tour Thro' the Whole Island of Great Britain. Divided into Circuits or Journies*, 6th edn, 4 vols (London: D. Browne, &c., 1762), vol. 3, pp. 132–239; quotation on p. 152.

195 *Reeth*: a village in the Yorkshire Dales.

ENDNOTES

196 *fashionable and titled Circe*: Circe is an enchantress of Greek mythology. The epithet is a foreshadowing reference to the high-born seductress who will be described in the next chapter.
197 *profusion*: extravagance.
198 *cognizable by the law*: liable to be tried in a court of law.
199 *be forbidden to have his humble dinner baked on the seventh day*: a reference to debates in the 1790s about Sunday baking. It was common for labourers to bring their food to bakeries and cooks' shops to be prepared and baked. A law dating to the time of Charles II prohibited trade on Sundays, but bakers were mostly exempt because they were needed to dress meat and bake pastries for the Sunday meal. When Delamere bemoans 'the fury of fanatical reform', he may have in mind the religious reformers who wanted bakeries to remain closed on Sundays or he may be referring to groups of bakers themselves who argued for the right to take Sundays off instead of being required to stay open. In 1794, the Master and Journeymen Bakers of London, Westminster and the Borough of Southwark published a pamphlet titled *Grounds of Complaint Against the Practice of Sunday Baking*. William Jolliffe, the Member of Parliament for Petersfield, 'lamented the situation of the journeymen bakers, but was of opinion, that if they did not bake of a Sunday, the poor could not eat'. See 'Journeymen Bakers', in *Jordan's Parliamentary Journal for the Year 1794* (London: J. S. Jordan, 1794), vol. 1, pp. 424–5; quotation on p. 425.
200 *profited by the Sunday schools . . . levelling principles*: Sunday schools offered free religious education and played a role in spreading literacy among the labouring classes. Delamere links the democratic ideas of the newly-educated working classes both to the Sunday schools and to the poor moral example set by the upper classes. M. O. Grenby uses this moment in Charlton's novel to group *Rosella* with conservative novels of this period that criticize the profligacy of the aristocracy because it 'add[s] grist to the levellers' mills'. See Grenby, *The Anti-Jacobin Novel: British Conservatism and the French Revolution* (Cambridge: Cambridge University Press, 2001), pp. 160–1.
201 *spunging-house*: a holding place for debtors.
202 *devoirs*: attentions.
203 *Cassinos*: Casinos were private establishments, or clubs, used by the wealthy. There were many near St. Mark's Square in Venice. The casinos were associated with gambling and licentiousness: 'they have the misfortune to labour under a very bad reputation', one contemporary author remarks; 'they are accused of being temples entirely consecrated to lawless love, and a thousand scandalous tales are told . . . concerning them'. See J. Moore, *A View of Society and Manners in Italy* (Dublin: Messrs. Price, Watson, Whitestone, &c., 1781), p. 170. When Sophia uses the term 'Cassinos', she means the women of fashion and questionable morality in London who attend private gambling parties.
204 *horrible periods of Newgate eloquence . . . placed the saddle upon the right horse*: Sophia concludes that George Mompesson belongs in a criminal biography after all. See note 194.
205 *German ocean*: historic name for the North Sea.
206 *Miss Beauclerc wished herself very vehemently on the celebrated banks of the Garonne, or gliding through the Rialto, encircled by dying cadencies, garnished with pauses, and swells, and ritornellos*: an allusion to the 'exotic' settings and diction characteristic of Radcliffe's works. Emily St. Aubert, the heroine of *The Mysteries of Udolpho* (1794), is born in a chateau on the banks of the Garonne in Southwestern France. Over the course of the novel, Emily travels to various locations, including Venice, where she twice hears songs and musical instruments reverberating over the Grand Canal. See A. Radcliffe, *The Mysteries of Udolpho*, ed. J. Howard (London: Penguin, 2001), pp. 168 and 193. The Rialto is one of the bridges that spans the canal.

207 *evasions*: excursions.
208 *mal-à-propos*: inopportune (French).
209 *quoined golden guineas*: The landlord speculates that Mompesson is a coiner of counterfeit guineas. A Yorkshire man, Thomas Denton, was tried and hanged for coining in 1789. Several decades earlier a group of counterfeiters known as the Yorkshire Coiners or Cragg Vale Coiners were active in the West Riding of Yorkshire. For more on coining in eighteenth-century England, see R. Norton, 'Coiners and Counterfeiters', in *The Georgian Underworld*, https://rictornorton.co.uk/gu12.htm.
210 *Cits*: inhabitants of a city; urbanites.
211 *passe-par-tout*: a key that opens many doors.
212 *'To storm and stare,/And load with curses the withdrawing fair'*: adapted from lines spoken by the servant in Richard Owen Cambridge's *A Dialogue between a Member of Parliament and his Servant* (1752), written in imitation of Horace: 'Tho' – begs you'll stay and vote,/And zealous – tears your coat./You damn your coachman, storm and stare;/And tear your throat to call a chair' (lines 71–4). The poem is included in the popular Romantic-period anthology *Elegant Extracts*, first published in 1789. See *Elegant Extracts; or, Useful and Entertaining Passages in Verse, Book the Fourth: Sentimental, Lyrical, and Ludicrous*, ed. V. Knox (London, T. Longman, 1796), pp. 791–3; quotation on p. 792.
213 in] 1799 and 1800 texts.
214 *Warkworth*: Warkworth is described by Defoe as being one of the villages in Northumberland that offer 'abundant business for an antiquary' due to their 'old castles' and 'ruins'. See D. Defoe, *A Tour Thro' the Whole Island of Great Britain*, ed. P. Rogers (London: Penguin, 1971), p. 537. Upcoming scenes will take place in Warkworth Castle and Hermitage, medieval ruins that have long attracted tourists to Warkworth. The castle dates to the twelfth century; the hermitage was built one hundred years later. The latter inspired Thomas Percy's popular poem *The Hermit of Warkworth, A Northumberland Ballad* (1771).
215 *hermitage up the river was the most curiousest place any gentlefolks might wish to see*: Warkworth Hermitage was built directly into the cliff above the River Coquet and is now accessible to tourists only by boat. The inner chambers consist of a small chapel and priest's dwelling.
216 *'The moon shining over the stream . . . Beating time to the echo's soft sound'*: an adaptation of 'The Gondolier', a popular song from Richard Tickell's comic opera *The Carnival of Venice* (1781): 'And while the moon shines on the stream,/And as soft music breathes around;/The feathering oar returns the gleam,/And dips in concert to the sound' (lines 5–8). The song has been attributed to Richard Brinsley Sheridan. See 'Song, Sung by Mr. Bannister, in the *Carnival of Venice*', *The Universal Songster, o Harmony and Innocence: An Elegant and Polite Selection of Modern and Approved Songs* (London: W. Lane, *c.* 1781), p. 28.
217 *'Plain Sense'*: an allusion to the popular Minerva Press novel *Plain Sense* (1795) by Frances Margaretta Jacson. See Hudson, 'Imitation, Intertextuality and the Minerva Press Novel', p. 160.
218 *olive-wreathed god*: presumably Apollo, the God of Music, although he is usually depicted wearing a laurel wreath, not an olive wreath.
219 *Northumberland Militia*: a military unit formed during the Seven Years' War (1756–63).
220 *'made up of shreds and patches'*: Hamlet refers to his uncle Claudius as 'A king of shreds and patches' (III.iv.117).
221 *'music is the food of love'*: Shakespeare's *Twelfth Night*: 'If music be the food of love, play on' (I.i.1).
222 *con molto spirito*: in a fast and lively manner.

223 *White Cockade*: a popular Scottish folk tune, the lyrics of which were rewritten by Robert Burns as 'A Highland lad my love was born' in *The Jolly Beggars; or, Love and Liberty: A Cantana* (1799).
224 *dunny*: hard of hearing.
225 *'Moll in the Wad,' – 'the Cameronian Rant,' and 'the Morgan Rattler'*: lively Irish and Scottish tunes.
226 *amours, and amourettes*: love affairs (French); the latter are 'brief or minor' affairs (*OED*).
227 *At the further end of the chapel a recumbent female figure caught her eye*: The recumbent statue in the chapel of Warkworth Hermitage is the imaginative leaping off point for Thomas Percy's 1771 ballad *The Hermit of Warkworth*. As explained in the advertisement, 'what principally distinguishes the Chapel is a small Tomb or Monument, on the south side of the altar; on the top of which lies a Female Figure extended in the manner that effigies are usually exhibited praying on ancient tombs'. The ballad opens with a framing narrative in which visitors to the chapel wonder over the reclining statue of the 'young and beauteous Maid'. Their questions about the 'hapless dame' prompt the hermit to launch into the romantic tale that is the poem proper. See T. Percy, *The Hermit of Warkworth. A Nothumberland Ballad* (London: T. Davies and S. Leacroft, 1771), pp. vi, 17, 18. The sight of the recumbent statue is likewise a cue for Sophia's Gothic flight of fancy.
228 *minutely surveying the ruins of the castle*: Warkworth Castle. See note 214.
229 *Brutus wigs and banded wigs*: The former is a kind of short-cropped wig that was fashionable in this period. Bandeaux (hairbands) were à la mode for women. The 'banded wig' is likely a hairpiece for ladies.
230 *a hap*: a fortunate turn.
231 *Jarmin oshin*: See note 205.
232 *the famous ballad that celebrates Chevy Chace*: a traditional English ballad about a party of English hunters in the Cheviot Hills on the border of England and Scotland who are taken for an invading force by the Scottish. The result is a battle led by the English Earl of Northumberland and the Scottish Earl of Douglas. The ballad is included in Thomas Percy's *Reliques of Ancient English Poetry* (1765). Defoe mentions it in his account of Northumberland: 'We had the Cheviot Hills so plain in view, that we could not but enquire of the good old women every where, whether they had heard of the fight at Chevy Chace'. See D. Defoe, *A Tour Thro' the Whole Island of Great Britain*, ed. P. Rogers (London: Penguin, 1971), p. 537.
233 *Northumberland wharle*: a pronounced 'r' sound or burr distinctive to the region.
234 *Berwick-upon-Tweed, whose stream has been so sweetly and so simply sung*: a reference to the song 'The Free and Easy English Traveller' by John Freeth (1731–1808), which begins: 'A Traveller full forty years I have been,/But never tript over to France,/All cities and most market towns have been in,/'Twixt Berwick-on-Tweed and Penzance' (lines 1–4).
235 *Press-Inn . . . Peas-bridge*: two of the travellers' stops or post-stages on the road from Northumberland to Edinburgh.
236 *she certainly much wished to behold, amongst other desirable objects, the apartments at the Palace, where she had lately read a beautiful young creature had been immured . . . envious cater cousins*: an allusion to the popular Minerva Press novel *The Beggar Girl and her Benefactors* (1797) by Anna Maria Bennett. Elizabeth Rose marked this passage in her copy of *Rosella* and wrote 'The Beggar girl by Mrs Bennet' [sic] in the margin. (See the Introduction for a discussion of Elizabeth Rose's marginalia. See also Hudson, 'Imitation, Intertextuality and the Minerva Press Novel', p. 162.) A 'cater-cousin' is a good friend (*OED*). The Calton is a hill in Edinburgh.
237 *the denouement may be selon l'usage*: the customary ending (French).

ENDNOTES

238 *Lady C —:* not identified.
239 *F — 's:* not identified.
240 *'sigh in shades, and sicken at the sun':* taken from Elegy XXVI ('Describing the sorrow of an ingenuous mind on the melancholy event of a licentious amour') by William Shenstone (1714–63) (line 48).
241 *à bonne marchée:* at a good price.
242 *the lions:* the tourist attractions. The expression refers to the historic menagerie or zoo that was located at the Tower of London from the late Middle Ages until the nineteenth century.
243 *cicerone:* Italian for 'guide'.
244 *compagnon du voyage:* travelling companion (French).
245 *charming new novel we lately read:* identified by Hannah Doherty Hudson as *The Beggar Girl and her Benefactors* (1797) by Anna Maria Bennett. See Hudson, 'Imitation, Intertextuality and the Minerva Press Novel', p. 160.
246 *confiteor:* a prayer of penance.
247 *Cheapside:* a busy commercial district in this period. In Austen's *Pride and Prejudice*, Caroline Bingley and Fitzwilliam Darcy look down on the Bennet sisters because their relatives (the Gardiners) live 'near Cheapside'. It was assumed that the families who resided there had earned their fortunes through trade. See J. Austen, *Pride and Prejudice*, ed. D. Gray (New York and London: W. W. Norton & Company, 2001), p. 25.
248 *the noble bridges over the Clyde, the Guildhall, the Tolbooth, the University, and the Cathedral. . .*: These important Glasgow attractions are included in the 1797 Scottish guidebook *A Guide from Glasgow*, and they remain points of interest for visitors today. The Merchant's Guildhall, however, was mostly demolished in 1817; all that is left of the building is its steeple, which is now incorporated into the Briggait, a magnificent former fish market built in the 1870s. See J. McNayr, *A Guide from Glasgow, to Some of the Most Remarkable Scenes in the Highlands of Scotland, and the Falls of the Clyde* (Glasgow: Courier Office, 1797), pp. 190–204.
249 *ruins of Bothwell Castle . . . the falls of the Clyde*: When William Wordsworth, his sister Dorothy and S. T. Coleridge visited South Lanarkshire around this time their itinerary included both Bothwell Castle and the Falls of Clyde. The Falls of Clyde were a particular draw for Romantic tourists. Wordsworth's poem 'Clyde, the River, Composed at Cora Linn' (1802) was one of several Romantic works inspired by the falls (another being J. M. W. Turner's 1801 painting *The Falls of Clyde*). In her travel memoir, Dorothy Wordsworth noted that Coleridge mused about the words that best described the falls, 'grand, majestic, sublime, etc.' (p. 37). See D. Wordsworth, *Recollections of a Tour Made in Scotland, A.D. 1803*, ed. J. C. Sharp (New York: G. P. Putnam's Sons, 1874) for her accounts of the party's visits to the ruins of the castle (pp. 48–51) and the falls (pp. 35–9).
250 *Naiades:* water nymphs.
251 *one which the name of the place they were visiting gave rise to . . . the luckless destiny of the Scottish Mary, over whose admitted faults he cast the veil of oblivion*: The 4th Earl of Bothwell was Mary, Queen of Scots's third husband and one of those suspected of murdering her second husband, Lord Darnley. Opinions were divided over Mary in the eighteenth century, with some believing her to be an adulteress and murderer and others regarding her as a tragic figure. The latter view is taken in Sophia Lee's hugely popular Gothic novel *The Recess: A Tale of Other Times* (1785), the heroines of which are Mary's fictional twin daughters.
252 *'fair young wanton lady'*: taken from the Scottish ballad 'The Gypsy Laddie'. It tells of a 'gypsy laddie' (John Faa) who persuades a noble lady to run away from her husband; the lord chases them down and kills John Faa and his gang: 'And we were fifteen well-made men,/Altho we were nae bonny;/And we were a' put down for ane,/A fair young wanton lady' (lines 37–40). Later versions of the ballad identify the lady as the Countess of

Cassilis, a sixteenth-century Scottish aristocrat. See 'The Gypsy Laddie' (ballad 200A), in *The English and Scottish Popular Ballads* (1882–98), 5 vols, ed. F. J. Child (Boston and New York: Houghton Mifflin and Company, 1890), vol. 4, pp. 61–74.

253 *'once how honoured!'*: possibly an allusion to Pope's 'Elegy to the Memory of an Unfortunate Lady' (1717): 'So peaceful rests, without a stone, a name,/What once had beauty, titles, wealth, and fame./How lov'd, *how honour'd once*, avails thee not,/To whom related, or by whom begot;/A heap of dust alone remains of thee,/'Tis all thou art, and all the proud shall be!' (lines 69–74; italics added).

254 *Lanerk*: the old spelling of Lanark, a town on the River Clyde.

255 *'like a certain heroine, of whom it was said that she was beautiful . . . whilst the rest of the family were wrapped in soft repose'*: a reference to Charlotte Smith's *The Old Manor House* (1793). The heroine is the servant Monimia Morysine; the 'young heir [whom she meets] clandestinely at midnight' is Orlando Somerive.

256 *Very reluctantly Miss Beauclerc left Bothwell Castle, to proceed to a celebrated Palace*: Hamilton Palace was a grand mansion built around the time of James Hamilton, 1st Lord Hamilton (*c*. 1415–79). It underwent extensive renovations in the late seventeenth and eighteenth centuries and was demolished in the 1920s. Given Sophia's taste for all things Gothic, it is not surprising that she would rather spend her time in the ruin of a thirteenth-century castle than in a renovated neoclassical building.

257 *Airshire Bard*: Robert Burns. The poet was born in Ayrshire in southwest Scotland.

258 *St. James's-Street fellow*: a dissolute man of fashion. Several fashionable gentlemen's clubs and tailors were located on St. James's Street.

259 Burn] 1799 and 1800 texts.

260 *factor*: agent.

261 *ad libitum*: at will (Latin).

262 *The fall that first presented itself to the view of the party, which is by far the most striking and considerable one, . . . deprived them of utterance*: Corra Linn is the largest of the waterfalls that comprise the Falls of Clyde, and the one that is captured in Turner's 1801 painting (see note 249). The speechless wonder of the party recalls Edmund Burke's description of the effect of the sublime: perceivers 'are commonly struck with an awe which takes away the free use of their faculties'. See E. Burke, 'Section V: Power', in *A Philosophical Enquiry into the Origin of Our Ideas of the Sublime and Beautiful (1757)*, ed. A. Phillips (Oxford: Oxford University Press, 2008), pp. 59–65; quotation on p. 62.

263 *Petrarch and Metastatio*: Petrarch (1304–74) was an Italian poet famous for his love sonnets. Pietro Metastasio (1698–1782) was a celebrated Italian librettist. Charles Burney's biography of the latter – *Memoirs of the Life and Writings of the Abate Metastasio. In which are incorporated, Translations of his Principal Letters* – was published in 1796.

Volume III

264 *guerre masquée*: a masked or hidden war (French).

265 *like a certain lady of devout memory, who lived like a good housewife in a small house by the side of the bourn) . . . flowing grey locks*: possibly a reference to Mrs. Walsingham in Bennett's *The Beggar Girl and her Benefactors* (1797).

266 'Most probably in the autumn;' but,] 1800 text.

267 *'af the leddies wad na gang tul the Castle to ken what a brae place it was'*: Dumbarton Castle is situated on a massive rock, which is why the landlord uses the Scots term 'brae' ('steep bank') to describe it.

268 *house of the Governor*: The Georgian structure known as the Governor's House was built near the base of Dumbarton Rock in 1735.

269 *even endeavoured to appear cheerful, to atone for having suffered herself to listen to idle and romantic apprehensions*: This exchange reminds one of Catherine Morland and Henry Tilney's carriage ride to Northanger Abbey, during which Henry teasingly plays on Catherine's Gothic expectations about the Abbey (II, ch. 5). Rosella soon recognizes that she is being teased, but Catherine naively persists in her romantic beliefs about the Abbey even after Henry's burlesque story is over. Nonetheless, Catherine (like Rosella) tries to compose herself and deny her superstitious fears. As the journey comes to an end, 'Catherine, recollecting herself, grew ashamed of her eagerness, and began earnestly to assure [Henry] that her attention had been fixed without the smallest apprehension of really meeting with what he related. . . . She was not at all afraid'. See J. Austen, *Northanger Abbey*, ed. M. Gaull (New York: Longman, 2005), p. 126.

270 *passablement idle and ennuyé*: passably idle and affected by ennui (French).

271 *en famille*: as one of the family.

272 *bog-trotter*: an insulting term for an Irish person.

273 *'as we walk down the cliff, I will give you my birth, parentage, and education: I know that a dying speech and confession should properly follow'*: Here, Charlton (or more properly Oberne) satirizes the long inset first-person narratives often found in Gothic novels. Austen takes aim at the same target in *Northanger Abbey* when her narrator gives a cursory introduction to the Thorpes and then notes, 'this brief account of the family is intended to supersede the necessity of a long and minute detail from Mrs. Thorpe herself, of her past adventures and sufferings, which might otherwise be expected to occupy the three or four following chapters; in which the worthlessness of lords and attornies might be set forth, and conversations, which had passed twenty years before, be minutely repeated' (I, ch. 4). See Austen, *Northanger Abbey*, p. 27.

274 *Killbegan, in the sister kingdom*: Killbegan is a town in County Westmeath, Ireland.

275 *dunned*: assailed.

276 dulcina] 1799 text. Dulcinea is Don Quixote's ideal woman in Cervantes's 1615 parody of romance.

277 dependance] 1799 and 1800 texts.

278 *'– Frowning he went . . . And kindle rivers in its course'*: taken from William Congreve's tragedy *The Mourning Bride* (1697), V.iii.

279 *amende*: a public admission of guilt (French).

280 *coup d'essai*: first shot (French).

281 *drover*: cattle driver.

282 *bawbees*: Scottish coins equivalent to halfpence.

283 symptoms] 1800 text.

284 *bairn*: child (chiefly Scots).

285 sic a brae young leddy] 1799 and 1800 texts. In her copy of the first edition of *Rosella*, Elizabeth Rose crossed out the 'e' in 'brae' and replaced it with 'w'. This edition follows her correction as it is likely that Charlton intended 'braw' ('brave') rather than 'brae' ('steep bank') here. The term 'brae' is used earlier to describe Dumbarton Castle (see note 267). See the Introduction for a discussion of Rose's marginalia.

286 *Kamschatska*: an old spelling of Kamchatka, a peninsula in northeastern Russia. The area was annexed to Russia in the late seventeenth century. Various explorers visited the Kamchatka Peninsula in the eighteenth century, including the British naval officer Charles Clerke who died there of tuberculosis in 1779. For a contemporary description of the huts of the indigenous people who lived there, see the entry on 'Kamtchatka', in *Encyclopaedia Britannica* (Dublin: James Moore, 1792), vol. 9, p. 429.

287 *waylaid at his return . . . by the hand of rapine*: He was robbed on the road of the money he had earned from selling his cow.

288 *the rapid Nith*: the River Nith in southwest Scotland.

289 *emigre*] 1800 text.
290 *yet she wondered much that the hut was not exquisitely neat and white-washed, . . . and a lute hung carelessly by a plaid ribbon upon a cane-bottomed London cottage-chair*: Charlton makes fun of the romanticized depictions of rural life found in popular novels. Maria Edgeworth also satirizes unrealistic portrayals of cottages in her female Quixote tale 'Angelina; or, L'Amie Inconnue' (1801) when the book-loving heroine visits a cottage and finds it is cramped, damp and altogether less charming than those she had read about: cottage life is 'not quite so satisfactory in actual practice, as in poetic theory'. See M. Edgeworth, 'Angelina', in *The Novels and Selected Works of Maria Edgeworth 10*, ed. Elizabeth Eger and Clíona ÓGallchoir (London and New York: Routledge, 2003), pp. 255–302; quotation on p. 268.
291 Lady Janos and Lady Jessy's] 1800 text.
292 *energy of feeling*: Here 'energy' means rhetorical energy (*energia*), 'effectiveness or power of expression' (*OED*).
293 isle of Arran] 1800 text. An island off the west coast of Scotland.
294 *first-sight sympathy*: sympathy at first sight. The term echoes Vicesimus Knox's moral criticism of sentimental fiction. He argues that Laurence Sterne's books have a 'pernicious influence on virtue' because they inspire 'That softness, that affected and excessive sympathy at first sight, that sentimental affection, which is but *lust, in disguise*'. See V. Knox, 'No. CXLV. On the Moral Tendency of the Writings of Sterne', in *Essays Moral and Literary*, 2 vols. (Dublin: R. Marchbank, 1783) vol. 2, pp. 251–4; quotation on p. 254.
295 *Inchdavan*: Inchtavannach is a large island in Loch Lomond.
296 *Inchmonger*: Inchmurrin, the largest island in Loch Lomond.
297 *bonny loon*: good-looking lad.
298 *the Erse language*: Gaelic.
299 *spalpeen*: 'A low or mean fellow; a scamp, a rascal' (*OED*).
300 champetre] 1800 text. *Champêtre* is French for 'rural' or 'pastoral'.
301 *in petto*: Italian for 'in secret'; 'in reserve' (*OED*).
302 *treillage paper*: wallpaper with a trellis or latticework pattern.
303 *rumbling brig . . . An Edinburgh painter had taken views to the extent of five miles round, which views were hung up in the cottage*: The Rumbling Bridge (or 'Rumbling Brig', as it was called in the period) is a stone bridge above the River Braan near Dunkeld. It is so called because of the noisy rapids and waterfalls beneath it. It is described, with a picture, in William Gilpin's *Observations, Relative Chiefly to Picturesque Beauty, Made in the Year 1776, On Several Parts of Great Britain; Particularly the High-Lands of Scotland* (London: R. Blamire, 1789), vol. 1, pp. 124–5. The Edinburgh artist mentioned here may be Alexander Campbell, whose *A Journey from Edinburgh through Parts of North Britain* includes descriptions and engravings of the 'Falls of the Brahan' and the 'Rumbling-brig over the Brahan'. See A. Campbell, *A Journey from Edinburgh through Parts of North Britain* (London: T. N. Longman and O. Rees, 1802), vol. 1, pp. 272–5.
304 Crauford] 1800 text.
305 *treillage*: trellis.
306 *fuel-shed*: a shed used to store firewood and coal.
307 *deal*: wood.
308 *Æolian harp*: a harp that produces eerie, musical sounds when wind blows over its strings. It was a popular Romantic instrument.
309 *the fascinating epithet of the cottage recurred to her*: Picturesque cottages are a common feature of sentimental and Gothic novels. Charlton likely has in mind such popular works as Elizabeth Helme's *Louisa; or the Cottage on the Moor* (London: George Kearsley, 1787). See note 290.

310 *cabriole chairs*: elegant chairs with curved legs.
311 *'the hare-bell and violet grew'*: a line adapted from Part II ('Hope') of William Shenstone's 'A Pastoral Ballad' (1733): 'I seldom have met with a loss,/Such health do my fountains bestow;/My fountains all border'd with moss,/Where the hare-bells and violets grow' (lines 5–8). See W. Shenstone, 'A Pastoral Ballad', in *The Poetical Works of Will. Shenstone* (London: C. Cooke, 1795), pp. 137–43; quotation on p. 138.
312 *'stole o'er the senses like the sweet south upon a bed of violets'*: taken from *Twelfth Night*, I.i.5–6.
313 *equally wild, but far more interesting than the subjects of Salvator's pencil*: Salvator Rosa (1615–73) is an Italian artist known for his sublime landscapes.
314 *in the unwelcome accoutrements of a winding-sheet, saucer-eyes, and marble hands*: In other words, Nancy believes that Menie and Sophia are dead and that they will return as ghosts to haunt her. Here and elsewhere Charlton makes fun of the comical superstitious servants often found in Gothic novels.
315 *cap-a-pie*: head to foot.
316 *Rosella declining at that moment, the opportunity of addressing vows of everlasting affection to Miss Livia, and of giving her a glowing portrait of every shelf in the cottage*: Charlton is making fun of epistolary fictions and characterizations of female friendships in sentimental novels. Austen uses hyperbole to parody the same targets in her juvenile work 'Love and Freindship' (1790) when Laura describes her first meeting with Sophia: 'We flew into each others arms & after having exchanged vows of mutual Freindship for the rest of our Lives, instantly unfolded to each other the most inward secrets of our Hearts'. See J. Austen, *Teenage Writings*, ed. Kathryn Sutherland and Freya Johnston (Oxford: Oxford University Press, 2017), pp. 69–95; quotation on p. 76.
317 *Wallace, the northern hero, described by a Scots painter*: the Scottish warrior Sir William Wallace (*c.* 1270–1305). The painter may be David Allan (1744–96): an engraving by Daniel Lizars after Allan's painting of Wallace is housed at the National Portrait Gallery in London.
318 *Padrona*: Italian for 'the mistress of a household' (*OED*).
319 *victuals*: food.
320 *unlading*: to unburden or unload.
321 *Niobe-like*: grief-stricken. Niobe is a bereaved mother of Greek mythology.
322 *lacrymalian*: tearful.
323 *menage*: household or housework (French).
324 *the stirrup in her petticoat*: a tear in the petticoat created by putting one's foot through the fabric, making it look like a stirrup. (I am indebted to fashion historian Hilary Davidson for suggesting this possible explanation.)
325 *smoaked*: ruined through contact with smoke; an archaic spelling of 'smoked'.
326 *changed du haut en bas*: turned upside down (French).
327 *Zantippean*: 'an ill-tempered woman . . . a shrew' (*OED*); after Xanthippe, Socrates's wife, who has been depicted with these qualities.
328 house!'] 1800 text.
329 *'on a fair mountain leave to feed, and batten on a moor!'*: adapted from *Hamlet*: 'Could you on this fair mountain leave to feed,/And batten on this moor?' (III.iv.69–70). Quotation marks are as they appear in the 1799 and 1800 texts.
330 *wear the myrtle*: a wedding crown or wreath. Myrtle is associated with the Greek goddess of love, Aphrodite.
331 *third table gentry*: At a royal dinner, the monarch would be seated at the first table. Guests seated at the second table would have higher social standing than those seated at the third table.
332 wind] 1799 and 1800 texts.
333 *wafered cover*: In this period, letters were usually sealed with wax or with a wafer. The latter is a disk of dried paste that is moistened and then pressed into the folded paper.

334 *deil's*: devil's (Scots).
335 *pauky*: chiefly Scots: 'Artful, sly, . . . roguish' (*OED*). Also 'pawky'.
336 *roombling brig*: See note 303.
337 *posse comitatus*: the 'force of the land' (Latin); a band of men who can be mobilized when help is needed.
338 *raree-show*: a picture or puppet show that is viewed by peering into a box; a spectacle, a peep show.
339 *stringing rhimes to celebrate the sentimental and interesting amours of the plants*: an allusion to *The Loves of the Plants*, one of two plant-themed poems that comprise Erasmus Darwin's *The Botanic Garden* (1791), the other being *The Economy of Vegetation*. A popular poem in the 1790s, *The Loves of the Plants* describes plants using the language of sex and love. Critics objected to the sexual language of the poem and expressed concern over its influence on female readers. In *The Unsex'd Females* (1798), satirist Richard Polwhele had the poem in mind when he ridiculed female botanists for their immodest interest in plant reproduction: 'With bliss botanic as their bosoms heave,/Still pluck forbidden fruit, with mother Eve,/For puberty in signing florets pant,/Or point the prostitution of a plant'. In a footnote he adds: 'Botany has lately become a fashionable amusement with the ladies. But how the study of the sexual system of plants can accord with female modesty, I am not able to comprehend'. His conservative satire provides context for Charlton's depiction of female botanists here and elsewhere in *Rosella*. See R. Polwhele, *The Unsex'd Females; A Poem* (New York: Wm. Cobbett, 1800), p. 10.
340 under-woods] 1800 text.
341 *like the head of Medusa, that of Maclean was so extraordinary, that it every moment attracted her regards*: An example of Charlton's comic treatment of horror, the simile compares Maclean to the monstrous Gorgon Medusa of Greek mythology who turned all those who gazed upon her to stone.
342 *mentha aquatica*: a species of mint. See note 349.
343 *mart*: market town; a place for buying and selling.
344 *the noble seat of 'Athol's Duke,' which it contains, and the ruins of the cathedral*: two tourist sites. The first is Dunkeld House, a grand seventeenth-century mansion that was built for John Murray, 1st Marquess of Atholl (1631–1703) and his heirs. His son and namesake (1660–1724) was made the 1st Duke of Atholl in 1703. The mansion was demolished in the early nineteenth century. Dunkeld Cathedral was built in medieval times and still serves as the town's parish church.
345 *homme d'affaires*: a businessman (French).
346 *salute*: greet, possibly with a kiss.
347 *come in pudding time*: an archaic expression meaning 'to come in good time, to come at a propitious moment' (*OED*); here, it is meant figuratively and literally.
348 *tout ensemble*: overall effect (French).
349 *Maister Meller*: Philip Miller (1691–1771) was an English gardener and botanist. In this paragraph Maclean is referring to the entry on 'Mentha' in Miller's popular work, *The Gardeners Dictionary* (1731), which appeared in many editions throughout the eighteenth century. See P. Miller, 'Mentha', in *The Abridgement of the Gardeners Dictionary*, 6th edn (London: Printed for the Author, 1771), n.p.
350 *'high in air' . . . 'maun na luk bot where his foot do tread'*: sources not identified.
351 *pladdie*: 'plaidie' (Scots for plaid).
352 *bastinado*: strike with a stick.
353 *pauky beastie*: Here, 'pauky' suggests slow and dawdling. See notes 335 and 362 for other uses of the term.
354 *'He glowr'd at me as he'd been daft . . . New hose and new shoon –'*: taken from the traditional Scottish tune 'The Carle he came o'er the Craft' about a fellow (the 'carle') who woos a lass who will not have him. See *The Scots Musical Museum* (Edinburgh: James Johnson, 1788) vol. 2, p. 141.

355 *jockied*: outwitted.
356 *'Curse his Brutus'*: 'Curse his Brutus wig' (see note 229); in other words, 'curse him'.
357 *Princesse des coulisses:* According to Thomas Deletanville's *New French Dictionary*, 'Une princess de coulisse' is 'an actress'. See T. Deletanville, 'Coulisse', in *A New French Dictionary, in Two Parts*, 3rd edn (London: Printed for F. Wingrave, 1794). Literally, the phrase means a 'princess behind the scenes'.
358 *chemin faisant*: en route (French).
359 *cup of Lethe*: Those who drink the waters of Lethe, a river in Hades, fall into complete forgetfulness.
360 *chef d'œuvre*: masterpiece (French).
361 *hobby*: a small horse.
362 *pauky toad of loomber*: likely Menie's epithet for the pony. 'Pauky' (also 'pawky') is Scots for 'sly' or 'roguish' (*OED*), although the term may carry the alternative meaning of 'dawdling', as in poky or 'slowpoke'. For comparison, see notes 335 and 353.
363 *communicated from the tiers-etat to the second etat, . . . to the etat majeur*: According to the social divisions of the Ancien Régime, the Third Estate consisted of the commoners, the Second Estate of the nobles and the First Estate of the clergy. 'Etat major' means top military staff.
364 *Linnæus*: the famous Swedish botanist and taxonomist Carl Linnaeus (1707–78).
365 *frightened by the shadow of a bush they had encountered in their* way . . . *and followed with all her might*: Again Charlton parodies the conventionally superstitious servants of Gothic fiction. (See note 314.)
366 *like other heroines, Miss Beauclerc extremely condemned in theory the folly of believing in the spiritual visitations . . ., but most devoutly subscribed to the doctrine in private*: a reference to Gothic novels that seem to deny the existence of the supernatural even though the heroines have many apparently supernatural experiences. Ann Radcliffe's ostensibly rational heroines are sceptical about ghosts; however, their superstitions are awakened by strange appearances and sounds, and the author's 'reasonable' explanations for the mysteries often fall short in accounting for them. The result is a teeter-tottering between rationalism and supernaturalism.
367 *she thought it would be proper, selon l'usage, to explore the burial-place belonging to the mansion*: Driven by curiosity and convention, Gothic heroines often explore gloomy crypts, secret chambers and other shadowy places.
368 unhandsomely,] 1799 and 1800 texts.
369 *led Captain*: 'a hanger-on, dependant, parasite' (*OED*).
370 the *Canon-gate*: The Canongate is one of the main streets in central Edinburgh. It forms the lower half of the famous Royal Mile.
371 criminal!'] 1800 text.
372 *non compos*: short for '*non compos mentis*': a person of unsound mind (Latin).
373 self-expressed] 1800 text.
374 *dressing-box*: a case that holds toiletries, combs and other personal items.
375 *castellum*: a small fortress.
376 *Caledonian*: Scottish. Caledonia was the ancient Roman name for Scotland.
377 *queue*: pigtail.
378 *sable-peruked*: black-wigged.
379 *milch-cow*: a source of income; literally, a milk-producing cow.

Volume IV

380 *cozened*: deceived or cheated. This is an allusion to Tobias Smollett's *The Expedition of Humphry Clinker* (1771). In volume two, a young coxcomb who is tricked into thinking a purgative drug has been added to his wine exclaims, 'He that would cozen

a Scot, mun get oop betimes, and take Old Scratch [the devil] for his counsellor –'. See T. Smollett, *The Expedition of Humphry Clinker*, ed. E. Gottlieb (New York and London: W. W. Norton & Company, 2015), p. 182.
381 *'maun ha got oop betimes, and ha ta'en auld scratch for his counsellor'*: See note 380.
382 *déjeuné*: French for 'breakfast' in this period. (In the nineteenth century, the morning meal became 'petit déjeuner' and the word 'déjeuner' came to mean 'lunch'.)
383 *'bull-faced, and freckled fair'*: taken from 'Fragment of a Character of Jacob Tonson, His Publisher' by John Dryden (*c.* 1705): 'With leering looks, bull-faced, and freckled fair,/With two left legs, and Judas-coloured hair,/And frowsy pores that taint the ambient air'.
384 *in alt*: in a high pitch.
385 *'if it had been less, 'twould have been none at all'*: source not identified.
386 *get shut of*: be free from.
387 *tacked about*: turned around.
388 *yestreen*: yesterday evening.
389 *speirs*: The *OED* defines 'speir' as 'Hope; expectation'. According to the *Dictionaries of the Scots Language*, the term means 'To ask', to 'make inquiries'. Both definitions seem possible here.
390 *'that within which passeth shew'*: taken from *Hamlet*, I.ii.85.
391 Solway Frith] 1799 and 1800 texts. The Solway Firth is an inlet at the border of England and Scotland.
392 *ain coontra kirk*: the Church of Scotland.
393 *running cash*: ready cash.
394 *a Diligence*: a large public stagecoach.
395 *kirks*: churches.
396 *delassement*: relaxation.
397 in my way?'] 1799 and 1800 texts.
398 Gallowway] 1799 and 1800 texts
399 *siller*: silver coin; money.
400 *'Can I not speak to him – can I not say I thank you!'*: adapted from lines spoken by Orlando in *As You Like It*, I.ii: 'I cannot speak to her' (line 259) and 'Can I not say "I thank you"?' (line 249).
401 *when I shan't have money to pay for your letters*: The recipient typically paid the postage in this period.
402 *carnying*: flattering, coaxing.
403 *surgeon*: physician in a general sense.
404 *fomentations*: poultices.
405 *Tabithise at Bath*: an allusion to Smollett's *The Expedition of Humphry Clinker* (1771), in which the spinster Tabitha Bramble seeks a husband in Bath.
406 *a croaker*: one who is prone to making gloomy prognostications.
407 *'loves of the plants'*: See note 339.
408 *parterre*: the lower part of the auditorium and those in it.
409 *Chairmen*: post-chaise drivers.
410 suaviter in modo] 1799 and 1800 texts. See note 125.
411 *en maitresse*: as the mistress of the house.
412 *King's Bench*: the Court of King's Bench, a former court of law in England.
413 *quarterage*: a sum received quarterly.
414 *fagging*: working hard.
415 *Bootle's*: Boodle's is a gentleman's club located on St. James's Street, Central London. It was founded in 1762.
416 *embrocation*: the act of applying a liniment on some part of the body.
417 *twenty thousand pounds*: For comparison's sake, Jane Austen's richest heroine, Emma Woodhouse, is 'a heiress of thirty thousand pounds' (II, ch. 16), whereas another one

of Austen's heroines, Catherine Morland, the daughter of a middle-class clergyman, 'would have three thousand pounds' for her dowry (II, ch. 16). See J. Austen, *Emma*, ed. G. Justice (New York and London: W. W. Norton & Company, 2012), p. 96; see also J. Austen, *Northanger Abbey*, ed. M. Gaull (New York: Longman, 2005), p. 198.

418 *to publish a key to their foolish mystery*: First popularized in the seventeenth century, *romans à clef* (French for 'novels with a key') are a kind of novel in which real people and events are presented in fictional guises. The 'key' to such a work, often sold separately, would identify the real people upon whom the characters were based.

419 *the review*: possibly a military review in Hyde Park, a spectacle that would have been a draw for the nobility and gentry, as well as the general public.

420 *gib*: [pronounced *jib*] a horse that 'gibs' is hard to control; it 'refuse[s] to draw' or 'shrinks from pulling' See O. Heslop, 'Gib', in *A Glossary of Words Used in The County of Northumberland and on the Tyneside* (London: Henry Frowde, 1894), vol. 2, p. 323.

421 *which he thought more safe than venturing it at so dangerous an hour as it must necessarily be before they reached his house*: Carriages travelling along lonely stretches of roads after dark were targets for highway robbers.

422 *fully expecting the usual demand, was preparing to transfer his cash without bond or obligation*: Mr. Mordaunt thinks that he is about to be robbed by a highwayman and he is ready to hand over his money.

423 *jammed my leg with the pole*: the pole suspended between the horses. Postilions on horseback often wore iron guards to protect their legs and feet from the centre pole. See J. Kloester, *Georgette Heyer's Regency World* (London: Sourcebooks, 2010), p. 177.

424 *hungary-water*: a distillation of alcohol and rosemary that was used for medicinal and restorative purposes.

425 *the bar of the chaise*: Typically, the driver of a post-chaise is mounted on one of the horses pulling the vehicle. Since the post-boy is injured and cannot ride a horse, his only option is to sit on the crossbar at the front of the chaise, near the luggage platform.

426 gentleman.'] 1799 and 1800 texts.

427 *Norebeton Common*: the original name for Norbiton, an area in southwest London.

428 *would in matters of opinion, almost turn Mahometan*: that is, espouse any convenient doctrine or opinion.

429 *rappee*: coarsely shredded (or 'rasped') snorting tobacco; snuff.

430 *'what maggot's in the wind now!'*: Here, 'maggot' is used in the archaic sense to mean a 'strange, or perverse notion or idea' (*OED*).

431 *enamorata*: a variant of 'inamorata', Italian for 'female lover'.

432 *'go seek his fortunes'*: a reference to, but not a direct quotation from, Shakespeare's *As You Like It*.

433 *tournure*: 'manner or bearing' (*OED*).

434 *French Directory*: the executive council that ruled revolutionary France from 1795 until its abolishment by Napoleon in 1799.

435 *coffre-fort*: chest or strongbox (French).

436 *who never made incomprehensible extracts from incomprehensible authors . . . or looked into Voltaire or Rousseau to improve her morality*: Charlton satirizes women who take a superficial interest in literature and ideas. Voltaire (1694–1778) and Jean-Jacques Rousseau (1712–78) were admired by French revolutionaries, and so those who opposed radicalism regarded their writings as harmful to morality. The 1801 French translation omits the reference to these philosophers.

437 *'She speaks and acts ('tis said) just as she ought; . . . As never yet to love, or be belov'd!'*: slightly adapted from Pope's 'Epistle to a Lady' (1735), lines 161–6.

438 *Brookes's*: Brooks's is a gentleman's club on St. James's Street that was founded in 1764.

439 *Bognor Rocks*: now Bognor Regis, a seaside resort in West Sussex. It was described in the September 1799 issue of *The European Magazine* as 'a new bathing place'

(p. 151). It was founded by Sir Richard Hotham who may be the model for Mr. Parker in Austen's unfinished novel *Sanditon* (1817).
440 '*Reformation comes in a flood,/With a strong heady current, scow'ring faults*': adapted from *Henry V*, I.i.35–6.
441 *sop to Cerberus*: See note 112.
442 *peccavi*: Latin for 'I have sinned'; to cry peccavi is to admit guilt.
443 *Philistines*: This term often means 'uncultured', but here it is used in the following sense: 'Frequently humorous. A member of a group regarded as one's enemies, or into whose hands one would not wish to fall; a foe, a persecutor' (*OED*). The Hebrew Bible describes the Philistines as the enemies of the Israelites.
444 'from till morn dewy eve'] 1799 text. Taken from Milton's *Paradise Lost* (1667): 'from morn/To noon he fell, from noon to dewy eve,/A summer's day; and with the setting sun/dropp'd from the zenith like a falling star' (I, 742–5).
445 *gave a loose to*: '[gave] full vent to' (*OED*).
446 *Monsieur Servise will tell you that a turn too much l'envoit au diable!:* Monsieur Servise is either their French cook or a generic name for a French cook. 'L'envoit au diable' means 'sends it to hell'. This line is left out of the 1801 French edition.
447 *merry as a grig*: exuberantly cheerful.
448 *déjeuné apparatus*: 'breakfast service' (*OED*). See note 382.
449 *Egyptian task*: a reference to Exodus 5:6–7, in which the Egyptian taskmasters expect the Israelites to make bricks without providing them with straw. Here, Lady Lucy is teasing Rosella because the task she set for her (to preside at the breakfast table) was merely a pretence to bring Rosella and Oberne together.
450 *ticket*: a visiting ticket or calling card; a card bearing one's name.
451 *first mourning*: the initial period of deep mourning. Traditionally, this is followed by the half-mourning period when black clothes are no longer required. Mr. Mordaunt has required the couple to wait a respectable time after Mrs. Delaval's death before getting married.
452 *a French Marquis, who offered to engage in her service as an aide-de cuisine*: The implication is that he is an émigré who fled France after the 1789 revolution. His property confiscated by the revolutionary leaders in France, he has been forced to seek employment as an assistant cook in England. The line is not included in the 1801 French translation.
453 *budgets of old stories*: A budget is a pouch or bundle. Here, the term is used figuratively to mean a stock or supply, a large collection.
454 *petit-maîtres*: fops, dandies; French for 'little masters'.
455 *tournure*: 'turning of language', 'mode of expression' (*OED*). He thanks Lady Lucy for her generous take on the matter.
456 *Lady's Magazine*: *The Lady's Magazine; or Entertaining Companion for the Fair Sex* was a popular Romantic literary periodical that published poetry, fiction, essays, reviews and other miscellaneous pieces written by women for a female readership. As 'the first recognisably modern women's magazine', *The Lady's Magazine* provided an important platform for aspiring and established female writers; however, it was disparaged by some critics for its 'association with amateurism, the ephemeral, the feminine and the non-intellectual and diverse offerings of its . . . unprofessional contributors'. For more, see J. Batchelor's excellent study, *The Lady's Magazine (1770–1832) and the Making of Literary History* (Edinburgh: Edinburgh University Press, 2022); quotations on pp. 3 and 7. Charlton's gibe about 'the sublime effusions' published in *The Lady's Magazine* suggests a dismissive attitude towards the publication.
457 *fam-de-sham*: a humourous term for a lady's maid or 'femme de chambre'.

GLOSSARY OF REPEATED TERMS

The following terms appear two or more times throughout the text. Each term is defined in a note upon its first occurrence.

airing   a 'walk or ride outdoors to take air or exercise' (*OED*).
amourette   a 'brief or minor love affair' (*OED*).
bairn   child (chiefly Scots).
band-box   a box designed to hold collars, caps and hats.
blunderbuss   a short-barreled gun.
chace   hunt; the hunting of animals for sport.
chairmen   post-chaise drivers.
chaise   see *post-chaise*.
cicerone   guide (Italian).
ci-devant   former (French).
congé   'Ceremonious dismissal or leave-taking' (*OED*); from the French.
courser   horse.
deil   devil (Scots).
déjeuné   French for 'breakfast' in this period. (In the nineteenth century, the morning meal became 'petit déjeuner' and the word 'déjeuner' came to mean 'lunch'.)
dressing-box   a case that holds toiletries, combs and other personal items.
dulcinea   Don Quixote's ideal woman in Cervantes's 1615 parody of romance.
ebullition   'a sudden outburst or . . . bubbling over' (*OED*). To 'ebulliate' is to boil or bubble up.
en attendant   'meanwhile'; 'while waiting' (French).
escrutoire **(an older spelling of *'escritoire'*)**   a writing desk, sometimes portable. Used interchangeably with secretaire in this text.
factor   agent.
fag, **also *'fagging'***   a hard task or errand; to perform an unpleasant job.
Faro, **also *'Pharaoh'* or *'Pharo'***   a gambling card game.
foresters   ponies native to New Forest in Southern England.
hackney, **or *'hack'* for short, as in *'hack-chaise'***   a horse-drawn carriage for hire.

house of public resort   an inn or a tavern.
hoyden   a high-spirited girl; a romp or tomboy.
in petto   Italian for 'in secret'; 'in reserve' (*OED*).
in propria persona   Latin for 'in the flesh' (*OED*).
Indiaman   any ship operating for the East India Company.
mal-à-propos   inopportune (French).
menage   household or housework (French).
peregrination, also *'peregrinate'*   a tour or journey. To 'peregrinate' is to travel, especially by foot; to walk.
post-chaise, also *'chaise'* or *'chair'*   a four-wheeled closed carriage drawn by two or four horses.
rencontre   meeting (French).
secretaire, see *escrutoire*.
ton, also *'tonish'*   members of high society; people of fashion.
victuals   food.
yestreen   yesterday evening.

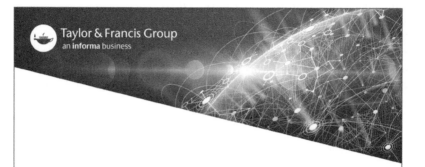